Florian Zemmin
Modernity in Islamic Tradition

Religion and Society

Edited by
Gustavo Benavides, Frank J. Korom,
Karen Ruffle and Kocku von Stuckrad

Volume 76

Florian Zemmin

Modernity in Islamic Tradition

The Concept of 'Society' in the Journal *al-Manar* (Cairo, 1898–1940)

DE GRUYTER

ISBN 978-3-11-071050-2
e-ISBN (PDF) 978-3-11-054584-5
e-ISBN (EPUB) 978-3-11-054486-2
ISSN 1437-5370

Library of Congress Control Number: 2018949466

Bibliographic information published by the Deutsche Nationalbibliothek
The Deutsche Nationalbibliothek lists this publication in the Deutsche Nationalbibliografie; detailed bibliographic data are available in the Internet at http://dnb.dnb.de.

This volume is text- and page-identical with the hardback published in 2018.
Printing and binding: CPI books GmbH, Leck

www.degruyter.com

Acknowledgments

> „What, do you imagine that I would take so much trouble and so much pleasure in writing, do you think that I would keep so persistently to my task, if I were not preparing – with a rather shaky hand – a labyrinth into which I can venture, in which I can move my discourse, opening up underground passages, forcing it to go far from itself, finding overhangs that reduce and deform its itinerary, in which I can lose myself and appear at last to eyes that I will never have to meet again. I am no doubt not the only one who writes in order to have no face."
>
> – Foucault

> "Truth is a journey not a destination."
>
> – Tea bag

This book is the slightly revised version of my PhD thesis, which I submitted in May 2016 to the Institute for Islamic and Middle Eastern Studies at the University of Bern. It thus is the outcome of a journey that began seven years ago, with an application to the Swiss National Science Foundation for a research grant. I am grateful to that institution for having provided the material basis for the greatest part of that journey, namely for having funded this research project – which was submitted initially under the working title "Socialization of Islam or Islamization of Society: Islam as a context of normative order in the Islamic public of *al-Manar*" – from November 2011 until October 2015.

Intellectually, I am most grateful and indebted to Prof. Dr. Reinhard Schulze, who was the principal applicant of the above-mentioned research project and the supervisor of my thesis. He inspired this journey, planned it with me, guided me back to my main path when I was in danger of losing myself in the woods, and (not least) let me venture into new paths on my own, and assured me of his trust in this regard. In an important sense, it was this combination of guidance and liberty that propelled me to walk the paths I walked and that led to the final destination of this journey – namely, this book.

Prof. Dr. Anke von Kügelgen, my second supervisor, joined me at crucial crossroads on this journey. She always offered good advice as to which direction to take, ensured that I was on the right track, and helped to restore my confidence when necessary. As to Reinhard Schulze, I am grateful to her both for her company during this journey and for having been my teacher before. I consider myself privileged for the training, knowledge, and inspiration I received already as an MA student in Bern.

As a student assistant, Esma Isis-Arnautovic was part of the above-mentioned research project for two years. Among other tasks, she was mainly respon-

https://doi.org/10.1515/9783110545845-001

sible for processing the electronic version of *al-Manar.* I could not have wished for a more pleasant and reliable travel companion.

Many other people whom I met at one point or another on this journey pointed me to particular spots, made me look in different directions, shared their experiences with me, or listened to mine – I am grateful to all of them. I especially benefitted from discussions of this project on the following occasions: "7. Schweizerische Nachwuchstagung der Asienwissenschaften" in Zäziwil in April 2013; "DAVO-Werkstattgespräche im Rahmen des 32. Deutschen Orientalistentags" in Münster in September 2013; "Forschungskolloquium Islamwissenschaft" (FoKI) in Basel in November 2013; the IASH (Insitute of Advanced Study in the Humanities and the Social Sciences, now part of the Walter Benjamin Kolleg) workshop on secularity with Prof. Dr. Volkhard Krech at the University of Bern in November 2013; "Forschungswerkstatt" at the Chair for the Study of Religion (Prof. Dr. Christoph Bochinger) at the University of Bayreuth in February 2014; and, last but not least, "Orient-Institut Beirut/Forum Transregionale Studien: Summer Academy: 'Language, Science, and Aesthetics'" in Beirut in September 2014. The variety of disciplinary contexts in which this project was discussed greatly shaped its itineary and its final outcome.

If I, in all humility, point out this study's interdisciplinary integration as a significant achievement in itself, I do so not least because it necessarily goes along with what some may perceive as a shortcoming – namely, the impossibility of adhering to the state-of-the-art of each discipline involved. I thus wish to clarify that, in drawing on sociology, historiography, linguistics, philosophy, or religious studies, I do not aspire to make original contributions to all of these fields. The primary discipline this study intervenes in is that of Islamic studies (*Islamwissenschaft*), which initially inspired this project. That said, I shall of course be glad and grateful if representatives of other disciplines also find parts of this study valuable. One set of debates beyond the field of Islamic studies that I do indeed hope to speak back to are theories and understandings of secularity and modernity.

I thank the editors of Religion and Society for including this book in their series, which I consider a very fitting venue also in terms of interdisciplinary outreach. Thanks are also due to Dr. Sophie Wagenhofer and Dr. Eva Frantz, who – on behalf of De Gruyter – guided the publishing process in the best manner imaginable. Dr. Alissa Jones Nelson joined this project in its final but crucial stage; she improved the English of this text far beyond the correction of mere factual errors. Naturally, all remaining mistakes are my own responsibility.

One very special little person started her own journey of life pretty much when I set out on the journey of this project, and it is certain that without her, my jour-

ney would have been an entirely different one. I can only apologize to you, Hannah, for not having included more pictures in this study, and I am very much looking forward to the day when I'll be able to share the experiences of my academic journeys with you.
Private journeys, I have come to learn, yield at least as many suprising turns as academic ones. In the end, it still is to you, Sonja, my closest traveling partner for so long, that I dedicate this book. Thank you.
All you other people dear to my heart, you know who you are...

For altogether different and easily guessable reasons, I am grateful to the developers of the writing program Scrivener and the application Freedom, which blocks access to the Internet.

Florian Zemmin
August 2017

Contents

Chapter 1 Introduction: Modernity, Islam, and Society – The Argument for a Heuristic Eurocentrism — 1
1 Hegemonic Modernity and Its Others — **1**
2 The Historicity and Normativity of 'Society' — **9**
3 Conceptual History of Another Language — **12**
4 The Contribution and Main Argument of This Book — **14**
5 The Approach of This Study: A Heuristic Eurocentrism — **17**
6 Rationale and Structure of the Book: Assumptions, Expectations, Findings — **26**
7 Locating Terms in *al-Manar* — **32**

Part A Assumptions: 'Society' and the Secular in European Modernity

Chapter 2 'Society' in European Modernity — 39
1 'Society' as a Basic Concept of (European) Modernity — **39**
1.1 Conceptual History and the Saddle Period — **39**
1.2 'Society' as the Most Constitutive Concept of Modernity — **44**
2 Society and the State: The Political Dimension of 'Society' — **48**
3 Society and Religion: The Secular and Metaphysical Dimensions of 'Society' — **57**
4 Society and Sociology: Institutionalizing 'Society' as an Autonomous Object — **64**
4.1 Sociology and the Social Sciences as a Response to the Modern Problématique of Socio-political Order — **64**
4.2 The End of the Social and the Loss of the Metaphysical Ground of Society — **69**

Chapter 3 *A Secular Age* as a Heuristic Tool — 73
1 *A Secular Age:* The Usefulness of One Particular Story — **73**
2 Modern Social Imaginaries, the Immanent Frame, and 'Society' — **77**
3 Islam: Absent from *A Secular Age*, Present in the Secular Age — **83**
4 Historical Self-understanding and Storytelling — **86**

Part B Expectations: Egyptian Modernity, *al-Manar*, and Arabic Concepts

Chapter 4 Modernity in Egypt: Nation, Society, Secularism, and the Press — 93
1 Egypt as a Modern Nation-State — **93**
1.1 Preliminaries: Writing about the Modern Egyptian Nation — **93**
1.2 Egypt Becomes a Nation-State: Nationalizing Politics and Nationalist Sentiments — **98**
2 Egypt as a Modern Society: Social Change, Social Groups, and Societal Reformists — **105**
2.1 Social Change and Social Groups — **105**
2.2 Spokespersons and Reformists of the Egyptian Nation and Society — **113**
3 A Modern Intellectual Arena: The Plural Landscape of the Press in Egypt — **118**
3.1 The Rise of Private Publishing in Egypt: A Public Arena of Intellectual Debate — **118**
3.2 Engaging the Secular: Islamic Reformists in the Public Sphere — **122**

Chapter 5 *Al-Manar:* The Mouthpiece of Islamic Reformism — 138
1 Foundation, Distribution, and Authors — **138**
2 An Islamic Journal on and for What? The Topics and Goals of *al-Manar* — **145**
3 The Prominence and Usual Depiction of *al-Manar* — **151**
4 Islamic Reformism, Religion, Secularity, and Society — **164**

Chapter 6 The Arabic Saddle Period and Arabic Terms for 'Society' — 177
1 The Arabic Saddle Period and Socio-Political Concepts — **177**
2 'Society' in Arabic: *al-Hay'a al-Ijtimāʿiyya* and *Mujtamaʿ* — **185**
3 *Al-Hay'a al-Ijtimāʿiyya:* Prominent Usages — **192**

Part C Findings: 'Society' in *al-Manar*

Chapter 7 *Al-Hay'a al-Ijtimāʿiyya* in *al-Manar:* Offering *Umma* as an Alternative — 199
1 Occurrences of *al-Hay'a al-Ijtimāʿiyya* in *al-Manar* — **199**

2 Rashid Rida: *Umma* as an Alternative to *al-Hay'a al-Ijtimāʿiyya* — **201**
3 Crucial Aspects of *al-Hay'a al-Ijtimāʿiyya* — **211**
3.1 A Social Body and a Social Order — **211**
3.2 *Al-Hay'a al-Ijtimāʿiyya* and Politics — **215**
3.3 *Al-Hay'a al-Ijtimāʿiyya*, Morals, and Religion — **222**
3.4 Work, Women, and Education: Specific Aspects of Society — **226**
4 Particular Societies Conceptualized as *al-Hay'a al-Ijtimāʿiyya* — **233**
4.1 Lord Cromer: Egyptian Society, Eastern Society, and the Socio-political Relevance of Islam — **233**
4.2 Niqula Dabana: Eastern Society, the Qur'an, and Republicanism — **237**
4.3 Muhyi al-Din Azad: Islamic Society and the Principle of *Jamāʿa* — **239**
4.4 Other Particular Societies Conceptualized as *al-Hay'a al-Ijtimāʿiyya* — **245**
5 Alternative Terms for Conceptualizing Particular Societies — **247**
6 Conclusion: *Umma* as a Less Specific Alternative to *al-Hay'a al-Ijtimāʿiyya* — **250**

Chapter 8 *Mujtamaʿ* in *al-Manar:* Avoiding the Established Meaning of 'Society' — 254
1 Overview, Semantic Range, and Authorship — **254**
2 A Seemingly Self-evident Term: The Meaning of *Mujtamaʿ* and Its Relation to *Umma* and *Shaʿb* — **261**
2.1 Rashid Rida: Early Usages of *Mujtamaʿ* in Relation to *Umma* and *Shaʿb* — **261**
2.2 Other Authors Using *Mujtamaʿ* in Relation to *Umma* and *Shaʿb* — **265**
3 *Mujtamaʿ* and *al-Hay'a al-Ijtimāʿiyya* — **269**
3.1 *Mujtamaʿ* and *al-Hay'a al-Ijtimāʿiyya* in *al-Manar* — **269**
3.2 *Mujtamaʿ* and *al-Hay'a al-Ijtimāʿiyya* in Niqula Haddad's Book on Sociology — **273**
4 Crucial Aspects of *Mujtamaʿ* — **275**
4.1 *Mujtamaʿ* and Politics — **275**
4.2 *Mujtamaʿ* and Religion — **278**
4.3 *Mujtamaʿ* and (Religious) Morals — **282**
4.4 *Mujtamaʿ* and (Religious) Law — **286**

5 Particular Societies and Social Orders — 291
5.1 Modern Society, Development, and Progress — 291
5.2 Particular Societies — 295
6 Conclusion: The Establishment and Normative Connotations of *Mujtamaʿ* — 299

Chapter 9 Rafiq al-ʿAzm: Islamic Reformist, Secular Historian, and Sociological Thinker — 303
1 The Life and Works of Rafiq al-ʿAzm (1865–1925) — 303
2 A Secular(ist) Islamic Intellectual — 310
3 *Al-Durus al-Hikamiyya:* An Anthropological and Sociological Argument for Society, Religion, and Government — 325
4 *Tanbih al-Afham:* Islam as (a Solution to the Problem of) Social Order — 336
5 Conclusion: Islam, Religion, Secularity, and Concepts of Society — 346

Chapter 10 Social Association Reified: *Ijtimāʿ*, *Ijtimāʿī*, and *Umma* in Articles by Rashid Rida — 350
1 *Ijtimāʿ* and *Ijtimāʿī(ya):* Ubiquity, Semantic Range, and Positive Connotation — 350
1.1 Social Association, Society, Concurrence, Unity – The Semantic Range and Normativity of *Ijtimāʿ* — 350
1.2 Societal Aspects and Social Reform: *Ijtimāʿī(ya)* in *al-Manar* — 359
2 Sociology and Soci(et)al Laws: Grounding the Social in Nature and God — 367
2.1 Sociology and Societal Thinkers: Rida's Positive but Vague Reception — 367
2.2 Sociology and the Qurʾan, Societal and Godly Laws: An Open Spin on the Immanent Frame — 373
2.3 *Umma* as the Object of Sociological Inquiry — 381
3 Islam, Religion, and Society — 385
3.1 Religion as a Natural Requirement of and a Superior Bond for Society — 385
3.2 Islam as a Societal Religion — 389
3.3 The Distinction and Subsequent Connection of Religion and Society — 397

4 Conclusion: *Umma* as 'Society' — **410**
4.1 Individuals Cooperating to Construct the Integrated Social Body of the *Umma* — **410**
4.2 The *Umma* as a National Society: *Al-Muslimun wa-l-Qubt* — **417**
4.3 *Umma* as 'Society' Beyond *al-Manar* — **420**

Chapter 11 Conclusion: Society, The Immanent Frame, and Modernity – Concepts, Spins, and Genealogies — 423
1 Summary of This Study — **423**
2 Modernity in Islamic Tradition: Spins on the Immanent Frame — **425**
3 Avenues for Future Research — **429**

Bibliography — 433
a) Articles from *al-Manar* — **433**
b) Other Arabic Publications — **448**
c) Publications in Other Languages — **453**

Appendix: Tables of Search Terms — 484

Index — 509

Chapter 1
Introduction: Modernity, Islam, and Society – The Argument for a Heuristic Eurocentrism

Islam and modernity. This prominent pair of terms often appears in questions such as "Are Islam and modernity compatible?" or "Is an Islamic modernity possible?" Islam here tends to be associated with tradition, whereas modernity is associated with certain concrete norms and values, which allegedly emanate from Europe or the West, or are even considered exclusive to it. Rather than positing Islamic tradition against modernity, this study discerns modernity *in* Islamic tradition by showing how the fundamental background understanding of modernity – signified by the concept of 'society' – was articulated from within the Islamic discursive tradition – namely, in the journal *al-Manar*, the mouthpiece of Islamic reformism. The fact that in *al-Manar* the classical term *umma* was a principal term used to conceptualize modern society supports a model of convergence of discursive traditions in modernity, over against one of diffusion of European concepts.

1 Hegemonic Modernity and Its Others

What, then, does it mean to be modern? At no point has there been a unanimously accepted answer to this question, which will recur in different elaborations throughout this study. Nevertheless, some four decades ago, two aspects figured prominently in most replies: being modern was associated with being secular and being Western(ized). Modernization was thus widely regarded as following the trajectory of the modern West, a key feature of which was secularization in the sense of the declining relevance of religion.[1] This understanding informs, for example, David Lerner's 1958 book, *The Passing of Traditional Society: Modernizing the Middle East.*[2] While this was not the first work referring to the

1 I am using 'secularization' to refer to the process leading to 'secularity' and 'secularism' to designate positions arguing for secularization. Likewise, 'modernization' designates the process leading to 'modernity' as its outcome, and 'modernism' argues for such a process.
2 Lerner, David. 1958. *The Passing of Traditional Society: Modernizing the Middle East.* New York: The Free Press.

https://doi.org/10.1515/9783110545845-002

idea of modernization in its title,[3] it was certainly an influential one, marking the heyday of modernization theories. An assumed binary between modern, secular, Western societies and traditional, religious, non-Western – not least Islamic – societies continues to inform some academic research.[4] However, it has come under serious pressure in different regards, three of which I want to recall here, leading up to my own research question: (1) modernity did not originate in Europe or the West[5] and gradually diffuse to other regions; (2) secularization is not to be understood as a continuous decline of religion in modernity; and (3) the secular is not a neutral category but is itself normative, as are concepts crucial to the modern self-understanding, such as 'religion' and 'society.'

(1) The concept of multiple modernities, chiefly associated with the name of the late Shmuel Eisenstadt,[6] is probably the most prominent – but ultimately unsatisfactory – attempt at correcting the understanding of a singular modernity, originating in Europe and leading to the same outcome everywhere.[7] While

---

3 This was suggested by: Knöbl, Wolfgang. 2013. "Aufstieg und Fall der Modernisierungstheorie und des säkularen Bildes 'moderner Gesellschaften'." In *Moderne und Religion: Kontroversen um Modernität und Säkularisierung* ed. by Ulrich Willems, Detlef Pollack, Helene Basu, Thomas Gutmann and Ulrike Spohn: 75–116. Bielefeld: transcript, 91. An earlier title is: Cooper, Clayton Sedgwick. 1914. *The Modernizing of the Orient.* New York: McBride, Nast & Company.

4 For critical discussions, see: Masud, Muhammad Khalid and Salvatore, Armando. 2009. "Western Scholars of Islam on the Issue of Modernity." In *Islam and Modernity. Key Issues and Debates* ed. by Muhammad Khalid Masud, Armando Salvatore and Martin van Bruinessen: 36–53. Edinburgh: Edinburgh University Press; Salama, Mohammad R. 2011. *Islam, Orientalism and Intellectual History: Modernity and the Politics of Exclusion since Ibn Khaldun.* London: I. B. Tauris.

5 In this study I often use 'Europe' and 'the West' interchangeably; this is due to their often being treated synonymously in primary and secondary sources alike. Neither 'Europe' nor 'the West' are fixed regions, but rather constructions that came to epitomize modernity. Which countries or regions are included in these constructions is subject to debate. At the beginning of the twentieth century, 'the West' for most constituted England and France, with the USA joining later, and Germany was excluded until basically after the Second World War.

6 Another prominent contribution in this vein is: Gaonkar, Dilip Parameshwar (ed.). 2001. *Alternative Modernities.* Durham, NC: Duke University Press.

7 For a programmatic text, see: Eisenstadt, Shmuel N. 2000. "Multiple Modernities." *Daedalus* 129/1: 1–29; for a subsequent elaboration: idem. 2003. *Comparative Civilizations and Multiple Modernities.* 2 vols. Leiden: Brill. A precursor is: idem. (ed.). 1987. *Patterns of Modernity; vol. 1: The West; vol. 2: Beyond the West.* London: Frances Pinter. For a (sympathetic) overview of the directions in which Eisenstadt's approach has been taken, as well as of alternative approaches, see: Schwinn, Thomas. 2009. "Multiple modernities: Konkurrierende Thesen und offene Fragen. Ein Literaturbericht in konstruktiver Absicht." *Zeitschrift für Soziologie* 38: 454–476. For a critical discussion, see: Patel, Sujata. 2013. "Are the Theories of Multiple Modernities

this approach accounts for different trajectories or "paths" of modernization, it still regards Europe as the origin of modernity, which was later appropriated differently by other "civilizations." The problematic assumption of different, rather self-contained civilizations is also operative in other recent attempts at rethinking modernity in a way that also accounts for non-Western experiences.[8] 'The West,' as with any civilization, is not a given unit but a historically contingent construction. The alleged contrast to an imagined Other, notably Islam, has played a significant role in consolidating Western self-understanding.[9]

In addition to attempts at non-Eurocentric or non-Western-centric[10] contributions, there have also been decidedly anti-Eurocentric contributions to the debate, which claim that central features of modernity – such as rational bureaucracy or capitalism – first evolved in other regions of the world.[11] More convincing is a polycentric understanding of modernity as advanced by a variety of research programs that can be grouped under the broad heading of "global" or "entangled history." Moreover, these approaches stress local, regional, or global connections over civilizational or national differences.[12] Indeed, modernity – which I take to be a certain self-understanding, crucial for which is the idea of

Eurocentric? The Problem of Colonialism and Its Knowledge(s)." In *Worlds of Difference* ed. by Saïd Amir Arjomand and Elisa Reis: 40–57. London et al.: Sage.

8 See, for example, Arjomand, Saïd Amir (ed.). 2014. *Social Theory and Regional Studies in the Global Age*. Albany: State University of New York Press. In this volume, Peter Wagner critically discusses the civilization paradigm employed by most of his co-contributors: Wagner, Peter. 2014. "World-Sociology Beyond the Fragments. Oblivion and Advance in the Comparative Analysis of Modernities." In *Social Theory and Regional Studies in the Global Age* ed. by Saïd Amir Arjomand: 293–311. Albany: State University of New York Press.

9 See, for example: Hurd, Shakman Elizabeth. 2010. "Appropriating Islam: The Islamic Other in the Consolidation of Western Modernity." *Critique: Critical Middle Eastern Studies* 12/1: 25–41.

10 'Europe' and the 'West' are much conflated in this regard. In a most basic sense, "Eurocentrism is a project to recentre the West, a project that is only possible when the West and the centre are no longer considered to be synonymous" (Sayyid, Bobby S. 1997. *A Fundamental Fear: Eurocentrism and the Emergence of Islamism*. London/New York: Zed Books, 128.) Five meanings of 'Eurocentrism' are distinguished in: Delanty, Gerard. 2006. "Modernity and the Escape from Eurocentrism." In *Handbook of Contemporary European Social Theory* ed. by Gerard Delanty: 266–278. London: Routledge, here 268.

11 For an overview of such arguments, see Pieterse, Jan Nederveen. 2006. "Oriental Globalization." *Theory, Culture & Society* 23/2–3: 411–413.

12 For a concise overview of this vast body of literature, see Schulz-Forberg, Hagen. 2014. "Introduction: Global Conceptual History: Promises and Pitfalls of a New Research Agenda." In *A Global Conceptual History of Asia, 1860–1940* ed. by Hagen Schulz-Forberg: 1–24. London: Pickering & Chatto, here 3–8.

human autonomy and mastery, in tension with social contingency –[13] only evolved in the "imperial encounter"[14] between Europeans and non-Europeans.

In addition to direct contact in the colonies, since the middle of the nineteenth century at the latest, there were significant global communicative networks,[15] even though the notion of a "global public sphere"[16] might exaggerate the degree of integration of this discourse. Moreover, in hindsight, we can discern commonalities between different elaborations of modern issues or *problématiques*, even though these had been articulated independently from each other. In any case, the European elaboration – or rather, one of several elaborations contested in Europe itself – of the modern self-understanding as "the commitment of modernity to autonomy and mastery"[17] became hegemonic.

This hegemonic European self-understanding[18] was significantly elaborated in the discipline of sociology, the major self-interpreting instance of modern European societies.[19] In 1977, Eckart Pankoke pointed to the importance of early modern discoveries of the "new world" and "natural peoples" for the evolution of the "sociological imagination" – namely, for questioning one's own societal order and for formulating universal social laws.[20] A collection of essays by Timo-

---

13 This widely shared conception of modernity as a certain self-understanding was developed in a most sophisticated manner by Peter Wagner; see esp.: Wagner, Peter. 2008. *Modernity as Experience and Interpretation.* Cambridge: Polity. Dietrich Jung and Kristine Sinclair draw principally on Wagner in developing a very fruitful theoretical framework for studying Muslim modernities. Their article only came to my attention after completing this study, with which it shares several premises and arguments: Jung, Dietrich, and Kristine Sinclair. 2015. "Multiple Modernities, Modern Subjectivities and Social Order: Unity and difference in the rise of Islamic modernities." *Thesis Eleven* 130/1: 22–42.

14 Van der Veer, Peter. 2001. *Imperial Encounters: Religion and Modernity in India and Britain.* Princeton, N.J.: Princeton University Press.

15 Even though such contacts also existed in earlier times, there is validity to the claim that they achieved a new quality in the nineteenth century, not least due to the spread of print capitalism.

16 Jung, Dietrich. 2011. *Orientalists, Islamists and the Global Public Sphere: a Genealogy of the Modern Essentialist Image of Islam.* Sheffield/Oakville: Equinox.

17 Wagner, "World-Sociology," 294.

18 For the sake of argumentation, and in order to avoid overly complicating matters, let us assume that there is something like a common European self-understanding. Differentiating between countries, classes, or any other categories would in the end lead to having to differentiate between individuals. Also, this self-understanding is not confined to Europeans, but shared by others.

19 See below: chapter 2 section 4.

20 Pankoke, Eckart. 1977. "Fortschritt und Komplexität. Die Anfänge moderner Sozialwissenschaft in Deutschland." In *Studien zum Beginn der modernen Welt* ed. by Reinhart Koselleck: 352–376. Stuttgart, here 354 f.

thy Mitchell substantiates the importance of colonialism, especially the colonial encounter in nineteenth- and twentieth-century Egypt,[21] for the evolution of the social sciences. In this process, Egyptian intellectuals drew on both European ideas and local discourses to develop their own conceptions of social sciences, as Omnia El Shakry has shown in a work building on Mitchell.[22] One may assume that the early modern process of discovery already induced similar questions among those people being discovered, to adopt Pankoke's premises. Since modernity proper only evolved in the colonial encounter, it seems clear that both colonizers and colonized people developed their understandings of modernity in and through that encounter.

(2) For modern European self-understanding – which is our focus for now – the narrative of secularization became crucial,[23] but in recent decades, it has lost its former status as a basically unquestioned paradigm. José Casanova authored what is probably the most influential deconstruction of secularization.[24] In his 1994 book *Public Religions in the Modern World*, Casanova distinguished three, often interwoven aspects of the paradigm: privatization of religion, decline of religious belief and practice, and differentiation of religion from other social spheres.[25] He argued that only the last aspect, social differentiation, could be maintained as a structural trend of modernity. The continuing relevance of religion in and for European societies has also now become widely acknowledged. Jürgen Habermas, the eminent secular[26] theoretician of the modern public sphere, expresses this acknowledgment[27] by characterizing these societies as

---

21 Mitchell, Timothy. 2002. *Rule of Experts: Egypt, Techno-Politics, Modernity.* Berkeley/Los Angeles/London: University of California Press.

22 El Shakry, Omnia. 2007. *The Great Social Laboratory: Subjects of Knowledge in Colonial and Postcolonial Egypt:* Stanford University Press.

23 For the genealogy of 'secularization,' see: Bremmer, Jan N. 2008. "Secularization. Notes Toward a Genealogy." In *Religion. Beyond a Concept* ed. by Hent de Vries: 432–437. New York: Fordham University Press; Borutta, Manuel. 2010. "Genealogie der Säkularisierungstheorie: Zur Historisierung einer großen Erzählung der Moderne." *Geschichte und Gesellschaft* 36: 347–376.

24 For a historical critique of secularization, see Clark, J. C. D. 2012. "Secularization and Modernization: The Failure of a 'Grand Narrative'." *The Historical Journal* 55/1: 161–194.

25 Casanova, José. 1994. *Public Religions in the Modern World.* Chicago: The University of Chicago Press.

26 Habermas said of himself that he had become "old but not pious" (Habermas, Jürgen. 2008. "Ich bin alt, aber nicht fromm geworden [Gespräch mit Michael Funken]." In *Über Habermas. Gespräche mit Zeitgenossen* ed. by Michael Funken: 181–190. Darmstadt: WBG, here 185).

27 Idem. 2001. *Glauben und Wissen. Friedenspreis des Deutschen Buchhandels 2001. Laudatio: Jan Philipp Reemtsma.* Frankfurt a.M.: Suhrkamp, 22; idem. 2001. "Einleitung." In *Zwischen Naturalismus und Religion. Philosophische Aufsätze:* 7–14. Frankfurt a.M.: Suhrkamp. I read Habermas as acknowledging not only a genealogical or temporary relevance of religions for the mod-

"post-secular."[28] Casanova, in turn, taking non-European societies into account as well, and in reaction to a critique by Talal Asad,[29] now also questions the universality of social differentiation as the core of modernity.[30]

As happens when a previously seemingly self-evident paradigm becomes questionable, some have even been calling for the wholesale abandonment of 'secularization.'[31] While these critical considerations motivate a reconceptualization rather than an abandonment of 'secularization,' the former standard sociological narrative and model concerning the relation between religion and society in modernity has forfeited much of its hegemonic standing. However, the basic categorical distinction between religion and society remains central to sociology and beyond, whether addressing European or non-European contexts.

(3) A major ongoing challenge for any analysis of non-European modern contexts consists of operative categories and concepts, insofar as these have largely been developed in, on, and for European history and societies. This challenge, which becomes ever more obvious as "the hegemony of the Western center

ern state, but the *continuing* relevance of religious positions. This reading has been put forward, for example, by Philipp, Thomas. 2009. "Gesellschaft und Religion. Eine kritische Auseinandersetzung mit Habermas' Zeitdiagnose der postsäkularen Gesellschaft." *Berliner Journal für Soziologie* 19/1: 55–78. For a contrasting reading, see: Endreß, Martin. 2011. "Postsäkulare Kultur'? Max Webers Soziologie und Habermas' Beitrag zur De-Säkularisierungsthese." In *Religionen verstehen. Zur Aktualität von Max Webers Religionssoziologie* ed. by Agathe Bienfait: 123–149. Wiesbaden: VS, esp. 131.

28 Habermas, "Glauben," 13. For an overview of the genealogy and various usages of the term 'postsecular,' see Beckford, James A. 2012. "SSSR Presidential Address: Public Religions and the Postsecular: Critical Reflections." *Journal for the Scientific Study of Religion* 51/1: 1–19.

29 Asad, Talal. 1999. "Religion, Nation-State, Secularism." In *Nation and Religion: Perspectives on Europe and Asia* ed. by Peter van der Veer and Hartmut Lehmann: 178–196. Princeton, NJ: Princeton University Press, here 179.

30 Casanova, José. 2008. "Public Religions Revisited." In *Religion. Beyond a Concept* ed. by Hent de Vries: 101–119. New York: Fordham University Press. On this point, see also, idem. 2006. "Rethinking Secularization: A Global Comparative Perspective." *The Hedgehog Review* 8/1–2: 7–22, esp. 9 f.

31 For an overview of such calls, see Gorski, Philip S. and Altınordu, Ateş. 2008. "After Secularization?." *Annual Review of Sociology* 34/1: 55–85. Gorski and Altınordu themselves argue that secularization may still, albeit with greater caution, be useful for integrating and relating a range of seemingly unconnected phenomena (ibid., 75 f.). See also Bruce, Steve. 2011. *Secularization: In Defence of an Unfashionable Theory.* Oxford: Oxford University Press. Peter Berger no longer defends the paradigm of secularization in general but maintains its continuous validity for Western Europe and a global, Westernized, elite culture (Berger, Peter. 1999. "Introduction." In *The Desecularization of the World. Resurgent Religion and World Politics* ed. by Peter Berger: 1–18. Washington, D.C.: Ethics and Public Policy Center, here 2, 9 f.).

of the world system wanes, and with it that of metropolitan social theory,"[32] has already been extensively addressed concerning the category of religion and the concept of 'religion,'[33] the normative claim of which is rather obvious. It is true in general that "[c]ategories are not simply containers of thought: they have an effect on the contents."[34] The power mechanisms at work in designating certain beliefs or practices as 'religion' and thus assigning them to the category of religion should be clear, not least in the legal and political consequences this entails.

Arguably less visible – but equally powerful and part of the same operation of constructing religion – is the construction of a secular realm, which is not a neutral sphere either, but is rather equally loaded with normative claims.[35] Post-colonial critics are joined by some European Christian theologians[36] in challenging claims to the neutrality and universality of the secular. Secular theoreticians have come to partly acknowledge the critique of a secular bias in social

---

32 Arjomand, Saïd Amir and Schäfer, Wolfgang. 2014. "Foreword: Pangaea II: Global/Local Studies." In *Social Theory and Regional Studies in the Global Age* ed. by Saïd Amir Arjomand: xi–xii. Albany: State University of New York Press, here xi.)

33 From among the vast literature on the matter, I want to highlight here the following works (in chronological order): Asad, Talal. 1993. *Genealogies of Religion: Discipline and Reasons of Power in Christianity and Islam.* Baltimore/London: The Johns Hopkins University Press; Balagangadhara, S. N. 1994. *"The Heathen in his Blindness...:" Asia, the West, and the Dynamic of Religion.* Leiden: Brill; Chidester, David. 1996. *Savage Systems: Colonialism and Comparative Religion in Southern Africa.* Charlottesivilee: University of Virginia Press; King, Richard. 1999. *Orientalism and Religion: Postcolonial Theory, India and the Mystic East.* London: Routledge; Dubuisson, Daniel. 2003. *The Western Construction of Religion: Myths, Knowledge and Ideology*; transl. William Sayers. Baltimore: Johns Hopkins University Press; Masuzawa, Tomoko. 2005. *The Invention of World Religions.* Chicago: Chicago University Press; Schalk, Peter (ed.). 2013. *Religion in Asien? Studien zur Anwendbarkeit des Religionsbegriffs.* Uppsala: Uppsala Universitet.

34 Godart, Gerard Clinton. 2008. "'Philosophy' or 'Religion'? The Confrontation with Foreign Categories in Late Nineteenth-Century Japan." *Journal of the History of Ideas* 69/1: 71–91, here 71.

35 Whether taking the secular or religion as a starting point, the constructed nature of the complementary category inevitably comes into view. For an eminent example of the first approach, see: Asad, Talal. 2008 [2003]. *Formations of the Secular: Christianity, Islam, Modernity.* Stanford: Stanford University Press, esp. 1–2; for the second, see: Fitzgerald, Timothy. 2000. *The Ideology of Religious Studies.* New York/ Oxford: Oxford University Press, esp. 5f., 8; idem. 2007. "Introduction." In *Religion and the Secular. Historical and Colonial Formations* ed. by Timothy Fitzgerald: 1–24. London/Oakville: equinox, esp. 7.

36 A powerful expression of this can be found in: Milbank, John. 1991. *Theology and Social Theory: Beyond Secular Reason.* Cambridge, Mass.: B. Blackwell. This book can be regarded as the founding text of Radical Orthodoxy. For examples of post-colonial critics, see the previous footnote.

and political theory.[37] If this bias affected the understanding of European societies, this seems even more true for non-European societies. To overcome this bias concerning Islamic contexts, some have raised the need for particular theoretical approaches. Calls for a sociology of Islam are a case in point, even though the exact approaches that fall under this heading differ greatly: some adhere to the idea of Islam as the Other of secular Western modernity,[38] while others aim at overcoming this contrast.[39] A similar distinction could be made among calls for an Islamic sociology, voiced by Muslim scholars.[40] In any case, particularism offers no convincing remedy for the secular bias and false universalism of European social theory, as such particularism is not only "paralyzing,"[41] but also mistaken, in view of the factual integration of the modern world.

The hegemony of European categories of knowledge and order is crucial for this factual integration – and whether one deplores this or not, we cannot write power out of history. I somehow picture Aziz al-Azmeh shrugging his shoulders when he states: "I take it as an accomplished fact that modern history is characterized by the globalization of the Western order."[42] Indeed, "one of the greatest changes in the intellectual history of the non-Western world was the grand reclassification of ideas into categories adopted from the West during the nine-

37 The concept of 'post-secular' mentioned above is a case in point. As another example, Hurd has shown how a secular bias in political theory led to misconceiving international relations (Hurd, Elizabeth Shakman. 2008. *The Politics of Secularism in International Relations*. Princeton: Princeton University Press).

38 See the discussion in Bracke, Sarah and Fadil, Nadia. 2008. *Islam and Secular Modernity under Western Eyes: A Genealogy of a Constitutive Relationship*. San Domenico di Fiesole: European University Institute, 4f. It should be clear that the actual lifeworlds of people identifying themselves as Muslims can combine religious and secular elements in manifold ways; see, for example: Gramling, David. 2012. "'You Pray like We have Fun:' Toward a Phenomenology of Secular Islam." In *Migration and Religion: Christian Transatlantic Missions, Islamic Migration to Germany* ed. by Barbara Becker-Cantarino: 175–191. Amsterdam/New York: Rodopi.

39 See, for example, Salvatore, Armando. 2013. "The Sociology of Islam: Precedents and Perspectives." *Sociology of Islam* 1: 7–13.

40 For example, Ba-Yunus, Ilyas and Ahmad, Farid. 1985. *Islamic Sociology: An Introduction*. London: Hodder & Stoughton; Younos, Farid. 2011. *Principles of Islamic Sociology*. Bloomington, IN: AuthorHouse; al-Samaluti, Nabil. 1970. *al-Manhaj al-Islami fi Dirasat al-Mujtama': Dirasat fi 'Ilm al-Ijtima' al-Islami*. Cairo: Dar al-Shuruq; Isma'il, Zaki Muhammad. 1981. *Nahwa 'Ilm al-Ijtima' al-Islami*. Alexandria: Dar al-Matbu'at al-Jadida; al-Fawal, Salah Mustafa. 2000. *al-Madkhal li-'Ilm al-Ijtima' al-Islami*. Cairo: Dar Gharuba li-l-Tiba'a wa-l-Nashr wa-l-Tawzi'. For an overview of additional contributions, see: Edipoğlu, Kerim. 2007. "Islamische Soziologie: Menschen- und Gesellschaftsbild." *Zeitschrift für Religionswissenschaft* 15/2: 131–153.

41 Bracke and Fadil, *Islam*, 8.

42 Al-Azmeh, Aziz. 1996. *Islams and Modernities*. London/New York: Verso, 80.

teenth century."[43] By now it has become almost impossible to make sense of non-European contexts without resorting to categories that are most markedly elaborated in European thought.[44] (I wish to reiterate here that these European categories themselves did not plainly evolve 'internally,' but were significantly shaped in the colonial encounter.) Regarding 'religion,' for example, José Casanova has pointed to the paradox that "scholars of religion are questioning the validity of the category of 'religion' at the very moment when the discursive reality of religion is more widespread than ever and has become for the first time global."[45] Against claims that analyses of non-European societies require different categories altogether, it thus seems more feasible – especially within the setting of a secular university – to try to integrate European and non-European trajectories and experiences into a more global understanding of modernity, and also to tentatively depart from categories of European modernity in developing such an integrative account.[46]

2 The Historicity and Normativity of 'Society'

More specifically, I deem it promising to attend to the very concepts carrying and expressing these categories and ideas, such as 'religion' and 'society,' to trace how they have travelled between thinkers, languages, and regions, and to discern how they have been understood and put to use in different (con-)texts. This line of inquiry only makes sense when the concept under consideration can plausibly be expected in the texts under study. The very relevance of identifying concepts of (European) modernity in a given (non-European) text results from the fact that these are not merely analytical, but historical and normative concepts.

---

43 Godart, "'Philosophy'," 71.

44 This has been stressed in a general sense by: Kaviraj, Sudipta and Khilnani, Sunil. 2001. "Introduction: Ideas of Civil Society." In *Civil Society: History and Possibilities* ed. by Sudipta Kaviraj and Sunil Khilnani: 1–8. Cambridge: Cambridge University Press, here 4 f.

45 Casanova, José. 2011. "The Secular, Secularizations, Secularisms." In *Rethinking Secularism* ed. by Craig Calhoun, Mark Juergensmeyer and Jonathan VanAntwerpen: 54–74. Oxford: Oxford University Press, here 62. For a fascinating example illustrating the sometimes very concrete occasions necessitating the translation of 'religion,' see Godart, "'Philosophy'," esp. 74 f.

46 In this regard, I share the approach formulated in: Arjomand, Saïd Amir. 2014. "Introduction. The Challenge of Integrating Social Theory and Regional Studies." In *Social Theory and Regional Studies in the Global Age* ed. by Saïd Amir Arjomand: 1–20. Albany: State University of New York Press, here 3. But for a criticism of this volume, see above: 3fn8.

This study considers the concept of 'society' as fundamental to and constitutive of the modern self-understanding most markedly developed in Europe. Only in modernity did men and women imagine their lives as ordered in and by society. To inquire into equivalents and alternatives to 'society' in non-European languages and thought is thus to ask whether the thinkers under consideration shared this modern self-understanding.

While I will elaborate on the normativity and historicity of 'society' in the second chapter of this study, some basic considerations might be helpful at this stage. It is quite true that 'society' has come to be used independently from its historical roots and its normative core, referring to very different social formations, such as 'feudal' or even 'monolithic societies.' While we do need language in the end, such seemingly descriptive usages of 'society' contain the danger of misunderstanding the social formation under study. This is also why sociologists attributing epistemological importance to the historical institution of 'society' are wary of using the term when speaking of pre-modern social formations.[47] At the very least, it is important not to conflate a (seemingly) descriptive usage of 'society' with the understanding pre-modern women and men themselves had of their social formations. The sociologist Armin Nassehi implicitly makes this distinction when he stresses the specifically modern self-understanding expressed by the concept of 'society': "[T]he fact that societies describe themselves *as societies* and not simply as world or order of creation or the like, is already a sign of their modernity. *As society* in the end means nothing other than that the living-together of human beings, their *form of association* becomes problematic unto itself, because it obviously had become shapeable."[48] In an important sense then, a social formation can be meaningfully designated as 'society' when its justification and organization has become a matter of continuous debate.

Therefore, when dealing with how pre-modern men and women have understood their social formation, a heuristic employment of 'society' is preferable to a (seemingly) descriptive or analytical one. This more cautious approach avoids imposing our own concepts, and thus our own epistemology, on contexts differing in these regards. Employing a present-day concept in a heuristic sense aims at making aspects of such different contexts understandable to us, while simul-

---

47 They thus question the assumption made by other sociologists, such as Talcott Parsons, that society was conceptualized only in modernity, but as an idea had already existed (Wagner, *A History*, 138.)

48 Nassehi, Armin. 2001. "Moderne Gesellschaft." In *Klassische Gesellschaftsbegriffe der Soziologie* ed. by Georg Kneer, Armin Nassehi and Markus Schroer: 208 – 245. München: Wilhelm Fink, here 209; transl. F.Z., all emphases in the original.

taneously asking how they were understood there and then, and thus identifying possible functional or substantial equivalents or alternatives to this present concept. Regarding historical processes, we may in this vein, and only in hindsight, trace kernels of our present concepts back to a certain historical point before which they no longer make sense. This procedure, which amounts to a "regressive genealogy,"[49] is markedly different from identifying the supposed roots and origins of our present concepts and tracing their evolution *forward* in time – forward from a wrongly assumed founding moment, that is.[50]

A different approach is again advisable when dealing with modern contexts for which the conceptualization of a certain idea, such as society, can plausibly be expected. Here, we have the basic choice between two well-known alternatives – namely, between using 'society' as an analytical or as an object category.[51] In the first case, we must work out the criteria for identifying textual passages as addressing society. This might seem obvious but is often neglected, supposedly assuming a somewhat implicit consensus on the meanings of 'society.' Since 'society' is a historical and normative category, I generally deem the alternative more fruitful – namely, to discern how the authors under consideration have themselves employed this concept. However, this procedure is again complicated when dealing with sources written in another language, especially when the correspondence of concepts in that language with 'society' is not yet

---

49 Reinhard Schulze, drawing upon Nietzsche and Foucault, has elaborated this approach concerning the concept of 'religion' in the Islamic tradition (Schulze, Reinhard. 2015. *Der Koran und die Genealogie des Islam*. Basel: Schwabe Verlag, esp. 109 ff., 117 f.; the original reads "rückläufige/restrospektive Genealogie"). For a brief mention of this argument in English, see: idem. 2016. "The Quest for the West in an Era of Globalization: Some Remarks on the Hidden Meaning of Charles Taylor's Master Narrative." In *Working with A Secular Age. Interdisciplinary Perspectives on Charles Taylor's Master Narrative* ed. by Florian Zemmin, Colin Jager and Guido Vanheeswijck: 175–203. Berlin/Boston: De Gruyter, esp. 191–197.

50 A rather explicit example in this regard, which moreover employs the notion of Islam as a separate entity, is: Black, Antony. 2011. *The History of Islamic Political Thought: from the Prophet to the Present*. Edinburgh: Edinburgh University Press. In a more subtle way, since the primary interest is in present appropriations of different "heritages," this understanding also informs: Cook, Michael. 2014. *Ancient Religions, Modern Politics. The Islamic Case in Comparative Perspective*. Princeton/Oxford: Princeton University Press. For the problems involved in locating 'religion' and 'state' in early Islamic history and the establishment of this view in nineteenth-century European historiography, see: Asad, Talal. 1997. "Europe against Islam: Islam in Europe." *The Muslim World* 87/2: 183–195, esp. 190 f.

51 Concerning early modern England, two studies nicely illustrate these alternatives: the first uses 'society' as an analytical category, the second as an object category: Clark, Peter. 2000. *British Clubs and Societies*. Oxford: Clarendon; Withington, Phil. 2010. *Society in Early Modern England. The Vernacular Origins of Some Powerful Ideas*. Cambridge, Malden/Mass.: Polity.

established. Here, as will become clear, attention to object categories has to be complemented by pre-configuring the concept under consideration.

3 Conceptual History of Another Language

The pioneering volume *A Global Conceptual History of Asia, 1860–1940*, edited by Hagen Schulz-Forberg,[52] combines attention to the globalization of concepts with a commitment to a polycentric conception of modernity. I cite this volume here because, firstly, my own study fills a research gap formulated therein and, secondly, because the considerations underlying my own approach become clearer in contrast with the procedure undertaken in that volume. The volume departs from a "polycentric, entangled approach," according to which "colonial modernities have been just as constitutional of European modernities as vice versa."[53] Eastern concepts have influenced Western concepts as much as the other way around, Schulz-Forberg maintains, and one should not always have to stress this reciprocity when dealing with the influence of one context upon another. This volume specifically traces how European "concepts of the social and the economic" have moved into different Asian languages.

Whether in Korean,[54] Chinese (via Japanese),[55] Malay,[56] Indonesian,[57] Siamese,[58] or Arabic,[59] European concepts of 'the social' and 'the economic' played a

52 Schulz-Forberg, Hagen (ed.). 2014. *A Global Conceptual History of Asia, 1860–1940.* London: Pickering & Chatto. See also the following reader, published after the completion of this study: Pernau, Margrit and Sachsenmeier, Dominic (eds.). 2016. *Global Conceptual History: A Reader.* London et al.: Bloomsbury.

53 Schulz-Forberg, "Introduction," 21.

54 Park, Myoung-Kyu. 2014. "How Concepts Met History in Korea's Complex Modernization: New Concepts of Economy and Society and their Impact." In *A Global Conceptual History of Asia, 1860–1940* ed. by Hagen Schulz-Forberg: 25–42. London: Pickering & Chatto.

55 Sachsenmeier, Dominic. 2014. "Notions of Society in Early Twentieth-Century China, 1900–25." In *A Global Conceptual History of Asia, 1860–1940* ed. by Hagen Schulz-Forberg: 61–74. London: Pickering & Chatto; Tian, Hailong. 2014. "Differing Translations, Contested Meanings: A Motor for the 1911 Revolution in China?." In *A Global Conceptual History of Asia, 1860–1940* ed. by Hagen Schulz-Forberg: 43–60. London: Pickering & Chatto.

56 Pannu, Paula. 2014. "From *Kerajaan* (Kingship) to *Masyarakat* (The People): Malay Articulations of Nationhood through Concepts of the 'Social' and the 'Economic', 1920–40." In *A Global Conceptual History of Asia, 1860–1940* ed. by Hagen Schulz-Forberg: 111–128. London: Pickering & Chatto.

57 Avonius, Leena. 2014. "Building Nation and Society in the 1920s Dutch East Indies." In *A Global Conceptual History of Asia, 1860–1940* ed. by Hagen Schulz-Forberg: 129–148. London: Pickering & Chatto.

formative role in the modern quest for social order. Schulz-Forberg repeatedly emphasizes that these European concepts did not simply diffuse to other parts of the world, but rather were appropriated quite consciously and very differently by local actors.[60] The case studies then illustrate such different ways of appropriation, which in fact serve as the *tertium comparationis* of his volume.[61] European concepts were employed to serve different interests, contested in meaning, connected to different related concepts, and creatively interwoven with vernacular concepts. Stressing these creative appropriations of European concepts and conceiving of modernity as a shared historical condition, global conceptual history aims at "establishing a transnational epistemological horizon, towards which European and Asian conceptualizations of society and economics are related on an equal basis."[62]

In her chapter "The Conceptualization of the Social in Late Nineteenth- and Early Twentieth-Century Arabic Thought and Language," Ilham Khuri-Makdisi focuses on Arab Christian, somewhat secular[63] thinkers based in Beirut and Cairo, who are known for their reception and mediation of European thought – namely, Butrus al-Bustani (d. 1883), Salama Musa (d. 1958), and, above all, Shibli Shumayyil (d. 1917). In a very learned and dense analysis, Khuri-Makdisi shows how these thinkers linked ideas of the social and of society to ideas of civilization, progress, the nation, (political) economy, reform, and justice. Khuri-Makdisi's identification of ideas of society and the social, however, does not always seem to be based on specific terms conceptualizing these ideas. I limit myself here to a discussion of her findings regarding such terms.

58 Meyer, Morakot Jewachinda. 2014. "Discordant Localizations of Modernity: Reflections on Concepts of the Economic and the Social in Siam during the Early Twentieth Century." In *A Global Conceptual History of Asia, 1860–1940* ed. by Hagen Schulz-Forberg: 149–168. London: Pickering & Chatto.

59 Khuri-Makdisi, Ilham. 2014. "The Conceptualization of the Social in Late Nineteenth- and Early Twentieth-Century Arabic Thought and Language." In *A Global Conceptual History of Asia, 1860–1940* ed. by Hagen Schulz-Forberg: 91–110. London: Pickering & Chatto.

60 Schulz-Forberg, "Introduction," 11, 13, 20. This point had already been made earlier; see, for example: Montgomery, Scott. 2000. *Science in Translation: Movements of Knowledge through Cultures and Time.* Chicago/London: The University of Chicago Press; Howland, Douglas. 2001. *Translating the West: Language and Political Reason in Nineteenth-Century Japan.* Honolulu: University of Hawaii Press; Richter, Melvin. 2005. "More Than a Two-Way Traffic: Analyzing, Translating, and Comparing Political Concepts from other Cultures." In *Redescriptions. Yearbook of Political Thought and Conceptual History* 9: 217–228.

61 Schulz-Forberg, "Introduction," 15.

62 Ibid., 24.

63 She notes that the label 'secular' might possibly be problematic in this context (Khuri-Makdisi, "The Conceptualization," 92).

According to Khuri-Makdisi, the social came to be conceptualized with the adjective *ijtimāʿī/ya* and the noun *ijtimāʿ*[64] in the 1860s, but at first mainly appeared as part of the composite *al-hayʾa al-ijtimāʿiyya*, which she translates as "the social body/social configuration." By the 1890s, however, "the social starts to stand out, and to stand conceptually on its own,"[65] and by 1908, it had even become an unavoidable concept.[66] For expressing the idea of society, *al-hayʾa al-ijtimāʿiyya* arguably remained the most widely used term throughout her period of study.[67] Concerning the concept of 'society,' she finds that "the term that is presently used to refer to society, *mujtamaʿ* [...], while not completely absent in that period, seems to have become dominant in the 1930s to early 1940s."[68] Her selection of thinkers appropriating European ideas of the social is in itself, of course, perfectly justified, even though it then amounts to a truism to identify familiarity with European and American ideas and languages as a crucial factor contributing to the prominence of 'the social.'[69] In any case, Khuri-Makdisi explicates the absence of Islamic reformists, such as Muhammad ʿAbduh and Rashid Rida, as the most "glaring" gap resulting from her selection of thinkers.[70]

4 The Contribution and Main Argument of This Book

As its most concrete contribution, this study fills the above-mentioned "glaring" research gap by attending to the concept of 'society' in the journal *al-Manar*, which Rashid Rida founded in Cairo in 1898 and edited until his death in 1935, and to which Muhammad ʿAbduh (d. 1905) also contributed significantly. *Al-Manar* is widely considered to be the mouthpiece of the intellectual trend known as 'Islamic modernism' or 'Islamic reformism.' While the latter label is somewhat more blurry than the former, I do prefer it, since it is closer to the reformists' own terminology.[71]

---

64 Ibid., 99.
65 Ibid., 99.
66 Ibid., 110.
67 Ibid., 187fn6.
68 Ibid., 187fn6.
69 Ibid., 99.
70 Ibid., 92.
71 The stress on the need for *iṣlāḥ* (reform) and the self-designation as *muṣliḥūn* (reformers) is ubiquitous in *al-Manar*. On the concept of *iṣlāḥ*, see: Voll, John O. 1983. "Renewal and Reform in Islamic History: *Tajdid* and *Islah*." In *Voices of Resurgent Islam* ed. by John L. Esposito: 32–47. New York/Oxford: Oxford University Press. The label 'Islamic modernism' was coined in analogy to Catholic modernism in the 1930s, mainly implying a harmonization of science and religion

Speaking of the authors of *al-Manar* as "the Islamic reformists," as I shall do from here on, is not to suggest that they were a homogeneous group or that they encompassed the whole spectrum of reformism, although they certainly stand in for the one trend that became dominant in the colonial period.[72] And I speak of "Islamic" instead of "Muslim" reformists, since I am concerned less with their personal identity as Muslims, but rather with the Islamic framing of their public discourse.

Islamic reformism is usually situated between traditionalism on the one hand and secularism on the other. Although the names assigned to these intellectual trends vary, the underlying logic remains the same: traditionalists wanted to preserve Islam as it was, ignoring modern challenges altogether; secularists oriented themselves toward the Western model, distancing themselves from Islamic tradition; and the reformists, occupying a middle ground, allegedly aimed at combining Islamic tradition with certain aspects of modernity.

This common classification, which will be dealt with in greater detail in chapter 5 section 3, is problematic in two respects. Firstly, it is formulated from the normative perspective of the reformists themselves, quite possibly inspired by self-descriptions found in *al-Manar*.[73] A second difficulty lies in the notions of Islam and modernity upon which the whole classification rests, as this

---

(Schulze, Reinhard. 2000. "Is there an Islamic Modernity?." In *The Islamic World and the West: An Introduction to Political Cultures and International Relations* ed. by Kai Hafez: 21–32. Leiden: Brill, here 23 f.; Elshakry, Marwa. 2013. *Reading Darwin in Arabic, 1860–1950*. London: The University of Chicago Press, 164). Subsequently, this term has been used for a range of trends (see: Masud, Muhammad Khalid. 2009. "Islamic Modernism." In *Islam and Modernity. Key Issues and Debates* ed. by Muhammad Khalid Masud, Armando Salvatore and Martin van Bruinessen: 237–260. Edinburgh: Edinburgh University Press, here 237 f.).

72 For eighteenth-century attempts at reform, see: Dallal, Ahmad S. 2010. "The Origins and Early Development of Islamic Reform." In *The New Cambridge History of Islam; vol 6: Muslims and Modernity; Culture and Society since 1800* ed. by Robert W. Hefner: 107–147. Cambridge: Cambridge University Press. For commonalities and differences between ʿAbduh, Rida, and other Islamic reformists (self-)designated as *salafiyya*, see: Griffel, Frank. 2015. "What Do We Mean By 'Salafī'? Connecting Muḥammad ʿAbduh with Egypt's Nūr Party in Islam's Contemporary Intellectual History." *Die Welt des Islams* 55: 186–220, esp. 213–218. For a critique of Griffel's treatment of *salafiyya* and 'salafism' as an analytical concept, see: Lauzière, Henry. 2016. "What We Mean Versus What They Meant by 'Salafi': A Reply to Frank Griffel." *Die Welt des Islams* 56: 89–96. For a comment on this debate, see now: Zemmin, Florian. 2018. "Wider die islamische Exzeptionalität: Zur (Inter-)Disziplinarität der Islamwissenschaft am Beispiel des Salafismus." In *Islam in der Moderne, Moderne im Islam. Eine Festschrift für Reinhard Schulze zum 65. Geburtstag* ed. by Florian Zemmin, Johannes Stephan and Monica Corrado: 159–186. Leiden/Boston: Brill, here 178 ff.

73 For references, see below: chapter 5 section 3.

presupposes a certain – albeit bridgeable – gap between Islamic tradition and (Western) modernity. Muslim thinkers appear more traditional the more they refer to Islam and more modern (and more Westernized) the more they approve of certain norms and values associated with (Western) modernity, such as freedom of science, gender equality, or a parliamentary system. Yet such specific norms and values can hardly be taken as definitive of modernity.

Attempts at more fundamental understandings of the process of Islamic reform mirrored in *al-Manar* stress its relation of religion to society. However, as I will substantiate in chapter 5 section 4, nowhere does any author explicate how they identified society in that Arabic journal – via a pre-configured understanding of 'society' or via Arabic terms for 'society.' This makes it even more relevant to identify the concept of 'society' in *al-Manar*. After all, my introductory considerations so far have stressed this relevance in relation to theories and (self-)understandings of modernity. From another angle, then, a critical assessment of the vast body of literature on *al-Manar* lends additional relevance to the project of discerning the concept of 'society' in *al-Manar*.

My main argument is that the authors writing regularly for *al-Manar* – and especially the journal's editor, Rashid Rida – employed the term *umma* as an equivalent and also alternative to the concept of 'society.' This is not to say that *umma* came to mean 'society,' but rather that the Islamic reformists conceptualized the modern idea of society with *umma*, which was a very flexible term at the time. In a period during which no single Arabic term for 'society' had yet been established, Rida avoided the terms predominantly used by secular thinkers and associated with the hegemonic European understanding of society – namely, *mujtamaʿ* and *al-hayʾa al-ijtimāʿiyya*. While English and French were "prestige languages"[74] for these thinkers, for Rida classical Arabic was the prestige language of Islam. Thus he tried to express the most constitutive concept of modernity – 'society' – from within the Islamic discursive tradition,[75] of which *umma* is firmly a part. Shifting between secular and religious connotations,

74 Karttunen, Klaus. 2014. "Sabhā-Samāj Society: Some Linguistic Considerations." In *A Global Conceptual History of Asia, 1860–1940* ed. by Hagen Schulz-Forberg: 75–90. London: Pickering & Chatto, here 77.

75 I here draw on Talal Asad's understanding of Islam as a discursive tradition: "An Islamic discursive tradition is simply a tradition of Muslim discourse that addresses itself to conceptions of the Islamic past and future, with reference to a particular Islamic practice in the present" (Asad, Talal. 1986. *The Idea of an Anthropology of Islam*. Washington, D.C.: Centre for Contemporary Arab Studies, Georgetown University, 14). This text has been reprinted: idem. 2009. "The Idea of an Anthropology of Islam." *Qui Parle* 17/2: 1–30. For a discussion, see: Anjum, Ovamir. 2007. "Islam as a Discursive Tradition: Talal Asad and His Interlocutors." *Comparative Studies of South Asia, Africa and the Middle East* 27/3: 656–672.

the concept of *umma* combined features of 'society' and aspects ideal-typically associated with 'community.' *Umma* was also the dominant term used to conceptualize the nation, and since the society to which *umma* refers is genealogical and value-based, 'society' is closely linked to (an Islamic) 'nation.' This I read as an attempt to conceive of modernity within Islamic tradition.

While the sub-arguments and individual findings of this study are given in the summaries of the individual chapters at the end of this introduction, it illustrates my conceptual approach to say here that my main argument emerged from what constitutes the first half of the empirical part of this study – namely, a comprehensive analysis of the supposedly pertinent terms for 'society,' *al-hay'a al-ijtimāʿiyya* and *mujtamaʿ*. This analysis also produced significant insights concerning these terms themselves, partly confirming and partly modifying Khuri-Makdisi's findings. Today's Arabic term for 'society,' *mujtamaʿ*, had already acquired its modern meaning by the end of the nineteenth century. In 248 of its 358 occurrences in *al-Manar*, *mujtamaʿ* refers to society as an overall social sphere or as an abstract entity, thus outpacing the composite *al-hay'a al-ijtimāʿiyya*, which occurs 142 times. This finding reverses Khuri-Makdisi's estimation regarding the currency of both terms.

5 The Approach of This Study: A Heuristic Eurocentrism

More fundamental than correcting some of Khuri-Makdisi's concrete estimations are the important differences between her approach and my own, as well as between the considerations underlying my study and those formulated by Schulz-Forberg in the introduction to the anthology of which Khuri-Makdisi's chapter is a part. I do want to stress that I am critically engaging with a selection of their arguments and considerations here, for the sake of elucidating my own approach. This would not be possible without a certain affinity with, and certainly a high esteem for, their approach. Clearly, some of these differences are due to the disciplinary approach from which I came to the subject matter[76] and the debates informing my approach. In the following discussion, I therefore also intro-

76 The contributors to the anthology edited by Schulz-Forberg come from different disciplines; the volume is presented as contributing to the field of global history (Schulz-Forberg, "Introduction," 1) but having "disciplinary roots within the interpretive sciences of philosophy, hermeneutics and literary criticism" (ibid., 9).

duce the implications of the three above-mentioned aspects concerning the identification of modernity with a secular West for this study.[77]

Directly engaging with Schulz-Forberg's and Khuri-Makdisi's contributions, but also deviating into more general discussions, I shall make the following five arguments: (1) The global conceptual history approach[78] only works when a correspondence between terms in two or more languages is established. (2) We need to distinguish a concept from a word/term as well as from the idea(s) it is expressing. Only then can we identify terms and concepts that correspond to the established ones. (3) Inevitably, we have to depart from European conceptualizations of society in order to identify possible equivalents in an Arabic discourse. (4) As the concept of 'society' is not a neutral one but expresses the hegemonic understanding of modernity, this procedure amounts to a heuristic Eurocentrism, which acknowledges that a purely descriptive conception of modernity is impossible. (5) While this heuristic Eurocentrism might be of a temporal nature and possibly give way to a more polycentric understanding of modernity, no academic study can avoid its *academicentrism*.

These five arguments combined result in the guiding thread of this study, which consists of interrogating the hegemonic academic understanding of 'society' for the purpose of investigating to what extent this understanding was present in the context of *al-Manar* and was, via Arabic equivalents to 'society,' voiced by the authors of the journal themselves. After having elucidated my approach via the above-mentioned five arguments, I will lay out how this guiding thread manifests itself in the structure of this book.

(1) A central precondition for the global conceptual history approach is "robust connections between historical spaces and languages," which allow us to look "at concepts as embedded in transnational and local discourses and semantic fields."[79] These connections – which were certainly present between France, England, and Egypt in the second half of the nineteenth century – thus allow us to trace how certain concepts travelled between languages and were put to use by different actors. This entails a focus on those non-European actors who were most closely in contact with Europeans and who most explicitly appropriated European thought. However, Schulz-Forberg stresses that, for example, "merely following the English concept of self-determination through a va-

---

77 Schulz-Forberg foregrounds the first of these three aspects. While the third aspect somewhat implicitly informs the volume he edited, the second one seems to be mostly absent.

78 Also, when speaking of "global conceptual history" in a general sense, it is the volume edited by Schulz-Forberg I am referring to.

79 Ibid., 10.

riety of source material and checking its appearance in foreign languages does not provide a sufficient level of sophistication. The Korean expression for – or equivalent to – self-determination must be taken into account as well."[80] The meaning of a concept will always differ between two languages, but Schulz-Forberg rhetorically asks, "[D]o we need complete symmetry to compare?"[81]

While I agree that we do not need such symmetry, the question remains as to how we identify the terms to compare in the first place. This seems rather unproblematic when dealing with related languages – for example, comparing meanings of *société* with those of 'society.'[82] It also is highly plausible for languages from different language groups if the term(s) corresponding to one's own are rather clearly established. In Arabic, however, *mujtamaʿ* only came to be established as corresponding with 'society' after the Second World War. What about other possible terms that could be compared with 'society' before then? Might these terms have been alternatives for conceptualizing the idea of society before the appropriation of the European concept of 'society' became hegemonic and standardized for expressing this idea? Did the idea of society, then, which is crucial to the modern self-understanding, only evolve in Europe and travel to other regions? Or did it also evolve elsewhere? Or, as a third possibility, was it established in a shared discourse in which the European concept of 'society' then became hegemonic?

(2) Attending to these questions requires, as a first step, distinguishing a concept from a word/term as well as from the idea(s) it expresses. To distinguish between a term/word and a concept, I follow the pragmatic approach of Adi Ophir, according to whom any word can be turned into a concept by problematizing its meaning.[83] In this sense, basic concepts are those words that can be most fruitfully turned into concepts. When they are at the center of debates and are hotly disputed, they are hardly usable as mere words. However, as established terms, they can well be used as mere words. Here 'society' is a primary example, as it became the generic term for social collectivities, but its normative connotations can still be brought to light by problematizing its meanings. One important aspect to consider is whether the authors under consideration have

---

80 Ibid., 9.
81 Ibid., 14
82 A comparison of closely related terms also naturally produces differences; see, for example, the different meanings of 'liberalism,' *liberalisme*, and *Liberalismus:* Leonhard, Jörn. 2001. *Liberalismus: Zur historischen Semantik eines europäischen Deutungsmusters.* München: Oldenbourg.
83 Ophir, Adi. 2011. "Concept." *Political Concepts – A Critical Lexicon* 1. http://www.politicalconcepts.org/2011/concept (accessed March 20, 2015).

themselves turned into concepts those terms that I am turning into concepts, or whether they have used them as mere words. Ophir's pragmatic distinction circumvents many problems inherent in the seemingly endless philosophical and hermeneutical attempts to consistently distinguish between word and concept.

The relation between concept and idea also needs to be addressed. The fact that Khuri-Makdisi does not explicate this relation makes it difficult to understand parts of her argument. She uses 'concept' to refer to both the idea or notion of the social and the term 'the social.'[84] Therefore, it remains somewhat unclear whether she takes the very idea of the social as developing during her period of study, or whether she wants to argue that a new concept of 'the social' was introduced into previously existing discourses on the social. And are these discourses thought to have evolved at an earlier historical moment, or are they considered a timeless anthropological given? I argue that not only the concept of 'the social' or 'society,' but also the idea of the social or society is historically contingent.[85]

As in the previous sentence, when I speak of a 'concept,' this refers to the concrete term, the meanings of which are under consideration. The ideas it expresses or the function it fulfills can also be expressed or fulfilled by other terms, some of which I am not turning into concepts. It seems logical to assume that an idea evolved before it was conceptualized – that is, before new meanings were expressed with an existing term or a new term was coined to that end. In hindsight, we may trace kernels of a certain idea back to a time before its conceptualization. However, in the end, it is much more convincing to claim that a historical person held this idea themselves, if they did conceptualize it. Importantly, they might have conceptualized this idea with a different term than the one that was eventually established.

(3) Therefore, we need to investigate the evolution of our present concept in order to identify equivalent concepts in another language that express the same essential ideas or answer to the same *problématique* – that is, fulfill the same function.[86] Herein lies a major difference from conceptual histories written in the same language as their source material. In that case, one can depart from a specific term, identify its etymology, and retrace its usages and meanings in

84 For example, Khuri-Makdisi, "The Conceptualization," 92, 110.

85 Khuri-Makdisi might well agree with this argument, although I could not discern it from her text.

86 For an exemplary study departing from the function of a concept to identify equivalents in other languages, see Pernau, Margrit. 2007. "Gab es eine indische Zivilgesellschaft im 19. Jahrhundert? Überlegungen zum Verhältnis von Globalgeschichte und historischer Semantik." *Traverse: Zeitschrift für Geschichte* 14/3: 51–65, esp. 57 f.

time, discerning synonymous, antonymous, or alternative terms along the way. Of course, one will also address the term's present meanings, but one can follow the term independently from the ideas it currently expresses and find very different meanings in its earlier usages. In other words, the primary research unit is the term (which one turns into a concept) and not the ideas it is conveying. However, this is not possible in a study written in English dealing with Arabic source material, for a very basic reason: my interest lies in the idea of society, which hegemonically came to be conceptualized as 'society,' yet not once does any author use the term 'society' in *al-Manar.*

The basic problem is thus one of translation, and it becomes central due to the normativity of the concept 'society.'[87] Unless one is writing a study on Arabic concepts in Arabic, there is no avoiding this problem. Hypothetically, I could posit *mujtamaʿ* instead of 'society' as my primary term of interest, even though this already naïvely suppresses the question of why I have become interested in that specific term in the first place. I then either have to translate *mujtamaʿ* directly, or at some point – rather early in the text – I have to circumscribe its meanings in English in order to make it comprehensible to my readers. In both cases, the English meanings are already forming in my mind when I read the Arabic terms, and at no point will I have made sense of them independently of these meanings.[88] Now, I might say that *mujtamaʿ* does not equal 'society' but that I do *understand* it as such, in that I understand (some of) its meanings as correlating with (some of) the meanings of 'society.' However, this only shifts the question to the criteria of my understanding. The basic problem thus remains: I cannot possibly know when to translate an Arabic term as 'society,' let alone identify Arabic equivalents to 'society,' without having pre-configured the central ideas this term has been expressing or the function it has been fulfilling.

It is not an option to abstain from such a pre-configuration in order to escape the charge of Eurocentrism – that is, of imposing one particular understanding of a concept on the source material. The attempt to escape this charge might ex-

---

87 On this aspect beyond 'society,' see also: Pernau, Margrit. 2012. "Whither Conceptual History? From National to Entangled Histories." *Contributions to the History of Concepts*, 7/1: 1–11, esp. 11; Juneja, Monica and Pernau, Margrit. 2009. "Lost in Translation? Transcending Boundaries in Comparative History." In *Comparative and Transnational History: Central European Approaches and New Perspectives* ed. by Heinz-Gerhard Haupt and Jürgen Kocka: 105–132. New York/Oxford: Berghahn, esp. 112–115.

88 In my case, in fact, the issue is even more vexed, as English is only my second language and Arabic my fourth. The basic problem remains the same, however, and as I have read Arabic texts for this study, I have thought about them in English.

plain the striking absence of this hermeneutic operation in Schulz-Forberg's theoretical considerations. Yet, even if one focuses on terms in another language whose correspondence with 'society' is rather clearly established, it significantly diminishes the relevance of tracing this concept if it is treated as merely a discursive unit, which can be used very differently. Moreover, one cannot assume an implicit consensus on the fundamental meanings of 'society' in English, neither at the time of one's own writing nor at the time during which one's source material was written.[89] Thus I need to inquire into the normativity and the historicity of 'society,' into its core meanings and its function, in order to question my own understanding of the concept and to identify the Arabic term(s) corresponding to 'society.'

This identification includes a tentative comparison, the purpose of which in my case is to familiarize the seemingly unfamiliar, but also to "de-familiarize the familiar."[90] A basic premise for such an identification, as with any comparison, consists of pre-configuring the unit to be identified or compared (e.g., 'society') in a way that is specific enough to meaningfully identify the unit of interest (e.g., Arabic equivalents to 'society') but broad enough to allow for differences. This preliminary pre-configuration, which will be undertaken in the next chapter, amounts to what I want to call a heuristic Eurocentrism.

(4) This heuristic Eurocentrism doubts that a purely descriptive understanding of 'modernity' is possible. Schulz-Forberg's attempt in that direction[91] conceives of modernity as "a web of connections both in space and over time," presumably established in "the last few centuries."[92] But, as such connections had always existed, why does 'modernity' designate the connections of a certain period? One may suspect that this is because, to employ Enrique Dussel's words, "modernity appears when Europe appears itself as the 'centre' of *World* history that it inaugurates; the periphery that surrounds this centre is consequently part

89 Klaus Karttunen problematizes this point in his contribution to the volume, which differs markedly from the other chapters (Karttunen, "Sabhā-Samāj").

90 This is one of the five potential methodological purposes of historical comparisons helpfully distinguished by: Kocka, Jürgen and Haupt, Heinz-Gerhard. 2009. "Comparison and Beyond: Traditions, Scope, and Perspectives of Comparative History." In *Comparative and Transnational History: Central European Approaches and New Perspectives* ed. by Heinz-Gerhard Haupt and Jürgen Kocka: 1–32. New York/Oxford: Berghahn, here 4. To avoid a potential misunderstanding on this issue, I do not aim at a full-fledged historical comparison. Rather, my identification of the concept of 'society' in *al-Manar* requires and implies a tentative comparison with European understandings of 'society.'

91 Schulz-Forberg, "Introduction," 13.

92 Ibid., 21.

of its self-definition."[93] Importantly, non-Europeans also regarded Europe or the West, which came to epitomize modernity, as such a centre. Of course, this centre was projected quite differently, often with the aim of developing alternative visions of modernity. It also remains true that the European self-understanding only evolved in contact with others. In this sense, "colonial modernities have [indeed] been just as constitutional of European modernities as vice versa."[94] In the English-Indian encounter, for example, "the boundaries between the self and the other are no longer recognizable."[95] This academic observation, however, must be distinguished from the understandings of historical actors, who may well have stressed boundaries between 'Islamic' or 'Western civilization.'

Moreover, when it comes to the ideas and terms expressing the modern self-understanding, the transfer of these ideas from Europe to other regions, unlike Schulz-Forberg suggests, is hardly just one side of the story, to which an equally expansive history of transfers *into* European thought and languages could be written. In spite of Schulz-Forberg's general emphasis on the reciprocity of exchanges, I doubt whether a non-European starting point could have served equally well for a *global* conceptual history.[96] And also in the volume edited by Schulz-Forberg, Europe appears as central in the end. Some hints at entanglements between non-European languages notwithstanding,[97] the authors deal with European concepts appropriated in Asian languages. Thus, in an attempted descriptive understanding of modernity as a polycentric web of connections, Europe still retains its central position.

Modernity is even more closely imbricated with European tradition regarding its epistemic, intellectual, and institutional features. Attempts to locate crucial aspects of modernity in earlier non-European contexts are actually a case in point. Their point of departure is features that are (allegedly wrongly) identified with European modernity, which are then located elsewhere. As long as 'modernity' is maintained as the overarching paradigm, Europe does indeed seem to be the hedgehog, who can always say to the non-European rabbit that it was there

93 Dussel, Enrique. 1993. "Eurocentrism and Modernity." *Boundary* 2/3: 65–76, here 65.
94 Schulz-Forberg, "Introduction," 21.
95 Juneja and Pernau, "Lost in Translation?," 116.
96 This could only be misunderstood as an implicit claim to European superiority if one upholds a positive assessment of modernity at large. I am, however, not interested in any normative evaluation of modernity. Should I be prompted to attempt one, it would hardly be an unambiguously positive one. The simple reference to fascism, communism, nationalism, and capitalism should suffice here.
97 For example: Avonius, "Building," 136.

first[98] – if not historically, then at least conceptually. There is thus no escaping a Eurocentric bias in 'modernity,' since – for the foreseeable future – there is no undoing the concept's particular genealogy and coinage.[99] Tellingly, we find the identification of modernity with the European tradition in even the most sophisticated attempts at conceiving of modernity as evolving from a plurality of traditions.[100] This can be read as being tricked by modernity's "false game"[101] of universalizing one particular tradition. A more fruitful reading, however, stresses that this particular European tradition had already incorporated other particularities and hegemonically elaborated features universal to modernity.[102]

A heuristic Eurocentrism therefore departs from a hegemonic, potentially universal understanding of (one aspect of) modernity and tries to discern the ways in which this is shared in the texts we are studying. My use of European conceptualizations of society as a starting point must not be confused with making society the proprium of European thinking, let alone European civilization. Such a postulate necessarily eventuates the deficiency of other contexts when compared to this standard.[103] Moreover, claims to a European – or Western, or Christian, but also Islamic or Chinese – exclusivism are hardly convincing, as long as other contexts have not been researched. The idea of society was certainly developed "most pronouncedly, but not without ambiguities"[104] in the European tradition which became hegemonic. However, its usage in a non-European context is not necessarily exclusively due to its having been appropriated from European thought, but might also be the outcome of convergent developments

---

98 Pflitsch, Andreas. 2012. *Zweierlei Barbarei. Überlegungen zu Kultur, Moderne und Authentizität im Dreieck zwischen Europa, Russland und arabischem Nahen Osten.* Würzburg: Ergon, 56f.

99 This sense of 'Eurocentrism' is not included in the five meanings distinguished by: Delanty, "Modernity," 268.

100 Compare Schulze, *Der Koran*, 16 and 26; Schulz-Forberg, "Introduction," 16, 22 (page 22 reads only "temporal logics," but it seems rather clear that also here, as on page 16, vertical temporal logics are referred to.)

101 Pflitsch, *Zweierlei Barbarei*, 57 (the original reads "falsches Spiel").

102 In a way, these two readings are put into dialogue in a debate between Dietze and Chakrabarty, in which I am siding with the latter: Dietze, Carola. 2008. "Toward a History on Equal Terms: A Discussion of Provincializing Europe." *History and Theory* 47/1: 69–84; Chakrabarty, Dipesh. 2008. "In Defense of Provincializing Europe: A Response to Carola Dietze." *History and Theory* 47/1: 85–96. See also Chakrabarty's preface to the new edition of *Provincializing Europe* (idem. 2000. *Provincializing Europe: Postcolonial Thought and Historical Difference*; with a new preface by the author. Princeton, NJ: Princeton University Press, esp. xiii–xiv).

103 As illustrated, for example, by: Black, Antony. 2001. "Concepts of Civil Society in Pre-Modern Europe." In *Civil Society: History and Possibilities* ed. by Sudipta Kaviraj and Sunil Khilnani: 33–38. Cambridge: Cambridge University Press.

104 Wagner, "World-Sociology," 294.

in both contexts.[105] The convergence of fundamental ideas certainly does not mean complete symmetry. The differences to be expected (as Schulz-Forberg rightly stresses)[106] are meant to inform the original understanding and might lead to a more universal understanding of 'society.' A heuristic Eurocentrism, then, investigates the universality of the hegemonic European understanding and, through integrating different particularities, possibly gives way to a more integrative understanding of modernity. While modernity will probably always be tainted by the historical fact of European hegemony, the above reasons for departing from European particularities – that is, for a heuristic Eurocentrism – might hypothetically be of a temporary nature.

(5) There is, however, a more fundamental reason why I am departing from European conceptualizations of society, amounting to what I want to term *academicentrism.*[107] To some extent, this academicentrism results from the problem of translation alluded to above, which has nothing to do with power constellations and equally exists when writing an Arabic study on English source material. On another level, this academicentrism results from the basic fact that every author understands their sources from within their epistemic moment and based on her or his implicit "background understandings."[108]

While the secular academy clearly plays an important, even hegemonic role in the formulation of the European self-understanding,[109] the two are not identical. When it comes to my understanding of *al-Manar*, I might thus more aptly speak of a heuristic academicentrism rather than of Eurocentrism. The deconstruction of 'secularization' mentioned above is an eminent example of the

---

105 For a model of convergence with regard to Islamic and European traditions in modernity, see Schulze, *Der Koran*, 26 f., 147–152; alternative models are mentioned in: Buessow, Johann. 2015. "Re-imagining Islam in the Period of the First Modern Globalization: Muhammad ʿAbduh and his *Theology of Unity*." In *A Global Middle East: Mobility, Materiality and Culture in the Modern Age, 1880–1940* ed. by Liat Kozma, Cyrus Schayegh and Avner Wishnitzer: 273–320. London: I.B. Tauris, here 275 ff.

106 Schulz-Forberg, "Introduction," 14.

107 Only after completion of this manuscript, I learned of earlier coinages of that term. If the following considerations overlap with these, this is coincidental.

108 I am using the concept here in the sense of: Taylor, Charles. 2007. *A Secular Age*. Cambridge, Mass./London: The Belknap Press of Harvard University Press.

109 Masuzwa shows that, in a way, the modern "transformation of the university may be said to epitomize the very process of 'becoming modern' and 'becoming secular'" (Masuzawa, Tomoko. 2011. "The University and the Advent of the Academic Secular: The State's Management of Public Instruction." In *After Secular Law* ed. by Winnifred Fallers Sullivan, Robert A. Yelle and Taussig-Rubbo. Mateo: 119–139. Stanford, CA: Stanford Law Books, here 119.)

bias at work in the secular academy – that is, of its adherents universalizing their particular experiences and interpretations and molding them into theories with allegedly greater general explanatory or interpretive value. As the secular academy holds a hegemonic position in the European interpretation of modernity, its ordering of the world does indeed have more general interpretive value than perhaps all other particular attempts.[110] Nevertheless, the particular assumptions of the secular academy have not gone unchallenged, also within Europe or the West. As the old narrative of secularization has lost its force, various alternative stories of the generation and self-understanding of Western modernity are now available.

To understand modernity in Islamic tradition, I chose a narrative of Western modernity that, presumably more than my own secular understanding, would have resonated with the understanding of modernity brought forward by the authors in *al-Manar.* This narrative is Charles Taylor's *A Secular Age,*[111] which serves as a tool to question and modify my own background understandings and, as such, most obviously forms part of the guiding thread running through this study.

6 Rationale and Structure of the Book: Assumptions, Expectations, Findings

The guiding thread of this study consists of interrogating my own understanding of 'society' and discerning how far this understanding can plausibly be shifted back onto the authors in *al-Manar.* In other words: How has the concept of 'society,' which is crucial for the hegemonic modern self-understanding, evolved? How far does it travel? Were the authors in *al-Manar* directly confronted with proponents of this understanding? How did they react to them? To what extent did they themselves share in the hegemonic conceptualization of society as 'society,' and in which respects did they bring forward an alternative? How does their alternative reflect back upon the hegemonic understanding? Does it modify the latter and contribute to a more integrative understanding of 'society' and thus of modernity?

This guiding thread and these questions manifest themselves in the three main parts of this study, which are entitled "Assumptions" (part A), "Expecta-

110 The reasons for this have been elaborated above: the universalization of the European or Western order, but also the shared discourse of modernity.
111 Taylor, *A Secular Age.*

tions" (B), and "Findings" (C). I shall now explicate the purposes of these parts and summarize their contents.

Part A, consisting of two chapters, inquires into, disorients, and subsequently (p)re-configures my own (i.e., the secular European) assumptions concerning the concept of 'society' and the modern self-understanding it has been expressing.

Chapter 2 inquires into the historicity and normativity of 'society' in order to get at its normative core and the function it has been fulfilling. I first introduce the heuristic tool of the saddle period (*Sattelzeit*) to depict the foundational conceptual changes on the threshold of modernity and then argue that no concept is more constitutive of the modern self-understanding than 'society.' It is only modern men and women who came to conceive of themselves as equal individuals forming one society, which comprises all members living under the jurisdiction of one state. In addition to being distinguished from the state, society was also distinguished from religion. The establishment of sociology further perpetuated the understanding of society as an autonomous order with independent social laws. The central function of 'society' was its response to a crisis of social and political order. I hermeneutically distinguish alternative concepts from 'society' in order to ideal-typically decide on one English term when translating Arabic terms. This second chapter is not a conceptual history in any narrow sense, but rather brings together pivotal moments demonstrating the historicity and normativity of 'society' in order to illuminate what is at stake when rendering an Arabic term as 'society.'

While the second chapter is based on a broad range of material, chapter 3 introduces one particular story of how the modern secular Western self-understanding, crystallized in the concept of 'society,' emerged. With the aim of understanding how secular modernity was framed in the Islamic discourse of *al-Manar*, a story maintaining a contrast between religion and the secular would not have been helpful. Over against such secularist accounts, I have chosen Charles Taylor's master narrative of Western modernity as told in *A Secular Age*. Taylor's story has been forcefully criticized for its Catholic bias and for drawing a boundary around an imagined West. I thus have to argue in some detail why I consider *A Secular Age* a greatly useful heuristic tool for my research. I am resorting to Taylor's story not because I deem it truer than secularist accounts of modernity, but rather because it resonates better with the Islamic reformists' vision of modernity. In a sense, Taylor's Catholic book, written from within the secular West in 2007, serves as a hermeneutic bridge between my own secular background and that of Islamic thinkers at the beginning of the twentieth century.

This first part also contains some references to *al-Manar* and its Egyptian-Arabic-Islamic contexts, even though these really are only addressed in part B. In addition to supporting the usability of *A Secular Age* and recalling the central question of this study, these references are intended to counter a potential misunderstanding of my presentation as suggesting a contrast between Europe and other regions. In fact, given that the modern self-understanding – as epitomized by Europe – only evolved in mutual exchange with other regions, parts A and B could have been presented together. There are three reasons for not having done so: firstly, the research I discuss in part A essentially limits itself to the European context. Secondly, the sources I bring together here are already quite disparate in many regards. Adding studies on the context of *al-Manar* to that discussion would have resulted in a rather confusing presentation. The third and most substantial reason is the following: because the challenge of discerning 'society' in *al-Manar* is not least one of translation, it makes sense to treat studies on 'society' and its established equivalents in other European languages separately.

Part B, which consists of three chapters (4–6), substantiates the expectation that one can discern counterparts to the modern concept of 'society' in *al-Manar* by presenting and discussing the existing research on the journal itself, on its socio-political and intellectual contexts, and on transformations in the Arabic socio-political vocabulary in the period under consideration.

Chapter 4 presents the socio-political and intellectual setting in which *al-Manar* was founded. I selectively draw on existing historiographical research, with the aim of showing the eminence and contestation of social questions in Egypt at the end of the nineteenth century. In that century, in hindsight, we can trace the process of Egypt's becoming a nation-state. This process was mainly initiated by centralizing governmental reforms. Governmental policies also partly accounted for changes in the makeup of Egyptian social arrangements. Increasingly, however, social actors themselves began to attend to the reform of society. The urban literati, in particular, regarded themselves as spokespersons of the Egyptian nation and society and as agents of reform. They enthusiastically embraced the press as a means for reform and for intellectual and political debates. In the increasingly plural landscape of the Egyptian press, various answers to eminent social questions were offered. The Islamic reformists were confronted with secular(ist) propositions for social and political order. On both the material and the interpretive level, this chapter substantiates the expectation that Arabic correspondents to the modern concept of 'society' in *al-Manar* should be identified.

Once chapter 4 has laid out the setting in which *al-Manar* was founded, chapter 5 presents the journal itself, along with existing research on it. After providing some factual information concerning the journal's foundation, distribution, and most prolific authors, I approach the topics broached in *al-Manar* by scrutinizing the journal's subtitles and the index compiled by Rashid Rida. After all, the (self-)designation of *al-Manar* as an "Islamic journal" does not reveal a great deal about its contents. While the journal's subtitles varied, in several volumes, *al-Manar* was presented as a journal on "the philosophy of religion and the affairs of social association (*ijtimāʿ*) and civilization." This again heightens the expectation that Arabic equivalents and alternatives to the concept of 'society' can be discerned in this journal. The vast body of literature on *al-Manar* attests to the prominence of the journal as the mouthpiece of Islamic reformism. Having critically discussed the general characterization of *al-Manar*, I briefly summarize existing research on specific aspects of and viewpoints advanced by the journal. More extensively, I then collect hints in existing studies that point to the centrality of society in *al-Manar*.

Chapter 6 widens the focus from *al-Manar* to transformations in nineteenth- and early twentieth-century Arabic in general. The centrality of this period for modern transformations in Arabic is rather well established, and today one can tentatively locate the Arabic 'saddle period' between 1860 and 1940. However, there is a striking lack of proper conceptual histories. Almost all the statements concerning Arabic terms for 'society' are instead made in passing. Our lack of knowledge in this regard is especially demonstrated in the fact that assessments concerning the evolution of *mujtamaʿ* vary greatly. More firmly established is the usage of *al-hayʾa al-ijtimāʿiyya* for conceptualizing society. To get an idea of this seemingly pertinent term for 'society' in the late nineteenth and early twentieth centuries, I point out its most prominent usages outside of *al-Manar*. In this chapter, I also explain which Arabic terms I searched for in *al-Manar* to identify conceptualizations of society.

My findings are organized in the four chapters of part C. The first two chapters are centered on what are allegedly the most pertinent Arabic terms for 'society' – namely, *al-hayʾa al-ijtimāʿiyya* and *mujtamaʿ*. Using these terms as guiding units of analysis is meant to foreground the terminological contestation of shared semantic fields and to identify potential rival terms. This means that topics such as the relation between society and morals or society and politics are not analyzed systematically, but reoccur across chapters. In the chapters on *al-hayʾa al-ijtimāʿiyya* and *mujtamaʿ*, I address the context of these terms only to the extent necessary for understanding their meanings, and I deviate into more general discussions and interpretations to the extent necessary to show the broader relevance of my conceptual findings. The following two chapters are then organized differently, each dedicated to one author's conceptualization of society – namely, to Rafiq al-ʿAzm, as the one regular contributor to *al-Manar* who most strikingly used *mujtamaʿ*; and to Rashid Rida, who most strikingly avoided both *al-hay'a al-ijtimāʿiyya* and *mujtamaʿ*. The chapter on al-ʿAzm is primarily interested in his socio-political views and epistemic premises, since his works have hitherto been studied sursprisingly rarely, whereas the chapter on Rida, whose views are well-researched, is primarily interested in terminological usage.

In general, I accessed the vast corpus of *al-Manar* via pertinent terms[112] and was guided by these terms, which I turned into concepts, to the ideas of society they are conveying. With historians (among others) in mind, I should stress that this is a work of theory, rather than of history. Hence, I have not arranged the pertinent terms conceptualizing society and thematic statements on society in a strict chronological order. Rather, I accessed the exemplary corpus of *al-Manar* with the aim of exploring a semantic and discursive field and arriving at a model for conceiving of modernity in Islamic tradition.

Chapter 7 analyzes the composite of *al-hay'a al-ijtimāʿiyya* in *al-Manar*. This composite – which, according to Khuri-Makdisi, was the standard term for conceptualizing society at the time – occurs a mere 142 times in *al-Manar*. An overview of the authors who use *al-hay'a al-ijtimāʿiyya* most strikingly, especially to refer to particular societies, tentatively confirms the term's Christian-secular roots and connotations. Still more evident is Rashid Rida's avoidance of *al-hay'a al-ijtimāʿiyya*. He uses the composite most prominently when paraphrasing non-religious philosophers, whereas he himself prefers to address the same aspects by employing *umma*. Based on its analysis of the authorship, main usages, and central aspects of *al-hay'a al-ijtimāʿiyya*, this chapter produces clear first hints that Islamic reformists expressed aspects of the idea of society with *umma*.

Chapter 8 attends to the present Arabic term for 'society,' *mujtamaʿ*. Contrary to previous estimations, I show that, in the first decade of the twentieth century, *mujtamaʿ* was already predominantly used to mean 'society' and occurred more frequently than *al-hay'a al-ijtimāʿiyya*. While *mujtamaʿ* was used to address similar aspects of society as *al-hay'a al-ijtimāʿiyya*, it more often conveyed the idea of an abstract legal order and was less often used to conceptualize an organic understanding of society. An analysis of the authors who use the term *mujtamaʿ* is again very interesting and in some ways overlaps with that of *al-hay'a al-ijtimāʿiyya*. *Mujtamaʿ* meaning 'society' was used most prominently in translations of European works and in articles originally published in journals other than *al-Manar*. Rashid Rida only rarely uses *mujtamaʿ* to refer to society as a whole, especially when it comes to particular societies. Of the authors writing regularly for *al-Manar*, Rafiq al-ʿAzm stands out for his prominent use of *mujtamaʿ*.

112 For my location of terms, see below: 33 ff.

Hence, chapter 9 investigates Rafiq al-ʿAzm's socio-political views and their underlying epistemological premises. The aim of this chapter is twofold: firstly, to test the hypothesis from the foregoing chapter concerning the secular connotations of *mujtamaʿ* through a particular focus on a central author in *al-Manar* and a close collaborator of Rida. Secondly, and in light of al-ʿAzm's œuvre having hitherto received surprisingly little attention, to present pertinent societal writings by this eminent "historiographical and sociological author," as he was characterized in *al-Manar*. I show that al-ʿAzm (a) clearly and remarkably early formulated an Islamic argument for the separation of religion and politics; (b) based his societal perspective on religion and politics on the anthropological premise that social association is a natural human tendency; and (c), in engagement with European schools of thought, constructed Islam as a principle of socio-economic order. Indeed, Rafiq al-ʿAzm was less interested in reforming Islam as a religion, so as to render it appropriate for society, but rather constructed Islam *as* society. If the integration of religion and society is characteristic of the Islamic reformists of *al-Manar*, then al-ʿAzm contributed the most clearly societal perspective to the journal.

Chapter 10, which attends to conceptualizations of the social and society in writings by Rashid Rida, builds on two insights from the previous chapters: firstly, that Rida avoided *al-hay'a al-ijtimāʿiyya* and *mujtamaʿ* in favor of *umma* and, secondly, that normative claims were derived from human beings' asserted natural need for social association (*ijtimāʿ*). As Rida's writings and views in comparison to those of al-ʿAzm are well researched, in this chapter – in contrast to the previous one – I am primarily interested in terms. Consequently, I access Rida's articles in *al-Manar* in a very selective manner, via the ubiquitous terms *ijtimāʿ* (social association, unity, concurrence) and *ijtimāʿī* (the social). Two aspects I pay particular attention to are Rida's adducement of sociology and societal laws and the relation between the social and the religious in his writings. This chapter gives greater substance to this study's main argument, which is already visible in chapters seven and eight – namely, that Rida used *umma* to express his vision of society. I show that for Rida, the ideal society of the *umma* is founded on human beings' natural yet divinely ordained need for social association; that it functions according to largely autonomous societal laws (which, however, are validated as the laws of God); and that it requires the guidance of a societal religion to attain perfection. By tightening the connetion between religion and society, in comparison to al-ʿAzm, Rida gave a different twist to modernity in Islamic tradition.

In a decidedly concise manner, the concluding chapter 11 summarizes this study's structure, interpretes its findings and discusses their implications, and sketches avenues for future research.

7 Locating Terms in *al-Manar*

In order to comprehensively locate terms in the vast corpus of *al-Manar*, with its approximate 30,000 pages, I had recourse to a digital version of the journal. The index of *al-Manar*, published in 1998, is generally a helpful tool for orienting ourselves within the journal.[113] It lists in alphabetical order some 11,000 entries of article titles, subjects, and author names, spanning all volumes until 1935. This index, however, does not contain any of the pertinent terms for 'society', other than for 'religion' (*dīn*) or *islām*. I thus mainly resorted to it for locating additional articles on a topic or by a specific author previously identified via my electronic search. The electronic version of *al-Manar*, released by al-Maktaba al-Shamila as Word files,[114] proved to be identical with the printed version,[115] with one minor and one major exception: as a minor exception, other than occasional typing mistakes, an author's name is given for each article, even though it is sometimes absent from the printed version. In some of these cases, the electronic version wrongly names Rashid Rida as the author. This is possibly due to the fact that Rida was the author of almost all the unsigned articles in *al-Manar*. At times, however, Rida seems to have assumed that his readers would be familiar with the author of a text, especially in longer series of articles.[116]

The major difference between the printed and the electronic versions consists in the latter excluding the Qur'an commentary, which accounts for more

---

113 Yasushi, Kusuji, Ibish, Yusuf Husayn and Khuri, Yusuf Quzma (eds.). 1998. *Fihris Majallat al-Manar, 1898–1935*. Beirut/Tokio: Turath/Mashruʿ Dirasat al-Hadara al-Islamiyya. For a review, see: Brunner, Rainer. 2001. "[Review of:] Yasushi, Kosugi; Ibis, Yusuf Husain; Huri, Yusuf Quzma (eds): *Fihris mağallat al-Manār, 1898–1935 – The Index of Al-Manar*. Beirut: Turāṯ/Tokio: Mašruʿ dirāsāt al-ḥaḍāra al-islāmīya/The Islamic Area Studies Project 1998." *Die Welt des Islams* 41/1: 132–133. On Rida's own index, see below: chapter 5 section 2.

114 This version is available here: http://shamela.ws/index.php/book/6947 (accessed Sept. 13, 2011); for information on this website, see Gilet, Julien. 2010. "al-Maktaba al-Shamela." In *Aldébaran, Collections numériques*, http://aldebaran.revues.orf/6597 (accessed Sep. 30, 2013).

115 To my knowledge, the different editions of the printed version are identical, with the exception of the first volume, to the 1909 reprint of which Rida added a new preface and from which he cut some articles from the first edition which he considered outdated. The electronic version is identical with this second edition, which is more widespread than the first and also the only one at my disposal.

116 An example is al-Kawakibi's work *Umm al-Qura*, serialized in volumes four and five of *al-Manar*. The printed version does not give the author, and the electronic version wrongly states Ridas as the author.

than one-fifth of the journal's overall content.[117] To fill this gap, I resorted to a digital version of the *Tafsir al-Manar*, also released by al-Maktaba al-Shamila.[118] The separate publication of the *Tafsir* engenders three disadvantages and one advantage: on the negative side, one must conduct the same search twice. What was not possible was to locate passages or even search terms present in the electronic version of the *Tafsir* in the printed version of the journal. Therefore, we cannot know for certain whether a passage or a term found in the *Tafsir* (in its printed and electronic versions) appeared identically in the journal.[119] As we also do not know the exact volume of *al-Manar* in which the terms found in the digital version of the *Tafsir* first appeared,[120] all chronological trends concerning the frequency of a term are based on the digital version of the journal, excluding the *Tafsir*. As an advantage, the two separate digital versions allow for a comparison of the frequency of a term in the overall journal and in the *Tafsir*, which presumably more clearly represents a religious discourse.

For extracting terms from the digital versions, as a first step, I used the program PowerGrep.[121] This program proved useful for locating less commonly used terms and for providing a rough quantitative overview of the frequency of terms as well as of trends in their usage over the lifespan of *al-Manar*. It informs us, for example, that the term *siyāsa* (politics) was less common than *taʿlīm* (education), with 3725 versus 4969 occurrences in the journal, excluding the *Tafsir*.[122]

117 I arrived at this figure by comparing the word counts of the Qur'an commentary and the rest of the journal (roughly 2.2 million compared to 7.5 million). This is to be taken as a rough estimate, since the count of Arabic words in Microsoft Word is not fully reliable.

118 This version is available here: http://shamela.ws/index.php/book/12304 (accessed July 28, 2012). It is based on the following edition: Rida, Rashid. 1990. *Tafsir al-Qur'an al-Hakim (Tafsir al-Manar)*. 12 vols. Cairo: al-Hay'a al-Misriyya al-ʿAmma li-l-Kitab. This printed edition was unavailable to me. I have, however, verified the accuracy of the electronic version – which, in contrast to the electronic version of the rest of the journal, includes exact page numbers – by selectively comparing it to the following printed edition: Idem. 1948–1961. *Tafsir al-Qur'an al-Hakim, al-Mushtahir bi-Tafsir al-Manar*. 12 vols. Cairo: Maktabat al-Qahira. Since the electronic version proved accurate but differs in page numbers from the printed edition at my disposal, I considered it an unjustifiably time-consuming task to locate all the passages identified electronically in that printed edition, whence I rely on the electronic version to refer to the edition on which it is based.

119 Jomier mentions some differences between the *Tafsir* as serialized in *al-Manar* and as it was published later (Jomier, Jacques. 1954. *Le Commentaire Coranique du Manār*. Paris: G.-P. Maisonneuve, 54).

120 One volume of the *Tafsir* was based on up to five volumes of the journal (see: ibid., xvi).

121 The software is available here: http://www.powergrep.com (accessed April 14, 2015).

122 See Appendix, tables 7 and 8.

In the *Tafsir*, *siyāsa* played a marginal role, with only 186 occurrences.[123] The question of belief, in turn, was more central to the *Tafsir*, as indicated by the 2938 occurrences of *īmān*, a term that appears less often – namely 2526 times – in the rest of the journal.[124] We also learn from this search that the term *thaqāfa* (culture) was first used in volume 26 of *al-Manar* and thereafter appears in every volume, albeit only 33 times in total.[125] Equally marginal is the term *ʿalmānī(ya)* (secular), which occurs only 21 times.[126] A look at the context of these occurrences then shows that *ʿalmānī* was primarily used in articles on 'secular' Christian schools in Lebanon.[127] These examples illustrate the potential of PowerGrep for locating marginal terms within the vast corpus of *al-Manar* and for producing broad statistical overviews of the number of ubiquituous terms.

The overviews in the appendix should, however, be taken with some caution, since the program displayed several limitations, which render it insufficient for producing completely reliable statistics, and which also required locating the central terms of this study by searching for them manually in Microsoft Word. With potential future users of the program in mind, I shall explain its major peculiarities and limitations for searching Arabic texts, using my central terms as examples. The search for *ijtimāʿ* also produces the adjective *ijtimāʿī* or the composite *al-hayʾa al-ijtimāʿiyya*. I thus manually disentangled the different terms including *ijtimāʿ*.[128] This would, however, be an overly time-consuming task for more common strings of letters, such as *dīn*, which mostly means 'religion' when it stands for itself, but the 39,176 results of which also include *madīna* (city) or the name of Jamal al-Din al-Afghani, among other words. When searching for *mujtamaʿ*, the results also include instances of the adjective *mujtamiʿ(a)* (together, combined, assembled) or *al-mujtamiʿūn* (those assembled). Of the 547 instances in the journal, excluding the *Tafsir*, 336 actually read *mujtamaʿ*, to which the *Tafsir* adds another 22. The fact that the electronic version of the *Tafsir*, unlike that of the rest of the journal, is vocalized, makes its search results unam-

---

123 See Appendix, table 7.
124 See Appendix, table 5.
125 See Appendix, table 10.
126 See Appendix, table 6.
127 Thus a review of publications by Salih Mukhlis Rida in 1910 presents a book entitled *The Secular French Schools* (*al-Madaris al-Fransawiyya al-ʿAlmaniyya*; Rida, Salih Mukhlis. 1910. "al-Taqariz." *al-Manar* 13/8: 634–635, here 635), and an article published the following year is dedicated to unbelief in secular schools (Hifar, Muhammad Najib. 1911. "al-Ilhad fi al-Madaris al-ʿAlmaniyya." *al-Manar* 14/7: 544–545).
128 See Appendix, table 2.

biguous.[129] Vocalization, however, also changes with the case of a noun, and concerning all words starting with a so-called sun letter also depending on whether the definite article *al-* is preceding the word. This means one has to search for differently vocalized versions of the same term.[130] Concerning composites, PowerGrep turned out to be disappointingly unreliable. Thus, of the 142 instances of *al-hay'a al-ijtimāʿiyya* in *al-Manar*, the program only found 107. For locating this composite, as well as for the other terms central to this study – namely, *mujtamaʿ* and *ijtimāʿ* – I therefore resorted to the search function in Microsoft Word. The electronic version of the journal (excluding the *Tafsir*) only states the start page of each article, whereas the electronic version of the *Tafsir* marks the beginning of each page. Thus for page reference to the *Tafsir*, I have relied on the electronic version, whereas for the rest of the journal, I have located all instances I am referring to in the printed version of the journal.

For transliteration of Arabic terms and names I used the IJMES system, mainly because it is reader-friendly for those who do not speak Arabic. With the same intention of reader-friendliness, I have, where necessary, adjusted transliterations in English quotations so as to conform to the IJMES system. I have deviated from this system in that I have also transliterated words commonly used in English when referring specifically to the Arabic term (e.g., "Rida considers the *ʿulamāʾ al-dīn,*" but "historians found that the ʿulamaʾ of Egypt").

I give full bibliographical references for the first mention of a publication and subsequently state the author's name and a short title. When the author is Rashid Rida, I state 'Rida' only in subsequent references; when the author is one of Rida's brothers, I add the first name. If an article forms part of a series, I restate the volume and issue of *al-Manar* with each reference.

---

129 Thus one has to search specifically for *mujtamaʿ* – that is, for مُجْتَمَع. A search without vocalization will not produce any result.

130 For example, to find all composites of *ummat al-* , one has to search for all cases of *umma* – that is, for أُمَّةُ, for أُمَّةَ, and for أُمَّةِ. Concerning Arabic words starting with a sun letter, the letter *lām* (*l*) of the definite article *al* preceding the word is assimilated to the first letter of the word. Thus, for example, *al-dīn*, is pronounced *ad-dīn*. In vocalized script, this is indicated with a *shadda* over the letter *dāl* (*d*). Thus, in order to find both versions of *dīn*, one has to conduct two searches, one for *dīn* with a *shadda* and one without – that is, one for دِّين and one for دِين.

Part A
Assumptions: 'Society' and the Secular in European Modernity

Chapter 2
'Society' in European Modernity

1 'Society' as a Basic Concept of (European) Modernity

1.1 Conceptual History and the Saddle Period

"The concept is not merely a sign for, but also a factor in, political or social groupings."
– Koselleck, *Futures Past*[1]

We live after the *Sattelzeit* (saddle period). With this metaphor, the German historian Reinhart Koselleck designated the threshold period of modernity,[2] in which concepts acquired new meanings, both reflecting and shaping fundamental changes in social, economic, and political organization. Modern human beings living after the saddle period struggle to grasp the meaning these concepts had before that period, whereas their new meanings, which would have been almost inconceivable to our ancestors living before that period, are seemingly intuitively understandable to us.[3] Koselleck introduced the saddle period as a heuristic device for the vast project on *Geschichtliche Grundbegriffe*, dealing with 130 German basic concepts of social and political language[4] and guided by the overarching aim of conceptually investigating the dissolution of the old world and the evolution of the modern world.[5] For German-speaking Europe, Koselleck provisionally dated this period between 1750 and 1850.

1 Koselleck, Reinhart. 2004. *Futures Past. On the Semantics of Historical Time*; translated and with an introduction by Keith Tribe. New York: Columbia University Press, 156.

2 In the English translation of the *Einleitung*, both the *Sattelzeit* and *Schwellenzeit* are rendered as 'threshold period.' However, while each epoch is preceded by a threshold period, the saddle period specifically designates the threshold of modernity: Koselleck, Reinhart and Richter, Michaela. "Introduction and Prefaces to the 'Geschichtliche Grundbegriffe'." *Contributions to the History of Concepts* 6, no. 1 (2011): 1–5, 7–25, 27–37, here esp. 9. The translation of the *Einleitung* is also available here: Koselleck, Reinhart. 2011. "Introduction (Einleitung) to the Geschichtliche Grundbegriffe." *Contributions to the History of Concepts* 6/1: 6+ (accessed from Academic OneFile. Web. Jan 19, 2016).

3 Idem. 1972. "Einleitung." In *Geschichtliche Grundbegriffe: Historisches Lexikon zur politisch-sozialen Sprache in Deutschland. Band 1: A-D* ed. by Otto Brunner, Werner Conze and Reinhart Koselleck: xiii–xvxii. Stuttgart: Ernst Klett, here xv; Koselleck and Richter, "Introduction," 9.

4 Koselleck, who co-edited the volumes of this project together with Otto Brunner and Werner Conze, is regarded as the theoretical mastermind behind it. This becomes ever more clear in his subsequent publications and their wide reception. Therefore, I focus on him here.

5 Koselleck, "Einleitung," xiv; Koselleck and Richter, "Introduction," 8f.

https://doi.org/10.1515/9783110545845-003

While space does not permit me to discuss either the "career"[6] of the saddle period or the wide reception of German conceptual history in general,[7] I should address two major points of criticism directed at the metaphor of the saddle period and explain why I nevertheless deem it useful for the purposes of this study.

Firstly, there is no denying that a modernist bias is built into the metaphor of the saddle period, which was formulated in 1972. If a threshold period also implies a certain continuity, in that it links the past with the present, Koselleck clearly stresses ruptures over continuities and thereby constitutes the saddle period leading up to modernity as part of modernity.[8] Thus, viewed critically, the saddle period functions as yet another means by which modernity itself asserts its own peculiarity as a radically new era, directed toward the future and breaking with tradition. However, as elaborated in the introduction, while today we may view this modernist bias as problematic, we still operate using the normative concepts of modernity. In this sense, the metaphor of the saddle period actually heightens awareness of the particular lenses through which we are looking at pre-modern concepts today.

A second major point of criticism directed at Koselleck's metaphor is its vagueness: the exact dating of this period is debatable, not only in the German-speaking context,[9] but even more so when we include other languages as well. Moreover, it is also not quite clear how one should picture the image of the saddle.[10] Koselleck notably never elaborated on his metaphor and once

6 Fulda, Daniel. 2016. "Sattelzeit. Karriere und Problematik eines kulturwissenschaftlichen Zentralbegriffs." In *Sattelzeit. Historiographiegeschichtliche Revisionen* ed. by Elisabeth Décultot and Daniel Fulda: 1–16. Berlin/Boston: De Gruyter.

7 Melvin Richter introduced an English-speaking audience to the project *Geschichtliche Grundbegriffe* and German conceptual history in general (Richter, Melvin. 1995. *The History of Political and Social Concepts. A Critical Introduction*. New York/Oxford: Oxford University Press). Richter also played a role in setting up the History of Political and Social Concepts Group in 1998, which now goes by the shortened name History of Concepts Group and which – along with its associated journal, *Contributions to the History of Concepts* – is the most obvious evidence of the expansion of the field.

8 See: Motzkin, Gabriel. 2005. "On the Notion of Historical (Dis)Continuity: Reinhart Koselleck's Construction of the Sattelzeit." *Contributions to the History of Concepts* 1/2: 145–158.

9 The *Geschichtliche Grundbegriffe* itself also contains concepts of later origin – for example, 'Faschismus.' Christian Geulen has even suggested that our present is in fact separated from the high times of modernity by yet another saddle period; see Geulen, Christian. 2010. "Plädoyer für eine Geschichte der Grundbegriffe des 20. Jahrhunderts." *Zeithistorische Forschungen/Studies in Contemporary History* 1: 70–97.

10 Fulda, "Sattelzeit," 2f.

even bluntly stated that he invented it "in order to make money."[11] That said, the saddle period might have been such a powerful metaphor precisely because of its vagueness, which facilitated its reception and elaboration in different fields of research.[12] Reference to the saddle period is thus also a means of facilitating the interdisciplinary reception and integration of research.

Concerning the specific context of this study, the saddle period seems even more useful as a heuristic tool than it is in conceptual histories of European languages, where the state of research is much more advanced. The conceptual history of Arabic is in its earliest stage, as I will show in chapter 6 section 1. This involves both methodological and theoretical debates, but also the establishment of historical processes, the availability of defined text corpora, and the technical means for searching these. For Arabic conceptual history, the question of "how we got there" – that is, to modernity – is still very much an open one, and it has to be answered by the relatively few people attending to it, while the majority of potential sources are unedited manuscripts, and with limited technical possibilities for searching those Arabic texts that are available in electronic versions.

Therefore it is only partially true that the conceptual history of Arabic today has to adhere to state-of-the-art debates between conceptual historians who study European languages. Given the state of research on Arabic concepts, it makes sense to appropriate foundational and basic insights from European conceptual history, even though these may have since come to be modified or criticized. For the purposes of this study, there are two additional reasons why, while resorting to the saddle period as a powerful heuristic tool, I refer to only the most general considerations of conceptual history: I am not attempting a conceptual history of Arabic terms for 'society' in the narrow sense,[13] and the pioneers of conceptual history also differed greatly in their methodological procedures[14] and were sometimes not quite faithful to their initial considerations.[15]

---

11 Koselleck, Reinhart and Dipper, Christoph. 1998. "Begriffsgeschichte, Sozialgeschichte, begriffene Geschichte. Reinhart Koselleck im Gespräch mit Christoph Dipper." *Neue Politische Literatur* 51: 187–205, here 195; transl. F.Z.

12 Fulda, "Sattelzeit," 3.

13 In a sense, this study is a precursor to such a potential attempt, as it aims to discern Arabic terms for 'society' in the first place. A conceptual history of these terms would then, among other things, require a much broader empirical basis, both diachronically and synchronically.

14 For the fundamental differences between the three pioneering projects of German conceptual history, see ibid., 9–21.

15 A recurring criticism directed at the *Geschichtliche Grundbegriffe* is that it relies on elite writing as sources, even though Koselleck had intended conceptual history to be a combination of intellectual and social history. While not focusing on eminent thinkers (as does the Cambridge

A central premise of conceptual history is that language is inherently social, whence concepts both grasp and shape social reality.[16] Social reality is thus always mediated by language but is presumed – although not if we follow the linguistic turn – to exist also in an unmediated form.[17] A concept is not to be identified with a specific term, but with a semantic range, which can be expressed by several terms. When this semantic range crystallizes into one term, the latter becomes a basic concept: "As distinguished from concepts in general, a basic concept [...] is an inescapable, irreplaceable part of the political and social vocabulary. Only after a concept has attained this status does it become crystallized in a single word or term such as 'revolution,' 'state,' 'civil society,' or 'democracy.' Basic concepts combine manifold experiences and expectations in such a way that they become indispensable to any formulation of the most urgent issues of a given time. [T]hey are always both controversial and contested."[18]

Conceptual analysis has to consider the different meanings of a term (semasiology) as well as different terms expressing a concept (onomasiology) – or rather (according to my usage of 'term,' 'concept,' and 'idea,' as stated in the introduction) the different meanings of a term by turning that term into a concept – and the different terms expressing (when they are turned into concepts) an idea.

A significant variety of terms expressing an idea is to be expected particularly in periods of rapid social change – such as the saddle period – during which

---

School), the *Grundbegriffe* project pays less attention to everyday publications than its initial aim suggests.

16 For the sake of brevity, I only refer to 'social reality.' Here, this is to be taken in a broad sense, including political life, economic life, etc.

17 Obviously, I am here simplifying rather complex considerations regarding the relation between language and history. For Koselleck's view of this relation, see Koselleck, Reinhart. 2006. "Sprachwandel und Ereignisgeschichte (erstmals erschienen 1989)." In *Begriffsgeschichten: Studien zur Semantik und Pragmatik der politischen und sozialen Sprache:* 32–55. Frankfurt a.M.: Suhrkamp; idem. 1998. "Social History and *Begriffsgeschichte.*" In *History of Concepts: Comparative Perspectives* ed. by Iain Hampsher-Monk, Karin Tilmans and Frank van Vree: 23–36. Amsterdam: Amsterdam University Press. For differences between German conceptual history and the Cambridge School in this regard, as well as a possible synthesis of the two, see: Leonhard, Jörn. 2004. "*Grundbegriffe* und *Sattelzeiten:* Languages and Discourses: Europäische und anglo-amerikanische Deutungen des Verhältnisses von Sprache und Geschichte." In *Interkultureller Transfer und nationaler Eigensinn. Europäische und anglo-amerikanische Perspektiven der Kulturwissenschaften* ed. by Rebekka Habermas and Rebekka von Mallinckrodt: 71–86. Göttingen: Wallstein.

18 Koselleck, Reinhart. 1996. "A Response to Comments on the Geschichtliche Grundbegriffe." In *The Meaning of Historical Terms and Concepts: New Studies on Begriffsgeschichte* ed. by Melvin Richter and Hartmut Lehmann: 59–70. Washington: German Historical Institute, here 64; taken from Richter, *The History,* 220.

formerly established ideas do not disappear all at once, but gradually lose their capacity to make sense of social reality, leading to new semantizations of terms or neologisms. Thus terminological variety and conceptual change can both alert us to social transformations and are themselves incomprehensible without considering the latter, as language is both an indicator of and a factor in history. Hence the interplay of conceptual and social history. My focus on conceptual change in this study results not from a general prioritization of ideal over material factors, of conceptual over social change, but rather from the latter having already been established in Egypt at the turn to the twentieth century.[19] What is more, conceptual change can also *precede* social change, as concepts alert us to the *envisioned* formation of social order, rather than to actual social structures.

This is especially true for modernity, in which visions of social and political order – as expressed by basic concepts – were the starting point for remaking or creating social and political structures and institutions; just think of 'racism,' 'communism,' or 'nationalism.' In fact, the very evolution of such '-isms' is crucial for the saddle period. Koselleck coined the term *Verzeitlichung* for this process, a term which may best be translated as 'temporalization,' in the sense of the "introduction of a temporal dimension."[20] *Verzeitlichung* indicates the progressive nature of concepts articulating historical time, such as 'development' or 'progress.' Moreover, collective terms (*Oberbegriffe*) were infused with a sense of expectation. Thus 'republic' was no longer a collective term designating all constitutions, but was identified with one true constitution. The expectation that this specific constitution would be realized is demonstrated even more clearly in 'Republicanism,' which, like all -isms, was coined as a term of expectation (*Erwartungsbegriff*). The expectation that a certain constitutional state would be realized is then, to a lesser extent, also infused into the term 'republic' itself. Thus, if the normativity of modern -isms is obvious, the terms from which these -isms are derived also acquire a normative dimension, even though – in non-ideologized contexts – a descriptive usage may be intended, as is the case with 'national' or 'social.'

Verzeitlichung is one of four characteristics of the saddle period; the other three characteristics Koselleck names are democratization, politicization, and the transformability of concepts into ideology (*Ideologisierbarkeit*). Democratization describes the increasing extension of concepts formerly confined to a specific estate to eventually include whole populaces. Through politicization, an in-

---

19 See below: chapter 4.

20 Koselleck, *Einleitung*, xvi–xviv; Koselleck and Richter, "Introduction," 11.

creasing number of people became involved in the political process, which itself came to revolve around terms of expectation. *Ideologisierbarkeit*, the "increasing extent to which many expressions could be incorporated into ideologies,"[21] results from the increasingly abstract scope of concepts, which no longer coalesce with observed reality and thus can be used to designate a variety of phenomena. This is, for example, what enabled the grouping of quite disparate sectors of reality under the new abstract noun 'religion.' Another abstract noun that only evolved in modernity is that of 'history' itself, whereas in the pre-modern period, there were only individual histories. In fact, the concept of 'history' expresses no less than the idea of a secular world, whose ends are located within this world.[22]

1.2 'Society' as the Most Constitutive Concept of Modernity

> "'Progress', 'civilization', 'toleration', 'utility': such keywords of enlightened philosophy are unthinkable without 'society' as their implied referent; they all assume its logical priority and moral value as the essential frame of collective human existence."
>
> – Baker, "Enlightenment," 84

Of the many basic concepts crucial to the modern understanding and structuring of the world, two candidates tend to be identified as the most constitutive: 'nation' and 'society.'[23] To some extent, whether 'society' or 'nation' is more fundamental does indeed depend on the historical context, as David Bell argues.[24] For

---

21 Ibid., 13.

22 Koselleck, *Futures*, 93–104. In relation to the concept of 'society,' see: Conze, Werner. 1992 [1964]. "Nation und Gesellschaft. Zwei Grundbegriffe der revolutionären Epoche." In *Gesellschaft – Staat – Nation: Gesammelte Aufsätze* ed. by Ulrich Engelhardt, Reinhart Koselleck und Wolfgang Schieder: 341–354. Stuttgart: Ernst Klett, here 342.

23 Conze stresses the commonalities between the two concepts, which he regards as best illustrating the modern idea of secular history (Conze, "Nation," 341, 343). Greenfield regards the idea of the 'nation' as "*the constitutive element of modernity,*" whereas he handles 'society' as a universal given (Greenfield, Liah. 1992. *Nationalism. Five Roads to Modernity.* Cambridge, Mass.: Harvard University Press, 18). Gordon, in turn, regards 'society' – or in his case, *société* – as more fundamental than 'nation' (Gordon, Daniel. 1994. *Citizens without Sovereignty. Equality and Sociability in French Thought (1670–1789).* Princeton: Princeton University Press, 7).

24 Bell, David A. 2001. *The Cult of the Nation in France: Inventing Nationalism, 1680–1800.* Cambridge, Mass./London: Harvard University Press, 231fn20; idem. 2003. "Nation et Patrie, Société et Civilisation: Transformations du vocabulaire social français, 1700–1789." In *L'invention de la société: Nominalisme politique et science sociale au xviiie siècle* ed. by Laurence Kaufmann and Jacques Guilhaumou: 99–120. Paris: École des Hautes Études en Sciences Sociales, here 102.

France, Bell names three concepts in addition to *société* and *nation* (namely *civilisation, patrie,* and *public*) which he regards as equally "illuminating of the overall phenomenon" – that is, of a "broad shift in the way the French imagined the world around them: from a perspective in which the human terrestrial order was seen as subordinated to exterior (particularly divine) determinations, to one in which it was seen as autonomous and self-regulating."[25] This aptly summarizes the shift to the autonomous modern self-understanding, which Bell dates between 1680 and 1800 for the French context.

The transition to modernity is illustrated in another sense by the parallel rise of the terms 'modern' and 'society' in "early modern England" and the shifting meaning of 'society' toward the end of that period, which Phil Withington dates between 1500 and 1700.[26] As Withington shows, 'society' was popularized in the 1570s by the same humanist authors who introduced the term 'modern.' However, "far from orientating its proponent forward in time 'modern' entailed a retrospective outlook."[27] Attention to contemporaneous usages of 'modern' thus allows Withington to grasp the (early) modernity of this period without imposing later understandings of the concept. The same is true for 'society,' which "was likewise pregnant with classical inference and resonance."[28] 'Society' was clearly popularized as a normative, even ideological term, the core reference of which was to "a kind of social interaction lying somewhere between the realms of 'the family' and 'the state' – a mode of collectivism best described as *voluntary and purposeful association.*"[29]

As a term of "Renaissance modernity," 'society' significantly overlapped in meaning with its older, "Gothic," rival term, 'company':[30] both pre-supposed an actual "communicable co-presence,"[31] referring to everyday sociability, networks, or corporations.[32] However, in contrast to 'company,' 'society' was also used "in a more abstract manner to invoke and philosophize about shared ways of life and the structures and values underpinning them."[33] These abstract references became more central in the second half of the seventeenth century,

25 Idem., *The Cult*, 26.

26 Withington, *Society*. Withington's corpus consists of "the title-pages of printed vernacular texts published between 1500 and 1700" (ibid., 7).

27 Ibid., 13.

28 Ibid., 13.

29 Ibid., 13.

30 Ibid., 107.

31 Ibid., 109.

32 Ibid., 113.

33 Ibid., 113.

when composites such as 'humane society,' 'civil society,' and 'political society' also came into wider usage.[34] Significantly, the normative core of 'society' as a "*voluntary and purposeful association*" was maintained even as the "spectrum of social interaction" referred to by the term was increasingly widened.[35] At the end of the seventeenth century, '(civil) society' had started to replace the older 'commonwealth,' which, in early modernity, had been the standard term for referring to the body politic in general.[36] As the normative connotations of 'society' show, this was not merely a change in terminology, but rather indicates the evolution of the autonomous modern self-understanding.

In this study, then, I take 'society' to be the most fundamental concept of modernity. While one may well assign this position to other concepts ('nation,' for instance, but also 'reason' or 'progress,' among others), the fundamental importance of 'society' for our modern self-understanding shows not least in us being hardly aware of its specificity. In other words, the modern idea of society has become so entrenched in our background understanding that we can hardly imagine our social life *not* taking place in and as society. It is in this vein that I read Keith Baker's argument, quoted in the epigram above: "'Progress', 'civilization', 'toleration', 'utility': such keywords of enlightened philosophy are unthinkable without 'society' as their implied referent; they all assume its logical priority and moral value as the essential frame of collective human existence."[37] The normativity of these keywords is thus easier to grasp but, in the end, less fundamental than that of 'society,' which forms "their implied referent." I would also argue that alternative political collectivities to the nation are more easily imaginable than forms of collective existence other than society. This might be why the imaginary nature of the nation has received greater attention than society,[38] which is equally an imaginary.

While the concept of 'society' does overlap significantly with 'nation,' I do need to distinguish hermeneutically between the two in order to decide for

34 Ibid., 129.

35 Ibid., 105.

36 Ibid., 129 f.

37 Baker, Keith Michael. 2001. "Enlightenment and the Institution of Society: Notes for a Conceptual History." In *Civil Society: History and Possibilities* ed. by Sudipta Kaviraj and Sunil Khilnani: 84–104. Cambridge: Cambridge University Press, here 84. This chapter was first published as idem. 1992. "Enlightenment and the Institution of Society: Notes for a Conceptual History." In *Main Trends in Cultural History* ed. by W Melching and W Velema: 95–120. Amsterdam/Atlanta: Rodopi.

38 Most notably, of course: Anderson, Benedict. 2006 [1982]. *Imagined Communities. Reflections on the Origin and Spread of Nationalism.* London/New York: Verso. Anderson briefly remarks on 'society' as well (ibid., 6, 25 f.).

one of the two terms in those cases where an Arabic term could be translated as either 'nation' or 'society.' To this end, I take 'nation' to foreground a common genealogy or the common characteristics of a group of people, whereas 'society' is continuously made and remade by a group of people – which may well be a 'nation.' The bonds of 'society' are to be created, whereas a 'nation' is constituted by imagined bonds, whether of religion, ethnicity, territory, or language. In a sense, then, 'society' addresses *how* the continuous modern problem of social order is to be dealt with, whereas 'nation' delineates the group of people *who* are to solve this problem. In the remainder of this chapter, I introduce additional hermeneutical distinctions between 'society' and related concepts, working out the main characteristics of 'society' in quite an extremely systematic manner.

After all, while we need a sense of the crucial features of the idea of society – as expressed by the concept of 'society' – in order to discern this concept in *al-Manar*, no definition of 'society' can be given. This is clear because there is no escaping Nietzsche's fundamental insight that "nothing that has a history can be defined."[39] In addition, I cannot possibly aim to summarize the history of 'society' in any way that would qualify as a conceptual history. The entries treating 'society' (*Gesellschaft*) in the *Geschichtliche Grundbegriffe* alone make up more than 140 pages.[40] Comparable results would be expected from similar comprehensive undertakings for other European languages. Between languages, the evolution, usages, and connotations of 'society' differ even more than is already the case within a single language. Here, I limit myself to examples from the English, French, and German languages.[41] More importantly, with the exclusive aim of discerning the concept of 'society' in *al-Manar*, I will work out the most fun-

39 Nietzsche, Friedrich. 1977. "Zur Genealogie der Moral." In *Sämtliche Werke. Kritische Studienausgabe*; ed. Giorgio Colli und Mazzino Montinari, vol. 5 München/Berlin: dtv/De Gruyter, 317.

40 Riedel, Manfred. 1975. "Gesellschaft, bürgerliche." In *Geschichtliche Grundbegriffe. Historisches Lexikon zur politisch-sozialen Sprache in Deutschland; Band 2 E-G* ed. by Otto Brunner, Werner Conze and Reinhart Koselleck: 719–800. Stuttgart: Klett; idem. 1975. "Gesellschaft, Gemeinschaft." In *Geschichtliche Grundbegriffe. Historisches Lexikon zur politisch-sozialen Sprache in Deutschland; Band 2 E-G* ed. by Otto Brunner, Werner Conze and Reinhart Koselleck: 801–862. Stuttgart: Klett. For a synthesis of the last-mentioned article in English, see: idem. 1984. "'State' and 'Civil Society': Linguistic Context and Historical Origin." In: *Between Tradition and Revolution*. Cambridge: Cambridge University Press, 129–158.

41 There are good reasons for doing so, besides the fact that I am most versed in these languages: of all European languages, English and French were the most influential in the context of *al-Manar*. While this is less true for German, German conceptual history has provided insights on the evolution of *Gesellschaft* and its Latin precursor, *societas*, which are not confined to the German trajectory.

damental characteristics of the concept, as acquired in modernity and as constitutive of the modern self-understanding.

The following three sections each foreground and substantiate a specific modern characteristic of 'society' – namely, its distinction from 'the state' (2) and from 'religion' (3) and the consolidation of society as an autonomous object of sociological study (4).

2 Society and the State: The Political Dimension of 'Society'

"L'ancien gouvernement n'est plus; le nouveau n'existe pas encore.
La république est proclamée, plutôt qu'établie; notre pacte social est à faire... ."
– Robespierre, 1792[42]

"There is no such thing as society.
There are individual men and women, and there are families."
– Margaret Thatcher, 1987[43]

In demonstrating that the distinction between society and the state is specifically modern, it is helpful to also attend to the concept of 'civil society,' which – especially in continental Europe[44] – is often used synonymously with 'society' as concerns the latter's political dimension. (The reference to polite, civil intercourse expressed by 'civil society' was also a dominant pre-modern meaning of 'society' tout court;[45] this, however, is of lesser concern to us here.) While 'society' tends to be used for pre-modern social formations as well, 'civil society' designates a specifically modern, predominantly liberal vision of society.[46] For reasons that should have become clear by now, I prefer to treat 'society' as a normative and historical concept. The specifically modern relation of society to the state is often negotiated under the heading of 'civil society.' Including the latter concept in this section therefore enhances our understanding of some of the for-

---

42 Quoted from: Kaufmann, Laurence. 2003. "Le Dieu Social: Vers une socio-logie du nominalisme en Révolution." In *L'invention de la société: Nominalisme politique et science sociale au xviiie siècle* ed. by Laurence Kaufmann and Jacques Guilhaumou: 123–161. Paris: École des Hautes Études en Sciences Sociales, here 132.

43 Quoted from: Bennett, Tony, Grossberg, Lawrence and Morris, Meaghan (eds.). 2005. *New Keywords. A Revised Vocabulary of Culture and Society.* Malden, Mass.: Blackwell, 326.

44 Outhwaite, William. 2006. *The Future of Society.* Oxford: Blackwell, 107.

45 Gordon, *Citizens*; Withington, *Society.*

46 See, for example: Kaviraj, Sudipta. 2001. "In Search of Civil Society." In *Civil Society: History and Possibilities* ed. by Sudipta Kaviraj and Sunil Khilnani: 287–323. Cambridge: Cambridge University Press, esp. 308 f.

mer's political connotations. While the concept of 'civil society' seems more specific than 'society,' its usages also differ significantly,[47] and I can here only point to pivotal moments illustrating the historicity and normativity of the concept. Central to the conceptual history of 'civil society,' which actually reaches back further than that of 'society,' is the distinction between society and the state in modernity.

The concept of 'civil society' – and its French and German counterparts, *société civile* and *bürgerliche Gesellschaft* – can be traced back, via their common Latin predecessor *societas civilis*, to the Aristotelian concept of *koinonìa politkè.*[48] For Aristotle, this 'political society' was that type of *koinonìa* (i.e., of human association) that took place in the city-state of the *polis.* It consisted exclusively of free men, who – as the heads of households (*oikos*) – came together to independently give themselves laws for the sake of common felicity. As such, the *koinonìa politkè* was regarded as superior to all other forms of human association. More importantly, it was contrasted with the sphere of households, rather than with the state. In fact, no distinct concept of the latter existed, and, by implication, there was also no distinct concept of its modern twin – society. Rather, society and the state were conflated in the concept of *koinonìa politkè.* (Of course, we can identify this conflation only retrospectively.) After the appropriation of the Aristotelian concept, the identification of a 'civil society' of free citizens with 'political society' basically remained in place until the institution of democratic political arrangements.

It was only in the eighteenth century that 'civil' and 'political society' came to be dissociated, leading to the modern distinction of (civil) society and the state. The formation of the latter as an abstract and relatively stable entity went hand in hand with society coming to include all members living in the territory and under the jurisdiction of a state, which was hegemonically conceived of as a nation-state. This distinction between state and society, together with the

---

47 For an overview of the literature on 'civil society,' which has mushroomed especially since 1990, see: Gosewinkel, Dieter. 2011. "Civil Society." In *European History Online (EGO), published by the Institute of European History (IEG), Mainz 2011–01–12,* http://www.ieg-ego.eu/gosewinkeld-2010-en (accessed March 20, 2015).

48 While Aristotle did not create the concept *ex nihilo*, of course, its specific formulation has not been identified as occurring earlier (Riedel, "Gesellschaft, bürgerliche," 721 f.). For summaries of the history of 'civil society' other than Riedel's extensive survey, see: Hallberg, Peter and Wittrock, Björn. 2006. "From *koinonìa politikè* to *societas civilis:* Birth, Disappearance and First Renaissance of the Concept." In *The Languages of Civil Society* ed. by Peter Wagner: 28–54. New York: Berghahn; Kocka, Jürgen. 2005. "Civil Society: Some remarks on the career of a concept." In *Comparing Modernities. Pluralism versus Homogenity* ed. by Eliezer Ben-Rafael and Yitzhak Sternberg: 141–149. Leiden/Boston: Brill.

increasing inclusiveness of society, had been a Europe-wide and even a global phenomenon.[49] However, when and how state and society came to be distinguished differed greatly according to context. With Phil Withington in the previous section, we sensed the origins of the encompassing reference of 'society' in early modern England. Yet for John Locke (d. 1704), 'civil' and 'political society' were still identical, with no distinction between society and the state in evidence.[50] Crucially, however, Locke prioritized human beings' natural tendency to socialize and to thereby form a polity. The social and political order, which was perceived as having reached a crisis, was thus not to be regrounded in God or the king, but in human beings' social nature, which was notably regarded as given by God.[51] Philosophically, the distinction between society and the state was first and most forcefully formulated by Hegel,[52] although his importance in this regard is not uncontested.[53]

In Britain, the relative success of the liberal tradition is regarded as a central reason why state and society have rarely been viewed as being opposed to one another, quite contrary to the revolutionary institution of society in France or Germany.[54] A closer look at the German context, where the dominant understanding continued to identify 'civil society' with the estate of free citizens until the middle of the nineteenth century, again reveals quite contradictory trends, which only temporarily culminated in calls to eliminate the state in a "social revolution" in the 1840s.[55] In France, by the time of the revolution in 1789, *société civile* had already given way to *société* tout court.[56] The revolutionaries advanced a nominalist understanding of politics and of society as a construct consisting of equal individuals bound together by contract, as Laurence Kauf-

49 Conze, Werner. 1992 [1958]. "Staat und Gesellschaft in der frührevolutionären Epoche Deutschlands." In *Gesellschaft – Staat – Nation: Gesammelte Aufsätze* ed. by Ulrich Engelhardt, Reinhart Koselleck und Wolfgang Schieder: 157–185. Stuttgart: Ernst Klett, here 157.
50 Withington, *Society*, 132; Seligman, Adam. 2002. "Civil Society as Idea and Ideal." In *Alternative Conceptions of Civil Society* ed. by Simone Chambers and Will Kymlicka: 13–33. Princeton: Princeton University Press, here 15.
51 Ibid., 14 ff.
52 Riedel, "Gesellschaft, bürgerliche," 779 ff.; Kocka, "Civil Society," 143.
53 See: Terrier, Jean and Wagner, Peter. 2006. "Civil Society and the Problématique of Political Modernity." In *The Languages of Civil Society* ed. by Peter Wagner: 9–27. New York: Berghahn.
54 Riedel, "Gesellschaft, bürgerliche," 721; Conze, "Staat," 157 f.; Kocka, "Civil Society," 143 f.
55 Conze, "Staat," 173.
56 Branca-Rosoff, Sonia and Guilhaumou, Jacques. 1988. "De 'société' à 'socialisme' (Sieyès): l'invention néologique et son contexte discursif. Essai de colinguisme appliqué." *Langage et société* 83–84: 39–77, here 50–59.

mann has argued.[57] Whether the notion of individual beings and of society appeared at the same historical moment, or whether the stress on individual rights was a precondition for the idea of society to evolve, cannot be discussed here.[58] In any case, prioritizing individuals (as members of society) was not only an attack on the monarchic, universalist understanding of socio-political order, but also on the cosmic, godly order sustaining it.[59]

However, the French Revolution's promise of equality had reached a crisis by 1848, and the Republic itself seemed to be a problem rather than the solution. It was really only then, as Jacques Donzelot has shown, that the social was promoted to explain and manage social differences and problems. 'The social,' which is synonymous with 'society' when "conceptualised as a realm between 'the private' and 'the political',"[60] thus became a means for the state itself to address the 'social question.'[61] Beyond the French context, the state also played a primary role in producing knowledge about the newly constructed object of the social or society.[62] Therefore a focus on society does not necessarily entail opposition to the state. Rather, once society and the state are distinguished, the two can be related in very different ways – either as mutually dependent or as prioritizing one of the two, possibly to the extent of attempting to make the other superfluous.

An attempt at making the state superfluous is most clearly visible in the program of socialism, which also terminologically illustrates the potential political force of the terms 'society' and 'the social,' from which it is derived.[63] The link between human beings' soci(et)al nature and socialism also finds a terminological expression in Arabic. The present Arabic term for socialism is *ishtirākiyya*,

---

57 Kaufmann, "Le Dieu."

58 Compare [Kaufmann, Laurence and Guilhaumou, Jacques]. 2003. "Présentation." In *L'invention de la société: Nominalisme politique et science sociale au xviiie siècle* ed. by Laurence Kaufmann and Jacques Guilhaumou: 9–20. Paris: École des Hautes Études en Sciences Sociales, here 10, 17; and Baker, "Enlightenment" [2001], 95–98.

59 Kaufmann, "Le Dieu," 124, 132; Gautier, Claude. 1993. *L'invention de la société civile. Lectures anglo-écossaises: Mandeville, Smith, Ferguson.* Paris: Presses Universitaires de France, 7.

60 Wagner, Peter. 2001. *A History and Theory of the Social Sciences.* London: Sage, 178fn63.

61 Donzelot, Jacques. 1994 [1984]. *L'invention du social. Essai sur le déclin des passions politiques.* Paris: Éditions du Seuil. The central chapter of this book has been translated into English: idem. 1988. "The Promotion of the Social." *Economy and Society* 17/3: 395–427.

62 On this, see: Wittrock, Björn, Wagner, Peter and Wollmann, Hellmut (eds.). 1990. *Social Sciences and Modern States.* Cambridge: Cambridge University Press; Rueschemeyer, Dietrich and Skopcol, Theda (eds.). 1994. *States, Social Knowledge, and the Origins of Modern Social Policies.* Princeton, NJ: Princeton University Press.

63 See Branca-Rosoff and Guilhaumou, "De 'société,'" esp. 59–77.

which refers to the idea of mutual sharing and cooperation. Before this term became established, however, socialism was also rendered as *ijtimāʿiyya*, which – to keep matters simple here[64] – drew upon the act of human beings' social association (*ijtimāʿ*).

In its most general sense, the concept of 'society' foregrounds social differentiation, whereas its rival term of 'the people,' which is preferred by nationalists, stresses an imagined unity.[65] The preference of sociologists for the concept of 'society,'[66] the primary interpreters and spokespersons of which they were to become, thus tends to go along with certain political convictions: "In fact, by far the majority of sociologists lie within a political arena which is fairly well defined by the central importance given to the concept of society. It is difficult to imagine a Nazi or Stalinist sociologist and almost impossible to imagine a racist sociologist."[67] Building on these different normative connotations of 'the people' and 'society,' we may add that the first tends to refer to actual persons and tends to be contrasted with 'the rulers' or 'the government,' whereas 'society' conveys a more abstract notion of order and is instead contrasted with 'the state.'

When discerning the concept of 'society' in *al-Manar*, particularly regarding its political relevance, it is important to keep these rival concepts in mind. In fact, my interest in 'society' rather than 'the people' is partly due to its having become hegemonic, especially in the secular academy, through whose lens I am looking at *al-Manar*. The journal's authors, as we will see, in fact conceived of the political collectivity in a way that combines aspects pre-dominantly associated with either 'society' or 'the people.' Still, in choosing one of these terms to translate individual instances, the above distinction is useful as a hermeneutic tool.

For the same purpose, an ideal-typical distinction between 'society' and 'community' needs to be introduced. Their history is conventionally taken to begin with Aristotle as well, with both concepts retrospectively identified as being conflated in his concept of *koinonìa*.[68] Bracketing the pre-modern history

64 For the different meanings of *ijtimāʿ*, see below: chapter 10 section 1.

65 Bielefeld, Ulrich. 2003. *Nation und Gesellschaft. Selbstthematisierungen in Frankreich und Deutschland.* Hamburg: Hamburger Edition, 250.

66 Ulrich Bielefeld, who regards the concept of 'the people' as central to modernity (ibid., 12), identifies German sociologists as initially preferring that concept but gradually dissolving it into 'society' (ibid., 53, 57).

67 Touraine, Alain. 2005. "The End of the 'Social'." In *Comparing Modernities. Pluralism versus Homogenity* ed. by Eliezer Ben-Rafael and Yitzhak Sternberg: 229–244. Leiden/Boston: Brill, here 231f.

68 As for 'civil society' (*bürgerliche Gesellschaft*), Manfred Riedel also provided the most extensive conceptual history of these two concepts; see: Riedel, "Gesellschaft, Gemeinschaft."

of 'society' and 'community,' for our purposes it only matters that both concepts were still used synonymously at the end of the nineteenth century.[69] Faced with what he perceived as a conceptual muddle, Ferdinand Tönnies then famously attempted to restrict the respective meanings of 'community' (*Gemeinschaft*) and 'society' (*Gesellschaft*) and to clearly distinguish between these concepts according to their alleged essence. His work *Gemeinschaft und Gesellschaft*, first published in 1887,[70] was also influential outside of the German-speaking world.[71] The central terms were translated into English differently, with 'community' and 'society' arguably being the most adequate renditions.[72] Tönnies's attempt to restrict the meanings of both concepts was eventually doomed to failure, as is hardly surprising in light of the plurality of meanings inherent to concepts. Nevertheless, his definitions clearly resonated in wider understandings. Tönnies defined 'life in community' as "all close, intimate, exclusive living together."[73] 'Society,' on the other hand, was defined as "the public sphere, the world."[74] 'Community,' with its romantic overtones, was thus associated with intimacy, collectivism, and tradition, whereas 'society' was associated with rationality, individualism, and modernity. This understanding of both concepts, which Tönnies presented as "basic concepts of pure sociology" in the subtitle of the 1912 edition,[75] became influential as an ideal-typical distinction in the social sciences and the humanities. It should be clear that community is imagined as a traditional form of social life only in modernity.

The contemporary distinction in Arabic between *jamāʿa* ('community') and *mujtamaʿ* ('society') – in a broad sense, and keeping in mind the polyvalence of concepts – resembles these ideal types. It remains to be seen whether such a broad distinction, which evolved in European languages only from the end of the nineteenth century onward and at no point came to be unambiguously established, can already be discerned in *al-Manar*. Equally possible is that a single

---

69 Ibid., 803.

70 Tönnies, Ferdinand. 1887. *Gemeinschaft und Gesellschaft. Abhandlung des Communismus und des Socialismus als empirischer Culturformen.* Leipzig: Fues.

71 For the English-speaking world, see: Bond, Niall. 2009. "Gemeinschaft und Gesellschaft: The Reception of a Conceptual Dichotomy." *Contributions to the History of Concepts* 5/2: 162–186. The reception of Tönnies's distinction in the English language somewhat undermines Riedel's argument of it being a German, anti-Western *Sonderweg* (Riedel, "Gesellschaft, Gemeinschaft," 859).

72 Bond, "Gemeinschaft," 165, 173. In fact, Tönnies himself had previously used the German terms to translate Hobbes's 'commonwealth' and Locke's 'political society' (ibid., 170).

73 Ibid., 168fn26.

74 Ibid., 168fn27.

75 The subtitle of the original edition read "communism and socialism as empirical forms of culture," associating the former with 'community' and the latter with 'society' (ibid., 169).

Arabic term may combine those aspects ideal-typically associated with 'community' and 'society.'[76] In European languages as well, societal aspects can be expressed by the term 'community,' as can communitarian aspects by 'society.'[77]

What is more, research on the intellectual and social history of India (which, compared with research on Arab countries, has yielded more thoroughly reworked European theories and concepts) has convincingly argued that the primary function of 'civil society' – to create social solidarity in a sphere autonomous from the state – has been fulfilled in India by forms of community, such as caste or *jamat* assemblies.[78] This goes hand in hand with questioning the universality of the European coinage of 'civil society' as consisting of free individuals, voluntary assembling. Partha Chatterjee maintains that the universalization of this understanding was crucial for the victory of capitalism and resulted in suppressing narratives of community.[79] Herein lies a supposed reason why anti-colonial nationalism then resorted to notions of community rather than of society.[80] As this research on India suggests, shifting from the ideas a concept has been expressing to the function it has been fulfilling enlarges the range of possible alternatives to the hegemonic concept. This shift can be characterized as a shift from a narrow to a broad understanding of the concept, and it is of interest to investigate whether the concept of 'society' in *al-Manar*, if discernible at all, corresponds to a narrow, hegemonic understanding or "only" to a broader conception of society.

An overly narrow understanding of (civil) society for our purposes would be to conceive of the concept not only as a sphere distinct from the state, but to identify it with individualism, pluralism, or democracy, as has been done in many debates on 'civil society' since the concept's forceful reappearance in the 1990s. In this vein, an anthology on *Alternative Conceptions of Civil Society,*[81]

---

76 Such was actually the case with *umma*, as will become apparent in part C; see especially chapter 10 section 4.2.

77 For usages of 'civil society' that stress the value of community, see: Seligman, "Civil Society," 18 f.

78 Randeria, Shalini. 2009. "Entangled Histories of Uneven Modernities: Civil Society, Caste Councils, and Legal Pluralism in Postcolonial India." In *Comparative and Transnational History: Central European Approaches and New Perspectives* ed. by Heinz-Gerhard Haupt and Jürgen Kocka: 77–104. New York/Oxford: Berghahn, esp. 82; see also: Pernau, "Gibt es."

79 Chatterjee, Partha. 1990. "A Response to Taylor's 'Modes of Civil Society'," *Public Culture* 3/1: 119–132, here 128.

80 Ibid., 132.

81 Chambers, Simone and Kymlicka, Will (eds.). 2002. *Alternative Conceptions of Civil Society.* Princeton: Princeton University Press.

while stressing differences within the liberal tradition itself,[82] asks whether, in fact, "a non-liberal or non-pluralist civil society (is) a contradiction in terms."[83] It is largely in this more recent context that the question of civil society in Islamic countries has been posed[84] and within which the Islamic intellectual tradition has been interrogated concerning its potential resources for civil society.[85] However, identifying a pre-modern Islamic civil society via actors and institutions that were allegedly autonomous from the state[86] unhelpfully blurs the modern specifics of (civil) society. For the same reasons, I am also highly skeptical concerning the identification of pre-modern equivalents or alternatives to the present Arabic term for 'civil society,' *al-mujtamaʿ al-madanī.*[87]

---

82 The volume actually opens with two different concepts of 'civil society' offered by thinkers who identify themselves as liberal; compare: Walzer, Michael. 2002. "Equality and Civil Society." In *Alternative Conceptions of Civil Society* ed. by Simone Chambers and Will Kymlicka: 34–49 Princeton: Princeton University Press; and Lomasky, Loren E. 2002. "Classical Liberalism and Civil Society." In *Alternative Conceptions of Civil Society* ed. by Simone Chambers and Will Kymlicka: 50–70. Princeton: Princeton University Press.

83 Chambers, Simone and Kymlicka, Will. 2002. "Introduction: Alternative Conceptions of Civil Society." In *Alternative Conceptions of Civil Society* ed. by Simone Chambers and Will Kymlicka: 1–10. Princeton: Princeton University Press, here 5.

84 See: Norton, August Richard (ed.). 1995. *Civil Society in the Middle East.* 2 vols. Leiden/New York/Köln: Brill.

85 See, for example: Hanafi, Hasan. 2002. "Alternative Conceptions of Civil Society: A Reflective Islamic Approach." In *Alternative Conceptions of Civil Society* ed. by Simone Chambers and Will Kymlicka: 171–189. Princeton: Princeton University Press. For an overview of debates, see: Hamzawy, Amr. 2002. "Normative Dimensions of Contemporary Arab Debates on Civil Society. Between the Search for a New Formulation of Democracy and the Controversy over the Political Role of Religion." In *Civil Society in the Middle East* ed. by Amr Hamzawy: 10–46. Berlin: Schiler; Zubaida, Sami. 2001. "Civil Society, Community, and Democracy in the Middle East." In *Civil Society: History and Possibilities* ed. by Sudipta Kaviraj and Sunil Khilnani: 232–249. Cambridge: Cambridge University Press. Stressing the transformation of Catholicism and its important role in the resurgence of 'civil society,' José Casanova asks whether Islam "could possibly play a similar role in the democratization of Muslim countries and in the emergence of Islamic civil societies" (Casanova, José. 2001. "Civil Society and Religion: Retrospective Reflections on Catholicism and Prospective Reflections on Islam." *Social Research* 68/4: 1041–1080, here 1042).

86 Hanafi, "Alternative," 173 ff. Other examples are: Kamali, Masoud. 2001. "Civil Society and Islam: A Sociological Perspective." *European Journal of Sociology* 42/3: 457–482; Moussalli, Ahmad S. 1995. "Modern Islamic Fundamentalist Discourses on Civil Society, Pluralism and Democracy." In *Civil Society in the Middle East* ed. by August Richard Norton: vol. 1: 79–119. Leiden/New York/Köln: Brill, here 82–88.

87 Drawing on a brief paper by Wajih Kawtharani, Amr Hamzawy suggests the term *al-mujtamaʿ al-ahlī* as classical (Hamzawy, "Normative," esp. 28). A danger of misunderstanding results from Hamzawy's failure to explain that *al-mujtamaʿ al-ahlī* was coined by Kawtharani, rather

In the broadest sense, '(civil) society' answers to the "problématique of political modernity."[88] Herein lies the common reason for the concept having gained prominence in the seventeenth century and again after the end of the Cold War. As Terrier and Wagner have succinctly put it, "the concept 'civil society' refers to a way of answering the question of how a configuration of social relations can find its adequate expression in a political form under conditions of political modernity, that is, of a commitment to collective self-determination, in a given historical context."[89] Thus the concept of 'civil society' has been answering to the problem of socio-political order, which had become questionable. As we have seen, its normative core was also expressed by 'society,'[90] which – in the French example (as *société*) – had already replaced 'civil society' (*société civile*) by the end of the eighteenth century. 'Society,' along with 'the social,' then gained particular importance in answering and managing social questions, as we shall see in greater detail in chapter 2 section 4, when dealing with the sociological institutionalization of society as an autonomous object with independent laws.

In addition to recalling the hermeneutic distinctions between 'society' and 'community' and 'society' and 'the people,' I also want to reiterate the following points from the foregoing presentation: (civil) society, after having been distinguished from the state, was only gradually conceived of as including all the members of a polity – hegemonically, the nation-state. The specifically modern distinction between (civil) society and the state presupposed that political order was no longer seen as mirroring the cosmic, godly order, but rather was grounded in human nature – that is, it was regarded as internal to society, even though human nature and social association might optionally be regrounded in God. While the distinction of society from the state already has secular implications,[91] these are increasingly obvious in the relation of society and religion, to which we now turn.

---

than being a classical term in itself. Kawtharani's paper can be found here: http://www.aljaredah.com/paper.php?source=akbar&mlf=interpage&sid=11515 (accessed Sept. 8, 2015).

88 Terrier and Wagner, "Civil."

89 Ibid., 24.

90 Elsewhere, Wagner himself speaks of 'society' instead of 'civil society' as answering to this problématique: Wagner, *Modernity*, 10.

91 Catherine Pickstock, who is affiliated with Radical Orthodoxy (see above: 7fn36), stresses both the fundamentally secular implications of the modern understanding of civil society and the origins of the concept in mediaeval scholasticism: Pickstock, Catherine. 2002. "The Mediaeval Origins of Civil Society." In *The Social in Question: New Bearings in History and the Social Sciences* ed. by Patrick Joyce: 21–43. London/New York: Routledge.

3 Society and Religion: The Secular and Metaphysical Dimensions of 'Society'

"La société civile est, pour ainsi dire, une divinité pour lui sur la terre."
– *Encyclopédie ou Dictionnaire raisonné des sciences*, 1765[92]

"Quelques moralistes modernes osent faire entendre que tous les devoirs de l'homme émanent du principe de la société, c'est-à-dire, que si nous vivions séparés de toute société, nous n'aurions point de devoirs. Doctrine détestable [...]"
– *Dictionnaire de Trévoux*, 1771[93]

"For us, too, civil society is, as it were, a divinity on earth. Society is our God, the ontological frame of our human existence."
– Keith Baker, 2001[94]

Concerning the inherently secular but in a sense also metaphysical dimension of 'society' and its relation to religion, Keith Baker's "Enlightenment and the Institution of Society" remains the most illuminating study at our disposal.[95] As the title indicates, 'society' was *instituted* at a particular historical moment – or, put otherwise, it was *invented:*[96] "Society is an invention not a discovery. It is a representation of the world instituted in practice, not simply a brute objective fact. This is not to deny, of course, that there is interdependence in human relations. It is simply to point out that there are many possible ways in which this interdependence might be construed. *Society* is the conceptual construction of that interdependence we still owe to the Enlightenment."[97]

---

92 Quoted from: Baker, "Enlightenment" [2001], 84.
93 Quoted from: Moras, Joachim. 1930. *Ursprung und Entwicklung des Begriffs der Zivilisation in Frankreich (1756–1830)* Hamburg: Seminar für romanische Sprachen und Kultur, 6.
94 Baker, "Enlightenment" [2001], 85.
95 Ibid. From a critical perspective, one may argue that Baker overstresses the contribution of Enlightenment thinkers, neglecting related or similar developments among "common people" (see [Kaufmann and Guilhaumou], "Présentation," 18 f.). Of course, this echoes a wider critique of the narrow focus on elite texts in conceptual history. However, for my purposes of foregrounding the normativity of 'society' and its related concepts, Baker's restricted focus is no impediment.
96 Tellingly, the German translation has *Erfindung* (invention) instead of 'institution' in its title (idem. 1995. "Aufklärung und die Erfindung der Gesellschaft." In *Nach der Aufklärung?* ed. by Wolfgang Klein and Waltraud Naumann-Beyer: 109–124. Berlin: Akademie Verlag).
97 Idem., "Enlightenment" [2001], 99 f.

Tellingly, Diderot and d'Alembert's mid-eighteenth century *Encyclopédie*, a masterpiece of the Enlightenment,[98] declared that the term *social* had been introduced only in recent years.[99] While the central terms of the debate around society were not quite as novel as they appeared to contemporaries,[100] the usage of *société* – along with its cognates *social*, *sociable*, and *sociabilité* – did indeed surge through the 1670s and 1680s, and then steadily increased throughout the following century.[101] This surge in usage went along with an ever more significant shift in the meaning of *société*, which Baker discerns from a range of dictionaries and encyclopedias. With regard to the beginning of the seventeenth century, Baker summarizes the meanings of *société* in a rather similar way as did Withington for 'society:' "At the beginning of the seventeenth century, *société* carried a range of essentially voluntaristic meanings, clustered around two poles: association or partnership for a common purpose, on the one hand; friendship, comradeship, companionability, on the other."[102] By the end of the seventeenth century, *société* had acquired the additional modern meaning that we are familiar with: the earlier meanings "are joined by a more general meaning of society as the basic form of collective human existence, at once natural to human beings and instituted by them, a corollary of human needs and a human response to those needs."[103]

The modern meaning of *société* was not only controversial in its institutional phase, but also entailed many debates concerning the more specific understandings and foundations of society. Even Enlightenment thinkers, who advanced the modern understanding of *société*, profoundly disagreed about central features of the concept. The different positions taken up in crucial debates in the eighteenth century can to some extent be discerned from the differing meanings assigned to *société:* "the semantic charge of *société* oscillates between the twin poles of freedom and necessity, between the voluntarism of free contract, on the one hand,

98 *Encyclopédie ou Dictionnaire raisonné des sciences, des arts et des métiers;* par une société de gens de lettres, mis en ordre & publié par M. Diderot ... & quant à la partie mathématique, par M. d'Alembert ...; 35 vols. 1751–1780. Paris/Neuchâtel/Amsterdam: [Various publishers].

99 Baker, "Enlightenment" [2001], 86 f. For an analysis of *société* and its cognates in that work, see also Branca-Rosoff and Guilhaumou, "De 'société'," 53–58.

100 The term *socialiser*, which is hardly conceivable without its implied referent *le social*, first appeared in 1786 (Martin, Xavier. 1989. "Révolution française et socialisation de l'individu." In *La Révolution française et les processus de socialisation de l'homme moderne* ed. by Claude Mazauric: 78–84. Paris: Messidor; referred to by Kaufmann, "Le Dieu," 126).

101 Baker, "Enlightenment" [2001], 85. Baker takes these statistics from Gordon, *Citizens*.

102 Baker, "Enlightenment" [2001], 86.

103 Ibid., 95. The first work foregrounding these modern meanings of 'society,' according to Baker, was Antoine Furetière's *Dictionnaire universal* from 1690.

and the constraints of collective human existence on the other. Chronologically, the transparence of society as free contract and open companionability thickens into the complex necessities of human interdependence. Philosophically, society as contract is opposed to society as bonds. Metaphysically, society replaces religion."[104] Here, we are interested in this last aspect, concerning the relation of society and religion, which, in the end, is more complex than the wording of the former "replacing" the latter might suggest.

The main controversy between Enlightenment thinkers themselves was whether society can be justified and instituted by purely natural means, or whether it requires religious foundations. A very explicit refutation of the first position can be found in an article in the *Encyclopédie méthodique* from 1790.[105] Here, it also becomes clear that even when the necessity of religious foundations is stressed, society has assumed primacy. In the first article, the author[106] agrees that "society is grounded in human needs," and as such, it is "natural to humankind."[107] However, he attacks in the strongest terms the position that society "owes its existence to a contract among individuals in pursuit of their common utility."[108] He maintains that the idea of such a social contract being possible without any obligations prior to human conventions is absurd, and he charges those philosophers upholding this idea with "pure atheism."[109]

For this author, it is God who, "in giving mankind the need to live in society, has also imposed upon it the obligation of social life. [...] Behind the necessity of society there lies, in this account, the necessity of religion. God, it turns out, is the ultimate founder of society."[110] Contrary to the claim that religion is dangerous for society, it is religion that guarantees social order, validating it as the "work of God himself."[111] The fact that this religious argument is made in reaction to secularist claims shows that religion is validated in its function for society, which has assumed primacy: "The necessity of society here becomes the essential argument for the indispensability of religion. Christianity assumes the

104 Baker, "Enlightenment" [2001], 95.

105 Another article in the same encyclopaedia approvingly cites Rousseau's *Du contrat social.* According to Baker, this reference was most likely inserted for editorial purposes (ibid., 94). In any case, it does further testify to the presence of antagonistic opinions, without adding anything of significance to the first article presented here, the author of which most probably regarded Rousseau as one of those modern philosophers to be refuted.

106 Baker does not give the name of this – possibly anonymous – author.

107 Ibid., 92.

108 Ibid., 92.

109 Ibid., 93.

110 Ibid., 93.

111 Ibid., 93.

form of a social gospel, a stage in the progressive advance of human civilization towards universal fraternity. Religion emerges as the guarantee of social order; but in the process the discourse of religion has been subordinated to the discourse of society. Religion is ultimately justified in the name of society, not vice versa."[112] To give a concrete example, which can be found in Christian apologetics as well as in *al-Manar*,[113] under the utilitarian premise resulting from the primacy of society, the purpose of religious fasting or alms-giving is not stated as cleansing one's own soul, but rather as contributing to social welfare or solidarity.

The mutual dependence of religion and society under the primacy of the latter becomes still clearer in Diderot and d'Alembert's *Encyclopédie* (which served as a model for the *Encyclopédie méthodique*). Drawing upon Claude Buffier's *Traité de la société civile* from 1726, the authors of the *Encyclopédie* argue that the principles of ethics would be unsustainable without religion.[114] This, however, does not posit an absolute authority or even primacy of religion. Firstly, "the goals and interests of religion must be strictly distinguished from those of civil society."[115] Secondly, "the resources of religion must be used in the manner most advantageous to society."[116] One can certainly interpret this as according primacy to society. The more fundamental point, however, is the mutual dependence of religion and society: "Neither could be thought without reference to the other: the institution of society as the conceptual frame of human collective existence required (indeed, it found its ultimate logic in) the displacement and reworking of the prior claims of the divine."[117] It was especially concerning questions of social order and ethics that religion and society were mutually dependent and initially almost necessarily invoked as a pair.

Regarding its jurisprudential relevance, 'society' was addressed independently of religion, which illustrates the term's overall "secular force."[118] The *Encyclopédie* contained two articles on *société* – one under the heading of 'ethics,' the other "largely devoted to the jurisprudential meaning of the term."[119] In fact, most encyclopedias and dictionaries of the seventeenth and eighteenth cen-

---

112 Ibid., 93 f.

113 See below: chapter 7 section 3.3, 8 section 4.2, and 10 section 3.2.

114 Baker, "Enlightenment" [2001], 91.

115 Ibid., 92. Following the discussion in the previous section, we sense that in this argumentation, (civil) society was not yet clearly distinguished from the state.

116 Ibid., 91 f.

117 Ibid., 92.

118 Ibid., 89

119 Ibid., 88.

turies expressed a certain disjunction of the legal and moral dimension of 'society' by including two articles on the term, each of which was primarily devoted to one of these dimensions.[120] The legal understanding of *société* expressed the broadest sense of the term – namely, as any union of people grouped around a common object. This included scientific as well as commercial or literary societies, religious congregations as well as political society, among others. The only *société* concerning which the *Encyclopédie* inserts a non-secular – that is here, a supra-temporal, timeless reference – is marriage, which is depicted as the most ancient of all societies and a divine institution.[121] In shifting from the ethical to the legal dimension, the *Encyclopédie* paid heed to the semantic range of *société* and showed its inherently secular – that is, temporal – notions in its legal dimension.

Concerning questions of ethics and social order, 'society' (as conceived of by early proponents of *société*) appears secular in the sense of abstaining from religious allusions to transcendence, while in another sense, 'society' – as well as 'the social' – can in fact be regarded as metaphysical. The metaphysical nature of 'society' results from its replacing "religion as the ultimate ground of order, the ontological frame of human existence."[122] Increasingly, then, society replaces God as the principle of moral evaluation. Crucially, this metaphysical dimension also is inherent in the social as an abstract notion. This point, which Baker hints at briefly,[123] is substantiated by Mary Poovey: "The concept of the social [...] ultimately functions to legitimate social arrangements that are no longer seen as resting on a providential ground."[124] Poovey shows how this understanding evolved from within a providential order in eighteenth-century British moral philosophy. Beyond this specific intellectual and historical context, it is important to bear in mind that, as with society as an abstract idea, "'the social' has become thinkable [only] as part of the long history of reification that we call modernity."[125]

120 Riedel, "Gesellschaft, Gemeinschaft," 811.
121 Baker, "Enlightenment" [2001], 88f.
122 Ibid., 99.
123 Ibid, 85.
124 Poovey, Mary. 2002. "The Liberal Civil Subject and the Social in Eighteenth-Century British Moral Philosophy." *Public Culture* 14/1: 125–145, here 135.
125 Ibid., 125. This article also appeared as: idem. 2002. "The Liberal Civil Subject and the Social in Eighteenth-Century British Moral Philosophy." In *The Social in Question: New Bearings in History and the Social Sciences* ed. by Patrick Joyce: 44–61. London/New York: Routledge.

At the same time, religion in a sense becomes secularized as its discourse is "subordinated to the discourse of society."[126] Here, we must not dwell on theoretical elaborations or historical manifestations of this fundamental constellation. The important point is that the basic problématique is historically contingent: it arose at a certain historical moment, and, as we will see in the following section, it might also come to an end. It should be clear, then, that asking about the relation between religion and society – a question not in much need of justification for modern men and women – only makes sense for historical contexts in which religion and society had come to be distinguished. After that historical moment, society and religion, in the same sense as society and the state, can be related to each other in manifold ways.

Once society had been instituted, it is certainly true that religious actors reacted to a secular discourse on society – in quite different ways, of course. For France in the nineteenth century, for example,[127] Michael Behrent has distinguished two main possibilities for religion entering the field of society – one based on a nominalist, the other on a realist premise. Nominalists invested religion in the individuals who made up society; realists came to see society itself as religious.[128] In Catholic discourses, the term *societas perfectas* arose in the eighteenth and nineteenth centuries to express the idea that the Church is a self-sufficient, independent society unto itself.[129] This was directed against the evolution of national churches under the auspices of the state, as well as against Protestant validations of the church as an order within the state.[130]

Importantly, even those theological discourses that opposed the autonomy of the state and of a secular realm were deeply oriented toward and shaped by the latter. Charles Davis has aptly formulated this fundamental point: "In general terms it can be said that the context for theology since the seventeenth century has been secular."[131] Stephan Conermann, in a rather similar way, formulat-

126 Baker, "Enlightenment" [2001], 99.

127 The following example is still a rough sketch. For an exemplary historiographical case study on a particular theological engagement with modernity and society in a concrete setting, see: Kuhlemann, Frank-Michael. 2002. *Bürgerlichkeit und Religion: Zur Sozial- und Mentalitätsgeschichte der evangelischen Pfarrer in Baden 1860–1914.* Göttingen: Vandenhoeck & Ruprecht.

128 Behrent, Michael C. 2008. "The Mystical Body of Society: Religion and Association in Nineteenth-Century French Political Thought." *Journal of the History of Ideas* 69/2: 219–243.

129 Granfield, Patrick. 1982. "Aufkommen und Verschwinden des Begriffs 'societas perfecta'." *Concilium* 18: 460–464.

130 Ibid., 462.

131 Davis, Charles. 1994. *Religion and the Making of Society: Essays in Social Theology.* Cambridge: Cambridge University Press, 6. Davis uses 'secular' and 'sacred' as a pair. It is historically more adequate and analytically more fruitful to distinguish between the following pairs: 'sa-

ed it as "decisive for the history of Islam in the twentieth century that Muslim intellectuals were prompted to develop models of society, which no longer served as counter conceptions to other religions but rather had to be coequal to a secular worldview."[132] Only at the end of the twentieth century – and somewhat paradoxically, rather shortly after having not only broadly accepted but also validated the autonomy of the secular order[133] – did Christian theological discourses shift from a "focus upon the secular" to a "focus upon the supernatural," as Davis observes.[134] This shift increasingly reveals the distinction and complementarity of religion and society as constitutive of modernity.

Having stressed the reactions of religious to secular discourses in modernity, I should add that, when looking at an earlier historical moment, the secular – in an important sense – reacted to or evolved out of the religious. While the orders of religion and society did *manifest* themselves in a common process and the concepts of 'religion' and 'society' did become central as a twin pair, 'society' might in fact have reproduced a transition in meaning that 'religion' had already undergone – namely, from particular instances to an abstract reality, quite detached from peoples or places. Based on such a reading of the historical record, John Bossy maintains that "one cannot therefore exactly call Religion and Society twins; but in other respects they are like the sexes according to Aristophanes, effects of the fission of a primitive whole, yearning towards one another across a great divide. The whole, for better or worse, was 'Christianity', a word which until the seventeenth century meant a body of people, and has since then, as most European languages testify, meant an 'ism' or body of beliefs."[135] Baker hypothesizes that the skepticism and Augustinianism of the sixteenth and seventeenth centuries were crucial for producing the problem to which the invention of society was suggested as a solution – that is, providing new ground for a common

---

cred'/'profane', 'transcendent/immanent', 'religious/secular'; see Casanova, José. 2012. "Religion, Secularization, and Sacralization." In *Dynamics in the History of Religions between Asia and Europe. Encounters, Notions, and Comparative Perspectives* ed. by Volkhard Krech and Marion Steinicke: 453–460. Leiden/Boston: Brill, here 453f.

132 Conermann, Stephan. 1996. *Muṣṭafā Maḥmūd (geb. 1921) und der modifizierte islamische Diskurs im modernen Ägypten.* Berlin: Klaus Schwarz, 51; transl. F.Z.

133 The decisive date for the Catholic Church here is, of course, the Second Vatican Council (1962–1965), which also made the term *societas perfectas* superfluous (Granfield, "Aufkommen," 464).

134 Davis, *Religion*, 1f.

135 Bossy, John. 1985. *Christianity in the West 1400–1700.* Oxford: Oxford University Press, 170f.

order.[136] As God was increasingly removed from this 'fallen world,' society was instituted as "the new divinity on earth."[137]

The main aim of Charles Taylor's *A Secular Age*, which will be presented in the next chapter, is to narrate the Christian roots and genealogy of Western secular modernity. Taylor offers his story as an allegedly superior alternative to supposedly hegemonic "subtraction stories" of secularization, elaborated most substantially in sociology. According to Taylor, these subtraction stories posit that the secular is a universal realm that was laid open once human beings freed themselves from the bonds of religion. Although I agree with him that, contrary to this view, the secular was historically instituted, Taylor ignores the fact that sociologists themselves have also come to acknowledge the historical institution of the secular. The following section shows how the modern construction of society, with autonomous and intelligible social laws, was indeed solidified in the discipline of sociology but has come under increasing pressure in the last few decades.

4 Society and Sociology: Institutionalizing 'Society' as an Autonomous Object

"Sociology has a foremost place in the thought of modern men. Approve or deplore the fact at pleasure, we cannot escape it."
– A.W. Small, 1895[138]

"In many respects, the twentieth century appears now, after its end, as the century of the social sciences."
– Peter Wagner, 2001[139]

4.1 Sociology and the Social Sciences as a Response to the Modern Problématique of Socio-political Order

The preceding two sections have highlighted the distinction of society as autonomous from the state and from religion. The discipline of sociology solidified both distinctions by elaborating society as an autonomous object with independ-

136 Overall, Baker distinguishes between epistemological, ethical, religious, and political problems that motivated the institution of society (Baker, "Enlightenment" [2001], 100 – 104).
137 Ibid., 104, see also 84, 85.
138 Small, A. W. 1895. "The Era of Sociology." *American Journal of Sociology* 1/1: 1–15, here 1.
139 Wagner, *A History*, 1.

ent laws. Again, I am here referring to the one conception that became hegemonic in the twentieth century, but which at no point was uncontested and which has increasingly come under pressure in the last few decades. The second subsection (4.2) will point to possible reasons for and consequences of the end of "The Era of Sociology," as Small's opening article for the *American Journal of Sociology* in 1895 was entitled. Before attending to the (possible) end of this era, I shall discuss when it began.

The term *sociologie* was really introduced by Auguste Comte in 1839, even though Sieyès had already used it in unpublished papers some sixty years earlier.[140] It was another Frenchman, namely Émile Durkheim, who founded the first department for sociology in 1895. Durkheim's intellectual influence was visible in the establishment of a sociological institute at the university of Istanbul in 1915[141] and the creation of a department for sociology at Cairo University a decade later.[142] In Germany, which lays claim to Weber as its own founding father of sociology, there was no sociological chair until after the First World War, even though sociology was taught at other chairs and sociological journals, programs, and societies did exist.[143] The varied formations and evolutions of sociology

---

140 Guilhaumou, Jacques. 2006. "Sieyès et le non-dit de la sociologie: du mot à la chose." *Revue d'Histoire des Sciences Humaines* 2/15: 117–134. For a contemporaneous observation on the controversies surrounding the term 'sociology' at the time of the establishment of sociology as an independent discipline, see: Branford, Victor V. 1903. "On the Origin and Use of the Word 'Sociology,' and on the Relation of Sociological to Other Studies and to Practical Problems." *American Journal of Sociology* 9/2: 145–162.

141 Özervarlı, M. S. 2007. "Transferring Traditional Islamic Disciplines into Modern Social Sciences in Late Ottoman Thought: The Attempts of Ziya Gokalp and Mehmed Serafeddin." *The Muslim World* 97: 317–330. Berkes dated the establishment of sociology, which had been taught earlier at Turkish institutes of higher learning, to 1912 (Berkes, Niyazi. 1936. "Sociology in Turkey." *American Journal of Sociology* 42/2: 238–246, here 242).

142 Roussillon, Alain. 1996. "Sociologie et société en Egypte : le contournement des intellectuels par l'Etat." In *Les intellectuels et le pouvoir* ed. by T. Al-Bishri [et al.] ; réalisé en collaboration par le SEDEJ et le CEROAC et placé sous la direction de G. Dalanoue: 93–138. Cairo: CEDEJ, here 101 f.; idem. 1991. "Projet colonial et traditions scientifiques : aux origines de la sociologie égyptienne." In *D'un Orient l'autre : les métamorphoses successives des perceptions et connaissances* ed. by CEDEJ: 347–388. Paris: Editions du CNRS et Idem., here esp. 363–366. On the first Egyptian who held the chair of sociology at Cairo University, see: idem. 1992. "La représentation de l'identité par les discours fondateurs de la sociologie turque et égyptienne: Ziya Gökalp et 'Ali 'Abd al-Wahid Wafi." In *Modernisation et mobilisation sociale II, Egypte-Turquie [Online]* ed. by CEDEJ. Cairo: CEDEJ – Égypte/Soudan. http://books.openedition.org/cedej/1047 (accessed July 23, 2017). The sociology department at Cairo University was closed in 1934; sociology was reinstitued in Alexandria in 1947, appropriating Anglo-Saxon rather than Durkheimian views (ibid., paragraphs 42–45).

143 Wagner, *A History*, 10.

across European countries significantly hinged on their different political and institutional settings, as Peter Wagner has magisterially shown.[144] Moreover, the conception and practice of the discipline differed greatly from "classical sociology" to "modern sociology," which was established after the Second World War. Based on these insights, Wagner forcefully contests the common view of the years between 1870 and 1930 as the founding period of sociology.[145] These qualifications notwithstanding, the origins of sociology as a discipline can be dated rather exactly.

The beginnings of sociological thinking more broadly are more controversial. The different estimations greatly hinge on whether society and the social are regarded as specifically modern or as a universal given. The origins of sociological thinking are sometimes shifted back as far as to the sixth century BCE.[146] More commonly, alongside to Greek philosophers,[147] the Arab philosopher of history Ibn Khaldun (d. 1406) is named as a forerunner or even the founder of sociology.[148] As such, he was also revered by Rashid Rida, as we shall see below;[149] Taha Husayn, in turn, in his doctoral thesis, written under the auspices of Durkheim, placed Ibn Khaldun firmly outside of modern thinking.[150] In the background of Rida's and Husayn's diverging opinions lies the far-reaching question of whether modern sociological thinking is external to the Islamic tradition or also has bases within it;[151] this is a question which tends to be answered accord-

---

144 Idem. 1990. *Sozialwissenschaften und Staat: Frankreich, Italien, Deutschland 1870–1980.* Frankfurt a.M.: Campus.

145 Idem., *A History*, 8–24, esp. 12.

146 Sica, Alan. 2012. "A Selective History of Sociology." In *The Wiley-Blackwell Companion to Sociology* ed. by Georg Ritzer: 25–54. Chichester: Wiley-Blackwell, here 26.

147 Ibid., 27 f.

148 See, for example, ibid., 28 f.; Abdullahi, Ali Arazeem and Salawu, Bashir. 2012. "Ibn Khaldun: A Forgotten Sociologist?." *South African Review of Sociology* 43/3: 24–40; Alatas, Syed Farid. 2006. "Ibn Khaldūn and Contemporary Sociology." *International Sociology* 21/6: 782–795; idem. 2014. *Applying Ibn Khaldūn: The Recovery of a Lost Tradition in Sociology.* London: Routledge; Baali, Fuad. 1986. *Ilm al-Umran and Sociology: A Comparative Study.* Kuwait: Kulliyyat al-Adab, Jamiʿat al-Kuwayt; Wafi, ʿAli ʿAbd al-Wahid. 1951. *al-Falsafa al-Ijtimaʿiyya li-Ibn Khaldun wa-Auguste Comte.* Cairo: Matbaʿat Lajnat al-Bayan al-ʿArabi; ʿIzzat, ʿAbd al-ʿAziz. 1947. *Ibn-Khaldoun et sa science sociale.* Cairo: C. Tsoumas.

149 See below: chapter 10 section 2.1.

150 Husayn, Taha. 1917. *La philosophie sociale d'Ibn-Khaldoun.* Paris: A. Pedone. On this work's Arabic translation, see below: 296.

151 I have already referred to calls for an Islamic sociology in the introduction. The relation between Islam and social sciences more broadly has received heightened attention in recent years. An extensive conference series on "Social Thought in the MENA" was held in Beirut, Istanbul, and twice in Teheran, between 2011 and 2015; for the program of this series' most recent

ing to personal convictions rather than historical evidence. In Europe, scholars of Christian affiliation in particular have stressed the mediaeval theological roots or even the continuous theological essence of modern sociology,[152] sometimes additionally attributing the national differences in sociological thinking to different religious heritages.[153] It will come as no surprise that my stress on the historical institution of 'society' goes along with an emphasis on the modern specificity of sociological thinking.

This is not at all to assert, as sociologists often do,[154] an abrupt rupture of modernity with the past. The modern understanding of the world, for which sociological thinking is crucial, has of course evolved from previous understandings and discourses. How far one goes back into the past in order to discern the roots or predecessors of sociological thought – a potentially infinite endeavor – obviously depends on the (hi)story and vision of modernity one wants to narrate. One such story is Charles Taylor's *A Secular Age*, which will be presented in the following chapter. Here, it suffices to note that religion has been a central topos for modernity and thus for sociology and that, moreover, early sociologists also picked up theological motifs and intervened in religious discourses. This intervention could mean envisioning explicit counter-models to revealed religions, such as Comte's vision for a positivist "religion of humanity." With more nuance, Durkheim, for whom religions were the product of society, intervened in the religious republican tradition.[155] The fact that Durkheim himself did not settle for one standard model concerning the relation of religion and society[156] is sufficient to caution us to abstain from trying to elaborate such a standard model for sociology in general. Equally important as sociologists' intervention in and continuation of religious discourses was their engagement with political economy.

---

event, see: https://www.aub.edu.lb/fas/cames/Documents/Abstracts%20and%20Bios%2025-26%20April%202015%20Conference%20AMPL%20CAMES%20SOAM.pdf (accessed June 4, 2015). See also: Senturk, Recep. 2007. "Intellectual Dependency: Late Ottoman Intellectuals between *fiqh* and Social Science." *Die Welt des Islams* 47/3–4: 283–318.

152 For an overview of the different conceptions of the relation between theology and sociology, see: Harrington, Austin. 2006. "Social Theory and Theology." In *Handbook of Contemporary European Social Theory* ed. by Gerard Delanty: 37–45. London: Routledge.

153 Mellor, Philip A. 2004. *Religion, Realism and Social Theory: Making Sense of Society.* London: Sage, esp. 122–126.

154 Peter Wagner is again the author to look to for a profound critical discussion of this view and a most sophisticated reconception of 'modernity' and its evolution; see Wagner, *Modernity.*

155 Behrent, "The Mystical."

156 Belier, Wouter W. 1999. "The Sacred in the Social Sciences: On the Definition of Religion by the *Année sociologique* Group." In *The Pragmatics of Defining Religion: Contexts, Concepts and Contests* ed. by Jan G. Platvoet and Arie L. Molendijk: 173–206. Leiden/Boston/Köln: Brill.

Political economy, as a direct predecessor of sociology, may be regarded as the link between theology and sociology,[157] but more importantly here, it alerts us to the origins of sociological thinking prior to the academic institution of sociology as a discipline – that is, to the origins of the social sciences. The need for the formation of the social sciences was created by the revolutionary dissolution of the old political order in France and America, which discredited metaphysically grounded moral and political philosophies.[158] The social sciences were thus a (temporary) response to the newly created contingencies of socio-political order and human life. It is constitutive of modernity that these contingencies are permanent and that the problem of socio-political order can only ever be solved provisionally. The social sciences rather quickly rejoined the social with the political and, in important ways, continued the legacy of political philosophy.[159] However, they attempted to ground new certainties in something within society or human beings rather than beyond them. To this end, they aimed at discovering – read: at postulating and instituting – stable social laws and firm social bonds. Fueled by the Enlightenment's enthusiasm for liberty and reason, the first such attempts at creating new certainties took the individual as their starting-point, as was most influentially the case in political economy.[160]

Classical sociology – now again in the more narrow sense of a discipline – can be regarded as a reaction to political economy's enthusiastic, liberal emphasis on the individual. The early proponents of sociology – Auguste Comte and his teacher, Claude-Henri de Saint-Simon – still shared the political economists' "Enlightenment optimism about the coming of a society in which the interests of its individual members would converge to thus enhance the well-being of all without any need for major force or complex organisation."[161] By the late 1800s, this optimism had ceased in the face of new uncertainties: industrialization and urbanization, as well as workers' and women's movements, made 'the social question' a primary one. In these uncertain times, the major figures of sociology reacted against liberal premises and aimed to establish the science of society on another basis. Their reconceptions then differed greatly: in France, Durkheim replaced individualism by giving primacy to social facts; in Italy, Pareto regarded sociology as complementing the economists' study of logical actions by investigating non-logical actions; and in Germany, Weber reformulated the utilitarian

---

157 Harrington, "Social," 37.
158 Wagner, *A History*, 2.
159 Idem. 2006. "Social Theory and Political Philosophy." In *Handbook of Contemporary European Social Theory* ed. by Gerard Delanty: 25–36. London: Routledge.
160 Ibid.
161 Idem., *A History*, 14.

categories of economics as ideal-types.[162] While these divergent reconceptions of the science of society point to the different ways in which sociology was conceived, the common reaction against (political) liberalism reminds us of the political dimension of sociology.

In fact, the 'social question' to which sociology attended was in a way also a national question. The different sociologies may have made universal claims concerning the working of human society, but they were not only shaped by national settings, they often moreover served as sciences of national societies. What is more, "[s]ociology [...] tended to conflate the specific historical form of the European nation-state with the general solution to, as it was often called, the problem of life in common, or the political *problématique*, which was expressed in the concept 'society'."[163] It was only in the last three decades that the concept of 'modernity' replaced modern (national) societies as the central object of sociological study, albeit often maintaining one standard (Western) model of modern social and political organization.[164] However, the perpetual modern question of how society is to be organized may also be answered in other than national terms.

This last point is worth remembering when we later turn to the concept of 'society' in the Islamic journal *al-Manar*, whose authors wrote from within a national setting but also envisioned social collectivities beyond the nation. It is also worth reiterating the following aspects from the foregoing discussion: the concept of 'society' was a response to a crisis of social and political order, which prompted the search for and postulation of social laws and bonds. Additionally, the social sciences sought answers to societal questions, paying heed to the goal of social and political unity. Finally, the perpetual modern question of socio-political order may also be answered from within discourses other than sociology.

4.2 The End of the Social and the Loss of the Metaphysical Ground of Society

We now jump from the period of sociology contemporaneous with *al-Manar* to more recent discussions about a possible "end of the social" and refutations of society as an abstract entity. While this conception of society, chiefly advanced by Durkheim, had not been shared by all early sociologists – with Weber and

162 Ibid., 12f.
163 Idem., *Modernity*, 10. See also Bielefeld, *Nation*, 97f.
164 Wagner, *Modernity*, 6f.

Simmel representing prominent alternatives[165] – it nevertheless became greatly influential. In a "thought experiment," Bruno Latour hinted at how sociology might have conceivably deveveloped very differently had Gabriel Tarde not lost his hegemonic position to Durkheim.[166] The more recent questioning of 'society' and 'the social' concerns an ontological level. Indeed, if the social was instituted at a certain historical moment, it might also come to an end, as Alain Touraine has forcefully argued.[167] Touraine recalls the link between the social and society when he states that the social vision "is primarily defined by recourse to the idea of society."[168] It should be noted that Touraine does not make this argument in a triumphant way, but rather warns of the potential alternatives that might replace the social, especially liberal capitalism. What is at stake here may be sensed from the fact that the following statement by Keith Baker, with whom we traced the institution of society and the social in the Enlightenment, presumably holds less true today than it did twenty-five years ago: "The social (as anyone who presumes to question its priority is reminded) is our name for the 'really real'. It secures the existential ground beneath our feet, presenting a bedrock of reality beneath the shifting sands of discourse."[169] With the crumbling of the social, we may indeed lose the former metaphysical ground of modernity.

While the concept of 'society' has become questionable from various angles,[170] this most fundamental, ontological level concerns the relation of society and religion. Above I sketched the evolution of this twin pair and theological reactions to the inherently secular but at the same time metaphysically grounded concept of 'society.' If the context of theology since the seventeenth century had been a secular one, as we saw with Charles Davis, this is no longer unanimously the case; Davis today observes a theological turn toward the supernatural.[171]

---

165 Outhwaite, *The Future*, 7; Joyce, Patrick. 2002. "Introduction." In *The Social in Question: New Bearings in History and the Social Sciences* ed. by Patrick Joyce: 1–18. London/New York: Routledge, here 1.

166 Latour, Bruno. 2002. "Gabriel Tarde and the End of the Social." In *The Social in Question: New Bearings in History and the Social Sciences* ed. by Patrick Joyce: 117–132. London/New York: Routledge.

167 See: Touraine, "The End;" and earlier: idem. 1980. "L'inutile idée de société." In *Philosopher* ed. by R. Maggiori and C. Delacampagne: 237–245. Paris: Fayard; idem. 1965. *Sociologie de l'action*. Paris: Seuil, 53. See also: Baudrillard, Jean. 1983. *In the Shadow of the Silent Majorities, or, The End of the Social and Other Essays*. New York: Semiotext(e), 67 f.

168 Touraine, "The End," 230.

169 Baker, "Enlightenment" [2001], 85.

170 Outhwaite, who defends 'society' in the end, has identified five such angles (Outhwaite, *The Future*, vii–viii).

171 Davis, *Religion*, 1.

There is a theological trend, which also fuels the religious critiques of secular reason mentioned above, toward no longer accepting the secular as a given context to be engaged with – that is, as the twin of religion –, instead positing "that there is only one concrete order and that is not secular but supernatural."[172]

In turn, those who regard society rather than religion as the "only one concrete order" yield to the understanding of a purely secular and immanent order. (There are then, of course, attempts to locate the transcendent within the immanent, and the line between both spheres is generally hard to draw and maintain; but let us here keep matters simple in order to grasp the basic issue at stake.) Indeed, as the concept of 'society' gained much of its power from its religious resonances, the increasing "disenchantment" of the modern world might well contribute to the declining force of 'society.' In 2001, David Bell observed such a decline of both 'society' and 'civilization,' which "are losing their centrality, in France and beyond. The word 'civilization' is spoken with irony more often than not. [...] 'Society,' as is often remarked, is steadily giving way to 'culture' in everything from the most abstruse academic discourse to the most popular media. We may not be at the 'end of history,' but we do seem to be at the end of a period in which reshaping human society into some sort of ideally harmonious order was seen as the central task for human beings to accomplish."[173]

Despite possible qualifications of this observation – such as 'civilization' returning as a research paradigm and the still abundant publications on 'society,' not a few of them pairing the term with 'religion' in their titles – it leads to two significant aspects: firstly, the quest for an "ideally harmonious order" was clearly central at the time of *al-Manar*'s publication. Under the then-reigning paradigm of progress, this quest was carried out in a utopian manner, even when the past – that is, a constructed tradition – was mobilized to that end. There was still room for alternative utopias of modernity, despite the secular, liberal order already having become hegemonic and thus an inevitable point of reference. Today, to give a very broad impression, ideal harmonious orders are instead alluded to in a nostalgic manner. Those doing so critically engage with what they perceive as present (dis-)order, which they either want to overthrow or to reground in a nostalgic past. Both options are markedly different from formulating a prospective alternative vision. Secondly, I am looking at *al-Manar* from within an epistemic moment, when the mutual dependence of society and religion – which, despite its manifold possible relations, has been constitutive of modernity – has become questionable, as has the concept of 'society' itself. However, I

---

172 Ibid., 14.
173 Bell, *The Cult*, 216.

agree only partially with Cabrera's statement: "The concept of society has been useful and effective as an epistemological tool for so long only because (social) historians and other social scientists have been thinking and working *within* the modern social imaginary itself."[174] While today we may question the concept of 'society' and its twin 'religion' since we are beyond the modern(ist) moment, these contingent modern concepts are still useful and even inevitable for research on previous modern(ist) self-understandings.

The modern self-understanding regards human beings as autonomously organizing their social life in a secular and increasingly self-sufficient "immanent frame." That self-understanding crystallizes in the normative core of 'society,' as this chapter has shown. We have also seen, partly in the introduction as well, that different stories are being told about how this modern self-understanding came about. According to some stories, the modern secular self-understanding had to fight against religious obstacles, whereas other stories stress that modern secularity was in fact the product of religious sources. The first type of stories suggest an opposition of religion and the secular (for which the concept of 'society' stands). Based on such a premise, the secular would be hard to identify in the Islamic-religious discourse of *al-Manar.* The following chapter thus introduces a story of the latter type as a heuristic tool – namely, Charles Taylor's *A Secular Age.*

---

174 Cabrera, Miguel A. 2005. "The Crisis of the Social and Post-social History." *The European Legacy* 10/6: 611–620, here 616.

Chapter 3
A Secular Age as a Heuristic Tool[1]

1 *A Secular Age:* The Usefulness of One Particular Story

Charles Taylor's *A Secular Age*, published in 2007,[2] clearly stands out among the many attempts at reconstructing secularity and secularization that have been put forward since the deconstruction of that formerly unquestioned paradigm. In the English language alone, I collected more than 120 academic reviews of or direct responses to *A Secular Age*, many praising it in the highest terms, but some also advancing very substantial points of critique.[3] I will address those points of critique relevant for this study below. Here I simply note that it is remarkable that the Canadian philosopher's book has been received in a wide range of disciplines, mainly philosophy, theology, sociology, and political science, but also religious studies, literary studies, area studies, social anthropology, and even musicology and cognitive science.[4] The reception of Taylor's previous œuvre had been rather confined to specialist discourses, even though it not only foreshadowed but also explicitly contained some of the central assumptions and arguments of *A Secular Age*. The success of *A Secular Age* is certainly due to the timeliness of its opening question: "What does it mean to say that we[5] live in a secular age?"[6] – but it is also the result of Taylor telling a story.

The story Taylor tells is fundamentally one of the Christian, more specifically Catholic, roots of secularity in the West.[7] Taylor explicitly limits his story to what

1 A different version of this chapter has appeared as: Zemmin, Florian. 2016. "*A Secular Age* and Islamic Modernism." In *Working with A Secular Age. Interdisciplinary Perspectives on Charles Taylor's Master Narrative* ed. by Florian Zemmin, Colin Jager and Guido Vanheeswijck: 307–329. Berlin/Boston: De Gruyter.

2 Taylor, *A Secular Age*.

3 Zemmin, Florian. 2016. "An Annotated Bibliography of Responses to *A Secular Age*." In *Working with A Secular Age. Interdisciplinary Perspectives on Charles Taylor's Master Narrative* ed. by Florian Zemmin, Colin Jager and Guido Vanheeswijck: 385–419. Berlin/Boston: De Gruyter.

4 Ibid. The broad interdisciplinary reception of *A Secular Age* shows most clearly in: Zemmin, Florian, Jager, Colin and Vanheeswijck, Guido (eds.). 2016. *Working with A Secular Age. Interdisciplinary Perspectives on Charles Taylor's Master Narrative*. Berlin/Boston: De Gruyter.

5 For a complication of Taylor's "we," as referring to (all) Westerners, see Tester, Keith. 2010. "Multiculturalism, Catholicism and Us." *New Blackfriars* 91/1036: 665–676.

6 Taylor, *A Secular Age*, 1.

7 The Catholic nature of *A Secular Age* has been pointed out in many reviews (Zemmin, "Annotated"). Taylor addressed the role of his own Catholic convictions in *A Secular Age* in: Taylor,

https://doi.org/10.1515/9783110545845-004

he imagines to be Western civilization and asserts that its secularity differs from that of all other world regions. Only in the West, Taylor argues, did religious belief become optional. Unbelief became not only a real alternative, but in some milieux, even the preferred option. Within this constructed West, whose demarcation I will discuss critically below, Taylor contrasts the present situation (he gives the year 2000 as a date) with a pre-modern counterfoil (he gives the year 1500, which is somewhat arbitrary but nevertheless important, insofar as it predates the Protestant Reformation).[8] In pre-modern times, as Taylor has it, religion was an inherent part of communal life and of reality as such, whence pre-modern men and women did not regard belief as optional. Taylor is less interested in explicit differences in belief than in a change in background understandings, which he deems the reason for belief having become optional.[9] Crucial for the modern background understanding – or, put otherwise, the "modern social imaginary" – is the imagination of a self-sufficient "immanent frame."

Before addressing these two metaphors of the social imaginary and the immanent frame – which, I argue, are expressed by 'society' – the contours of Taylor's story ought to be outlined, along with its central aim. Taylor aims at countering and replacing what he dubs "subtraction stories."[10] These allegedly still-dominant stories (nevermind that Taylor is to some extent building a straw man here)[11] contend that the modern secular realm was laid open once human beings freed themselves from former illusions that had obstructed their view in favor of this universally given realm and of true human nature. For Taylor, modern secularity was not discovered, but historically constructed and instituted. His "Reform Master Narrative" identifies the roots of this institution in theological arguments of the late Middle Ages. Paradoxically, secularization originated in the theological impulse to make over the secular world outside of the monasteries to conform to the spiritual standards of monastery life: "[P]eculiar to Latin Chris-

Charles. 2010. "Afterword: Apologia pro Libro suo." In *Varieties of Secularism in a Secular Age* ed. by Michael Warner, Jonathan VanAntwerpen and Craig Calhoun: 300 – 321. Cambridge, Mass.: Harvard University Press, here 319 ff. See also: idem. 1999. *A Catholic Modernity? Charles Taylor's Marianist Award Lecture;* with responses by William M. Shea, Rosemary Luling Haughton, George Marsden, Jean Bethke Elshtain; edited and with an Introduction by James L. Heft, S. M. New York/Oxford: Oxford University Press.

8 Taylor, *A Secular Age*, 13, 25 f.

9 Ibid., 3 f.

10 Ibid., 22.

11 See: Koenig, Matthias. 2016. "Beyond the Paradigm of Secularization?." In *Working with A Secular Age. Interdisciplinary Perspectives on Charles Taylor's Master Narrative* ed. by Florian Zemmin, Colin Jager and Guido Vanheeswijck: 23 – 48. Berlin/Boston: De Gruyter, esp. 23 ff.

tendom is a growing concern with Reform, a drive to make over the whole society to higher standards."[12]

Beyond what its initiators hoped for, this theological impulse accorded increasing value to the secular world in its own right. Via the catalyst of the Protestant Reformation and the crucial stages of Deism and natural law theories, an "exclusive humanism" eventually became possible. This exclusive humanism, which regarded the secular world as completely self-sufficient, became a viable option in the nineteenth century. Once this basic option was instituted, both religious and non-religious alternatives – that is, the different options for the location of "fullness"[13] – multiplied. The increasingly dramatic multiplication of options after the Second World War, which Taylor allegorizes as a "super-nova," are basically a consequence of these previous developments. Taylor's aim is to recall the Christian roots of this secular age and, amid the wide range of available options, to strengthen the plausibility of locating fullness not within, but beyond this world. He wants to convince his readers that a fundamental dimension of human life is lost when the immanent frame is regarded as all that there is.

Yes, this is a Catholic story, and both Taylor's conception of the immanent frame and his metaphor of the fullness toward which all human beings strive have been criticized for their underlying Christian bias.[14] Indeed, in the end, Taylor does conceive of the immanent frame in such a way that its non-religious reading appears deficient, and fullness can only be truly achieved when it involves striving for something beyond this world. So Taylor is not speaking from nowhere – but who is? Taylor rightfully points to academia as the milieu where unbelief most clearly became the hegemonic option, with most academics reading the immanent frame as closed off from transcendence. This reading is even more dominant when it comes to theorizing, when personal beliefs are expected to be put aside: if one wants to presume an open reading, one has to do theology. Taylor's book can complement secular(ist) theories. Rejecting a religiously informed conception such as Taylor's due to its underlying bias would

---

12 Taylor, *A Secular Age*, 63.

13 Ibid., 5 – 12.

14 For powerful examples of this critique, see: Connolly, William E. 2010. "Belief, Spirituality, and Time." In *Varieties of Secularism in a Secular Age* ed. by Michael Warner, Jonathan VanAntwerpen and Craig Calhoun: 126 – 144. Cambridge, Mass.: Harvard University Press; Gordon, Peter E. 2008. "The Place of the Sacred in the Absence of God: Charles Taylor's 'A Secular Age'." *Journal of the History of Ideas* 69/4: 647 – 673; Schweiker, William. 2009. "Our Religious Situation: Charles Taylor's *A Secular Age*." *American Journal of Theology & Philosophy* 30/3: 323 – 329; Sheehan, Jonathan. 2010. "When Was Disenchantment? History and the Secular Age." In *Varieties of Secularism in a Secular Age* ed. by Michael Warner, Jonathan VanAntwerpen and Craig Calhoun: 217 – 242. Cambridge, Mass.: Harvard University Press.

prematurely inhibit this complementary potential. Secular research on religious contexts in particular can benefit from recourse to Taylor's views, as they make the objects of research more intelligible. In short, Taylor's depiction of modernity and secularity allows for the integration of religious self-understandings, including Islamic ones, into a common framework of understanding.

If I am making quite selective use of Taylor's impressively rich and complex work, this is because the interdisciplinary task is not about getting Taylor right (in all his details); it is rather about using *A Secular Age* to get one's primary object of study 'right' – that is, to grasp it more adequately and portray it more comprehensibly. Such an approach might sound unsatisfactory to participants in theoretical debates, who strive for consistency and systematization. However, research on Islamic contexts in general has to resort to theories elaborated in, on, and for a Western context. Sticking wholeheartedly to these theoretical models runs the risk of distorting the phenomena at hand. For this reason, I advocate a pragmatic and selective usage of such theories as means, not ends unto themselves. It remains desirable, of course, not to pull the theory out of its original shape, in order to facilitate conversation with other usages of the theory and to circumscribe the potentials and limits of the theory itself. In the particular case of *A Secular Age*, moreover, we need to keep in mind that Taylor is not offering a theory in the conventional sense, but rather a story containing both a descriptive and a normative level.

While crucial concepts or metaphors in Taylor's story contain both of these levels, they nevertheless also make sense beyond his story. It is quite true that most of Taylor's concepts and descriptions would require testing in Western contexts, as well. This particularly concerns the distinction between immanence and transcendence,[15] but also assertions such as the contemporary hegemony of secular stances.[16] Here, it is important to remember that the landmarks of Taylor's story are not really situated on the level of empirical reality, but rather try to capture a certain self-understanding. Taylor describes himself not as a historian, but

---

15 In response to Hauerwas and Cole, Taylor acknowledged that he had portrayed immanence and transcendence in too binary a way: Hauerwas, Stanley and Coles, Romand. 2010. "'Long Live the Weeds and the Wilderness Yet': *Reflections on A Secular Age.*" *Modern Theology* 26/3: 349–362; Taylor, Charles. 2010. "Challenging Issues about the Secular Age." *Modern Theology* 26/3: 404–416, here 411.

16 For empirical questionings of Taylor's assessment of the dominance of secularism, see: Miller, James. 2008. "What Secular Age?." *International Journal of Politics, Culture, and Society* 21/1: 5–10; Abbey, Ruth. 2010. "*A Secular Age:* The Missing Question Mark." In *The Taylor Effect. Responding to a* [sic] *Secular Age* ed. by Ian Leask, Eoin Cassidy, Alan Kearns, Fainche Ryan and Mary Shanahan: 8–25. Newcastle upon Tyne: Cambridge Scholars Publishing.

as "a mapper of social imaginaries."[17] Taken in this sense, the central metaphors of the immanent frame or of modern social imaginaries are giving voice to a widely shared (self-)understanding of modernity, whose crystallization in the concept of 'society' has been demonstrated in the previous chapter.

The following section properly introduces these two metaphors, which I selectively adopt from Taylor's story for the sake of better grasping the background understandings of modernity.

2 Modern Social Imaginaries, the Immanent Frame, and 'Society'

The story of *A Secular Age* is essentially the story of a fundamental change in the background understandings informing and limiting the ways in which we make sense of ourselves, of the world, and of our relations with others. As far as this latter aspect is concerned, these background understandings are "social imaginaries." Taylor first elaborated this concept, drawing on Castoriadis,[18] in an article from 2002.[19] This article was part of a special journal issue on "New Imaginaries," which did much to advance the concept of "social imaginaries" on the research agenda. Since then, the concept has often been put to use, culminating in the foundation of the journal *Social Imaginaries* in 2015. In 2004, Taylor himself published a small book on "modern social imaginaries,"[20] which evolved into a chapter with that title in *A Secular Age.*[21]

The social imaginary differs from other background understandings, such as "the cosmic imaginary," in that it is not only shared *by* a collectivity of people, but is also an imaginary *about* that collectivity of people, for which Taylor uses the short-hand 'society': "The social imaginary consists of the generally shared background understandings of society, which make it possible for it to function as it does. It is 'social' in two ways: in that it is generally shared, and in that it is about society."[22] While this background, which is normative insofar as it regu-

17 Taylor, "Afterword," 314.

18 Castoriadis, Cornelius. 1987 [1975]. *The Imaginary Institution of Society*; transl. Kathleen Blamey. Cambridge, Mass.: MIT Press. For a comparison of Castoriadis's, Taylor's, Lacan's, and Benedict Anderson's usage of the concept, see: Strauss, Claudia. 2006. "The Imaginary." *Anthropological Theory* 6/3: 322–344.

19 Taylor, Charles. 2002. "Modern Social Imaginaries." *Public Culture* 14/1: 91–124.

20 Idem. 2004. *Modern Social Imaginaries.* Durham/London: Duke University Press.

21 Idem., *A Secular Age*, 159–211.

22 Ibid., 323.

lates social life, cannot be clearly delimited, "one way of defining a social imaginary is as the kind of collective understanding that a group has to have in order to make sense of their practices."[23] For Taylor, it is different social imaginaries that most profoundly account for cultural differences across regions and ages. Taylor's multiple modernities are, in the end, due to multiple social imaginaries, with the modern Western imaginary differing from all previous imaginaries and from all non-Western imaginaries. It is the difference in imaginaries that allegedly makes 'us' secular and 'them' not. In a sense, then, and recalling the shift from 'society' to 'culture' discussed at the end of the last chapter, these are cultural imaginaries, since culture is considered the primary constituent for the different background understandings of social life and society.[24]

While this underlying primacy of culture is merely an observation, I suggest departing from Taylor's general employment of social imaginaries on two other points: firstly, Taylor distinguishes social imaginaries from theories because he aims to discern the unreflectively held background understandings of ordinary people rather than the reflective theories of elites. Yet surely the latter also hold a certain social imaginary, even when writing theories. That is to say, texts written by elites (and for most of human history, that means all texts) are valid sources from which to discern a social imaginary. In the end, Taylor mainly relies on such texts too, positing that the modern social imaginary originated in theory. Secondly, Taylor, in line with his broad focus on Western civilization in general, tends to speak of *the* social imaginary held by a society or "the Western social imaginary."[25] However, as tentatively acknowledged by Taylor himself in discussions on *A Secular Age*,[26] we can hardly expect a uniform imaginary throughout the West – nor, obviously, for all Muslims.[27] A first attempt at discerning the modern Islamic imaginary should therefore limit itself to a rather

---

23 Ibid., 315.

24 Taylor has long favored "cultural" theories of modernity; see: idem. 1993. *Modernity and the Rise of the Public Sphere.* Salt Lake City: University of Utah Press; idem. 1995. "Two Theories of Modernity." *The Hastings Center Report* 24/2: 24–33. Sara Maza, in one of the earliest usages of the concept by a historian, explicitly foregrounds this cultural dimension: "I would define the social imaginary simply as 'the cultural elements from which we construct our understandings of the social world'" (Maza, Sarah. 2003. *The Myth of the French Bourgeoisie: An Essay on the Social Imaginary, 1750–1850.* Cambridge, Mass.: Harvard University Press, 10).

25 Taylor, "Afterword," 314.

26 Idem. 2010. "Charles Taylor replies [to Tester, 'Multiculturalism']." *New Blackfriars* 91/1036: 677–679, here 677 f.; idem., 2011. "Response." *The Australian Journal of Anthropology* 22: 125–133, here 128.

27 But compare: Barre, Elizabeth A. 2012. "Muslim Imaginaries and Imaginary Muslims. Placing Islam in Conversation with *A Secular Age.*" *Journal of Religious Ethics* 40/1: 138–148.

specific group of people, such as the authors in *al-Manar*, as the actual carriers of that imaginary[28] and not claim validity for an overall Islamic civilization.

As to the modern social imaginary, Taylor illustrates it via three more specific "forms of social self-understandings" – namely, the market economy, the public sphere, and democratic self-rule.[29] Recalling the lack of distinction between society and the state in pre-modern concepts of 'civil society,'[30] he suggests that "the economic was perhaps the first dimension of 'civil society' to achieve an identity independent from the polity. But it was followed shortly afterwards by the public sphere."[31] The public sphere is radically secular in the sense of standing not only "in contrast with a divine foundation for society, but with any idea of society as constituted in something which transcends contemporary common action."[32] This "purely secular time-understanding" also underlies the ideal of a sovereign people and democratic self-rule, as it "allows us to imagine society 'horizontally,' unrelated to any 'high points,' where the ordinary sequence of events touches higher time, and therefore without recognizing any privileged persons or agencies – such as kings or priests – who stand and mediate at such alleged points."[33]

Such mediation between higher and ordinary times is no longer required in modernity because human beings imagine their lives to take place in an "immanent frame," which increasingly closes itself off to transcendental interference. Indeed, the increasing separation of the immanent and the transcendent, of the natural and the supernatural, is a guiding thread running through Taylor's story (whence also the importance of Deism). The "immanent frame," another of Taylor's powerful metaphors, largely coincides with what could more conventionally be depicted as the outcome of disenchantment: the idea of a divinely created "cosmos" gives way to an intelligible natural "universe" with stable laws; the pre-modern "porous self," sensitive to spirits and magic, gives way to a modern "buffered self"; and these buffered selves autonomously (re-)create their social-political order, which is historical by nature and no longer mirrors a timeless cosmic order. Taylor's story of the immanent frame's evolution shows the different degrees of openness to and entanglement with transcendence. But even after the immanent frame is established as fully self-sufficient, it is

28 On the carriers of a social imaginary, see also: Strauss, "The Imaginary."

29 Taylor, *A Secular Age*, 176.

30 Taylor has given greater attention to the concept of 'civil society' elsewhere: idem. 1990. "Modes of Civil Society." *Public Culture* 3/1: 95–118.

31 Idem., *A Secular Age*, 185.

32 Ibid. 192.

33 Ibid, 209.

still understood differently: some (those believing in God) read it as open, while others (those believing that the immanent frame is all there is) read it as closed.[34]

Crucial for the modern social imaginary in general is the idea of an immanent social sphere composed "of rights-bearing individuals, who are destined (by God or nature) to act for mutual benefit."[35] (The resonance of natural law and contract theories here is rather clear. Indeed, Taylor argues that it was these theories, as articulated by Grotius or Locke, which pushed "older theories of society, or newer rivals, to the margins of political life and discourse"[36] and eventually became entrenched in the background understandings of whole societies.) Since "we are well installed in the modern social imaginary" today, this makes it "easy to forget" the specificity of this imaginary.[37] For our pre-modern ancestors, in turn, a secular understanding of society as composed of individuals would have been quite impossible. There was no individual life before life in common, and life in common was founded upon the existence of God, and belief was not merely an option: "It is this facet, God's existential-foundational role in [pre-modern] society, which perhaps best explains how difficult it was to get our minds around the possibility that a society might exist which was not grounded in common religious beliefs."[38]

Taylor here stresses how tremendously difficult – if not utterly impossible – it is to detach oneself from one's social imaginary. Recalling the possible end of the social,[39] the fact that he does such a good job of depicting the modern social imaginary raises the question of whether we are still firmly entrenched in this imaginary today. Indeed, Taylor might "be recognized as the last philosopher of secular modernity and as the visionary prophet of the dawn of a postsecular age."[40] In any case, his effort to address the level of implicit background understandings convincingly shows what all modern human beings have in common. These fundamental commonalities underlying different and potentially contradictory convictions and thoughts inevitably remain somewhat vague – or in

34 Ibid., 543 f.; idem., "Afterword," 306 f.

35 Ibid., 305.

36 Idem., *A Secular Age*, 160.

37 Ibid., 168.

38 Ibid., 43.

39 See above: chapter 2 section 4.2.

40 Casanova, José. 2010. "A Secular Age. Dawn or Twilight?." In *Varieties of Secularism in a Secular Age* ed. by Michael Warner, Jonathan VanAntwerpen and Craig Calhoun: 265–281. Cambridge, Mass.: Harvard University Press, here 281.

other words, the social imaginary is as fundamental as it is hard to pin down and delineate.

For all its vagueness, the modern social imaginary does help produce the actual order of modern society – not least due to its seeming self-evidence and thus self-sustainability: "Like all earlier notions of the moral basis of social order – like the orders of hierarchical complementarity, or ancient law – the modern idea of moral order tends to be seen by its adherents as self-stabilizing. That is, conformity to it lends cohesion to society, which becomes self-sustaining. In modern society, this stability is meant to be based on the basic principle of the modern idea, that is, that the properly ordered society brings together individuals in such a way that their reciprocal action redounds to their mutual benefit."[41] Taylor maintains that the shift in social imaginaries was equally important for the rise of modern society as were structural changes – for example, the institution of print capitalism, the importance of which was demonstrated by Benedict Anderson: "Modern society also required transformations in the way we figure ourselves as societies."[42] To this I wish to add that not only "the way," but also the very fact that "we figure ourselves as societies" is specifically modern, whence the significance of discerning the concept of 'society' in *al-Manar.*

In *A Secular Age*, Taylor identifies "images, stories, legends, etc." as the carriers of social imaginaries[43] and does not give much attention to concepts. Concerning 'religion,' he settles for a pragmatic definition in terms of a distinction between transcendence and immanence,[44] without tracing the concept's evolution over time. This is indeed somewhat surprising, as Matthias Koenig points out, given that "the creation of the immanent frame was reflected in the conceptual history of 'religion' itself."[45] The same can be said for the conceptual history of 'society,' as the previous chapter should have made clear. In *A Secular Age*, where 'society' appears only slightly less often than 'religion' (692 vs. 820 times), Taylor makes only brief references to the modern specificity of the term.[46] He uses 'society' predominantly to refer to the whole social formation

41 Taylor, *A Secular Age*, 690.

42 Idem. 1998. "Modes of Secularism." In *Secularism and Its Critics* ed. by Rajeev Bhargava: 31–53. New Delhi: Oxford University Press, here 42.

43 Idem., *A Secular Age*, 171f.

44 Ibid., 15f.

45 Koenig, "Beyond," 36.

46 Taylor, *A Secular Age*, 25, 181, 183, 191. Taylor places the question of concepts more centrally in: idem., "Modes of Civil Society;" idem., "Modes of Secularism;" idem. 2009. "The Polysemy of the Secular." *Social Research* 76/4: 1143–1166.

or social order at a given time, whether pre-modern or modern. However, Taylor diverges from a seemingly descriptive usage of 'society' in that he focuses upon the (self-)understanding of society as an imaginary. At one point, he defines the social imaginary itself as "the ways we are able to think or imagine the whole of society."[47] In this sense, *A Secular Age* is the story of the shifting background understandings of society, the specifically modern understanding of which, I would add, is expressed by the concept of 'society.' Briefly, what Taylor characterizes as specific to modern societies is in fact characteristic of 'society' tout court.

The major advantage of *A Secular Age* over most accounts of secularity lies in Taylor's deconstruction of the oft-presumed binary between religion and secularity, as is especially demonstrated in the concept of the immanent frame. Taylor convincingly shows that the understanding of an immanent frame is what modern religious and secular Westerners fundamentally share. This understanding might, however, also be shared by non-Western men and women. In fact, Taylor's story, while explicitly confined to the West, has already been applied to other contexts.[48] Scott Appleby, for example, has depicted Islamic fundamentalists as upholding an "open spin" on the immanent frame.[49] Considering that the modern character of fundamentalists is often exclusively illustrated by their use of technology and media, this application of Taylor's concept offers a more foundational reading. It allows us to ask, for example, how the authors in *al-Manar* engaged with those advancing a closed reading of the immanent frame, to what degree they shared this reading, and at which points they stressed references to transcendence.

Having shown the desirability of using *A Secular Age* as a heuristic tool for my study on 'society' in *al-Manar*, I will now further establish the plausibility of doing so. Indeed, while Islam is absent from the genealogy of secularity as narrated by Taylor, it is present in our common secular age, as I shall now argue.

---

47 Idem., *A Secular Age*, 156.

48 Previous works which use *A Secular Age* for research on Islamic and other non-Western contexts are: Appleby, Scott R. 2011. "Rethinking Fundamentalism in a Secular Age." In *Rethinking Secularism* ed. by Craig Calhoun, Mark Juergensmeyer and Jonathan VanAntwerpen: 225–247. Oxford: Oxford University Press; Madsen, Richard. 2011. "Secularism, Religious Change, and Social Conflict in Asia." In *Rethinking Secularism* ed. by Craig Calhoun, Mark Juergensmeyer and Jonathan VanAntwerpen: 248–269. Oxford: Oxford University Press. See now also (published after completion of this manuscript): Bilgrami, Akeel (ed.). 2016. *Beyond the Secular West*. New York: Columbia University Press.

49 Appleby, "Rethinking."

3 Islam: Absent from *A Secular Age*, Present in the Secular Age

"Above all, I have neglected the way in which Western understandings of religion were informed through the pre-colonial and then the colonial encounter with other parts of the world."[50] With this statement, Taylor acknowledges a central criticism directed at *A Secular Age* – namely, that the story of Western secularization cannot be told without taking into account the contributions of Latin Christendom's others, both within and beyond the North Atlantic world. The introduction to this study has shown the fundamental role of entanglements and mutual encounters in the formation of the modern self-understanding. Reacting to *A Secular Age* specifically, this point has been most forcefully argued by Saba Mahmood.[51] Mahmood also advances another point of criticism – namely, that the civilization Taylor limits his story to, which he alternately designates as the "North Atlantic world," "Latin Christendom," or "the West," is not a given, but is itself a historical construction. This is why "[t]he boundary Taylor draws around Latin Christendom is difficult, if not impossible, to sustain for both historical and conceptual reasons."[52] Indeed, Taylor rather uncritically adopts discursive categories that evolved from and strengthen Western hegemony; however, to be fair, he did not himself construct 'the West' or its hegemony.

What is more, Taylor's intention behind "drawing a boundary around Latin Christendom" is less to exclude others than to isolate this previously constructed civilization with the aim of better understanding it. Taylor advocates the idea of multiple modernities, according to which crucial features of modernity – notably secularity – are constituted and expressed differently in different "civilizations." He defends his decision to limit *A Secular Age* to the West on the basis of a desire to avoid premature universalization: only after an in-depth study of one civilization could one attempt comparisons with other contexts.[53] Taylor is quite consistent in his self-imposed limitation: there are only few allusions to the non-West in the pages of *A Secular Age*, most notably parallels between Christianity and Buddhism. The few times Islam is mentioned in Taylor's story, it is both as a

50 Taylor, "Afterword," 301.

51 Mahmood, Saba. 2010. "Can Secularism Be Other-wise?." In *Varieties of Secularism in a Secular Age* ed. by Michael Warner, Jonathan VanAntwerpen and Craig Calhoun: 282–299. Cambridge, Mass.: Harvard University Press.

52 Ibid., 296.

53 Taylor, *A Secular Age*, 21; idem. 2011. "Western Secularity." In *Rethinking Secularism* ed. by Craig Calhoun, Mark Juergensmeyer and Jonathan VanAntwerpen: 31–53. Oxford: Oxford University Press, here 36 f.

counter-example[54] and to illustrate commonalities.[55] In contrast to many contemporary debates on secularity, the central counterfoil to contemporary Western societies in *A Secular Age* is not Islam, but rather the West's own past,[56] and Taylor explicitly criticizes the practice of othering Islam for the sake of assuring oneself of one's own secularity.[57]

Then again, Taylor's interest in understanding the secularity that is allegedly specific to the West goes hand in hand with an exclusion of the non-West, including Islam. At the beginning of *A Secular Age*, Taylor names two common characterizations of secularity: secularity 1, "emptying" public spaces of God, or what would more commonly be termed social differentiation; and secularity 2, "the falling off of religious belief and practice."[58] According to the latter understanding, the United States, Pakistan, and Jordan – exemplary cases for the West and the non-West – would be classed "as the same,"[59] so this is not the secularity in which he is interested. Taylor is interested in an understanding of secularity that brings out the alleged specifics of Western societies, with Muslim societies serving as contrast cases. The West's specific secularity (secularity 3), according to Taylor, consists of the asserted fact that belief in God is no longer axiomatic, but has become a mere option. If these supposedly specific characteristics then serve as the benchmark for whether "an age or society" is "secular or not,"[60] the answer is a given – only 'we' are secular. Therefore, while Taylor names characteristics of secularity that extend to the non-West, he advances an understanding that turns 'secularity' into a placeholder for 'our' alleged exclusivity.[61]

However, while perhaps less obviously than with secularities 1 and 2, Taylor's own characterization (secularity 3) is not all that exclusive to the West either. One can hardly doubt the predominance of secularity 1 throughout the Is-

---

54 Idem., *A Secular Age*, 102, 283, 419.
55 Ibid., 770, 834fn19.
56 This is why Taylor cannot acknowledge those historians who complicate his image of past societies as holistically and harmoniously grounded in transcendence (Gordon, "The Place;" Sheehan, "When").
57 Taylor, *A Secular Age*, 770, 834fn19.
58 Ibid., 1f.
59 Ibid., 3.
60 Ibid., 3.
61 Read more sympathetically, one could argue that Taylor often means "Western secularity" when he writes "secularity" in general. In that case, Western secularity would not be the benchmark for secularity in general, but only one version of it. Or does Taylor view the West as most obviously secular according to secularity 3, with the possibility of this secularity extending to non-Western contexts, too? Both readings seem to bend the text too far.

lamic world. Gudrun Krämer, in an article that also draws on Taylor, leaves no doubt that this is a historical fact: "A close look at modern political thought and practice (including notably Islamic discourse), economics, law, art and education would reveal that secularization processes form an integral part of Middle Eastern history and society."[62] As Krämer notes, the question is rather how Muslims position themselves with regard to this factual secularity. Regarding secularity 2, the decline of religious beliefs and practices, Taylor himself has stated that the United States (as a crucial example of the West) is on the same level as the Islamic countries Jordan and Pakistan.[63] This assessment is supported by comparative empirical studies.[64] The issue is indeed less clear regarding secularity 3, the optionality of belief. Of course, Taylor has not settled on this understanding without reason, pointing out Muslim societies as clear counter-cases. Yet even in most Islamic societies, belief is no longer axiomatic; these societies might instead appear as counter-cases because belief is the hegemonic option.

Let us approach this argument from its least controversial side: Nilüfer Göle has indisputably shown that migrant Muslims, especially in a European setting, use Islam as a means of individual "self-fashioning."[65] As Krämer argues, the spread of new media might also multiply the availability of options in Muslim majority societies.[66] But unbelief as an option has not only recently become available. Samuli Schielke reminds us that "nonreligion and atheism have long had supporters among Muslim peoples too."[67] These supporters may be few in number, but contemporary Islamic revival movements should not deceive one into thinking that belief is axiomatic. Rather, these very movements testify to the fact that belief is an option and, through failing to deliver on their compre-

---

62 Krämer, Gudrun. 2013. "Modern but not Secular: Religion, Identity and the *ordre public* in the Arab Middle East." *International Sociology* 28/6: 629–644, here 630). This point is mostly undisputed, and had already been made earlier (for example: Zubaida, Sami. 2005. "Islam and Secularization." *Asian Journal of Social Sciences* 33/3: 438–448).

63 Taylor, *A Secular Age*, 3.

64 For example: Fish, M. Steven. 2011. *Are Muslims Distinctive? A Look at the Evidence*. Oxford: Oxford University Press.

65 Göle, Nilüfer. 2010. "The Civilizational, Spatial, and Sexual Powers of the Secular." In *Varieties of Secularism in a Secular Age* ed. by Michael Warner, Jonathan VanAntwerpen and Craig Calhoun: 243–264. Cambridge, Mass.: Harvard University Press, here 261. One could fully attribute this fact to the European environment. However, for cultural accounts stressing the importance of religious traditions, such as Taylor's, Muslims within European civilization are relevant signifiers of an Islamic self-understanding.

66 Krämer, "Modern," 635.

67 Schielke, Samuli. 2012. "Being a Nonbeliever in a Time of Islamic Revival: Trajectories of Doubt and Certainty in Contemporary Egypt." *International Journal of Middle East Studies* 44: 301–320, here 302.

hensive agenda, may even motivate people to embrace unbelief.[68] While Schielke here focused on contemporary Egypt, Daniel Kinitz has shown the contingency of religious positions in Egypt in the first half of the twentieth century.[69] It is true that, in Muslim majority societies, even fewer people than in the West are put in that "Jamesian open space" where one is pulled first to belief and then to unbelief.[70] But at least since the colonial era, which the following chapter deals with in greater detail, a naive, unreflective belief has become unavailable in many milieux in Islamic societies.[71] Since then, religion as a basis for society has been disputed even more extensively, with secularism, nationalism, and socialism representing major competitors to religious agendas.

This rough sketch suggests that, while Islam is absent from Taylor's story, it does participate in our common secular age, as conceived of in *A Secular Age*. The background understandings which, according to Taylor, made possible and continue to support the secular age, and which are more fundamental than the degree to which belief is an option, are thus very useful in research on Islamic contexts. Interestingly, Taylor himself tentatively suggests Islam as the one tradition (next to Western Christendom) that produced a crucial landmark of his story – namely, the division between a natural and a supernatural order.[72]

While the factual secularity of Egypt at the turn to the twentieth century will be illustrated in the next chapter, the following section suggests that the Islamic reformists also understood themselves historically.

4 Historical Self-understanding and Storytelling

Why does Charles Taylor tell a story? On the normative side, he wants to show the Christian roots of our secular age, so as to render plausible the existence of a transcendent reality and to strengthen the option of belief in a Christian God today. With regard to the underlying epistemology, Taylor's reason for resort-

68 Ibid., 302.

69 Kinitz, Daniel. 2015. "Deviance as a Phenomenon of Secularity: Islam and Deviants in Twentieth-century Egypt – A Search for Sociological Explanations." In *Multiple Secularities Beyond the West* ed. by Marian Burchardt, Monika Wohlrab-Sahr and Matthias Middell: 97–120. Boston/Berlin: DeGruyter.

70 Taylor, *A Secular Age*, 549, 551, 592.

71 This is not only true for urban areas; see for example: Loeffler, Richard. 1988. *Islam in Practice: Religious Beliefs in a Persian Village*. New York: State University of New York Press.

72 Taylor, *A Secular Age*, 781fn19.

ing to storytelling is his assumption that "we (modern Westerners) can't help understanding ourselves in these terms [i.e., via master narratives]. I'm not claiming this for all human beings at all times."[73] Indeed, the Islamic reformists at the turn to the twentieth century did not narrate a continuous, autochthonic genealogy of modernity. Yet this was due less to a different epistemology than to colonial power structures. After all, why *can* Taylor tell the story he is telling? This is surely facilitated by the fact that he, in contrast to the reformists of *al-Manar*, lives after the heyday of modernity. However, why does his exclusivist Western story work, despite its lack of attention to the historical role of the non-West in shaping our present self-understandings? It only works because of the West's political, economic, and cultural hegemony and its seeming self-sufficiency.

Try to imagine being a reformist Muslim intellectual at the beginning of the twentieth century, like Rashid Rida, who wants to describe an exclusivist genealogy of an autochthonic Islamic modernity. He cannot – that is, his story would not be very convincing, since Europe's contribution to the present state of affairs is too obvious to ignore. The potential alternative of telling a common story – which would probably best mirror historical reality – was inhibited by colonialists' exclusivist claims to modernity. The Islamic reformists wanted to participate in modernity, but they wanted their own Islamic version instead of following the allegedly areligious European model. They are buying into European subtraction stories when they maintain that, in Christendom, liberation from religious bonds was necessary for the achievement of modernity. They then argue that this is not true for Islam, since its fundamentals – mainly the Qur'an – already contain all the positive aspects of modernity.

What might sound contradictory at first actually brings to light the Islamic reformists' mode of legitimizing and critiquing modernity: all the positive elements of modernity were already present in the fundamentals of Islam, while the negative aspects of Western modernity were absent. In other words, the Islamic fundamentals embody modernity to perfection. The envisioned modernity is most profoundly manifested in the harmonization of religion and reason, of spiritually guided ethics and material progress. Whereas in Christendom reason had to free itself from religion, in Islam reason had always been free within a religious framework. Whereas Christianity did indeed necessitate secularization, Islam neither allows for nor requires secularization, as it has always been secu-

73 Taylor, "Afterword," 300.

lar. Muhammad ʿAbduh, in a book first serialized in *al-Manar*,[74] offers an elaborated version of this oft-recurring argument – although he, unlike present Muslim reformists,[75] does not yet use the term 'secular' or its Arabic equivalent, ʿ*almānī*. This argument, which buys into the subtraction stories criticized by Taylor, is of course ahistorical and apologetic; yet it is also a way of appropriating modernity. Equally important, the Islamic reformists' use of Islamic points of reference and of an Islamic discourse to address both religious and secular domains makes it harder to see the factual secularity of their thinking. Taylor refers to a similar problem regarding Christian thinkers turning to worldly affairs: "It became hard for many to answer the question, what is Christian faith about? The salvation of humankind, or the progress wrought by capitalism, technology, democracy?"[76]

The fact that the Islamic reformists appropriated modernity via the Islamic fundamentals and thereby negated the supposed need for secularization – that is, for history – might seem to support Taylor's contention that storytelling is not a universal mode. However, while the reformists negated the need for one history (secularization) and one story (subtraction), they outlined the contours of another story, which reminds us of what Taylor calls an "Intellectual Deviation story."[77] After all, the reformists needed to explain why, if the Islamic fundamentals had always contained a perfect modernity, Muslims were now behind Europeans in so many fields. The answer was that Muslims had been betraying the Islamic message and teachings: even directly after the time of the pious forefathers, political strife corrupted the Islamic community, and intellectual life had come to a standstill by the thirteenth century, with most scholars blindly following tradition. Colonialism then allegedly served as a wake-up call to return to the core teachings of Islam. While even in its longer version, this narrative of deviation and its envisioned remedy does not match the complexity of Taylor's Reform Master Narrative, it shows that the Islamic reformists also resorted to (hi)storytelling to make sense of themselves and their present state of affairs.

---

74 ʿAbduh, Muhammad. 1323 h [1905/1906]. *al-Islam wa-l-Nasraniyya maʿa al-ʿIlm wa-l-Madaniyya*. Cairo: Matbaʿat al-Manar.

75 For a prominent example, see: Ramadan, Tariq. 1998 [1994]. *Les musulmans dans la laïcité: responsabilités et droits des musulmans dans les sociétés occidentales*. Lyon: Tawhid, 59–61, 76–81, 114 f.; idem. 2001. *Islam, the West and the Challenges of Modernity*; transl. Saïd Amghar. Leicester: The Islamic Foundation, 89 f., 261, 332 f. For a comprehensive overview of literature on Ramadan and an analysis of changes in his reformist discourse, see: Zemmin, Florian. 2015. "Integrating Islamic Positions into European Public Discourse: The Paradigmatic Example of Tariq Ramadan." *Journal of Religion in Europe* 8/1: 121–146.

76 Taylor, *A Secular Age*, 736.

77 Ibid., 774.

Moreover, even though not only the narratives themselves, but also the point of narration, the state of modernity narrated, and the alternative modernity envisioned differ greatly between Taylor and the Islamic reformists, there are important commonalities between the two. While the extent to which Taylor's book is a Catholic one, a nostalgic one, or even an anti-democratic one[78] is debatable, what is rather uncontroversial is his basic goal – to recall the religious roots and essence of the present secular age, and thus to subsume secular reality under a religious standpoint. Compare this with how Aziz al-Azmeh summarized the basic goals of Islamic reformism: "Islamic Reformism was founded on the postulation of a possible equivalence between the reality of a secular age and normative religion: theorizing that, given its innate nature, normative religion preceded the reality of today, and consequently should reclaim today as its very own."[79] If we hypothetically picture Rashid Rida walking into a bookstore where Taylor's story and a subtraction story were both on display, it seems rather clear which of the two he would have spent his money on, which would have resonated more with his own understanding of modernity, and with which story we can thus better grasp this understanding today.

If the last two sections have already formulated some expectations and even tentative findings in order to show the usability of *A Secular Age* as a heuristic tool, the following part further substantiates the expectation that one can discern the concept of 'society' in *al-Manar*.

---

78 See: Thomas, Günter. 2016. "The Temptation of Religious Nostalgia. Protestant Readings of *A Secular Age*." In *Working with A Secular Age. Interdisciplinary Perspectives on Charles Taylor's Master Narrative* ed. by Florian Zemmin, Colin Jager and Guido Vanheeswijck: 49–70. Berlin/Boston: De Gruyter.

79 Al-Azmeh, *Islams*, 106.

Part B

Expectations: Egyptian Modernity, *al-Manar*, and Arabic Concepts

Chapter 4
Modernity in Egypt: Nation, Society, Secularism, and the Press

1 Egypt as a Modern Nation-State

> "Egyptians! [...] I only came to you in order to rescue your religion and your rights from the hand of tyrants. I am more than the slave-soldiers [i.e., the Mamluks] worshipping God, may He be praised and exalted. And I respect His prophet, Muhammad, and the glorious Qur'an."
>
> – Napoleon Bonaparte, 1798[1]

> "Egypt is no longer part of Africa. It is part of Europe."
>
> – Khedive Ismail, 1867[2]

1.1 Preliminaries: Writing about the Modern Egyptian Nation

This study understands modernity as an interpretation of the world for which the concept of 'society' is a constitutive signifier. However, no interpretation is detached from institutional and material socio-political developments. Material and idealist aspects are always interdependent, and my focus on the latter is only possible due to the former being rather firmly established for modern Egypt, as the following sketch of socio-political developments between 1805 and 1940 will show. Prior to outlining those developments, however, I shall briefly discuss the beginnings of modernity in Egypt – and the extent to which Egypt in the nineteenth and early twentieth centuries can meaningfully be designated as a modern 'nation-state.'

Under the classical paradigm of modernization, which equated modernization with Westernization, a concrete date symbolized the onset of modernity in Egypt – and the Middle East at large – namely, the landing of Napoleon's

1 Quoted from: Cole, Juan Ricardo. 2010. "Playing Muslim: Bonaparte's Army of the Orient and Euro-Muslim Creolization." In *The Age of Revolutions in Global Context, c. 1760–1840* ed. by David Armitage and Sanjay Subrahmanyam: 125–143. Basingstoke/New York: Palgrave Macmillan, here 128.

2 Quoted from: Berman, Nina. 2004. *Impossible Missions? German Economic, Military, and Humanitarian Efforts in Africa*. Lincoln: University of Nebraska Press, 45.

https://doi.org/10.1515/9783110545845-005

army and scientific corps in Alexandria on July 1, 1798.[3] Many contemporaries, including members of the French scientific corps, had still assumed a "coevalness" between Egypt and France, allowing for the possibility of mutual learning and exchange.[4] A couple of decades later, however, the majority of European thinkers had come to deny Egyptians' coevalness. Even though the French withdrew from Egypt after only three years, they were said to have incited modernity in Egypt by introducing political ideas and also scientific methods and the printing press. This once-popular view went hand in hand with depicting the previous centuries in Egypt and the wider 'Islamic world' – if there was such an entity before modernity – as dark ages, in which intellectual life had come to a complete standstill and economic and political conditions had deteriorated.

In reality, the most important impact of the French invasion was probably the end of Mamluk rule in Egypt,[5] as it opened the path to Muhammad ʿAli's reorganization of political, economic, and social structures – even though, between 1768 and 1775, the Mamluk rulers ʿAli Bey and Muhammad Bey had already pursued a similar path in many regards.[6] Namely, they had attempted to centralize power in a new way by bringing both political-military institutions and economic resources under the unified control of their household. Moreover, they had sought to expand Egyptian control into neighboring regions, thus heightening the importance of Egypt to European powers. Economic and political decline is thus not characteristic of the eighteenth century at large, but rather of the last two decades of that century. It was then that ʿAli Bey's and Muham-

3 For a solid summary of Napoleon's mission, which also discusses the impact of the French invasion, see: Dykstra, Darrell. 1998. "The French Occupation of Egypt." In *The Cambridge History of Egypt. Volume 2: Modern Egypt, from 1517 to the End of the Twentieth Century* ed. by M.W. Daly: 113–138. Cambridge: Cambridge University Press. Well researched and at the same time very enjoyable to read is: Cole, Juan Ricardo. 2008. *Napoleon's Egypt: Invading the Middle East.* New York: Palgrave Macmillan. A major primary source observing the events from the perspective of an Egyptian chronicler is: al-Jabarti, ʿAbdarrahman. 1994. *ʿAbd al-Raḥmān al-Jabartī's History of Egypt = ʿAjāʾib al-āthār fī'l-tarājim wa'l-akhbār*; ed. by Thomas Philipp and Moshe Perlmann. 3 vols. Stuttgart: Steiner; al-Jabarti, ʿAbdarrahman. 1975. *Al-Jabartī's chronicle of the first seven months of the French occupation of Egypt : Muḥarram-Rajab 1213, 15 June – December 1798 = Tārīkh muddat al-faransīs bi-miṣr*; edited and translated by S. Moreh. Leiden: Brill.

4 Ze'evi, Dror. 2004. "Back to Napoleon? Thoughts on the Beginning of the Modern Era in the Middle East." *Mediterranean Historical Review* 19/1: 73–94, here 77. For the notion of "coevalness," see: Fabian, Johannes. 1983. *Time and the Other: How Anthropology Makes Its Object* New York: Columbia University Press, esp. 31.

5 For a discussion of the French impact on various levels, see: Dykstra, "The French," 134 ff.

6 Crecelius, Daniel. 1998. "Egypt in the Eighteenth Century." In *The Cambridge History of Egypt. Volume 2: Modern Egypt, from 1517 to the End of the Twentieth Century* ed. by M.W. Daly: 59–86. Cambridge: Cambridge University Press, here 79–82.

mad Bey's efforts were discontinued and political strife and economic deterioration added to plagues haunting the population.[7] On the intellectual plain, the French presence in Egypt had a greater impact on France than on Egypt, mainly due to the knowledge and experience the French had gathered there. Moreover, Egyptian intellectual life had hardly come to a standstill in the centuries preceding the Napoleonic invasion. Indeed, whether on the intellectual, the political, or the economic plain, the picture of an Egyptian (or Ottoman, or Islamic) decline that was only brought to an end by European influence does not stand the test of historical evidence.

In a highly recommendable discussion of Western historiographical writing on Egypt and the Middle East,[8] Dror Ze'evi discusses how "revisionist" narratives and historical case studies since the 1970s have been challenging this "decline paradigm," which accompanied the paradigm of modernization.[9] The revisionist arguments stress pre-Napoleonic internal developments of modernity in Egypt or the Ottoman Empire, which were then interrupted by Western influence. While revisionist studies have done an important job in revealing the decline paradigm as obviously mistaken, they failed to produce a convincing alternative narrative of internal modernization.[10] Such a narrative, however, is not to be expected in the first place if one argues, as I have done in the introduction to this study, that the modern self-understanding was significantly shaped in the colonial encounter and was not an internal development – neither in Europe, from which it was arguably then exported, nor in Egypt, where it was then supposedly superseded by Western influence. Ze'evi shares this general understanding of modernity concerning the case of the Middle East.[11] Against both the decline and the revisionist views, the importance of the Napoleonic invasion thus lies in its having created a moment of encounter, which contributed to the emergence of the modern self-understanding.

The year 1798, moreover, became a crucial date for the Egyptian "experience and interpretation"[12] of modernity. Since Europe was regarded as epitomizing

---

7 Ibid., 82–86.

8 See also: Hathaway, Jane. 2004. "Rewriting Eighteenth-Century Ottoman History." *Mediterranean Historical Review* 19/1: 29–53; Humphreys, Stephen R. 2006. "The Historiography of the Middle East: Transforming a Field of Study." In *Middle East Historiographies. Narrating the Twentieth Century* ed. by Israel Gershoni, Amy Singer and Erdem Y. Hakan: 19–36. Seattle/London: University of Washington Press.

9 Ze'evi, "Back."

10 Ibid., 86.

11 Ibid., 86f.

12 Wagner, *Modernity.*

modernity, modernity was experienced as something external, even if one subsequently asserted the roots of modernity in one's own tradition or proclaimed that from this tradition a better, more sustainable version of modernity would evolve. Thus, if in Europe modernity was experienced as a rupture with tradition, in Egypt, as in other non-European settings, modernity was experienced as a double rupture: internal and external.[13] As mentioned in chapter 3 section 4, Islamic reformists shared the view of decline and stagnation in the "dark ages," attributing this situation to a neglect of Islamic teachings. Moreover, they regarded the European invasion and domination as a wake-up call to return to an allegedly true Islam. Egyptian nationalist historiographies, which tend to attribute the supposed "decline" to foreign Ottoman influence rather than to an absence of Islam, have also given credit to the Napoleonic invasion for inciting modernity.[14]

Particularly in nationalist historiography, but also beyond, another man is considered to be the actual founding father of the modern Egyptian nation – namely, Muhammad[15] ʿAli. ʿAli was an Albanian officer who emerged from the political turbulence after the French withdrawal as ruler of Egypt in 1805 and whose dynasty was in power until the revolution of 1952, even though the British actually administered the country from 1882 on. The role and title of "founder of modern Egypt" was only assigned to Muhammad ʿAli from the early twentieth century on. Crucial in this regard were the 1905 celebrations of the centenary of his ascension to power. These celebrations were organized by the Egyptian palace in an attempt to construct its own nationalist historical narrative over against both British and anti-monarchical versions.[16] This attempt proved rather successful, as Muhammad ʿAli has since been widely regarded as the founder of modern Egypt, bringing the supposedly ancient Egyptian nation to independence and maturity. If every nation, as an "imagined community,"[17] projects its essence back into the past and constructs an almost timeless essence, it can in-

13 Idem., "World-Sociology," 308 f.; Pflitsch, *Zweierlei*, esp. 54 f.

14 Ze'evi, "Back," 79 f., 84.

15 The name of 'Muhammad' instead of 'Mehmet' ʿAli stresses the Egyptian rather than the Ottoman identity of that ruler, who spoke Albanian and Turkish.

16 Cuno, Kenneth M. 2000. "Muhammad Ali and the Decline and Revival Thesis in Modern Egyptian History." In *Reform or Modernization? Egypt under Muhamed Ali. Symposium Organized by The Egyptian Society of Historical Studies, 9–11 March 1999* ed. by Raouf ʿAbbas: 93–119. Cairo: al-Majlis al-ʿAmm li-l-Thaqafa, here 107 f. Cuno mentions an article by ʿAbduh in *al-Manar* as the "most famous criticism of the role of Muhammad Ali by an Egyptian." This has to be seen in the context of what ʿAbduh, in 1905, perceived as excessive celebrations of the centenary of Muhammad ʿAli's reign.

17 Anderson, *Imagined.*

deed be argued that Egypt was positioned rather well for such a construction,[18] not least due to its geographical setting and the rich history within its geographical boundaries.

However, throughout the nineteenth century, the identity of the Egyptian nation was still not fixed, either politically or legally, or indeed concerning sentiments of belonging. Despite having had a significant degree of autonomy before the British took over the actual administration of the country, Egypt was still officially part of the Ottoman Empire, and most of its subjects identified themselves as both Egyptian and Ottoman.[19] The picture becomes increasingly complicated as other loyalties and sentiments of belonging enter into the frame, be it identification with perceived European values and ways of life or, more significantly, with an imagined Arab[20] or Muslim community. Such identifications were not at all mutually exclusive.[21] Rashid Rida, one of many who left their Syrian homeland[22] to pursue their journalistic ambitions in Egypt, also displayed multiple senses of belonging. Thus my focus on the Egyptian nation should not suggest a fully autonomous Egyptian state or a clearly bounded Egyptian national identity. Rather, what is significant is that the authors in *al-Manar* were writing from within the setting of a modern nation-state and interpreted its conditions accordingly.

---

18 Baron, Beth. 2005. *Egypt as a Woman: Nationalism, Gender, and Politics.* Cairo: American University in Cairo Press, 3.

19 See: Hanley, Will. 2013. "When did Egyptians stop being Ottomans? An Imperial Citizenship Case Study." In *Multilevel Citizenship* ed. by Willem Maas: 89–109. Philadelphia: Pennsylvania University Press.

20 For the evolvement of the idea of an 'Arab nation,' see: Schaebler, Birgit. 2007. "Writing the Nation in the Arabic-Speaking World, Nationally and Transnationally." In *Writing the Nation. A Global Perspective* ed. by Stefan Berger: 179–196. New York: Palgrave Macmillan.

21 See Gershoni, Israel and Jankowski, James P. 1995. *Redefining the Egyptian Nation, 1930–1945.* Cambridge/New York: Cambridge University Press; and, as an insightful rejoinder: idem. 1999. "Print Culture, Social Change, and the Process of Redefining Imagined Communities in Egypt. Response to the Review by Charles D. Smith of *Redefining the Egyptian Nation.*" *International Journal of Middle East Studies* 31/1: 81–94.

22 For the evolution of Syrian national identity, see: Beshara, Adel (ed.). 2011. *The Origins of Syrian Nationhood. Histories, Pioneers and Identity.* Oxon/New York: Routledge.

1.2 Egypt Becomes a Nation-State: Nationalizing Politics and Nationalist Sentiments

Since 1517, when Ottoman Turks conquered the Mamluk Sultanate, Egypt had been a province of the Ottoman Empire, with the Mamluks remaining the ruling class. The French invaders deliberately portrayed themselves to Egyptians as friends of Islam and liberators of Egypt from the Ottoman and Mamluk yoke.[23] The French withdrawal in 1801 followed their surrender to British forces, which, in collaboration with the Sublime Porte in Istanbul, had entered Egypt in order to restore Ottoman sovereignty over it. After four years of power struggles between various factions, with British forces leaving Egypt in 1803, Muhammad ʿAli, an Albanian military commander of the Ottoman army backed by a politicized urban population, emerged as the ruler of Egypt.[24]

Egypt officially remained a province of the Ottoman Empire until 1914, but Ottoman sovereignty was in reality reduced to suzerainty. The Porte had awarded the title of governor (*walī*) to Muhammad ʿAli in 1805. It did not recognize his self-designation as viceroy (*khedive*) but eventually granted this title to his successor, Ismaʿil, in 1867. Exact designations and legal status notwithstanding, beginning with his consolidation of power in 1811,[25] Muhammad ʿAli rather firmly ruled and reformed the country. (The previous Mamluk rulers had already been gaining increasing autonomy from the Sublime Porte since the seventeenth century.[26]) It was only under British pressure – and in return for being granted the hereditary right to rule over Egypt in 1841 – that Muhammad ʿAli put a halt to his

---

23 Cole, "Playing," esp. 128 f.

24 For a concise overview of the main factions involved in Muhammad ʿAli's ascent to and consolidation of power, see: Dykstra, "The French," 132 ff.; Fahmy, Khaled. 1998. "The Era of Muhammad ʿAli Pasha." In *The Cambridge History of Egypt. Volume 2: Modern Egypt, from 1517 to the End of the Twentieth Century* ed. by M.W. Daly: 139 – 179. Cambridge: Cambridge University Press, here 139 – 147.

25 That year, Muhammad ʿAli got rid of his Mamluk rivals by executing hundreds of their fighters. He also diminished the power of rural landowners by reforming land laws and confiscating territories.

26 This trend was enforced in the eighteenth century, as Crecelius shows. He also briefly looks back at the previous century, which is dealt with more extensively in the chapter preceding his own (Crecelius, "Egypt."). It could be added that the Ottoman Empire in the seventeenth century more generally witnessed a certain decentralization of power: "Ottoman military-administrative elites [became] localized, while the local elites gradually became ottomanized" (Toledano, Ehud, R. 1998. "Social and Economic Reform in the Long Nineteenth Century." In *The Cambridge History of Egypt. Volume 2: Modern Egypt, from 1517 to the End of the Twentieth Century* ed. by M.W. Daly: 252 – 284. Cambridge: Cambridge University Press, here 257).

expansionist plans, which had led to major victories over Ottoman forces up until that time.

Muhammad ʿAli's plans for the reform and development of Egypt were primarily driven by military interests[27] but went well beyond the military itself. His expansionist ambitions, culminating in the temporary annexation of Northern Sudan and occupations of Syria and parts of Arabia and Anatolia, not only prompted a modernization of the army,[28] but also infrastructural projects, the initiation of a modern bureaucracy, and the establishment of government schools. While Muhammad ʿAli also founded a few factories, these did not last long, and further large-scale industrialization only occurred in Egypt after the First World War.[29] His military reform efforts were partly modeled on earlier Ottoman reforms,[30] especially the New Order (Nizam-ı Cedid) of Sultan Selim III (r. 1789–1807), which itself drew on French models. With the aim of collecting scientific, medical, technical, military, and administrative skills and knowledge, Muhammad ʿAli dispatched student missions to Europe – first to Italy and then, beginning in 1826, to France.[31] Inspired mainly by French models, he then founded government schools to teach this knowledge.[32] These schools became rivals to

27 The following glimpses of Muhammad ʿAli's policy and reform efforts are based, unless indicated otherwise, on: Fahmy, "The Era" and Cuno, Kenneth M. 2010. "Egypt to c. 1919." In *The New Cambridge History of Islam. vol. 5: The Islamic World in the Age of Western Dominance* ed. by Francis Robinson: 79–106. New York: Cambridge University Press, here 79–88. See these encyclopedic articles for further references.

28 For Muhammad ʿAli's creation of a modern army and its role in building the modern nation of Egypt, see: Fahmy, Khaled. 1997. *All the Pasha's Men. Mehmed Ali, His Army and the Making of Modern Egypt.* Cambridge: Cambridge University Press.

29 Toledano, "Social," 273; Baer, Gabriel. 1968. "Social Change in Egypt: 1800–1914." In *Political and Social Change in Modern Egypt. Historical Studies from the Ottoman Conquest to the United Arab Republic* ed. by P. M. Holt: 135–161. London: Oxford University Press, here 139 (this chapter in general gives a good summary of the major developments depicted more substantially in: Baer, Gabriel. 1969. *Studies in the Social History of Modern Egypt.* Chicago/London: The University of Chicago Press). Although Baer's analysis is at times weakened by his adoption of a developmentalist paradigm, his factual historical findings remain relevant and, in part, unsurpassed.

30 It was Selim's successors who undertook more comprehensive reform efforts, known as the Tanzimat (1839–1876).

31 For divergent opinions as to the date of the first student missions, see Sawaʿi, Muhammad. 2013. *al-Hadatha wa-Mustalahat al-Nahda al-ʿArabiyya fi al-Qarn al-Tasiʿa ʿAshar. Dirasa fi Mufradat Ahmad Faris al-Shidyaq fi Jaridat ʻal-Jawaʾibʼ.* Beirut: al-Muʾassasa al-ʿArabiyya li-l-Dirasat wa-l-Nashr, 14fn1.

32 Raouf, Abbas. 2005. "French Impact on the Egyptian Educational System under Muhammad Aly and Ismail." In *La France & l'Égypte à l'époque des vice-rois 1805–1882* ed. by Daniel Panzac and André Raymond: 91–99. Cairo: Institut français d'archéologie orientale.

the classical religious institutions of learning, the *kuttāb* and the *madrasa*. Moreover, Muhammad ʿAli brought major religious institutions under government control: in 1812, he asserted his right to appoint the Shaykh of al-Azhar and granted authority over Sufi orders to the Shaykh of the Bakriyya order; in 1835, he created the office of a state mufti, whose rulings should have sole authority in official affairs.[33] To generate revenue, Muhammad ʿAli conducted land reforms, set up industries, and transformed most of Egyptian agriculture into a cash-crop culture under his control. The export of a large portion of its produce, especially cotton, significantly advanced the integration of Egypt's economy with European markets.[34] Under Muhammad ʿAli's successors, this economic integration led to increasing control of Egyptian commerce by Europeans. Nevertheless, Muhammad ʿAli's sons and grandsons retained control over trade and infrastructure and, more significantly, shifted the focus from military to administrative advancement.[35]

Thus, during the successive reigns of ʿAbbas (1848–1854), Saʿid (1854–1863), and Ismaʿil (1863–1879), "Egypt's civil bureaucracy emerged as the preeminent state institution,"[36] signifying an increasingly centralized and encompassing public authority and consequently the national integration of a society living under its jurisdiction. This is illustrated, for example, in the fact that murder cases were no longer resolved by village shaykhs as arbiters, but instead by governmental courts.[37] However, the outreach of the central authorities still had its limits, and this was not an all-encompassing state confronting a homogeneous populace.[38] Moreover, the distinction between state and society in general simplifies the actual relations between political and societal actors.[39] And while the state in nineteenth-century Egypt began to represent itself as an abstract order,[40] it was still mainly embodied by the ruling dynasty. In any case, the tendency to centralize government authority and thereby nationalize its populace remains significant. This was facilitated by the construction of railways and telegraphs from the 1860s onward. The administration itself was also in-

33 Cuno, "Egypt," 82f.

34 Already in the second half of the eighteenth century, European markets had become more significant for Egyptian trade (Crecelius, "Egypt," 68).

35 Hunter, Robert F. 2000. "State-Society Relations in Nineteenth-Century Egypt: The Years of Transition, 1848–79." *Middle Eastern Studies* 36/3: 145–159, here 145.

36 Ibid., 145.

37 Ibid., 148f.

38 See, for example: Chalcraft, John. 2005. "Engaging the State: Peasants and Petitions in Egypt on the Eve of Colonial Rule." *International Journal of Middle East Studies* 37/3: 303–325.

39 Toledano, "Social," 256.

40 Mitchell, Timothy. 1988. *Colonising Egypt*. Cambridge: Cambridge University Press.

creasingly (albeit slowly) nationalized, with Arabic replacing Turkish as the official language in 1856[41] and Arabic-speaking graduates of government educational programs taking up official positions. While government educational programs had a limited reach, the attention to social, civilizing reform is aptly demonstrated in family politics[42] or the improvement of sanitary conditions and hygiene. The rationale behind this was that "healthy bodies meant agricultural prosperity, hence greater tax returns."[43] More generally, it is true that government social reforms were undertaken with a primary interest not in improving social conditions, but in shaping a national society to better serve the state.[44]

Foreign – namely French and British – control over Egyptian politics increased in the second half of the nineteenth century, and after the failed ʿUrabi revolt of 1881–1882, which was the first powerful manifestation of nationalist sentiments, the English occupied and subsequently administered the country. ʿUrabi was an Egyptian officer and, for a brief time, the war minister in the newly formed cabinet of 1882 – the first cabinet to include a significant number of Egyptians.[45] One major reason for the revolt was the dearth of opportunities for Egyptian army personnel to get promoted in a military hierarchy in which the upper ranks were dominated by Turks. Another was the growing discontent with foreign control over the country.[46] It is worth mentioning in the context of this study that Muhammad ʿAbduh was expelled from Egypt in 1882, due to his support for the ʿUrabi movement. After his redemption and return to Egypt in 1888, ʿAbduh first served as a judge in the civil courts. From 1899 until his death in 1905, he occupied the office of the Grand Mufti of Egypt. After the English defeated the nationalist forces headed by ʿUrabi, they restored Khedive Tawfiq (1879–1892) to power.

If Tawfiq was the first ruler who was clearly endorsed by the English, foreign control had already severely limited khedival power prior to 1882. A major factor that contributed to this situation was Egypt's large external debt, which in 1878 prompted the installation of French and English ministers in the Egyptian cab-

---

41 Hunter, "State-Society," 148, 156.

42 Pollard, Lisa. 2005. *Nurturing the Nation: The Family Politics of Modernizing, Colonizing, and Liberating Egypt (1805–1923)*. Berkeley: University of California Press.

43 Hunter, "State-Society," 148.

44 Ibid., 156 f.

45 Prior to 1882, there had been only one lone Egyptian minister in the khedival cabinet – namely, ʿAli Mubarak (1823–1898).

46 For the more complex set of reasons leading to the ʿUrabi revolt, see: Cole, Juan Ricardo. 1991. *Colonialism and Revolution in the Middle East: Social and Cultural Origins of Egypt's ʿUrabi Movement*. Princeton, N.J.: Princeton University Press; and, concisely discussing different interpretations: Toledano, "Social," 267–270.

inet, whose major task was to control public spending. English influence in – and later control over – Egypt did not begin with the occupation of 1882, and it also did not end with the proclamation of Egyptian independence in 1922. Since 1879, Lord Cromer had been the British controller-general in Egypt, and during his tenure as British Consul-General of Egypt from 1882 to 1907, it is hardly an exaggeration to consider him the de-facto ruler of the country. Foreign control of the country heightened national sentiments, and Tawfiq's successor ʿAbbas II (1892–1914) was strongly opposed to British rule. When the Ottoman Empire, of which Egypt still was officially a part, joined the Allied forces in 1914, the English disposed of ʿAbbas II and turned their "veiled protectorate" (a term coined by Lord Cromer) into an official one, installing Hussein Kamel, ʿAbbas's uncle, as Sultan of Egypt – a title that stressed Egypt's independence from the Ottoman Empire.

Nationalist sentiments grew under the British occupation and lead to the formation of nationalist parties in 1907 and the nationalist revolution of 1919. The most significant single event catalyzing this general trend was the execution of peasants in the village of Dinshaway in 1906. The colonial authorities collectively punished these peasants for the death of a British officer, who had actually died of heat stroke. This event led to the formation of three political parties the following year, which represented the political stances of the time rather well. The outburst of colonial violence and the public anger that ensued first motivated a group around Ahmad Lutfi al-Sayyid (d. 1963) to found the moderately nationalist Umma Party (Hizb al-Umma), which favored cooperation with the British until the accomplishment of certain reforms to ready Egypt for independence. This in turn prompted Mustafa Kamil (d. 1908) to found the Nationalist Party (al-Hizb al-Watani), which demanded an immediate end to the British occupation.[47] A different political stance was presented by ʿAli Yusuf's (d. 1913) Constitutional Reform Party (Hizb al-Islah ʿala al-Mabadiʿ al-Dusturiyya), also founded in 1907, which sided with the khedive. The mouthpiece of Hizb al-Umma was the journal *al-Jarida*, that of al-Hizb al-Watani was the journal *al-Liwaʾ*, and ʿAli Yusuf owned the daily *al-Muʾayyad*, which included articles by Muhammad ʿAbduh and Rashid Rida; ʿAli Yusuf's press also printed the first issues of *al-Manar.* If Rida increasingly displayed anti-British sentiments, especially after 1914, he was part of a much wider trend. Shortly after the First World War, Egypt witnessed massive nationalist demonstrations, culminating in the Egyptian Revolution of 1919. The emblematic figure of this revolution was Saʿd Zaghlul (d. 1927), a leading member of the nationalist Wafd party. Not only did the Wafd enjoy tremendous sup-

47 Cuno, "Egypt," 101 ff.

port among the Egyptian populace, but many social groups played an active role in this revolution, including peasants,[48] ordinary Egyptians,[49] and feminists.[50] The role of the press[51] was also crucial for the evolution of a national sense of belonging and national popular culture.[52] The imagined nation also requires images, and – especially in the context of rather low levels of literacy – paintings, cartoons, monuments, and photography were vital for imagining Egypt as a nation.[53]

Faced with growing nationalist sentiments and acute unrest and hostilities, the British government unilaterally declared Egypt's nominal independence in February 1922, although it retained significant influence in the country. In particular, Britain secured for itself control over four vital areas, the so-called "reserve points": foreign relations, communications, the military, and issues concerning the Sudan. One might even say that "for the British the 1922 declaration marked a return to the preferred imperial methods of informal control."[54] English influence and partial control remained strong, even though the official structure of political power changed significantly. Two weeks after the declaration of independence, Fu'ad, who had been Sultan of Egypt and the Sudan since 1917, awarded himself the title of king. The Egyptian Constitution of 1923 established a representative parliamentary system, with the cabinet now accountable to the elected parliament. A repeating pattern over the following decades saw the

48 Schulze, Reinhard. 1992. "Kolonisierung und Widerstand. Die ägyptischen Bauern-Revolten von 1919." In *Die ägyptische Gesellschaft im 20. Jahrhundert* ed. by Alexander Schölch and Helmut Mejcher: 11–41. Hamburg: Deutsches Orient-Institut.

49 Fahmy, Ziad. 2011. *Ordinary Egyptians. Creating the Modern Nation through Popular Culture, 1870–1919.* Cairo: AUC Press.

50 Badran, Margot. 1995. *Feminists, Islam, and Nation: Gender and the Making of Modern Egypt.* Princeton: Princeton University Press; Baron, Beth. 1994. *The Women's Awakening in Egypt.* New Haven: Yale University Press; idem., *Egypt*, 105–214.

51 Benedict Anderson pointed out the general role of print capitalism in the construction of the nation as an imagined community and in nationalist senses of belonging (Anderson, *Imagined*). An illustrative case study concerning the nationalization of previously locally confined events is: Lopez, Shaun T. 2005. "Madams, Murders, and the Media: Akhbar al-Hawadith and the Emergence of a Mass Culture in 1920s Egypt." In *Re-Envisioning Egypt 1919–1952* ed. by Arthur Goldschmidt, Amy J. Johnson and Barak A. Salmoni: 371–397. Cairo: The American University in Cairo Press. The landscape of the Egyptian press will be properly depicted in chapter 4 section 3.

52 Fahmy, *Ordinary.*

53 For the visual depiction of Egypt, which was mainly imagined as a woman, see: Baron, *Egypt*, 57–104.

54 Daly, M.W. 1998. "The British Occupation, 1882–1922." In *The Cambridge History of Egypt. Volume 2: Modern Egypt, from 1517 to the End of the Twentieth Century* ed. by M.W. Daly: 239–251. Cambridge: Cambridge University Press, here 251.

Wafd party win in free elections, get into conflicts with the palace, and subsequently be dismissed.

While the three decades from 1923 onward have been termed "the liberal age"[55] due to political pluralism, regular elections, and constitutionalism, this must still be taken with some caution, as the more circumspect designation of these decades as 'the liberal experiment' indicates.[56] The liberal elites in political power considered themselves not as equal with the population at large, but rather as guiding the masses toward modernity.[57] With the onset of the Second World War, communist groups appeared as a political force to be reckoned with, even though their support base among the wider populace was rather limited. Islamic political movements, which had already made themselves heard in the 1920s, reached a wider following. In 1928, Hasan al-Banna (1906–1949) founded the Muslim Brotherhood, which is still the most popular Islamist movement even today.[58] It was under the auspices of al-Banna that the last six issues of *al-Manar*, from 1939 to 1940, appeared.[59] Al-Banna's view of a plural party system remained somewhat ambivalent; he seems to have regarded its benefits as being rather temporary in nature.[60] It was not only communists and Islamists

---

55 Botman, Selma. 1998. "The Liberal Age, 1923–1952." In *The Cambridge History of Egypt. Volume 2: Modern Egypt, from 1517 to the End of the Twentieth Century* ed. by M.W. Daly: 285–308. Cambridge: Cambridge University Press.

56 For a recent example, considering this experiment as ultimately failed, see: Gordon, Joel. 2010. "Egypt from c. 1919." In *The New Cambridge History of Islam. vol. 5: The Islamic World in the Age of Western Dominance* ed. by Francis Robinson: 372–401. New York: Cambridge University Press, here 373 f.

57 See, for example: Ryzova, Lucie. 2005. "Egyptianizing Modernity through the 'New Effendiya': Social and Cultural Constructions of the Middle Class in Egypt under the Monarchy." In *Re-Envisioning Egypt 1919–1952* ed. by Arthur Goldschmidt, Amy J. Johnson and Barak A. Salmoni: 124–163. Cairo: The American University in Cairo Press, here 132.

58 On the early years of the Muslim Brotherhood founded by Hassan al-Banna, see: Mitchell, Richard P. 1993 [1969]. *The Society of the Muslim Brothers*. New York: Oxford University Press; Brynjar, Lia. 2010 [1998]. *The Society of the Muslim Brothers in Egypt: the Rise of an Islamic Mass Movement, 1928–1942*. Reading: Ithaca Press. For al-Banna's life and activities specifically, see: Commins, David. 1988. "Hasan al-Banna (1906–1949)." In *Pioneers of Islamic Revival* ed. by Ali Rahnema: 125–153. London/New Jersey: Zed Books; Krämer, Gudrun. 2010. *Hasan al-Banna*. Oxford: Oneworld, esp. 23 concerning the relation with Rida. For a translation of selected writings by al-Banna, see: al-Banna, Hasan and Wendell, Charles. 1978. *Five Tracts of Ḥasan Al-Bannā' (1906–1949): a Selection from the Majmū 'at Rasā' il al-Imām al-Shahīd Ḥasan al-Bannā'*. Berkeley/Los Angeles: University of California Press.

59 See below: chapter 5 section 1.

60 Against the tenor of scholarship and in a rather apologetic manner, al-Banna's grandson, Tariq Ramadan, attributed democratic convictions to al-Banna (Ramadan, Tariq. 1998. *Aux sour-*

who challenged liberal political structures; landowners and industrial elites also opposed a more democratic distribution of power, the king frequently exerted the right to dissolve parliament, and continuing foreign influence inhibited democratic representation in practice. The withdrawal of British troops from Egypt was agreed upon in the Anglo-Egyptian Treaty of 1936, the year Farouk inherited Fu'ad's throne. British troops, however, remained at the Suez Canal and used Egypt as a military base during the Second World War. It was only after the revolution of 1952, which overthrew the monarchy, that British forces were expelled from the country[61] and the modern Republic of Egypt was established.

This section has focused on political developments, showing how Egypt was transformed into a nation-state in the colonial context of French and especially English dominance and in a complex relationship with the Ottoman Empire. I also mentioned European dominance in the field of economics and the importance of European models as templates for military, legal, bureaucratic, and educational reforms. The following section shifts the focus from the political to the societal plain, keeping in mind that the changing structure of Egyptian society cannot be explained without considering political measures, and that the very distinction between state and society simplifies the actual relations between political and social actors.[62]

2 Egypt as a Modern Society: Social Change, Social Groups, and Societal Reformists

2.1 Social Change and Social Groups

> "It is no exaggeration to say that, by 1860, the pre-existing social order that had regulated life within the Ottoman Empire for all its subjects was coming to an end."
> – Khuri-Makdisi, "The Conceptualization," 93

Somewhat paradoxically, governmental reforms helped create not only a national society, but also new social groups that came to challenge the government on questions of social and political order. While the following subsection will focus on the activities and forms of association of the urban intelligentsia, who regarded themselves as spokespersons and reformers of the Egyptian nation and soci-

ces du renouveau musulman: d'al-Afghānī à Ḥassan al-Bannā. Un siècle de réformisme islamique. Paris: Bayard Editions/Centurion, esp. 214 ff., 439).

61 The last British troops left Egypt in 1956.

62 Toledano, "Social," 256.

ety, this subsection gives an overview of social groups and broader changes in the makeup of Egyptian social formation during the (long) nineteenth century.

The population of Egypt increased from 4.5 million inhabitants in 1800 to almost 10 million at the close of the century, with substantial growth beginning in the 1840s.[63] Urbanization was not a major phenomenon, and the rural population still accounted for 90% of the populace at the end of the century. Still, Alexandria emerged as a new urban center, next to Cairo, and both cities roughly doubled in size during the second half of the century, with Alexandria then being home to 320,000 and Cairo to 570,000 people.[64] By 1947, Cairo and Alexandria were home to over three million people, and the overall Egyptian population numbered 19 million.[65] An influx of Europeans contributed to this growth in population. Whereas at the beginning of the nineteenth century only a few hundred foreigners resided in Egypt, their number rose to 140,000 by 1907, ninety percent of whom lived in the two urban centers.

The impact of Europeans as a new and disproportionately powerful element of Egyptian society[66] most clearly manifested itself on the economic level, whereas it is much harder to assess on the intellectual and cultural plains. Foreigners not only owned 15% of Egyptian land, but also controlled most of the country's trade and industry.[67] Backed by colonial power, which had directly shaped the country's political and administrative structures since 1882, the economic standing and influence of Europeans residing in Egypt was much higher than their actual share of the population. Concerning the intellectual and cultural level, I have repeatedly stressed the hegemony of those European ideas which are considered to epitomize modernity. However, these ideas were selectively and creatively appropriated by Egyptians, rather than plainly implemented by Europeans. What is more, Europeans can hardly be straightforwardly regarded as the major force behind modernization, as wanting to spread modern ideas. Thus,

---

63 Toledano, "Social," 253.

64 Ibid., 254.

65 Beinin, Joel. 1998. "Egypt, Society and Economy, 1923–1952." In *The Cambridge History of Egypt. Volume 2: Modern Egypt, from 1517 to the End of the Twentieth Century* ed. by M.W. Daly: 309–333. Cambridge: Cambridge University Press, here 313.

66 While we conventionally speak of pre-modern 'Egyptian society,' the introduction to this study stressed that this is somewhat misleading concerning 'society,' and chapter 4 section 1.1 showed that it is also misleading concerning 'Egyptian.' A more adequate way of formulating it is: In hindsight, how would we sketch the social structure of the people who later came to form Egyptian society – that is, the inhabitants of the land which later became the territory of the Egyptian nation-state? Here, I follow conventional parlance in order not to burden the reader too much with complicated, though more adequate, terminology.

67 Toledano, "Social," 254; Cuno, "Egypt," 90.

for example, the British deliberately kept the Egyptian education budget to a minimum, and it only increased significantly after independence in 1922.[68] Nevertheless, as we shall see below, the appropriation of European ideas, notably via translations, factored into intellectual debates in the increasingly plural arena of the press.

While the presence of Europeans was the most clearly visible change in the structure of Egyptian society, other new social groups also emerged, and existing groups underwent significant changes. The emergence of the household of Muhammad ʿAli as the central(izing) power constitutes the most significant change in the makeup of Egypt's military-political and economic elite. Next to this elite, in 1835, Clot Bey identified four main social groups during the reign of Muhammad ʿAli: the shaykhs and ʿulamaʾ; proprietors, merchants, and traders; artisans and, still in very limited numbers, industrial workers; and, finally, the fellahin, who made up ninety percent of Egypt's population.[69] Missing from this list are slaves, who – until the end of the century – served in agricultural production, government development projects, and domestic households.[70] One could also add Beduins as a separate group, many of whom settled down during the century, partly incited or forced by the ruler.[71]

The fellahin, the last group on Clot Bey's list, were greatly affected by government conscription, agricultural measures, and land reforms, in addition to plagues, floods, and droughts. By 1815, Muhammad ʿAli had put an end to the previous *iltizām* system, in which the ruling household granted tax farmers (*multazims*) the right to collect taxes or shares of agricultural produce from the land they were assigned. Muhammad ʿAli's household now directly taxed the land. It also ordered the peasants to plant certain crops, thereby ending the rather autonomous organization of peasants and village communities. The distribution of land to various officials and members of the ruling household, along with other government measures and economic developments, resulted in between

---

68 Toledano, "Social," 279f.; Cuno, "Egypt," 103.

69 Tomiche, Nada. 1968. "Notes sur la hiérarchie sociale en Égypte à l'époque de Muḥammad ʿAlī." In *Political and Social Change in Modern Egypt. Historical Studies from the Ottoman Conquest to the United Arab Republic* ed. by P. M. Holt: 249–263. London: Oxford University Press.

70 For a brief overview, see: Baer, "Social," 150–154. See also: Toledano, Ehud, R. 1993. "Shemsigul: A Circassian Slave in Mid-Nineteenth-Century Cairo." In *Struggle and Survival in the Modern Middle East* ed. by Edmund Burke: 59–74. Berkeley, CA etc.: University of California Press; Troutt Powell, Eve M. 2006. "Will That Subaltern Ever Speak? Finding African Slaves in the Historiography of the Middle East." In *Middle East Historiographies. Narrating the Twentieth Century* ed. by Israel Gershoni, Amy Singer and Erdem Y. Hakan: 242–261. Seattle/London: University of Washington Press.

71 Baer, "Social," 138f.

one and two million peasants becoming landless by the end of the century.[72] In terms of economic conditions and the development of infrastructure and educational institutions, Upper Egypt had an additional disadvantage, due to its distance from the administrative and economic center in Cairo. This situation contributed to upheavals and revolts among the peasantry, but also to migration to the urban centers and the dissolution of village communities.[73]

Partly due to urban migration, towns and cities also witnessed an increasing dissolution of previous forms of social organization, not least affecting two other groups mentioned by Clot Bey – namely, artisans and merchants. Most significant in this regard was the supersession of guilds by new forms of economic and administrative organization toward the end of the century.[74] Following his general policy of government expansion and centralization, Muhammad ʿAli had increasingly brought the guilds under government control.[75] One could debate whether the concept of 'guild' adequately captures the organized groups at hand. Moreover, there were significant differences between these guilds (*ṭawāʾif*, sg. *ṭāʾifa*), and Baer's seminal work, on which I am drawing here, has been modified on several points.[76] However, for our purposes here, it is not necessary to enter into these discussions and nuances. It remains safe to say that a guild was composed of urban people with a similar occupation, and that the functions of the guilds' shaykhs included mediation between the government and the guilds' members, arbitration in disputes between members, and the collection of taxes.

In the 1880s, the guilds still comprised "almost the whole indigenous gainfully occupied population" in Cairo and other Egyptian towns,[77] as both the government and – despite decreasing autonomy – the guilds benefitted from this system and had no interest in discontinuing it. Subsequently, however, several factors weakened the significance of the guilds: the expansion and greater efficiency of the government bureaucracy decreased the need for guilds and their shaykhs as mediators; European control of Egyptian trade and commerce weakened the standing of Egyptian merchants and deprived the previous retail system, the *sūq*, of its organizing function; and entrepreneurs, merchants, and in-

---

72 Ibid., 141.
73 Ibid., 141 f.
74 On guilds in Egypt in our period of interest, see: Chalcraft, John. 2004. *The Striking Cabbies of Cairo and Other Stories: Crafts and Guilds in Egypt, 1863–1914.*
75 For a concise depiction and further literature, see: ibid., 30–34.
76 Ibid., 18–23.
77 Baer, "Social," 142.

dustrialists increasingly bypassed the guilds as suppliers of workers, resorting instead to rural migrants who were not affiliated with guilds.[78]

The disappearance of the guilds, of course, does not imply the disappearance of their members, who could effectively maintain their ties informally and who also came to express their interests via new organizational forms – for example, trade unions.[79] In general, there are continuities between pre-modern and modern arrangements, with the latter hardly ever instantly and completely replacing the former. That said, new forms of social and commercial organization clearly altered the structure and interpretation of Egypt's society and economy. At the beginning of the twentieth century, trade unions emerged as a new form of professional organization for urban wageworkers.[80] A strike by coal heavers in Port Said in 1882 was the first known manifestation of workers' collective action, and the first trade union was founded in 1899. In the nationalist uprising of 1919, the labor movement expressed its political demands in a way that renders its designation as a (self-conscious) "working class" meaningful. An Egyptian business class manifested itself in the early 1920s, with the foundation of Bank Misr (1920), the Agricultural Syndicate (1921), and the Egyptian Federation of Industry (1922). The concept of 'class' thus becomes a plausible category for interpreting the structure of Egyptian society (only)[81] since the beginning of the twentieth century.

Before introducing the new socio-cultural group known as the *effendiyya*, which may be understood as middle class in a qualified sense, I should attend to changes in the first group mentioned by Clot Bey – the ʿulamaʾ. As mentioned in the previous subsection, Muhammad ʿAli restricted the ʿulamaʾ's autonomy and influence by bringing leading religious institutions under government control.[82] In addition, the personal economic standing of many ʿulamaʾ deteriorated, especially among those who had previously made a substantial fortune as *mul-*

78 Ibid., 143f.

79 Chalcraft, *Striking*, 105–190.

80 On trade unions and the Egyptian worker movement in general, see: Beinin, Joel and Lockman, Zachary. 1998. *Workers on the Nile: Nationalism, Communism, Islam and the Egyptian Working Class, 1882–1954.* Cairo: The American University in Cairo Press.

81 Nelly Hanna, in a generally fascinating study, blurs the characteristics of 'middle class' by projecting the concept back into the Cairo of the sixteenth to eighteenth centuries (Hanna, Nelly. 2003. *In Praise of Books. A Cultural History of Cairo's Middle Class, Sixteenth to Eighteenth Century.* Syracuse, NY: Syracuse University Press). Only under modern social-political conditions can we expect a more meaningful application of the concept; see, for example: Watenpaugh, Keith David. 2006. *Being Modern in the Middle East. Revolution, Nationalism, Colonialism, and the Arab Middle Class.* Princeton, NJ: Princeton University Press.

82 Cuno, "Egypt," 82f.

tazims. "In 1831 the mufti of Mansura complained that the 'ulama' had become poor people, and in 1863 von Kremer wrote that they had completely lost their former influence and importance, and that many of the 'ulama' originated from the peasant population."[83] Whereas many 'ulama' came from peasant families, better-off families increasingly sent their children to the newly founded government schools, and later to secular institutions of higher learning – such as Cairo University,[84] which was founded in 1909.

The decicion to send one's child to a secular institution was in many cases the result of assessing prospective professional and economic opportunities: "While in the 1880s one would still hesitate whether to send his son through the Azhar curriculum or a secular one, and would ideally combine both, at the beginning of the twentieth century the more well-to-do families started leaving al-Azhar for the government secondary schools and higher institutes, which offered much better career prospects, and came increasingly to be regarded as gates of entrance to 'power and influence.'"[85] Conflicts between secularly educated *mutarbashūn* (tarbush wearers) and *muʿammamūn* (turban wearers) educated at al-Azhar or other religious institutions of higher learning were thus not only motivated by (non-)religious convictions, but also fueled by competition over jobs and influence. Reacting to the demands of new knowledge and qualifications, various attempts were made to reform the curricula of al-Azhar, so as to include modern disciplines, or to formalize its examination procedures.[86] Despite resistance to these attempts at reforming al-Azhar, change was ultimately inevitable, since insistence on maintaining previous structures would have rendered the institution as a whole meaningless – that is, would have deprived it of its social function.

The *muʿammamūn* also had to engage with modern questions and premises of socio-political order, so as not to leave the field to the *mutarbashūn*. This engagement significantly altered the contents and function of religious discourse. Countering the view of unchanging traditionalism, recent research has stressed such alterations in the conservative camp.[87] Changes in the content of religious

83 Baer, "Social," 147.

84 Reid, Donald Malcolm. 1990. *Cairo University and the Making of Modern Egypt*. Cambridge: Cambridge University Press.

85 Ryzova, "Egyptianizing," 129.

86 Luizard, Pierre-Jean. 1995. "al-Azhar: Institution sunnite réformée." In *Entre reforme sociale et mouvement national: Identité et modernisation en Egypte (1882–1962)* ed. by Alain Roussillon: 519–547. Cairo: CEDEJ.

87 For Egypt, see: Gesink, Indira Falk. 2010. *Islamic Reform and Conservatism: Al-Azhar and the Evolution of Modern Sunni Islam*. London: I.B. Tauris.

discourse are inseparable from the form and social location in which this discourse is formulated. In order to make their voices heard, the ʿulamaʾ had to enter the emerging arena of the public sphere, the discourse of which was centered around notions of the common good. Bringing forward their own notions of the common good in this plural arena had two main consequences: firstly, it obviously altered the content of 'religion'; and, secondly, it meant that the ʿulamaʾ's interpretation was only one among several competing interpretations.[88] The founding of a journal by al-Azhar in 1931[89] illustrates the acceptance of these modern challenges by what is often considered a bulwark of Islamic traditionalism. However, it remains true that al-Azhar's journal was a latecomer to the arena of the press, which had emerged as a central forum of public debate beginning in the 1870s.

While many producers of journals and newspapers were Syrian immigrants, the commercial success of print media in Egypt would have been highly unlikely without the broadening of education and the emergence of a new social and cultural group as potential consumers of journalistic production – namely, the social and cultural group that, in the 1920s, came to be designated as the *effendiyya*.[90] Since the second half of the nineteenth century, the most stable characteristic of this group had been the modern-style education of its members.[91]

Muhammad ʿAli and his successors not only recruited men with modern skills and knowledge, but had also created – via education – a professional

---

88 Zaman, Muhammad Qasim. 2004. "The ʿUlama of Contemporary Islam and their Conceptions of the Common Good." In *Public Islam and the Common Good* ed. by Armando Salvatore and Dale F. Eickelman: 129–156. Leiden/Boston: Brill.

89 On this journal, see: Corrado, Monica. 2011. *Mit Tradition in die Zukunft. Der taǧdīd-Diskurs in der Azhar und in ihrem Umfeld.* Würzburg: Ergon.

90 For a conceptual, social, and cultural history of the Egyptian *effendiyya*, see: Ryzova, "Egyptianizing;" idem. 2014. *The Age of the Efendiyya: Passages to Modernity in National-Colonial Egypt.* Oxford: Oxford University Press. Shechter complements Ryzova's commanding work with an illustrative insight into effendi lifestyle and identity: Shechter, Relli. 2006. *Smoking, Culture and Economy in the Middle East. The Egyptian Tobacco Market 1850–2000.* London/New York: I.B. Tauris, 133–154 ["The Cigarette and Efendi Identity"]. For a brief overview of the concept *effendiyya* in various Arab countries, see: Eppel, Michael. 2009. "Note About the Term Efendiyya in the History of the Middle East." *International Journal of Middle East Studies* 41: 535–539. The following is based on Ryzova, "Egyptianizing."

91 The fact that the term *effendiyya* only appears in the 1920s is arguably attributable to the more general appearance of Arabic collective nouns designating human groups, rather than to such a social and cultural group only being identified and self-identifying itself at that time, as the preceding (self-)identification of *effendi*s and *mutarbashūn* indicates.

group serving its modernizing policies. Until the turn to the twentieth century, most effendis worked as teachers and especially as bureaucrats in government institutions. Increasingly, however, the *effendiyya* also comprised merchants, students, engineers, lawyers, and journalists.[92] Moreover, many effendis who aimed at a career in government institutions were forced to reorient themselves once the government was no longer able to offer jobs to all the members of this increasingly large workforce. This failure on the part of the government to provide jobs for the graduates of its own schools led to a deteriorating economic and social status and an increased politicization of the *effendiyya* beginning in the 1910s.

The changing socio-economic status of the *effendiyya* is one reason why its designation as a 'middle class' fails to capture the group's constitutive characteristics. If anything, being an effendi did not mean being part of the middle class, a socio-economic stratum meaningfully identifiable since the 1920s, but rather aspiring to a middle-class existence. Still more fundamentally, however, "[t]he concept effendi is not a class situation but a cultural term, and one that is related to social mobility, but more importantly, to passages from non-modernity to modernity in its many forms."[93] Most significant for the effendis' cultural self-identification was their distinction from both traditionalist social groups and colonial elites, going along with their claim that only they combined authentic Egyptian or Arab roots with the skills and knowledge needed to master modernity.[94]

There is, however, an important generational break within the *effendiyya:* after 1923, many of the old effendis, who had primarily striven for independence from Britain, advanced to central government positions. From these positions, they tried to construct a liberal order in which the effendi embodied the role of the "ideal citizen."[95] A new generation of effendis – beginning in the 1930s, the term *effendī* became conflated with the recent category 'youth' – was disappointed that their educational level did not lead to adequate employment opportunities, and therefore they opposed the existing political order. Striving for a middle-class existence, they worked for the reform of society and politics from below.[96] As such, they presented a potentially troublesome political force, as can be seen in British officers' discussion of "the effendi problem" in the 1930s.[97]

92 Ryzova, "Egyptianizing," 125, 129.
93 Ibid., 125.
94 Ibid., 126.
95 Ibid., 131.
96 Ibid., 133, 141, 149.
97 Ibid., 134f.

There thus exists a clear trajectory in the long nineteenth century from governmental attempts to construct an Egyptian nation and reform society to societal actors emerging as spokespersons and protagonists of reform, as shown by the emergence of the *effendiyya*.

2.2 Spokespersons and Reformists of the Egyptian Nation and Society

> "[C]'est seulement d'un point de vue et en termes réformistes que le réferent identitaire de la société égyptienne, institué comme le garant des gestions contemporaines, est susceptible de faire problème."
> – Alain Roussillon, 1995[98]

Without denying the agency of other societal groups, my focus is on those urban literati elites who considered themselves reformers. These reformists tended to regard workers – and especially peasants – as central objects of their internal civilizing mission.[99] Reconfiguring the role and status of women was also central to envisioning a modern, civilized, and moral nation and society. In this reconfiguration, bourgeois and aristocratic women played an active role.[100] The roles and images of peasants, workers, and women formed crucial social questions in reformists' visions of the Egyptian nation and society as a whole. It is important to keep this common impetus of the reformists in mind, as well as their rather similar social and educational background, as compared to the non-literate populace.[101]

---

98 Roussillon, Alain. 1995. "Introduction: La modernité disputée: Réforme sociale et politique en Egypte." In *Entre reforme sociale et mouvement national: Identité et modernisation en Egypte (1882–1962)* ed. by Alain Roussillon: 9–35. Cairo: CEDEJ, here 18.

99 On the role of peasants in reformists' visions of a civilized nation and society, see: Gasper, Michael Ezekiel. 2009. *The Power of Representation. Publics, Peasants, and Islam in Egypt.* Stanford, CA: Stanford University Press; idem. 2013. "Public Deliberations of the Self in *fin-de-siècle* Egypt." In *The Making of the Arab Intellectual (1880–1960): Empire, Public Sphere and the Colonial Coordinates of Selfhood* ed. by Dyala Hamzah: 40–62. London: Routledge; El Shakry, *The Great*, 89–144. On workers in this regard, see: Beinin, "Egypt," 311f.; Beinin and Lockman, *Workers*.

100 See: Baron, *Egypt*, 15–104; Beinin, "Egypt," 316; Toledano, "Social," 277f.; Noorani, Yaseen. 2010. *Culture and Hegemony in the Colonial Middle East*. New York: Palgrave Macmillan, 107–148.

101 These underlying communalities are, for example, stressed in the following comparisons of two reformists with overtly differing programs of reform: Roussillon, "Introduction," esp. 17f.; Noorani, *Culture*, 71–106, esp. 74.

The concrete visions of society and programs of reform differed greatly between nationalist, socialist, and Islamist reformists. These differences played out most overtly in the plural landscape of the press. While this plural landscape manifests the emergence of an Egyptian public sphere, it ought to be kept in mind that literacy levels were still rather low in Egypt at the turn to the twentieth century, as will be shown below. And indeed, the self-declared spokespersons of the Egyptian nation and society thought of themselves as forming the public.[102] Whereas the following subsection will focus on the press as a limited public sphere in that sense, this subsection sketches other arenas for socio-political debates and other forms of social activities on the part of the urban literati.

Intellectuals, oppositional nobles, and political activists in the 1870s founded or belonged to a number of political clubs, salons, and secret societies. These were crucial for networking, forming political opinion, and planning activities, especially before the foundation of political parties in 1907. Juan Cole partly bases his overview of these organizations on papers confiscated from none other than Jamal al-Din al-Afghani.[103] This anti-colonial activist, revered by Rashid Rida,[104] was a member of several masonic lodges and temporarily presided over the Star of the East Lodge in Cairo.[105] Rida himself (co-)founded a number of political societies and societies for the promulgation of Islam; among them were The Society of the Ottoman Council (Jamʿiyyat al-Shura al-ʿUthmaniyya) in 1907,[106] The Association for Missionary Activity and Guidance (Jamaʿat al-Daʿwa wa-l-Irshad) in 1911,[107] and in 1913, when Rida had lost faith in Ottomanism, The Society of the Arab Union (Jamʿiyyat al-Jamiʿa al-ʿArabiyya).[108] Next to clubs and societies, coffeehouses were attractive places for socio-political debates and networking.[109]

---

102 Cole, *Colonialism*, 115; Elshakry, *Reading*, 22.

103 Cole, *Colonialism*, 133–163.

104 For more on the connection between Rida and al-Afghani, see below: chapter 5 section 3.

105 Cole, *Colonialism*, 138 ff. On Freemasonry and Islamic reformists in Egypt, see: Kudsi-Zadeh, A. Albert. 1972. "Afghānī and Freemasonry in Egypt." *Journal of the American Oriental Society* 92/1: 25–35.

106 Tauber, Eliezer. 1993. *The Emergence of the Arab Movements*. London: Frank Cass, 51 ff.

107 Ibid., 113 f.

108 Ibid., 114–117.

109 We are still lacking a profound analysis of coffeehouses in Egypt specifically. A German doctoral dissertation promisingly entitled "A Cultural History of Coffee Houses in Cairo as Places of Social and Political Innovation" (transl. F. Z.) unfortunately does not live up to its title (El-Deeb, Mohamed Nagib. 2009. *Kulturgeschichte der Kaffeehäuser "makahi" in Kairo. Orte der sozialen und politischen Innovation im Ägypten des 19. und 20. Jahrhunderts*. Dissertation, Universität Freiburg). For coffeehouses in Istanbul, see: Işin, Ekrem. 2003. "Coffeehouses as Places of

Another type of association focused primarily on social rather than political questions – namely, the social welfare organizations and benevolent societies that became active beginning in the 1880s. Prior to the nineteenth century, it was mainly wealthy families and religious institutions that cared for the poor. In tune with his general centralizing efforts, Muhammad ʿAli restricted the scope of such activities and took charity into government hands. Financial constraints in the 1870s, however, limited the government's resources to provide for the poor. The British administration attended to assistance for the needy only in a limited and scattered manner, largely leaving the field to private charity organizations. These organizations ran hospitals, orphanages, and schools and provided food, clothes, and financial assistance.[110] The government, however, interacted with these organizations, aiming to maintain some control over their activities.[111] Members of the khedival household also financed such organizations themselves. Mostly, however, it was wealthy landowners, members of the *effendiyya*, and – in significant numbers – elite women who funded and ran these organizations.[112] Muhammad ʿAbduh was involved in the 1892 opening of a Cairene branch of the Islamic Benevolent Society (al-Jamʿiyya al-Khayriyya al-Islamiyya), which had been founded in Alexandria in 1879 by ʿAbd Allah al-Nadim, who drew on his experiences as a Freemason and a member of a political society.[113]

Charitable organizations increasingly became concerned with Egyptian society as a whole, fostering reform and becoming politically active, especially in the build-up to the revolution of 1919. "Such changes were reflected in the language used by the associations to describe their mission. At the turn of the 20th century, benevolent societies claimed to provide charitable services (*khidmāt khayriyya*) to the poor. In the years leading up to the 1919 uprisings, some associations

---

Conversation." In *The Illuminated Table, the Prosperous Hose. Food and Shelter in Ottoman Material Culture* ed. by Suraiya Faroqhi and Christoph K. Neumann: 199–208. Würzburg: Ergon; and, especially: Kırlı, Cengiz. 2004. "Coffehouses: Public Opinion in the Nineteenth-Centruy Ottoman Empire." In *Public Islam and the Common Good* ed. by Armando Salvatore and Dale F. Eickelman: 75–98. Leiden/Boston: Brill.

110 Ener, Mine. 2003. *Managing Egypt's Poor and the Politics of Benevolence, 1800–1952.* New Haven, CT: State University of New York Press.

111 Pollard, Lisa. 2014. "Egyptian by Association: Charitable States and Service Societies, circa 1850–1945." *International Journal of Middle East Studies* 46/2: 239–257, here 244f.

112 Ibid., 244. On women's activities in particular, see: Baron, Beth. 2005. "Women's Voluntary Social Welfare Organizations in Egypt." In *Gender, Religion and Change in the Middle East. Two Hundred Years of History* ed. by Inger Marie Okkenhaug and Ingvild Flaskerud: 85–102. Oxford/New York: Berg.

113 Pollard, "Egyptian," 241f.

announced that their services were both charitable and social (*ijtimāʿiyya*), offering service to Egyptian society. Sometimes such social services were linked with the Egyptian nationalist movement."[114] This trend became stronger over the following decades, and it eventually prompted King Faruq to issue "a decree separating charitable societies from political parties and from paramilitary organizations" in 1938.[115] In 1939, the Ministry of Social Reform was created to bring charitable societies more firmly under government control and to reinstate the state as the guarantor of social assistance. Still, a more comprehensive government program of social welfare would have to wait until the revolution of 1952.[116]

Scientific societies also attended to the question of social reform and contributed to the understanding of society as an abstract entity, beginning at the latest in the first decades of the twentieth century. The Royal Geographic Society of Egypt, founded in 1875, was the first scientific society founded under the patronage of the Egyptian state. Scientific societies and the social sciences became instrumental in the implementation of development projects and population policies.[117] It was arguably in the period after the First World War that "'society' itself [was formulated] as an entity – an object of scientific study, social control and management."[118] Under the reigning paradigm of social reform in the 1930s, private scientific societies and nationalist researchers then formulated "social-scientific agendas" for the reform of Egyptian society, which centered around reform of the peasantry.[119]

The societies sketched above, to which cultural and literary societies could be added, represented a new type of associational life in Egypt, which – beginning at the end of the nineteenth century – gained increasing importance over against previous forms. Related to the declining importance of the guilds, migration to the cities, and urban planning, "the town-quarter had lost its significance as a social unit" by the end of the nineteenth century.[120] Religious festivals, many organized by Sufi orders, had been a significant form of temporary associational life. Reformists criticized such festivals for what they portrayed as irra-

114 Ibid., 246.
115 Ibid., 240.
116 Baron, "Women's," 98 ff.; Pollard, "Egyptian," 248–251.
117 The definitive study on the emergence of Egyptian scientific societies and the development of the sciences of anthropology, human geography, and demography in Egypt is: El Shakry, *The Great*.
118 Ibid., 8.
119 Ibid., 114.
120 Baer, "Social," 145.

tional practices.[121] Rashid Rida was especially critical of the *mawālid* (sg. *mawlid*) festivals held in honor of saints.[122] Due to their strange mixture of religious and worldly aspects, he argued, they could not achieve the societal benefits inherent in associational life in general.[123] The success of European nations, Rida maintained, was also due to their superior form of associational life – that is, to the manifold and diverse but mutually complementary religious and civil associations and societies.[124] This is not at all to say that Rida devalued confessional solidarity or organizations based on religious affiliation. Such organizations in general remained important in twentieth-century Egypt, and many of the benevolent societies were also community-based.[125] Nevertheless, the new types of voluntary social organizations, which were secular in the sense of temporarily bringing people together for the sake of mutual benefit, represented an important new type of associational life in Egypt at the end of the nineteenth century.

While in hindsight one may detect the seeds of a civil society in these associations, it was only in the 1950s and 1960s that voluntary associations really gained autonomy from the state and began to multiply.[126] Equal caution must be exercised as to the question of whether the plural landscape of the press, to which we now turn, can meaningfully be designated as constituting a 'public sphere.'

---

121 See, for example: Hatina, Meir. 2007. "Religious Culture Contested: The Sufi Ritual of *dawsa* in Nineteenth-Century Cairo." *Die Welt des Islams* 47/1: 33 – 62.

122 On the *mawālid*, see: Schielke, Samuel. 2007. "Hegemonic Encounters: Criticism of Saints-Day Festivals and the Formation of Modern Islam in Late 19th and Early 20th-Century Egypt." *Die Welt des Islams* 47/3 – 4: 319 – 355.

123 Rida, Rashid. 1898. "al-Mawalid aw al-Maʿarid " *al-Manar* 1/5: 79 – 87.

124 For a pertinent example, see: Idem. 1329 h. [1911]. *al-Muslimun wa-l-Qubt wa-l-Mu'tamar al-Islami: Majmuʿ Maqalat Ijtimaʿiyya Nushirat fi al-Mu'ayyad wa l-Manar.* Cairo: Matbaʿat al-Manar, 114 ff.

125 Pollard, "Egyptian," 242.

126 Al-Sayyid, Mustapha K. 1995. "A Civil Society in Egypt?." In *Civil Society in the Middle East* ed. by August Richard Norton: 269 – 293. Leiden/New York/Köln: Brill, here 271 f. For the applicability of the concept of 'civil society,' see above: chapter 2.2.

3 A Modern Intellectual Arena: The Plural Landscape of the Press in Egypt

3.1 The Rise of Private Publishing in Egypt: A Public Arena of Intellectual Debate

> "Some readers may be alarmed at the rapid progress of the press in Egypt. But there is no cause for alarm. Could the world progress too rapidly?"
> – Martin Hartmann, 1899[127]

> "[T]he genesis and massive distribution of renowned literary-scientific Arabic journals such as *al-Jinan, al-Muqtataf, Misr* (*Egypt*), *al-Liwa'*, *Misbah al-Sharq* (*Lantern of the East*), *al-Manar* (*The Lighthouse*), *al-Hilal, and al-Jami'a* (*The Federation*), among others, produced the intellectual, political, and social conditions for modernity in the Arab world."
> – Stephen Sheehi, 2005[128]

The mushrooming of newspapers and journals in Egypt since the late 1870s demonstrates most clearly the multiplication of political, ideological, and religious stances. Questions of political and social order were equally pressing in Europe and in Egypt, as parts of the modern world. However, colonized contexts were distinct in that the answers to these questions were generated through engagement with the colonizers' propositions. Thus, in the marketplace of ideological and intellectual propositions, European hegemony comes back in: European economic, political, and military superiority lent authority to the intellectual premises allegedly supporting it and thus turned these premises into a hegemonic standard that inevitably had to be engaged. I shall now paint the contours of the plural arena of the press in late nineteenth-century Egypt, and the follwing subsection will turn more specifically to the position of Islamic reformists in the emerging public sphere.

During the last three decades of the nineteenth century, Egypt witnessed a rapid expansion and diversification of socio-political discourse, which manifested itself in the advent of private publishing. In 1860, private publishing was still basically non-existent in Egypt. Between 1876 and 1914, a total of 849 newspapers and journals were founded in Arabic alone.[129] In the last two decades of

127 Hartmann, Martin. 1899. *The Arabic Press of Egypt*. London: Luzac & Co, 51.
128 Sheehi, Stephen. 2005. "Arabic Literary-Scientific Journals: Precedence for Globalization and the Creation of Modernity." *Comparative Studies of South Asia, Africa and the Middle East* 25/2: 438–448, here 440.
129 Ayalon, Ami. 2010. "The Press and Publishing." In *The New Cambridge History of Islam; vol 6: Muslims and Modernity; Culture and Society since 1800* ed. by Robert W. Hefner: 572–596.

the nineteenth century, Egypt clearly replaced Lebanon as the center of private Arabic publishing.[130] Syrian and Lebanese journalists and publishers, most of them Christians, who moved to Egypt in order to escape the stricter censorship in their homelands and to reach a potentially larger market, sparked the advent of private publishing in Cairo and Alexandria. The rather favorable conditions for private publishing in Egypt that attracted Syrio-Lebanese journalists were due to at least three factors: a rise in literacy, widespread interest in socio-political events and developments, and the breakdown of government censorship.

Let us take the point of censorship first.[131] In the first place, it was Muhammad ʿAli who brought publishing to Egypt. After having sent people to Europe to collect relevant skills in the 1810s, in 1821 he set up the Bulaq Press, initially to publish military manuals and translations.[132] That same year, Muhammad ʿAli founded the *Jurnal al-Khidiw*, a bilingual Turkish-Arabic paper containing mainly official announcements.[133] This also largely held true for its successor, *al-Waqaʾiʿ al-Misriyya* (*Egyptian Affairs*), founded in 1828 and circulated to government officials only. Its range of topics, however, was expanded under Ismaʿil's reign in the 1870s.[134] (In 1880, none other than Muhammad ʿAbduh, who then also headed the government censorship offices, became editor-in-chief of *al-Waqaʾiʿ al-Misriyya*. The premier Riyad Pasha had awarded this position to ʿAbduh, not only due to their personal relationship, but also in the hope of controlling nationalist sentiments among those opposed to the reign of Khedive Tawfiq. However, ʿAbduh became sympathetic to these sentiments and allowed their greater expression. These nationalist sentiments then manifested themselves in the ʿUrabi revolt of 1881, in the wake of which ʿAbduh was exiled.[135]) Due to budget-

Cambridge: Cambridge University Press, here 579. In 1899, Michael Hartmann gave a list of 168 journals and newspapers published in Egypt (Hartmann, *The Arabic*). For a recent list of (not only Egyptian) Arabic newspapers and journals founded in the eighteenth and nineteenth centuries, including their availability in libraries or online, see: http://www.zmo.de/jaraid/index.html (accessed Oct. 10, 2015).

130 Ayalon, "The Press," 578; idem. 1995. *The Press in the Arab Middle East: a History.* New York/Oxford: Oxford University Press, 28–62.

131 For censorship in Egypt before 1881, see: Cole, *Colonialism*, 213–233. For later years and other Arab countries, see: Ayalon, *The Press*, 109–137.

132 Idem., "The Press," 575; Fahmy, "The Era," 170.

133 Ayalon, *The Press*, 14 f.

134 Idem., "The Press," 575, 577; idem., *The Press*, 15–20.

135 Cole, *Colonialism*, 231, 233. In an article in *al-Waqaʾiʿ al-Misriyya* from 1881, ʿAbduh argued for greater freedom of publication, stressing the benefits of (certain) publications: ʿAbduh, Muhammad. 2006 [1881]. "al-Kutub al-ʿIlmiyya wa-Ghayruha." In Rashid Rida: *Tarikh al-Ustadh al-Imam al-Shaykh Muhammad ʿAbduh*, vol. 2: 153–157. Cairo: Dar al-Fadila.

ary constraints, in 1879 the government had cut subsidies for publications, thus depriving itself of a means to control and direct journalistic work by offering incentives. No longer fearing the loss of subsidies, journalists subsequently voiced their opinions more freely and demanded the right of freedom of the press in general. After all, "[u]nremunerated servility would give pleasure to few, and a stick without a carrot would as likely inspire defiance as abject obedience."[136] Since the middle of the 1870s, and before budgetary constraints limited governmental control of the press in 1879, Tawfiq's less European-oriented predecessor Isma'il had already allowed greater freedom in the coverage of political events, since he regarded Egyptian newspapers as useful for opposing imperial policies.[137]

If journalists had the skills and the means to cover political events and affairs, interest in politics was not at all confined to a literate elite; rather, it was shared by an increasingly politicized wider populace. As Juan Cole aptly put it: "I do not believe the intellectuals were more awake than anyone else, and most artisans and peasants needed no newspaper to tell them that their taxes were high, that their government was autocratic, and that foreigners were penetrating their country's economy and administration at dizzying speed."[138] The political stance of individual publications was often due to their being sponsored by nobles and notables. As such, "divisions within the ruling elite tended to get aired in the press."[139] However, these divisions were not the only dividing line in an increasingly diverse and open political discourse. After all, "[m]any journalists, moreover, genuinely believed in parliamentary government, as liberal small-time capitalists in a society whose quasi-feudal political institutions seemed increasingly archaic."[140] From its beginnings in the mid-1870s, political journalism in Egypt – which was complemented by cultural and scientific journals, as we shall see below – expanded steadily, with only temporary setbacks. The expansion of political journalism answered the demands of a populace that remained highly interested in politics during colonial times and whose level of literacy rose significantly during that period.

Even though solid statistical figures are missing, one may deduce from other historical findings that "Egypt's literacy rate in 1800 probably did not exceed 1 percent, whereas in 1880 it may well have stood around 4 or 5 percent."[141] By

136 Cole, *Colonialism*, 227.
137 Ibid., 225 f.
138 Ibid., 134.
139 Ibid., 231.
140 Ibid. 231.
141 Ibid., 114.

1917, this rate rose to some 15 percent among men and 2 percent among women,[142] with literacy rates among men in Cairo and Alexandria having already reached circa 20 percent in 1897.[143] The publishers interacted with their readers, opening their journals for inquiries and debates, which were decidedly transregional in nature. As an example, "between 1876 and 1908 the literary scientific quarterly *al-Muqtataf* handled questions by no fewer than 2,612 people identified by place of residence and mostly also by name, from Fez to Delhi, and a still bigger number by unidentified inquirers. They asked about every matter, from pre-Islamic poetry to photography, with answers often coming from other readers."[144] Some Egyptian journalists deliberately took up the concerns of workers or peasants, and some partly used colloquial Arabic instead of standard Arabic, which was easier for Egyptians with no or a low level of formal education to understand.[145] Moreover, illiterate Egyptians had access to the press insofar as it became customary to read newspapers and journals aloud in coffeehouses and other public spaces. The press thus connected people on an unprecedented scale, allowing them to form a public opinion, which often implied demands made of the state. This fulfills a central criteria of the ideal-typical public sphere, as coined by Habermas, and, despite potentially alternative genealogies and structures of Arab public spheres,[146] one can apply the concept much more meaningfully to late nineteenth-century Egyptian society than to previous "Muslim societies."[147]

Still, it should be added that, even though the journalists interacted with their readers and took up the concerns of ordinary people, they (governmental restrictions aside) concentrated in their own hands the power to decide what was actually published. In an important sense, the public is an imagination and a construction of publicists, who claim to represent and guide the public,

---

142 Cuno, "Egypt," 104.

143 El Shakry, *The Great*, 22. Ayalon basically confirms these statistics: Ayalon, *The Press*, 141, 143 f.

144 Idem., "The Press," 585.

145 Cole, *Colonialism*, 124.

146 LeVine, Mark and Salvatore, Armando. 2009. "Religious Mobilization and the Public Sphere: Reflections on Alternative Genealogies." In *Publics, Politics and Participation. Locating the Public Sphere in the Middle East and North Africa* ed. by Seteney Shami: 65–90. New York: Social Science Research Council; Salvatore, Armando. 2007. *The Public Sphere: Liberal Modernity, Catholicism, Islam.* Basingstoke et al.: Palgrave Macmillan.

147 As with 'civil society,' I see the specificities of the 'public sphere' blurred if the concept is projected back into pre-modern history, as is the case in: Hoexter, Miriam, Eisenstadt, S. N. and Levtzion, Nehemia (eds.). 2002. *The Public Sphere in Muslim Societies.* Albany: State University of New York Press.

even though this constructed public then shapes their own discourse as well.[148] And while newspapers were a powerful means of forming national public opinions directed toward the state, the debates in journals published in Egypt in the nineteenth and early twentieth centuries were also stunningly transregional in nature. The press allowed intellectuals to establish and maintain connections across regions and lanuages on an unprecedented scale. Might we thus better understand these public debates as constituting not a national, but "a global public sphere"?[149] While stressing an important aspect of the situation, this notion might be misleading nevertheless, in that it suggests a greater density and inclusivity of existing networks. I prefer to regard journals – and books, which were often printed by the journals' own publishing houses – as forming a transregionally connected arena of intellectual debate.

3.2 Engaging the Secular: Islamic Reformists in the Public Sphere

> "Les solutions proposées par les partisans d'une 'réforme de la société par la science' et par ceux d'une 'réforme de la société par la religion' peuvent bien diverger, la structure même de l'interrogation demeure inchangée, autorisant toutes les 'conversions' d'une option à l'autre."
>
> Roussillon, "La représentation", paragraph 38

> "Rashīd Riḍā and others of his school found it difficult to accept certain modern practices because they bore a secular label, but it proved equally difficult to put anything else in their place. Thus what passed for an Islamic revival became, in practice, an uneasy process of ideological assimilation."
>
> Kerr, *Islamic Reform*, 201

When *al-Manar* was founded in 1898, it entered an intellectual arena and an economic marketplace dominated by newspapers and journals run by Syrian Christians, who played a central role in the appropriation of European scientific knowledge and European ideas of social and political organization. Here, I can present only the most significant publications. However, it should not go unmentioned that, next to newspapers and journals run by Christian Syrians, other Egyptian publications in Arabic were edited by Coptic Christians, Jews, Armeni-

148 Hamzah, Dyala. 2013. "Introduction: the Making of the Arab Intellectual (1880–1960): Empire, Public Sphere and the Colonial Coordinates of Selfhood." In *The Making of the Arab Intellectual (1880–1960): Empire, Public Sphere and the Colonial Coordinates of Selfhood* ed. by Dyala Hamzah: 1–19. London: Routledge, here 1.
149 Jung, *Orientalists.*

ans, and Kurds.[150] Depending on their individual language skills, the Egyptian public could also select from French, Greek, Italian, Turkish, English, and bilingual journals and newspapers published in Cairo and Alexandria, as well as from foreign publications in different languages, which were smuggled into the country.

Al-Ahram, which remains Egypt's leading daily newspaper even today, was founded in 1876 by Salim and Bashara Taqla, two Maronite Christians from Beirut. A major competitor of *al-Ahram* in the late nineteenth century was *al-Muqattam*, which basically favored the occupation and was supported by the British authorities.[151] *Al-Muqattam* was founded by three graduates of the American Protestant College in Beirut – namely Faris Nimr, Yaʿqub Sarruf, and Shahin Makariyus. When they came to Egypt in 1884, Nimr and Sarruf brought with them their cultural-scientific journal *al-Muqtataf*, founded in Beirut in 1876 and published until 1952.[152] *Al-Muqtataf* is known for popularizing modern scientific knowledge.[153] In fact, its editors had left Beirut after an *éclat* at the Syrian Protestant College, which was caused by their defense of Darwin's theory of evolution.[154] After leaving Syria, Nimr and Sarruf increasingly attended to socio-philosophical theories, above all those of Herbert Spencer: "From the very start of its transfer to Egypt, *al-Muqtataf* shifted its focus from Darwin to Spencer, from the laws of biology to the evolutionary laws of society, and its reliance on *Popular Science Monthly* [an American journal dedicated to disseminating Spencer's thought] grew."[155]

---

150 Hartmann, *The Arabic*, 30–33, 44.

151 ElShakry, *Reading*, 80.

152 The definitive study on the organization and contents of this journal is: Glaß, Dagmar. 2004. *Der Muqtaṭaf und seine Öffentlichkeit. Aufklärung, Räsonnement und Meinungsstreit in der frühen arabischen Zeitschriftenkommunikation. Erster Band: Analyse medialer und sozialer Strukturen. Zweiter Band: Streitgesprächsprotokolle.* Würzburg: Ergon.

153 In addition to Glaß's comprehensive work (mentioned above), see on this aspect specifically: idem. 1994. "Popularizing Sciences through Arabic Journals in the Late 19th Century: How al-Muqtaṭaf Transformed Western Patterns." In *Changing Identities: The Transformation of Asian and African Societies under Colonialism* ed. by Joachim Heidrich: 323–364. Berlin: Das Arabische Buch.

154 Philipp, Thomas. 2010. "Progress and Liberal Thought in al-Hilāl, al-Manār, and al-Muqtaṭaf before World War I." In *Nationalism and Liberal Thought in the Arab East: Ideology and Practice* ed. by Christoph Schumann: 132–144. London: Routledge, here 135, 137. On the reception of Darwinist thought in Arabic in general, see: ElShakry, *Reading.*

155 Ibid., 82. For a series of articles on sociology that is presented as an excerpt (*mulakhkhaṣ*) from Spencer's books, see: Birbari, Nasim Efendi. 1897. "al-Susiyulujiyya ay 'Ilm al-Ijtimaʿ al-Insani." *al-Muqtataf* 21/8: 574–579, 21/9: 674–679, 21/11: 825–830.

In 1890, *al-Muqtataf* also became the first journal to use the term *ishtirākiyya* for 'socialism,'[156] and it played a significant role in the early dissemination of socialist ideas, as did *al-Hilal*, which was founded by Jurji Zaydan.[157] Zaydan[158] knew Nimr and Sarruf from the Syrian Protestant College and had also been involved in the aforementioned *éclat*.[159] *Al-Hilal*, founded in 1892 and depicted by Hartmann in 1899 as "by far the best organ in the hands of Syrian Christians,"[160] is still published today. Less popular, but worth mentioning as a disseminator of secular and socialist ideas, is *al-Jami'a*, which Farah Antun (1874–1922) published from Alexandria and then New York.[161] Antun was one of the first, along with other Syrian Christians,[162] to actually propagate European socialist ideas,[163]

---

156 Reid, Donald M. 1974. "The Syrian Christians and Early Socialism in the Arab World." *International Journal of Middle East Studies* 5/2: 177–193, here 179. The noun *al-ishtirāk* had been used by other Lebanese and Egyptian journals in the preceding decade (Wahba, Mourad Magdi. 1990. "The Meaning of Ishtirakiyah: Arab Perceptions of Socialism in the Nineteenth Century." *Alif: Journal of Comparative Poetics* 10: 42–55). On the various convictions and views that could be expressed with *ishtirākiyya* and rivalling concepts, see: Kerr, Malcolm. 1968. "Notes on the Background of Arab Socialist Thought." *Journal of Contemporary History* 3/3: 145–159.

157 Reid, "The Syrian," 179 f.; Khuri-Makdisi, Ilham. 2013. "Inscribing Socialism into the Nahḍa: al-Muqtaṭaf, al-Hilāl, and the Construction of a Leftist Reformist Worldview, 1880–1914." In *The Making of the Arab Intellectual (1880–1960): Empire, Public Sphere and the Colonial Coordinates of Selfhood* ed. by Dyala Hamzah: 63–89. London: Routledge; idem. 2014. "Fin-de-Siècle Egypt: A Nexus for Mediterranean and Global Radical Networks." In *Global Muslims in the Age of Steam and Print* ed. by James L. Gelvin and Nile Green: 78–102. Berkeley/Los Angeles: University of California Press.

158 For translations of Zaydan, see: Zaydan, Jurji. 1990. *The Autobiography of Jurji Zaidan: Including four Letters to his Son*; transl., ed. and introduced by Thomas Philipp. Washington: Three Continents Press; Dupont, Anne-Laure. 2006. *Ǧurǧī Zaydān (1861–1914): écrivain réformiste et témoin de la Renaissance arabe.* Damas: IFPO; Philipp, Thomas. 2014. *Jurji Zaydan and the Foundations of Arab Nationalism.* New York: Syracuse University Press.

159 Idem., "Progress," 139.

160 Hartmann, *The Arabic*, 35.

161 On Antun, see: Reid, Donald Malcolm. 1975. *The Odyssey of Farah Antun: a Syrian Christian's Quest for Secularism.* Minneapolis [etc.]: Bibliotheca Islamica.

162 Two other pioneers of socialism in the Arab world were the Syrian Christians Shibli Shumayyil and Niqula Haddad, who will be referred to below; for now, see: idem., "The Syrian." One intellectual generation later, a very outspoken propagator of socialist and areligious views was Salama Musa. By and on him, see: Musa, Salama. 1962 [1913]. *al-Ishtirakiyya.* Cairo: Salama Musa li-l-Nashr wa-l-Tawzi'; idem. 1961. *The Education of Salama Musa*; translated by L. O. Schuman. Leiden: Brill; Egger, Vernon. 1986. *A Fabian in Egypt. Salamah Musa and the Rise of the Professional Classes in Egypt, 1909–1939.* Lanham: University Press of America; Reid, "The Syrian," 188 ff.

163 The explicitness of their stances and references to European socialist thinkers distinguish these Christian pioneers of socialism from Muslim thinkers, in whose writings basic socialist

which the editors of *al-Muqtataf* had portrayed rather accurately but had not subscribed to themselves. Without forming a homogeneous group, the aforementioned Syrian Christians knew each other well and regularly contributed to each other's journals, which dominated the intellectual arena of the press in Egypt by the time *al-Manar* was founded in 1898.

While Muslims in Egypt entered the business of printing rather late and in proportionally small numbers,[164] Rida was not the first to do so, nor was *al-Manar* the first explicitly 'Islamic journal.' In fact, among the daily newspapers, the major rival to *al-Ahram* and *al-Muqattam* was *al-Mu'ayyad*, founded by the Egyptian Muslims Ahmad Madi and ʿAli Yusuf in 1890 and edited by Yusuf alone from 1893 onward. By the end of the nineteenth century, *al-Ahram*, *al-Muqattam*, and *al-Mu'ayyad* each boasted around 6,000 subscribers.[165] Rashid Rida contributed some articles to *al-Mu'ayyad*, whose press would also print the first issues of *al-Manar*. *Al-Manar* then quickly became the most prominent Islamic journal. However, it hardly marked the beginnings of Islamic journalism in Egypt.[166] The first journal to carry *islām* in its title was *Majallat al-Islam*, founded in 1894. The editor of this monthly journal of "science, literature, and history" carried the title 'al-Azhari' after his name, as did the editors of two other publications, even though this was allegedly "merely for the pleasure and proud satisfaction of being reckoned as belonging to the Ultra-Islamic party."[167] The self-designation of a journal as 'Islamic' signified the identity of its editor, but was equally a marketing factor.

While these Islamic journals gave special attention to religious topics and alluded to Islamic references, they also – as we shall see in the case of *al-Manar* – attended to a host of non-Islamic or secular issues and also adopted secular premises. It is quite true that the distinction between religious and secularist worldviews does not adequately account for the dynamics in the intellec-

ideas may be identified in hindsight (see, for example: Hanna, Sami A. 1967. "al-Afghani: a Pioneer of Islamic Socialism." *The Muslim World* 57/1: 24–32).

164 Here, we must not enter into the debate on why, in general, Muslims appropriated techniques of printing rather late (see: Ayalon, "The Press," 573).

165 Sheehi, "Arabic," 442. This is a reasonably secure figure, even though the number of subscriptions was often dramatically exaggerated (Ayalon, *The Press*, 146 ff.).

166 Next to *al-Manar*, *Rawdat al-Madaris* (1870–1878) and *al-Waqa'iʿ al-Misriyya* (under the editorship of ʿAbduh) have been named as marking the beginning of Islamic journalism (Glaß, *Der Muqtataf*, vol. 1: 151).

167 Hartmann, *The Arabic*, 19.

tual landscape of turn-of-the-century Egypt.[168] Additionally, the present Arabic term for 'secular' – *'almānī* – was hardly used in the first decades of the twentieth century.[169] Nevertheless, it was mainly Syrian Christians, along with Europeans, who openly advocated positions that, in hindsight, may meaningfully be designated as 'secularist.'[170] Next to journals like *al-Muqtataf* and *al-Hilal,* whose editors were versed in French and/or English, translations of European works into Arabic played a crucial role in the dissemination of modern scientific knowledge and modern social, philosophical, and historical theories.

If newspapers and journals constituted the most lively arena of public debate in the medium of print, this debate was also stimulated by an equally expansive market of book publications: "Three fifths of all Arabic books published in the nineteenth century were printed in the 1880s and 1890s, and the number published in the first quarter of the new century surpassed what had been published up to 1900. Islamic books were the most numerous, being well over a fourth of what was published between 1822 and 1925."[171] The print market transformed the production and status of Islamic knowledge. It was in this process that an Islamic tradition was constituted and solidified: the medium of printing connoted modern, useful, and public knowledge, whereas manuscripts were associated with traditional, private, and specialized knowledge.[172] Selecting Islamic manuscripts for publication thus meant constituting a good and useful (and marketable) tradition over against a bad and useless (and unmarketable) tradition that should not be publicized.[173] *Al-Manar*'s press played a part in constituting this good tradition: about one-third of the more than 100 publications it issued between 1900 and 1936 were editions of texts from before the eighteenth century. Among the pre-modern authors published,[174] Ibn Taymiyya (d. 1328) fig-

168 Gasper, "Public," 40. On the Turkish context in this regard, see: Dressler, Markus. 2015. "Rereading Ziya Gökalp: Secularism and Reform of the Islamic State in the Late Young Turk Period." *International Journal of Middle East Studies* 47: 511–531.

169 In *al-Manar,* the term *'almānī(ya)* appears only 21 times (see appendix, table 6).

170 This historical fact can, however, hardly be explained by the assertion that the Christian tradition, in sharp contrast to Islam, is inherently secular, in contrast to what is assumed by: Yared, Nazik Saba. 2002. *Secularism and the Arab World (1850–1939).* London: Saqi Books.

171 Cuno, "Egypt," 99, see also 92.

172 Schulze, Reinhard. 1997. "The Birth of Tradition and Modernity in 18th and 19th Century Islamic Culture: The Case of Printing." *Culture and History* 16: 29–72, here 29 f.

173 Ibid., 59 f.

174 Among the contemporary publications, Rida himself accounted for 19 and 'Abduh for 10 works.

ured most prominently, with eleven published works.[175] Today, the fourteenth-century logician and Hanbali[176] jurist is known as a central reference point of modern fundamentalist thought (which, I may add, could not possibly make him the founder of Islamic fundamentalism). Here, however, we are concerned more with the modern non-Islamic publications with which *al-Manar* was confronted – especially with translations of European works.

Translations of European works were first initiated by Muhammad ʿAli, who founded a school for translators in 1835, with the aim of using European military, technical, medical, and scientific knowledge for his expansionist plans. By the time of the First World War, some 700 published translations existed in Egypt. The largest group was 270 scientific and medical works, followed by 200 works of literature, 160 philosophical, pedagogical, or sociological books, and 82 historical, geographical, and archeological works.[177] The intention of translating scientific, technical, and medical works was to appropriate useful knowledge. More subtly, translating literature was a means by which European-oriented literati could conceal their own "Europeanness" by clothing it in Arabic language.[178] It enabled them, as Shaden Tageldin concludes in her analysis of Muhammad al-Sibaʿi's 1911 translation of Carlyle's *On Heroes*, "to view secular literature (English especially) as religion, [and] it also enabled them to subsume religion (Islam especially) within the secular and thus to reconcile religion to the political project of colonial modernity."[179] Whether or not contemporary readers of al-Sibaʿi's translation would have shared Tageldin's sophisticated analysis, translating literature was a highly creative exercise, in which Arab translators and their readers experimented with different identities.

---

175 For example: Ibn Taymiyya, Ahmad ibn ʿAbd al-Halim. 1349 h [1930]. *Haqiqat Madhhab al-Ittihadiyin wa-Wahdat al-Wujud, wa-Bayan Butlanuhu bi-l-Barahin al-Naqliyya wa-l-ʿAqliyya.* Cairo: Matbaʿat al-Manar; idem. 1349 h [1930]. *Kitab Madhhab al-Salaf al-Qawim fi Tahqiq Mas'alat Kalam Allah al-Karim: Majmuʿ Fatawa Ibn Taymiyya wa-Ma Haqqaqahu fi Mawadiʿ min Kutubihi wa-Mu'allafatihi*; ed. Rashid Rida. Cairo: Matbaʿat al-Manar.

176 *Al-Manar*'s press played a central role in the publicization of Hanbali works in general, as a contemporary observed: Schacht, Joseph. 1928. "Zur wahhābitischen Literatur." *Zeitschrift für Semitistik und verwandte Gebiete* 6: 200–212, here 200.

177 These statistics are taken from the following article, which, I caution the reader, follows the outdated paradigm of modernization and decline: Khoury, R. G. 1971. "Die Rolle der Übersetzungen in der modernen Renaissance des arabischen Schrifttums. Dargestellt am Beispiel Ägyptens." *Die Welt des Islams* 13/1: 1–10, here 4f.

178 Tageldin, Shaden M. 2011. *Disarming Words. Empire and the Seductions of Translation in Egypt.* Berkeley, CA: University of California Press, 2.

179 Idem. 2011. "Secularizing Islam: Carlyle, al-Sibāʿī, and the Translations of 'Religion' in British Egypt." *PMLA* 126/1: 123–139, here 128.

The practices of translation in Egypt also show that hegemonic European discourses were not simply imposed on colonized men and women. Rather, these practices, as Tageldin brilliantly argues, "sugges[t] that cultural imperialism might be better understood as a politics that lures the colonized to seek power *through* empire rather than against it, to translate their cultures into an empowered 'equivalence' with those of their dominators and thereby repress the inequalities between those dominators and themselves."[180] This is not to say that Arab intellectuals denied these inequalities or the perceived backwardness of their own society as a whole, but they certainly denied the inequality of their own socio-cultural group in particular. After all, they regarded themselves as the protagonists of an internal civilizing mission. Moreover, works that shared the reigning paradigm of European superiority also supposedly contained *universal* social laws, which, if heeded, would arguably incite progress.

This certainly lent attraction to some European, mainly French, historical or socio-philosophical works translated into Arabic. Gustave Le Bon (1841–1931) was the European author most widely translated and most prominently received by Egypt's urban intelligentsia at the turn to the twentieth century.[181] Worth mentioning here are his historical-anthropological works *La civilisation des Arabes*[182] and *Les premières civilisations*[183] and his socio-psychological studies *Psychologie des foules*[184] and *Lois psychologiques de l'évolution des peuples*[185]. The last two titles were translated in 1909 and 1913, respectively, by Ahmad Fathi Zaghlul, brother of the nationalist leader Sa'd Zaghlul. Ahmad Fathi Zaghlul also translated Rousseau, Bentham, Spencer, and Demolins into Arabic.[186] Demolins's work *A quoi tient la superiorité des Anglo-Saxons* from 1897[187] had been quickly

180 Idem., *Disarming*, 10.
181 On the popularity of Le Bon and the major ideas that attracted Egyptian intellectuals, see: Mitchell, *Colonising*, 122–125.
182 Le Bon, Gustave. 1884. *La civilisation des Arabes*. Paris: Firmin-Didot. The translation was serialized in the Cairene journal *al-Mufid* (Mitchell, *Colonising*, 201fn113).
183 Le Bon, Gustave. 1889. *Les premières civilisations*. Paris: Marpon et Flammarion; idem. n.d. *al-Hadara al-Misriyya*; transl. Muhammad Sadiq Rustum. Cairo: al-Matba'a al-'Asriyya.
184 Idem. 1900. *Psychologie des Foules*. Paris: Librairie Félix Alcan; idem. 1909. *Ruh al-Ijtima'*; transl. Ahmad Fathi Zaghlul. Cairo: Matba'at al-Sha'b; reprint: Cairo: al-Majlis al-A'la li-l-Thaqafa, 2005. In this title, *ijtimā'* refers more to the act of associating than to its outcome. For the latter meaning, in this translation, Zaghlul preferred the term *jamā'a*.
185 Idem. 1894. *Lois psychologiques de l'évolution des peuples*. Paris: Felix Alcan; idem. 1913. *Sirr Tatawwur al-Umam;* transl. Ahmad Fathi Zaghlul. Cairo: Matba'at al-Ma'arif.
186 Mitchell, *Colonising*, 200fn111.
187 Demolins, Edmond. 1897. *A quoi tient la supériorité des Anglo-Saxons*. Paris: Firmin-Didot.

translated into almost a dozen languages.[188] Zaghlul's Arabic translation appeared in 1899,[189] and in 1902 Muhammad 'Umar, a functionary at the Egyptian post office, was already applying Demolins's questions concerning the reasons for social progress and backwardness to Egyptian society.[190]

As with the translation of Demolins's book,[191] *al-Manar* in general tended to publish short reviews of notable translations but did not accord prominent space to them, especially compared to the rather close monitoring of European thought in journals such as *al-Muqtataf* or *al-Hilal*. A notable exception is the translation of Alphonse Esquiros's *L'Émile du dix-neuvième siècle*,[192] which was fully serialized in *al-Manar*[193] and later published as a book by *al-Manar*'s press.[194] This translation – notably of a work by an author who had been convicted for his alleged areligious views in France – was undertaken upon the suggestion of 'Abduh.[195]

'Abduh himself attempted a translation of Herbert Spencer's *On Education*,[196] even though it was never published,[197] although another Arabic transla-

---

188 For the Turkish, Persian, and English translations, see: idem. 1330 h. [1912]. *Anglosaksonların esbab-ı faikiyeti nedir?: Anglosaksonlar hakkında tedkikat-ı ictimaiye*; transl. A. Fuad. Dersaadet: Kitabhane-i Askeri/İbrahim Hilmi; idem. [1923]. *Tafawwuq-i Angluksaksun marbut bi-či'st?*; transl. 'Ali Dashti. Teheran: Husain Kushan-Pur; idem. 1898. *Anglo-Saxon Superiority: To What it is Due*; transl. Louis Bertram Lavigne. London: Leadenhall.
189 Idem. 1899. *Sirr Taqaddum al-Injliz*; transl. Ahmad Fathi Zaghlul. Cairo: Matba'at al-Ma'arif.
190 'Umar, Muhammad. 1320 h./1902. *Hadir al-Misriyin aw Sirr Ta'akhkhurihim*. Cairo: al-Muqtataf. On this work, see the following excellent analysis: Roussillon, Alain. 1995. "Réforme sociale et production des classes moyennes: Muhammad 'Umar et 'l'arriération des Egyptiens'." In *Entre reforme sociale et mouvement national: Identité et modernisation en Egypte (1882–1962)* ed. by Alain Roussillon: 37–89. Cairo: CEDEJ.
191 For reviews and discussions of Demolins's book in *al-Manar*, see Rida, Rashid. 1899. "al-Kitaban al-Jalilan." *al-Manar* 2/18: 282–286; Ha'. 'Ayn. 1899. "Radd 'ala Bahith fi Kitab Sirr Taqaddum al-Inkliz al-Saksuniyin." *al-Manar* 2/30: 465–470; Rida, Rashid. 1908. "Athar 'Ilmiyya Adabiyya." *al-Manar* 11/7: 528–539, here 537 f.
192 Esquiros, Alphonse. 1869. *L'Emile du dix-neuvième siècle*. Paris: Librairie Internationale.
193 Serialized in *al-Manar*, vol. 2–9, mostly under the title "Amil al-Qarn al-Tasi' 'Ashar," occasionally with section titles instead.
194 Idem. 1331 h. [1913]. *al-Tarbiya al-Istiqlaliyya aw Amil al-Qarn al-Tasi'a 'Ashar*; transl. 'Abd al-'Aziz Muhammad. Cairo: Matba'at al-Manar.
195 Thus the translator 'Abd al-'Aziz Muhammad stated in his preface (ibid., yā').
196 Spencer, Herbert. 1861. *Education: Intellectual, Moral, And Physical*. New York: D. Appleton And Company.
197 This translation is mentioned in: Shahin, Emad Eldin. 1993. *Through Muslim Eyes: M. Rashīd Riḍā and the West*. Herndon, Virginia: The International Institute of Islamic Thought, 26fn33; Azmeh, *Islams*, 102; ElShakry, *Reading*, 161. 'Abd al-'Aziz Muhammad refers to it in his preface to Esquiros's *Émile* (Esquiros, *al-Tarbiya*, yā').

tion of that work eventually was.[198] Spencer's organicist understanding of society had been tremendously influential in the last four decades of the nineteenth century – in Europe and beyond.[199] In Europe, Spencer's fame and influence had declined rapidly since the turn to the twentieth century, and his organic conception of society was replaced by a view of society as organized (sic) by a division of labor. In Egypt, it was mainly secular scientific journals run by Syrian Christians that popularized Spencer's thought,[200] but Rashid Rida also revered Spencer as the greatest European social philosopher (*al-faylusūf al-ijtimāʿī*)[201] and founder of sociology (*muʾassis ʿilm al-ijtimāʿ*).[202]

Next to Spencer and Le Bon, both of whom he had met in person,[203] ʿAbduh drew on a number of other European works. Guizot's *Histoire de la civilisation en Europe*[204] inspired him concerning the role of religion in civilization and the importance of a reformation. Regarding the relation of science and religion, he appropriated the ideas of John William Draper, which *al-Muqtataf* had disseminated.[205] Rida, as the editor of a major journal, was also well-informed about socio-political intellectual developments in Europe, and about Arabic translations of European works in particular. However, Rida appropriated European or Christian authors rather selectively when it suited his arguments.[206]

Three more nuanced strokes ought to be added to the above-painted picture of Islamic reformists engaging with modern secular knowledge and theories via

198 Spencer, Herbert. 1308 h. [1890)]. *al-Tarbiya;* transl. Muhammad as-Sibaʿi. Cairo: al-Jarida.
199 See now (published after the completion of this study): Lightman, Bernard. 2015. *Global Spencerism: The Communication and Appropriation of a British Evolutionist.* Leiden: Brill.
200 ElShakry, Marwa. 2015. "Spencer's Arabic Readers." In *Global Spencerism: The Communication and Appropriation of a British Evolutionist* ed. by Bernard Lightman: 35–55. Leiden: Brill.
201 Rida, Rashid. 1918. "al-Mutafarnijun wa-l-Islah al-Islami (1)." *al-Manar* 20/8: 340–345, here 341.
202 Idem. 1923. "Fatihat al-Kitab al-Khilafa aw al-Imama al-ʿUzma." *al-Manar* 24/6: 459–465, here 463.
203 On the personal meeting between ʿAbduh and Spencer: ElShakry, *Reading*, 161 ff.; with Le Bon: ibid., 190, but compare Mitchell, *Colonising*, 201fn124. On ʿAbduh appropriating ideas from Le Bon: ibid., 124 f.; and from Spencer: ElShakry, *Reading*, 195 ff.
204 Adams, Charles. 1933. *Islam and Modernism in Egypt. A Study of the Reform Movement Inaugurated by Muḥammad ʿAbduh.* London: Oxford University Press, 44; Hourani, Albert. 1983 [1962]. *Arabic Thought in the Liberal Age, 1798–1939.* Cambridge/New York: Cambridge University Press, 132.
205 ElShakry, *Reading*, 191.
206 For Rida's views on the West and his employment of European sources, see: Shahin, *Through.* For his engagement with Christianity and Christian thinkers, see: Ryad, Umar. 2009. *Islamic Reformism and Christianity: A Critical Reading of the Works of Muhammad Rashīd Riḍā and His Associates (1898–1935).* Leiden: Brill.

rival journals edited by Syrian Christians and via translations of European works: (1) these channels were not the only ones though which Islamic reformists were confronted with secular views, which, moreover, did not induce modernity, but were one interpretation of it; (2) while Christian secular thinkers and Islamic reformists fought out many prominent controversies, they did not constitute two sharply delineated, antagonistic groups; (3) debates about the adoption of European norms and values and of secular premises also took place between Muslim intellectuals.

(1) Translations of European works and the dissemination of European thought via secular journals were not the sole avenues through which Islamic reformists were confronted with modern secular knowledge and ideas. Publications in Ottoman Turkish and institutional developments in Istanbul presumably played a role in the mediation of European ideas to Egypt,[207] both for geographic and linguistic reasons, even though thus far, we know too little about the concrete channels and networks of transmission in this regard. Travels and personal encounters also had an impact on Rida's and ʿAbduh's perceptions of the world, their society, and themselves, albeit this impact is hard to pin down. Rida mainly travelled in Ottoman and Arab lands, but also once visited Europe.[208] ʿAbduh had been in France for a prolonged period, where he changed his traditional turban for a modern hat, illustrating his experimentation with religious and secular layers of identity. Above all, socio-political developments interplayed with or even prompted intellectual propositions. Whether in Europe or in Egypt, rapid material and socio-political changes were visible to everyone who wanted to see. Modern secular ideas were advanced as one intellectual proposition for how to cope with these changes and how to construct a future order. European intellectual influences thus presented only one, albeit hegemonic, interpretation

207 The first sociological institute in Istanbul was founded in 1915. For the appropriation of French sociological thought by Turkish Muslim modernists around Ziya Gökalp (1876–1924), see: Özervarlı, "Transferring;" see also: idem. 2010. "The Reconstruction of Islamic Social Thought in the Modern Period: Nursi's Approach to Religious Discourse in a Changing Society." *Asian Journal of Social Sciences* 38: 532–553. For the appropriation of German materialist philosophy by mid-nineteenth century Ottoman intellectuals, see: Hanıoğlu, Şükrü. 2005. "Blueprints for a Future Society: Late Ottoman Materialists on Science, Religion, and Art." In *Late Ottoman Society: The Intellectual Legacy* ed. by Elisabeth Özdalga: 28–116. London/New York: RoutledgeCurzon.

208 On Rida's European journey, see: Sajid, Mehdi. 2013. "Rashīd Riḍā in Europe: A monomythic reading of his travel narrative." In *Venturing beyond Borders: Reflections on Genre, Function and Boundaries in Middle Eastern Travel Writing* ed. by Bekim Agai, Olcay Akyıldız and Caspar Hillebrand: 179–202. Würzburg: Ergon; Shahin, Emad Eldin. 1989. "Muḥammad Rashīd Riḍā's Perspectives on the West as Reflected in *al-Manār*." *The Muslim World* 79/2: 113–132, here 114fn8.

of the common modern problématique. Islamic reformists, in their answers to modern questions, drew rather selectively upon hegemonic European interpretations and upon classical Arabic sources.

(2) It is quite true that it was often Christian or secular thinkers who challenged Islamic reformists with secularist propositions. The first prominent debate between a secular thinker and a Muslim intellectual in the medium of journalism took place in 1881, in the Parisian *Journal des Débats*, between the French historian Ernest Renan and Jamal al-Din al-Afghani.[209] Against Renan's allegations to the contrary, al-Afghani tried to show that the Arabs – race was a primary category in this debate – were very capable of rational thinking and inquiry and that the Islamic religion was not more opposed to reason than any other religion. Another prominent debate took place between Muhammad ʿAbduh and Farah Antun in *al-Manar* and *al-Jamiʿa.*[210] Antun, who had been Rida's travel companion to Egypt[211] and had introduced Rida to Jurji Zaydan,[212] was an admirer of Renan and drew upon his work on Averroes (Ibn Rushd) in a series of articles seemingly dealing with this twelfth-century Spanish-Muslim philosopher. Antun's real aim was to argue for the distinction between religion and reason or science and for a purely civil political order. He claimed that Christianity allowed for such an order, whereas Islam did not. It was mainly this claim that prompted ʿAbduh's response. The Grand Mufti turned the tables on Antun by arguing that Islam was in fact superior to Christianity in that it accorded religion, science, and politics their appropriate autonomy and thus ensured sustainable progress.

Importantly, these debates were not exclusively motivated by differing worldviews, but also by concerns for the contender's own prominence, intellec-

209 Keddie, Nikki R. 1983. *An Islamic Response to Imperialism: Political and Religious Writings of Sayyid Jamāl ad-Dīn "al-Afghānī"*. Berkeley: University of California Press, 181–190.

210 Flores, Alexander. 1995. "Reform, Islam, Secularism: Farah Antûn and Muhammad Abduh." In *Entre reforme sociale et mouvement national : identité et modernisation en Egypte (1882–1962)* ed. by Alain Roussillon: 565–576. Cairo: CEDEJ; Langner, Joachim. 2015. "Religion in Motion and the Essence of Islam: Manifestations of the Global in Muhammad ʿAbduh's Response to Farah Antūn." In *A Global Middle East: Mobility, Materiality and Culture in the Modern Age, 1880–1940* ed. by Liat Kozma, Cyrus Schayegh and Avner Wishnitzer: 356–364. London: I.B. Tauris.

211 Ryad, Umar. 2009. "A Printed Muslim Lighthouse in Cairo: *al-Manār*'s Early Years, Religious Aspiration and Reception (1898–1903)." *Arabica* 56/1: 27–60, here 38.

212 Hamzah, Dyala. 2013. "From *ʿilm* to *Ṣiḥāfa* or the Politics of the Public Interest (*maṣlaḥa*): Muḥammad Rashīd Riḍā and his Journal al-Manār." In *The Making of the Arab Intellectual (1880–1960): Empire, Public Sphere and the Colonial Coordinates of Selfhood* ed. by Dyala Hamzah: 90–127. London: Routledge, here 99.

tual authority, and material standing. Thus Farah Antun openly challenged ʿAbduh, the prestigious Grand Mufti of Egypt, also in order to raise the public profile of his journal.[213] Another case in point are Rida's attacks on his former friend, Jurji Zaydan. Rida argued that the Christian author Zaydan, with his work *Tarikh al-Tamaddun al-Islami* (*The History of Islamic Civilization*),[214] had entered a field in which he did not have any authority.[215] This argument was motivated not only by concerns for preserving the truth of Islam, but also, I suggest, by concerns about securing Rida's own share in a highly competitive market of print publications. After all, the success of *al-Hilal*, as Hartmann observed in 1899, was also due to its catering for an Islamic readership, as well.[216] Twenty years later, the label *salafiyya* was used for marketing purposes.[217] Unless they were financially completely independent, the editors of journals and newspapers had to take market demands into account when positioning their publications and when selecting materials for individual issues.

Nevertheless, Rida, like other editors, regularly included material from competing publications and continuously – and in most cases uncritically – informed his readers about the appearance of new journals. After all, and this recalls the rather similar socio-cultural background of the urban literati mentioned above,[218] despite intellectual and ideological controversies, many journalists shared the basic aim of social reform and the belief in printing as a means toward that end. Moreover, Islamic reformists also entertained respectful or even

---

213 Reid, *The Odyssey*, 81.

214 Zaydan, Jurji. 1901–1906. *Tarikh al-Tamaddun al-Islami*. 5 vols. Cairo: Dar al-Hilal.

215 Ende, Werner. 1973. *Arabische Nation und islamische Geschichte: die Umayyaden im Urteil arabischer Autoren des 20. Jahrhunderts*. Beirut/Wiesbaden: Orient-Institut der DMG/Franz Steiner, 46. Rida discussed, more or less extensively, all five volumes of Zaydan's work: Rida, Rashid. 1902. "al-Hadaya wa-l-Taqariz." *al-Manar* 5/14: 551–553, here 551 f.; idem. 1904. "al-Taqriz." *al-Manar* 7/4: 149–153, here 149–152; idem. 1904. "Athar ʿIlmiyya Adabiyya." *al-Manar* 7/13: 514–518; idem. 1905. "Athar ʿIlmiyya Adabiyya." *al-Manar* 8/13: 507–516, here 511 f. (right after the presentation of the main historiographical work by Rafiq al-ʿAzm, a close colloborator and friend of Rida); idem. 1906. "[Athar ʿIlmiyya Adabiyya]." *al-Manar* 9/11: 872–879, here 873 f. In volume fifteen of *al-Manar*, the Indian reformist Shibli al-Nuʿmani (1858–1914) presented a more extensive critique of Zaydan's work. On al-Nuʿmanis critique and Rida's role in its publication, see Ende, *Arabische*, 42–47.

216 Hartmann, *The Arabic*, 35 f.

217 Lauzière, Henry. 2010. "The Construction of Salafiyya: Reconsidering Salafism from the Perspective of Conceptual History." *International Journal of Middle East Studies* 42: 369–389, here 383 f. Lauzière's more extensive study appeared after the completion of this manuscript (idem. 2016. *The Making of Salafism: Islamic Reform in the Twentieth Century*. New York: Columbia University Press).

218 See above: chapter 4 sections 2.2 and 3.1.

friendly personal relationships with secular Christian thinkers and journalists. Thus Rida is said to have been friends with the Christian scientific-socialist and the most important Arab disseminator of Darwinism, Shibli Shumayyil (c. 1850 – 1917), who regularly contributed to *al-Muqtataf*.[219] Rida defended Shumayyil and his Darwinist views against charges of anti-religiosity,[220] and when Shumayyil died, Rida wrote an unusually long and appreciative eulogy.[221] On another occasion, Rida stressed that the worldview of *al-Muqtataf*'s editors did not actually differ profoundly from his own: Nimr and Saʿrruf, whom he had previously wrongly suspected of atheism, had also expressed belief in a higher being.[222] Moreover, Rida also cooperated with Shumayyil in political activities: both were members of the Ottoman Party for Administrative Decentralization (Hizb al-Lamarkaziya al-Idariya al-ʿUthmani), founded by Rafiq al-ʿAzm in 1912,[223] and open to both Christian and Muslim Syrians.[224] Overall, not only were intellectual debates between Muslim and Christian intellectuals partially fueled by non-religious disagreements, but respectful relations and friendships between Islamic reformists like Rida and non-Muslim journalists and thinkers also existed.

(3) Differences in socio-political or religious views also played out between Muslim thinkers themselves – for example, in the seminal social question concerning the role of women and the family in and for society. Here, Qasim Amin's (1863 – 1908) works *Tahrir al-Mar'a* (*The Liberation of the Woman*) from 1899 and *al-Mar'a al-Jadida* (*The New Woman*) from 1901,[225] which propagated a European, bourgeois family ideal and the equality of women in private and

219 On Shumayyil's Darwinist views, see: ElShakry, *Reading*, passim; on his socialist ideas, see: Reid, "The Syrian," 183 ff.

220 Rashid Rida commenting upon Qabani, ʿAbd al-Qadir. 1909. "al-Duktur Shibli Efendi Shumayyil." *al-Manar* 12/8: 632 – 637, here 634 – 637. A favorable review of a collection of Shumayyil's works is: Rida, Husayn Wasfi. 1910. "Taqriz al-Matbuʿat al-Jadida." *al-Manar* 13/5: 374 – 383, here 374 ff.

221 Rida, Rashid. 1917. "al-Duktur Shibli Shumayyil." *al-Manar* 19/10: 625 – 632. Funeral eulogies indicate the shift toward a bourgeois conscience, in that they praise spokespersons of the bourgeois public instead of rulers (Noorani, *Culture*, 51 – 57).

222 Rida, Rashid. 1911. "al-Ishtirakiyya wa-l-Din wa-l-Ilhad: Nasara al-Muqtataf al-Iman ʿala al-Taʿtil." *al-Manar* 13/12: 913 – 921.

223 Tauber, *The Emergence*, 123.

224 Ibid., 126.

225 Amin, Qasim. 1899. *Tahrir al-Mar'a*. Cairo: Maktabat at-Taraqqi; idem. 1901. *al-Mar'a al-Jadida*. Cairo: Matbaʿat al-Maʿarif. These two books are translated into English: idem. 2000. *The Liberation of Women and The New Woman: Two Documents in the History of Egyptian Feminism*; transl. Samiha Sidhom Peterson. Cairo: American University in Cairo Press.

in public, incited great controversies.[226] Rida initially presented Amin's first work as an outstanding contribution to pressing debates about social questions and reform,[227] but engaged more critically with Amin's views when he put forward his own stance on one central aspect of "the woman question" – namely, that of the hijab,[228] which Amin wanted to see removed. Here, as in his reaction to *The New Woman*, Rida warned of moral chaos resulting from the propagation of new practices.[229] While Rida was not among the harshest critics of Amin, who was himself a disciple of Muhammad ʿAbduh, their diverging views illustrate different Muslim intellectuals' positions concerning "the woman question."

An even greater controversy was sparked, this time concerning the question of political order, by ʿAli ʿAbd al-Raziq's 1925 book *al-Islam wa-Usul al-Hukm* (*Islam and the Foundations of Power*).[230] ʿAbd al-Raziq was yet another disciple of ʿAbduh,[231] who had been a regular guest at his family's house. Writing a year after the abolition of the Caliphate, ʿAli ʿAbd al-Raziq argued for the apolitical nature of Muhammad's message, which, he asserted, left the question of political organization open to the demands of the time. Implicitly, ʿAbd al-Raziq suggested democracy as the model best suited to the demands of modernity. That Rashid Rida also forcefully attacked ʿAbd al-Raziq for his secular views[232] is hardly surprising, given that just two years earlier, Rida had advocated the necessity of retaining the caliphate in his work *al-Khilafa aw al-Imama al-ʿUzma*[233].

However, Malcolm Kerr has revealed that, in fact, Rida often shares the secular premises he overtly rejects, even though he backs away from spelling out the

226 See: Noorani, *Culture*, 125–147.

227 Rida, Rashid. 1899. "Athar ʿIlmiyya Adabiyya." *al-Manar* 2/11: 173–174, here 174 (announcing the publication and referring to an upcoming discussion); idem. 1899. "al-Nahda al-Islamiyya fi Misr." *al-Manar* 2/16: 241–248, here 247 f.; idem., "al-Kitaban."

228 Idem. 1899. "Kalima fi al-Hijab." *al-Manar* 2/24: 369–379.

229 Idem. 1901. "al-Marʾa al-Jadida." *al-Manar* 3/32: 850–854; idem. 1901. "al-Marʾa al-Jadida: Tatimmat al-Taqariz." *al-Manar* 4/1: 26–34.

230 ʿAbd al-Raziq, ʿAli. 1925. *al-Islam wa-Usul al-Hukm: Bahth fi al-Khilafa wa-l-Hukuma fi al-Islam.* Cairo: Matbaʿat Misr. This book has been translated into French and German: idem. 1994 *L'Islam et les fondements du pouvoir*; transl. Abdou Filali-Ansary. Paris/Cairo: Éditions La Découverte/CEDEJ; ʿAbd al-Raziq, ʿAli, Hans-Georg Ebert, Assem Hefny. 2010. *Der Islam und die Grundlagen der Herrschaft: Übersetzung und Kommentar des Werkes von Alî ʿAbd ar-Râziq.* Frankfurt a.M. et al.: Peter Lang. An extensive, sympathetic summary and a discussion in English is: Ali, Souad T. 2009. *A Religion, Not a State: Ali ʿAbd al-Raziq's Islamic Justification of Political Secularism.* Salt Lake City: The University of Utah Press.

231 Ibid., 55–79.

232 Rida, Rashid. 1925. "al-Islam wa-Usul al-Hukm." *al-Manar* 26/3: 212–217, 230–232.

233 Idem. 1922. *al-Khilafa aw al-Imama al-ʿUzma: Mabahith sharʿiyya siyasiyya ijtimaʿiyya islahiyya.* Cairo: Matbaʿat al-Manar.

consequences of these premises.[234] The fact that Islamic reformists shared secular premises in their turn to society will be further substantiated in chapter 5 section 4, and in chapter 9 section 2, we will see that Rafiq al-ʿAzm, one of Rida's close collaborators, had in fact already expressed ʿAbd al-Raziq's core arguments 20 years earlier in *al-Manar*. For now, we may rely on Kerr's pointed observation that "Rashīd Riḍā and others of his school found it difficult to accept certain modern practices because they bore a secular label, but it proved equally difficult to put anything else in their place. Thus what passed for an Islamic revival became, in practice, an uneasy process of ideological assimilation."[235] This observation provokes the question of whether profound alternatives to the hegemonic socio-political and economic order are possible at all.[236]

This question, however, is not our concern here. Rather, this section established one fundamental point: if we can meaningfully speak about 'society' when life in common becomes a problem of continuous debate, then this is clearly a given in the plural Egyptian public at the turn to the twentieth century.

The centrality of social questions in this public arena reflects itself terminologically in many journals' subtitles. Subtitling a journal as dealing with 'social' (*ijtimāʿī*) topics both served marketing purposes and expressed sincere concerns over societal issues.[237] After all, if financial motives or the quest for personal fame had brought some literati to publishing in the first place, many also believed in their necessary role as educators of society.[238] It is interesting to consid er that *ijtimāʿī* in some cases was intended to mean 'sociological' rather than 'social,' especially when editors oriented themselves toward French terminology. Thus Mirza Muhammad al-Baqir, the editor of the Beirutian journal *al-Muntaqid*, presented his journal in Arabic as a *Majalla ʿilmiyya ijtimāʿiyya* (etc.) and in French as a *Revue scientifique, sociologique* (etc.). Editors also experimented with various subtitles, which did not necessarily imply a clear shift in the topics

---

234 Kerr, Malcolm. 1966. *Islamic Reform. The Political and Legal Theories of Muḥammad ʿAbduh and Rashīd Riḍā*. Berkeley, CA: University of California Press, 158–186.

235 Ibid., 210.

236 On proposed Islamic alternatives to a capitalist system, whose logic they nevertheless adopt, see: Tripp, Charles. 2006. *Islam and the Moral Economy. The Challenge of Capitalism*. Cambridge: Cambridge University Press.

237 A dedication to such issues was of course also possible under other headings, and the presentation of journals as 'literary,' 'scientific' or 'historical' was equally popular. My stress on *ijtimāʿī* is due to this study's interest in specific Arabic terms for the social and for society. More detail on the identification of 'social' issues via *ijtimāʿī* will be provided in chapter 10 section 1.2.

238 Ayalon, Ami. 2008. "Private Publishing in the *Nahḍa*." *International Journal of Middle East Studies* 40: 561–577, here 564, 568f.

addressed. Farah Antun, for example, first published *al-Jami'a* as a "political, literary, scientific, and moral journal" (*majalla siyāsiyya adabiyya 'ilmiyya tahdhībiyya*) but, after dropping the 'political' rather early, introduced the 'social' in the journals's fifth year, presenting it as "a sociological, scientific, moral, and historical journal" (*majalla ijtimā'iyya, 'ilmiyya, tahdhībiyya, tārīkhiyya*).

As we shall see now in greater detail, Rashid Rida also changed the subtitles of *al-Manar* several times – the most prominent and suggestive reads: "a monthly journal examining the philosophy of religion and the affairs of social association and civilization" (*majalla shahriyya tabḥuth fī falsafat al-dīn wa-shu'ūn al-ijtimā' wa-l-'umrān*).

Chapter 5
Al-Manar: The Mouthpiece of Islamic Reformism

1 Foundation, Distribution, and Authors

As is true for studies of *al-Manar*'s socio-political and intellectual context, there is also no lack of studies on the journal itself. Early on, *al-Manar* caught the attention of contemporaneous European observers; it continues to be revered by present-day Muslim thinkers, mainly of salafi orientation; and for scholars from a range of disciplines, it remains both an object of research in itself as well as an important source for writing the modern intellectual and socio-political history of Egypt, the Arab world, and the Islamic world. This section deals with the foundation and distribution of *al-Manar* and introduces its central authors, while the following section will present the topics dealt with in *al-Manar* and discuss the journal's position in the public arena of the press. More specifically following from the interest of this study, the subsequent two sections will then critically examine the usual characterization of Islamic reformism (5.3) and foreground hints that further heighten the expectation that one can discern Arabic conceptualizations of society in *al-Manar* (5.4).

The foundation of *al-Manar*, which is well researched,[1] starts with a journey: Rashid Rida was one of those Syrians leaving for Egypt in order to benefit from the more favorable conditions for journalistic projects.[2] Apart from journalism being the medium of the age, Rida was drawn to this profession by two more concrete influences: his teacher, Husayn al-Jisr (1845–1909), and the short-lived but influential journal *al-ʿUrwa al-Wuthqa*, published by ʿAbduh and al-Afghani during their Parisian exile.[3] After having been affiliated with the Naqshbandi Sufi order in his youth and having received a diploma in the study of hadith, Rida joined the National Islamic School in Tripoli, founded by Husayn al-Jisr, who put emphasis on the transmission of modern sciences alongside a more classical religious education. It was also al-Jisr who introduced Rida to the (rath-

---

1 The definite source in this regard is: Ryad, "A Printed." For Rida's autobiography of his Syrian years (written in 1934), see: Sirriyeh, Elizabeth. 2000. "Rashid Rida's Autobiography of the Syrian Years, 1865–1897." *Arabic and Middle Eastern Literatures* 3/2: 179–194.

2 See above: chapter 4 section 3.1.

3 Ryad, "A Printed," 33 f. A selection of articles from that journal was published as: al-Afghani, al-Sayyid Jamal al-Din al-Husayni and ʿAbduh, Muhammad. 2002. *al-ʿUrwa al-Wuthqa*; ed. Sayyid Hadi Khusr Wishahi. Cairo: Maktabat al-Shuruq al-Duwaliyya.

https://doi.org/10.1515/9783110545845-006

er limited) journalistic circles of Tripoli, where he came to write his first articles, in addition to being active as a preacher.

Rida himself, who would later disagree with his former teacher al-Jisr on certain issues,[4] stresses the tremendous influence *al-ʿUrwa al-Wuthqa* had on him.[5] This journal was read aloud on the streets of Tripoli by Egyptian refugees.[6] According to Rida, it was like "an electric current passing through his body" when, in 1892/1893, he found some copies of *al-ʿUrwa al-Wuthqa* among his father's papers.[7] Even though such autobiographical testimonies should be taken with caution, Rida's motivation for going into journalism is credible in light of his ensuing activities: "All I wanted to do before I read *al-ʿUrwa al-Wuthqa* was to teach the tenets of Islam and the transitory nature of life on earth. Now I saw a new light: to work for the unification of the Muslim world. My duty, I now knew, lay in guiding the faithful to the ways of progress and modern civilization."[8] To achieve this goal, newspapers and journals seemed to be the most appropriate and powerful means. In 1897, while still in Tripoli, Rida signed a contract with ʿAbd al-Halim Murad, the future manager of *al-Manar*, concerning the founding and financing of a journal in Egypt[9] – and two months later, he boarded a ship to Alexandria.

Upon his arrival in Egypt, Rida lost no time in pursuing his journalistic ambitions. After meeting previous acquaintances and establishing new contacts in Alexandria and other Northern Egyptian cities,[10] Rida first met Muhammad ʿAbduh, who had already been informed about Rida's journalistic plans, in Cairo some two weeks after his arrival. Despite his initial skepticism concerning the prospects of this endeavor, ʿAbduh eventually offered his advice and his networks to help establish the journal. It was also ʿAbduh who chose the title *al-Manar* from a list of names suggested by Rida.[11] This title refers back to the following hadith: "Just like the road, Islam has its landmarks (*ṣuwan*) and a lighthouse (*manār*)." This hadith appears below the journal's title in every issue of *al-Manar* from the third volume onward. Two Qur'anic verses embellish the left and

---

4 ElShakry, *Reading*, 158.

5 Rida's self-stylization is rather uncritically adopted by: Abu-Zahra, Nadia. 2007. "Al-Manar (1898): A Journal Inspired by Afghani and ʿAbduh." *Maghreb Review* 32/2–3: 218–232.

6 Ryad, "A Printed," 34.

7 Sirriyeh, "Rashid Rida," 187.

8 Rashid Rida quoted in: Ahmed, Jamal Mohammed. 1968. *The Intellectual Origins of Egyptian Nationalism*. London: Oxford University Press, 29.

9 Ryad, "A Printed," 35, 50.

10 Ibid., 38 ff.

11 Ibid., 40.

right sides of the title.[12] Thus the design of the journal's title page gives us the first hints as to how Rida wanted to position *al-Manar* in the contested arena of the Egyptian press.

The first issue of *al-Manar* was published in mid-March 1898. For the first two years the journal appeared weekly, with individual issues rarely exceeding eight pages.[13] Henceforth, *al-Manar* was published as a monthly journal. The issues of each Islamic year (the Gregorian equivalents are given for each number) are numbered consecutively, with the yearly volumes usually ranging between 800 and 960 pages.[14] After the first few modest years, with only some 300 to 400 subscribers, *al-Manar* gained popularity in its fifth year, and Rida would reprint the first volume in 1907.[15] Muhammad ʿAbduh had helped to increase the popularity of *al-Manar* both by promoting the journal in his circles and by contributing his own writings.[16] After Rida's death in August 1935, *al-Manar* appeared quite irregularly: two numbers were published in 1936, under the editorship of the Syrian Muhammad Bahjat al-Bitar (1894–1976), and another six numbers in 1939 and 1940, under the auspices of Hasan al-Banna, the founder of the Muslim Brotherhood. The continued prominence of *al-Manar* is demonstrated by the founding of *al-Manar al-Jadid* (*The New Manar*)[17] exactly 100 years after Rida founded his journal; the first issue reprinted Rida's programmatic preface.

Al-Manar's prominence and influence extends not only temporally to the present day, but also spatially across regions and countries, making the journal a predestined source for transnational historiography. In its founding year, *al-Manar* had already attracted the attention of the Syrian-Lebanese emigrant community in Brazil,[18] and Rida could eventually boast of subscriptions from Russia, Tunisia, India, Sudan, Sierra Leone, Bosnia, China, and America.[19] The intended transregional readership is already discernible from the subscription prices stated in the first volume of *al-Manar:* the price for one year was 60 qurush in Egypt

12 The Qur'anic verses are (parts of) 39:16 f. and 2:269.

13 Ryad, "A Printed," 43.

14 Exceptions are volumes 19 to 21 (1916–1918), which only contain 640, 448, and 560 pages, respectively.

15 Ibid., 43 f.

16 Ibid., 44.

17 On this journal, see: Hamzawy, Amr. 2004. "Exploring Theoretical and Programmatic Changes in Contemporary Islamist Discourse: The Journal *al-Manar al-Jadid.*" In *Transnational Political Islam. Religion, Ideology and Power* ed. by Azza Karam: 120–146. London/Sterling, Virginia: Pluto Press.

18 Ryad, "A Printed," 46.

19 Ibid., 44.

and the Sudan, 3.5 reals in the Ottoman Empire, 18 francs abroad (*al-khārij*), 15 shillings in India, and 7 rubels in Russia. While we have only broad hints at the overall composition of *al-Manar*'s readership,[20] the journal's global reception and influence has been especially well documented for Southeast Asia,[21] but also for Russia,[22] Turkey,[23] and Syria.[24] This transregional record becomes even more substantial when we add the reception of individual thinkers affiliated with *al-Manar.*[25] In initiating this global outreach, Rida's journal might have benefitted from resorting to *al-Mu'ayyad*'s "cosmopolitan" network of subscribers.[26]

---

20 Laoust remarked that *al-Manar* appealed to "a cultivated and liberal minority" (Laoust, Henri. 1932. "Le Réformisme orthodoxe des 'Salafiya' et les caractères généraux de son orientation actuelle." *Revue des Études Islamiques* 6: 175–224, here 177). For testimonies by Rida in this regard, see Ryad, "A Printed," 44.

21 Abaza, Mona. 1998. "Southeast Asia and the Middle East: Al-Manār and Islamic Modernity." In *From the Mediterranean to the Chinese Sea: Miscellaneous Notes* ed. by Claude Guillot, Denys Lombard and Roderich Ptak: 93–111. Wiesbaden: Harrasowitz; Abushouk, Ahmed Ibrahim. 2007. "Al-Manār and the Ḥadhramī Elite in the Malay-Indonesian World: Challenge and Response." *Journal of the Royal Asiatic Society of Great Britain & Ireland* 17/3: 301–322; Azra, Azyumardi. 2008. "The Transmission of *al-Manār*'s Reformism to the Malay-Indonesian World: the Case of *al-Imām* and *al-Munīr*." In *Intellectuals in the Modern Islamic World. Transmission, Transformation, Communication* ed. by Stéphane A. Dudoignon, Komatsu Hisao and Kosugi Yasushi: 143–158. London/New York: Routledge; Bluhm, Jutta E. 1997. "*al-Manār* and Aḥmad Soorkattie: Links in the Chain of Transmission of Muhammad 'Abduh's Ideas to the Malay-Speaking World." In *Islam: Essays on Scripture, Thought and Society* ed. by Peter G. Riddell and Tony Street: 295–308. Leiden: Brill; Burhanudin, Tajat. 2005. "Aspiring for Islamic Reform: Southeast Asian Requests for *Fatwās* in *al-Manār*." *Islamic Law and Society* 12/1: 9–26.

22 Dudoignon, Stéphane A. 2008. "Echoes to al-Manār among the Muslims of the Russian Empire: a Prelimenary Research Note on Riza al-Din b. Fakhr al-Din and the Šūrā (1908–1918)." In *Intellectuals in the Modern Islamic World. Transmission, Transformation, Communication* ed. by Stéphane A. Dudoignon, Komatsu Hisao and Kosugi Yasushi: 85–116. London/New York: Routledge.

23 Gen, Kasuya. 2008. "The Influence of al-Manār on Islamism in Turkey: the Case of Mehmed Âkif." In *Intellectuals in the Islamic World: Transmission, transformation, and communication* ed. by Stéphane A. Dudoignon, Komatsu Hisao and Kosugi Yasushi: 74–84. London/New York: Routledge.

24 Commins, David. 2008. "Al-Manār and Popular Religion in Syria, 1898–1920." In *Intellectuals in the Islamic World: Transmission, transformation, and communication* ed. by Stéphane A. Dudoignon, Komatsu Hisao and Kosugi Yasushi: 40–54. London/New York: Routledge.

25 See, for example: Benite, Zvi Ben-Dor. 2014. "Taking 'Abduh to China: Chinese-Egyptian Intellectual Contact in the Early Twentieth Century." In *Global Muslims in the Age of Steam and Print* ed. by James L. Gelvin and Nile Green: 249–268. Berkeley/Los Angeles: University of California Press.

26 Hartmann, *The Arabic*, 12.

While this fascinating transregional record points to an altogether different research project on global connections, here it is significant to note that *al-Manar* also received – and in fact reprinted – articles from a variety of other journals and publications as well as from individual readers, both Egyptian and foreign. Articles by other contributors, especially those who did not regularly write for *al-Manar*, do not necessarily reflect Rida's assumptions and positions.[27] Moreover, in addition to critical references to other journals, more than one controversy played out within *al-Manar* itself,[28] and Rida explicitly invited criticism of his journal.[29] While the range of contributors implies the advantage of other voices being present in the journal, a certain core of contributors, alongside Rida and ʿAbduh, can be identified.

Rashid Rida, who not only wrote most of the journal's articles but also selected the other contributions, was the clear center of *al-Manar*'s discourse. Literature on Rida will be presented together with literature on his journal below (5.3), as the two tend to overlap. Muhammad ʿAbduh not only helped to establish *al-Manar*, but also significantly contributed to the journal until his death in 1905. The Qurʾan commentary, which makes up more than a fifth of *al-Manar*'s overall content, is based upon lessons given by ʿAbduh up to sura 4:125.[30] Rida transcribed these lessons faithfully,[31] and after ʿAbduh's death, he continued the *Tafsir* up to sura 12. Overall, the *Tafsir* should be regarded as Rida's œuvre, comprising

---

27 See: Rida, Rashid. 1906. "Abuna Adam wa-Madhhab Darwin." *al-Manar* 8/23: 920; Haddad, Mahmoud. 2008. "The Manarists and Modernism. An Attempt to Fuse Society and Religion." In *Intellectuals in the Modern Islamic World. Transmission, Transformation, Communication* ed. by Stéphane A. Dudoignon, Komatsu Hisao and Kosugi Yasushi: 55–73. London/New York: Routledge, here 55.

28 See, for example, the debate between Rafiq al-ʿAzm (more on him at the end of this section and especially in chapter 9) and the Indian scholar al-Yafiʿi: al-ʿAzm, Rafiq. 1904. "Hadha Awan al-ʿIbar." *al-Manar* 7/7: 269–271, *al-Manar* 7/8: 304–312; al-Yafiʿi, Salih bin ʿAli. 1904. "Asbab Daʿf al-Muslimin wa-ʿAlajuhu." *al-Manar* 7/14: 540–550, *al-Manar* 7/15: 581–590; al-ʿAzm, Rafiq. 1904. "Daʿf al-Muslimin bi-Mazj al-Siyasa bi-l-Din." *al-Manar* 7/17: 660–667; al-Yafiʿi, Salih bin ʿAli. 1905. "Shakl Hukumat al-Islam wa-Daʿf al-Muslimin bi-Istibdad al-Hukkam." *al-Manar* 7/23: 899–912. This debate is dealt with in detail in chapter 9.2.

29 Rida created a section specifically for criticism directed at his journal; see: Rida, Rashid. 1905. "Bab al-Intiqad ʿala al-Manar." *al-Manar* 8/7: 279–280. The section inviting criticism of the views presented in *al-Manar* then reoccurs in several volumes, often prominently placed right after the prefatory article of the volume: Idem. 1907–1928. "al-Daʿwa ila Intiqad al-Manar." *al-Manar* 10/1: 9, *al-Manar* 11/1: 6–8, *al-Manar* 16/1: 9, *al-Manar* 17/1: 11, *al-Manar* 18/1: 31, *al-Manar* 19/1: 64, *al-Manar* 22/1: 74, *al-Manar* 24/1: 8, *al-Manar* 25/2: 160, *al-Manar* 29/1: 114.

30 Jomier, *Le Commentaire*, 50.

31 Ibid., 51.

numerous, well-marked passages by 'Abduh.[32] Two more of 'Abduh's seminal works were first serialized in *al-Manar:* his *Risalat al-Tawhid* (*Theology of Unity*),[33] which has been translated into both English[34] and French,[35] and his *al-Islam wa-l-Nasraniyya ma' al-'Ilm wa-l-Madaniyya* (*Islam and Christianity in Relation to Science and Civilization*),[36] of which a German translation exists.[37] In tune with 'Abduh being revered as the greatest Muslim reformist of modern times, it is hard to keep track of the literature on him, both in European languages[38] and in Arabic.[39] I am not attempting a comprehensive overview of this literature on 'Abduh here, but I will appeal to some of its individual insights along the way.

In addition to 'Abduh and Rida himself, authors worth mentioning for their regular contributions to *al-Manar* are Muhammad Tawfiq Sidqi (1881–1920), Rafiq al-'Azm (1865–1925), 'Abd al-Hamid al-Zahrawi (1855–1915), and Shakib Arslan (1869–1946). Rashid Rida's brothers, Salih Mukhlis and Husayn Wasfi Rida, also contributed to the journal, mainly presenting and reviewing other

---

32 Ibid., 52.

33 Haddad stresses important differences between the first edition of this work from 1892 and the later and much more widespread editions published by *al-Manar*'s press (Haddad, Mohamed. 1997. "Les Œuvres de 'Abduh: Histoire d'une manipulation." *Institut de Belles Lettres Arabes* 60/180: 197–222, here 209–215).

34 'Abduh, Muhammad. 1966. *The Theology of Unity*; transl. Ishaq Musa'ad and Kenneth Cragg. London: Allen & Unwin.

35 Idem. 1925. *Rissalat al Tawhid (Exposé de la religion musulmane).* Paris: Geuthner. trad. de l'arabe avec une introd. sur la vie et les idées du cheikh Mohammed Abdou par B. Michel et Moustapha Abdel Razik.

36 Idem., *al-Islam wa-l-Nasraniyya.*

37 Hasselblatt, Gunnar. 1968. *Herkunft und Auswirkungen der Apologetik Muhammed 'Abduh's (1849–1905), untersucht an seiner Schrift: Islam und Christentum im Verhältnis zu Wissenschaft und Zivilisation.* Dissertation, Göttingen.

38 The first major study in English, and still a useful one, is: Adams, *Islam.* For a recent, easily accessible sketch of 'Abduh's life and works, see: Sedgwick, Mark J. 2010. *Muhammad Abduh.* Oxford: Oneworld.

39 The first major study in Arabic is: Amin, 'Uthman. 1944. *Muhammad 'Abduh.* Cairo: Dar Ihya' al-Kutub al-'Arabiyya. This has been translated into English: Amin, Osman [= idem.]. 1953. *Muhammad 'Abduh*; transl. Charles Wendell. Washington, D.C.: American Council of Learned Societies. A noteworthy recent collection is: Ghanim, Ibrahim al-Bayyumi and al-Jawhari, Salah al-Din (eds.). 2009. *al-Imam Muhammad 'Abduh: Mi'at 'Am 'ala Rahilihi, 1905–2005: A'mal wa-Munaqashat al-Nadwa al-Fikriyya allati Nazamatha Maktabat al-Iskandriyya 4–5.12.2005.* Cairo/Alexandria/Beirut: Dar al-Kitab al-Misri/Maktabat al-Iskandriyya/Dar al-Kitab al-Lubnani. 'Abduh's collected works have been published as: 'Abduh, Muhammad. 1993. *al-A'mal al-Kamila li-l-Imam al-Shaykh Muhammad 'Abduh;* taḥqīq wa-taqdīm Muhammad 'Imara. 5 vols. Cairo: Dar al-Shuruq.

publications. Sidqi, "considered to be the most prolific polemicist in al-Manar,"[40] was an Egyptian physician who wrote on medical and scientific issues but dedicated much of his efforts to studies of the Qur'an and comparisons between Islam and Christianity.[41] Al-'Azm was a Syrian intellectual, historian, and political activist. His political activities included the founding of The Society of the Ottoman Council (Jam'iyyat al-Shura al-'Uthmaniyya) together with Rida in 1907.[42] Al-'Azm is the one regular contributor to *al-Manar* who most prominently uses *mujtama'* and most clearly represents a societal perspective, whence a separate chapter will be dedicated to him below.[43] Damascus was the hometown of both al-'Azm and 'Abd al-Hamid al-Zahrawi, who, in 1915, was hanged along with fifteen other journalists and political activists on the order of a commander of the Ottoman Army in Syria. Rafiq al-'Azm and Rashid Rida, as well as the secular Christian journalists Faris Nimr and Shibli Shumayyil, were among those tried in absentia.[44] The fact that Damascus was the hometown of both al-'Azm and al-Zahrawi might go some way toward explaining why al-Zahrawi also repeatedly used *mujtama'* in *al-Manar*, as he did in his series of articles on "Khadija Umm al-Mu'minin" ("The Mother of the Believers"), which was later published as a book.[45] Shakib Arslan is probably the most prominent of the aforementioned thinkers. His book on the supposed reasons for Muslims' backwardness,[46] first serialized in *al-Manar*,[47] has been translated into English.[48] Ar-

40 Ryad, *Islamic*, 243.

41 His most substantial contributions were two series of articles: Sidqi, Muhammad Tawfiq. 1905. "al-Din fi Nazar al-'Aql al-Sahih." *al-Manar* 8/9: 330–335, *al-Manar* 8/11: 417–427, *al-Manar* 8/13: 495–500, *al-Manar* 8/18: 693–700, *al-Manar* 8/19: 721–744, *al-Manar* 8/20: 771–783; idem. 1913. "Nazra fi Kutub al-'Ahd al-Jadid wa-fi 'Aqa'id al-Nasraniyya." *al-Manar* 16/4: 281–299, *al-Manar* 16/5: 353–378, *al-Manar* 16/6: 433–449, *al-Manar* 16/7: 521–534, *al-Manar* 16/8: 588–600, *al-Manar* 16/9: 689–703, *al-Manar* 16/10: 777–789, *al-Manar* 16/11: 833–838.

42 Tauber, *The Emergence*, 51.

43 See below: chapter 9.

44 Ayalon, *The Press*, 71.

45 Al-Zahrawi, 'Abd al-Hamid. 1328 h. [1910/11]. *Khadija Umm al-Mu'minin.* Cairo: Matba'at al-Manar. Another series of articles by al-Zahrawi is: idem. 1903–1904. "Nizam al-Hubb wa-l-Bughd." *al-Manar* 6/7: 270–274, *al-Manar* 6/8: 298–302, *al-Manar* 6/9: 335–341, *al-Manar* 6/13: 513–517, *al-Manar* 6/14: 552–558, *al-Manar* 6/16: 621–625, *al-Manar* 6/19: 745–752, *al-Manar* 6/20: 795–799, *al-Manar* 6/22: 863–869, *al-Manar* 6/23: 910–916, *al-Manar* 7/4: 147–149, *al-Manar* 7/5: 187–193, *al-Manar* 7/6: 229–233, *al-Manar* 7/7: 261–266, 271–275.

46 Arslan, Shakib. 1936. *Limadha Ta'akhkhara al-Muslimun wa-Limadha Taqaddama Ghayruhum.* Damascus: Matba'at Ibn Zaydun; a re-edition is: idem. n.d. *Limadha Ta'akhkhara al-Muslimun wa-Limadha Taqaddama Ghayruhum.* Beirut: Dar Maktabat al-Hayat.

47 Idem. 1931. "Limadha Ta'akhkhara al-Muslimun, wa-Limadha Taqaddama Ghayruhum." *al-Manar* 31/5: 353–370, *al-Manar* 31/6: 449–464, *al-Manar* 31/7: 529–553.

slan was not only Rida's friend, providing him with information from his French exile, but also composed the most extensive contemporary account of Rida's life and work.[49] Rida himself honored those of his above-mentioned collaborators whom he survived with substantial biographies.[50] In contrast to research on ʿAbduh and Rida, the literature on Sidqi,[51] al-ʿAzm,[52] al-Zahrawi,[53] and Arslan[54] has not exploded yet.

Having answered the questions of when, why, and how *al-Manar* was founded and distributed and who contributed significantly to the journal, the following section shows what the journal was actually concerned with.

2 An Islamic Journal on and for What? The Topics and Goals of *al-Manar*

The (self-)description of *al-Manar* as an "Islamic journal"[55] does not tell us very much about its actual contents. Without going into the details of individual ar-

48 Idem. 1952. *Our Decline and Its Causes: A Diagnosis of the Symptoms of the Downfall of the Muslims*, transl. M. A. Shakoor. Lahore: Sh. Muhammad Ashraf.

49 Idem. 1937. *al-Sayyid Muhammad Rashid Rida aw Ikha' Arbaʿin Sanna*. Damascus: Matbaʿat Ibn Zaydun.

50 Rida, Rashid. 1916. "al-Sayyid ʿAbd al-Hamid al-Zahrawi." *al-Manar* 19/3: 169–182; idem. 1920. "Tarjamat al-Tabib Muhammad Tawfiq Sidqi." *al-Manar* 21/9: 483–495; idem. 1925. "Rafiq al-ʿAzm: Wifatuhu wa-Tarjamatuhu." *al-Manar* 26/4: 288–300. The last biography also appeared in a collection of works by al-ʿAzm (see below: 305 f.).

51 On him, see: Adams, *Islam*, 240 ff.; Ryad, *Islamic*, 54–57, 243–262.

52 The most extensive study on al-ʿAzm's life and works is: al-Batush, Basam ʿAbd al-Salam. 2007. *Rafiq al-ʿAzm: Mufakkiran wa-Muslihan; Dirasa fi Fikrihi wa-Dawrihi fi al-Haraka al-Islahiyya al-ʿArabiyya*. For other studies, see below: chapter 9 section 1.

53 See: Hallaq, Muhammad Ratib. 1995. *ʿAbd al-Hamid al-Zahrawi: Dirasa fi Fikrihi*. Damascus: Ittihad al-Kuttab al-ʿArab. His collected works were published as: al-Zahrawi, ʿAbd al-Hamid. 1995–1997. *al-Aʿmal al-Kamila*; iʿdād wa-taḥqīq ʿAbdallah Nubhan. 5 vols. Damascus: Wizarat al-Thaqafa.

54 See: Cleveland, William L. 1985. *Islam against the West: Shakib Arslan and the Campaign for Islamic Nationalism*. Austin: University of Texas Press; Adal, Raja. 2008. "Constructing Transnational Islam. The East-West Network of Shakib Arslan." In *Intellectuals in the Modern Islamic World. Transmission, Transformation, Communication*. ed. by Stéphane A. Dudoignon, Komatsu Hisao and Kosugi Yasushi: 176–210. London/New York: Routledge. Concerning Arslan's contributions to *al-Manar*: Ryad, *Islamic*, 43–49.

55 As already mentioned, *al-Manar* is sometimes regarded as the beginning of the Islamic press (see above: chapter 4 section 3.2). Its characterization as an "Islamic journal" is found in *al-Manar* itself, for example: al-Hadi, Shaykh bin Ahmad. 1905. "al-Manar al-Islami wa-l-Liwa' al-Watani." *al-Manar* 8/12: 478–479; Rida, Rashid. 1908. "Muqaddimatuna li-Kitab al-Tarbiya

ticles at this point, let us approach the journal's overall topics by looking at its subtitles and the indices Rida compiled, which also provide glimpses into the production and organization of *al-Manar.*

As a paratext, the subtitles on the cover of the yearly volumes[56] characterize and thus position *al-Manar* according to the topics its editor aimed to address. These subtitles vary in an interesting way. On the covers of volumes 2 through 10, *al-Manar* is presented as "A Scientific, Literary, Moral, Confessional, and Informative Journal" ("Majalla ʿIlmiyya Adabiyya Tahdhibiyya Milliyya Akhbariyya"), as was most likely also the case with the first volume, of which I possess only the reprint edition from 1907. On the cover of that reprint edition, *al-Manar* is advertised as "A Monthly Journal Exploring the Philosophy of Religion and the Affairs of Social Association and Civilization" ("Majalla Shahriyya Tabhuth fi Falsafat al-Din wa-Shuʾun al-Ijtimaʿ wa-l-ʿUmran").[57] This suggestive subtitle reappars in volumes 11 through 28.[58] Volume 29 then presents *al-Manar* as an "Islamic Journal Exploring all Matters of Religious and Civil Reform" ("Majalla Islamiyya Tabhuth fi Jamiʿ Shuʾun al-Islah al-Dini wa-l-Madani"). To the aspects of religious and civil reform is added the goal of political reform ("al-Islah al-Dini wa-l-Madani wa-l-Siyasi") in volumes 30 through 32. Volume 34 then again adds to this subtitle the "Religious Duties of Calling to and Defending Islam and Uniting the Forces of Muslims" ("Taqum bi-Faridatay al-Daʿwa ila al-Islam wa-l-Difaʿ ʿanhu wa-Jamʿ Kalimat al-Muslimin").[59] These varying subtitles do not correspond to a significant shift in the topics actually addressed in the respective volumes, as a comprehensive search for the subtitles' terms within these volumes reveals.[60] While the subtitles overall heighten the expectation that one will encounter social affairs and conceptualizations of society in *al-Manar,*

al-Istiqlaliyya aw Amil al-Qarn al-Tasiʿ ʿAshar." *al-Manar* 11/6: 427–431, here 429. In later volumes, this self-characterization also appears in the subtitle of the journal itself, as will be shown in the following paragraph.

56 These covers are missing in the printed version of *al-Manar* at my disposal, most likely due to them being bound in hardcover. They are, however, reproduced in the indices of *al-Manar* published by Rida.

57 Some literature mentions this subtitle only. It is also the one taken up by *al-Manar al-Jadid.* It is highly unlikely that this was the subtitle of the original first volume – firstly, because the reprint edition was published in 1907, the same year that volume 11 appeared, which carries the same subtitle, and I can see no reason as to why the subtitle would have been changed for volumes 2 to 10, and then picked up again. Secondly, and even more suggestively, *al-Manar* was initially published as a weekly journal but is announced as "a monthly journal" in that subtitle.

58 The index to volume 13 does not reproduce the cover; for volume 23, no index was published.

59 The index to volumes 33 does not reproduce the cover; for volume 35, no index was published.

60 See appendix, tables 2a, 3, 5–11.

marketing may have been a major consideration underlying these changes to the subtitles, as potentially was censorship, especially where 'the political' was concerned.

The experimental character of *al-Manar* is also certainly relevant in this regard, as becomes evident in Rida's various attempts to order the journal's topics and articles in an index. The indices to the first four volumes mainly state the titles and section headings of the individual articles; the following two indices then also list the subjects or persons dealt with in the articles. Volumes seven and eight have three indices each: one of "questions and studies" (*masāʾil wa-mabāḥith*), one of the Qurʾanic verses addressed, and one of *aḥādīth* (the plural of *ḥadīth*, the alleged sayings and deeds of the prophet Muhammad). Volume nine adds to these the names of hadith scholars and a list of reviewed publications. For the following two volumes, there is an index of "all subject matters" (*jamīʿ al-mawwād*) and one of publications; the indices of the Qurʾan and the hadith are no longer included. Volume 15 is the first to contain a separate index of individual sections of the journal, highlighting the Tafsir and the Fatwa section next to other "articles" (*maqālāt*) and "news" (*akhbār*). Again there is a separate index of reviewed publications included, thus placing an intellectual journalistic discourse right next to Qurʾan commentary. In addition to its interaction with other journals and intellectuals, *al-Manar* also interacted with its readers, not only in the above-mentioned section inviting criticism of *al-Manar*, but also in the Fatwa section and in a section on "debate and correspondence" (*al-munāẓara wa-l-murāsala*), which was first indexed in volume 17 and again in the following volume. While volumes 19 through 22 only include a general index, volumes 24 and 25 resort to a new mode of organization, listing the articles in order of appearance and summarizing some of them.

The index to volume 26 may be regarded as the most substantial, and, for the sake of not losing ourselves in details, it will be the last one mentioned here.[61] After listing the articles in order of appearance, this index distinguishes between five sections, some with additional subsections: (1) on the doctrinal and scientific bases of religion and its practical rulings (*fī uṣūl al-dīn al-iʿtiqādiyya wa-l-ʿilmiyya wa-aḥkāmihi al-ʿamaliyya*); (2) on unbelief, the turning away from Islam, fabricating harmful innovations, mysticism, and Sufi orders; (3) on Islamic reform in its religious, social, historical, and political aspects (*al-iṣlāh al-islāmī min dīni wa-ijtimāʿī wa-tārīkhī wa-siyāsī*); (4) on moral and intellectual education

61 The indices to volumes 27 and 28 list the articles in order of appearance; the following three volumes add an alphabetical index to that. The index to volume 32 is again more substantial, differentiating between ten sections. The indices to volumes 33 and 34 are threefold, distinguishing between Qur'an, fatwas, and an alphabetical list.

(*al-tarbiya wa-l-taʿlīm*); and (5) on miscellaneous questions and studies (*masāʾil wa-mabāḥith shittā*). In contrast to this overview, section (3) itself is then entitled "on historical, social, and political Islamic affairs" (*fī al-shuʾūn al-islāmiyya min tārīkhiyya wa-ijtimāʿiyya wa-siyāsiyya*), with 'religion' no longer mentioned. Without putting too much emphasis on this different wording, it points to a more fundamental question concerning the Islamic or religious nature of the topics dealt with in *al-Manar* and the reforms it attempted.[62]

Before discussing this question, let me summarize the insights emerging from these glances at *al-Manar*'s title, subtitles, and indices: firstly, these indices, due to their extremely varied organization and comprehensiveness, are hardly useful as a proper research tool – that is, they are a quite insufficient means for identifying specific subjects or authors, let alone concepts. Moreover, whatever limited use they might have had has been superseded by the index published in 1998.[63] Secondly, alongside the experimental character of the journal, the indices also show that is is clearly modeled on modern publications.[64] Thirdly, *al-Manar* participated in a journalistic discourse not only in its layout and style, but also dedicated significant space to reviewing and interacting with other publications. This intra-journalistic discourse followed upon the Qurʾan commentary, which, when included, was placed at the beginning of the individual issues. *Al-Manar*'s generally broad range of subjects makes it difficult to pin down and differentiate between the fields it engaged with. Fourthly, despite this difficulty, *al-Manar*'s subtitles and index leave no doubt that the journal also tackled social questions, even though these might be scattered over different sections.

It was not only Rashid Rida himself who struggled to pin down and name the fields and questions tackled by *al-Manar*; so, too, have external observers. Umar Ryad stands for many others when he repeatedly avoids this question by adding an "etc." to central topics addressed by Rida – for example, depicting *al-Manar* as "one of the newest and most significant printed platforms for Muslim writers to disseminate their reflections and knowledge on a wide range of re-

---

62 After all, in the overview of sections, "the religious" is identified as a part of "Islamic reform," as are "the societal, the historical, and the political." Does this indicate that "the societal, the historical, and the political" are non-religious parts of Islamic reform? In the section title, "Islamic affairs" are then divided into "the historical, the societal, and the political" only. Is this because Islamic affairs – and therefore also "the historical, the societal, and the political" – are considered "religious" per se?

63 Yasushi, Ibish and Khuri, *Fihris*; see above: 32.

64 Shahin mentions that Rida admired and partially adapted the index to a book by Margoliouth (Shahin, "Muhammad Rashid," 114).

ligious matters, such as theology, law, historiography, Qur'ānic exegesis, etc."[65] Here, historiography is notably grouped under "religious matters," thus suggesting a holistic nature of the Islamic religion. The allegedly holistic character of Islam is often more overtly alluded to in explaining the wide range of topics tackled by Muslim reformists. Thus Charles Adams, in his influential work on Islamic modernism, stresses that "it should be remembered that the religion of Islam embraces all departments of life of its adherents, the civil, social, and political as well as the religious; hence the inclusive character of the reforms attempted."[66]

This statement boils down to the still-ubiquitous and seemingly contradictory idea that "Islam is [a] a religion that is [b] more than just religion." One way of understanding this phrase is to read it as referring (a) to a seemingly universal abstract category of religion and (b) to a normative standard of what religion proper ought to be. Another related reading would be that Islam foregrounds what is actually true for every religion: they all also contain social and political values, and in Christianity as well, the privatization of religion is merely a secularist claim. In both cases, the question remains as to how these other, not properly religious, but rather social and political aspects can be identified in an overall Islamic discourse, and whether they can be meaningfully distinguished from (Islamic) religion proper. One approach to partially answering this question is to identify 'society' in *al-Manar.*

Against the common characterization of Rida as a religious reformist, Dyalah Hamzah suggested that Rida should be regarded primarily as a journalist,[67] which would explain the variety of topics covered in *al-Manar* by virtue of their journalistic relevance. Hamzah argues that scholars have too uncritically accepted Rida's self-styling as a reformer (*muṣliḥ*)[68] and that his self-designation as a religious savant (*'ālim*) was also mainly intended to raise the standing of his journal in a competitive market.[69] According to her, Rida did not strive for theological reforms himself, but left those to the proper 'ulama',[70] which amounts to a "paradigm shift from Islamic knowledge to journalism."[71] Rida's overarching

65 Ryad, "A Printed," 55, see also 28, 41.
66 Adams, *Islam*, 187.
67 Hamzah, Dyala. 2008. "Muhammad Rashid Ridâ (1865–1935) or: The Importance of Being (a) Journalist." In *Religion and Its Other. Secular and Sacral Concepts and Practices in Interaction* ed. by Heike Bock, Jörg Feuchter and Michi Knecht: 40–63. Frankfurt/New York: Campus.
68 Ibid., 45 f.
69 Ibid., 51.
70 Ibid., 57.
71 Ibid., 42.

dedication, as Hamzah elaborates elsewhere,[72] was to the "public interest," which he addressed via a broadened, secularized version of the legal concept *maṣlaḥa*. She convincingly argues that Rida considered the press to be the most appropriate means for realizing the public interest, and the journalist to be the most qualified figure in this regard.

While Hamzah perceptively points to problematics in the common classification of Rida as a religious reformist and interestingly foregrounds the secular, societal dimension of Rida's activities, the alternative she offers is questionable in two aspects: firstly, Hamzah herself puts too much emphasis on Rida's self-styling as a journalist, a procedure she criticizes concerning his self-designation as *muṣliḥ* and *ʿālim*. Secondly, religious knowledge or reform and journalism are difficult to compare as fields or professions on one level; still more significantly, they are hardly mutually exclusive options. Rather, the new possibilities of journalism were also a means to voice concerns for religious reform. As form impacts content, religious discourses were transformed by adopting this new medium, but this did not make them less religious, except possibly in the eyes of stakeholders involved in established forms of religious discourse. Some religiously educated Muslims, like Rida, chose the press as a means to realize the goals of modern religion, which had come to be judged in utilitarian terms, according to its contribution to society, civilization, and progress. Rida's own statements concerning the function of the press in general further testify to the equally religious and social dimensions of his discourse. While Hamzah foregrounds the social contract as a central topic for which Rida employed the press,[73] her very source for this statement, immediately prior to the section she is referring to, recalls three other functions which Rida assigned to the press, and which are drawn from classical religious vocabulary – namely, "to teach, to preach and to 'promote good and forbid evil'" (*taʿlīm, khaṭāba, iḥtisāb*).[74] The fact, then, that *al-Manar* represents a socio-politico-religious discourse in the medium of journalism, and that Rida was both a journalist and a religious reformist concerned with social and political affairs, makes it difficult to label the journal's program or its editor's position in any non-reductionist way.

Jakob Skovgaard-Petersen has provided the most convincing characterization of Rida's role so far – namely, in understanding him as a "consciously reli-

72 Hamzah, "From *ʿilm*."

73 Ibid., 100.

74 Skovgaard-Petersen, Jakob. 1997. *Defining Islam for the Egyptian State: Muftis and Fatwas of the Dār al-Iftā*. Leiden/New York/Köln: Brill, 69.

gious Muslim modern intellectual."[75] Rida was an intellectual who, in a public sphere marked by competition between differing agendas for reform and progress, voiced the need for Islamic belief, identity, and references. For Rida, the social collectivity to which the intellectual dedicates his efforts shifted between the Egyptian nation, Syria, the Ottoman Empire, the Arab world, and the community of Muslims. In yet another self-designation, Rida did indeed position himself as a *mufakkir* (thinker, intellectual). He thus stressed the importance of active, critical thinking over against a passive reception of knowledge, which he associated with the 'ulama'.[76] Next to traditional men of learning, Rida also distinguished himself from the *effendiyya*, the new middle class of office-workers and bureaucrats, whom he regarded as Westernized. His repeated stylization of the *muqallid* (traditionalist) and *mutafarnij* (Westernized) can be seen as a way to make sense of the social order he encountered in Egypt, as Hamzah has argued.[77] It was in contrast to those ideal-typical figures that Rida stylized himself as a *muṣliḥ*, who – as the *effendiyya* also claimed to do – pursues the reasonable middle way, combining Islamic tradition and (Western) modernity.

The three figures of the traditionalist, the reformist, and the Westernized Muslim as stylized by Rida are taken up in the academic characterization of *al-Manar* and of Islamic reformism at large. Focusing on this common characterization, the following section also mentions studies on more specific aspects of *al-Manar*, while those aspects substantiating this study's quest for 'society' in *al-Manar* will be highlighted in the subsequent section.

3 The Prominence and Usual Depiction of *al-Manar*

Contemporary European observers rather quickly noticed the importance of *al-Manar*. George Swan, the Secretary of the General Mission in Egypt, remarked in 1911: "Of the religious magazines, El-Minar undoubtedly holds the first place and has done so for thirteen years."[78] Three years later, Arthur Upson called *al-Manar* "the leading Moslem magazine for all the world."[79] Serving at

75 Idem. 2001. "Portrait of the Intellectual as a Young Man: Rašīd Riḍā's Muḥāwarāt al-muṣliḥ wa-al-muqallid (1906)." *Christian-Muslim Relations* 12/1: 93–104, here 93.
76 Skovgaard-Petersen, "Portrait," 94. On the distinction between *mufakkir* and *ʿālim* and the designation as "intellectual," see also: Hartung, Jan-Peter. 2013. "What Makes a "Muslim Intellectual"? On the Pros and Cons of a Category." *Middle East – Topics & Arguments* 1: 35–43.
77 Hamzah, "Muhammad Rashid Rida," 55.
78 Swan, George. 1911. "The Moslem Press in Egypt." *The Moslem World* 1: 147–154, here 153.
79 Upson, Arthur T. 1914. "A Glance at 'al-Manār'." *The Moslem World* 4: 392–395, here 392.

the Nile Mission, Upson also engaged directly with Rida, who had reprinted and refuted an article by a Muslim convert to Christianity who worked at that mission.[80] In 1920, the French Orientalist Louis Massignon stressed the importance of *al-Manar* as the only Islamic journal in Arabic that regularly informed readers during the First World War about the "social problems in the different countries of Islam."[81] Massignon then confines himself to listing and very briefly commenting on articles in *al-Manar*, which he groups according to different subjects. It was Ignaz Goldziher who first engaged more thoroughly with a specific aspect of *al-Manar* – namely, the theological premises and views discernible in its Qur'an commentary.[82] To Goldziher, the "Manar-party"[83] represented a "theological modernism" fueled by three factors: "the ultra-conservative tendency of Ibn Taymiyya, al-Ghazali's ethical conception of religion, and the requirements of the progressive development."[84] These three factors, together with the label "Manar-party," are taken up in Charles Adams's 1928 dissertation on the *Reform Movement Inaugurated by Muhammad ʿAbduh*,[85] which was tremendously influential in the further characterization of *al-Manar*.

Two aspects central to the common description of *al-Manar* are that it represents a middle way between traditionalism and Westernism and that it is the disseminator of ʿAbduh's ideas. Both of these aspects require critical discussion, and I shall tackle the latter first.

Islamic intellectual history is predominantly written based on individual figures. The major advantage of this approach is of a practical nature, as it provides access points to a vast field of unexplored source materials. A crucial disadvantage, in addition to its marginalization of other thinkers and non-elite thought, is that the focus on intellectual genealogies, and especially on teacher-student re-

---

80 Idem. 1915. "al-Manār as Open Court." *The Moslem World* 5: 291–295. The article translated in *al-Manar* is: Rida, Rashid. 1914. "Bab al-Murasala wa-l-Munazara." *al-Manar* 17/10: 793–800, here 795–797.

81 Massignon, Louis. 1920. "La Presse Arabe." *Revue du Monde Musulman* 38: 210–216, here 210.

82 Goldziher, Ignaz. 1920. *Die Richtungen der islamischen Koranauslegung.* Leiden: Brill, 310–370. The book is based on lectures given in 1913. In the meantime, Max Horten had presented and analyzed the life and theological-philosophical thought of ʿAbduh in two extensive articles: Horten, Max. 1915–1916. "Muhammad Abduh: Sein Leben und seine theologisch-philosophische Gedankenwelt." *Beiträge zur Kenntnis des Orients* 13: 83–114, *Beiträge zur Kenntnis des Orients* 14: 174–128.

83 Goldziher also speaks of "ʿAbduh Manar school," "Manar school," and "Manar people;" transl. F.Z.

84 Goldziher, *Die Richtungen*, 342; transl. F.Z.

85 Adams, *Islam*.

lationships,[86] tends to sideline or even ignore the importance of socio-political circumstances and epistemic conditions. Among modern Muslim thinkers, Muhammad ʿAbduh is regarded – whether to an exaggerated extent or not[87] – as the towering figure, and Rashid Rida as his most eminent pupil, or even as a loyal disseminator of ʿAbduh's thought.

While Adams stresses that ʿAbduh's thought was taken up by a wide range of intellectual and ideological thinkers,[88] he regards Rida as his most faithful successor, calling him "the chief disciple of ʿAbduh, who has carried on his tradition" and describing *al-Manar* as "the monthly journal of the ʿAbduh party"[89] and "the mouthpiece for the propagation of ʿAbduhs doctrines and the accomplishment of his reforms."[90] Albert Hourani basically shares this assessment in his seminal work on *Arabic Thought in the Liberal Age* from 1962.[91] In a revised edition of that work, Hourani critically contemplates his own focus on individual thinkers and their influence[92] and mentions other pupils of ʿAbduh who contested Rida's successorship, but he defends Rida's loyalty to his teacher, despite certain differences in their views.[93]

---

86 From a sociological perspective, Weisman has stressed the influence of socio-political circumstances on ʿAbduh's thought, over against the personal influence of al-Afghani (Weismann, Itzchak. 2007. "The Sociology of 'Islamic Modernism': Muḥammad ʿAbduh, the National Public Sphere and the Colonial State." *The Maghreb Review* 32/1: 104–121, here 110–120).

87 Monica Corrado names voices questioning ʿAbduh's importance and, interestingly, she herself thinks that the orientalists' attention to ʿAbduh might have significantly increased his prominence among Muslims (Corrado, *Mit Tradition*, 80 f., see also 149).

88 Adams, *Islam*, 2.

89 Ibid., vii.

90 Ibid., 177. A contemporaneous reviewer of Adams argued that the younger generation of modernists, whom Adams devoted little space to and whose connection with ʿAbduh's thought he considered less strong than Rida's (ibid., 248 f.), in fact "carrie[d] on more truly the ʿAbduh spirit of critical inquiry and reform" (Jeffery, Arthur. 1933. "Modernism in Islam. [Review of] *Islam and Modernism in Egypt. A Study of the Modern Reform Movement Inaugurated by Muhammad ʿAbduh* by Charles C. Adams." *The Journal of Religion* 13/4: 469–470, here 470). Adams's book was translated into Arabic during Rida's lifetime, and Rida spoke favorably about it (van Nispen Tot Sevenaer, Christian. 1996. *Activité humaine et agir de Dieu. Le concept de "Sunan de Dieu" dans le commentaire coranique du Manār.* Beirut: Dar al-Machreq, 12fn7). Rida stated the title of Adams's works as *al-Islam wa-Ruh al-ʿAsr bi-Misr* (Rida, Rashid. 1933. "al-Haja ila Hadhihi al-Tarjama." *al-Manar* 33/7: 536–542, here 537).

91 Hourani, *Arabic*. On this work's tremendous influence, see: Reid, Donald M. 1982. "*Arabic Thought in the Liberal Age* Twenty Years After." *International Journal of Middle East Studies* 14/4: 541–557.

92 Hourani, *Arabic*, v, 222.

93 Ibid., 224, 226 f.

While Rida himself not only stressed his loyalty to ʿAbduh in several articles, but also produced a three-volume biography of his teacher,[94] contemporaries had already contested Rida's claim to succeed ʿAbduh.[95] More recently, Mohamed Haddad has criticized the established view of Rida as ʿAbduh's successor as having fallen prey to Rida's manipulating self-stylization.[96] In the end, asking who most faithfully carried on ʿAbduh's ideas and preserved his heritage is quite a speculative question, one which can only be answered hypothetically and by positing an allegedly true understanding of ʿAbduh. While it is safe to say that *al-Manar* represents an immensely prominent line of reception of ʿAbduh's thought, it should be clear that such a reception always amounts to a selective and creative appropriation in the light of present socio-political and intellectual contexts and concerns.

Rida creatively appropriated not only ʿAbduh's thought, but also that of premodern thinkers.[97] One increasingly important figure of reference for Rida was Ibn Taymiyya, several of whose works were reprinted by *al-Manar*'s press.[98] This went along with Rida's turn toward the Saudi Wahhabi movement, which was motivated by political-strategic more than theological concerns.[99] A concrete difference between Rida and ʿAbduh is evident in the former resorting more often to hadiths in his Qurʾan commentary. While Rida thus validated tradition, it ought to be stressed that he did so selectively and pragmatically, on the basis of present concerns. In the end, in Rida's usage of tradition, utility and public interest overruled the soundness of a hadith.[100]

Concerning political positions, it has been observed that, after ʿAbduh's death, Rida became more conservative[101] and abandoned his teacher's advice

---

94 Rida, Rashid. 1926. *Tarikh al-Ustadh al-Shaykh Muhammad ʿAbduh.* 3 vols. Cairo: Matbaʿat al-Manar.

95 Busool, Assad Nimer. 1976. "Shaykh Muḥammad Rashīd Riḍā's Relations with Jamāl al-Dīn al-Afghānī and Muḥammad ʿAbduh." *The Muslim World* 66/4: 272–286, here 284; see also above: 153fn90.

96 Haddad, Mohamed. 1997. "ʿAbduh et ses lecteurs: Pour une histoire critique des 'lectures' de M. ʿAbduh." *Arabica* 45/1: 22–49; idem., "Les Œuvres." Weisman criticizes the common genealogy of al-Afghani, ʿAbduh, and Rida (Weismann, "The Sociology," 105–110).

97 Dallal, Ahmad. 2000. "Appropriating the Past: Twentieth-Century Reconstruction of Pre-Modern Islamic Thought." *Islamic Law and Society* 7/3: 325–358.

98 See above: 127fn175.

99 Lauzière, *The Making*, 60–94; Thompson, "Rashid Rida," 253f.

100 Azmeh, *Islams*, 114.

101 See, for example: Griffel, "What," 198.

to keep out of politics.[102] The increasing politicization of *al-Manar* is indeed indicated by the journal's editorship being handed over to the Muslim Brotherhood, founded by Hasan al-Banna in 1928, after Rida's death. This is not the place to further discuss the lines drawn from al-Afghani and ʿAbduh via Rida and al-Banna to the present[103] or to engage with alternative claims to the succession of ʿAbduh. The most important difference between al-Afghani and ʿAbduh was a shift from politics to education. In 1932, Laoust had already pointed out the evolution of reformist thought from al-Afghani via ʿAbduh to Rida: "Tout réformisme s'atténue en évoluant: Jamāl Al Dīn Al Afġānī était franchement révolutionnaire; Muḥammad ʿAbduh était déjà plus modéré. Le disciple Rašīd Riḍā est presque conservateur."[104] The experience of colonial repression and unkept political promises as well as the failure of previous attempts at reform certainly played a role in the shifting of the reformists' priorities between revolutionary, educational, and political means.

Overall, despite differences in their views, and in spite of alternative lines of reception, al-Afghani, ʿAbduh, and Rida are regarded as the core of Islamic reformism[105] and *al-Manar* as the mouthpiece of that intellectual trend; this brings us to the second aspect of the journal's common characterization.

As the mouthpiece of Islamic reformism, *al-Manar* is commonly situated between traditionalism and Westernism. This tri-partition of the intellectual field has become widely standardized in representing possible Muslim reactions to (Western) modernity, both in European-language[106] and Arabic[107] literature. A glance at other intellectual traditions suggests this tripartite scheme to be

102 See, for example: Badawi, Muhammad Zaki. 1978. *The Reformers of Egypt*. London: The Muslim Institute, 99fn13.

103 See, for example: Ramadan, *Aux sources*; Malla, Ahmad Salah. 2013. *Judhur al-Usuliyya al-Islamiyya fi Misr al-Muʿasira: Rashid Rida wa-Majallat al-Manar*. Cairo: Misr al-ʿArabiyya li-l-Nashr wa-l-Tawziʿ.

104 Laoust, *Le Réformisme*, 185.

105 See, for example: Kurzman, Charles. 2002. *Modernist Islam, 1840–1940: A Sourcebook*. Oxford/New York: Oxford University Press, 5; Sharabi, Hisham. 1970. *Arab Intellectuals and the West: The Formative Years, 1875–1914*. Baltimore/London: The Johns Hopkins Press, 24; al-Batush, Basam ʿAbd al-Salam. 2004. *al-Fikr al-Ijtimaʿi fi Misr: Dirasa fi al-Khitab al-Ijtimaʿi al-Islami wa-l-Libarali wa-l-Yasari fi Misr Khilal Fitra ma bayna al-Harbayn al-ʿAlamiyyatayn*. al-Urdun: ʿAlam al-Kutub al-Hadith, 253 ff.

106 For an example of its popular usage, see: Ansary, Tamim. 2009. *Destiny Disrupted. A History of the World Through Islamic Eyes*. New York: Public Affairs, 251.

107 See, for example: al-Shawabika, Ahmad. 1989. *Muhammad Rashid Rida wa-Dawruhu fi al-Hayat al-Fikriyya wa-l-Siyasiyya*. ʿAmman: Dar ʿAmmar, 34; ʿImara, Muhammad. 2011. *Al-Shaykh Muhammad Rashid Rida wa-l-ʿAlmaniyya wa-l-Suhyuniyya wa-l-Taʾifiyya*. Cairo: Dar al-Salam li-l-Tibaʿa wa-l-Nashr wa-l-Tawziʿ wa-l-Tarjama, 29.

even more widespread in classifying reactions to (Western) modernity. With regard to the Islamic field, according to this common scheme, traditionalists wanted to preserve Islam as it supposedly was; Westernized Muslims advocated wholehearted adoption of the allegedly successful secular Western path; and, between these two extremes, the reformists aimed at harmoniously combining (Islamic) tradition and (Western) modernity. While this standard characterization of reformism as a middle way between traditionalism and Westernism is useful for a tentative orientation in a complex intellectual landscape, it is not a neutral historical description, but rather a normative depiction, formulated from the perspective of the reformists.

The two most influential works on Islamic reformism, by Adams and Hourani, in fact draw upon Rida's self-depiction as seeking a reasonable middle way between what he portrayed as rigid traditionalists and Westernized Muslims.[108] These seminal works helped to turn Rida's normative self-depiction into a seemingly objective description. Rida, who referred to this scheme on several other occasions,[109] was probably himself inspired by European politicians and orientalists, who also distinguished between three intellectual or political trends and tentatively suggested the middle course as superior – as Martin Hartmann had already done in 1899.[110] In fact, Rida elaborated this prominent threefold scheme when he engaged with Lord Cromer's characterization of ʿAbduh and his party as representing a middle position between conservative and Europeanized Muslims.[111] Regardless of its exact genealogy, the uncritical adoption of the

108 Adams, *Islamic*, 99, 185: Hourani, *Arabic*, 242f.

109 Rida's designations of the three trends vary. Most prominent is his depiction of the reformer (*muṣliḥ*) as representing the superior middle way between the traditionalist (*muqallid*) and the Europeanized (*mutafarnij*). Two examples in which Rida expresses this threefold scheme by using different terminology are the following: in the opening article of volume eleven, it is "the clear-sighted people (*ahl al-baṣīra*) representing a middle-way between those Muslims clinging to tradition (*muslimī al-taqlīd*) and those adhering to nationalism (*muslimī al-jinsiyya*)" (Rida, Rashid. 1908. "Fatihat al-Sanna al-Hadiyya ʿAshara." *al-Manar* 11/1: 1–6). In volume fifteen, concerning Muslim attitudes toward European education, Rida distinguishes between those exclusively adhering to either the old (*qadīm*) or the new (*jadīd*) and the moderate (*muʿtadil*) middle way (idem. 1912. "al-Tarbiya wa-Wajh al-Haja ilayha wa-Taqasimiha." *al-Manar* 15/5: 567–586, here 585f.) Rida himself referred to the difficulty of upholding the middle position, due to attacks from both sides; see: Sirry, Munʾim. 2011. "Jamāl al-Dīn al-Qāsimī and the Salafi Approach to Sufism." *Die Welt des Islams* 51: 75–108, here 83f.

110 Hartmann, *The Arabic*, 5.

111 Baring, Evelyn. 1908. *Modern Egypt*. 2 vols. London: Macmillan, vol. 2: 180; Rida, Rashid. 1906. "al-Shaykh Muhammad ʿAbduh." *al-Manar* 9: 276–288, here 276f.; and again in idem. 1908. "Kitab Misr al-Haditha li-l-Lurd Krumir." *al-Manar* 11/2: 81–113, here 90; see also: idem. "al-Mutafarnijun;" see also below: chapter 7 section 4.1.

reformists' own normative ordering of the intellectual landscape is problematic for rather obvious reasons.[112]

A somewhat less obvious difficulty lies in the notions of Islam and modernity on which the whole classification rests. To give a recent example, in his 2008 article "Al-Manār Revisited," Yasushi states that the reformists would alter their own positions depending on changes to the extremes between which they were located. In a conceptually very dense but, on second glance, almost meaningless formulation, Yasushi depicts the reformists' basic goal as combining the "two substances" of Islam and modernity: "What is certain at the macro level is, however, the general position of the Islamic reformers, who tried to find a middle ground where they could combine Islam and modernity. The combination was that of two substances, contradicting each other, 'Islam and modernity,' 'revelation and reason,' 'religion and modern civilization,' 'Islam and modern society,' and the like, and therefore a way had to be found in between."[113]

Indeed, despite their centrality, 'Islam' and 'modernity' are rarely defined systematically, but rather tend to stand in for whatever the one who employs these terms associates with them. Islam is commonly equated with tradition, and Muslim thinkers appear the more traditional the more they refer to Islam. Against the equation of Islam with tradition, the understanding of Islam as a discursive tradition, which I adopted in my introduction, is by now firmly established and hardly in need of further explanation.

While I have also elaborated on my understanding of 'modernity' in the introduction, a few more words ought to be said on the usage of this concept with regard to the characterization of Islamic reformism and the threefold scheme concerning us here. In this context, modernity is often associated with concrete norms and values – such as freedom of science, gender equality, or a parliamentary system – all of which tend to be seen as more or less exclusively Western. Accordingly, Muslim thinkers appear more modern (and more Westernized) the more they approve of these norms. Thus, for example, Albert Hourani assesses the degree of Rida's modernity according to his approval of rather concrete modernist convictions: "The limits of his sympathy with the modern world and the strength of his roots in tradition, were shown most clearly perhaps in his discus-

---

112 If, for example, Adams regards Rida's claim to represent a middle way as only partially justifiable and sees him as often siding with the traditionalist position (Adams, *Islam*, 185 f.), he is still upholding the threefold scheme.

113 Yasushi, Kosugi. 2008. "Al-Manār Revisited. The 'lighthouse' of the Islamic revival." In *Intellectuals in the Modern Islamic World. Transmission, Transformation, Communication* ed. by Stéphane A. Dudoignon, Komatsu Hisao and Kosugi Yasushi: 3–39. London/New York: Routledge, here 24 f.

sion of the rights of women."[114] Also in early twentieth-century Europe, demands for women's equality were hardly broadly supported, but remained a particular modernist position. Unless one overtly equates modernity with modernism, such specific norms and values can hardly be taken as definitive of modernity. Moreover, stances on such specific norms may change over time. Before the First World War, Rida mainly stressed the positive aspects of European nations, especially their scientific progress, institutional arrangements, and political systems. Tellingly, his three articles on "The Benefits and Harms of Europeans" ("Manafiʿ al-Urubiyin wa-Madarruhum"), published in 1907, mention only benefits.[115] Yet one could hardly be more modern in 1905 than in 1915 – unless, again, modernity is overtly identified with a specific modernist position, which one may embrace only temporarily. It should have become clear that I favor an understanding of modernity which gets at the common background understandings underlying the more specific positions in modernity, of which modernism is but one.

While I have thus far, for the sake of argument, focused on problematic aspects of the common description of *al-Manar*, I shall now add three qualifications to the above picture, also so as to do justice to the existing literature. Based on my identification of 'the social' in *al-Manar*, I will then suggest in chapter 10 section 1.2 that we should understand Rida's middle position not as one between (Islamic) tradition and (Western) modernity, but rather between religious and societal perspectives.

(1) Sometimes four trends are named rather than three,[116] and the names assigned to the individual trends also vary: 'traditionalism' is sometimes called 'fundamentalism'; 'Westernized' Muslims have been called 'secularists' or 'modernists'; and the 'reformists' are also known as 'modernists,' 'fundamentalists,' or *salafiyya*.[117] As mentioned in the introduction, I prefer the term 'reformists,' as it

---

114 Hourani, *Arabic*, 238.

115 Rida, Rashid. 1907. "Manafiʿ al-Urubiyin wa-Madarruhum fi al-Sharq." *al-Manar* 10/3: 192–199, *al-Manar* 10/4: 279–284, *al-Manar* 10/5: 340–344); see also Haddad, "The Manarists," 62.

116 See: Badawi, *The Reformers*, 13–16; Binder, Leonard. 1963. *Religion and Politics in Pakistan*. Berkeley/Los Angeles: University of California Press, 7 ff. Tellingly, Binder then elaborates on only the three main trends mentioned, and Badawi only really attends to al-Afghani, ʿAbduh, and Rida.

117 Other examples could be added: Thomson, writing shortly after Rida's death, designated the "ʿAbduh party" as "moderate modernists" positioned between "fundamentalists" and "ultra-modernists" (Thomson, William. 1937. "The Renascence of Islam." *The Harvard Theological Review* 30/2: 51–63, here 58). Twenty years earlier, ʿAbduh was called "the founder of Neo-Islam in Egypt," steering "a middle course between the Europeanized Egyptians and the conser-

is closest to the self-description of *al-Manar*'s protagonists. Despite what one might think, this is not so unambiguously the case with *salafiyya*, which Rida began to employ only at the end of the 1920s.[118] (This insight does not necessarily render Salafism unusable as an *analytical* category with which to designate the thought and programs of al-Afghani and ʿAbduh.[119]) While constituting a first qualification of the above picture, these extensions of the classical scheme and the variations in terminology do not alter the scheme's underlying premise – namely, that there is a contrast between Islamic tradition and Western modernity.

(2) This contrast has been questioned by recent literature attending to transformations in the so-called traditionalist camp[120] – which also provides further evidence of the normative bias built into the common characterization of traditionalists.

(3) Despite its problematic aspects, the common depiction rightfully foregrounds two fundamental aspects of the reformists' program – namely, their ambiguous view of (what they perceived as) the West and the rejection of accumulated tradition in favor of an alleged essence of Islam. Rida partook of the view of many Arab and also European thinkers when he identified materialism as the major negative or even destructive characteristic of the West, which needed to be complemented or even redeemed by the spiritualism preserved in the East. Rida's increasingly negative view of European nations after the First World War can, to a large extent, be attributed to experiences of colonial oppression and to unfulfilled hopes for the independence of Arab nations. The reformists' engagement with Islamic tradition was equally as ambiguous or nuanced as their view of the West, but was less prone to shifts. In their search for appropriate answers to contemporary questions, the reformists rejected the bulk of tradition – that is, of what they devalued as historically contingent elaborations – and instead focused on an alleged universal essence of Islam, which they saw as embodied mainly in the Qur'an. This essentialist view of Islam again corre-

vatives" (Wilson, Samuel Graham. 1916. *Modern Movements among Moslems*. New York/Chicago: Fleming H. Revell, 158).

118 Lauzière, "The Construction."

119 Against Lauzière, mentioned in the previous footnote, Griffel maintains the usefulness of Salafism as an analytical concept (Griffel, "What"). In a rejoinder to Griffel, Lauzière defends his arguments respecting his interest in *salafiyya* as used by actors (Lauzière, "What"). See also: Zemmin, "Wider," 178 ff.

120 For the Egyptian context, see: Gesink, *Islamic*. See also: Hatina, Meir. 2010. *ʿUlamaʾ, Politics, and the Public Sphere: an Egyptian Perspective*. Salt Lake City: University of Utah Press. Hatina's aim of demonstrating the continuing public relevance of the ʿulamaʾ in modernity is, I would like to caution, premised on the essentialist assumption of an inherent connection between religion and politics in Islam.

sponds with and was inspired by the essentialist view of religion that became dominant in modern European – and especially in Protestant – discourses.[121] Without discussing its exact genealogy here, the construction of an essential core of religion was indeed fundamental to the reformists' program, something which is aptly captured by the common depiction, even though the reformists' construction is sometimes confused with the actual existence of such an essence.[122]

Whether or not they problematically contrast Islam and the West or employ the scheme of traditionalists-reformists-Westernized, many studies on *al-Manar* and Rida in European languages are extremely useful for their analysis of specific viewpoints or topics. Theological and philosophical questions have mainly been analyzed based on the *Tafsir al-Manar.* Jacques Jomier offers the most extensive study on this Qur'an commentary,[123] with important rejoinders and additions provided by Christiaan van Nispen tot Sevenaer.[124] Several studies focus on Rida's political activities and ideas,[125] especially his views on the caliphate and an Islamic government.[126] Rida's seminal work in this regard, *al-Khilafa aw al-*

121 Jung, *Islam.*

122 I will come back to this in the following section.

123 Jomier, *Le Commentaire.*

124 Van Nispen tot Sevenaer, *Activité*; idem. 2002. "Le commentaire coranique du Manâr. Un siècle plus tard." In *En hommage au père Jacques Jomier* ed. by Marie-Thérèse Urvoy: 247–257. Paris: Les Editions du Cerf.

125 Jomier, Jacques. 1973. "Les raisons de l'adhésion du Sayyed Rashid Riḍā au nationalisme arabe." *Bulletin de l'Institut d'Égypte* 53: 53–61; Tauber, Eliezer. 1989. "Rashid Riḍā as Pan-Arabist before World War I." *The Muslim World* 79/2: 102–112; idem. 1995. "Rashid Riḍā and Political Attitudes during World War I." *The Muslim World* 85/1–2: 107–121; idem. 1998. "The Political Life of Rashīd Riḍā." *The Arabist: Budapest Studies in Arabic* 19–20: 261–272; Dupont, Anne-Laure. 2008. "The Ottoman Revolution of 1908 as seen by al-Hilāl and al-Manār: The Triumph and Diversification of the Reformist Spirit." In *Liberal Thought in the Eastern Mediterraneaen: Late 19th Century until the 1960s* ed. by Christoph Schumann: 123–146. Leiden: Brill; Zisser, Eyal. 2011. "Rashid Rida: On the Way to Syrian Nationalism in the Shade of Islam and Arabism." In *The Origins of Syrian Nationhood. Histories, Pioneers and Identity* ed. by Adel Beshara: 123–140. Oxon/New York: Routledge; Thompson, Elizabeth F. 2015. "Rashid Rida and the 1920 Syrian-Arab Constitution: How the French Mandate Undermined Islamic Liberalism." In *The Routledge Handbook of the History of the Middle East Mandates* ed. by Cyrus Schayegh and Andrew Arsan: 244–257. London/New York: Routledge.

126 Seferta, Yusuf H. R. 1985. "Rashid Rida's Quest for an Islamic Government." *Hamdard Islamicus* 8/35–50; Haddad, Mahmoud. 1997. "Arab Religious Nationalism in the Colonial Era: Rereading Rashīd Riḍā's Ideas on the Caliphate." *Journal of the American Oriental Society* 117/2: 253–277; Enayat, Hamid. 2005. *Modern Islamic Political Thought: the Response of the Shîʿî and the Sunnî Muslims to the Twentieth Century.* London: I.B. Tauris, 69–83; Ivanyi, Katharina A. 2007. "Who's in Charge? The Tafsir al-Manar on Questions of Religious and Political Authority."

Imama al-ʿUzma (*The Caliphate or the Great Imamate*), was analyzed and translated into French just three years after his death.[127] Concerning Rida's thought in the field of law, Malcolm Kerr's seminal work from the 1960s[128] has been complemented by a couple of insightful recent studies.[129] Emad Eldin Shahin has focused on Rida's views on the West and his employment of European sources,[130] and Umar Ryad even more extensively studied Rida's views on Christianity.[131] As one important document in this regard, Rida's work on *Shubahat al-Nasara wa-Hujjat al-Islam* (*Christian Criticisms and Islamic Proofs*)[132] has been translated into English.[133] Another topic repeatedly addressed is Rida's views on and relations with Sufi orders.[134] These popular topics are complemented by individual

---

Maghreb Review 32/2–3: 175–195; Willis, John. 2010. "Debating the Caliphate: Islam and Nation in the Work of Rashid Rida and Abul Kalam Azad." *The International History Review* 32/4: 711–732.

127 Rida, *al-Khilafa*; Laoust, Henri. 1986 [1938]. *Le Califat dans la doctrine de Rašīd Riḍā. Traduction annotée d'al-Ḫilāfa au al-Imāma al-ʿuẓmà (Le Califat ou l'Imāma suprême).* Paris: Librairie d'Amérique et d'Orient.

128 Kerr, Malcolm. 1960. "Rashīd Riḍā and Islamic Legal Reform. An Ideological Analysis; Part I: Methodology; Part II: Application." *The Muslim World* 50: 99–108, 170–181; idem., *Islamic.*

129 Dallal, "Appropriating;" Ibrahim, Yasir S. 2006. "Rashīd Riḍā and Maqāṣid al-Sharīʿa." *Studia Islamica* 102–103: 157–198; idem. 2007. "Muḥammad ʿAbduh and Maqāṣid al-Sharīʿa." *The Maghreb Review* 32/1: 2–30.

130 Shahin, "Muḥammad Rashīd;" idem., *Through*; see also: Ryad, Umar. 2010. "Islamic Reformism and Great Britain: Rashīd Riḍā's Image As Reflected in the Journal Al-Manār in Cairo." *Islam and Christian Muslim Relations* 21/3: 263–285.

131 Idem., *Islamic.* See also: Bormans, Maurice. 1975. "Le commentaire du Manar à propos du verset coranique sur l'amitié des Musulmans pour les Chrétiens (5, 82)." *IslamoChristiana* 1: 71–86; Wood, Simon A. 2010. "Researching 'The Scripture of the Other': Niqula Ghabriyal's *Researches of the Mujtahids* and Rashid Rida's Rejoinder." *Comparative Islamic Studies* 6/1–2: 181–216.

132 These articles appeared in volumes four to six of *al-Manar* and were later published as a book: Rida, Rashid. 1322 h. [1904]. *Shubahat al-Nasara wa-Hujaj al-Islam: Maqalat fi al-Radd ʿala al-Nasara Tunshar fi Majallat ʿal-Manarʾ al-Islami.* Cairo: Matbaʿat al-Manar.

133 Rida, Rashid. 2008. *Christian Criticisms, Islamic Proofs. Rašīd Riḍā's Modernist Defence of Islam*; translation and analysis by Simon A. Wood. Oxford: Oneworld.

134 Hourani, Albert. 1977. "Rashid Rida and the Sufi orders: a footnote to Laoust." *Bulletin d'études orientales* 29: 231–241; idem. 1981. "Sufism and Modern Islam: Rashid Rida." In *The Emergence of the Modern Middle East:* 90–102. Berkeley/Los Angeles: University of California Press; van Leeuwen, Richard. 2013. "Reformist Islam and Popular Beliefs: Rashīd Riḍā's Attack against the Cult of Shrines." In *Sources and Approaches Across Disciplines in Near Eastern Studies. Proceedings of the 24th Congress, Union Européenne des Arabisants et Islamistes, Leipzig 2008* ed. by Verena Klemm and Nuha al-Shaʿar: 141–154. Leuven/Paris/Walpole, Mass.: Uitgeverij Peters/Departement Oosterse Studies; see also: Scharbrodt, Oliver. 2007. "The Salafiyya and Sufism: Mu-

studies on rather specific questions, such as the question of whether women should learn to write (which Rida answered positively),[135] Rida's views on the Arabic and Turkish languages,[136] his relation to the short-lived Hashimite kingdom of 1920,[137] his earlier Syrian journey,[138] his depiction of his European travels as a "hero's journey,"[139] his view of progress,[140] and his engagement with scientific and materialist arguments.[141]

The bulk of Arabic literature I have found on Rida and *al-Manar* does not add much to these studies in European languages and would mainly be of interest for an altogether different study tracing the reception of Rida's thought. Since the publication of Ahmad al-Sharabasi's three books on Rida's life and work in the 1970s, which continue to be widely referenced,[142] the body of Arabic literature on Rida has become increasingly large. Next to innumerable reprints of

---

hammad ʿAbduh and his Risalat al-Waridat (Treatise on Mystical Inspirations)." *Bulletin of the School of Oriental and African Studies* 70: 89–115.

135 Ende, Werner. 1994. "Sollen Frauen schreiben lernen? Eine innerislamische Debatte und ihre Widerspiegelung in Al-Manār." In *Gedenkschrift Wolfgang Reuschel: Akten des III. Arabistischen Kolloquiums, Leipzig, 21.–22. November 1991* ed. by Dieter Bellmann: 49–57. Stuttgart: Steiner.

136 Brunner, Rainer. 2016. "Lātinīya lā-dīnīya: Muḥammad Rašīd Riḍā über Arabisch und Türkisch im Zeitalter des Nationalismus." In *Osmanische Welten: Quellen und Fallstudien. Festschrift für Michael Ursinus* ed. by Johannes Zimmermann, Christoph Herzog and Raoul Motika, 73–114. Bamberg: University of Bamberg Press. Concerning the question of translatability of the Qur'an, see also: Abou Sheishaa, Mohamed Ali Mohamed. 2001. "A Study of the Fatwa by Rashid Rida on the Translation of the Qur'an." *Journal of the Society for Qur'anic Studies* 1/1 https://www.academia.edu/6481246/A_STUDY_OF_THE_FATWA_BY_RASHID_RIDĀ_ON_THE_TRANSLATION_OF_THE_QURĀN (accessed Aug. 17, 2017).

137 Tauber, Eliezer. 1995. "Rashīd Riḍā and Fayṣal's Kingdom in Syria." *The Muslim World* 85: 235–245.

138 Van Leeuwen, Richard. 2012. "Mobility and Islamic Thought: The Syrian Journey of Rashīd Riḍā in 1908." In *Centre and Periphery within the Borders of Islam. Proceedings of the 23rd Congress of L'Union Européenne des Arabisants et Islamisants* ed. by Giuseppe Contu: 33–46. Leuven/Paris/Walpole, MA: Uitgeverij Peeters.

139 Sajid, "Rashīd Riḍā."

140 Philipp, "Progress."

141 Stolz, Daniel A. 2012. "'By Virtue of your Knowledge': Scientific Materialism and the *fatwās* of Rashīd Riḍā." *Bulletin of the School of Oriental and African Studies* 75/2: 223–247.

142 Al-Sharabasi, Ahmad. 1970. *Rashid Rida, Sahib al-Manar: ʿAsruhu wa-Hayatuhu wa-Masadir Thaqafatihi.* Cairo: Matabiʿ al-Ahram al-Tijariyya; idem. 1976. *Rashid Rida: al-Adib al-Katib al-Islami.* Cairo: al-Hay'a al-ʿAmma li-Shu'un al-Matabiʿ al-Amiriyya; idem. 1977. *Rashid Rida: al-Sahafi, al-Mufassir, al-Shaʿir, al-Lughawi.* Cairo: al-Hay'a al-ʿAmma li Shu'un al-Matabiʿ al-Amiriyya.

Rida's works,[143] collections of selected writings have also been published.[144] These reprints and collections already testify to Rida's prominence and continued relevance, which becomes ever more clear from the large number of publications – often in the format of small booklets,[145] but also as hardbound books[146] or university theses[147] – that appropriate Rida's thought for what they perceive as solutions to current socio-political problems. The two non-academic English translations of his work *al-Wahy al-Muhammadi*[148] (*The Muhammadan Revelation*)[149] may be included among the literature that upholds the relevance of Rida's thought for present concerns. These translations and the bulk of Arabic literature would thus be of potential value as primary sources rather than as academic studies. I should at least point to three more substantial recent publications on *al-Manar*, concerning the fields of law,[150] politics,[151] and theology.[152] Overall, however, and for the reasons mentioned above, in this study I make very limited use of Arabic literature on *al-Manar*.

---

143 For example: Rida, Rashid. 1406 h. [1985/86]. *al-Wahy al-Muhammadi: Thubut al-Nubuwa wa-l-Qur'an wa-Da'wat Shu'ub al-Madaniyya ila al-Islam Din al-Akhira li-l-Insaniyya wa-l-Salam*. Beirut: Mu'assasat 'Izz al-Din li-l-Tiba'a wa-l-Nashr; idem. 2007. *Nida' li-l-Jins al-Latif: fi Huquq al-Nisa' fi al-Islam wa-Hazzuhunna min al-Islah al-Muhammadi al-'Amm*. Cairo/Minneapolis: Dar al-Nashr li-l-Jami'at/Dar Almanar; idem. 2008. *Muhawarat al-Muslih wa-l-Muqallid wa-l-Wahda al-Islamiyya*. Cairo/Minneapolis: Dar al-Nashr li-l-Jami'at/Dar Almanar.

144 For example: idem. 1970–1971. *Fatawa al-Imam Muhammad Rashid Rida*; jama'aha wa-ḥaqqaqaha Salah al-Din al-Munajjid wa-Yusuf Q. Khuri. Beirut: Dar al-Kitab al-Jadid; al-Kawtharani, Wajih. 1980. *Mukhtarat Siyasiyya min Majallat al-Manar*. Beirut: Dar al-Tali'a; [Rida, Rashid]. 1983. *Muhammad Rashid Rida*; ikhtara al-nuṣūṣ wa-qaddamaha Adunis wa-Khalida Sa'id. Beirut: Dar al-'Ilm li-l-Milayin.

145 For example: Abu Hamdan, Samir. 1992. *al-Shaykh Rashid Rida wa-l-Khitab al-Islami al-Mu'tadil*. Beirut: al-Sharika al-'Alamiyya li-l-Kitab; al-Fahdawi, Khalid. 2007. *al-'Alama Muhammad Rashid Rida: 'Asruhu, Tahdiyatuhu, Manhajuhu al-Islahi*. Damascus: Dar Safahat.

146 For example: al-Samahan, Faysal bin 'Abd al-'Aziz. 2011. *al-Imam al-Sayyid Muhammad Rashid Rida fi Mayadin al-Muwajaha*. Kuwayt: Maktabat Ahl al-Athr li-l-Nashr wa-l-Tawzi'.

147 For example: Al Hamza, Khalid bin Fawzi bin 'Abd al-Hamid. 1415 h. [1994/95]. *Muhammad Rashid Rida: Tawd wa-Islah, Da'wa wa-Da'iyya, 1282–1354 h.: Jihaduhu fi Khidmat al-'Aqida wa-Athruhu fi al-Ittijahat al-Fikriyya al-Mu'asira*. Alexandria: Dar al-'Ulama' al-Salaf.

148 Rida, Rashid. 1933. *al-Wahy al-Muhammadi*. Cairo: Matba'at al-Manar.

149 Idem. 1960. *The Revelation to Muhammad*; transl. Abdus-Samad Sharafuddin. Bhiwandi [India]: Ad-Darul-Qayyimah; idem. 1996. *The Muhammadan Revelation*; transl. Yusuf T. DeLorenzo. Alexandria: Al-Saadawi.

150 Mahmud, Ra'd Muhammad. 2013. *al-Imam Muhammad Rashid Rida wa-Ikhtiyaratuhu al-Fiqhiyya min Khilal Tafsirihi al-Manar*. Baghdad: Diwan al-Waqf al-Sunni.

151 Malla, *Judhur*.

152 Al-Din, Hazim Zakariyya Muhy. 2007. *Mafhum al-Sunan al-Ilahiyya fi al-Fikr al-Islami: al-Sayyid Muhammad Rashid Rida Namudhajan*. Damascus: Dar al-Nawadir li-l-Nashr wa-l-Tawzi'.

Mainly based on studies in European langauges, the following section collects indications of the evolving understanding of an autonomous social sphere and of the centrality of society in *al-Manar*, before the next chapter then attends to hints at Arabic concepts of 'society.'

4 Islamic Reformism, Religion, Secularity, and Society

The major premises of this section have already been introduced, and some of its insights have also already been touched upon: in chapter 2 section 3, we have seen how, in Europe, questions of society and social order also gained primacy for religious actors, who then transformed discourses and understandings of religion accordingly. In order to substantiate the usability of *A Secular Age* as a heuristic tool, in chapter 3 section 4, I mentioned that the Islamic reformists developed an Islamic discourse to address both religion and society. Chapter 4 section 2 established the importance of social questions in Egypt in the nineteenth century, and chapter 4 section 3 showed that the reformists were directly confronted with secular stances and also drew upon European thought. Not surprisingly, then, a first glance at the topics of *al-Manar* in chapter 5 section 2 showed that social questions were prominently addressed in the journal. Building on that foundation, this section brings together insights and hints from secondary sources to show that *al-Manar* was an eminent instance of the turn to society – a turn characteristic of the modern transformation of religion.

Other than substantiating this fact, I am presenting these insights with three major purposes in mind: firstly, to stress (again) that the reformists' comprehensive understanding of Islam as an abstract entity addressing all the spheres of life does not follow from the (allegedly) essentially comprehensive nature of Islam, but rather mirrors a decidedly modern transformation. Secondly, the fact that the reformists' Islamic discourse addresses both religion and society raises the question of whether these two spheres can be clearly distinguished as separate entities. Relatedly, and most importantly for our purposes, it, thirdly, will transpire that the literature on the prominence of society in *al-Manar* does not reflect upon the concept of 'society.'

While one can already trace the increasing primacy of social questions in Islamic discourses in the eighteenth century,[153] it here suffices to go back to Jamal

153 One noteworthy figure is the Indian scholar Shah Wali Allah (1703–1762). For a brief presentation and further literature, see Dallal, "The Origins," 118–120.

al-Din al-Afghani, the early teacher of Muhammad ʿAbduh, who was greatly revered by Rashid Rida. Al-Afghani most strikingly illustrates the primacy of social questions in his famous *Refutation of the Materialists* (*al-Radd ʿala al-Dahriyin*), translated into Arabic under the auspices of ʿAbduh.[154] (As we are interested here in fundamental conceptual and epistemic transformations, we may leave aside diverging statements which the political activist al-Afghani made in other settings.)[155] Arguing against what he portrayed as the circle of materialists around the Indian Sayyid Ahmad Khan,[156] al-Afghani stresses the continuous validity and necessity of Islamic religion. Significantly, al-Afghani values religion almost exclusively for its creation of solidarity and unity – that is, for its social and political function.[157] For one reader, it even became hard to discern whether al-Afghani might not in fact mean the "order of society" or "civilization" when he talks about "religion."[158]

Abdulkader Tayob has recently suggested that we should generally understand al-Afghani's and ʿAbduh's reconception of Islam as a "functionalist approach"[159] to religion: "They were less concerned about the essence of religion, and more attentive to its social and political values. Religion was a means for achieving progress, development and happiness in community and society."[160] Malcolm Kerr illustrates the novelty of ʿAbduh's approach by contrasting it

---

154 Al-Afghani, Jamal al-Din. 2002. "al-Radd ʿala al-Dahriyin." In *Rasaʾil fi al-Falsafa wa-l-ʿIrfan* (= *al-Athar al-Kamila*, vol. 2): 127–198. Cairo: Maktabat al-Shuruq al-Duwaliyya; Keddie, *An Islamic.*

155 In his debate with Renan, for example, al-Afghani depicted philosophy as superior to religion, Islam being only a temporary necessity for guiding the Arabs to philosophy (al-Afghani, Sayyid Jamal al-Din. 2002. "Lecture on Teaching and Learning *and* Answer to Renan." In *Modernist Islam, 1840–1940: A Sourcebook* ed. by Charles Kurzman: 103–110. Oxford/New York: Oxford University Press, here 107–110).

156 On him and the debate with al-Afghani, see: Troll, Christian W. 1978. *Sayyid Ahmad Khan. A Reinterpretation of Muslim Theology.* New Delhi: Vikas Publishing House; Ahmad, Aziz. 1960. "Sayyid Aḥmad Khān, Jamāl al-dīn al-Afghānī and Muslim India." *Studia Islamica* 13: 55–78.

157 This striking feature has been recognized repeatedly; a commendable recent reading is: Tayob, Abdulkader. 2009. *Religion in Modern Islamic Discourse.* London: Hurst, 50–57. Tellingly, the title of the first edition of the Arabic translation of the *Radd* in 1885 was: *A Treatise Invalidating the School of the Materialists and Explaining their Harmfulness and Establishing that Religion is the Foundation of Civil Order and that Unbelief is the Corruption of Civilization* (*Risala fi Ibtal Madhhab al-Dahriyin wa-Bayan Mafasidihim wa-Ithbat anna al-Din Asas al-Madaniyya wa-l-Kufr Fasad al-ʿUmran*) (see: Rida, *Christian*, 155fn146).

158 Ende, Werner. 1969. "Waren Ǧamāladdīn al-Afġānī und Muḥammad ʿAbduh Agnostiker?." *ZDMG* Supplement 1/17: 650–659, here 655; transl. F.Z.

159 Tayob, *Religion*, 24.

160 Ibid., 17.

with that of al-Ghazali (d. 1111), the most important pre-modern reference for ʿAbduh. Compared to al-Ghazali, ʿAbduh reverses the priorities ascribed to religion and the world, as Kerr perceptively observes: "ʿAbduh describes material well-being as having an importance of its own which even 'takes precedence' over acts or expressions of devotion. What he seeks to show is that religion is no impediment to worldly prosperity. For Ghazali, the need is to show that worldly prosperity is no impediment to religion, and is in fact necessary for it as a means to an end; and the end is faith."[161]

Embedding the reformists' transformation of Islam in the broader epistemic developments of modernity, as Tayob and Kerr do, surpasses previous attempts at trying to grasp this markedly novel understanding of Islam. Such attempts included characterizing ʿAbduh as a humanist[162] or asking whether al-Afghani and ʿAbduh were in fact agnostics[163] or even unbelievers.[164] While Rida's religious convictions have not been questioned, Juan Cole has shown that, more than ʿAbduh,[165] Rida explained the spread of religions "in terms of organization and efficiency rather than in terms of the intrinsic truth of the message or the intervention of a supernatural agency."[166] Rida thus resorted to social explanations in his utilitarian view of religion. The integration of sociological, historiographical, and theological premises and arguments is indeed characteristic of the reformists' discourse at large.[167] I suggest that we understand this not as a *combination* of (Islamic, traditional) religion and (Western, modern) secular thought, as the common depiction of Islamic reformism does, but rather as a *transformation* of religion within the epistemic framework of modernity.

---

161 Kerr, *Islamic*, 118.

162 Vatikiotis, P. J. 1958. "Muhammad Abduh and the Quest for a Muslim Humanism." *Islamic Quarterly* 4/4: 145–161. It should not go unmentioned that Vatikiotis also recognized ʿAbduh's turn to social affairs: "The starting-point of Abduh's 'humanist' approach to Islam and an Islamic 'feeling of unity' is his idea that Islam is a 'social religion', which has combined in its message the welfare of man in this world and in the hereafter" (ibid., 151).

163 Ende, "Waren." Lord Cromer was rather certain that ʿAbduh was an agnostic (Cromer, *Modern*, vol. 2: 179 f.). Cromer's decree containing this statement was translated in *al-Muʾayyad* and reprinted in *al-Manar* (Rida, "Kitab Misr"). *Al-Muʾayyad* refuted Cromer's assessment (ibid., 99), as did Rashid Rida in a more extensive discussion of it (idem. 1908. "al-Radd ʿala al-Lurd Krumir." *al-Manar* 11/3: 185–207, here 193–196). See also below: chapter 7 section 4.1.

164 Kedourie, Elie. 1966. *Afghani and Abduh. An Essay on Religious Unbelief and Political Activism in Islam.* London.

165 Cole, Juan Ricardo. 1983. "Rashid Rida on the Bahaʾi Faith: A Utilitarian Theory of the Spread of Religion." *Arab Studies Quarterly* 5: 276–291, here 282.

166 Ibid., 276.

167 As one concrete example, Johann Buessow has recently stressed this integration in ʿAbduh's famous *Risalat al-Tawhid* (Buessow, "Re-imagining," esp. 284).

The turn to society as an autonomous, inner-worldly order presupposes the modern understanding of religion as an abstract entity – a presupposition that has been rather firmly established for the Islamic tradition,[168] and that also reflects itself conceptually in the pertinent Arabic term for 'religion,' *dīn*. While we lack a proper conceptual history of that term, there are clear hints that, from the sixteenth century onward, *dīn* came to be understood as a system of belief independent from its inner-worldly realization[169] and increasingly was conceived of as an autonomous, transcendent sphere.[170] Much is to be said, then, for a convergence of the conceptual history of *dīn* and the much better-researched history of 'religion'[171]. In any case, the Islamic reformists' understanding of *dīn* rather clearly corresponds to the modern concept of 'religion.' The subsumption of Islam under the modern category of religion is also indicated by the 898 instances of *(al-)dīn (al-)islāmī* in *al-Manar*. Hence, it is rather unproblematic to translate *dīn* in *al-Manar* as 'religion.'

Things are very much complicated, however, by the fact that the reformists' conception of *dīn* does not fully encompass their understanding of *islām*, which poses the question of whether "Islam is a religion that is more than just religion"[172] – and, if yes, as what else it then is to be understood. Before discussing systematic attempts to contemplate Islam as a religion, let us first look at studies on the very concept of *islām*. Whereas several studies – of quite varyied quality and with quite divergent findings – have attended to the meaning of *islām* and related words in the Qur'an,[173] we know astonishingly little about the subsequent conceptual history of *islām*.

---

168 See: Tayob, *Religion*.

169 Schulze, Reinhard. 2010. "Die Dritte Unterscheidung: Islam, Religion und Säkularität." In *Religionen – Wahrheitsansprüche – Konflikte: Theologische Perspektiven* ed. by Walter Dietrich and Wolfgang Lienemann: 147–206. Zürich: TVZ, here 178, 199.

170 For a case study on the relegation of 'religious matters' to transcendence in Egypt at the turn to the twentieth century, see: Quadri, Junaid. 2016. "Religion as Transcendence in Modern Islam: Tracking 'Religious Matters' into a Secular(izing) Age." In *Working with A Secular Age. Interdisciplinary Perspectives on Charles Taylor's Master Narrative; with an Afterword by Charles Taylor* ed. by Florian Zemmin, Colin Jager and Guido Vanheeswijck: 331–348. Berlin/Boston: De Gruyter.

171 See: Feil, Ernst. 1986–2007. *Religio* [different subtitles for the individual volumes]. 4 vols. Göttingen: Vandenhoeck & Ruprecht; Glei, Reinhold and Reichmuth, Stefan. 2012. "Religion between Last Judgement, Law and Faith: Koranic *dīn* and its Rendering in Latin Translations of the Koran." *Religion* 42/2: 247–271.

172 See above: 149.

173 Most commendable concerning Qur'anic terms are the studies by Izutsu: Izutsu, Toshihiko. 1965. *The Concept of Belief in Islamic Theology. A Semantic Analysis of îmân and islâm*. Toyko/Yokohama: The Keio Institute of Cultural and Linguistic Studies/Yurindo Publishing; idem.

Over three decades ago, Wilfried Cantwell Smith traced the shifting meaning of *islām* based on a sample of book titles including the term. He observed "a tendency over the centuries and especially in modern times for the connotation of the word 'Islām' gradually to lose its relationship with God, first by shifting from a personal piety to an ideal religious system, a transcendent pattern, then to an external, mundane religious system, and finally by shifting still further from that religious system to the civilization that was its historical expression."[174] While W.C. Smith himself essentially understood Islam as a religion, the term thus also came to denote a civilization. Despite the superficiality of Smith's sources, this observation goes a long way toward explaining why modern Islamic discourses may correspond more with European or Western discourses than with Christian ones.

In a much less widely recognized but more substantial study than the one by W.C. Smith, his namesake and student, Jane Idleman Smith, traced the changing understanding of *islām* based on commentaries on the eight occurrences of *islām* in the Qur'an. Smith selected one Qur'an commentary for each century, choosing for the twentieth century the *Tafsir al-Manar*, which she rightfully regards as the first modern commentary. Smith alerts us to the distinction in this commentary between a "religious Islam" (*al-islām al-dīnī*) and a mere "ethnic or customary Islam" (*al-islām al-jinsī/al-ʿurfī*).[175] For the authors of the *Tafsir al-Manar*, only the "religious Islam" – Islam as a religion – is the true Islam: "Truly *al-dīn*, which is at once the commandment of God and the way in which man responds to that commandment, is *al-islām al-ḥaqīqī* [the true Islam]. In absolute contrast to *al-islām al-ʿurfī*, the conventional religion characterized by *taqlīd* [traditionalism] and *jinsiyya* [ethnicity], true *islām* is the personal submission of the individ-

1966. *Ethico-Religious Concepts in the Qurʾān*. Montreal: McGill University Press. Other studies on *islām* include: Lidzbarski, Mark. 1922. "Salām and Islām." *Zeitschrift für Semitistik und verwandte Gebiete* 1: 85–96; Künstlinger, David. 1935. "'Islām', 'Muslim', 'aslama' im Kurān." *Rocznik Orientalistyczny* 11: 128–137; Ringgren, Helmer. 1949. "Islam, 'aslama and muslim." *Horae Soederblomianae* 2: 1–34; Robson, James. 1954. "'Islām' as a Term." *The Muslim World* 44: 101–109; Kazi, Abdul Khaliq. 1966. "The Meaning of Īmān and Islām in the Qurʿān." *Islamic Studies* 5/3: 227–237; Abdul Rauf, Muhammad. 1967. "Some Notes on the Qur'anic use of the terms Islām and Imān." *The Muslim World* 57: 94–102; Baneth, D. Z. 1971. "What did Muhammad Mean when he Called his Religion Islām? The Original Meaning of Aslama and its Derivatives." *Israel Oriental Studies* 1: 183–190.

174 Smith, Wilfred Cantwell. 1981. "The Historical Development in Islām of the Concept of Islām as an Historical Development." In *On Understanding Islam. Selected Studies:* 41–77. The Hague et al.: Moutin Publishers, here 64f.

175 Smith, Jane Idleman. 1975. *An Historical and Semantic Study of the Term 'islām' as seen in a Sequence of Qur'ān Commentaries.* Montana: Scholars Press of the University, 196f.

ual to God and the universal spirit in which all religions share, the educator of the natural disposition [*al-fiṭra*] and the ideal society attainable when the *dīn* of all men is perfected."[176] Significantly, the validation of religious over customary Islam is not to be understood as negating the worldly and societal relevance of the Islamic religion.

Rather, in the *Tafsir al-Manar*, Islam was defined as a religion detached from its contingent historical manifestations; however, via its internalization by believing Muslims, Islam was also to produce an ideal society. Care has to be taken to avoid understanding this conception in an overly systematic manner. Not only did the Qur'an commentary differ from other writings, but also, and still more fundamentally, the relation of religion and society – and thus the demarcation of these categories – was hotly contested. Nevertheless, Jane Idleman Smith's analysis seems to support the argument that the reconstruction of Islam as *dīn*, and thus as a religion, was modeled on a Protestant template. Johann Buessow, following Reinhard Schulze and others, has recently substantiated this argument of a Protestantization of Islam based on his reading of ʿAbduh's *Risalat al-Tawhid.*[177] The expression 'Protestantization of Islam' foregrounds the fundamental understanding of religion as a transcendent, supra-temporal order, which then – via the believers' conscience and moral behavior – finds its realization in the worldly order.

Concerning the more specifically liberal Protestant template of religion as mere private belief, Dietrich Jung showed that the Islamic reformists directly engaged with but rejected this template: "In their efforts to define the particularities of Islam, Muslim reformers and Islamist thinkers took the universalized model of liberal Protestantism as a major conceptual reference. They juxtaposed Islam against this subjective, spiritual and strongly transcendental construction of modern religion; a process of religious reconstruction in which the idea that Islam is 'more than a religion,' that it, in contradistinction to the Christian faith, represents an all-encompassing way of life, gained hegemony."[178] Significantly, Jung does not follow those essentializing views that maintain the all-encompassing nature of Islam per se, but rather shows how this "essentialist image of Islam" was only constructed in modernity – and this in close interaction between European orientalists and our Islamic reformists.

A holistic discourse addressing all the spheres of life was not peculiar to Islamic reformists, it should be added, but is rather constitutive of intellectual and

176 Ibid., 221; emphases adjusted.
177 Buessow, "Re-imagining," esp. 274.
178 Jung, *Orientalists*, 270.

ideological discourses operating within the setting of the modern expansive nation-state. Khuri-Makdisi identifies the conception of "reform as a total project" as the common core of all *nahḍa* thinkers, in spite of their differing intellectual and political affiliations.[179] The reformists' construction of an essentialist, holistic, and timeless image of Islam, which revolved around the Qur'an as its core, may be regarded as the crucial move for this comprehensive conception of reform. In this process, modern epistemological and secular premises were projected onto the alleged essence of Islam. The integration of modern knowledge was facilitated by positing reason as part of Islam's essence and by even defining Islam as "the religion of reason" (*dīn al-ʿaql*) and "the natural religion" (*dīn al-fiṭra*). In a rather trivial sense, it was argued that the Qur'an already contained the discoveries of modern science. More significantly, Islamic reformists also read the Qur'an as a text about modern society, corresponding to modern sociological theories.[180]

If a "certain permeability of Islamic reformism and contemporary social systems"[181] had already been recognized during Rida's lifetime, the understanding of Islam as a discursive tradition further facilitated the identification of analogies between Islamic reformism and secular European discourses. Aziz al-Azmeh encourages us to look at the actual premises operative in a seemingly purely Islamic discourse centered around the Qur'an: "Islamic reformism's appropriation of what was known as social Darwinism was conditional upon the concepts of social Darwinism, even though the discourse assumed the form of argumentation based on interpreting verses of the Koran: yet these verses were, in this context, nevertheless nothing more than occasions for linking the imperative intellectual authority of the West with the symbolic authority of Islam as represented by the Koran."[182] Using Islamic tradition – and above all its founding text, the Qur'an – as a symbolic authority to articulate modern views obviously also transforms the understanding of that tradition itself. In a profound sense, the expansion of the reformists' Islamic discourse to include all areas of modern life implies a certain secularization of their understanding of Islamic religion itself.

Several authors have pointed to this factual secularization of Islamic discourse under the conditions of the modern nation-state. Thus Sami Zubaida stressed: "Crucially, what is called Islamic reform of *ʿaṣr al-nahḍa* (the Arab Ren-

---

179 Khuri-Makdisi, "The Conceptualization," 93.
180 Van Nispen tot Sevenaer, *Activité*, esp. 121; see below: chapter 10 section 2.2.
181 Laoust, "Le Réformisme," 194.
182 Azmeh, *Islams*, 105f.

aissance) from the nineteenth century includes elements of secularization of religion itself as well as the social spheres of its operation."[183] This is evident especially in the field of law, where, as Ahmad Dallal has shown, Rida reconstructed the views of Islamic authorities to serve his own novel aim of developing "a jurisdiction that covered 'all aspects of life'," thus matching the modern nation-state's jurisdiction.[184] Zubaida, too, refers to Rida's expansion of "religious and Shari'a competence, in theory, to all areas of modern life at the cost of emptying it of its religious content."[185] Or as Aziz al-Azmeh put it: Rida "secularized the shariʿa, and refused to see in this secularization anything but a validation of the shariʿa."[186] Crucial in this regard was a transformation of two concepts of classical Islamic legal theory, the *maqāṣid al-sharīʿa* (ends of the shariʿa) and *maṣlaḥa* (common benefit, public interest). This amounts to a fundamental epistemic shift in the principles of Islamic law,[187] which, it may be added, was increasingly turned into ethics.[188] Ironically, whereas in pre-modern legal theory the *maqāṣid* restrained the possibility of new rulings, in modernity they served to expand this possibility.[189] And the previously rather marginal notion of *maṣlaḥa* was then conceived of as overall public interest, which may overrule individual legal prescriptions. The identification of shariʿa with a continuously negotiable public interest allowed the Islamic reformists to introduce shariʿa as a meta-norm for public discourse, as Armando Salvatore has argued.[190] Subsequently, non-Muslim participants in this discourse also addressed Islamic questions[191] and even appropriated the tropes of Islamic discourse for their own arguments. This additional reference to Islam as culture further complicates the plain

183 Zubaida, "Islam," 444; transliteration adjusted.
184 Dallal, "Appropriating," 357.
185 Zubaida, "Islam," 445.
186 Azmeh, *Islams*, 114; transliteration adjusted.
187 Johnston, David. 2004. "A Turn in the Epistemology and Hermeneutics of Twentieth Century Uṣūl al-Fiqh." *Islamic Law and Society* 11/2: 233–282.
188 Concerning the case of the contemporary Islamic reformist Tariq Ramadan, see: March, Andrew F. 2011. "Law as a Vanishing Mediator in the Theological Ethics of Tariq Ramadan." *European Journal of Political Theory* 10/2: 177–201; Zemmin, "Integrating."
189 Emon, Anver M. 2010. *Islamic Natural Law Theories*. New York: Oxford University Press, 195, also 35f., 187f., 194f., 204f.
190 Salvatore, Armando. 2000. "The Islamic Reform Project in the Emerging Public Sphere: The (Meta-)Normative Redefinition of Shariʿa." In *Between Europe and Islam: Shaping Modernity in a Transcultural Space* ed. by Armando Salvatore and Almut Höfert: 89–108. Brüssel/Berlin/Oxford: Presses Interuniversitaires Europeénnes.
191 Partly due to *al-Manar*'s powerful articulation of a comprehensive Islamic discourse, the Christian editors of *al-Muqtataf* also increasingly addressed Islamic topics (Glaß, *Der Muqtaṭaf*, vol. 1: 190f., vol. 2: 591).

identification of Islam as religion.[192] But even within the reformists' discourse itself, as we have seen, "Islam now addressed two realities simultaneously: religion and secularity."[193]

The reformists did distinguish between religion and secularity – religion and the social – within this overall Islamic discourse. Conceptually,[194] they updated the classical distinction between *ʿibādāt* (matters of worship, religious matters) and *muʿāmalāt* (worldly, social matters) to address the modern order. Qur'anic verses relating to *ʿibādāt* were to be taken literally, whereas concerning the *muʿāmalāt*, God illustrated his intentions by clothing them in historically contingent examples. Here, it was the task of human reason to elaborate answers appropriate for the contemporary context, in the light of God's underlying intentions. These intentions are arguably discernible from, if not identified with, public interest (*maṣlaḥa)* and the ends (*maqāṣid*) of the shariʿa. The reformists validated the use of human reason as *ijtihād*. In pre-modern Islamic legal theory, *ijtihād* was a method of arriving at rulings, which was subject to strict conditions. The reformists both significantly relaxed these conditions and expanded the realm of *ijtihād* far beyond the field of law. Its central counterpart was *taqlīd* – a notion which, in pre-modern times, positively connoted faithfulness to one's own school of law and its founding father, and which was devalued by the reformists as blind, traditionalist, irrational imitation. This opposition between *taqlīd* and *ijtihād* was central to the Islamic reformists; on the political and cultural plain, as well, they attributed Muslims' perceived backwardness to the practice of *taqlīd* at the expense of *ijtihād*.

Abdulkader Tayob has shown that the distinction between *ʿibādāt* and *muʿāmalāt* corresponds with that between *dīn* and *sharʿ* in Rida's political thought.[195] Thus, while Rida rejected a *separation* of religion and politics, as argued by ʿAli ʿAbd al-Raziq,[196] he nevertheless introduced a *distinction* between the two in his conception of an Islamic republic:

"He recognized the deeply religious from the merely religious. He defined *dīn* as something general related to this life and the hereafter, values, and general prin-

---

192 Schulze, Reinhard. 2013. "On Relating Religion to Society and Society to Religion." In *Debating Islam. Negotiating Religion, Europe, and the Self* ed. by Samuel M. Behloul, Susanne Leuenberger and Andreas Tunger-Zanetti: 333–356. Bielefeld: transcript, here 346 ff.

193 Ibid., 347.

194 For a more systematic discernment of this distinction, see below: chapters 9 section 2 and 10 section 3.

195 Tayob, *Religion*, 110 f.

196 See above: 135 f.

ciples. This was religion at a personal, devotional level. The *shar'*, on the other hand, was also religious but was marked by general values and flexibility. One gets the impression that, with respect to this *shar'*, Rida was more concerned about emphasizing the changing character of the latter than the permanent features of *dīn*. Politics was engaged with issues marked by change and temporality, while *dīn* was concerned about the permanent. The *shar'* of Rida could be compared with the politics of 'Abd al-Raziq, while they both agreed on the meaning of *dīn*."[197]

While a related example of the distinction between religion and politics and between a religious and a secular sphere in an Islamic reformist discourse will be discussed below,[198] three points ought to be considered here: firstly, the categories of religion and society were operative, and the Islamic reformists basically distinguished between them, however these categories were then related to each other. Secondly, as the demarcation of the religious and the secular – of religion and society – was hotly contested and may moreover shift within a single author's writings, no such fixed demarcation can necessarily be expected. After all, the ideal secularist distinction between religion and society is also difficult to maintain when looking more closely at discursive practices or institutional arrangements. Thirdly, with Charles Taylor, we have seen that the secular may well be embedded in a theological framework. Since an open reading of the immanent frame is equally as possible as a closed one, the primary question is whether such an immanent frame was imagined and, subsequently, conceptualized, not least as 'society.'

The Islamic reformists' validation of immanent natural and social laws based on theological premises – that is, based on an open reading of the immanent frame – is demonstrated most clearly in the concept of *sunan allāh* (God's laws or ways; sg. *sunnat allāh*), to which the *Tafsir al-Manar* gave unprecedented importance. In his comprehensive analysis of that concept,[199] van Nispen tot Sevenaer has shown how 'Abduh, but especially and more systematically Rida,[200] attributed an ontological status to these *sunan*. 'Abduh and Rida foregrounded these laws as underlying the whole of God's creation and determining not only the natural, but also the social world, as well as human beings' destiny

197 Tayob, *Religion*, 111.
198 See below: chapter 9 section 2; for an analogy between Rida and Gökalp in this regard, see: Dressler, "Rereading," 522.
199 Van Nispen tot Sevenaer, *Activité*; see also, briefly but pointedly: Kerr, *Islamic*, 130.
200 Van Nispen tot Sevenaer, *Activité*, esp. 98.

in the afterworld.[201] These *sunan* were thought to be stable and unchanging. While almighty God can theoretically intervene in this world at will, he would do so based on these *sunan*,[202] which are explicitly equated with natural laws in the *Tafsir al-Manar.*[203] Relatedly, Rida does not rule out the hypothetical possibility of miracles, which he understands as God's temporary deviation from his *sunan*. But he stresses that no such miracles have occurred since the time of the Prophet, whose credibility God wanted to thus underwrite.[204] This essentially amounts to a natural universe governed by internal laws of cause and effect, which can and shall be discerned and acted upon by human reason. Significantly, these stable natural, but also social laws are not seen as questioning the existence of God – as a subtraction story would have it – but rather are validated as confirming it.[205]

This view of a stable and intelligible universe is closely connected to the imagination of an autonomous social order. Thus, departing from Rida's criticism of the continued belief in miracles, Richard van Leeuwen discerned "the re-definition of the concepts of religion and society as interacting, but separate entities"[206] as central to Rida's "program of religious reform."[207] The *Tafsir al-Manar* is indeed mainly interested in those *sunan allāh* explicitly addressing social life. Here, the concept of *sunan ijtimāʿiyya* is used synonymously with *sunan allāh*, especially to "indicate the 'sociological laws' of modern sociology."[208] If human society is based on firm and unchanging laws, which can be discovered and acted upon by human beings, then every group of people is responsible for their own state of society.

This understanding shows itself most clearly in the new interpretation and prominence Islamic reformists gave to verse 13:11, which states, "God does not change a people until they change themselves." In pre-modern times, this verse was almost exclusively interpreted as meaning that God punishes sinful people. The Islamic reformists foregrounded this verse as proving that a people will be successful if they, as moral beings created by God, adhere to their innate

---

201 Ibid., esp. 26ff.
202 Ibid., esp. 142.
203 Ibid., esp. 79, 84.
204 Ibid., 74f.; see also: Kerr, *Islamic*, 119f.
205 Van Nispen tot Sevenaer, *Activité*, esp. 77f., 101.
206 Van Leeuwen, Richard. 2008. "Islamic Reformism and the Secular: Rashid Ridâ's Theory on Miracles." In *Religion and Its Other. Secular and Sacral Concepts and Practices in Interaction* ed. by Heike Bock, Jörg Feuchter and Michi Knecht: 64–78. Frankfurt/New York: Campus, here 77.
207 Ibid., 67.
208 Van Nispen tot Sevenaer, *Activité*, 106, transl. F.Z., see also 115, 139fn45.

natural disposition (*fiṭra*) and follow his *sunan*. Thus the reformists did not attribute the allegedly sad state of Muslim society to God's punishment, but rather to the Muslims' neglect of his *sunan*. Complementarily, the success of European societies is attributed to their acting according to these *sunan*. This illustrates the presumed "objective and basically secular character" of these *sunan*.[209] Islamic reformists, pointing to European success and progress, often add that this will not last, since Europeans have detached themselves from a firm religious basis. According to the reformists, it is thus up to Muslims to combine the respect for God's *sunan*, now epitomized by European societies, with the religious conscience they preserved and thus to construct a lasting, prosperous, and ideal society.

I have drawn on existing literature to substantiate – from various angles – my argument that the protagonists of *al-Manar* imagined a distinct, inner-worldly order and conceived of human society as a rather autonomous sphere. Indeed, in a general manner, one may conclude that "anybody who now studies modern Islamic traditions will see that the categorial (non-institutional) separation of religion and society is constitutive for their interpretation of the world."[210] Mahmood Haddad maintained that "what the Manarists/Salafists were after was a fusion or unity of religion and society rather than of religion and state."[211] However, while these assessments are very convincing indeed, nowhere does any author explicate how they identified 'society' in *al-Manar*.

While studies in Arabic do not have to confront the hermeneutic problem of translation,[212] they unfortunately do not provide substantial insights concerning the transpiring of the pertinent Arabic concepts for society and the social. Arabic literature does indeed point to the duality of religious and social reforms (*al-iṣlāḥ al-dīnī wa-l-ijtimāʿī*) in *al-Manar* and also speaks of *mujtamaʿ*, the present Arabic term for 'society,' as a central object of the reformists' efforts.[213] However, these studies do not locate *mujtamaʿ* within *al-Manar*, but rather project this now-established term back onto these texts, or even into the reformists' minds – very much analogous to the now-universal usage of 'society.'

---

209 Ibid., 125, transl. F.Z.

210 Schulze, "On Relating," 345.

211 Haddad, "The Manarists," 57. Especially for ʿAbduh, a focus on societal reform rather than politics had been discerned some time ago (for example: Kerr, *Islamic Reform*, 152).

212 See above: 21f.

213 For example: Qarni, ʿIzzat. 2006. *Tarikh al-Fikr al-Siyasi wa-l-Ijtimaʿi fi Misr al-Haditha (1834–1914)*. Cairo: al-Hayʾa al-Misriyya al-ʿAmma li-l-Kitab, 423.

Thus, whereas chapter 2 has shown that the conceptual history of 'society' is rather well established, even if the concept's historicity and normativity is often ignored, the following chapter underwrites how little we know about the conceptual history of *mujtama*ʿ or other Arabic terms corresponding to 'society.'

Chapter 6
The Arabic Saddle Period and Arabic Terms for 'Society'

1 The Arabic Saddle Period and Socio-Political Concepts

> "[A]ll cognitive experience and its classification is conveyable in any existing language. Whenever there is deficiency, terminology may be qualified and amplified by loanwords or loan-translations, neologism or semantic shifts, and finally, by circumlocutions."
> – Robert Jakobsen, 1959[1]

In recent years, heightened attention has been paid to concepts in non-European languages, a vast but hitherto remarkably unexplored field of research. Such research is facilitated by the digitization of large text corpora, and it will certainly receive a further boost from the ongoing development of search tools handling non-Latin scripts. However, while technical possibilities facilitate research programs, they hardly account for their inception. The intellectual – and potentially political – interest in non-European concepts can largely be attributed, I suggest, to acknowledging the particularity of secular European modernity and thus of concepts in European languages.

This acknowledgment has been prompted from various sides, as I showed in the introduction, where I also elaborated on my own approach to concepts via a discussion of the pioneering volume *Global Conceptual History in Asia.* I engaged with this volume for two reasons: firstly, because it combines conceptual history with theoretical considerations of Eurocentrism and "multiple modernities"; secondly, because Khuri-Makdisi's contribution on "The Conceptualization of the Social" in Arabic is very relevant to this study. In my discussion of both Khuri-Makdisi's contribution and the overall volume, I also expounded my own handling of 'word,' 'concept,' and 'idea.' It was necessary to elaborate these points, which intersect with the problem of translation, at the beginning of this study, in order to demonstrate why I then departed from particular European concepts.

The one point worth recalling here is that the contributors to *Global Conceptual History* agreed that the time between 1860 and 1940 constituted a saddle pe-

1 Jakobsen, Robert. 1959. "On Linguistic Aspects of Translation." In *On Translation* ed. by Reuben A. Brower: 232–239. Cambridge, Mass.: Harvard University Press, here 233.

https://doi.org/10.1515/9783110545845-007

riod across Asian languages, including Arabic.[2] A current project at the University of Bonn – digitizing Arabic, Persian, and Turkish newspapers and journals – also focuses on this "Neareastern and Asian 'saddle period' between 1860 and 1945."[3] A saddle period designates a time when condensed conceptual change and terminological contestation over shared semantic fields intersects with rapid social and political transformations.[4] In the case of colonial Egypt, such transformations were partly induced by European powers. Since, as we have seen in chapter 4, European influence and hegemony was visible on the military and political, social and economic, cultural and intellectual levels, it should come as no surprise that it also left traces in the Arabic language. In fact, previous literature on changes in Arabic socio-political vocabulary during the modern saddle period very much focused on this impact of European-language terminology, based on the now-untenable equation of modernization with Westernization.

This is most clearly the case in Ami Ayalon's study *Language and Change in the Arab Middle East*, published in 1987,[5] which is still the only English-language monograph dedicated to terminological change in modern Arabic.[6] More overtly than in his works on the Arabic press, which I had referred to above for their useful collection of factual pieces of information, Ayalon here contrasts traditional, static, Middle Eastern with modern, dynamic, European societies.[7] "The evolution of modern political discourse," as the subtitle of this book reads, is thus solely attributed to the integration of European terms into Arabic vocabulary during the nineteenth century. What is more, in Ayalon's view, Arab writers may misunderstand the meanings and ideas expressed by these European

---

2 See esp.: Schulz-Forberg, *Global*, 5 (interconnections and conceptual innovation then became especially significant since the 1880s).

3 http://www.translatio.uni-bonn.de/arabische-persische-und-osmanisch-tuerkische-zeitschriften (accessed Oct. 24, 2015).

4 For Koselleck's metaphor of the saddle period and its usefulness for this study, see above: chapter 2 section 1.1.

5 Ayalon, Ami. 1987. *Language and Change in the Arab Middle East: The Evolution of Modern Political Discourse*. New York: Oxford University Press.

6 Wael Abu-'Uksa most recently suggested the decades between 1820 and 1860 as the formative period of modern political concepts (Abu-'Uksa, Wael. 2016. *Freedom in the Arab World: Concepts and Ideologies in Arabic Thought in the Nineteenth Century*. Cambridge: Cambridge University Press). His work appeared after the completion of this study and cannot be integrated here. Suffice it to say that it does not alter the core premises and arguments of this chapter, and that one may still locate the Arabic saddle period in the second half of the nineteenth and first half of the twentieth centuries. See my forthcoming review of Abu-'Uksa's book in *Die Welt des Islams*.

7 See Ayalon, *Language*, esp. 3.

terms.[8] This presumes an original, self-sufficient standard and a deficient imitation, quite in contrast to a view of entangled histories and creative appropriation. Ayalon's basic premises lead to his rather narrow focus on the adoption of European ideas and terms. He thus largely leaves out potential alternative avenues of modern Arabic political discourse, as well as factors accounting for the specificities of this discourse (other than the alleged constraints of tradition). Despite these major points of criticism, Ayalon's study yields several insights, which will be presented below in conjunction with findings from other studies.

Like Ayalon, Helga Rebhan – in her German dissertation on *The History and Function of some Political Termini in Nineteenth-Century Arabic*, published in 1986 – focuses on the Arabic reception of European political terms.[9] Like Ayalon, she mainly studies texts published in Cairo and Beirut, the two hubs of Arab printing at the time. Unlike Ayalon, who repeatedly stresses the Arabic language's resistance to change, Rebhan recalls the reception of Greek writings in the ninth century,[10] often dubbed the 'first wave of translation.' Also unlike Ayalon, she mentions that changes in the meaning of Arabic terms, which led to their modern semantic range, sometimes predated European influence.[11] However, her interest also lies in the Arabic reception of European political vocabulary. She, too, finds that Arab writers sometimes misunderstood European terms or did not render them adequately, while the Arabic terms mostly conveyed the same meanings as the European terms they were intended to express.[12] Attending primarily to the use of specific Arabic terms to render specific European terms, Rebhan only occasionally and in a secondary sense elaborates on the meanings these terms conveyed. Herein lies a major difference between her approach and my own, which departs from the modern self-understanding and treats specific terms as secondary manifestations of this self-understanding.

In addition to the two monographs by Ayalon and Rebhan, English-language research dedicated to Arabic socio-political concepts includes a very broad study by Bernard Lewis and two rather specific articles by Leon Zolondek. Lewis gives an overview of terms central to "the political language of Islam" – which, according to him, originates in the Qur'an and the Sunna.[13] Using Arabic, Persian, and

8 See ibid., esp. 68.

9 Rebhan, Helga. 1986. *Geschichte und Funktion einiger politischer Termini im Arabischen des 19. Jahrhunderts (1798–1882)*. Wiesbaden: Otto Harrassowitz.

10 Ibid., 1.

11 Ibid., 7.

12 Ibid., 4.

13 Lewis, Bernard. 1988. *The Political Language of Islam*. Chicago, Ill. et al.: University of Chicago Press.

Turkish sources, Lewis traces these terms into the present; that is, into the year 1986, when the Islamic Revolution in Iran was a major concern for scholars of Islam. Due only in part to the vastness of his corpus, Lewis's study amounts to an overly schematic presentation of Islamic political thought, which is contrasted with an equally simplified view of secular Christian or Western political thought.[14] While Lewis mentions the impact of the West on the modern transformation of Islamic languages, he only briefly attends to this period and does not add significantly to the studies by Ayalon and Rebhan.

In the 1960s, Leon Zolondek offered the first considerations concerning "The Language of the Muslim Reformers of the Late Nineteenth Century,"[15] followed by an article specifically dedicated to the term *al-shaʿb* (the people).[16] Many of Zolondek's arguments must be taken with caution, due to his rather selective approach to quite scattered sources. Aiming at systematic findings, Zolondek hardly allows for divergent usages of a term by a single writer – whence, for example, he suggests a clear contrast between Muhammad ʿAbduh's and al-Kawakibi's usages of *umma*.[17] While such overly systematic statements are unconvincing, I shall refer to some of Zolondek's findings concerning the usage of *al-shaʿb* below.

These few studies in English and German explicitly dedicated to conceptual change in nineteenth-century Arabic can be complemented with a number of studies on linguistic and lexical changes, which, however, are of little value for our core interest.[18] A number of Arabists have attended to grammatical or morphological changes in modern Arabic.[19] Among the Arabic literature on the subject, the work of Muhammad Sawaʿi stands out. In addition to providing a general overview, his work on *The Crisis of the Arabic Terminology in the Nineteenth Century* (*Azmat al-Mustalah al-ʿArabi*) focused on Rifaʿa Rafiʿa al-Tahtawi's and Ahmad Faris al-Shidyaq's use of terminology and their contributions

14 This contrast between Western and Islamic political thought reigns supreme, even though Lewis mentions some commonalities due to the common human predicament (ibid., 8 ff., 22 f.).
15 Zolondek, Leon. 1963. "The Language of the Muslim Reformers of the late Nineteenth Century." *Islamic Culture* 37/3: 155–162.
16 Idem. 1965. "Ash-Shaʿb in Arabic Political Literature of the 19th Century." *Die Welt des Islams* 10/1–2: 1–16.
17 Idem., "The Language," 156 ff.
18 In chapter four, I have already mentioned studies attending to the concepts of *islām* and *dīn* ('religion'); see above: 167.
19 See, for example: Stetkevych, Jaroslav. 1970. *The Modern Arabic Literary Language*. Chicago: Chicago University Press.

to lexical change.[20] Sawaʿi substantiated his findings in an English article on al-Tahtawi[21] and a monograph on al-Shidyaq[22]. In the latter work, he does pay some attention to notions of civilization and progress.[23] However, Sawaʿi is mainly interested in how these two pioneering translators rendered into Arabic rather specific legal, technical, or cultural terms they encountered in French literature, such as *journal, théatre, académie, télégraph*, or *boulevard.*

Literature that is not primarily dedicated to terminological change, but rather interested in the evolution and representation of modern socio-political order in the Arab world, tends to be more sensitive to the epistemic relevance of concepts. Thus in the following section I will collect tentative hints concerning Arabic terms for 'society' from this literature. First, however, I shall summarize the relevant insights contained in the above-mentioned studies.

Among the European languages from which Arabic authors appropriated terms, Italian figured most prominently at the beginning of the nineteenth century, but was replaced rather quickly by French, which continued to be the dominant European language throughout the nineteenth and early twentieth centuries, with English gaining importance toward the end of the nineteenth century.[24] These languages were also used, in the order just mentioned, as sources for Ottoman Turkish, which was a major mediator for terms from European languages into Arabic throughout the period, not least due to its having been the official language of the Egyptian government until 1856.[25] The reorientation from Italian to French was closely associated with Muhammad ʿAli sending his student missions, which he had initiated in the 1810s, to France rather than to Italy. The government school of translation – and especially its director, Rifaʿa Rafiʿ al-Tahtawi (1801/1802–1873), who had been the imam of the 1826 student mission to Paris – played an important role in rendering European-language terms into Arabic.[26]

20 Sawaʿi, Muhammad. 1999. *Azmat al-Mustalah al-ʿArabi fi al-Qarn al-Tasiʿ ʿAshar: Muqaddima Tarikhiyya ʿAmma.* Damascus/Beirut: al-Maʿhad al-Fransi li-l-Dirasat al-ʿArabiyya bi-Dimashq/ Dar al-Gharb al-Islami.
21 Sawaie, Mohammed [= idem]. 2000. "Rifaʿa Rafi al-Tahtawi and His Contribution to the Lexical Development of Modern Literary Arabic." *International Journal of Middle East Studies* 32/3: 395–410.
22 Sawaʿi, Muhammad [= idem]. 2013. *al-Hadatha wa-Mustalahat al-Nahda al-ʿArabiyya fi al-Qarn al-Tasiʿa ʿAshar. Dirasa fi Mufradat Ahmad Faris al-Shdyaq fi Jaridat "al-Jawa'ib"*. Beirut: al-Mu'assasa al-'Arabiyya li-l-Dirasat wa-l-Nashr.
23 Ibid., 277–297.
24 Rebhan, *Geschichte*, 12 f.
25 Ayalon, *Language*, 5 f.; Rebhan, *Geschichte*, 11 f.
26 Sawaie, "Rifaʿa;" Ayalon, *Language*, esp. 18, 36–40, 70–77.

In addition to direct translations, lexicographical projects, and travel accounts, journals were instrumental in the spread of new terminology,[27] in tune with their vital role in the appropriation and dissemination of European ideas, as shown in chapter 4 section 3.1. Rebhan and Zolondek convincingly stress the pioneering role of Syrian Christians in the appropriation of European socio-political concepts.[28] Ayalon and Rebhan agree that semantic and lexical change had slowed down significantly by the last decade of the nineteenth century, when Arabic terms had basically acquired their new meanings.[29] This assessment, however, cannot possibly mean that these terms and meanings were no longer contested. Rather, by the end of the nineteenth century, modern socio-political terms and meanings had become readily available to writers of Arabic, who nevertheless made quite various use of them and thus contributed to their continuing contestation, evolution, and dissemination.

Concerning the ways of integrating terms and concepts from European languages into Arabic, Muhammad Sawaʿi distinguishes four different means: (1) using existing Arabic terms, which acquire new meanings; (2) transcribing European terms, such as *jūrnāl* (for *journal*) or *iliktrisītīh* (for *eléctricité*); (3) translating European terms literally – for example, *Dīwān rusul al-ʿummālāt* for *chambre des députés*; (4) designating places or countries with European names instead of their previous Arabic names.[30] The first two options are those most often resorted to and, in fact, are the only two means distinguished by Rebhan.[31] Particularly in their initial attempts to translate European terms, Arabic authors – not least al-Tahtawi – resorted to phonematic borrowings of European terms. This method was criticized by al-Shidyaq (1805–1887), who advocated the usage of existing Arabic vocabulary to render new meanings and preferred to stick to Arabic morphology when creating neologisms.[32] This approach increasingly became much more dominant, and Arabic terms replaced phonemetic borrowings rather quickly.[33] Thus, *jūrnāl* was replaced by *majalla*, *iliktrisītīh* by *kahrabāʾ*, and *barlamān* (parliament) by *majlis al-shaʿb/al-umma/niyābī*. At first, there were three alternatives in Arabic for rendering 'socialism' – the transcription *sūsiyālism* and two

27 Ayalon, *Language*, 13 f.; Rebhan, *Geschichte*, 4 ff.

28 See, for example, Zolondek, "ash-Shaʿb," esp. 14; Rebhan, *Geschichte*, 32. Ayalon found a rather homogeneous usage of terminology across Arab countries and between Muslim and Christian thinkers (Ayalon, *Language*, 9 f.).

29 Rebhan, *Geschichte*, 120; Ayalon, *Language*, 8 f.

30 Sawaʿi, *Azmat*, 85 f.

31 Rebhan, *Geschichte*, 3; Ayalon distinguishes three modes (Ayalon, *Language*, 6).

32 Sawaʿi, *al-Hadatha*, 10 f.

33 Rebhan, *Geschichte*, 3; Ayalon, *Language*, 7.

neologisms modeled on classical Arabic morphology, *ijtimāʿiyya* and *ishtirākiyya*. As mentioned above, it was the latter term, derived from the root *sh-r-k* (to share), which won the day over *ijtimāʿiyya*, derived from the root *j-m-ʿ* (to gather or unite).[34] Overall, the increasingly dominant means for expressing new terms and ideas was not to coin neologisms, but rather to re-semantize classical Arabic terms.

A prime example in this regard is the term *umma*, which, in the second half of the nineteenth century, came to mean 'nation.'[35] Talal Asad stresses the fundamental epistemic shift underlying the acquisition of this new meaning:

"The fact that the expression *al-umma al-ʿarabiyya* is used today to denote the 'Arab nation' represents a major conceptual transformation by which *umma* is cut off from the theological predicates that gave it its universalizing power and made to stand for an imagined community that is equivalent to a total society, limited and sovereign like other limited and sovereign nations in a secular (social) world. The *ummat al-muslimīn* (the Islamic *umma*) is ideologically not 'a society' onto which state, economy, and religion can be mapped. It is not limited nor sovereign: not limited, for unlike Arab nationalism's notion of *al-umma al-ʿarabiyya*, it can and eventually should embrace all of humanity, and not sovereign for it is subject to God's authority. It is therefore a mistake to regard it as an 'archaic' (because 'religious') community that predates the modern nation."[36]

It was only modern Islamic thinkers engaging the nation-state who appropriated and remodeled the concept of *umma* so as to represent a sovereign entity "onto which state, economy, and religion can be mapped."[37]

That said, pre-modern meanings of *umma* included references to both religious and secular collectivities – if I may, for the sake of argument, project back this categorical modern distinction. The point is that it would be misleading to consider the second major meaning *umma* carries today, next to 'nation' – that

---

34 Rebhan, *Geschichte*, 103–106; Reid, "The Syrian," 190; see above: 51f., 124.

35 See Rebhan, *Geschichte*, 24–35; Ayalon, *Language*, 26–28.

36 Asad, "Religion," 189f.; transliteration adjusted.

37 This insight, formulated by Asad, does not yet inform Charles Wendell's study on *The Evolution of the Egyptian National Image*, which assumes a primitive *socio-political* community of Muslims founded by Muhammad and presents Ahmad Lutfi al-Sayyid's liberalist ideal of the nation-state as the most advanced emancipation from this original notion of *umma* (Wendell, Charles. 1972. *The Evolution of the Egyptian National Image from its Origins to Ahmad Luṭfī al-Sayyid*. Berkeley: University of California Press).

of a 'religious community' – as the only traditional one. The classical semantic range of *umma*, which is not to be understood as the term's true meaning,[38] was indeed not at all limited to designating a 'community of believers.' Rather, the term could also refer to a group with common characteristics other than belief, along with its additional references to the beliefs of a group itself, to a single exemplary person, or to a certain time span.[39] The major constituents of a collectivity other than common belief or unbelief included ethnicity and language, but also locality.[40] Furthermore, in the famous Constitution of Medina, the *umma* does not refer to an exclusive community of Muslims, but also includes Jews.[41] The liberal-leaning philosopher Nasif Nassar even maintains that, in pre-modern times, an *umma* was always constituted mainly by secular characteristics.[42] Other contemporary authors, in turn, understand *umma* as a community of Muslims only, and they see belonging to this community as fundamentally contradicting the idea of belonging to a nation(-state).[43] However, it seems that these religious and secular dimensions of *umma* were only categorically distinguished in modernity.

---

38 But compare: Giannakis, Elias. 1983. "The Concept of Ummah." *Graeco-Arabica* 2: 100 – 111.

39 See: al-Ahsan, Abdullah. 1992. *Ummah or Nation? Identity Crisis in Contemporary Muslim Society.* Leicester: The Islamic Foundation, 10 – 26; Nassar, Nasif. 2003 [1978]. *Mafhum al-Umma bayna al-Din wa-l-Tarikh: Dirasa fi Madlul al-Umma fi al-Turath al-ʿArabi al-Islami.* Beirut: Dar al-Taliʿya li-l-Tibaʿa wa-l-Nashr, 16 – 20. This plurality of meanings already in the Qur'an is ignored by: Massignon, Louis. 1946. "L'Umma et ses synonymes: notion de 'communauté sociale' en Islam." *Revue des Études Islamiques* 2: 151 – 157.

40 Haarmann distinguishes three classical meanings of *umma:* The community of Muhammad; antithetical to that, a collectivitiy of unbelievers or barbarians; and, neutrally, reference to an ethnic collectivity (Haarmann, Ulrich. 1996. "Glaubensvolk und Nation im islamischen und lateinischen Mittelalter." In *Berichte und Abhandlungen* ed. by Berlin-Brandenburgische Akademie der Wissenschaften, vol. 2: 161 – 199. Berlin: Akademie-Verlag, here 176 ff.) For the centrality of language in pre-modern and modern understandings of *umma* alike, see: Suleiman, Yasir. 2003. *The Arabic Language and National Identity: A Study in Ideology.* Edinburgh: Edinburgh University Press. The secular constitution of a collectivity might, in view of the following quotation, even have been the precondition for mapping a common belief onto it: "Those who linguistically or ethnically or locally belonged together in such a way that God can make known to them His will by one envoy form an *umma*" (Hurgronje, Christiaan Snouck. 1957. *Selected Works of C. Snouck Hurgronje, ed. in English and in French by G.-H- Bousquet and J. Schacht.* Leiden: Brill, 10).

41 For a discussion of different estimations concerning the exact status of the Jews and the meaning of *umma* in the constitution, see: Humphreys, Stephen R. 1991. *Islamic History: A Framework for Inquiry.* Princeton, NJ: Princeton University Press, 92 – 98.

42 Nassar, *Mafhum.*

43 Al-Ahsan, *Ummah*; al-Barghouti, Tamim. 2008. *The Umma and the Dawla: The Nation-State and the Arab Middle East.* London: Pluto Press.

Equally important, and of even more immediate relevance for my argument, *umma* in the nineteenth and early twentieth centuries was a very flexible term, used not only to render the meanings of 'nation' and 'community of believers,' but also to express a number of other concepts. Zolondek argued that Islamic reformists preferred to use *umma* to express the rights of 'the people,' deliberately avoiding the term *al-shaʿb*, due to its secular connotations.[44] My analysis of *al-Manar* will somewhat modify this interpretation by showing that Islamic reformists also appropriated the term *al-shaʿb*. Zolondek, however, points to a significant phenomenon – namely, the Islamic reformists' advancement of religiously connoted terms from a classical Arabic-Islamic vocabulary as a deliberate alternative to secularly connoted terms.

While the flexibility and broad semantic range of *umma* has been recognized, the possibility that the term also expresses the concept of 'society' – as I argue in this study – has not yet been explored, as transpires from the following section, which collects existing hints at Arabic terms for 'society.'

2 'Society' in Arabic: *al-Hay'a al-Ijtimāʿiyya* and *Mujtamaʿ*

The modern social imaginary of society can be expressed via – and thus discerned from – a range of concepts, as well as from "images, stories, legends, etc."[45] more broadly. However, the tendency of the modern social imaginary not only to interpret, but also to order social reality hinges on the conceptualization of categories of meaning and order. And, as shown in part A, the concept of 'society' is most constitutive of the modern self-understanding. In this section, I first collect hints from literature on Arabic terms conveying the European concept of 'society' and then complement these by looking at how contemporaneous dictionaries rendered the supposedly pertinent Arabic terms for 'society' into French and English, and which Arabic terms they gave for *société* and 'society.'

If one was interested in the conception of society laid down in a contemporary Arabic text, one would certainly focus on the term *mujtamaʿ*, which today is rather firmly established for expressing the concept of 'society' – whether in its relation to religion,[46] to the state,[47] or for envisioning an Islamic order of soci-

44 Zolondek, "The Language," 156–160; idem., "Ash-Shaʿb," 1; see also: Ayalon, *Language*, 51.
45 Taylor, *A Secular Age*, 172.
46 For example: Saʿb, Adib. 1995. *al-Din wa-l-Mujtamaʿ: Ruʾya Mustaqbaliyya*. Beirut: Dar al-Nahar.

ety.[48] While the establishment of *mujtamaʿ* in the sense of 'society' can be traced back to the 1960s,[49] we are basically left with educated guesswork concerning the term's evolution. I should add that of the vast literature dealing with Arab views on society in the nineteenth and twentieth centuries, almost no author states the Arabic terms based on which he or she discerned these views. Moreover, some authors refer to the allegedly predominant Arabic terms for 'society,' even though the terms are not present in the texts from which they claim to discern an understanding of society.[50] This goes some way toward explaining the rather preliminary character of the following estimations concerning the evolution of *mujtamaʿ*.

Discussing the shariʿa court reforms proposed by ʿAbduh in 1899, Talal Asad suggests: "The modern Arabic word for society (*mujtamaʿ*) [was] not yet linguistically available, nor [was] the modern concept to which it now refers."[51] According to Asad, at that time, *mujtamaʿ* only meant 'meeting place' – he writes that *mujtamaʿ* as an expression of the distinctly modern concept of society "gained currency only in the 1930s."[52] Here, Asad refers to a finding by Jaroslav Stetkevych, who, based on his analysis of dictionaries, argued that "the term *mujtamaʿ* does not become current until some time around 1930."[53] Reinhard Schulze, in

---

47 For example: al-Raʿi, al-Ab Basim. 2011. *al-Mujtamaʿ wa-l-Dawla: Ashkaluhuma wa-Tahawwuluhuma fi al-Falsafa al-Siyasiyya al-Gharbiyya al-Muʿasira*. Beirut: Dar al-Farabi.

48 For example: al-Samaluti, Nabil. 2007. *Binaʾ al-Mujtamaʿ al-Islami wa-Nuzumuhu*. Beirut: Dar wa-Maktabat al-Hilal.

49 A German-Arabic dictionary from 1964 distinguishes between various senses of the German *Gesellschaft* ('society'). *Mujtamaʿ* exclusively renders the meanings of 'society' as overall social sphere and as a social order (Krahl, Günther. 1964. *Deutsch-Arabisches Wörterbuch*. Leipzig: VEB, 176).

50 For example, Marwa ElShakry writes, concerning ʿAbduh's understanding of social laws (*sunan al-ijtimāʿ*): "These 'social laws' were also absolute natural laws, though in this case they governed the operations of 'society' (*al-hayʾa al-ijtimāʿiyya* or *al-mujtamaʿ*) (an increasingly popular nineteenth-century neologism in Arabic, as in English and French)" (ElShakry, *Reading*, 176; transliteration adjusted). The article in *al-Manar* which she refers to – of which the author, in view of the lack of a signature or other reference, seems to have been Rida – does indeed speak of *sunnat al-ijtimāʿ* and *al-sunan al-ijtimāʿiyya*, but not of the alleged terms for 'society' (Rida, Rashid. 1906. "al-Haqq, al-Batil wa-l-Quwa." *al-Manar* 9/1: 52–65, here 55). ElShakry (346fn59) also refers to an article by Shibli Shumayyil, allegedly entitled "Tarikh al-Ijtimaʿ al-Tabiʿi" and published in *al-Muqtataf* 9 (1884): 523–593. However, in the ninth volume of *al-Muqtataf*, published in 1885, we find instead two articles by Shumayyil entitled "al-Ijtimaʿ al-Bashari wa-l-ʿUmran" (Human Society and Civilization) and starting on pages 523 and 593.

51 Asad, *Formations*, 229.

52 Ibid., 198fn24; idem., "Religion," 195fn25.

53 Stetkevych, *The Modern*, 25.

turn, maintains that *mujtamaʿ* had already been established since the middle of the nineteenth century.[54] Allegedly related to the reception of the English concept of 'society,' according to Schulze, *mujtamaʿ* gradually replaced the notions of *ijtimāʿ* and *al-hay'a al-ijtimāʿiyya*, which he translates as 'assembly' and 'social cosmos.'[55] Resting on rather thin empirical bases, the above assessments thus differ greatly as to when *mujtamaʿ* was established. However, Schulze and Asad both suggest that *mujtamaʿ* came into usage specifically for the purpose of expressing the modern concept of 'society.' While not uncontested,[56] this hypothesis is worth testing. My analysis of *al-Manar* will thus consider the possibility that an epistemic shift was involved in *mujtamaʿ* replacing *al-hay'a al-ijtimāʿiyya*.[57]

In any case, several authors suggest that *al-hay'a al-ijtimāʿiyya* continued to be the dominant Arabic term for 'society' throughout the nineteenth and well into the twentieth century. Ilham Khuri-Makdisi, whose analysis of "Conceptualizations of the Social in Nineteenth-Century Arabic" I discussed in the introduction, finds – in tune with Asad – that "the term that is presently used to refer to society, *mujtamaʿ* [...], while not completely absent in that period, seems to have become dominant in the 1930s to early 1940s."[58] Prior to that, the term predominantly used to conceptualize society, according to Khuri-Makdisi, was *al-hay'a al-ijtimāʿiyya*,[59] which she translates as "the social body/social configuration." I will come back to her findings on the usage of that composite by Christian thinkers in the following section. For now, it is worth noting that Khuri-Makdisi seems to suggest that *al-hay'a al-ijtimāʿiyya* could express the modern idea of society equally as well as *mujtamaʿ*. Helga Rebhan, whose aforementioned study ends in the year 1882, only briefly mentions that "'society' in the nineteenth century was designated as *al-hay'a al-ijtimāʿiyya* (social organization) or *al-ijtimāʿ*

---

54 Schulze, *Der Koran*, 144f. Schulze here (144fn76) refers to a single usage of *mujtamaʿ* in a work by al-Tuwayrani. I did not find any further instances in that work (al-Tuwayrani, Hasan Husni. 1888. *al-Nashr al-Zahri fi Rasa'il al-Nasr al-Dahri*. [Istanbul]: Mahmud Bey).

55 Schulze, *Der Koran*, 144; idem., "On Relating," 346; idem., "Die Dritte," 200.

56 Marilyn Booth is skeptical concerning the relevance Asad attributes to the establishment of *mujtamaʿ* (Booth, Marilyn. 2004. "[Review of:] Talal Asad, Formations of the Secular: Christianity, Islam, Modernity." *Bryn Mawr Review of Comparative Literature* 4/2. http://www.brynmawr.edu/bmrcl/Summer2004/Asad.html [accessed May 30, 2014]).

57 See below: chapter 8 section 3.

58 Khuri-Makdisi, "The Conceptualization," 187fn6. Khuri-Makdisi does not refer to Asad or Stetkevych.

59 Ibid., 187fn6.

al-insānī (human society)."[60] Khuri-Makdisi takes *ijtimāʿ* as a stand-alone term which conceptualizes 'the social' instead of 'society.'[61]

Timothy Mitchell, who estimates "that the notion of 'society' or 'social form' had first been introduced in the writings of the 1870s,"[62] mentions several composites expressing these notions: "Phrases such as *al-intiẓām al-ʿumrānī* (social organisation) and *al-jamʿiyya al-muntaẓima* (organised association) were used, but the sort of phrase that became common was *al-hay'a al-mujtamaʿiyya* – *hay'a*, meaning 'form' itself, in the sense of visible shape or condition, qualified with the adjective from the word *mujtamaʿ*, collective."[63] I myself have encountered very few instances of *al-hay'a al-mujtamiʿa*[64] and have not come across any occurrence of *al-hay'a al-mujtamaʿiyya*. Mitchell himself also gives a reference for *al-hay'a al-ijtimāʿiyya* only.[65] If secondary sources thus primarily suggest *al-hay'a al-ijtimāʿiyya* and *mujtamaʿ* as pertinent Arabic terms for 'society' in the period we are considerating, contemporaneous dictionaries add two additional terms worth considering – namely *jamʿiyya* and *jamāʿa*.

As a source, dictionaries must be approached with some caution. The terms registered partly follow from the interests of the dictionary's compiler and the material they consulted. The fact that dictionaries tend to include only terms that were more or less widely used implies one advantage and one disadvantage: it is advantageous insofar as it testifies to those terms being established, but on the downside, it implies that new terms or meanings may well have been in

60 Rebhan, *Geschichte*, 104 f.; transliteration adjusted.
61 Khuri-Makdisi, "The Conceptualization," 99.
62 Mitchell, *Colonising*, 119.
63 Ibid., 120; transliteration adjusted.
64 In *al-Manar*, *al-hay'a al-mujtamiʿa* occurs only twice (al-Siyadi, Abu al-Huda quoted in Rida, Rashid. 1906. "Athar 'Ilmiyya Adabiyya." *al-Manar* 9/4: 309–316, here 309; al-Zahrawi, "Nizam," *al-Manar* 6/9: 337 f.). Al-Tuwairani uses *al-hay'a al-mujtamiʿa* right next to *al-hay'a al-ijtimāʿiyya:* al-Tuwayrani, Hasan Husni. 1891. *Maqala fi Ijmal al-Kalam ʿala Mas['Jalat al-Khilafa bayna Ahl al-Islam*. Cairo: Matbaʿat al-Mahrusa, 14. The attribute *al-mujtamiʿa* seems to positively qualify *al-hay'a*, which I here take to be a short form of *al-hay'a al-ijtimāʿiyya*. There are no additional occurrences of either composite in that work.
65 If we assume that Mitchell did not invent *al-hay'a al-mujtamaʿiyya* himself, but that this composite was at least marginally used by Arabic authors in the nineteenth century, this would support the suggestion that the stand-alone term *mujtamaʿ* did replace the composites *al-hay'a al-mujtamaʿiyya* and *al-hay'a al-ijtimāʿiyya*. Then again, in contrast to *al-hay'a al-ijtimāʿiyya*, society could seemingly also be conceptualized with *al-hay'a* only (see Zolondek, Leon. 1966. "Socio-Political Views of Salim al-Bustani (1848–1884)." *Middle Eastern Studies* 2/2: 144–156, here 146, 147). This decreases the practical advantage of the single term *mujtamaʿ* as an explanatory factor for the term's establishment.

use at the time a dictionary was composed but not included in that dictionary. With these considerations in mind, a look at two early nineteenth-century French-Arabic dictionaries provides the following Arabic terms for *société.*

In his French-Arabic dictionary of 1828, Bocthor distinguishes five meanings of *société.*[66] For *société* in the sense of "assemblage d'hommes unis par la nature et les lois," he noted *jamʿiyya* and *ijtimāʿiyya*; for *société* referring to "union des hommes, leur commerce naturel," he has *ulfa, ṣaḥba, maʿāshira,* and *ʿushra*; *société* as "compagnie, reunion des hommes" is *jamāʿa* and, again, *jamʿiyya*; the Arabic term which is today mainly used for 'company' or 'firm,' *sharika*, is given for *société d'intérêts, association*; and, finally, a *société* in the sense of "personnes avec qui l'on vit" is *jamʿiyya* and *ṣaḥba.* In distinguishing these five senses of *société,* Bocthor attests to the French term's semantic range and does not necessarily imply that these senses were similarly distinguished in Arabic. At the very least, there was obviously not one Arabic term yielding the semantic range of *société.* Of the meanings distinguished by Bocthor, the first is certainly the most relevant, suggesting the Arabic terms *jamʿiyya* and *ijtimāʿiyya.* Stetkevych assumes that, in the latter term, which was later proposed for rendering 'socialism,' "Bocthor had in mind a fuller form of the same, *al-ḥayāt al-ijtimāʿiyya* [social life]."[67] Belot's French-Arabic dictionary, published in 1913, gives *jamʿiyya* and *jamāʿa* for *société* in the sense of "réunion d'hommes ayant mêmes lois."[68] While the other meanings of *société* and their Arabic expressions as distinguished by Belot largely confirm those identified by Bocthor, Belot adds *jamʿiyya* for *société religieuse* and includes *niẓām al-hay'a al-ijtimāʿiyya* for *ordre social.*

A look at Arabic-French and Arabic-English dictionaries of the late nineteenth and early twentieth centuries also suggests that *jamʿiyya* and *jamāʿa* conveyed the meaning of 'society' and shows that some authors noted this modern meaning of *mujtamaʿ* rather early, while others remained unaware of it decades later. In 1860, Kazimirski discerned the following meanings of *jamāʿa:* "troupe d'hommes, quelques hommes, compagnie, réunion, société." For *jamʿiyya* he gives "réunion, rassemblement, assemblée," and for *ijtimāʿ*, "réunion, état de ce qui est réuni, vie sociale."[69] In 1881, Dozy states only "conjonction, rencontre

66 Bocthor, Ellious. 1828. *Dictionnaire français-arabe; revu et augmenté par A[rmand] Caussin de Perceva.* Paris: Didot, 324 f.

67 Stetkevych, *The Modern*, 25.

68 Belot, P. J.-B. 1913. *Dictionnaire Français-Arabe; 4ième édition revue et corrigée; Seconde Partie.* Beyrouth: Imprimerie Catholique, 1404.

69 Biberstein Kazimirski, Albert de. [ca. 1900; original: Paris 1860]. *Qamus al-Lughatayn al-ʿArabiyya wa-l-Fransawiyya = Dictionnaire arabe-français : contenant toutes les racines de la langue*

apparente des astres, incorporation" for *ijtimāʿ*.[70] He notes "société, assemblage d'hommes unis par la nature et les lois" as the meaning of *ijtimāʿiyya* based on Bocthor's entry from 1828.[71] For *mujtamaʿ*, Dozy only gives *réunion, assemblée.*[72] Hava's Arabic-English dictionary from 1915 does not list *mujtamaʿ* at all, but only the adjective *mujtamiʿa*, as meaning "in the strength of life." *Ijtimāʿ* here is asserted to mean 'reunion,' 'social life'; *jamāʿa* is 'party of men,' 'society'; and *jamʿiyya* is 'congregation,' 'religious confraternity.'[73]

To bring secondary sources back into our discussion, Rebhan and Ayalon concluded that *jamāʿa* and especially *jamʿiyya* were predominantly used to convey meanings other than 'society.' According to Rebhan, in the nineteenth century, *jamʿiyya* was mainly used to designate political congregations or institutions. In the second half of the century, the term – while also used as a synonym to 'conference' or 'congress' – predominantly referred to voluntary associations founded for political, scientific, literary, or benevolent purposes.[74] Ayalon considers that the meaning 'voluntary associations' was dominant throughout the century and that *jamʿiyya* was also used to refer to political bodies only in the last third of the century. According to Ayalon, *jamāʿa* – similarly to *jamʿiyya* – rather unspecifically "indicat[ed] a group or gathering of people."[75] Since at least the 1960s, *jamāʿa* may be used to connote 'community' in contrast to *mujtamaʿ*, 'society.' However, this connotation obviously only becomes meaningful when a contrasting term connoting 'society' is established. Based on these findings and considerations, I will not focus on *jamʿiyya* or *jamāʿa* in my search for Arabic terms for 'society' in *al-Manar* but will pay attention to their usage in the journal along the way.

Elias's Arabic-English dictionary from 1922 is the first to give the meaning 'society' for *mujtamaʿ*.[76] Entitled *Elias' Modern Dictionary* and published by Cairo's al-Matbaʿa al-ʿAsriyya (The Modern Press), this dictionary was very sensitive to recently coined terms and meanings. Thus it not only lists *mujtamaʿ* in

---

arabe, leurs dérivés, tant dans l'idiome vulgaire que dans l'idiome littéral ainsi que les dialectes d'Alger et de Maroc; tome premier. Beyrouth: Librairie du Liban, 328.

70 Dozy, R. 1967 [1881]. *Supplément aux Dictionnaires Arabes; tome premier.* Leyde/Paris: Brill/G.-P. Maisonneuve et Larose, 215.

71 Ibid., 217.

72 Ibid., 217.

73 Hava, J. G. 1915. *al-Faraʾid.* Beirut: Dar al-Mashriq, 98. Rebhan also noted that *jamʿiyya* originally designated Christian congregations (Rebhan, *Geschichte*, 84).

74 Ibid., 85.

75 Ayalon, *Language*, 117.

76 Elias, Elias A. 1922. *Elias' Modern Dictionary Arabic-English.* Cairo: al-Matbaʿa al-ʿAsriyya bi-Misr.

the sense of 'society,' but also *al-niẓām al-ijtimāʿī* as 'the existing order of society' and *ʿilm al-ijtimāʿ* as 'sociology, social science.' *Al-hay'a al-ijtimāʿiyya* is here given to mean 'the human society.'[77] The fact that Barthelemy, in his Arabic-French dictionary from 1935, does not list *mujtamaʿ* at all may be explained by his focus on Syrian dialects.[78] Yet an Arabic-French-English dictionary from 1976 still gives "place of convergence, of assembly, junction" as the primary meanings of *mujtamaʿ*.[79] The fact that dictionaries differed in noting the meaning of *mujtamaʿ* as 'society' reminds us of their limited value for registering lexicographical and semantic changes, on the one hand. On the other hand, the fact that *Elias' Modern Dictionary* was the first to note the new meaning of *mujtamaʿ*, in 1922, attests to the recency of this meaning, which gradually found its way into other dictionaries as well.

The discussion of existing studies and the consultation of contemporaneous dictionaries thus suggest *al-hay'a al-ijtimāʿiyya, mujtamaʿ*, and to a lesser extent *ijtimāʿ* as the most pertinent – albeit potentially not exclusive – terms corresponding to 'society.' Of special interest will be the emergence of *mujtamaʿ* as meaning 'society' and the question of whether a fundamental conceptual shift was involved in that term replacing *al-hay'a al-ijtimāʿiyya*. The term *ijtimāʿ*, it will transpire, was not used to conceptualize the modern idea of particular societies, but rather referred to the underlying premise of social association. Also, as *ijtimāʿ* occurs a total of 2,722 times in *al-Manar*, questions of authorship are far less interesting concerning *ijtimāʿ* than they are with regard to *al-hay'a al-ijtimāʿiyya* and *mujtamaʿ*, which occur only 142 and 358 times, respectively. I will thus illustrate the semantic range of *ijtimāʿ* based only on writings by Rashid Rida (in chapter 10), whereas I will comprehensively analyze the 142 occurrences of *al-hay'a al-ijtimāʿiyya* and the 358 instances of *mujtamaʿ* in *al-Manar* (in chapters 7 and 8 below).

Before narrowing my focus to *al-Manar* in part C, I want to highlight the earliest prominent usage of *al-hay'a al-ijtimāʿiyya* to mean society and summarize Khuri-Makdisi's findings on this composite's usage in the close context of *al-Manar*. For *mujtamaʿ*, no such prominent usage has yet been established.

---

77 Ibid., 90.

78 Barthélemy, A. 1935. *Dictionnaire Arabe-Français: Dialectes de Syrie: Alep, Damas, Liban, Jérusalem*. Paris: Librairie Orientaliste Paul Geuthner, 120 f.

79 Blachère, Régis, Pellat, Charles, Chouémi, Moustafa and Denizeau, Claude. 1976. *Dictionnaire Arabe-Français-Anglais (Langue classique et moderne); tome troisième*. Paris: G.-P. Maisonneuve et Larose, 1714 f.

3 *Al-Hay'a al-Ijtimāʿiyya:* Prominent Usages

The earliest known usages of *al-hay'a al-ijtimāʿiyya* are by Christian authors known for disseminating secular knowledge and ideas about socio-political order appropriated from French and English sources.

The one nineteenth-century author who first prominently used *al-hay'a al-ijtimāʿiyya* was Butrus al-Bustani (1819–1883)[80] in his *Treatise on Society and a Comparison between Arab and European Customs* (*Khitab fi al-Hay'a al-Ijtimaʿiyya wa-l-Muqabala bayna al-ʿAwa'id al-ʿArabiyya wa-l-Ifranjiyya*) from 1869.[81] Due to his pioneering encyclopedic and journalistic projects, al-Bustani is well known as a protagonist of the *nahḍa*, the Arab cultural and literary renaissance of the nineteenth and early twentieth centuries. Born into a Maronite Christian family in Mount Lebanon, al-Bustani converted to Protestantism after having been employed at the American Syrian Protestant College in Beirut, the same institution which the editors of *al-Hilal* and *al-Muqtataf* had also attended.[82] Al-Bustani was educated in several biblical as well as modern European languages. His dictionary *Da'irat al-Maʿarif*[83] and his encyclopedia *Muhit al-Muhit*[84] aimed at integrating European and Arabic knowledge into a common body of knowledge. He thus pursued the overarching goal of the *nahḍa* to revive Arab literary and scientific culture and to enhance the relevance of Arabic for addressing modern subjects. Next to his concerns for an Arab identity, al-Bustani also advocated the vision of a common Syrian polity, especially in the wake of tensions between Maronites and Druzes in Mount Lebanon in 1860.[85] In an editorial entitled "Ruh al-ʿAsr" ("The Spirit of the Age") – published 1870 in his jour-

---

80 On him, see: Abu-Manneh, Butrus. 1980. "The Christians between Ottomanism and Syrian Nationalism: The Ideas of Butrus Al-Bustani." *International Journal of Middle East Studies* 11/3: 287–304; Sheehi, Stephen. 2011. "Butrus al-Bustani. Syria's Ideologue of the Age." In *The Origins of Syrian Nationhood. Histories, Pioneers and Identity* ed. by Adel Beshara: 57–78. Oxon/New York: Routledge.

81 Al-Bustani, Butrus. 1981 [1869]. "Khitab fi al-Hay'a al-Ijtimaʿiyya wa-l-Muqabala bayna al-ʿAwa'id al-ʿArabiyya wa-l-Ifranjiyya." In *al-ʿAlim Butrus al-Bustani. Dirasa wa-Watha'iq* ed. by Jan Daya: 163–187. Beirut: Manshurat Majallat Fikr.

82 See above: 123 f.

83 Al-Bustani, Butrus. 2000 [1876]. *Da'irat al-Maʿarif: Encyclopedie Arabe.* Beirut: Dar al-Maʿrifa.

84 Idem. 1977 [1870]. *Muhit al-Muhit: Qamus Mutawwal li-l-Lugha al-ʿArabiyya.* Beirut: Maktabat Lubnan.

85 On these events and al-Bustani's view of them, see: Makdisi, Ussama. 2002. "After 1860: Debating Religion, Reform, and Nationalism in the Ottoman Empire." *International Journal of Middle East Studies* 34/4: 601–617.

nal, *al-Jinan* – al-Bustani argued that socio-political organization should be based on patriotic rather than religious affiliations.[86]

His *Treatise on Society,* written in view of both these sectarian tensions and the heightened numbers of Europeans residing in Beirut, consists of three chapters, entitled "*al-hay'a al-ijtimāʿiyya*" (society), "*al-ʿāda*" (custom), and "*muqābalat ʿādāt al-ʿArab wa-l-Ifranj*" (comparison of Arab and European customs). The chapter on society begins with a definition of the term:

"By society (*al-hay'a al-ijtimāʿiyya*) is meant the inhabitants of a country or city, who have shared interests (*ṣawāliḥ mushtaraka*), or, better put, it is the state resulting from human social association (*al-ijtimāʿ al-basharī*). And the true and natural basis (*asās*) of human social association is the needs of individuals and their fears (*iḥtiyājāt al-afrād wa-makhāwifuhum*). Therefore, the larger and more important these needs are and the more manifold and the stronger these fears, the more solid is this basis and the stronger its [i.e., the association's] bonds and relations."[87]

In the remainder of the first chapter, al-Bustani identifies the different needs of social association, whose complexity, he maintains, increases as human beings associate in ever-larger collectivities; he then inquires into the necessities of the present state of society in Beirut. The second chapter stresses the variation in suitable customs between different groups of people and portrays European customs as the most refined, in tune with their current level of civilization (*tamaddun*).[88] Chapter three compares current European and traditional Arab customs, from eating and greeting to morals and the critical evaluation of practices. Al-Bustani explains that he focused on the original Arab customs, since the current practices deviate too greatly from them,[89] mainly because Arabs are adopting outward European customs and habits. In doing so, according to al-Bustani, they are wrongly conflating these particular practices – which might not all be suitable for Arabs – with the core of civilization (*tamaddun*).[90]

This brief insight into the remainder of al-Bustani's treatise must suffice here, and we now return to his initial definition of *al-hay'a al-ijtimāʿiyya.* In it, al-Bustani addresses two senses of 'society' – the first referring to a delineated collectivity of people (with common interests) and the second to the state result-

86 Abu-Manneh, "The Christians," 269.
87 Al-Bustani, "Khitab," 163 f.
88 Ibid., 173 f.
89 Ibid., 185.
90 Ibid., 186, 172.

ing from human beings' natural tendency toward social association. In *Muhit al-Muhit*, which was published a year later, he reproduced and thus solidified the latter, clearly normative sense of *al-hay'a al-ijtimāʿiyya* as "the condition arising from the association of a people with common interests" (*al-ḥāla al-ḥāṣila min ijtimāʿ qawm la-hum maṣāliḥ mushtaraka*).[91] Al-Bustani did not yet use – at least in the writings that I have consulted – the term *mujtamaʿ*. In his *Da'irat al-Maʿarif*, we find an entry on "*jamʿiyya, société*, society." However, the societies al-Bustani addresses here are exclusively scientific and educational societies. He stresses the spread of such societies in Europe and America and regretfully notes that not much is left of attempts to found such societies in Asia and Africa.[92]

In a similar vein, Butrus al-Bustani's son, Salim al-Bustani, depicted *ijtimāʿ* as human beings' innate need for socialization, which results in the creation of societies (*hay'āt ijtimāʿiyya*) to facilitate cooperation and to ward off external threats. We do not find peace in our society (*hay'atunā al-ijtimāʿiyya*), Salim al-Bustani argues, because our social association (*ijtimāʿunā*) is intended for segregation and dispute rather than for unity and consent. In this brief excerpt, *ijtimāʿ* also expresses the act of associating rather than connoting an objectified society, whereas *al-hay'a al-ijtimāʿiyya* refers to both a social body and a social order.[93] The foregoing statement is included in a series of lexicons on exemplary usages of central concepts of Arabic thought between 1700 and 1940. These lexicons also include examples of Muslim thinkers, including Muhammad ʿAbduh, using *al-hay'a al-ijtimāʿiyya*.[94] Still, it is clearly Christian authors – more specifically Syro-Lebanese Christians, such as Butrus and Salim al-Bustani, but also Fransis Marrash (1836–1873)[95] – who account for the earliest and most prominent usages of the composite.

This rough sketch suggests three factors that possibly contributed to the coining of *al-hay'a al-ijtimāʿiyya* to conceptualize society: denominational back-

91 Idem., *Muhit*, 123.
92 Idem., *Da'irat*, 524 f.
93 Al-Bustani, Salim. n.d. *Iftitahat Majallat al-Jinan, vol. 2 (1872–1884)* ed. Yusuf Qizman Khuri. Beirut: Dar al-Hamra', 390, 10, taken from: Dughaym, Samih (ed.). 2000. *Mawsuʿat Mustalahat al-Fikr al-ʿArab wa-l-Islami al-Hadith wa-l-Muʿasir; al-Juz' al-Awwal: 1700–1890.* Beirut: Maktabat Lubnan Nashirun, 1202 f.
94 Ibid., 1202 ff.; al-ʿAjm, Rafiq (ed.). 2002. *Mawsuʿat Mustalahat al-Fikr al-ʿArabi wa-l-Islami al-Hadith wa-l-Muʿasir; al-Juz' al-Thani: 1890–1940.* Beirut: Maktabat Lubnan Nashirun, 1107 f.
95 Dughaym, *Mawsuʿat*, 1203 f. On Marrash, see, with further literature: Stephan, Johannes. 2016. "Reconsidering Transcendence/Immanence. Modernity's Modes of Narration in Nineteenth-Century Arabic Literary Tradition." In *Working with A Secular Age. Interdisciplinary Perspectives on Charles Taylor's Master Narrative* ed. by Florian Zemmin, Colin Jager and Guido Vanheeswijck: 349–367. Berlin/Boston: De Gruyter.

ground; regional socio-political events and parlance; and acquaintance with European languages and ideas of social order. *Al-hay'a al-ijtimāʿiyya* might indeed have been coined in order to render the English concept of 'society' and the French *société*. After all, Ilham Khuri-Makdisi, in her analysis of appropriations of European concepts of 'society' in Arabic, which I discussed in the introduction, had good reasons for focusing on writings by secular Christian authors.

Khuri-Makdisi's main findings concerning these authors' employment of *al-hay'a al-ijtimāʿiyya* include the concept's initial subsumption under the dominant idea of civilization and its later elaboration as a living organism resting on the natural cooperation of its individual members. In the writings of Lebanese Christians, such as Butrus al-Bustani in the 1860s and 1870s, a healthy social body and a functioning social organization were considered prerequisites for attaining civilization. The health of the social body itself necessitated the awareness of common interests and their realization via collaboration. This again depended on the dissemination of knowledge and education.[96] In the last two decades of the nineteenth century, the idea of society – conceptualized as *al-hay'a al-ijtimāʿiyya* – was further developed, most significantly as a living organism: "This conception of society as a living organism, whose health depended on the health of its every part and on the good functioning of the whole, became central to the thinkers of the *nahḍa*, who called for a social reform that would rid society of various internal as well as external 'diseases' threatening its cohesion."[97] Shibli Shumayyil in particular promoted the necessary cooperation between members of society by presenting it as part of human nature. However, in contrast to what Khuri-Makdisi suggests,[98] this did not do away with older older views of competition and rivalry as inevitable. Thus socialist agendas, like those of Shumayyil and Niqula Haddad, could be built on both the premise of human beings' natural tendency toward social cooperation and the need for a strong government to keep competitive tendencies at bay.[99] It was not only these socialist visions that were contested, but also the very concepts of labor and capital, whose increasing importance can also be discerned in the construction of political economy (*al-iqtiṣād al-siyāsī*) as a field of inquiry in the 1880s.[100]

Although it was secularly oriented Christians familiar with European languages and thought who first coined an Arabic equivalent to the concept of 'society,' *al-hay'a al-ijtimāʿiyya* and related concepts had become unavoidable by

---

96 Khuri-Makdisi, "The Conceptualization," 95 ff.
97 Ibid., 101.
98 Ibid., 100.
99 Reid, "The Syrian," 187.
100 Khuri-Makdisi, "The Conceptualization," 106.

1908, as Khuri-Makdisi finds, adducing a conservative Christian periodical's usage of *al-hay'a al-ijtimāʿiyya* as a case in point:

"For some factions, the social was the most important of these concepts; for others, it was political economy, and for yet another group, it was civilization. However, one would be hard pressed to find pieces written on either one of these topics around 1908 which did not rely conceptually on the other concepts as well. Significantly, even *al-Mashriq*, a Beiruti pro-Jesuit, conservative periodical, used a very similar terminology. While *al-Mashriq*'s authors saw religious education as central to *al-hay'a al-ijtimāʿiyya* and often did not make a distinction between *al-hay'a al-ijtimāʿiyya* and *al-waṭan* (i. e., between society and homeland), asserting that 'God...(is) the creator of *al-hay'a al-ijtimāʿiyya*, and people are its members', they still used the same concepts, and they still used the analogy of the social body as an organism and as the human body."[101]

This example reminds us of how European Christian authors reacted to and appropriated the concept of 'society' coined by secularly minded authors.[102] The fact that the Beiruti Christian paper *al-Mashriq* picked up the composite *al-hay'a al-ijtimāʿiyya* and connected it to other modern concepts and ideas, however differently elaborated in detail, raises the question of whether the concept had also become unavoidable in the Cairo-based Islamic journal *al-Manar*; indeed, Khuri-Makdisi herself mentions the lack of attention to Islamic reformists, such as ʿAbduh and Rida, as the most glaring gap in her research.[103]

---

101 Ibid., 110; transliteration adjusted.

102 See above: chapter 2 section 3.

103 Khuri-Makdisi, "The Conceptualization," 92.

Part C
Findings: ‘Society’ in *al-Manar*

Chapter 7
Al-Hay'a al-Ijtimāʿiyya in *al-Manar:* Offering *Umma* as an Alternative

1 Occurrences of *al-Hay'a al-Ijtimāʿiyya* in *al-Manar*

The preceding section, concluding part B and thus addressing our *expectations* concerning the concept of 'society' in *al-Manar*, has shown that *al-hay'a al-ijtimāʿiyya* was supposedly the most established term for conceptualizing society in nineteenth- and early twentieth-century Arabic. This first chapter of part C, which presents my *findings* on conceptualizations of society in *al-Manar*, is thus dedicated to *al-hay'a al-ijtimāʿiyya*. This first section gives an overview of the occurrences of *al-hay'a al-ijtimāʿiyya* in *al-Manar* and those authors who most prominently use the composite; the subsequent sections of this chapter then turn to more specific aspects of the usage and meanings of *al-hay'a al-ijtimāʿiyya* in our Islamic journal.

In *al-Manar*, *(al-)hay'a (al-)ijtimāʿiyya* occurs 142 times. This includes seven usages of *hay'at al-ijtimāʿ* by contemporaneous authors, but not the eleven cases in which that composite is used by the fourteenth-century legal scholar al-Shatibi. In his *Kitab al-Iʿtisam*, which was printed by *al-Manar*'s press and excerpted at length in the journal, *hay'at al-ijtimāʿ* – and once, synonymously, *al-hay'a al-ijtimāʿiyya* – is used when discussing the permissibility of invoking God during a gathering (*al-duʿā' bi-hay'at al-ijtimāʿ*).[1] Rashid Rida employs *hay'at al-ijtimāʿ* in the same sense as al-Shatibi only once.[2] The only pre-modern author other than al-Shatibi who is quoted in *al-Manar* as using *al-hay'a al-ijtimāʿiyya* is Ibn Taymiyya.[3] He uses the term to refer to the integrated or unified structure of the various aspects of the concept of belief (*īmān*).[4] Such references to a unified or unifying structure or principle in philosophical and logical discourse seem to have been the generally predominant employment and meaning of *hay'a (ijtimāʿiyya)*

1 Al-Shatibi, Abu Ishaq. 1913. "al-Bab al-Awwal min Kitab al-Iʿtisam." *al-Manar* 17/1: 54–63, here 57; idem. 1914. "Fasl." *al-Manar* 17/6: 433–454, here 444, 447, 448, 453, 454, *al-Manar* 17/7: 513–534, here 521, *al-Manar* 17/8: 593–615, here 600; idem. 1914. "Dukhul al-Ibtidaʿ fi al-ʿAdiyyat." *al-Manar* 17/10: 753–772, here 767.

2 Rida, Rashid. 1917. "Bidaʿ al-Jumʿa wa-l-Adhan wa-Khatm al-Salat wa-l-Janaza." *al-Manar* 19/9: 538–544, here 542.

3 See above: 126 f.

4 Ibn Taymiyya quoted in Rida, Rashid. 1906. "al-Iman Yazid wa-Yanqus." *al-Manar* 9/3: 196–204, here 201.

https://doi.org/10.1515/9783110545845-008

prior to modernity.[5] The modern authors of *al-Manar*, in turn, use *al-hay'a al-ijtimāʿiyya* exclusively to refer to society.

While the composite is used less often in the second half of *al-Manar*'s life span,[6] this cannot be said to constitute a clear tendency, since *al-hay'a al-ijtimāʿiyya* occurs relatively few times in total. After all, its 142 instances are spread over almost 30,000 pages. To put this number into perspective, the term *al-shaʿb* (the people), for example, appears 2,949 times, and *umma* a total of 11,586 times.[7] As *al-hay'a al-ijtimāʿiyya* was clearly not a ubiquitous term in *al-Manar*, the question of which authors did use it becomes especially interesting.

Rashid Rida accounts for roughly one-fourth of the composite's occurrences – namely, for 34 instances, 13 of which are in the *Tafsir*. However, this does not mean that Rida used *al-hay'a al-ijtimāʿiyya* prominently. After all, he accounts for the bulk of *al-Manar*'s articles. Moreover, his 21 usages of *al-hay'a al-ijtimāʿiyya* – excluding the *Tafsir* – are scattered over 18 articles. And more often than using the composite himself, Rida quotes someone else doing so or introduces an article that contains the composite, namely in 50 additional cases. Most remarkably, Rida himself presents *al-hay'a al-ijtimāʿiyya* as an expression used by others.

Of the other authors employing *al-hay'a al-ijtimāʿiyya* in *al-Manar*, whether quoted by Rida or in an original article, (translations of) Lord Cromer account for 14 instances in seven articles; (translations of) Muhyi al-Din Azad for eight instances in a series of five articles, and Muhammad ʿAbduh accounts for six instances of usage spread over five articles. No other author accounts for more than three instances of usage. I will thus group the most relevant instances not by authorship, but according to the meaning of *al-hay'a al-ijtimāʿiyya* the authors are conveying. Exceptions to this grouping are the usages of Cromer and Azad and an article by Niqula Dabana, which is the only one to use the composite in its title. Some articles in which both *al-hay'a al-ijtimāʿiyya* and *mujtamaʿ* are used will be dealt with in the following chapter. Before turning to other authors and usages of *al-hay'a al-ijtimāʿiyya*, let us first look at how Rida employed the composite.

---

5 For possible differences between *hay'a ijtimāʿiyya* and *hay'a* as a stand-alone term, see: Ibrahim, Bilal. 2013. *Freeing Philosophy from Metaphysics: Fakhr al-Dīn al-Rāzī's Philosophical Approach to the Study of Natural Phenomena.* PhD, McGill University, http://digitool.library.mcgill.ca/webclient/StreamGate?folder_id=0&dvs=1447165198658~26 (accessed Nov. 10, 2015), 8, 149–159.

6 See appendix, table 2.

7 See appendix, table 3.

2 Rashid Rida: *Umma* as an Alternative to *al-Hayʾa al-Ijtimāʿiyya*

Rashid Rida not only more often quotes others using *al-hayʾa al-ijtimāʿiyya* than he uses the composite himself, he also explicitly qualifies the composite as being used by others and offers *umma* as an equivalent and also alternative. In volume six of *al-Manar*, Rida finds that sensual relations between men and women are a spiritual vice (*maḍarra rūḥiyya*) which, so long as they do not overstep certain boundaries, do not have an influence on society – that is, "on *al-umma* or on *al-hayʾa al-ijtimāʿiyya* as they say" (*ka-mā yaqūlūn*).[8] In a similar manner, in the *Tafsir*, Rida speaks of the positive influence of almsgiving on individuals, on the community of believers (*jamāʿat al-muʾminīn*), and on "what in the usage of this age is being called the social body" (*al-hayʾa al-ijtimāʿiyya*).[9] One may question whether in the first instance *al-hayʾa al-ijtimāʿiyya* denotes the same idea as *umma*, whereas in the *Tafsir*, it refers to an additional idea – namely, to the order of society rather than to the collectivity of believers (*jamāʿat al-muʾminīn*). In the remainder of this chapter, we will once encounter *jamāʿa* as the main term for conceptualizing the social order,[10] whereas *umma* is used most frequently for discussing major aspects of *al-ḥayʾa al-ijtimāʿiyya*. This is not at all to say that both terms were identical in meaning. *Umma* was a much more prominent and flexible term than *al-hayʾa al-ijtimāʿiyya*, and the concluding section of this chapter will point out a major difference between them. The possibility of them being used to conceptualize the same ideas is, however, more striking. The one instance in which Rida most clearly uses *umma* as an explanatory synonym to *al-hayʾa al-ijtimāʿiyya* is to be found in volume eight of *al-Manar*, where he explains that "by what they term *al-hayʾa al-ijtimāʿiyya* is meant the *umma* as a whole and not its parts" (*mā yusammūnahu al-hayʾa al-ijtimāʿiyya wa-hiya al-umma fī majmūʿihā lā ajzāʾihā*).[11]

Looking at how Rida uses the composite himself, it is remarkable that he does so by far most extensively – namely ten times on two pages – when engaging a philosophical argument, thus offering a first hint as to whom he might have had in mind when qualifying *al-hayʾa al-ijtimāʿiyya* as a term used by "them." It is in his commentary on sura 4:114 that Rida refers to his debate with an anon-

8 Rida, Rashid. 1904. "al-Asʾila wa-l-Ajwiba." *al-Manar* 6/23: 902–907, here 904.
9 Idem., *Tafsir*, vol. 11: 21.
10 See below: chapter 7 section 4.3.
11 Rida, Rashid. 1905. "al-Hayat al-Milliya bi-l-Tarbiya al-Ijtimaʿiyya." *al-Manar* 8/21: 811–819, here 813.

ymous philosopher about the motives for good deeds. This verse reads: "No good [*khayr*] comes, as a rule, out of secret confabulations [*najwā*] – saving such as are devoted to enjoining charity [*ṣadaqa*], or equitable dealings [*al-maʿrūf*], or setting things to rights between people [*al-iṣlāḥ bayna al-nās*]: and unto him who does this out of a longing for God's goodly acceptance [*ibtighāʾ marḍāt allāh*] We shall in time grant a mighty reward."[12] Rida first elucidates why, in the three exceptions mentioned, the good effects of these deeds might become harmful if displayed or talked about in public.[13] He then attends to the second part of the verse, which states that a godly reward is promised to those who perform these deeds with the purpose of receiving this reward. To Rida, this incentive is what makes a believer superior to a philosopher in his deeds – less prey to deceptions, more honest, and seeking the good of people (*al-nās*) over against personal desires or inclinations.[14]

According to Rida, this superiority results from the philosophers – especially the contemporary ones – saying that what is good and virtuous consists in human beings doing good because it is beneficial for the society (*al-hay'a al-ijtimāʿiyya*) of which they are part,[15] whereas belief (*īmān*) surpasses this insight, which it also contains, by adding the dimension of recompense in the next world. Striving for this recompense arguably elevates the soul, since the believer performs good deeds with this higher purpose in mind, not caring – unlike those who are guided merely by philosophy – for lower purposes, such as his reputation.[16]

Rida then recalls a conversation he had with a distinguished Egyptian (*baʿḍ kubarāʾ al-miṣriyīn*) about the meaning of virtue (*al-faḍīla*). When the other man, who was speaking in philosophical terms (*yatakallim bi-lisān al-falsafa*), delineated what is beneficial for society (*al-hay'a al-ijtimāʿiyya*), Rida, who spoke in Islamic terms, combining religion (*dīn*) and wisdom (*ḥikma*), inquired about the motive (*al-bāʿith*) for human beings (*nufūs*) to act accordingly. The philosopher responded that this motive consists in every person believing that what is beneficial for society (*al-hay'a al-ijtimāʿiyya*) is also beneficial for himself. According to this, as Rida reiterates his interlocutor's argument, virtue means that human beings strive for what is beneficial for themselves, while also paying heed

---

12 This is the following translation of the Qur'an, into which I have inserted the original Arabic terms: Asad, Muhammad. 1980. *The Message of the Qur'ān*. Gibraltar: Dar al-Andalus.

13 Rida, *Tafsir*, vol. 5: 331 f.

14 Ibid., vol. 5: 332.

15 Ibid., vol. 5: 332.

16 Ibid., vol. 5: 332.

to the benefits of the society (*al-hay'a al-ijtimāʿiyya*) they live in.[17] But, Rida objects, human beings disagree considerably about what is beneficial for society (*al-hay'a al-ijtimāʿiyya*) and one might, for example, justify stealing someone else's money because one considers oneself more capable using that money to benefit society (*al-hay'a al-ijtimāʿiyya*). According to Rida, his interlocutor agreed that theft or adultery could indeed constitute a virtue if one commits these deeds in the honest belief that they are beneficial for society (*al-hay'a al-ijtimāʿiyya*). Clearly then, Rida maintains, this new way of thinking in practical philosophy (*al-madhhab al-jadīd fī al-falsafa al-ʿamaliyya*), which even justifies murder and turns vices into virtues, is very harmful. Moreover, while the early philosophers did expound many wise and virtuous insights, they were not able to guide people's hearts and souls or to prompt a reform of the affairs of social association (*iṣlāh shu'ūn al-ijtimāʿ*) in the way revelation does. Therefore, Rida concludes, religion is more beneficial for human beings than philosophy.[18]

The foregoing debate yields additional noteworthy points beyond the fact that Rida introduces the concept of *al-hay'a al-ijtimāʿiyya* when paraphrasing his philosophical interlocutor. The latter, according to Rida's depiction – which might not have portrayed his opponent's view fully adequately – gave primacy to the interests of society and trusted the individual to discern and respect those interests. Over against this position, Rida stresses the necessity of religious guidance for the individual and for social affairs. In the specific context of this conversation, Rida uses *al-hay'a al-ijtimāʿiyya* as a seemingly self-evident term for conceptualizing society and does not offer any alternative term.

However, Rida elaborates his argument about social morals requiring religion in another article, in which he – having previously used *umma* extensively – again introduces *al-hay'a al-ijtimāʿiyya* when presenting an antagonist's view, this time characterized as one held by "unbelievers in Western countries" (*afrād min al-mulāḥida fī al-bilād al-gharbiyya*), "their Westernized imitators" (*muqallidatuhum min al-mutafarnijīn*), and "materialist philosophers" (*al-falāsifa al-māddiyūn*).[19] The article in question consists of a lecture Rida gave at the Aligarh College, which was founded on the initiative of the Indian reformist Sayyid Ahmad Khan in 1875.[20] It was also during his Indian journey that Rida wrote the above-mentioned section of the *Tafsir*. While written at the same time and

17 Ibid., vol. 5: 333.

18 Ibid., vol. 5: 333.

19 Idem., "al-Tarbiya wa-Wajh," 578 ff.

20 For al-Afghani's criticism of Khan, see above: 165. At the end of his talk, and in a conciliatory tone, Rida praises Khan's efforts, but suggests that they are in need of complementation (ibid., 584 f.).

making a similar argument as the commentary on sura 4:114, in this article, Rida substantially elaborates on his own understanding of education as a central aspect of society and the nation, both of which are conceptualized as *umma*.

Having stressed moral and intellectual education (*al-tarbiya wa-l-taʿlīm*) as a requirement of human nature, which is fulfilled by the Islamic religion as the religion of humanity's innate natural disposition (*dīn al-fiṭra*), Rida elaborates on the instruction (*tarbiya*) of peoples (*umam*) as opposed to individuals (*afrād*). He defines the goal of this instruction as producing a complete transformation (*inqilāb ʿāmm*) in societies, carrying them to a higher level of material and intellectual life (*al-ḥayāt al-māddiyya wa-l-maʿnawiyya*).[21] This transformation can only be brought about gradually, and no one ever affected so rapid a change as Muhammad, Rida asserts. The fact that Muhammad belonged to a practically illiterate people and converted other peoples to Islam through righteousness and morality rather than by force is, for Rida, a superlative testimony of his prophethood. After all, in Rida's time, powerful states were conquering whole regions and trying to adapt the education (*tarbiya*) of peoples according to the laws (*al-sunan*) of the sciences of society and politics (*ʿulūm al-ijtimāʿ wa-l-siyāsa*). But Rida argued that these states have not succeeded in diverting the conquered people from the constituents and characteristics of their society (*muqawwimāt wa-mushakhkhiṣāt ummatihim*). The fact that Islam diverted several peoples (*umam*) from their religion, language, and customs in one generation – without resorting to schools, newspapers, or other artificial means demonstrated by the social sciences (*al-ʿulūm al-ijtimāʿiyya*) – is for Rida the clearest proof that God supported Muhammad in his mission.[22]

Rida then addresses education in the family (*tarbiyat al-buyūt*) as the smallest unit of society. To fulfill their central role as mothers in that smallest unit of society, women ought to be educated properly, Rida maintains. To think that one could match Europeans in worldly affairs by imitating their ways of educating women displays great ignorance of the science of the social (*ʿilm al-ijtimāʿ*) and the nature of societies (*ṭabāʾiʿ al-umam*). Moreover, Rida warns, such imitation would destroy one's own religious and national constituents and characteristics (*muqawwimātunā wa-mushakhkhiṣātunā al-milliyya wa-l-qawmiyya*), and it would not enable one to form such social constituents as the Europeans have (*muqawwimātuhum al-ijtimāʿiyya*). The education of girls thus needs to be based on the morals of our religion, its virtues, and its rules (*ādāb dīninā wa-faḍāʾiluhu wa-aḥkāmuhu*), Rida insists, and he adds that those pupils educated by

21 Ibid., 569.
22 Ibid., 569–572.

European women might be superior in contemporary social manners (*al-ādāb al-ijtimāʿiyya al-ʿaṣriyya*) but that one can only form a united, strong, advanced, and lively nation (*umma mutaḥidda, ʿazīza, rāqiyya, ḥayya)* based on common education.[23]

Rida briefly stresses the need to improve spiritual and intellectual education (*al-tarbiya al-nafsiyya wa-l-ʿaqliyya*) in schools – with intellectual education consisting mainly of forming free and critical minds[24] – and then dwells on the necessity of self-education. He asserts that many graduates of European schools become thieves or anarchists (*fawḍiyūn*), even though European schools and nations are superior in civilization (*ḥaḍāra*) and the sciences. For Rida, this demonstrates that the mere acquisition of knowledge is insufficient.[25] Acquiring worldly knowledge in order to make a living is of course necessary, Rida maintains, and everyone fulfilling a task required by society (*umma*) is to be thanked for it.[26] By contributing to the benefits and interests of the nation (*umma*), one not only becomes a useful member of society, contributing to the nation's strength, but actually represents the nation as a whole.[27] More than ordinary workers, teachers in higher schools are obliged to serve the nation (*umma*) by being role models of virtues and morals and by heeding public interests (*al-maṣāliḥ al-ʿāmma*) and common benefits (*al-manāfiʿ al-mushtaraka*). In order to fulfill that role, they have to educate themselves on the basis of and toward (*ʿalā*) moral excellence (*faḍīla*) and piety, lest they become a negative influence on society (*umma*).[28] Thus, Rida cautions his audience, one's self-education has to increase one's affinity with one's nation (*umma*) and vice versa, until all groups (*ṭabāqāt*) and members (*afrād*) of society (*umma*) are connected, differences in knowledge notwithstanding. Resorting to an analogy in nature, Rida compares this interconnected structure of society with that of a honeycomb.[29]

The overarching goal of a strong nation – Rida identifies himself in this talk with the nation or the community (*maʿāshir*) of Easterners in general, and Muslims in particular[30] – thus depends on virtuous and useful members of society, who collaboratively use their knowledge and skills to contribute to the interests of society and the nation. In order to form such virtuous, morally upright mem-

23 Ibid., 572f.
24 Ibid., 573f.
25 Ibid., 574.
26 Ibid., 575.
27 Ibid., 576ff.
28 Ibid., 575.
29 Ibid., 575f.
30 Ibid., 576.

bers of society, Rida considers religious education indispensible. Here, he depicts the production of moral virtues as the central and lasting function of religion: some people who were brought up according to religious virtues and morals might become doubtful concerning religion, and might even extricate (*tafallut*) themselves from all religious doctrines (*'aqā'id*). However, they will always possess a core of religious virtues (*faḍā'il*). Those who support their argument that unbelief is compatible with virtues by pointing to virtuous persons who enjoyed a religious upbringing but then abandoned religion ignore this lasting effect of religion, Rida maintains. To substantiate his point, he engages the same antagonizing, secularist view he refuted in the above-mentioned section of his *Tafsir.* It is here – eleven pages into his article, when portraying his virtual opponent's argument – that Rida introduces the concept of *al-hay'a al-ijtimā'iyya,* in a similar sense to that in which he had previously used *umma:*

"Some unbelievers in Western countries declare that it is possible to dispense with religion in education of the self (*tarbiyat al-nafs*), that virtue is built on the bases of science and reason only, that the educator (*murabbī*) can convince the one whom he is educating that vices (*radhā'il*) are harmful for the one who is committing them or for the society (*al-hay'a al-ijtimā'iyya*) in which he lives, and that virtues are the pillars (*da'ā'im*) of interests (*maṣāliḥ*) and benefits (*manāfi'*),[31] as though it is said to him that lying is repugnant [only] when a man knows that it makes trust in him untenable, and that he who is not trusted is deprived of many benefits [...]. And they think that this kind of education is preferable to and more beneficial than religious education, the basis of which according to them is intimidation of otherworldly punishments. We have indeed heard one of their Europeanized imitators repeating imperfectly the likes of these phrases and bragging with them, thinking that they would speak with wisdom (*ḥikma*) and would exalt the principles of philosophy."[32]

To Rida, this grounding of virtues merely on reason and personal or public interests represents a secularist societal perspective.

Rida tries to discredit and marginalize this perspective – not only in his own society, where it is allegedly upheld only by Europeanized imitators, but also in Europe itself – so as to devalue the argument that secular education underlies the success of European nations. In Europe, Rida suggests, the emergence of

---

31 Rida implies that virtues are tantamount to and thus discernible from what serves interests and benefits.
32 Ibid., 578.

this standpoint was due to the clergy having suppressed men of learning and independent thinkers. However, despite these thinkers' wholesale reaction against religion, the vast majority of European peoples continue to educate their children according to religious morals and virtues.[33] Rida paraphrases Herbert Spencer, whom he praises as the greatest scholar of society and of education (*akbar ʿulamāʾ al-ijtimāʿ wa-l-tarbiya*) in his age, as saying that changing the basis of education in virtues (*tarbiyat al-faḍīla*) from religion to science would result in great moral chaos (*fawḍā adabiyya*).[34] Attesting to the range of thinkers he selectively appropriates for his own arguments, in a footnote to his paraphrase of Spencer, Rida cites the twelfth-century Spanish-Arab philosopher Ibn Rushd as saying that "the true philosopher does not allow religion to be made the object of doubt and proof (*shakk wa-ithbāt*) and to be placed as the object of investigation, because this would imply making virtue and its basis the object of doubt, which would be a destruction of virtue."[35]

Rida then implicitly connects to a classical philosophical distinction between the masses and the elite (*al-ʿāmma wa-l-khāṣṣa*) when he goes on to argue that an elite might, to some extent, base their moral insights on reason, whereas the masses definitely require religion. Rida first contests reason's capacity to induce virtuous behavior and establish a moral consensus. As in the above-mentioned *Tafsir*, he refers to the possibility of justifying theft via the alleged benefits of society (*al-hay'a al-ijtimāʿiyya*). As people – including members of the elite – will necessarily disagree about what is beneficial, he suggests the necessity for a "religion whose book arbitrates (*yaḥkum*) between the people concerning what they differ in."[36] The absolute necessity of religion for the moral behavior of ordinary people is then illustrated with the example of a poor man finding a suitcase full of money and giving it back to its owner, even though the latter belongs to a social group of ill repute and moreover had been unaware that the poor man was in possession of his suitcase. When asked why he returned it nevertheless, the poor man replies that God was well aware that he had the suitcase. Do you think, Rida asks his audience rhetorically, that he would have returned the suitcase "if he had been told by a materialist philosopher (*baʿḍ falāsifa al-māddiyīn*) that there is no God, no religion, and no life after this life, and that security is a rational duty because without it society (*al-hay'a al-ijtimāʿiyya*) is not set right?"[37] For Rida, this proves that "education of the self

33 Ibid., 578.
34 Ibid., 579.
35 Ibid., 579fn1.
36 Ibid., 579.
37 Ibid., 580.

(*tarbiyat al-nafs*) toward virtue cannot be achieved except through religion, and that every single religion (*kull dīn min al-adyān*) – even those containing superstitions and pagan traditions that are an incentive to vices – supports this education more than this defective philosophy, which can never be universal (*ʿāmma*)."[38] Thus, against a secularist view that bases social morals on reason and inner-worldly interests alone, Rida – who uses *al-hay'a al-ijtimāʿiyya* only when paraphrasing that view – defends the necessity of religion in general as the guarantor of moral consensus, virtuous behavior, and a functioning social order.

Unsurprisingly, from this general argument for religion, Rida proceeds to advocate the benefits of the Islamic religion in particular, which he, in a noteworthy twist, promotes as a quasi-philosophy based on reason and general interests. Rida maintains that those European scholars who oppose a religious education do so based on the religions they are familiar with, and that they would change their opinions if they knew the truth of the Islamic religion – based on the Qur'an and the Sunna, not on the current practices of Muslims. In fact, the principles (*uṣūl*) of Islam contain everything the European proponents of a secular, rational education regard as beneficial. After all, Rida suggests, "the construction of rules (*aḥkām*) and practices (*aʿmāl*) on the basis of warding off what is corrupting and harmful (*al-mafāsid wa-l-maḍārr*) and bringing about what is beneficial and complies with the general interests (*al-manāfiʿ wa-murāʿāt al-maṣāliḥ*) is an agreed-upon Islamic basis (*qāʿida*)."[39] Here, it is useful to recall that Rida employed the concept of *maṣlaḥa* in general in a quasi-secular sense, equating it with public interest.[40] In this speech, he stresses that the Qur'an connects individual religious duties (*ʿibādāt*), such as fasting and almsgiving, to their overall benefits and advantages (*manāfiʿ wa-fawā'id*) or even justifies (*yuʿallil*) the former via the latter.[41] So how, Rida rhetorically asks, could the Qur'an "refuse to justify worldly rules and social morals (*al-ādāb al-ijtimāʿiyya*) with advantages and benefits?"[42] The "principles of Islam and its branches" are clearly "in agreement with reason, the human innate disposition, and the common interests of the people and their benefits," whence an Englishman to whom Rida explained this truth of Islam even exclaimed that "this is a philosophy, not a religion."[43]

38 Ibid., 581.
39 Ibid., 581.
40 See above: 171 f.
41 Ibid., 581 f.
42 Ibid., 582.
43 Ibid., 582.

This strategy of criticizing secular elaborations of certain premises and arguments and then ascribing those same premises and arguments to the Islamic religion is quite typical of a modernizing reformist discourse. There is a defensive and often apologetic tone to this strategy, insofar as it aims to show the continuing validity of Islam in an age when secular premises are considered the only means to social order, national strength, and progress. The reformists' incorporation of secular premises into an Islamic discourse can be explained to some extent as a means of preserving an Islamic identity. However, Islamic references are not merely a discursive cloth used to dress up modern secular premises for the sake of authenticity.

Rather, in Rida's understanding, belief adds something essential to the rational premises of worldly interests, which Islam also contains: since Islam is "in agreement with the innate disposition of mankind and their general interests" *and* since human beings "require religion due to their innate disposition," Rida envisions Islam eventually spreading among all Western and Eastern peoples.[44] Religion complements secular knowledge with moral guidance, without which the worldly order is arguably unsustainable. Based on this assertion, Rida reminds the students at Aligarh College: "if you need the English language for the sake of your world (*li-ajl dunyākum*), you need the Arabic language for the sake of your religion and your world, because formal-material life (*al-ḥayāt al-ṣūriyya al-māddiyya*) is not established, solidified, and advanced, except through moral-spiritual life (*al-ḥayāt al-adabiyya al-ma'nawiyya*)."[45]

I suggest that this aim and strategy also underlies Rida's use of *umma* instead of *al-hay'a al-ijtimā'iyya*. Rida resorts to *umma* as a central concept of classical Islamic discourse with the aim of preserving an authentic frame of reference and identity. As concerns content, Rida refutes the vision of a purely rational, non-religious social order associated with *al-hay'a al-ijtimā'iyya* – in other words, he refutes a closed reading of the immanent frame. He argues against the need to adopt this vision by showing that its aims are better realized by Islamic religion: the immanent frame can only be truly sustained in an open reading based on religious belief. Rida thus instills secular principles of moral and social order – which in themselves, as conceptualized in *al-hay'a al-ijtimā'iyya*, he regards as insufficient – in the concept of *umma*, with its enduring connotation of a moral community guided by religion. This is not to say that *umma* was then equivalent to 'society,' but rather that Rida used *umma* to convey, within a moral-religious framework, notions of social order that were other-

44 Ibid., 582f.
45 Ibid., 583.

wise expressed in the concept of *al-hay'a al-ijtimāʿiyya*, which was associated with a more secular framework.

While Rida overwhelmingly uses *al-hay'a al-ijtimāʿiyya* to paraphrase a secular view of moral order, he once makes prominent use of the concept to express his own view – possibly for the purpose of clarifying to his Lebanese audience that he would subsequently use *umma* to conceptualize society. Note Rida's employment of *al-hay'a al-ijtimāʿiyya* and *umma*, and also *mujtamaʿ*, in the very first sentences of a speech he gave in Tripolis in 1898:

"Unity (*ittiḥād*) and coherence (*ilti'ām*) are the life of the social body (*ḥayāt li-l-hay'a al-ijtimāʿiyya*), by means of which [i.e., this life] [society] is in its proper condition, and [unity and coherence are] the axis of [society's] formal and spiritual felicity, around which [i.e., this axis] it revolves. Unity and coherence in society (*al-umma*) are like that which is essential (*al-faṣl al-muqawwam*) in the natural sphere (*al-hay'a* [sic] *al-nawʿiyya*). Therefore, that member of society (*man min afrād al-umma*) who deviates from unity is considered outside society, and must be deprived of its rights, in the same way as a member of the human species who has lost the rational capability (*al-quwa al-nāṭiqa*) is considered to have left humanity and joined the beasts. Unity and coherence in human society (*al-mujtamaʿ al-insānī*) are like gravitation and attraction in the world of elements."[46]

Rida elaborates the last analogy between the order of stars in the cosmos and of members in society by resorting to *umma* only,[47] and then adds another analogy, this time between the body of a person and the body of society (*umma*, *al-hay'a al-ijtimāʿiyya*): it is necessary, he suggests, that "man senses that the whole society (*majmūʿ al-umma*) is like one person, and that all of its working parts (*aṣnāf*) are like a main organ (*ʿuḍw ra'īsī*) in the physical constitution of a person (*al-bunya al-shakhṣiyya*), and that the difference of the parts in appearances and ranks does not affect them being equal in merit with regard to the social body (*al-hay'a al-ijtimāʿiyya*)."[48] Rida goes on to stress the need for proper education (*tarbiya*) of all strata of society (*jamīʿ ṭabaqāt al-umma*) so as to produce the sentiment of belonging to an overall social body.[49]

---

46 Idem. 1898. "al-Ittihad." *al-Manar* 1/29: 547–551, here 547 f.
47 Ibid., 548 f.
48 Ibid., 549.
49 Ibid., 549 ff. For more instances in which Rida conceives of the *umma* as a social body, see chapter 10 section 4.1.

If this article substantiates the hypothesis of *umma* serving as a synonym for *al-hay'a al-ijtimāʿiyya*, it also suggests that it is worth considering whether *al-hay'a a-ijtimāʿiyya* was more firmly established in the Syro-Lebanese region, where it had first been coined. After all, other than the two articles discussed above, this speech from Tripolis is the sole article in which Rida uses *al-hay'a al-ijtimāʿiyya* twice, particularly in the very first sentence.

The analysis of Rida's usage of *al-hay'a al-ijtimāʿiyya* thus provides us with the first hints at the main argument of this study – namely, that Rida used *umma* to convey aspects of 'society.' This argument will be further established in chapter 10; for now, we will refocus our attention on *al-hay'a al-ijtimāʿiyya*. In all three of the texts by Rida discussed here, (religious) education and individuals working together were central requirements of society, and the last article added the image of society as a social body. These aspects are also central in other authors' usage of *al-hay'a al-ijtimāʿiyya* in *al-Manar*, as the following analysis of the composite's meanings and the topics it addresses will show.

3 Crucial Aspects of *al-Hay'a al-Ijtimāʿiyya*

3.1 A Social Body and a Social Order

"The organic concept of society finds its chief strength and support in the phenomena of co-operation."
– S. N. Patten, 1894[50]

An organic understanding of society, which underlies the conception of *al-hay'a al-ijtimāʿiyya* or *umma* as a social body, was almost unique to the last article by Rida discussed above. Khuri-Makdisi pointed out that the secular authors she analyzed, especially Shibli Shumayyil, employed *al-hay'a al-ijtimāʿiyya* to give voice to such an organic understanding.[51] Additionally, the composite *al-jism al-majmūʿī* (the collective body) was supposedly a forerunner of *al-hay'a al-ijtimāʿiyya* for conceptualizing society.[52] In future research attending to the predecessors of the modern concepts of society, one should also consider early modern Ottoman Turkish conceptions of *heyet-i içtimaiye* in analogy to the human

50 Patten, S. N. 1894. "The Organic Concept of Society." *Annals of the American Academy of Political and Social Science* 5: 88–93, here 88.
51 See above: 195 f.
52 Gasper, "Public," 58fn26. I have not come across this composite myself.

body.[53] To confine ourselves to fully modern times here, Mary Poovey has shown how the understanding of society as a social body emerged in England in the 1830s.[54] It connoted a social sphere distinct from politics and was a major competitor to the understanding of society as a social machine.[55] It was the self-proclaimed task of English reformists to cure the illnesses of the social body, which either referred to society as an organic whole or to the poor specifically.[56] In *al-Manar, al-hayʾa al-ijtimāʿiyya* consistently – and with only one potential minor exception, written by Rida[57] – refers to society as a whole. Rida was also not alone in elucidating the meaning of *al-hayʾa al-ijtimāʿiyya* as "the whole society" (*majmūʿ al-umma*). We find the same explanation in *The Tale of Isa ibn Hisham*, written by Muhammad al-Muwaylihi in 1898, which is considered one of the first Arabic novels. In that story, it is explained to the Pasha that "the social body" (*al-hayʾa al-ijtimāʿiyya*) on whose behalf a prosecutor acts is "the whole society" (*majmūʿat al-umma*).[58]

In *al-Manar,* we find a few additional pertinent usages of *al-hayʾa al-ijtimāʿiyya* in the sense of a social body, with the latest instance stemming from 1911. In 1900, Rida stresses that "for every illness (*marḍ*), there is a cure, and the social body (*al-hayʾa al-ijtimāʿiyya*) like the personal body (*al-hayʾa al-shakhṣiyya*) falls ill for a reason."[59] Following this statement, he addresses the illness of Islamic society (*marḍ al-umma al-islāmiyya*) and, earlier in the same article, he explains that the "meaning of man being a social creature (*khalq ijtimāʿī*) is that he senses that he is a member of a society" (*ʿuḍw min umma*).[60] Muhammad Tawfiq Sidqi argues that trying to deviate from the fact that some men are elevated over others in God's creation produces "the illness of mutual hatred in

---

53 For the organic understanding of society by the Ottoman polymath Katip Celebi and further literature, see: Zemmin, Florian. 2011. *Islamische Verantwortungsethik im 17. Jahrhundert. Ein weberianisches Verständnis der Handlungsvorstellungen Kātib Čelebis (1609–1657).* Schenefeld: E. B. Braun, 99 ff.

54 Poovey, Mary. 1995. *Making a Social Body: British Cultural Formation.* Chicago: University of Chicago Press.

55 Ibid., 8, 37.

56 Ibid., 7 f.

57 See: Rida, Rashid. 1918. "Radd al-Manar ʿala al-Naqid li-Dhikra al-Mawlid al-Nabawi." *al-Manar* 20/9: 395–403, here 400.

58 Mitchell, *Colonising,* 120.

59 Rida, Rashid. 1900. "al-Muhawarat bayna al-Muslih wa-l-Muqallid (al-Muhawara al-Ula)." *al-Manar* 3/28: 665–670 [misprinted as 635–640], here 669 (misprinted as 639). Note: pages 634–663 exist twice in this volume of *al-Manar*; this is the second occurrence of page 635 (thus actually page 665).

60 Ibid., 666 (misprinted as 636).

the body of society" (*jism al-hay'a al-ijtimāʿiyya*).[61] An organic understanding of society in analogy to the human body seems to also underly phrases like the following, which Rida quotes in 1911 from an article by Hibat al-Din (1884–1967), the editor of the Baghdad-based *Majallat al-ʿIlm:* "by harm usually is meant a matter (*amr*) drawn from the property (*khāṣṣiyya*) of a thing which [i.e., the property] has an effect that is contrary to health, like poison, or that is contrary to the social body (*al-hay'a al-ijtimāʿiyya*), like envy or injustice, etc."[62]

While the view of society as a social body implies and informs a vision of social order, the organic analogy often stands behind that vision of order or is dissolved into it. Thus the foregoing quotation continues: "and the exact opposite to [harm] is benefit, and this is a matter drawn from the property of a thing which [i.e., the property] has an effect that is favorable to health, like water, or that is favorable to the order of social association (*niẓām al-ijtimāʿ*), like justice and the performance of good deeds, etc."[63] In *al-Manar* in general, the understanding of *al-hay'a al-ijtimāʿiyya* as a social order is more prevalent than that of a social body, keeping in mind that the organic understanding of society also contains and informs notions of order.

The order(ing) of society is most explicitly addressed when authors refer to *tanẓīm//intiẓām al-hay'a al-ijtimāʿiyya* – which, however, is the case in only three instances. In the first volume of *al-Manar*, Rida quotes a certain Monsieur Coutard's opinion on the reports about "our"[64] clubs: "they are obstacles on the road to our advancement and dense darknesses [overshadowing] the appearance of the order of our society" (*intiẓām hay'atinā al-ijtimāʿiyya*).[65] In 1899, ʿUmar Khayri Zaghlul says that those drowning their reason in wine and songs can only gain true happiness when "the state of [the overall] society is brought into the right order (*tanẓīm ḥāl al-hay'a al-ijtimāʿiyya*), since the general condition (*al-ḥāla al-ʿāmma*) has an impact on individuals."[66] Most pertinently, a Lebanese writer, in a speech he gave in India, upholds the Islamic religion as the guarantor of the social order: "The Islamic religion (*al-diyāna al-islāmiyya*) guards all types of human needs and guarantees the duration of the order of society (*intiẓām al-hay'a al-ijtimāʿiyya*); and it did indeed set forth the worldly and

---

61 Sidqi, "al-Din," *al-Manar* 8/19: 734 f.

62 Majallat al-ʿIlm quoted in Rida, Rashid. 1911. "Munazarat ʿAlim Muslim li-Duʿat al-Brutistant fi Baghdad." *al-Manar* 14/12: 914–922, here 919.

63 Ibid., 919.

64 Rida here refers to either Egyptians or Arabs.

65 Monsieur Coutard quoted by Rashid Rida in ʿAbduh, Muhammad. 1898. "Muntadiyatuna al-ʿUmumiyya wa-Ahadithuha." *al-Manar* 1/20: 361–368, here 368.

66 Zaghlul, ʿUmar Khayri Efendi. 1899. "Kana Ya Ma Kana." *al-Manar* 2/23: 360–363, here 361.

otherworldly interests (*al-maṣāliḥ al-dunyawiyya wa-l-ukhrawiyya*), so that those who hold onto it will obtain the greatest felicity and the most exalted glory."[67]

In a number of other instances, *al-hay'a al-ijtimā'iyya* is not coupled with a term conceptualizing order, but most clearly addresses the specific contemporary order of society. The Indian Muslim reformist Amir 'Ali, best known for his work *The Spirit of Islam*,[68] accounts for the earliest of these cases, in an article translated from the English and published in *al-Mu'ayyad* in 1913. Discussing the topic of polygyny, 'Ali points out that this practice remained common in Europe until "the modern society (*al-hay'a al-ijtimā'iyya al-ḥadītha*) disapproved of it and abandoned it."[69] He twice mentions "the contemporary society" (*al-hay'a al-ijtimā'iyya al-ḥāḍira*) – once in the sense of modern society in general, the second time referring to the current state of order: in 1921, the decree of a conference in Geneva, of which Rida was the vice-president, stresses that the Arab culture (*al-ḥaḍāra al-'arabiyya*) is "a branch of the tree of civilization (*al-madaniyya*), which – together with the Greek and the Roman branches – is the root of the present social order (*al-hay'a al-ijtimā'iyya al-ḥāḍira*) and the reason for its flourishing."[70] And in 1930, Rida quotes an anonymous Indian writer as demanding both a political revolution (*inqilāb siyāsī*) and "certain changes in the current social order" (*al-hay'a al-ijtimā'iyya al-ḥāḍira*).[71] Finally, in 1924, Rida quotes from an unspecified book, noting that it will take at least a century until "the scientific, philosophical, contemporary social order (*al-hay'a al-ijtimā'iyya al-'ilmiyya al-falsafiyya al-'aṣriyya*) in the East" is formed.[72]

As we have seen, most explicit references to the order of society are found in quotations in articles by Rashid Rida, although he did not originate any of these instances himself. However, Rida does account for some of the following

---

67 Muhammad 'Arif Salhab al-Tarabulusi quoted in Rida, Rashid. 1926. "al-'Alam al-Islami." *al-Manar* 26/7: 540–547, here 545 f. Other instances in which Islam is related to *al-hay'a al-ijtimā'iyya* are dealt with in chapter 7 section 3.3.

68 Ali, Ameer. 1952 [1891]. *The Spirit of Islam: a History of the Evolution and Ideals of Islam; with a Life of the Prophet.* London: Christophers.

69 'Ali, Amir [= idem.]. 1913. "al-Mar'a qabl al-Islam wa-ba'duhu." *al-Manar* 16/12: 933–941, here 935. On this article see also below: 292.

70 Decree of a conference held in Geneva quoted in Rida, Rashid. 1922. "al-Rihla al-Urubiyya (4)." *al-Manar* 23/6: 441–459, here 450.

71 Anonymous Indian writer quoted in Rida, Rashid. 1932. "al-Tajdid wa-l-Tajaddud wa-l-Mujaddidun (3)." *al-Manar* 32/3: 226–231, here 227.

72 Anonymous author quoted in Rida, Rashid. 1926. "Abna' al-'Alam al-Islami." *al-Manar* 27/6: 471–477, here 476. The author is reacting to Taha Husayn's work *al-Shi'r al-Jahili* and to the alleged spread of unbelief in Turkey and Egypt.

uses of *al-hay'a al-ijtimā'iyya* that also convey the idea of a social order, if less explicitly than the foregoing examples.

3.2 *Al-Hay'a al-Ijtimā'iyya* and Politics

In the earliest noteworthy article concerning the relation of *al-hay'a al-ijtimā'iyya* to the political sphere, written by Rafiq al-'Azm[73] in 1899 and substantially commented upon by Rida, *umma* again is used much more prominently than *al-hay'a al-ijtimā'iyya.* Rida mentions the concept of *al-hay'a al-ijtimā'iyya* only in the very last sentence of his comment, after both he and al-'Azm have extensively employed *umma*, with al-'Azm even using it to refer to the order of society (*niẓām al-umma*). The topic and main argument of the article is indicated in its title: "The Islamic Reform will come about through the Justice of the Custodian or through Common Mutual Solidarity/Responsibility" (al-Islah al-Islami bi-'Adl al-Qawwam aw al-Takaful al-'Amm).[74] Without the realization of at least one of these two conditions, even a just legal order catering to the interests of the people – as the Islamic laws ideally do – cannot realize its goal, al-'Azm argues. It is worth following al-'Azm's line of argumentation closely; as the beginning of the article makes clear, it is premised on the social nature of human beings:

"Since God endowed human beings with the love for social association (*ḥubb al-ijtimā'*), the laws of communal existence (*al-wujūd al-madanī*) require that the general bonds of affection (*awākhī al-ulfa al-'umūmiyya*) are solidified by a complete order (*niẓām shāmil*) in which the beneficent inclinations find reassurance and subject to which (*dūnahu*) the desires leaning toward evil are destroyed. The necessary anchor (*manāṭ*) of this order are laws (*sharā'i'*) founded on justice and based on public interest (*al-maṣlaḥa al-'āmma*), with nothing following from personal desires (*aghrāḍ al-nufūs*) interspersed in them. And these laws only guarantee the felicity of nations (*umam*) and the continuation of the order of affection (*niẓām al-ulfa*) by one of two conditions: the justice of the custodian (*'adl al-qawwām*) or the solidarity/responsibility of the people (*takāful al-aqwām*). And when both of these two conditions are no longer given, it is impossible to benefit from the laws, however just they may be in themselves."[75]

---

73 Al-'Azm was the most eminent sociological thinker who wrote regularly for *al-Manar*, and as such will be dealt with extensively in chapter 9.
74 Al-'Azm, Rafiq. 1899. "al-Islah al-Islami bi-'Adl al-Qawwam aw al-Takaful al-'Amm." *al-Manar* 2/6: 81–88.
75 Ibid., 81.

Al-ʿAzm thinks that this causal chain is proven by the social history (*al-tārīkh al-ijtimāʿī*) of all past states (*duwal*) and peoples (*shuʿūb*) and suggests that the loss of these two conditions also occurred in the history of Islam (*tārīkh al-islām*), the laws of which, in the beginning, were perfectly just and were erected on the basis of common mutual solidarity (*al-takāful al-ʿāmm*).[76] From events in Islamic history, al-ʿAzm derives his argument that

"there is a power higher than respect for the caliph entrenched in the spirits (*nufūs*) of Muslims, and this is the power of common mutual responsibility for protecting the laws of Islam. Subjected to this force, each person (*nafs*) became like a venerable guardian (*raqīb ʿatīd*), inciting the other Muslims to knowledge of the rights and duties that compel every one of them (*kull fard minhum*) not to transgress (*al-wuqūf ʿind*) the ordinance of obedience to the caliph and to comply with his command, as long as he does not violate the domain (*jānib*) of the religious law (*al-sharʿ*) or upset the order of this great Islamic society (*niẓām dhalik al-mujtamaʿ al-islāmī al-ʿaẓīm*). It is obvious what this implies for the prestige (*nufūdh*) of the authority (*kalima*) of the caliph and the soundness (*salāma*) of the life of society (*umma*)."[77]

In a historical sketch, al-ʿAzm criticizes the alleged loss of mutual responsibility and the exaggerated obedience to the caliph under the Umayyads, and especially under Persian rule, whereas he judges the Abbasids more favorably.[78] When the latter came to power in 750, they immediately tried to reestablish the basis of common mutual responsibility, and for that purpose they even appointed the first minister (*wazīr*) of the Islamic state (*dawlat al-islām*). However, al-ʿAzm says, this was a ministry of implementation (*wizārat tanfīdh*), not a ministry of entrustment (*wizārat tafwīḍ*).[79] The meaning of this rather cryptic term becomes clear from its subsequent elaboration and from an analogy al-ʿAzm draws to modern forms of government. According to him, it was Harun al-Rashid (r. 786–809) who

"saw that it is closer to the basis of general mutual responsibility and better for the ordering of the affairs of the state (*tanẓīm shuʾūn al-dawla*) and the soundness (*salāma*) of laws (*aḥkām al-sharʿ*), to turn the ministry [which had been a

---

76 Ibid., 81f.
77 Ibid., 82.
78 Ibid., 83ff.
79 Ibid., 83f.

ministry of implementation] into a ministry of entrustment that is responsible before the people (*al-nās*) and the caliph for everything it does in the state (*fī al-dawla*); and thus it happened. And this ministry of entrustment equals what they today call the accountable ministry (*al-wizāra al-mas'ūla*) in the moderate governments (*al-ḥukūmāt al-muʿtadila*)."[80]

From the moment of its foundation, al-ʿAzm argues, "this ministry has had proper effects (*āthār ṣāliḥa*) on the order of the state (*niẓām al-dawla*), which [i.e., the effects] prompted an unprecedented advancement (*al-taraqqī*) of the nation (*umma*) on the ladder of civilization (*maʿārij al-tamaddun*)."[81] The negative influence of the Persians, al-ʿAzm suggests, did not matter a great deal as long as other states were also weak – something that changed drastically with the rise of the West, which then deprived Eastern peoples of their freedom.[82]

The attempts of some leaders to ward off this threat have not been fruitful, al-ʿAzm argues,

"due to their remoteness from what Islam is erected upon and from that by which the order of society (*niẓām al-umma*) is protected, and this is common mutual responsibility and the justice of the custodian. These are the two basic elements on whose pillars the Islamic states (*duwal al-islām*) are erected, and only through their life do societies (*umam*) revive. The backsliding that inflicted Muslims and the weakness of their states is only due to the weakness of these two conditions and not due to the weakness of the law (*qānūn*) or the need of the nation (*umma*) to found new principles (*awḍāʿ*) or advantageous arrangements (*tarātīb mufīda*) for the order of society (*niẓām al-umma*) and for the proper arrangement of the affairs of the state (*intiẓām shu'ūn al-dawla*); after all, if drawing up laws and writing down registers would dispense with this terrible regression and this sudden weakness, then the Islamic law (*sharīʿa*) in itself would be sufficient, as it is the most just and most great of all laws, leading to the benefits of mankind (*maṣāliḥ al-bashar*) and leading to the ways of felicity (*ṭuruq al-saʿāda*). However, [the Islamic shariʿa] is only sufficient for this when its custodian is just, and this [justness] is lost with the loss of accountability (*al-mas'ūliyya*)."[83]

80 Ibid., 84.
81 Ibid., 84.
82 Ibid., 85.
83 Ibid., 85.

Al-ʿAzm thus ends his article with a plea for a participatory, accountable government – a plea that points to his political views and activities, which will be presented in chapter 9 section 1. Of greater relevance to our question here is the fact that al-ʿAzm conceptually distinguishes between an order of society and an order of the state.

The other insights this article yields concerning terminological usage and the relation between society and politics will be discussed in conjunction with Rida's comment, which begins by elucidating the meaning of the principle of *al-takāful al-ʿāmm* – a principle that was central to al-ʿAzm's formulation of Islam as a socio-political order.[84] While we are specifically interested in al-ʿAzm's and Rida's terminological usage, it is worth noting that al-Batush, the author of the only substantial monograph on al-ʿAzm, translates al-ʿAzm's terminology into contemporary parlance: he explains *ʿadl al-qawwām* as meaning "*al-sulṭa al-siyāsiyya al-ʿādila*" (just political power) and *al-takāful al-ʿāmm* as "*al-mujtamaʿ al-mutakāfil*" (solidary society).[85]

According to Rida, al-ʿAzm's use of

"common mutual solidarity (*al-takāful al-ʿāmm*) means: true knowledge of the whole society (*majmūʿ al-umma*) of its general rights and its shared interests (*maṣāliḥihā al-mushtaraka*), in such a way as to incite agreement among them [i.e., the members of society] about the protection (*ḥifẓ*) of these rights and the preservation (*ṣiyāna*) of these interests, insofar that it incites the whole [society] (*al-majmūʿ*) when a transgressor (*ʿābith*) violates [these rights and interests] or an oppressor (*ẓālim*) damages them and [the whole society] embarks on defending them and preserving their existence (*kiyānihā*), and this is the political spirit of Islam (*rūḥ siyāsat al-islām*)."[86]

This spirit was weakened, Rida maintains, whenever "religion was weakened by the spread of illegitimate innovations (*bidaʿ*), immoral behavior (*fusūq*), and corrupted teachings and by its [i.e., religion's] scholars pursuing the desires of rulers and kings."[87] He agrees with al-ʿAzm that "reform either occurs through the justice of the custodian or through common mutual responsibility" and maintains: "this is [exactly] what I meant when I repeatedly stressed that reform will either be initiated by the rulers (*al-ḥukkām*) or by the people (*al-umma*).

84 See also below: chapter 9 section 3 and esp. 4.

85 Al-Batush, *Rafiq al-ʿAzm*, 49; more will be said on al-Batush's interpretation of al-ʿAzm's usage of *al-takāful al-ʿāmm* in chapter 9 section 4.

86 Rashid Rida in al-ʿAzm, "al-Islah," 86.

87 Ibid., 86f.

And as my hope in the rulers has been weak, I have been focusing much more on the education of the people (*tarbiyat al-umma*) in such a manner that it knows its rights (*ḥuqūqahā*) and takes upon itself their protection through cooperation (*taʿāwun*), and this is what the author [i.e., al-ʿAzm] called 'common mutual solidarity/responsibility'."[88]

After mentioning some minor points of disagreement with al-ʿAzm concerning events in Islamic history, Rida concludes:

"Thus, there is no doubt that the felicity of peoples (*umam*) only comes about through the knowledge (*ʿilm*), practice (*ʿamal*), and virtues (*faḍā'il*) of their members in total (*majmūʿ afrādihā*). And the justice of the rulers is merely a means to this felicity, because it helps the society (*umma*) to advance in what has just been mentioned by those things it is removing (*yadfaʿ ʿanhā*) from it which hinder it from advancing. Therefore the task (*waẓīfa*) of the rulers concerning the social body (*fī al-hay'a al-ijtimāʿiyya*) is like the task of doctors and physicians with regard to individuals (*bi-l-nisba li-l-ashkhāṣ*), and complete felicity is only realized by the propriety (*ṣalāḥ*) of both parties (*farīqayn*) [i.e., the rulers and the people] together."[89]

While it is rather clear that, in this last sentence, Rida uses *al-hay'a al-ijtimāʿiyya* synonymously with *umma*, more needs to be said about both concepts as referring to an order of society distinct from the state.

This was most explicit when al-ʿAzm distinguished between *niẓām al-umma* and *intiẓām shu'ūn al-dawla*. Previously, he had notably employed *mujtamaʿ* to refer to the order of Islamic society, which ought to be respected by the caliph. Al-ʿAzm thus indicates an abstract sense of order – an order (*niẓām*) that is required by human beings' natural inclination toward social association (*ijtimāʿ*) and that needs to be supported by a just legal system,[90] protecting the rights and interests of the people. When the relation to the ruler is addressed, *umma* may indeed be translated as 'the people' rather than as 'society.' Al-ʿAzm also once addresses this relation as that between the custodian (*al-qawwām*) and the people (*al-aqwām*), and once terminologically refers back to the pre-modern notion of the shepherd and his flock (*al-rāʿī wa-l-raʿiyya*). However, he dissolves

---

88 Ibid., 87.

89 Ibid., 87 f.

90 This legal system is a requirement of that order (*niẓām*) but not identical with it, in contrast to what one may suspect, given the meaning of the term in Ottoman Turkish, with which al-ʿAzm was quite familiar.

this classical understanding into the modern distinction between the people and the government, and even between society and the state.[91]

We can hardly interpret such an understanding of society and the state as two abstract orders on the basis of Rida's comment; here, *umma* and also *al-hay'a al-ijtimāʿiyya* rather refer to the people (*Volk*) or society, in distinction from the rulers or the government. One may thus ask whether and when *umma* is best translated as 'society,' and when it is best rendered 'the people.' The point remains, however, that Rida used *umma* to express notions otherwise expressed by *al-hay'a al-ijtimāʿiyya* – in this case, most notably the shared interests (*maṣāliḥ mushtaraka*) of society. I will discuss the differences between *umma* and *al-hay'a al-ijtimāʿiyya* in section 6. For now, we conclude that Rida once uses *al-hay'a al-ijtimāʿiyya* to address the relation between the ruler and the people or between the government and society, but that both he and al-ʿAzm employ *umma* to elaborate their interpretation of that relation, and that al-ʿAzm even distinguishes between the orders of society and the state.

In only few other instances in *al-Manar* is *al-hay'a al-ijtimāʿiyya* related to politics, although the discussion of particular societies in section 4 will add to the following examples. In two articles in a series published in volume two of *al-Manar*, an anonymous Syrian author conceptualizes the order of society as *hay'at al-ijtimāʿ:* he compares four Islamic governments concerning their level of order (*intiẓām*) and the coherence of society (*ittisāq hay'at al-ijtimāʿ*),[92] and in addressing the rights of the people (*shaʿb*) with respect to the government, he attests to a lack of knowledge among the Arabs concerning the order of society (*niẓām hay'at al-ijtimāʿ*).[93] To what extent the author actually distinguishes between social and political order, or even society and the state, could only be assessed based on a more detailled analysis.[94]

---

91 With reference to another text by al-ʿAzm, al-Batush also discerns different normative connotations in al-ʿAzm's use of *raʿiyya* and *umma* in relation to the government: *raʿiyya* in the pre-modern sense of 'the flock' expresses the view of absolutist governments (*al-ḥukūmāt al-istibdādiyya*), whereas constitutional governments (*al-ḥukūmāt al-dustūriyya*) regard the people as an *umma* (al-Batush, *Rafiq al-ʿAzm*, 62).

92 Ahad al-Kuttab min Suriya [an author from Syria] 1899. "Istinhad Himam (6)." *al-Manar* 2/13: 199–204, here 203.

93 Idem. 1899. "Istinhad Himam (13)." *al-Manar* 2/20: 312–316, here 315.

94 I did consider the possibility of *hay'at al-ijtimāʿ* here referring to a governmental assembly. While this cannot be ruled out completely, the following statements by that author made me decide in favor of 'society,' even though this may include the political sphere: the author speaks of the peoples constituting the order (*hay'a*) of a state (*al-shuʿūb al-mukawwina li-hay'atihā*) and

This also applies to the following statement, which is found in the translation of a decree by the Ottoman Sultan from 1876. In this decree, he explains the intentions of the constitution (*al-qānūn al-asāsī*) drawn up in that year and stresses, among other things, the necessity of a civil social order for a just government: The government, which now is founded on a secure and orderly basis (*asās maʾmūn muntaẓam*), ought to prevent "the bad comportments resulting from personal despotic rule or the rule of a small number of persons, so that all the people (*jamīʿ aqwām*) from which our body is composed (*al-murakkaba hayʾatunā minhum*) may benefit from the blessing of liberty, justice, and equality without exception. And this is the right (*ḥaqq*) and the interest (*manfaʿa*) appropriate for civil society (*al-hayʾa al-ijtimāʿiyya al-madaniyya*)."[95] This central passage envisaging a civil society (*al-hayʾa al-ijtimāʿiyya al-madaniyya*) is quoted again in the same volume of *al-Manar* from 1909 – namely, as an argument against despotism and against Europeans portraying Islamic governments as theocratic (*al-thiyūqrāṭiyya*).[96]

The only additional instance in which *al-hayʾa al-ijtimāʿiyya* is related to politics is a quotation from Faris Nimr, the editor of *al-Muqattam* and *al-Muqtataf*, who was one of several intellectuals who briefly stated their opinions concerning the means to reform the Egyptian sultanate[97] in volume 17 of *al-Manar*. Nimr explains that 'sultanate' (*al-salṭana*) means

"the government and the people (*al-umma*) in their present condition, which is constitutional (*dustūriyya*). The means to reviving it are numerous, some material (*māddī*), some ethical (*adabī*). And every means (*wāsiṭa*) is conditional upon a certain ability (*qūwa*), especially the means of knowledge and capital (*māl*). Both in the government and in society (*fī al-umma*) there are indeed knowledgable and wealthy persons, who are in no need of intelligence (*idrāk*) or wealth (*yasār*); but what we are lacking is instruction (*tarbiya*) of the government about proper morals and about those characteristics ordering and advancing the affairs of society (*al-ṣifāt al-munaẓẓima wa-l-muraqqiyya li-shuʾūn al-hayʾa al-ijtimāʿiyya*), until we as groups (*jamāʿāt*) are capable of unity and of mutual

---

the competition between states to complete the social order (*istitmām al-niẓām al-ijtimāʿī*) (idem., "Istinhad," *al-Manar* 2/13: 200).

95 Sultan ʿAbd al-Hamid II quoted in Rida, Rashid. 1908. "al-Qanun al-Asasi wa-l-Khatt al-Sultani bi-hi." *al-Manar* 11/6: 424–431, here 430.

96 Sultan ʿAbd al-Hamid II quoted in al-Maqdisi, Muhammad Ruhi al-Khalidi. 1908. "al-Inqilab al-ʿUthmani." *al-Manar* 11/9: 646–672, here 647 f.

97 This was the official designation of Egypt under the English protectorate between 1914 and 1922.

cooperation for the organization (*tadbīr*) of our affairs and the success of our works, in the same way as many of us are presently capable of as individuals (*afrād*)."[98]

The importance of morals for socio-political order, mentioned only briefly in this quote, is a recurrent topic in the pages of *al-Manar.* Above we saw that Rashid Rida stressed the necessity of religious education for social morals and social order, but that he rarely conceptualized society as *al-hay'a al-ijtimāʿiyya*, instead infusing notions of social order into the concept of *umma.*[99] The following subsection collects the rather few instances in *al-Manar* in which morals, religion, or Islamic prescriptions are explicitly related to *al-hay'a al-ijtimāʿiyya.*

3.3 *Al-Hay'a al-Ijtimāʿiyya*, Morals, and Religion

The earliest instance of stressing the importance of morals and virtues for society conceptualized as *al-hay'a al-ijtimāʿiyya* in *al-Manar* is found in the reprint of an article from *al-ʿUrwa al-Wuthqa,* the short-lived but influential paper al-Afghani and ʿAbduh founded in Paris in 1884.[100] In this article, the author of which is not identified, virtues (*faḍā'il*) – such as generosity, righteousness (*ʿifa*), and modesty (*ḥayā'*) – are upheld as "the anchor of union (*waḥda*) of the social body (*al-hay'a al-ijtimāʿiyya*) and the bond of unity (*ittiḥād*) between individuals (*al-āḥād*)."[101] In another article, written latter but published in the first volume of *al-Manar,* ʿAbduh charges that those who do not know the true meaning of values such as justice are a burden on society (*shu'm ʿalā al-hay'a al-ijtimāʿiyya*).[102]

Also in the first volume from 1898, an otherwise unknown author criticizes a common misunderstanding of *ḥurriyya* as absolute liberty, which condones the commitment of crimes (*mūbiqāt*) in public. According to him, this misunderstanding has led to disrespect for morals and the loss of inhibition (*ḥayā'*), which is absolutely required for society (*al-hay'a al-ijtimāʿiyya*) and for the

98 Faris Nimr quoted in Rida, Rashid. 1914. "Afdal al-Wasa'il li-Inhad al-Saltana." *al-Manar* 17/4: 303–312, here 304.
99 See above: chapter 7 section 2.
100 See above: 138 f.
101 Al-ʿUrwa al-Wuthqa. 1901. "al-Fada'il wa-l-Radha'il [the title is Rida's]." *al-Manar* 4/2: 41–50, here 42.
102 ʿAbduh, Muhammad. 1898. "Ma Akthar al-Qawl wa-Ma Aqall al-ʿAmal." *al-Manar* 1/9: 143–149, here 148.

order of humanity (*niẓām al-insāniyya*). True liberty, he maintains, is conditional upon inhibition and upon each person knowing their rights and duties.[103]

The last example explicitly relating morals to *al-hay'a al-ijtimāʿiyya* stems from an anonymous Muslim author writing from Marrakesh in 1927. He depicts one group of unbelievers as "knowing the truth of Islam and the worldly and otherworldly benefits it has set forth, knowing that it is appropriate (*ṣāliḥ*) for every time and place, and that it is the religion of humankind's innate disposition (*dīn al-fiṭra*) sought for and desired by humanity." However, among those aspects of Islam which these unbelievers allegedly have trouble accepting are the obligations concerning "abstention (*turk*) from forbidden and reprehensible actions (*al-munkarāt*) that lacerate the face of the social body (*takhdish wajh al-hay'a al-ijtimāʿiyya*)."[104]

Concerning the relation of Islam to *al-hay'a al-ijtimāʿiyya*, a most interesting occurence is a definition of the bases of Islam in a text by Rida from 1908. He again uses the composite in a Syro-Lebanese setting – namely, in a talk he gave in Beirut, which was summarized by an anonymous group of students but corrected by Rida before going to print.[105] He first explains that Islam, being a universal religion for all humankind, was sent to the ignorant people (*al-umma al-jāhilā*) – the Arabs – and not to a civilized people (*umma mutamaddina*) precisely because of the Arabs' simplicity and their independence of thought and will, which had not yet been impaired by existing teachings or corrupted rulers.[106] Sent to that simple people, Islam is itself "a very simple matter, namely it is tantamount to the return to humankind's innate disposition (*al-fiṭra al-bashariyya*) – and what is this innate disposition? It is that by which your soul longs to submit (*idhʿān*) to the invisible power (*al-salṭana al-ghaybiyya*) and to choose what you believe to be the good and beneficial."[107] If the promotion of Islam as the natural religion (*dīn al-fiṭra*) is a recurring topos in *al-Manar*,

103 Al-Mahami, Hamuduh Efendi. 1898. "Taqwim al-Afkar." *al-Manar* 1/34: 661–665, here 665.
104 Muslim Ghayur [a zealous Muslim]. 1927. "al-Islah al-Islami fi al-Maghrib al-Aqsa (3)." *al-Manar* 28/3: 196–201, here 200. The second group of unbelievers, characterized as being ignorant about the truth of Islam, is depicted in the following part (idem. 1927. "al-Islah al-Islami fi al-Maghrib al-Aqsa (4)." *al-Manar* 28/4: 285–288).
105 Rida, Rashid. 1908. "al-Khutba al-Ula min Khutabina al-Islamiyya fi al-Diyar al-Suriyya." *al-Manar* 11/9: 641–646.
106 Ibid., 641ff.
107 Ibid., 643.

Rida's statement also resonates strongly with modern Protestant understandings of religion as inner feeling and as submission to an unseen force.[108]

Rida goes on to suggest that, in order to fulfill human beings' natural needs, "Islam is built upon three bases: first, reform of the intellect (*'aql*) through a creed (*'aqīda*) cleansing the spirit (*janān*) and built upon rational proof (*burhān*); second, reform of the self (*nafs*) through purifying and cleansing it of vices and embellishing it with virtues; third, reform of practices concerning those acts of devotion (*'ibādāt*) and rights (*ḥuqūq*) by which the matter of individuals is in order (*yastaqīm bi-hā amr al-afrād*) and the social body advances (*tartaqī al-hay'a al-ijtimā'iyya*)."[109] Since, in his elaboration of that third basis, Rida only refers to the practice of prayer, *al-hay'a al-ijtimā'iyya* here seems to refer to the communal dimension of Islamic practices rather than to an order of society. (We also recall al-Shatibi's – and, in a single instance, Rida's – usage of the composite to refer to prayer in a gathering, mainly in the form of *hay'at al-ijtimā'*.)[110] While this particular usage of *al-hay'a al-ijtimā'iyya* to refer to communal religious practices might inform an evolving understanding of a religiously underpinned society, *al-hay'a al-ijtimā'iyya* itself has rarely been employed in that sense in *al-Manar.*

The benefits of the Islamic religious practice of zakat (alms-giving) for *al-hay'a al-ijtimā'iyya* are mentioned only three times in *al-Manar* – once predominantly conveying the idea of a social, observable body, and the second time very clearly conveying the idea of social order.[111] In the first volume of the journal, in an article on "That Which Is Inevitable" ("Ma La Budda Minhu"), Rida again stresses the fundamental importance of moral and intellectual education (*al-tarbiya wa-l-ta'līm*) and lists twelve branches of knowledge that everyone needs to be familiar with in his age.[112] Among these is sociology (*'ilm al-ijtimā'*), Rida's validation of which will be dealt with below.[113] For now, suffice it to say that Rida stresses the need for every person to know about the benefits of religious practices, including the benefit (*fā'ida*) of zakat concerning "the reform of the condition of the social body (*iṣlāḥ ḥāl al-hay'a al-ijtimā'iyya*) and the accomplishment of the rights of humanity (*al-qiyām bi-ḥuqūq al-insāniyya*). And he

108 In 1830, the Protestant theologian Friedrich Schleiermacher famously defined religion as "Gefühl schlechthinniger Abhängigkeit" – a feeling and sense of absolute dependence (on the unseen godly reality).
109 Ibid., 644.
110 See above: 199.
111 In addition to the two examples dealt with here, see: idem., *Tafsir*, vol. 11: 21.
112 Rida, Rashid. 1898. "Ma La Budda Minhu." *al-Manar* 1/30: 567–574.
113 See below: chapter 10 section 2.1.

[who has that knowledge] notices in pilgrimage the benefit of equality between the people, insofar as without distinction they are of the same appearance (*hay'a*), without embellishment or perfume, and with no difference between king and slave or between nobleman and beggar."[114] While connected to a notion of order, here *al-hay'a al-ijtimāʿiyya* primarily refers to observable social conditions, especially as Rida also uses the term *hay'a* to refer to the physical appearance of persons. A student of the Islamic Benevolent Society (al-Jamʿiyya al-Khayriyya al-Islamiyya) in Cairo in 1901 more clearly explicates a sense of order. He upholds the benefits of zakat "for the alms-giver and the poor and for society (*al-hay'a al-ijtimāʿiyya*), whence it is the remedy against the disease of disorder (*fawḍā*) and socialism (*al-ishtirāk*);"[115] he then ends his talk by stressing that "there is no anarchism (*fawḍiyya*) in Islam."[116]

Except for a very brief mention of a discussion about the influence of godly and positive laws in society,[117] there are only two cases in *al-Manar* that more generally stress the necessary benefit of religion in general – or of the Islamic religion in particular – for *al-hay'a al-ijtimāʿiyya*. One counterargument, however, precedes these two cases: in volume 19, Rida quotes the teacher of a military school in Istanbul, who suggests that "Turkism (*al-turkiyya*) is better for us than Islam, and ethnic solidarity (*al-taʿaṣṣub li-l-jinsiyya*) is among the greatest advantages (*al-faḍā'il*) for society (*al-hay'a al-ijtimāʿiyya*)."[118] In volume 25, Alfred Nelson, a priest residing in Damascus, asks rhetorically: "Is our present age (*ʿaṣrunā al-ḥāḍir*) not for every religion the age of *ijtihād*; and are the adherents of religion (*aṣḥāb al-dīn*) thus not required to stick to [religion]; not because they thus found their fathers to be, but because they have investigated the matter with utmost care (*tadaqqaqū*) and have found that religion is beneficial for themselves and for society (*al-hay'a al-ijtimāʿiyya*), more than any other thing in

114 Ibid., 571. The last part of the sentence is a quote from Qur'an 22:25, which I have omitted, since it would add nothing new in content, but would require explanation.

115 Here, *ishtirāk* seems to have been an early attempt to convey 'socialism,' for which *ishtirākiyya* then became established.

116 Student of the school of the Islamic Benevolent Society in Cairo quoted in Rida, Rashid. 1901. "Ihtifal Madrasat al-Jamʿiyya al-Khayriyya al-Islamiyya bi-Misr." *al-Manar* 4/9: 347–350, here 348.

117 Ahmad Zaki quoted in Rida, Rashid. 1904. "al-Su'al wa-l-Fatwa." *al-Manar* 7/10: 371–380, here 372.

118 Ustadh al-Tarbiya al-ʿAskariyya fi al-Madrasa al-Harbiyya fi al-Asitana [a teacher at the military school in Istanbul] quoted in Rida, Rashid. 1917. "al-Jamʿiyyat al-Ittihadiyya li-Takwin al-ʿAsabiyya al-Turkiyya." *al-Manar* 19/9: 555–562, here 561.

the world?"[119] To update Nelson's wording slightly, he rather clearly pleads for the basis of the modern social order on (modern) religion. In his response to Nelson, Rida stresses that the Qur'an commanded *ijtihād* and independence in the understanding of religion and that the need for this has never been greater than it is in his age.[120] Finally, in the journal's last volume, a reader praises Rida's book *The Muhammadan Revelation* (*al-Wahy al-Muhammadi*) for showing that "the obligation of the people to believe in and thus follow Muhammad is the remedy (*al-dawā'*) for the diseases (*al-adwā'*) of the social body (*al-hay'a al-ijtimāʿiyya*)."[121] Overall then, *al-hay'a al-ijtimāʿiyya* was rarely used to conceive of a social order in relation to religion.

The following subsection addresses two other specific social questions debated under the heading of *al-hay'a al-ijtimāʿiyya* – namely, the role of women and the value of work. Concerning both "the woman" and "the workers' question" as well as those societal issues dealt with already, education is repeatedly upheld as an underlying requirement, whence I will end the following subsection by recalling the fundamental importance societal reformists attributed to education.

3.4 Work, Women, and Education: Specific Aspects of Society

Given Egypt's increasing integration into global capitalist markets in the nineteenth century, its first attempts at industrialization, and its changing structures in the organization of labor,[122] it seems rather trivial to assert that thinking about the structure of society involved the question of work. Of interest here, however, is the extent to which *al-hay'a al-ijtimāʿiyya* was used to conceptualize a modern understanding of society as requiring a division of labor and the fruitful cooperation of its productive members.

The earliest instance of stressing the necessity of social cooperation and the value of work is a reprint of an article by Muhammad ʿAbduh that had appeared in the Alexandrian newspaper *Jaridat Misr* in 1879, which was itself based on the

---

119 Alfred Nelson quoted in Rida, Rashid. 1924. "Fatawa al-Manar: al-Tabshir wa-l-Mubashirun fi Nazar al-Muslimin." *al-Manar* 25/3: 188–194, here 188.

120 Ibid., 191f.

121 Mustafa Ahmad al-Rifaʿi al-Laban quoted in Rida, Rashid. 1935. "Kitab al-Wahy al-Muhammadi." *al-Manar* 35/1: 55–63, here 56.

122 See above: chapter 4 sections 1.2 and 2.1.

lessons of al-Afghani.[123] The argument for societal work rests on the anthropological premise that human beings, due to their natural weakness, need to invent tools to cooperate in society.[124] This premise – which here is firmly grounded in nature – recurs often in *al-Manar* and was shared much more widely in the late nineteenth and early twentieth centuries. The German anthropologist Helmuth Plessner, for example, identified *natürliche Künstlichkeit* (natural artificiality) as one of three anthropological laws in 1928.[125] Based on the premise of the human need for crafts and social cooperation, ʿAbduh, paraphrasing al-Afghani, stresses the need for organizing the skills of individuals in society, perceived as a social body: "[T]he principle of work in the [social] body is what we call craft or vocation (*ṣināʿa*), and he who is not capable of that true work (*ʿamal*) which benefits human society (*al-mujtamaʿ al-insānī*) and is not out for the order of the whole structure (*intiẓām al-hay'a al-kulliyya*), he is like a paralyzed limb from which derives no benefit for the body (*badn*), except that carrying its burden might be better than feeling the pain of its removal; whence it is preferable to cut it off."[126] Those who are not working and are moreover deterring others from work are like contagious diseases, and therefore "it is advisable to have done with them and cleanse the social body (*al-hay'a al-ijtimāʿiyya*) from their filth (*daran*)."[127] Thus, if nature prompts human beings toward social association and cooperation, the functioning of society – perceived as a social body – depends on the productive contribution of all of its members, whence society must be protected against and even cleansed of non-productive members.

This raises the question of which role the government ought to play in protecting the social order. In this text, a just government (*al-ḥukūma al-ʿādila*) is mentioned only briefly – namely, as belonging to that group of vocations whose exclusive goal is the benefit of human beings.[128] Philosophy (*ḥikma*), which is "the investigator into what human beings need to adopt in their works, thoughts, and morals," also belongs to this group.[129] Due to the broad range of its remit and the vastness of its benefits, philosophy is portrayed here

123 Muhammad ʿAbduh: "al-Sinaʿa" (1879) quoted in Rida, Rashid. 1906. "Maqalatan li-l-Ustadh al-Imam." *al-Manar* 9/4: 265–275, here 269–275.

124 Ibid., 269–273.

125 Plessner, Helmuth. 1928. *Die Stufen des Organischen und der Mensch: Einleitung in die historische Anthropologie.* Berlin: De Gruyter.

126 ʿAbduh quoted in Rida, "Maqalatan," 273.

127 Ibid., 274, in conjunction with 273 f.

128 Ibid., 275.

129 Ibid., 275.

as the most elevated of all crafts or vocations.[130] The practical aspect of philosophy is intended not only to elucidate moral virtues and vices, but also to set down practical systems of regulations. The other crafts mentioned are of a more practical nature, as is the case with writing and trade, and especially with smithing, tailoring, and agriculture. The most noteworthy aspect of this article is the fact that it grounds social order in human nature and views cooperation between the professions as constitutive for the functioning of society. On a terminological level, it is remarkable that in 1879, this article already conceptualized human society in general as *al-mujtamaʿ al-insānī*. It should also be noted that *mujtamaʿ* here seems to refer to the general social collectivity in which human beings naturally live, whereas the order of society is conceived of as a functioning body and conceptualized as *al-hayʾa al-ijtimāʿiyya*.

Interestingly, in volume one of *al-Manar*, Rashid Rida presents newspapers as the connector in a society (*wuṣlat al-hayʾa al-ijtimāʿiyya*) made up of different professional groups.[131] Those groups named explicitly are politicians, tradesmen, and craftsmen or workers. They are more knowledgable in their respective fields than journalists, Rida finds, adding that this is hardly surprising, since crafts (*ṣināʾiʿ*), which are a basic pillar of human livelihood, have become increasingly refined and complex, in accordance with the progress of the human species (*taraqqī al-nawʿ*). For Rida, the essential role of the press consists mainly in connecting the different groups of society and in serving as a forum for exchanging ideas.[132] After briefly interjecting that the Islamic religion is sufficient for both worlds and that morals are necessary for social cohesion, Rida bemoans the falling behind of Muslims in all fields.[133] Picking up a common topos of Islamic reformist writings, Rida presents the corruption of religion and politics as the two main reasons for this state of affairs.[134] To remedy this situation, some people allegedly favor the reform of the rulers, whereas others prioritize the encouragement of works and crafts.[135] Rida himself stresses the fundamental need

---

130 Al-Afghani elsewhere conceived of philosophy as a meta-science, integrating and guiding the particular sciences (al-Afghani, "Lecture," 103–106).

131 Rida, Rashid. 1899. "al-Sanaʾiʿ wa-l-Taʿlim wa-l-Tarbiya." *al-Manar* 1/47: 901–905, here 901. Newspapers "informing about the conditions of society (*al-hayʾa al-ijtimāʿiyya*)" is also briefly mentioned as one of their benefits by an Indian imam writing to Rida in 1908 (Ahmad Musa al-Manufi quoted in Rida, Rashid. 1908. "Raʾy al-Shaykh Ahmad al-Manufi fi al-Islah wa-Rijalihi." *al-Manar* 10/12: 941–943, here 942).

132 Rida, "al-Sanaʾiʿ," 901.

133 Ibid., 902.

134 Ibid., 902ff.

135 Ibid., 904.

for moral and intellectual education (*al-tarbiya wa-l-taʿlīm*). A proper education incites people to work, unites them, and familiarizes them with their rights and duties, whence they will also advance a just government. It is with this end in mind that he founded *al-Manar*, Rida maintains.[136] He adds that he never claimed that moral and intellectual education alone were sufficient, but rather has continuously been calling for the additional formation of financial corporations (*al-sharikāt al-māliyya*) to establish beneficial programs in the fields of agriculture, trade, and industry – programs that do not contradict, but rather preserve and strengthen religion.[137]

In this article, Rida takes the requirements of society as the starting point for his argument, and he brings in Islamic religion to endorse those requirements. This is a common move among Islamic reformists, who often apologetically uphold the continued validity of Islam in the face of modern secular propositions. There is a nuanced difference in whether reformists claim that Islam does not contradict these propositions, or whether they argue that Islam itself has contained them since its foundation. The first option may potentially evolve into an Islamic endorsement of secularism and the second into the elaboration of a holistic Islamic system comprising the realms of politics and economics. However, these options are to be understood as ideal-types and, as such, are hard to disentangle in actual writings. Thus, in this article, Rida complements his stress on the fact that the formation of financial corporations does not contradict religion (option 1) with the quotation of a hadith allegedly calling for such activities (option 2). As both options imply the validation of secular propositions and their embedding in a religious framework, this strategy generally amounts to an open reading of the immanent frame.

Concerning the importance and the value of work for society conceptualized as *al-hay'a al-ijtimāʿiyya*, there are three additional examples from *al-Manar*. In an excerpt from Muhammad al-Mahami's book *The Principles of Political Economy* (*Mabadi' ʿIlm al-Iqtisad al-Siyasi*)[138] in the eleventh volume of the journal, we read that God commanded "every single member (*fard*) of society (*al-hay'a al-ijtimāʿiyya*) to work in order to gain his livelihood, especially when he is physically healthy."[139] Three years later, Rida mentions "farmers and craftsmen, each one

136 Ibid., 904.
137 Ibid., 904 f.
138 This book is presented in: Rida, Rashid. 1908. "Athar ʿIlmiyya Adabiyya." *al-Manar* 11/8: 617–621, here 617 ff.
139 Al-Mahami, Muhammad Fahmi Husayn. 1908. "al-ʿAmal." *al-Manar* 11/9: 673–680, here 673.

contributing their small amount of work to society (*al-hay'a al-ijtimāʿiyya*)."[140] In this article, he repeats his point about knowledge only being fruitful for society when it is guided by morals. Finally, in volume 26 of *al-Manar*, Rida laments that a poor Azhari student who is not given a position or assistance after graduation cannot become "a useful member (*ʿuḍwan nāfiʿan*) of society (*al-hay'a al-ijtimāʿiyya*)."[141] Overall then, questions of productivity and the division of labor were clearly on the table, but in order to address these questions, society was only rarely conceptualized as *al-hay'a al-ijtimāʿiyya.*

Next to work and the division of labor, a primary social question at the turn to the twentieth century was "the woman question" – not only in European countries and North America, but also in Arab countries. As mentioned in part B, in Egypt at the turn to the twentieth century, debates about the role of women in the family and in society manifested themselves in feminist movements and in the controversy surrounding Qasim Amin's book *The Liberation of Women.*[142]

In *al-Manar, al-hay'a al-ijtimāʿiyya* is used most prominently to address the role of women in society in an article by ʿAtifa Jalal from Istanbul, one of the very few female authors published in the journal. This article first appeared in *Tharwat al-Funun* and was translated into Arabic in *al-Jarida.* Husayn Wasfi Rida included it in his overview of the Ottoman press, which, according to him, had come to focus solely on politics, neglecting moral and social studies, especially the topic of women.[143] ʿAtifa Jalal also calls for attention to the rights and education of women, who have a significant role to play in progress and reform. Some authors, she laments, write about the state of shipping companies but not about the reform of the woman (*iṣlāḥ al-mar'a*) – as if they consider the latter issue of lesser importance for society (*al-hay'a al-ijtimāʿiyya*) than the former.[144] "We women," Jalal exclaims, "consider ourselves to belong to humankind, and we demand that we have a share in society (*naṣīb fī al-hay'a al-ijtimāʿiyya*)."[145] Jalal stresses the need to educate women, so that they can obtain their rights and fulfill their roles in society and for the homeland (*waṭan*).[146] The

---

140 Rida, Rashid. 1911. "Ta'bin Riyad Basha." *al-Manar* 14/8: 633–635, here 635.
141 Idem. 1925. "Madi al-Azhar wa-Hadiruhu wa-Mustaqbaluhu (4)." *al-Manar* 26/2: 123–131, here 124.
142 See above: 134 f.
143 ʿAtifa Jalal. "A laysa la-Na Nasib fi al-Raqqi," quoted in Rida, Husayn Wasfi. 1908. "al-Suhuf fi al-Bilad al-ʿUthmaniyya." *al-Manar* 11/8: 634–638, here 636 ff.
144 Ibid., 636 f.
145 Ibid., 637.
146 Ibid., 637 f.

fact that the article's title asks rhetorically whether "we do not have a share in progress" indicates the connection between an envisioned social order and progress.

Let me briefly note three other cases of addressing the role of women in society with reference to *al-hay'a al-ijtimā'iyya*. In 1907, Rashid Rida announces a book with the title *The Life of the Married Couple* (*Hayat al-Zawjayn*), printed by *al-Manar*'s press and containing a chapter on "the influence of woman in society" (*ta'thīr al-mar'a fī al-hay'a al-ijtimā'iyya*).[147] A year later, Rida recommends the translation of Esquiros's *Émile* in part because it addresses "the place of the mother at the heart of the social body" (*makān al-umm min qalb al-hay'a al-ijtimā'iyya*).[148] Outside of *al-Manar*, the Lebanese weekly *Lisan al-Hal*, founded by the Maronite Christian Khalil ibn Khattar, had already printed an article on "Woman in Society" ("Al-Mar'a fi al-Hay'a al-Ijtima'iyya")[149] in 1894.

While the fundamental importance of moral and intellectual education (*al-tarbiya wa-l-ta'līm*) for society is evident in several of the preceding cases, there is only one additional instance in *al-Manar* of stressing this importance by employing *al-hay'a al-ijtimā'iyya*. An article from 1913 collects the answers of four students at the Dar al-Da'wa wa-l-Irshad, founded by Rida, to the question of whether moral or intellectual education has a greater effect on the reform of individuals and societies (*umam*).[150] All four agree that moral education (*tarbiya*) is more fundamental. The first student explains that those who have had a bad moral upbringing (*tarbiya*) will only accept knowledge (*'ilm*) that conforms to their upbringing. Thus their knowledge will not be beneficial, but rather harmful for society (*al-hay'a al-ijtimā'iyya*).[151] Hence he regards it as proven that "moral education is the first basis on which the reform of individuals (*iṣlāḥ al-afrād*) is built and by which the substance of societies (*kiyān al-umam*) is protected."[152] As

---

147 Rida, Rashid. 1907. "Athar 'Ilmiyya Adabiyya." *al-Manar* 10/5: 382–397, here 388.
148 Rida, "Muqaddimatuna," 430.
149 Jawish, Fathulla. 1894. "al-Mar'a fi al-Hay'a al-Ijtima'iyya." *Lisan al-Hal* 1601 (April 4): 4, taken from: Zachs, Fruma. 2014. "Growing Consciousness of the Child in Ottoman Syria in the 19th Century: Modes of Parenting and Education in the Middle Class." In *The Ottoman Middle East: Studies in Honor of Amnon Cohen* ed. by Eyal Ginio and Elie Podeh: 113–128. Leiden/Boston: Brill, here 117fn14.
150 Rida, Rashid. 1913. "Namudhaj min Insha' Talabat al-Sanna al-Tamhidiyya li-Madrasat Dar al-Da'wa wa-l-Irshad." *al-Manar* 16/9: 709–715, here 709–713.
151 Muhammad 'Ali Abu Zayd al-Misri al-Bahrawi (student at Dar al-Da'wa wa-l-Irshad) quoted in ibid., 710.
152 Ibid., 710.

in this last sentence, *al-Manar* in general stresses the importance of moral and intellectual education for society, the social order, the community, the nation, and the people by employing *umma* rather than *al-hay'a al-ijtimāʿiyya*. The central role of *tarbiya* and *taʿlīm* is also demonstrated in statistics: *tarbiya* and *taʿlīm* occur a total of 3,221 and 5,276 times in *al-Manar*, respectively.[153]

Beyond *al-Manar*, we should recall that almost all the reformists of the nineteenth and early twentieth centuries – whether Islamic, Christian, or secular – emphasized the fundamental importance of education for societal reform, national strength, and progress. These self-appointed spokespersons of the nation, however, differed greatly as to which type of education and which subjects of knowledge were required by and for society. A major subject of debate was the relative importance of religious and secular knowledge. As shown in part B, this manifested itself in the institutional setting, in which students had a choice between religious and secular institutions.[154] The Islamic reformists' stance may broadly be characterized as upholding the necessity of a religious upbringing and basic religious education and as exhibiting a desire to integrate contemporaneous and secular knowledge into updated curricula in religious institutions.

The aim of this section (3) has been to identify the central aspects of society conceptualized as *al-hay'a al-ijtimāʿiyya*. After all, according to the existing literature discussed above,[155] this composite was the established term for 'society.' However, the authors who wrote regularly for *al-Manar* discussed these central aspects of *al-hay'a al-ijtimāʿiyya* by employing alternative terms, most notably *umma*. The latter term is thus suggested as an alternative to convey central aspects of 'society.' Before we come to a crucial difference in meaning and usability between *umma* and *al-hay'a al-ijtimāʿiyya*, we must first examine those authors who used *al-hay'a al-ijtimāʿiyya* to refer to a particular society – that is, to a delineated and particular social collectivity "onto which," as Talal Asad put it,[156] "state, economy, and religion can be mapped."

---

153 Both terms are used more frequently in the journal's first fifteen years than in later years. See appendix, table 7. Comparative figures are, for example, the 942 instances of *falsafa* (philosophy) or the 3,911 instances of *siyāsa* (politics).
154 See above: 110.
155 See above: chapter 6 sections 2 and 3.
156 See above: 183.

4 Particular Societies Conceptualized as *al-Hay'a al-Ijtimāʿiyya*

4.1 Lord Cromer: Egyptian Society, Eastern Society, and the Socio-political Relevance of Islam

Translations of works by Lord Cromer are not only the one source accounting for the most instances of *al-hay'a al-ijtimāʿiyya* in *al-Manar* (other than articles by the journal's editor), they are the only texts that use the composite to speak of 'Egyptian society' (*al-hay'a al-ijtimāʿiyya al-miṣriyya*). As the British consul general in Egypt, Cromer's decisions, decrees, and opinions had been repeatedly discussed in *al-Manar* since the journal's foundation.[157] Particularly in 1908, the year in which Cromer's book on *Modern Egypt* was published[158] and immediately translated into Arabic in *al-Mu'ayyad*,[159] *al-Manar* accorded extensive space to debates about Cromer's views on Egypt and Islam. His opinions on Muhammad ʿAbduh and the Pan-Islamic movement (al-Jamiʿa al-Islamiyya), in particular, had already been discussed in two long articles over the two preceding years. Rida's engagement with *Modern Egypt* is also largely devoted to discussing Cromer's view of ʿAbduh and his reformist party. Overall, translations of Cromer's writings account for 14 instances of *al-hay'a al-ijtimāʿiyya* in *al-Manar* in six articles published between 1906 and 1908 – all except one in quotations in Rashid Rida's articles.

In a decree from 1905, quoted in volumes nine and eleven of *al-Manar*, Cromer pays his respects to the recently deceased ʿAbduh as a "prominent man in the social and political sphere in Egypt" (*rajulan mashhūran fī al-hay'a al-siyāsiyya wa-l-ijtimāʿiyya bi-Miṣr*).[160] Time will show, Cromer goes on, whether or not the opinions of the reformist trend led by ʿAbduh will permeate Egyptian society (*tatakhallil al-hay'a al-ijtimāʿiyya al-miṣriyya*).[161] Expressing his sympathy with the reformist stance, Cromer hypothesizes that the larger society (*al-hay'a al-ijtimāʿiyya*) might well accept them over time.[162] Rida discusses at length, also quoting extensively from *al-Mu'ayyad*, whether Cromer was actually friends with

157 See for example: Rida, Rashid. 1899. "Khitab al-Lurd Krumir fi al-Sudan." *al-Manar* 1/42: 827–828; idem. 1904. "Sabab Thana' Riyad Basha ʿala al-Lurd Krumir." *al-Manar* 7/8: 317–320.
158 Baring, *Modern*.
159 Rida refers to this translation, which he also used, in: Rida, Rashid. 1908. "al-Radd ʿala Kitab al-Lurd Krumir." *al-Manar* 11/5: 354–360, here 354.
160 Lord Cromer quoted in Rida, "al-Shaykh," 276 and again in idem., "Kitab Misr," 90.
161 Lord Cromer quoted in Rida, "al-Shaykh," 277 and again in idem., "Kitab Misr," 91.
162 Rida, "al-Shaykh," 277; idem., "Kitab Misr," 91.

'Abduh and refutes Cromer's characterization of 'Abduh as an agnostic (*lā-adrī*).[163] Rida also engages Cromer's characterization of 'Abduh and his party as representing a middle position between conservatives and Europeanized Muslims.[164] It is here that Rida elaborates the prominent threefold scheme of Islamic reformists (*muṣliḥūn*) representing a middle way between following rigid conservatives (*al-muḥāfiẓūn al-jāmidūn*) and imitating Europeanized Muslims (*al-mutafarnijūn al-muqallidūn*).[165] Rida identifies the overall goal of reformers as achieving social reform while preserving religion (*iṣlāḥ ḥāl al-muslimīn al-ijtimā'iyya ma' al-muḥāfiẓa 'alā al-dīn*).[166]

The context of the following occurrences of *al-hay'a al-ijtimā'iyya* is also of interest in itself, as it consists of Cromer's assessment of Pan-Islamism (al-Jami'a al-Islamiyya) and Rida's discussion of that assessment. In a decree from 1906, translated in *al-Muqattam* and quoted extensively in *al-Manar* the following year, Cromer suggests that the Pan-Islamic movement should be monitored closely, as it aims at the unification of Muslims around the world against the forces of Christian states.[167] However, according to Cromer, the greater danger consists in nationalism, and it is in a nationalist disguise that Pan-Islamic sentiments might gain popularity.[168] Thus far, Cromer argues, these sentiments have not yet permeated Egyptian society (*al-hay'a al-ijtimā'iyya al-miṣriyya*),[169] and it is doubtful whether they will succeed, for three reasons: firstly, because Muslims will hardly cooperate in practice on a large scale; secondly, because European states continue to be strong; and thirdly, because the program of Pan-Islamism is against the requirements of the age and will inhibit progress in Muslim lands.[170] After all, its proponents want to reform Islam by returning to principles laid down over a thousand years ago and intended to guide a still-primitive and simple society (*hay'a ijtimā'iyya fī ḥālat al-fiṭra wa-l-sadhāja*).[171]

---

163 Ibid., 96–111, esp. 96–104; see also: Cromer, *Modern*, vol. 2: 180.

164 Rida, "al-Shaykh," 276 f.; idem., "Kitab Misr," 90; see also: Cromer, *Modern*, vol. 2: 180; see above: 157 f.

165 Rida, "Kitab Misr," 203, 205; idem., "al-Shaykh," 281 f.

166 Ibid., 282.

167 Lord Cromer quoted in Rida, Rashid. 1907. "al-Jami'a al-Islamiyya." *al-Manar* 10/3: 200–234, here 215.

168 Ibid., 217.

169 Ibid., 215.

170 Ibid., 216 f.

171 Ibid., 217; and again Lord Cromer quoted in a quote of al-Mu'ayyad in: Rida, Rashid. 1908. "al-Qur'an wa-Najah Da'wat al-Nabi 'alayhi al-Salat wa-l-Salam wa-Ara' 'Ulama' Uruba fi Dhalik." *al-Manar* 11/1: 9–31, here 19; and again in: Rida, Rashid. 1923. "al-Khilafa al-Islamiyya (5)." *al-Manar* 24/4: 257–272, here 267.

In his response to Cromer in 1907, Rida notably denies the existence of a political Pan-Islamic movement. He considers it impracticable, due to the differences between regional Islamic reform movements, and maintains that – contrary to popular opinion – Jamal al-Din al-Afghani, the protagonist of al-Jami'a al-Islamiyya, did not aspire to the unification of Muslims under one political ruler, but rather under the Qur'an as their common guide.[172] Moreover, stressing the flexibility of the basic Islamic principles that were to be returned to, Rida suspects that Cromer could not possibly have criticized the return to these principles as inhibiting progress, but rather must have been referring to the strict adherence to concrete legal precedents.[173] This point is extremely important to Rida, and he refers to a letter he sent to Cromer inquiring whether he was referring to the basic universal principles, as laid down in the Qur'an and the Sunna, or to the human-made body of law, the *fiqh*.[174] According to Rida, Cromer replied that he did indeed have the latter in mind and that he was sympathetic toward those Muslims who aimed at reform by embracing civilization (*madaniyya*) while preserving the basics of religion (*uṣūl al-dīn*).[175] If it seems here that Rida stretched Cromer's wording to confirm his own convictions, some passages in *al-Mu'ayyad*'s translation of Cromer's *Modern Egypt*, excerpted in *al-Manar*, do in fact point to underlying assumptions shared by Rida and Cromer.

In an excerpt on "Islam and Muslims," Cromer stresses the commonalities between the English and the Egyptian people in their desire to build civilization on the basis of the Christian and the Islamic faiths, respectively.[176] The main tenets of the latter, as laid down in the Qur'an, are exclusively positive, inciting truthfulness and righteousness, among other virtues.[177] Indeed, "it cannot be doubted," Cromer asserts, "that a primitive society (*al-hay'a al-ijtimā'iyya al-aṣliyya*) benefits greatly by the adoption of the faith of Islam."[178] Unfortunately, however, "the great Arabian reformer" Muhammad tried to establish not only a religion, but also a social system (*niẓām ijtimā'ī*).[179] Approvingly quoting Lane-Poole, Cromer maintains that, "as a religion, Islam is great [...]. As a social sys-

172 Rida, "al-Jami'a al-Islamiyya," 218 f.
173 Ibid., 226–231.
174 Ibid., 231 f. Rida refers to this again in: idem., *Tafsir*, vol. 1: 171.
175 Idem., "al-Jami'a al-Islamiyya," 232.
176 Idem., "al-Radd," *al-Manar* 11/5: 354 f. For the original passage, see: Cromer, *Modern*, vol. 2: 132.
177 Idem. vol. 2: 133; Rida, "al-Radd," *al-Manar* 11/5: 355.
178 Cromer, *Modern*, vol. 2: 134; Rida, "al-Radd," *al-Manar* 11/5: 355.
179 Cromer, *Modern*, vol. 2: 134; Rida, "al-Radd," *al-Manar* 11/5: 355.

tem, it is a complete failure."[180] Cromer views the strict adherence to an inflexible social law as a major reason for this asserted failure: "If to this day an Egyptian goes to law over a question of testamentary succession, his case is decided according to the limited principles (*al-mabādī' al-ḍayyiqa*) which were laid down as applicable to the primitive society (*al-hay'a al-ijtimāʿiyya al-ūlā*) of the Arabian Peninsula in the seventh century."[181] Rida, who does not comment on this excerpt, likely approved of the grounds on which Cromer based his assertion of the inappropriateness of Islam as a social system today. He differs from Cromer in that he did not consider Islam an irremediable failure as a social system, but rather called for its reform (that is, from my perspective as an academic observer, for the construction of Islam as a social system in the first place, since no such system had existed in pre-modern times). The exchange between Rida and Cromer recalls the colonial setting in which the modern demand to construct a systematic social order was formulated.

Attending to the more narrow question of this study, it is important to note that, in translations of Cromer's texts, this order of society is conceptualized as *al-hay'a al-ijtimāʿiyya*, and that the composite refers to the particular social bodies or orders of 'primitive society,' 'Egyptian society,' and, as we shall see here, 'Eastern society.' In a speech he gave to the British parliament, Cromer observes that religious sentiments everywhere contend with agnosticism (*lā-adriyya*) or what approaches agnosticism.[182] He has no doubt that "the West's getting in contact with the East (*ittiṣāl al-gharb bi-l-sharq*) leads to the concussion of the moral pillars (*zaʿzaʿt al-arkān al-adabiyya*) on which is built the whole strucutre of the Eastern society (*taqūm ʿalayhā binā' al-hay'a al-ijtimāʿiyya al-sharqiyya kulluhā*)."[183] Rida quotes this statement in his response,[184] warning those calling for nationalism (*al-waṭaniyya wa-l-jinsiyya*) that tearing down old pillars is much easier than erecting new ones. Although here, as in the above instances, Rida does not think that these usages of *al-hay'a al-ijtimāʿiyya* to refer to a particular society require any explanation, he never once appropriates this usage himself.

---

180 Cromer, *Modern*, vol. 2: 134; Rida, "al-Radd," *al-Manar* 11/5: 356.

181 Cromer, *Modern*, vol. 2: 135; Rida, "al-Radd," *al-Manar* 11/5: 356.

182 Lord Cromer quoted in Rida, Rashid. 1908. "Ra'y Kibar Sasat al-Gharb fi al-Haraka al-Madaniyya al-Jadida fi al-Sharq." *al-Manar* 10/12: 916–919, here 916.

183 Ibid., 916.

184 Ibid., 919.

4.2 Niqula Dabana: Eastern Society, the Qur'an, and Republicanism

The only author besides Lord Cromer who substantially addresses 'Eastern society' (*al-hayʾa al-ijtimāʿiyya al-sharqiyya*)[185] is Niqula Yusuf Dabana, who is also the only one to include *al-hayʾa al-ijtimāʿiyya* in the (sub-)title of an article.[186] In addition to the title, the composite appears twice in his text "The Reasons for the Downfall of the East: The Eastern Social Order." This article by the otherwise unknown Dabana, who is introduced as a lawyer and whose name suggests that he is a Christian, was first published in *al-Muqattam*. Rida presents it to substantiate a central argument he himself made in the preceding pages:[187] Islam set forth all the teachings required for societies (*umam*) to ascend to the highest spheres, and while Europe prospered after adopting central Islamic teachings, it still falls short of fully realizing them.[188] Thus, according to Rida's example, the French – as leaders of European civilization (*madaniyya*), who pride themselves on justice and equality – continue to suppress Jews. Since principles such as justice are allegedly most fully realized in true Islam, Rida concludes that the condition of a people (*umma*) which has these bases as its religion can only be set right (*yuṣliḥ*) by adhering to them. He stresses that he is not ascribing any unfounded merit to Islam, but rather that all historians, as well as non-Muslim legal and religious scholars, concur on these traits. Rida then presents the article by Dabana as exemplary proof of this argument;[189] it is indeed remarkable how the non-Muslim Dabana validates Islam as a cultural resource in 1899.

---

185 There is a brief mention of *al-hayʾa al-ijtimāʿiyya al-sharqiyya* in an article from 1936 (al-Harawi, Husayn. 1936. "al-Mustashriqun wa-l-Islam." *al-Manar* 35/4: 249–260, here 258).

186 Dabana, Niqula. 1899. "Asbab Inhitat al-Sharq (al-Hayʾa al-Ijtimaʿiyya al-Sharqiyya)." *al-Manar* 1/46: 886–889. The composite also appears in the subtitle or the section titles of three books briefly reviewed in *al-Manar:* Niqula Haddad included *al-hayʾa al-ijtimāʿiyya* in the subtitle of his book on sociology (see below: chapter 8 section 3.2); Husayn Wasfi Rida presents two books containing chapter titles including *al-hayʾa al-ijtimāʿiyya:* Muhammad al-Khidr bin al-Husayn, a scholar at the Zaytuniyya University in Tunis entitled a chapter "the role of language in society (*taʾthīr al-lugha fī al-hayʾa al-ijtimāʿiyya*)"; and Ahmad ʿUmar al-Mahmasani has a section on "the harm of false testimony for the witness himself and for society (*al-hayʾa al-ijtimāʿiyya*)" (Rida, Husayn Wasfi. 1910. "Taqriz al-Matbuʿat al-Jadida." *al-Manar* 13/2: 131–144, here 141).

187 Rida, Rashid. 1899. "al-Islam wa-l-Taraqqi." *al-Manar* 1/46: 885–886. In the electronic version of *al-Manar*, Dabana's article is included as part of Rida's article; in the print version, both are quite clearly separated, whence I list them as seperate articles here.

188 Ibid., 885.

189 Ibid., 886.

At the beginning of his article, Dabana asserts that it was the Qur'an that bound the kings of the East to legal precepts at a time when their Western counterparts only knew the law of despotism,[190] and that the East is the cradle of republican principles (*al-mabādīʾ al-jumhūriyya*) and constitutional government (*al-ḥukūma al-dustūriyya*).[191] Historical examples to the contrary do not affect the basic principles in which he is interested, Dabana maintains, and thus he stresses that, "the principles of the Eastern social order (*mabādīʾ al-hayʾa al-ijtimāʿiyya al-sharqiyya*) are founded upon republicanism and equality."[192] The principles of republicanism and participation of the populace (*ishtirākiyya*, also: socialism), which are now spreading in the West and which the latter regards as a civilizational advancement (*taqadduman wa-tamaddunan*), have been present in the East since the beginning. These principles consist of the civil rights of women (*ḥuqūq al-marʾa al-madaniyya*); assistance for the poor via a compulsory tax, which in the East had long been instituted in the form of zakat;[193] governments not interfering with religion;[194] and the abolition of associations (*jamʿiyyāt*) autonomous from society (*al-mustaqilla ʿan al-hayʾa al-ijtimāʿiyya*), such as the clergy and monastic orders.[195]

According to Dabana, if the East would adhere to these basic principles, it would ascend to the highest levels of progress and civilization (*al-taqaddum wa-l-tamaddun*). However, the rulers had not adhered to them for such a long time that oppressive rule had even become customary.[196] At the time of writing, Dabana regards the main barriers to progress as the fact that the subjects (*al-maḥkūmūn*) have lost knowledge of their rights, that the rulers (*al-ḥukkām*) continue to suppress the people whose rise they fear (*qiyām al-shaʿb al-maẓlūm*), and that respected and powerful families are absent in the East.[197] Here we must not enter into a discussion of Dabana's diagnoses and arguments, which interest us only as the context for his use of *al-hayʾa al-ijtimāʿiyya*. In that regard, it is remarkable that Dabana identifies a particular – if ideal – Eastern society, that *al-hayʾa al-ijtimāʿiyya* clearly connotes 'society' in the sense of an overall so-

190 Dabana, "Asbab," 886.
191 Ibid., 887.
192 Ibid., 887.
193 Ibid., 887.
194 The Arabic "ʿ*adam taʿarruḍ al-ḥukūmāt li-l-adyān*" could also be read as the non-exposure of the government to religious interference.
195 Ibid., 888.
196 Ibid., 888.
197 Ibid., 888 f.

cial order, and that the adherence to common and just laws is crucial to the maintenance of this order.

4.3 Muhyi al-Din Azad: Islamic Society and the Principle of *Jamā'a*

There is only a single attribution of *al-hay'a al-ijtimā'iyya* that refers to 'Islamic society,' but it occurs in an entire book dedicated to advancing an Islamic socio-political order – namely, in Muhyi al-Din Azad's *al-Khilafa al-Islamiyya* (*The Islamic Caliphate*), whose translation from Urdu was serialized in volume 23 of *al-Manar*.[198] Maulana Abu al-Kalam Muhyi al-Din Azad (1888–1958) was an Indian Muslim reformist, political activist, author, and journalist with Pan-Islamic and then increasingly nationalist convictions. He played a central role in the Indian Caliphate movement and later became the country's first minister of education.[199] The Arabic translation of his *al-Khilafa al-Islamiyya* was undertaken by 'Abd al-Razzaq al-Mulih Abadi, the editor of the Indian newspaper *Baygham* and a pupil at the Dar al-Da'wa wa-l-Irshad, the Islamic school founded by Rida in 1911. In this book, Azad argues for the necessity of the caliphate to ensure Muslims' unity and strength.

Here we must not concern ourselves with Azad's more detailed conception of the caliphate – which would, for example, include the idea that the caliph, contrary to Rida's opinion, did not necessarily need to be of Qurayshi descent.[200] These details are elaborated in the last four articles of this nine-part series. Much more relevant for us are the series' first five articles, in which the composite *al-hay'a al-ijtimā'iyya* occurs eight times and in which, moreover, Islam is presented as a societal religion, with *jamā'a* as the main term used for conceptualizing the normative order of society.

---

198 Azad, Muhyi al-Din. 1922. "al-Khilafa al-Islamiyya; transl. 'Abd al-Razzaq al-Mulih Abadi." *al-Manar* 23/1: 45–56, *al-Manar* 23/2: 102–106, *al-Manar* 23/3: 193–201, *al-Manar* 23/4: 282–289, *al-Manar* 23/5: 361–372, *al-Manar* 23/6: 466–471, *al-Manar* 23/7: 509–512, *al-Manar* 23/9: 691–702, *al-Manar* 23/10: 753–757.

199 On him, see: Dabla, Bashir Ahmad. 2007. "Muslim Political Thought in Colonial India: a Comparative Study of Sir Sayyid Ahmad Khan and Mawlana Abu al-Kalam Azad." In *Challenges to Religions and Islam: A Study of Muslim Movements, Personalities, Issues and Trends* ed. by Hamid Naseem Rafiabadi, vol. 2: 788–815. New Delhi: Sarup & Sons, here 791, 798–812; Douglas, Ian Henderson. 1988. *Abul Kalam Azad: an Intellectual and Religious Biography*; ed. by Gail Minault and Christian W. Troll. Delhi: Oxford University Press.

200 For a contextualizing summary of some of Azad's main arguments, see: Pankhurst, Reza. 2014. *The Inevitable Caliphate? A History of the Struggle for Global Islamic Union, 1924 to Present.* New York: Oxford University Press, 38 ff.; Willis, "Debating."

A major premise on which Azad promotes Islam as a societal religion is his characterization of the present as "the age of coherence and concord" (*ʿahd al-ijtimāʿ wa-l-iʾtilāf*):

"This is that age in which the active collective forces (*al-quwā al-ijtimāʿiyya al-faʿʿāla*) join (*tajtamiʿ*) in one place (*makān*), in one spot (*nuqṭa*), in one chain (*silsila*), in one being (*dhāt*), and in one hand, through a natural arrangement (*tartīb ṭabīʿī*) suitable for them, so that all collective substances, forces, and deeds, and all members of society (*afrād al-umma*) become firmly connected and entangled (*mutamāsika mutashābika*), until we see no interstice (*khalal*; also: defect, disorder) between them and no disruption or crack but rather find them all to be like the links of a chain which are firmly joined together so that they appear as one thing."[201]

The principle of coherence and concord could not be more fundamental for Azad, who stresses that it is operative not only in societal life, but also in the formation of matter and the body of a person.[202]

According to Azad, the opposites of coherence and concord are dispersion and diffusion (*al-tashattut wa-l-intishār*),[203] and indeed, in the social sphere, Islam represents the principle of social cohesion (*jamāʿa*) as opposed to the *jāhiliyya*, the pre- or un-Islamic age of ignorance, representing division (*firqa*).[204] For Azad, coherence and concord are the prerequisites for the greatness of a people (*umma*) and even, as the Qurʾan repeatedly stresses, for the life of societies (*umam*) as such.[205] Based on this insight, the Prophet allegedly created Islam and the Islamic life (*al-ḥayāt al-islāmiyya*) in a communal form (*fī al-jamāʿa*).[206] According to the Qurʾan, Azad maintains, "life itself only is possible in community (*jamāʿa*), and individuals (*afrād*) and their deeds in its opinion only matter insofar as the social body (*al-hayʾa al-ijtimāʿiyya*) is formed from them."[207] Azad's eagerness to promote Islam as a societal religion is also demonstrated in his presentation of the Fatiha, the first sura of the Quran, as a "social call" (*duʿāʾ ijtimāʿī*). He emphasizes the fact that this sura calls upon God to "guide *us* on the straight path," not to "guide me." This communal principle al-

201 Azad, "al-Khilafa," 23/1: 45–56, here 51.
202 Ibid., 51f.
203 Ibid., 52.
204 Idem., "al-Khilafa," 23/5: 361–372, here 361.
205 Idem., "al-Khilafa," 23/1: 45–56, here 52.
206 Ibid., 53.
207 Ibid., 55.

legedly also underlyies the shariʿa as a whole, all the rules of which are "built on this principle, the principle of coherence and concord."[208] Communal prayer and the pilgrimage arguably testify to this, as does the duty of zakat, "which has only been created for the sustenance of the social body" (*qiyām al-hay'a al-ijtimāʿiyya*).[209]

According to Azad, the sole reason for the downfall of Muslims and the disintegration of their society was their deviation from the principle of coherence and concord[210] and their failure to entrust all power into the hands of one ruler, as the natural (sic) law of centrality (*nāmūs al-markaziyya*) demands. Azad justifies his argument for a strong, central caliph via analogies with natural phenomena, pointing to the sun as the center of the universe and the heart as the center of the human body.[211] "Exactly as the order of the universe (*niẓām al-kawn*) rests on the law of centrality, so does the order of Islam (*niẓām al-islām*) rest on the law of centrality," he maintains, comparing the role of the Prophet with that of the sun.[212] Muhammad had arguably been the clear center of Islamic society, holding both religious and political authority, in accordance with the fact that the Islamic order (*al-niẓam al-islāmī*) did not distinguish between this world and the next and demanded that the forces of society (*quwā al-umma*) should be combined in one center.[213] Arguably, however, this combination only persisted under the Four Rightly Guided Caliphs, after whom the caliphate was wrongly turned into a purely worldly government.[214] As an exception to this, I might add, Azad points to the constitutional government of Sultan Abdülhamid II as having approached the original idea of the caliphate resting on consultation (*shūrā*).[215] Additionally, Azad elsewhere limits the power of the caliph, possibly implicitly arguing against the charge of theocracy, by stressing that the caliph is subjected to religious legislation, over which he has no authority.[216] These qualifications aside, Azad deplores the alleged disintegration of religious and worldly authority, bemoaning that "the prophetical caliphate and Islamic society (*al-hay'a al-ijtimāʿiyya al-islāmiyya*) did not remain in this form (*minwāl*) for long but ended with ʿAli [r. 656–661]. Diffusion and dispersion then pervaded

208 Ibid., 55.
209 Ibid., 55.
210 Idem., "al-Khalifa," 23/2: 102–106, here 102, 105.
211 Idem., "al-Khilafa," 23/3: 193–201, here 193f.
212 Ibid., 194.
213 Idem., "al-Khalifa," 23/2: 102–106, here 102f.
214 Ibid., 103ff.
215 Ibid., 105.
216 Idem., "al-Khalifa," 23/1: 45–56, here 48.

all affairs of the community (*umma*), so that the social structure of the community (*bināyat al-umma al-ijtimāʿiyya*) trembled."[217] Next to the allegedly natural and social law of centrality, Azad thus also adduces (his interpretation of) the historical record to demonstrate the alleged need for a strong power center in society.

Having demonstrated this need, Azad elaborates on the envisioned social order of Islam (*niẓām al-islām al-ijtimāʿī*) based on a hadith, while explicitly stressing the universality of this order's principles and constituents. According to the hadith he adduces to elucidate the Islamic social order, Muslims are obliged to accomplish five things: a firmly integrated society (*jamāʿa*), compliance and obedience (*al-samʿ wa-l-ṭāʿa*), emigration (*hijra*), and struggle (*jihād*) on the path of God.[218] Azad argues that, while some might reject these Islamic concepts, all people of sound mind agree upon these five things, on which the lives of societies (*umam*) depend.[219] He downplays disagreement as merely a matter of terminology, likening the concept of *hijra* to the discoveries of European colonialism and depicting *jihad* as conveying the insights of social Darwinism.[220] Here, we are most interested in Azad's elaboration of the concept of *jamāʿa*, which is named as the first obligation in the hadith cited above.

The concept of *jamāʿa* in Azad's usage is not applicable to just any group of people, but only to that cluster of individuals (*kutlat al-āḥād*) that fulfills the following requirements: they have to be connected by unity and concord (*al-ittiḥād wa-l-i'tilāf*), have to be assimilated (*al-imtizāj*), and have to have an order (*niẓām*).[221] This reminds us of Gustave Le Bon's definition of a *foule* ('crowd') in his *Psychologie des Foules.*[222] In his Arabic translation of Le Bon, Ahmad Fathi Zaghlul notably rendered the original French term as *jamāʿa.*[223] One may assume that Azad's Arabic translator was familiar with that translation of Le Bon, given its popularity. I do not know whether Azad himself also had a translation of the work at his disposal, or which Urdu term underlies *jamāʿa* in the Arabic translation of his work. In any case, like Le Bon, Azad applies the concept of *jamāʿa* to a range of social associations: whether households, parties, clubs, meetings, associations (*jamʿiyyāt*), the parliament, or the military – all are in need of social cohesion (*jamāʿa*) and coherence (*ijtimāʿ*). This is all the more

217 Idem., "al-Khalifa," 23/2: 102–106, here 105
218 Idem., "al-Khilafa," 23/4: 282–289, here 282.
219 Ibid., 286.
220 Ibid., 286–289.
221 Ibid., 282f.
222 Le Bon, *Psychologie.*
223 Idem., *Ruh.*

true for the larger social collectivities of the nation (*umma*) and the homeland (*waṭan*). Moreover, Azad maintains, the requirements of a *jamāʿa* can only be fulfilled when someone is presiding over the collectivity in question, and when – and here the aforementioned obligations of *samʿ* and *ṭāʿa* are picked up – this person is listened to and obeyed. Thus, for Azad, the order of a household, as the most pertinent example, depends on the family obeying the head of the household. A household without social cohesion (*jamāʿa*), compliance, and obedience (*al-samʿ wa-l-ṭāʿa*) cannot thrive – nor can an umma without these three conditions.[224] On the level of the whole society, then, *jamāʿa* signifies the duty of the umma to rally (*tajtamiʿa*) around the imam, who is its unifying societal center (*markaz ijtimāʿī*).

It is worth quoting Azad's sketch of the envisioned Islamic social order at length, the translation of which brings together the key terms *al-hay'a al-ijtimāʿiyya*, *jamāʿa*, *ijtimāʿ*, and *umma*. The above-mentioned four requirements of a *jamāʿa*, Azad maintains,

"cannot be realized unless there is a sovereign power controlling social coherence (*ijtimāʿ*) and an authoritative hand conducting the integrated social collectivity (*jamāʿa*), uniting (*tuwaḥḥid*) the scattered individuals (*al-āhād al-muntashara*), joining them together (*tu'allif baynahum*), blending them with each other (*tamzuj baʿḍahum bi-baʿḍ*), and binding them closely together (*tukhriṭuhum*) in the order of the well-integrated social collectivity (*niẓām al-jamāʿa*). An imam and caliph therefore is indispensable, and the members of society (*afrād*) inescapably have to obey him and submit to him if they want to live a good social life (*ḥayāt ijtimāʿiyya ṭayyiba*). The place of the imam or caliph in the social order (*al-hay'a al-ijtimāʿiyya*) is like the pivotal point in a circle (*nuqṭa min al-dā'ira*), and his governors (*ʿummāl*) have the rank of the circle. The individual members of society (*āḥād al-umma*) are revolving around this circle, which itself is revolving around this pivotal point. In the manner here illustrated (*bi-hadhihi al-ṣūrā*) an integrated social collectivity (*jamāʿa*) is formed from the social association of individuals (*ijtimāʿ al-afrād*), so that they become a single mass (*kutla*) and one living body (*jisman ḥāyyan*) [...]. This is the kind of social collectivity (*jamāʿa*) which Islam calls for, and [Islam] orders Muslims to create their society (*yajʿalū hay'atahum al-ijtimāʿiyya*) according to its [i.e., this *jamāʿa*'s] method (*uslūb*)."[225]

224 Azad, "al-Khilafa," 23/4: 282–289, here 287.
225 Ibid., 283 f.

Both this passage and the preceding discussion convey several insights concerning the terms with which society, and especially the Islamic socio-political order, are conceptualized in the translation of Azad's book. The concept of *al-hay'a al-ijtimāʿiyya* is used to denote a particular Islamic society; this, however, is not in distinction from the state, but rather comprises the people and the ruler, who is the focal point of that society. Moreover, while *al-hay'a al-ijtimāʿiyya* is clearly a normative term which refers to the desirable order of society, *jamāʿa* is the dominant term used to elaborate on this desired type of social association. As such, *jamāʿa* may refer to a collectivity of people, in the sense of a 'community' or 'society,' but above all, it indicates the integrated nature of that collectivity and even stands in for the principle of social cohesion as such. *Umma*, in turn, for the most part, is the generic term used to designate social collectivities, especially the community of Muslims, and refers less to the manner in which these collectivities are organized. In some cases, however, *umma* also denotes a social order, as when the social structure of the community (*bināyat al-umma al-ijtimāʿiyya*) is thought to tremble, or when the absence of a legitimate caliph is thought to destroy the social structure (*al-hay'a al-ijtimāʿiyya*) and to shake the pillars of the community (*arkān al-umma*).[226]

The following two quotations illustrate the difference between the dominant meaning of *umma* and the normative senses of *al-hay'a al-ijtimāʿiyya* and, especially, *jamāʿa:* "The integrated social collectivity (*jamāʿa*) is like an unbreakable chain of steel and the members of the community (*āḥād al-umma*) are like the links [of that chain]."[227] And furthermore: "With this verse God obliged the Islamic community (*al-umma al-islāmiyya*) to obey the caliph and imam, as on him depends the sustenance of the integrated social collectivity (*qiyām al-jamāʿa*) and the continuation of the social body (*biqā' al-hay'a al-ijtimāʿiyya*)."[228] We may thus conclude that, in this translation from 1923, the Islamic order of a communitarian, authoritarian society is mainly conceptualized using the normative concepts of *al-hay'a al-ijtimāʿiyya* and, especially, *jamāʿa*, while *mujtamaʿ* is not used at all. The dominant meanings of *ijtimāʿ* – 'concurrence' and 'unity' – play into the term's reference to society, insofar as the latter ought to be coherent or unified. However, the usage of *ijtimāʿ* as 'society' has been marginal in this translation, in which even the adjective *ijtimāʿī* often denotes 'collectively' or 'coherent' rather than 'social.'[229]

---

226 Idem., "al-Khilafa," 23/5: 361–372, here 368.
227 Idem., "al-Khilafa," 23/1: 45–56, here 54.
228 Idem., "al-Khilafa," 23/3: 193–201, here 201.
229 I lay out the semantic range of *ijtimāʿ* more systematically in chapter 10 section 1.1.

The remaining articles that use *al-hay'a al-ijtimāʿiyya* to designate a particular society are far less fruitful concerning the conceptualization of a socio-political order, and can thus be presented briefly.

4.4 Other Particular Societies Conceptualized as *al-Hay'a al-Ijtimāʿiyya*

While *al-hay'a al-ijtimāʿiyya* is only used to refer to two other particular societies by name in *al-Manar*, the very idea of particular societies is discernible from a few other usages as well. The two societies identified by name are Christian and Jewish society, both of which are mentioned only once, and very briefly: Muhammad al-Asram and Monsieur de Dianous, in a jointly authored decree, presented to a conference in Marseille and translated by a Tunisian journal, note that "Christian society" (*hay'at al-ijtimāʿ al-masīḥiyya*) was in a deplorable state in the seventh century;[230] and an article in *al-Hilal*, which Rida reprinted, refers to Zionists aiming at advancing "Jewish society" (*al-hay'a al-ijtimāʿiyya al-yahūdiyya*).[231] The idea of a particular society is also clearly referenced when speaking of Muslims and their social order (*al-muslimīn wa-hay'atihim al-ijtimāʿiyya*).[232] One may also include the six references to "our society,"[233] the two references to "their society,"[234] and one mention of "the society to which he belongs."[235] A plurality – and thus supposedly a distinctiveness – of social orders also informs the usage of *al-hay'a al-ijtimāʿiyya* in the plural –

230 Al-Asram, Muhammad. 1907. "Uruba wa-l-Islam." *al-Manar* 10/10: 774–780, here 774.
231 Al-Hilal. 1914. "al-Sahyuniyya." *al-Manar* 17/5: 385–390, here 390.
232 Al-Maqdisi, Muhammad Ruhi al-Khalidi. 1908. "al-Inqilab al-ʿUthmani wa-Turkiya al-Fata (3)." *al-Manar* 11/11: 842–859, here 846.
233 ʿAbduh, "Muntadiyatuna," 368; Wajdi, Muhammad Farid. 1902. "Kayfa Yakun al-Mustaqbal li-l-Muslimin." *al-Manar* 5/17: 656–667, here 666; Rida, Rashid. 1912. "Fatihat al-Mujallad al-Khamis ʿAshar." *al-Manar* 15/1: 1–8, here 4; Chatelet, Monsieur. 1912. "al-Ghara ʿala al-ʿAlam al-Islami [translated from the French by al-Mu'ayyad]." *al-Manar* 15/4: 259–269, here 260; Saʿid Halim Basha quoted by Murasil Jaridat al-Akhbar fi al-Asitana in Rida, Rashid. 1922. "Saʿid Halim Basha." *al-Manar* 23/2: 147–153, here 151; al-Maghribi, ʿAbd al-Qadir. 1924. "Tazwij al-Muslim bi-Ghayr al-Muslima." *al-Manar* 25/2: 120–124, here 123 (here *hay'at ijtimāʿinā*).
234 Baʿd al-Fudala' fi Dar al-Saʿada quoted in Rida, Rashid. 1898. "Ra'y fi Mawduʿ al-Manar [transl. from the Turkish]." *al-Manar* 1/24: 453–460, here 457 (the Arabic translation expands on the preceding Turkish original. I could not detect a term for *al-hay'a al-ijtimāʿiyya* in the original); Muhammad ʿAbduh (in an article which originally appeared in al-Waqa'iʿ al-Misriyya in 1880) quoted in Rida, Rashid. 1906. "al-Maʿarif fi Misr qabl al-Thawra al-ʿUrabiyya." *al-Manar* 9/7: 505–514, here 505.
235 Al-Kawakibi, ʿAbd al-Rahman. 1902. "Baqiyyat al-Ijtimaʿ al-Thalith li-Jamʿiyyat Umm al-Qura." *al-Manar* 5/5: 183–190, here 188.

which, however, occurs only twice in *al-Manar,*[236] once relating "our social order and the other orders" (*al-hay'āt al-ukhrā*).[237]

Twice *al-hay'a al-ijtimāʿiyya* is used to refer to human society at large (*al-hay'a al-ijtimāʿiyya al-bashariyya*), in clear distinction from the individual peoples (*umam*) which constitute and are part of overall human society. In an article from 1882, which was reprinted in *al-Manar*, Muhammad ʿAbduh writes that, when we inquire into the affairs of peoples (*umam*), it becomes obvious that human society (*al-hay'a al-ijtimāʿiyya al-bashariyya*) did not attain a certain level of civilization and culture (*al-tamaddun wa-l-ḥaḍāra*) all at once. Rather, it is inevitable that one nation (*umma min al-umam*) takes the lead in reaching the heights of civilization (*ghāya fī al-madaniyya*).[238] Subsequently, ʿAbduh conceptualizes human society and its individual parts differently, when he writes that the above situation has been the case since human society (*al-jamʿiyya al-bashariyya*) has come to be divided into different peoples (*aqwām*) and tribes (*qabā'il*).[239]

Rashid Rida accounts for only one usage of *al-hay'a al-ijtimāʿiyya* to refer to a particular society – namely, when he complains that "our society" does not acknowledge the importance of newspapers. Rida stresses Riyad Basha's vital support for Egyptian newspapers and journals, taking care to point out that *al-Manar* does not receive special support. Without such assistance, these publications would possibly not have grown well in Egypt, he maintains. "This is because ignorance, weak morals, and corruption of the social order (*niẓām al-ijtimāʿ*) made our country like a salt swamp, in which the tree of knowledge can not grow except through especial care by the elite. We who have been reading the daily papers for decades have come to consider them indispensible for culture and civilization (*al-ḥaḍāra wa-l-madaniyya*). But our society (*hay'atunā al-ijtimāʿiyya*) due to its weak spirits (*ḍaʿf al-nufūs*) and sick morals (*marḍ al-akhlāq*) is still incapable or neglectful of undertaking what they [i.e., these papers] are entitled to, to the extent that many men of our upper class (*al-ṭabaqa al-ʿulyā fīnā*), like teachers, writers, or judges, postpone the subscription fee they ought to pay."[240]

---

236 Al-Mughira, ʿAbdallah. 1920. "Wasf Bilad al-ʿArab al-Janubiyya allati Yusammuha al-Yunan al-ʿArabiyya al-Saʿida." *al-Manar* 21/8: 415–422, here 417; Saʿid Halim quoted by Murasil Jaridat al-Akhbar fi al-Asitana in Rida, "Saʿid Halim," 151.

237 Ibid., 151.

238 ʿAbduh, Muhammad. 1906 [1882]. "al-Tamarrun wa-l-Iʿtiyad." *al-Manar* 9/8: 605–610, here 608.

239 Ibid., 609.

240 Rida, "Fatihat al-Mujallad al-Khamis ʿAshar," 4.

In *al-Manar* overall, *al-hay'a al-ijtimāʿiyya* was used to designate a particular society by name, but the authors who wrote regularly for the journal did not appropriate this usage. This is most obvious in the fact that Rida did not pick up the concept of *al-hay'a al-ijtimāʿiyya al-miṣriyya* in his discussion of Lord Cromer's translated writings. Indeed, Rida did not originate any instance of *al-hay'a al-ijtimāʿiyya* to conceptualize a particular society, except for the one mention of 'our society' (*hay'atunā al-ijtimāʿiyya*) cited above. This obviously raises a question regarding alternative terms used to designate particular societies.

5 Alternative Terms for Conceptualizing Particular Societies

In order to identify terms used to designate particular societies in *al-Manar*, I have searched the journal for instances in which terms conceptualizing social collectivities are attributed so as to refer to a particular collectivity – for example, 'the Egyptian,' 'the Jewish,' 'the French society/community/nation,' etc. The terms I searched for in this manner are *al-hay'a al-ijtimāʿiyya*, *mujtamaʿ*, *ijtimāʿ*, *umma*, *shaʿb*, *milla*, *jamʿiyya*, *jamāʿa*, and *qawm*.[241]

A few words are required on the terms *qawm* and *jamāʿa*, for which no table is included, since the search, remarkably, did not produce a single instance of either of them. The term *qawm* predominantly refers to a group of people who advocate a certain opinion (e.g., one *qawm* says..., whereas another says...) or allegedly hold a certain conviction (e.g., an unbelieving people, *al-qawm al-kāfirūn*). The term *jamāʿa* is mainly used in a generic sense to refer to a group of people, but may also indicate – as we have seen in chapter 7 section 4.3 – the firm integration of that social collectivity in a community. This is hardly surprising, given that the conceptual pair *jamāʿa* and *mujtamaʿ* came to mirror that of 'community' and 'society' in the sense of *Gemeinschaft* and *Gesellschaft*.[242] At the end of the 1920s, the Muslim Brotherhood was the first major movement to present itself as a *jamāʿa*, in distinction from society at large, which was dominated by colonial elites.[243] In turn, the Lebanese philosopher Nasif Nassar has been validating *mujtamaʿ* over *jamāʿa* since the 1970s – this in the sense of validating the whole, rationally organized society over against particular ideologi-

---

241 See appendix, tables 4a-h.

242 See above: 53.

243 Al-Anani has suggested a reading of the Muslim Brotherhood as presenting a *jamāʿa* paradigm (al-Anani, Khalil. 2013. "The Power of the Jama'A [sic]: The Role of Hasan Al-Banna in Constructing the Muslim Brotherhood's Collective Identity." *Sociology of Islam* 1: 41–63).

cal communities.[244] In *al-Manar*, the composite *al-jamāʿa al-islāmiyya* occurs only twice, and in these instances it refers to Islamic communities in Freetown[245] and Berlin,[246] respectively, rather than to an overall Islamic society or social order.

The main usages of *jamʿiyya* and *milla* largely confirm our expectations.[247] The first term refers mainly to specific societies in the sense of associations – whether welfare societies, political societies, literary societies, or religious societies. *Jamʿiyya* thus occurs mainly in the context of contemporaneous social and political events and activities, which explains why the term is used remarkably rarely in the *Tafsir.*[248] In light of this dominant usage, the few attempts to employ *jamʿiyya* to conceptualize human society or even an Islamic society are quite marginal. While *jamʿiyya* almost exclusively refers to worldly associations with specific socio-political aims, the attributions of *milla*, in turn, testify to the term's religious connotations. Five negligible occurrences of an Ottoman, Arab, or Egyptian *milla* aside, the term only refers to religious or denominational communities or convictions, most often to the Islamic *milla*, followed by the Hanafite *milla.*[249] *Milla* refers not only to a community, but also to a certain conviction or creed, as shown by the results of a search for *millat al-*, which are dominated by instances of *millat Ibrahim.*[250]

Things get more interesting concerning *mujtamaʿ* and *ijtimāʿ*. A first overview of attributed usages of *mujtamaʿ* already shows that these mainly conceptualize human society in general, in the form of *al-mujtamaʿ al-basharī* (six times) and *al-mujtamaʿ al-insānī* (42 times).[251] *Mujtamaʿ* is used to conceptualize Islamic society (*al-mujtamaʿ al-islāmī*) 18 times, and only in a very few other cases does *mujtamaʿ* refer to another particular society by name. The authorship of these instances, however, is remarkable, as will be demonstrated in the following chapter. Attributions of *ijtimāʿ* almost exclusively pertain to human society in

---

244 Nassar, Nasif. 1995 [1970]. *Nahwa Mujtamaʿ Jadid: Muqaddimat Asasiyya fi Naqd al-Mujtamaʿ al-Taʾifi.* Beirut: Dar al-Taliʿa, esp. 77–99, 179–207; idem. 2009 [1975]. *Tariq al-Istiqlal al-Falsafi: Sabil al-Fikr al-ʿArabi ila al-Hurriyya wa-l-Ibdaʿ.* Beirut: Dar al-Taliʿa. I owe these references to my colleague Michael Frey, whose forthcoming PhD dissertation includes an analysis of the relation of *mujtama*ʿ and *jamāʿa* in Nassar's writings.

245 Saʾih Muhibb li-l-Manar. 1903. "Siraliyun." *al-Manar* 6/19: 756–760, here 756.

246 Rida, Rashid. 1926. "al-Jamaʿa al-Islamiyya fi Berlin." *al-Manar* 27/4: 309–314. Rida was most probably referring to the *Islamische Gemeinde zu Berlin*, founded in 1922 as a *Verein.*

247 See above: 190.

248 See appendix, table 4f.

249 See appendix, table 4g.

250 See appendix, table 4h.

251 See appendix, table 4b.

general.[252] In its three main – and related – strands of meaning, *ijtimāʿ* refers to meetings, conventions, or gatherings; to unity, concurrence, or coherence; and to human beings' natural tendency toward social association, as will be substantiated in chapter 10 section 1.1.

The two main terms used to conceptualize particular societies are *shaʿb* (the people) and, above all, *umma* (society, nation, community, the people). The term *shaʿb*, whose usage increases in the second half of *al-Manar*'s life span, mainly refers to national or ethnic societies – with *al-shaʿb al-islāmī* occurring less often than *al-shaʿb al-inklīzī* or, especially, *al-shaʿb al-turkī*.[253] Combined with the rare usage of the term in the *Tafsir*, this seems to confirm Zolondek's above-mentioned evaluation of the term as carrying secular connotations.[254] It also indicates that *shaʿb* refers less to an abstract social order and more to a collectivity of actual people, often in opposition to the government.

Of all the terms discussed here, *umma* is by far the most frequent in *al-Manar*, both in general and concerning references to particular societies.[255] Of course, the term did convey a range of meanings – including community, the people, nation, and society – and it was often used in a generic sense, without normatively addressing a particular social order. However, it is remarkable that the composite *al-umma al-ʿarabiyya* (the Arab people/nation/society) occurs more frequently than *al-umma al-islāmiyya* in *al-Manar*, and also that the Egyptian nation or society was conceptualized as *al-umma al-miṣriyya* beginning in the first volume of the journal. The usage of *umma* to refer to an Arab or Egyptian social collectivity is especially noteworthy, in the light of its above-mentioned quasi-secular connotations.[256] This statistical overview thus quantitatively suggests that *umma* was the major term for conceptualizing society in *al-Manar*, and it complements this chapter's qualitative analysis of *al-hay'a al-ijtimāʿiyya*, which also pointed to *umma*.

The concluding section reiterates the extent to which the central authors in *al-Manar* used *umma* as an equivalent and alternative to *al-hay'a al-ijtimāʿiyya*, but it also points out a major difference between the two concepts: whereas *al-hay'a al-ijtimāʿiyya* always conveyed a normative sense of social order, *umma* carried a range of meanings and was a more generic term for referring to social collectivities.

---

252 See appendix, table 4c.
253 See appendix, table 4e.
254 See above: 185.
255 See appendix, table 4d.
256 See above: 183.

6 Conclusion: *Umma* as a Less Specific Alternative to *al-Hayʾa al-Ijtimāʿiyya*

In this chapter, we have repeatedly seen that central authors in *al-Manar* used the term *umma* as an alternative to *al-hay'a al-ijtimāʿiyya* – which was a clearly normative, tendentiously secularly connoted term for conceptualizing society. Despite occurring only 142 times in *al-Manar*,[257] *al-hay'a al-ijtimāʿiyya* alerts us not only to central aspects of society, but also to *umma* as a major alternative for conceptualizing society. Rashid Rida explicitly put forward *umma* as a synonym for *al-hay'a al-ijtimāʿiyya* and characterized the composite as a term "used by them." Equally remarkably, he most frequently employed *al-hay'a al-ijtimāʿiyya* when paraphrasing secular philosophers, himself preferring *umma* to address the same questions of social morals.[258] In addition, other central aspects of society conceptualized as *al-hay'a al-ijtimāʿiyya* were discussed by resorting to *umma*.[259] Concerning the usage of *al-hay'a al-ijtimāʿiyya* to refer to particular societies, the use of this composite by particular authors has been especially remarkable: Rida avoided this meaning entirely, and it was most prominently conceived in translations of works by Lord Cromer and also by Niqula Dabbana.[260] The identification of particular authors who use *al-hay'a al-ijtimāʿiyya* in *al-Manar* thus tentatively[261] confirms the composite's Christian-secular connotations, as suggested by prominent usages outside of *al-Manar*.[262] Nevertheless, while the authors who wrote regularly for our Islamic journal tended to avoid *al-hay'a al-ijtimāʿiyya*, they did occasionally make use of it themselves. In issues of *al-Manar* published after the First World War, we find supposedly conservative Azhari authors appropriating the concept in their writings, without qualifying or elaborating on it.[263] Thus, while *al-hay'a al-ijtimāʿiyya* was not so secularly charged as to be off limits to religious authors, these authors still preferred the alternative term *umma* when addressing the same aspects of society.

---

257 See above: chapter 7 section 1.

258 See above: chapter 7 section 2.

259 See above: chapter 7 section 3.

260 See above: chapters 7 sections 4.1 and 4.2.

261 I do not know the background of the translator of Cromer's texts, the translation of which appeared in the Muslim-owned newspaper *al-Mu'ayyad*.

262 See above: chapter 6 section 3.

263 See: Lajnat Mashyakhat al-Azhar. 1920. "Taqrir Lajnat Mashyakhat al-Azhar al-Sharif al-Mu'allafa li-Fahs Mashruʿ Taʿmim al-Taʿlim al-Ula [2]." *al-Manar* 21/8: 423–427, here 425; Ra'is Majallat al-Azhar quoted in Rida, Rashid. 1930. "al-Haqiqa wa-l-Tarikh." *al-Manar* 31/5: 371–389, here 382.

This is not to say that *umma* and *al-hay'a al-ijtimāʿiyya* both came to mean 'society,' but rather that Islamic reformists writing in *al-Manar* conveyed the same notions of society in their use of *umma* that somewhat secular authors conceptualized as *al-hay'a al-ijtimāʿiyya.* Moreover, *umma* had also been a much more prominent and flexible term than *al-hay'a al-ijtimāʿiyya*. This flexibility underlies the main semantic difference between the two concepts: whereas *al-hay'a al-ijtimāʿiyya* carried clear normative connotations of social order in almost all instances, *umma* was also used as a generic term to refer to social groups or collectivities. This main difference between the two terms was briefly demonstrated in several passages analyzed in this chapter above, but I shall now spell it out more explicitly.

To start with, let us take the following two examples, which use *al-hay'a al-ijtimāʿiyya* in the sense of the social order of a people or a nation (*umma*) – the first concerning the division of labor, the second concerning the relation of the people and the government. In the first year of *al-Manar*, an anonymous author from Damascus argues that "there is no life for a nation (*umma*) without money (*māl*), and no existence, and no independence. And it is known that the wealth (*tharwa*) of every state stems from the wealth of its people (*ummatihā*), and the wealth of the people from that of its individual members (*afrād*), whence the riches of a state depend on those of the people (*umma*), which in turn depend on those of individuals (*afrād*)."[264] In order to achieve national prosperity and strength, he deems it "necessary that traders, craftsmen, and farmers occupy the first place (*al-maqām al-awwal*) in society (*al-hay'a al-ijtimāʿiyya*), as on them rests the extent of wealth and power."[265]

In 1908, Rashid Rida – and this is the second example – criticizes, as he did repeatedly, the expectation that all reform should be carried out by the government. Here, he argues that the government ought to represent the people and act in their interest, instead of guiding them like a shepherd guides his sheep: "the government (*ḥukūma*), in the first sense, consists predominantly of members of the people (*afrād min al-umma*), who engage its services for the accomplishment of specific tasks (*aʿmāl makhṣūṣa*) that are indispensable for society (*al-hay'a al-ijtimāʿiyya*); and this in a manner determined by its shariʿa (that is, the shariʿa of the nation [*umma*]) and by [the nation's] laws which have been laid down by the representatives (*nuwwāb*) [the nation] has chosen for this purpose. And in its second sense, [the government] is tantamount to the shepherds (*ruʿā*) and the

---

264 An anonymous author from Damascus quoted in Rida, Rashid. 1898. "al-Quwa fi al-Mal." *al-Manar* 1/13: 225–230, here 226.
265 Ibid., 227.

people (*umma*) are their flock (*raʿiyya*)."[266] In these two examples, then, *umma* refers to the social collectivity of the nation or the people in distinction from the government, whereas *al-hayʾa al-ijtimāʿiyya* conceptualizes the social order of that collectivity.

In five other articles in *al-Manar*, the authors assess the degree of social order (*al-hayʾa al-ijtimāʿiyya*) attained by a nation or a people (*umma*, but also once *shaʿb*), predominantly that of the Arab people. In the first volume of the journal, Ahmad Hafiz Efendi stresses that Egyptian youths ought to get to know their own country before traveling abroad, "so that they are informed about the conditions of their nation (*aḥwāl ummatihim*) and its stage (*daraja*) concerning the social structure (*al-hayʾa al-ijtimāʿiyya*) and the civilized world (*al-ʿālam al-mutamaddin*)."[267] ʿAbd al-Rahman al-Kawakibi – in his famous book *Umm al-Qura*, about a fictional Muslim convention, which was first serialized in volumes four and five of *al-Manar* – writes that "the Arabs are the most advanced people (*aqdam al-umam*), adhering to the principles of equality of rights and [the principles of] mutual approximation (*taqārub*) of the ranks in society (*al-marātib fī al-hayʾa al-ijtimāʿiyya*)."[268] In volume 16 of *al-Manar*, al-Baghdadi reproduces this argument using the same terminology: "Oh, you Arab people (*al-umma al-ʿarabiyya*), [...], you, the most ancient of peoples (*umam*) concerning culture and civilization (*al-ḥaḍāra wa-l-madaniyya*), and the first in laying down the bases of the equality of rights and of the mutual approximation (*taqārub*) of the ranks in society (*al-marātib fī al-hayʾa al-ijtimāʿiyya*)."[269] Again in a similar vein, in volume 21 of *al-Manar*, al-Mughira maintains that "the Arabs belong to the first peoples (*asbaq al-umam*) having attained culture and civilization (*al-ḥaḍāra wa-l-madaniyya*), because they founded states (*duwal*) and constructed cities, ordered the governments (*naẓẓamū al-ḥukūmāt*) and established laws (*sannū al-sharāʾiʿ*), built schools and temples (*hayākil*), and advanced social structures (*raqqū al-hayʾāt al-ijtimāʿiyya*) so as to elevate the cause of the woman (*tarqiyat shaʾn al-marʾa*); and this four thousand years ago."[270] Finally, an article taken from an English journal published in Sierra Leone positively evaluates the societal integration of the Muslim people: "the Muslims are the only people

---

266 Rida, Rashid. 1908. "Iftitah Majlis al-Mabʿuthan." *al-Manar* 11/11: 860 – 872, here 867.
267 Ahmad Hafiz Efendi quoted in Rida, Rashid. 1898. "Riwayat al-Yatim." *al-Manar* 1/7: 129 – 133, here 132.
268 Al-Kawakibi, ʿAbd al-Rahman. 1903. "Tatimmat al-Ijtimaʿ al-Thani ʿAshar li-Jamʿiyyat Umm al-Qura." *al-Manar* 5/22: 859 – 864, here 863.
269 Al-Baghdadi, ʿAbd al-Haqq. 1913. "al-ʿArab wa-l-ʿArabiyya: bi-Hima Salah al-Umma al-Islamiyya." *al-Manar* 16/10: 753 – 771, here 765.
270 Al-Mughira, "Wasf," 417.

(*shaʿb*) enlightened with the light of civilization (*madaniyya*) and forming a social body (*hay'a ijtimāʿiyya*) in these dark regions."[271] Next to illustrating the main difference between *al-hay'a al-ijtimāʿiyya* and *umma*, this group of five examples nicely demonstrates the interconnectedness of the central ideas of society and civilization.

As a whole, the foregoing instances substantiate the point that *al-hay'a al-ijtimāʿiyya* was clearly a normative concept connoting a social order, whereas *umma* was used much more flexibly. While *umma* could well convey notions of order, as seen throughout this chapter, it was also used as a generic term to designate social collectivities. Put otherwise, if *al-hay'a al-ijtimāʿiyya* in almost all cases refers to the order of a social collectivity, *umma* could refer either to that collectivity or to its order. As a basic insight, then, it is safe to say that during the lifespan of *al-Manar*, no one Arabic term was established for conceptualizing society, and that *umma* was a major option to this end.

While this argument will be further substantiated in chapter 10, the following chapter shows which authors in *al-Manar* were already using *mujtamaʿ* – the term that later became the standard term for 'society' – and discusses whether this term carried distinct normative connotations.

271 Majallat Siraliyun quoted in Rida, Rashid. 1904. "al-Taʿlim al-Islami fi Siraliyun." *al-Manar* 7/4: 153–159, here 154.

Chapter 8
Mujtamaʿ in *al-Manar:* Avoiding the Established Meaning of 'Society'

1 Overview, Semantic Range, and Authorship

In addition to establishing the central aspects of society conceptualized as *mujtamaʿ* and the authors who most prominently used the term in that sense, this chapter[1] also points out commonalities and differences between *mujtamaʿ* and its alleged predecessor, *al-hayʾa al-ijtimāʿiyya*. One such crucial difference is that *mujtamaʿ* did not refer to society in the sense of a social order or overall social collectivity in all cases, but rather was used to mean different things, as this first section shows.

The search for *mujtamaʿ* in *al-Manar* produced 358 occurrences, 22 of which are in the *Tafsir.* Most of these instances could be translated as 'society,' bearing in mind the semantic range of that term. For the sake of clarity, however, I have only translated *mujtamaʿ* as 'society' when it refers to society as the overall social sphere or collectivity, and I have distinguished the following meanings of *mujtamaʿ*: reference to something non-human (19 instances); a place of assembly (12); a gathering, assembly, or get-together (58); instances that could fit into either of the last two categories (13); a club or association (8); human society or society in general (138); and a particular society or societies (110).

While *mujtamaʿ* was hardly a ubiquitous term in *al-Manar*,[2] it had been remarkably firmly established in the sense of 'society' since the first volume of the journal.[3] As such, it was also appropriated by authors who wrote regularly for *al-Manar*, including its editor, Rashid Rida. However, reprints of articles from other journals and translations of European works account for a strikingly large share of pertinent usages of *mujtamaʿ*, especially to designate particular societies. Rida, in turn, more frequently uses *mujtamaʿ* in meanings other than 'society,' and his share of the various categories differs significantly: whereas Rida accounts for 66 percent of the instances in which *mujtamaʿ* does *not* mean 'society,'

---

1 Some findings of this chapter have already been presented in: Zemmin, Florian. 2016. "Modernity without Society? Observations on the term *mujtamaʿ* in the Islamic Journal *al-Manār* (Cairo, 1898–1940)." *Die Welt des Islams* 56/2: 223–247.

2 Compare the number of occurrences of *mujtamaʿ* with that of *umma* (11,586) or *shaʿb* (2,949) (see appendix, table 3).

3 See appendix, table 2a.

https://doi.org/10.1515/9783110545845-009

his share drops to 27 percent of usages indicating society in a general sense and to a mere 10 percent of cases referring to a particular society.[4]

The last two categories of meanings, which are obviously the ones that interest us most, will be dealt with in the following sections. This section gives exemplary instances from the other categories, so as to establish the semantic range of *mujtamaʿ*; names the authors who acount for most instances of usages in the individual categories; and states my criteria for distinguishing between society in general and particular societies.

In nineteen cases, *mujtamaʿ* refers to an assembly or conjunction of things rather than of persons. The most common of these is the reference to a confluence of water, which occurs seven times[5] – three times in Rida's own words[6] and four times when he is quoting someone else.[7] In four cases, *mujtamaʿ* refers either to a particular joint of certain body parts or to the body part as a whole; in all of these, Rida explains the meaning of words in ancient poems.[8] Examples of other things assembled or collected include stars in a zodiac,[9] trees in a forest,[10] or money in an offertory.[11] This rather marginal usage of *mujtamaʿ* in *al-Manar* echoes a dominant meaning of the term in classical Arabic, which can be discerned from Edward Lane's *Arabic-English Lexicon* from 1865. Lane gave as the sole meaning of *mujtamaʿ* "[a] place in which a thing becomes collected, brought together, or the like; or in which things have become so; where they collect them-

4 See appendix, table 2b.

5 The digital version once wrongly has *mujtamaʿ al-anhur*, where it is *majmaʿ al-anhur* in the printed version (Rida, Rashid. 1929. "al-Istiftaʾ fi Haqiqat al-Riba." *al-Manar* 30/4: 273–291, here 283).

6 Idem. 1898. "al-Shiʿr wa-l-Shuʿaraʾ." *al-Manar* 1/10: 170–177, here 176; idem. 1922. "al-Rihla al-Urubiyya (2)." *al-Manar* 23/4: 306–313, here 308; idem. 1930. "Fatawa al-Manar." *al-Manar* 31/1: 46–58, here 50.

7 Three times it is the identical quote of an official decree concerning a possible Arab state and its borders – which, on one side, are determined by the confluence of the Euphrates and the Tigris: idem. 1921. "Wathaʾiq Tarikhiyya fi al-Masʾala al-ʿArabiyya." *al-Manar* 22/3: 232–240, here 236; idem. 1922. "al-Wathaʾiq al-Rasmiyya li-l-Masʾala al-ʿArabiyya." *al-Manar* 23/8: 612–616, here 614; idem. 1924. "Khitab ʿAmm fima Yajib ʿala al-Muslimin li-Bayt Allah al-Haram." *al-Manar* 25/1: 33–63, here 38. The fourth instance is to be found in: idem. 1903. "Namudhaj min Dalaʾil al-Iʿjaz." *al-Manar* 6/11: 418–421, here 419.

8 Rashid Rida commenting on: al-Taʿi, Abu Zabid. 1906. "Wasf al-Asad." *al-Manar* 9/3: 214–218, here 216 (two occurrences), 217; Rida, *Tafsir*, vol. 8: 151.

9 Al-Tunisi, Muhammad al-Khidr. 1921. "al-Khayal fī l-Shiʿr al-ʿArabī (2)." *al-Manar* 22/3: 218–227, here 218; Rida, *Tafsir*, vol. 2: 194.

10 Ibid., vol. 8: 268.

11 Idem. 1911. "ʿAridat al-Shukr min al-ʿUthmaniyin al-Mustakhdimin fī Afghanistan ila Amiriha." *al-Manar* 14/12: 943–944, here 944; idem., *Tafsir*, vol. 10: 12.

selves, come together, or unite; or in which they are comprised or contained; a place in which is a collection of things."[12]

When it comes to human beings associating, the meaning of *mujtamaʿ* as a place of assembly, which had been established according to the dictionaries mentioned above,[13] occurs only twelve times in *al-Manar.* The fourteenth-century jurist al-Shatibi accounts for two of these instances.[14] Of potential interest are the four cases in which the place of assembly is characterized as common or public (*ʿāmm*).[15] In an additional thirteen cases, the context does not provide sufficient information to determine whether the place of gathering or the gathering itself is referred to.[16]

Overall, the latter meaning was clearly predominant over the former: 58 times *mujtamaʿ* refers to the gathering, assembly, or get-together itself. In most of these instances, I found neither much ambiguity in meaning, nor any further interesting information.[17] This is different for the following cases: Rashid Rida

---

12 Lane, Edward William. 1863–1893. *An Arabic-English Lexicon: Derived from the Best and most Copious Eastern Sources*; 8 vols., vol. 6–8 compiled by S. Lane-Poole. London: Williams & Norgate, vol. 2 [1865]: 459.

13 See above: 189 ff.

14 Al-Shatibi, "Fasl," *al-Manar* 17/8: 604, 605.

15 Rida, Rashid. 1899. "Athar 'Ilmiyya Adabiyya: al-Kitaban al-Jalilan." *al-Manar* 2/18: 282–286, here 285; Shaykh Mashayikh al-Turuq. 1905. "Islah al-Turuq al-Sufiyya." *al-Manar* 8/9: 353–355, here 353; Abu al-Kalam. 1923. "Wasf Thawrat al-Hind al-Siyasiyya al-Salbiyya wa-Intisaruha li-l-Khilafa wa-l-Dawla al-Turkiyya wa-l-Bilad al-ʿArabiyya (2)." *al-Manar* 24/2: 121–128, here 122; Rida, Rashid. 1929. "Jamiʿ Baris." *al-Manar* 29/10: 793–794, here 793.

16 The instances that originate with Rida are: idem. 1898. "Kayfa al-Sabil?!." *al-Manar* 1/7: 112–119, here 115; idem., "al-Shiʿr," 176; idem. 1912. "Akhbar al-ʿAlam al-Islami." *al-Manar* 15/5: 386–391, here 391; idem. 1928. "Haqa'iq fi ʿAdawat Malahidat al-Turk li-l-Islam." *al-Manar* 29/6: 464–474, here 468. Instances by other authors include: al-Khuli, Muhammad ʿAbd al-ʿAziz. 1921. "Tarikh Funun al-Hadith (5)." *al-Manar* 22/5: 353–369, here 369; idem. 1926. "al-Irshad." *al-Manar* 27/4: 251–260, here 257.

17 Instances that originate with Rida include: Rida, Rashid. 1898. "Nahdat Muslimi al-Hind." *al-Manar* 1/20: 369–371, here 370; idem. 1898. "Ma'thara Jalila." *al-Manar* 1/25: 481–482, here 481; idem. 1899. "al-Akhbar al-Tarikhiyya: al-Daʿwa ila al-Din." *al-Manar* 2/9: 140–144, here 140; idem. 1901. "al-Akhbar al-Tarikhiyya." *al-Manar* 4/13: 509–520, here 512, 513; idem. 1905. "Tatimmat Mulakhkhas Sirat al-Ustadh al-Imam." *al-Manar* 8/11: 401–416, here 414, 415 (passage identical with the foregoing reference); idem. 1907. "al-Ihtifal bi-l-ʿAqd al-Awwal min ʿUmr al-Manar." *al-Manar* 10/9: 715–720, here 717; Rashid Rida in Tahir, Muhammad. 1914. "Maqam ʿIsa (Yasuʿ) al-Masih ʿalayhi al-Salam fi al-Nasraniyya wa-l-Islam." *al-Manar* 17/2: 142–147, here 147; Rida, Rashid. 1931. "Fatawa al-Manar." *al-Manar* 31/10: 732–744, here 734. Instances by other authors include: Bahithat bi-l-Badiyya [pseudonym of Malak Hifni Nasif]. 1910. "al-Mar'a al-Misriyya wa-l-Mar'a al-Gharbiyya." *al-Manar* 13/4: 265–284, here 276; Katib min al-Bahrayn [an author from Bahrain]. 1910. "al-Bidaʿ wa-l-Khurafat wa-l-Taqalid wa-l-ʿAdat ʿind al-

uses *mujtamaʿ* for the great or general congregation of Muslims in Mecca (*mujtamaʿ ʿaẓīm/ʿāmm*) seven times. Rida thereby mainly refers to Muslims getting together on the occasion of the hajj;[18] but in other cases, he seems to have a more institutionalized assembly in mind.[19] Rida uses *mujtamaʿ* for saint festivals (*mawālid*, sg. *mawlid*) five times.[20] In one article, he portrays these festivals as counterparts to fairs and exhibitions in Europe, albeit with a crucial difference: in the *mawālid*, religious and worldly aspects are strangely mixed, testifying to a lack of civilization in Egypt.[21] As with public places above, there are also a few references to public gatherings (sg. *mujtamaʿ ʿāmm*), which are twice contrasted with private gatherings (sg. *mujtamaʿ khāṣṣ*).[22] Four times *mujtamaʿ* refers to the coming-together or uniting of a man and a woman in marriage,[23] thereby attesting the broad applicability of the term and its echoing the semantic range of *société*.[24]

As the last category of meaning other than 'society' in the sense of overall social sphere or collectivity, there are eight cases in which *mujtamaʿ* denotes a more clearly delineated and institutionalized association – for example, student

Shiʿa." *al-Manar* 13/4: 303–313, here 312; Sidqi, Muhammad Tawfiq. 1910. "Hijab al-Mar'a fi al-Islam." *al-Manar* 13/10: 771–778, here 775; Chatelet, Monsieur. 1912. "al-Ghara ʿala al-ʿAlam al-Islami aw Fath al-ʿAlam al-Islami (10 [and 11])." *al-Manar* 15/10: 764–780, here 773; Jaridat Umm al-Qura. 1929. "al-Mu'tamar al-Najdi al-Shuri al-ʿAmm." *al-Manar* 29/9: 696–711, here 700; ʿAlim Kabir [a great scholar]. 1932. "Namudhaj min Kitab al-Injil wa-l-Salib." *al-Manar* 32/10: 745–752, here 752.

18 Rida, Rashid. 1902. "Bab al-As'ila wa-l-Ajwiba." *al-Manar* 5/18: 699–703, here 702; idem. 1932. "al-Mu'tamar al-Islami al-ʿAmm fi Bayt al-Muqaddas." *al-Manar* 32/2: 113–132, here 114.

19 Idem. 1900. "Fransa wa-l-Islam." *al-Manar* 3/7: 151–157, here 154, 155; idem. 1907. "Bahth fi al-Mu'tamar al-Islami li-Taʿaruf al-Muslimin wa-l-Bahth ʿan Asbab Daʿfihim wa-Tariq ʿAlajihi wa-Tarikh al-Daʿwa ilayhi." *al-Manar* 10/9: 673–682, here 674.

20 On these festivals, see: Schielke, "Hegemonic." For Rida's criticism of the *mawālid* and his fatwas in this regard, see: van Leeuwen, "Reformist," 147 f.; Abu-Zahra, "Al-Manar," 227 ff.

21 Rida, "al-Mawalid," here 81, 82. The other instances of *mujtamaʿ* referring to a *mawlid* are: idem. 1898. "Munkarat al-Mawalid." *al-Manar* 1/6: 93–101, here 99; idem., "Kayfa al-Sabil," 114; idem. 1900. "Kayfa Nantafiʿ bi-l-Mawalid wa-l-Mawasim." *al-Manar* 3/22: 525–527, here 525.

22 Idem. 1900. "Jamʿiyyat Shams al-Islam fi al-Qahira." *al-Manar* 2/48: 765–766, here 765; Lajnat Mashyakhat al-Azhar. 1920. "Taqrir Lajnat Mashyakhat al-Azhar al-Sharif al-Mu'allafa li-Fahs Mashruʿ Taʿmim al-Taʿlim al Ula." *al-Manar* 21/7: 362–371, here 369.

23 Sidqi, "al-Din," *al-Manar* 8/20: 777; Rida, Rashid. 1930. "Munazara fi Musawat al-Mar'a li-l-Rajul fi al-Huquq wa-l-Wajibat." *al-Manar* 30/7: 535–545, here 540, 545; idem. 1930. "Munazara fi Musawat al-Mar'a li-l-Rajul fi al-Huquq wa-l-Wajibat (3) [and 4–6]." *al-Manar* 30/8: 610–624, here 619.

24 Baker, "Enlightenment," 88.

clubs[25] or welfare organizations (*al-mujtamaʿāt al-khayriyya*).[26] This usage, albeit rather marginal, is not insignificant considering the origins of the English term 'society' and its normative core as a "voluntary and purposeful association,"[27] a definition that was maintained as the range of people addressed by 'society' increasingly widened and the term came to denote the overall social collectivity we are now familiar with. The standard term for such organizations, which also in Egypt increasingly attended to society as a whole,[28] was clearly *jamʿiyya* – and indeed, none of the admittedly few instances of *mujtamaʿ* in this meaning occurs after 1907.

Up to this point, Rida's share in the various categories has reflected the fact that he wrote most of the articles in *al-Manar.* Rida accounts for a total of 47 of the 58 cases of the most prominent meaning of *mujtamaʿ* so far – namely, its reference to a gathering, assembly, or get-together; he also accounts for about half of the cases in the other categories. This picture changes significantly now that we come to the usage of *mujtamaʿ* as 'society.' Here, I will name the most prolific authors for this usage and state my criteria for distinguishing between society in general and particular societies, before the following sections actually analyze the most pertinent instances of usage.

For the meaning of *mujtamaʿ* as society in general, Rida still accounts for more occurrences than any other author in *al-Manar* – namely, for 38 out of 138 instances. Yet not only is his share significantly less than in the previous categories, he also nowhere accords specific importance to *mujtamaʿ* – as indicated by the fact that these thirty-eight usages are spread out over thirty articles. The one author who most prominently uses the term in the sense of society in general is Hamid Mahmud Muhaysin – he uses the term fourteen times in a single article.[29] This text, which is also the only one to include *mujtamaʿ* in its title, was first published in *al-Siyasa*, the journal of the Liberal Constitutionalist Party (Hizb al-Ahrar al-Dusturiyin), which Rida notably characterized as areligious.[30] Of the other authors originally writing in Arabic, no one uses *mujtamaʿ* in the

25 For example: Rida, Rashid. 1907. "Khutbat al-Duktur Diyaʾ al-Din Ahmad." *al-Manar* 9/12: 933–939, here 933.

26 For example: Sidqi, "al-Din," *al-Manar* 8/20: 778.

27 Withington, *Society*, 12, 105; see above: 45.

28 See above: 115 f.

29 See below: 290 f.

30 Rida, Rashid. 1926. "al-Ladiniyun fi Tunis wa-Misr wa-Kitab ʿAli ʿAbd al-Raziq." *al-Manar* 26/7: 548–551, here 550 f.; idem. 1929. "al-Ilhad wa-Duʿatuhu fi Majallat al-Rabita al-Sharqiyya wa-l-Ustadh Ahmad Amin." *al-Manar* 29/9: 718–720, here 719; Rashid Rida commenting upon al-Ghamrawi, Muhammad Ahmad. 1926. "al-ʿIlm wa-l-Din (2)." *al-Manar* 27/7: 521–530, here 530.

sense of society in general more than four times. In translations, this usage appears twenty-five times, almost half of them in ʿAbd al-ʿAziz Muhammad's translation of Esquiros's *l'Émile du dix-neuvième siècle*.[31]

Concerning the reference of *mujtamaʿ* to particular societies, Rashid Rida accounts for a mere eleven of the 110 instances. There are 18 instances in which Rida quotes someone using *mujtamaʿ* in that sense, yet does not pick up the term himself. Two authors originally writing in Arabic use *mujtamaʿ* more prominently – namely, the Syrian-born intellectuals and political activists Rafiq al-ʿAzm and ʿAbd al-Hamid al-Zahrawi, with seventeen and eighteen instances respectively, spread over six articles each. Even more pertinently, the Egyptian writer Muhammad ʿAbdallah ʿAnan (1896–1986) uses *mujtamaʿ* nine times to signify a particular society, in two articles originally written for *al-Siyasa*. No other author writing in Arabic accounts for more than four instances. Translations into Arabic figure prominently in this category, too: of the 26 instances, Esquiros's *Émile* accounts for ten; an article by the Indian jurist and politician Ameer Ali (1849–1928) for six; and texts by the French sociologist Gustave Le Bon for five occurrences. I have formed a separate category for the 110 cases in which *mujtamaʿ* refers to particular societies, as here the modern sense tends to become most obvious. I have distinguished these references to particular societies from the 138 instances in which *mujtamaʿ* refers to society in general according to the following criteria.

The reference to human society in general is most obvious in cases where the authors add the attribute 'human' to *mujtamaʿ*: six times we find the composite *al-mujtamaʿ al-basharī*,[32] and 42 times *al-mujtamaʿ al-insānī*.[33] I have not

31 See above: 129.

32 Bin Fakhr al-Din, Rida' al-Din. 1907. "Matalib Muslimi Rusya min Dawlatihim; transl. Musa ʿAbdallah al-Qazani [2]." *al-Manar* 10/6: 444–455, here 446; Muhammad ʿAbduh quoted in Rida, "Athar," *al-Manar* 11/7: 532; Muhammad ʿAbduh quoted by Hafiz Ibrahim in Rida, Rashid. 1908. "Kitaban Siyasiyyatan li-l-Ustadh al-Imam al-Shaykh Muhammad ʿAbduh aw Matalib Misr min Inklitira." *al-Manar* 10/11: 834–848, here 846 (identical with the foregoing quote); Jaridat al-Afkar al-ʿArabiyya. 1915. "al-Haqq wa-l-Quwa: Bahth Falsafi ʿAnhuma bi-Munasibat al-Harb al-Hadira aw: Dars Daruri li-Nahnu al-Suriyin Khususan wa-l-Sharqiyin ʿUmuman." *al-Manar* 18/2: 141–152, here 142; ʿAnbarat Salam quoted in Rida, Rashid. 1921. "al-Rihla al-Suriya al-Thaniyya." *al-Manar* 22/5: 390–397, here 394; Khalid Shildrik quoted in Rida, Rashid. 1935. "al-Mawlid al-Nabawi." *al-Manar* 34/7: 549–552, here 550.

33 The ten instances authored by Rida are: Rida, Rashid. 1898. "Tabsira wa-Dhikra li-Qawm Yuʿqilun: fi Bayan anna Saʿadat al-Umma fi al-Tahdhib." *al-Manar* 1/4: 69–77, here 75; idem. 1898. "al-Namima wa-l-Siʿaya." *al-Manar* 1/14: 236–242, here 236; idem. 1899. "Ayyuha al-Fata." *al-Manar* 2/3: 43–46, here 44; idem. 1899. "al-Hayat al-Milliya." *al-Manar* 2/20: 305–310, here 309; idem. 1901. "As'ila Diniyya wa-Ajwibatuha." *al-Manar* 4/6: 221–225, here 224; idem. 1901. "al-Rijal wa-l-Nisa'." *al-Manar* 4/13: 481–489, here 486; idem. 1909. "Khitab Sahib al-Manar

turned these composites into a separate category because they largely overlap in meaning with the other cases in this category, in which *mujtamaʿ* stands alone. A potential but very marginal exception is two cases in which *al-mujtamaʿ al-insānī* refers to human society as a whole, as distinct from particular societies.[34] I have also considered those instances where the possessive pronoun 'his' or 'our' attached to society refers to all men (e.g., *al-insān wa-mujtamaʿuhu*) as referring to human society in general.

ʿala Tulab al-Kuliyya al-Amrikaniyya al-Muslimin fi Beirut." *al-Manar* 12/1: 16–18, here 16; idem. 1932. "Nidaʾ li-l-Jins al-Latif: Yawm al-Mawlid al-Nabawi al-Sharif." *al-Manar* 32/5: 352–400, here 352; idem. 1932. "Nidaʾ li-l-Jins al-Latif [...]: al-Talaq." *al-Manar* 32/8: 607–624, here 620; idem., *Tafsir*, vol. 4: 294. Among the instances by other authors, the translation of Esquiros's *Émile* accounts for nine cases: Esquiros, Alphonse. 1899–1900. "Amil al-Qarn al-Tasiʿ ʿAshar [; transl. ʿAbd al-ʿAziz Muhammad]." *al-Manar* 2/38: 598–603, here 601, *al-Manar* 2/42: 666–670, here 666, 670, *al-Manar* 2/43: 679–682, here 682 (twice), *al-Manar* 3/11: 253–257, here 255, *al-Manar* 3/13: 294–301, here 298, *al-Manar* 3/15: 345–351, here 345, *al-Manar* 3/26: 607–610 here 609. Other instances include: al-ʿUrwa al-Wuthqa, "al-Fadaʾil," 42; al-Dimashqi, Muhammad Efendi Kurd ʿAli. 1901. "al-Istiqlal wa-l-Ittikal." *al-Manar* 4/16: 601–615, here 613; al-Bakri, Muhammad Tawfiq. 1902. "al-Mustaqbal li-l-Islam." *al-Manar* 5/16: 601–634, here 623; ʿAlim ʿAmil wa-Katib Fadil [an active scholar and a noble writer]. 1903. "Raʾy fi ʿIlm al-Kalam wa-Tariqa fi Ithbat al-Wahy." *al-Manar* 5/19: 726–759, here 729; Sidqi, "al-Din," *al-Manar* 8/19: 735; Muhammad ʿAbduh: "al-Sinaʿa" (1879) quoted in Rida, "Maqalatan," 273; Bin Fakhr al-Din, "Matalib," *al-Manar* 10/6: 454; Sidqi, Muhammad Tawfiq. 1912. "Bashaʾir ʿIsa wa-Muhammad fi al-ʿAhdayn al-ʿAtiq wa-l-Jadid (3)." *al-Manar* 15/7: 494–510, here 498; Jaridat al-Afkar al-ʿArabiyya, "al-Haqq," 142, 145; Sidqi, Muhammad Tawfiq. 1915. "Madrasat Dar al-Daʿwa wa-l-Irshad, Durus Sunan al-Kaʾinat (7)." *al-Manar* 18/5: 353–371, here 365; Shaykh al-Azhar quoted in Rida, Rashid. 1925. "Hukm Hayʾa Kibar al-ʿUlamaʾ fi Kitab al-Islam wa-Usul al-Hukm." *al-Manar* 26/5: 363–382, here 381; Muhammad ʿAbduh quoted in Rida, Rashid. 1926. "Tarbiyat Umaraʾ al-ʿArab qabl al-Islam wa-Kayfa Nastafid minha fi Hadhihi al-Ayam?." *al-Manar* 26/8: 600–612, here 601; Ghandi, Mahatma. 1926. "al-Sihha (4); transl. ʿAbd al-Razzaq." *al-Manar* 27/1: 48–54, here 53; Abu al-ʿAyun. 1926. "Muharabat al-Bighaʾ." *al-Manar* 27/3: 233–235, here 233; Faruq, Sayf al-Rahman Rahmat Allah (Lord Headley). 1928. "Yaftarun ʿala Allah Kidhban." *al-Manar* 29/5: 344–351, here 350; Abd Allah ʿAfifi quoted in Rida, Rashid. 1933. "Thawrat al-Marʾa al-Ibahiyya wa-Khataruha ʿala al-Usra fa-l-Umma." *al-Manar* 33/6: 462–472, here 464; Arslan, Shakib. 1933. "Kalimatan fi al-Shaykh Muhammad ʿAbduh wa-l-Sayyid Rashid Rida." *al-Manar* 33/8: 635–638, here 636; ʿAbd al-ʿAziz al-Bishri quoted in Rida, Rashid. 1934. "Taqariz Kitab al-Wahy al-Muhammadi." *al-Manar* 33/10: 768–791, here 777; Muhammad Mustafa al-Maraghi quoted in Rida, Rashid. 1935. "Khitab al-Shaykh al-Akbar fi al-Jamiʿ al-Azhar." *al-Manar* 35/1: 41–46, here 43; al-Maraghi, Muhammad Mustafa. 1936. "Khutbat al-Ustadh al-Akbar Shaykh al-Jamiʿ al-Azhar." *al-Manar* 35/3: 186–188, here 186.

34 Bin Fakhr al-Din discusses important matters "for Muslims and even human society as a whole (*al-mujtamaʿ al-insānī bi-usarihi*)" (Bin Fakhr al-Din, "Matalib," *al-Manar* 10/6: 454. And Muhammad Tawfiq Sidqi names vices that destroy "first the pillars of the family, secondly of the nation, and thirdly of human society (*al-mujtamaʿ al-insānī*)" (Sidqi, "Madrasat," 365).

Among the 110 cases in which *mujtamaʿ* refers to a particular society or societies, the least specific instances are those in which the authors speak of 'societies' (*mujtamaʿāt*) or of 'every society' (*kull mujtamaʿ*). These usages refer to a plurality of different societies, although they tend to indicate traits common to all societies rather than specifics. A reference to the specifics of a particular society is already addressed in wordings such as 'this society' (*hadha al-mujtamaʿ*) or 'the society which...' (*al-mujtamaʿ alladhī...*). The same goes for those instances in which the possessive pronoun 'his' or 'our' (etc.) attached to society refers to a specific group of people. Things get most interesting when a society is clearly distinguished from others and given a specific name, such as 'Turkish society' (*al-mujtamaʿ al-turkī*) or 'Islamic society' (*al-mujtamaʿ al-islāmī*). While these last cases will be discussed separately (section 5), the foregoing, less pertinent instances of particular societies are merged with instances of society in general, because they tend to address the same central aspects of society.

Before getting to these central aspects of society conceptualized as *mujtamaʿ*, the following section shows that the reference of *mujtamaʿ* to an overall society or social order had indeed been firmly established since the first volume of *al-Manar.*

2 A Seemingly Self-evident Term: The Meaning of *Mujtamaʿ* and Its Relation to *Umma* and *Shaʿb*

2.1 Rashid Rida: Early Usages of *Mujtamaʿ* in Relation to *Umma* and *Shaʿb*

The establishment of *mujtamaʿ* in the sense of 'society' as an overall social sphere or collectivity and as connoting a social order is best demonstrated in cases where authors employ *mujtamaʿ* in relation to other concepts connoting social collectivities, such as *umma* or *shaʿb*. This subsection collects the most pertinent of such passages written by Rashid Rida, and the following subsection gathers those of other authors.

Let us begin, however, with the two earliest usages of *mujtamaʿ* as 'society' in *al-Manar*, which are to be found in reprints of two articles already discussed in the previous chapter concerning their employment of *al-hayʾa al-ijtimāʿiyya* – one written by ʿAbduh in 1879, the other taken from *al-ʿUrwa al-Wuthqa*, the short-lived journal ʿAbduh and al-Afghani published in Paris in 1884. ʿAbduh conceived of society conceptualized as *al-hayʾa al-ijtimāʿiyya* as an organic structure, all the limbs of which ought to work together for the good of human society (*al-mujtamaʿ al-insānī*) and to strive for the order of the whole structure (*intiẓām al-hay'a al-kulliyya*).[35] Whereas *al-hay'a al-ijtimā'iyya* specifies the order of society as functioning like a body, *al-mujtama' al-insānī* here seems to refer to the basic fact of human beings living in society. This basic fact, however, is not trivial, insofar as 'Abduh derives social norms from human beings' social nature. This also holds true for the article taken from *al-'Urwa al-Wuthqa.* It posits social association (*ijtimā'*) as distinguishing humans from animals and as leading to a comprehensive structure (*al-bunya al-jāmi'a*). This structure is again conceived of as a body, and, as seen above,[36] virtues are upheld as "the anchor of union (*waḥda*) of the social body (*al-hay'a al-ijtimā'iyya*)." The subsequent paragraph then elaborates on the function of virtues in human society (*al-mujtama' al-insānī*) as inciting every member to carry out their task in the proper manner.[37] Important to us here is the fact that Islamic reformists in 1879 and 1884 were already using *mujtama'* as a seemingly self-evident term for conceptualizing human society.

In the very first volume of *al-Manar*, Rashid Rida even employs *mujtama'* to explain the meaning of another term – namely of *al-sha'b* (the people). His article "The Authority of the Sheykhdom of the Spiritual Path" ("Sultat Mashyakhat al-Tariqa al-Ruhiyya")[38] was seemingly central to Rida. He quoted it at length in another article, "Religious and Civil Authority in Islam" ("Al-Sultatayn al-Diniyya wa-l-Madaniyya"),[39] which forms part of his series of articles on "Christian Criticisms and Islamic Proofs," which was later published as a book[40] and translated into English by Simon Wood[41]. Rida refers to this article from the first volume of *al-Manar* mainly to substantiate his argument that there is no religious authority in Islam, since all Muslims are equal before God and there are no clergy. Here, however, we are interested in the very beginning of this article, where he addresses the requirements of the order of social association (*niẓām al-ijtimā'*) and explains the meaning of *al-sha'b* via *mujtama'* (and *umma*):

"Various stages have come over man concerning the condition of his social association (*ṭawr ijtimā'ihi*). Eras and ages have passed over him, while his will

35 Preceding this passage, which has already been quoted (See above: 227), 'Abduh states that "the human collective (*al-majmū' al-insānī*) is like a body with limbs" ('Abduh, "al-Sina'a" (1879) quoted in Rida, "Maqalatan," 273).

36 See above: 222.

37 Al-'Urwa al-Wuthqa, "al-Fada'il," 42.

38 Rida, Rashid. 1898. "Sultat Mashyakhat al-Tariq al-Ruhiyya." *al-Manar* 1/22: 404–410.

39 Idem. 1903. "al-Sultatan al-Diniyya wa-l-Madaniyya." *al-Manar* 5/22: 841–859, here 844–847.

40 Idem., *Shubahat.*

41 Idem., *Christian.* The translation of the article in question is found on pages 193 ff.

was fettered and his physical forces were shackled by two great, strong powers. Those possessing these powers had complete influence over individuals (*afrād*) and the unrestricted right of disposal over them. These two powers are those of religion and politics (*sulṭat al-dīn wa-l-siyāsa*), or, as the people of this age call them, the spiritual and the temporal power (*al-sulṭa al-rūḥiyya wa-l-zamaniyya*), two powers without which the order of social association (*niẓām al-ijtimāʿ*) will not be completed and without which felicity is not attainable. Yes, even societies (*umam*) and peoples (*shuʿūb*) are not formed (*tatakawwan*) except by one of these two powers or both of them, because the meaning of the people (*al-shaʿb*) is: the integrated social collectivity (*mujtamaʿ*) or the civilized social collectivity (*al-umma al-mutamaddina*); individuals of one class (*ṣinf*) and of various classes (*aṣnāf*), brought together and integrated by a bond (*rābiṭa*) uniting all of them through unity of belief (*iʿtiqād*) and deed or unity of rule (*ḥukm*) and order (*niẓām*)."[42]

Rida goes on to stress the need for power to ensure unity, and the fact that it must do so by implementing and respecting civil and religious laws (*al-qawānīn wa-l-sharāʾiʿ*) that meet the requirements of the people (*umma*). He finds it problematic to entrust all power to one person, as the felicity and misery of a nation (*umma*) is then absolutely dependent on that person. Rida's argument that there is no clergy in Islam follows up on this alleged need for power to be restrained and controlled by laws.[43]

Most significantly for our purposes here, Rida took the meaning of *mujtamaʿ* as self-evident when using the term to explain the meaning of *al-shaʿb*, based on the following assumptions: spiritual and temporal power are necessary for the order of social association (*niẓām al-ijtimāʿ*). They are also necessary for forming a people (*shaʿb*), since a *shaʿb* is that social collectivity whose association is solidified and integrated by belief or by rule and legal order. This type of social collectivity is expressed by *mujtamaʿ*, which is the orderly result of social association (*ijtimāʿ*). We also note that, while Rida employed *umma* as a synonym to *al-hayʾa al-ijtimāʿiyya*, as shown in the previous chapter, *al-umma al-mutamaddina* here connotes the same type of ordered and integrated social collectivity as *mujtamaʿ*, whether one wants to render *umma* as 'nation,' 'people,' or 'society.'

As elaborated above,[44] however, one may hermeneutically distinguish these English terms, positing 'society' as focusing on the functioning of the social

---

42 Idem., "Sultat Mashyakha," 410. My translation differs from that of idem., *Christian*, 193.
43 Idem., "Sultat Mashyakha," 404f.
44 See above: chapter 2 section 2.

sphere, whereas 'nation' alludes to common bonds constituting a social collectivity, and 'the people' foregrounds the relation to the government, often stressing the need for a strong ruler. According to this distinction, *umma* might best be translated here as 'the people.' This then also holds true for *mujtamaʿ*. In other words, the entity in which human beings' social association (*ijtimāʿ*) is reified is here conceptualized as *shaʿb*, *mujtamaʿ*, and *umma*. In English, this entity has conventionally come to be conceptualized as 'society,' and we may also translate it here as such. The concept of 'the people' has served as a functional equivalent to 'society' in addressing the *problématique* of social order, albeit foregrounding different normative connotations. Rida here uses the Arabic terms *umma*, *mujtamaʿ*, and *shaʿb* as functional equivalents to 'society' and its own rival term 'the people,' foregrounding aspects ideal-typically associated with the latter.

While in the article just discussed, Rida uses *al-umma al-mutamaddina* and *mujtamaʿ* as synonyms, in two other articles he wrote in the first two years of *al-Manar*, *mujtamaʿ* refers to the whole society of the *umma* and thus also to the social order of the *umma*. In an article from the first volume of *al-Manar*, Rida adduces several Qurʾanic verses to support his main argument, which is contained in the article's sub-title: "Elucidation that the Felicity of the *umma* rests on Moral Refinement (*tahdhīb*)."[45] He begins this article by saying that "these verses (*āyāt*) of wisdom are read aloud to the whole social collectivity of this nation (*mujtamaʿ hadhihi al-umma*)."[46] The following year, Rida maintains that almsgiving (zakat) is one of the greatest wisdoms if not the greatest wisdom of the Islamic legislation, for it ensures "the support for eight groups (*ṭawāʾif*) of Muslims[47] without whom the whole social collectivity of the community (*mujtamaʿ al-umma*) will not be in proper order (*yuṣliḥ*)."[48] Earlier in the same article, Rida refers to the whole nation as *majmūʿ al-umma*,[49] suggesting that *mujtamaʿ* here does not specifically convey the idea of social order. Nevertheless, also in light of the topics dealt with in these two articles, such an idea of order is implicitly given in the reference to the social collectivity (of the nation or community) as a whole. Rida does not pick up the wording *mujtamaʿ al-umma* in subsequent volumes of *al-Manar*. Quite possibly, then, Rida came to use *umma* to express tout court what he had previously expressed with *mujtamaʿ al-umma*.

---

45 Rida, "Tabsira."

46 Ibid., 69.

47 This refers to the eight categories of people entitled to receiving alms. See Qurʾan 9:60.

48 Rida, Rashid. 1900. "al-Zakat wa-l-Tamaddun wa-l-Iman wa-l-Insaniyya." *al-Manar* 2/45: 705–713, here 712.

49 Ibid., 706.

However, both terms could be related in different ways, as an example from the *Tafsir* demonstrates, in which *mujtamaʿ* is used as the generic term for social collectivities. Rida posits it as "obligatory for the people of the village (*ahl al-qarya*) to choose a group (*jamāʿa*) which may rightfully be designated by the term *umma*, and that [the people] are doing what [this group] is doing, with unity and force, so that they assume the responsibility of establishing this duty [i.e., the duty of propagation (*daʿwa*)], as this is obligatory [not only in the village but] in every Islamic society (*mujtamaʿ islāmī*), urban or beduin. For the meaning of *umma* comprises the meaning of connection (*irtibāṭ*) and union (*waḥda*)."[50]

Concerning Rida's use of *mujtamaʿ*, this subsection established that he already regarded the term's reference to society as self-evident in the first volume of *al-Manar*. In fact, in all the cases in which Rida uses *mujtamaʿ* in this meaning, he does so without explaining or qualifying the term. This will be further demonstrated in the subsequent sections of this chapter, which include several additional examples written by Rida. However, before we come to those examples, the following subsection gathers examples from other authors concerning the generic usage of *mujtamaʿ* as well as its reference to a social order and its relation to *umma* and *shaʿb*.

2.2 Other Authors Using *Mujtamaʿ* in Relation to *Umma* and *Shaʿb*

In the *Tafsir al-Manar*, a section written by ʿAbduh[51] provides a telling example of *mujtamaʿ* being used in a generic sense. Addressing the relation of men and women, ʿAbduh posits that "men are responsible to provide [a livelihood] for women, to protect them, and to assume the task of general leadership (*al-riyāsa al-ʿāmma*) in the social collectivity of the clan (*mujtamaʿ al-ʿashīra*), which comprises the household (*manzil*). After all, every social collectivity (*mujtamaʿ*) inevitably requires a head (*raʾīs*) on whom it depends for the unification of the common interest (*al-maṣlaḥa al-ʿāmma*)."[52] Here as elsewhere, *mujtamaʿ* can be used to designate social collectivities from the size of a household to that of a nation. *Mujtamaʿ* is also used in a generic sense in later volumes of *al-Manar*, where

---

50 Idem., *Tafsir*, vol. 4: 31.

51 While Rida claims to have edited this section, the argument is definitely ʿAbduh's, and presumably the major terms are, too.

52 Ibid., vol. 5: 56.

mention is made of "the noise of society (*mujtamaʿ*)"[53] or "the society (*mujtamaʿ*) in which one lives."[54]

In another statement by ʿAbduh, quoted twice by Rida, which addresses the relation between the people (*shaʿb, umma*) and the ruler, the meaning of *mujtamaʿ* oscillates between a general reference to the social collectivity and a sense of order: "This is the pillar on which is based [the people's (*al-nās*)] collective life (*ḥayātuhum al-ijtimāʿiyya*), and no weakness and feebleness befell them except when this pillar was absent from their society (*mujtamaʿihim*). And this [pillar] is the distinction between the government's right to the obedience of the people (*al-shaʿb*) and the people's right to the justice of the government. Yes, I was among those inciting the Egyptian people (*al-umma al-miṣriyya*) to knowing their right over its ruler (*ḥākimihā*)."[55] The normativity of *mujtamaʿ* here results from this double reference to a social collectivity and to a sense of integration and order.

This sense of integration and order is more or less prominently visible in the following four examples, which further attest to the double reference of *mujtamaʿ* and its relation to *shaʿb* and *umma*. In volume four, an otherwise unknown author writes: "Every nation (*umma*) which threw itself into the arena (*miḍmār*) of life inevitably requires a system of rules (*qānūn*) [...] by which [the nation] protects its order (*niẓām*) and clears the roads of progress (*taraqqi*) for its society (*mujtamaʿihā*)."[56] He then argues that the law brought by Islam, which instituted legal principles but leaves the particularities to human beings, is most suitable for civilization (*al-madaniyya*) and social life (*al-ḥayāt al-ijtimāʿiyya*).[57] Rafiq al-ʿAzm, in an excerpt from his book on *Pan-Islamism* (*al-Jamiʿa al-Islamiyya*), asserts that "the natural laws of social association (*qawānīn al-ijtimāʿ al-ṭabīʿiyya*) compel the peoples (*shuʿūb*) to protect their society (*mujtamaʿihā*) and to defend its independence."[58] In volume 33, Farid Wajdi (1878–1954) writes that "the French nation (*al-umma al-fransiyya*) ventured to eradicate religion as a root

53 Rida, Salih Mukhlis. 1919. "Taqriz al-Matbuʿat al-Jadida." *al-Manar* 21/6: 327–336, here 331.
54 Al-Mawla, Muhammad Ahmad Jad. 1935. "Ma Ahwajuna fi hadha al-Zaman ila Hadayat al-Qur'an." *al-Manar* 35/5: 42–48, here 43 (page number 42 occurs twice in this volume; this is the second occurrence).
55 Muhammad ʿAbduh quoted in Rida, Rashid. 1906. "Tatimmat Sirat al-Ustadh al-Imam [2]." *al-Manar* 8/23: 891–901, here 893; identical: Muhammad ʿAbduh quoted in Rida, Rashid. 1927. "Saʿd Zaghlul (1)." *al-Manar* 28/8: 584–592, here 589.
56 Al-Marghinani, Kamal al-Din. 1901. "al-Fiqh al-islami." *al-Manar* 4/4: 132–140, here 133.
57 Ibid., 133.
58 Al-ʿAzm, Rafiq. 1907. "al-Jamiʿa al-Islamiyya." *al-Manar* 10/8: 589–594, here 590. This article consists of the following pages of the book: idem. 1907. *al-Jamiʿa al-Islamiyya wa-Uruba*. Cairo: Matbaʿa Hindiyya, 7–14.

of their society (*mujtamaʿihā*)."[59] And finally, in the journal's last volume, Hasan al-Banna characterizes his times as "the mechanical age (*al-ʿaṣr al-mīkānīkī*), in which the problem of unemployment and inactivity of men became one of the most complicated problems of human societies (*al-mujtamaʿāt al-bashariyya*) in every people (*shaʿb*) and state (*dawla*)."[60] As these examples show, *mujtamaʿ* could equally refer to a social collectivity such as the people (*umma*, *shaʿb*) or to the social order of that collectivity, and often the concept's meanings oscillate between these two senses.

A speech Ismaʿil Efendi Hafiz gave at a celebration of the Ottoman Constitution in Tripolis in 1909 further attests to *mujtamaʿ* referring to the whole, integrated collectivity and thereby to the order of the *umma*, which itself comprises the as yet hardly differentiated meanings of 'society,' 'the people,' and 'nation.'[61] It is worth quoting this speech at length, since it is so rich in content and terminology:

"On this day, the Ottoman sensed that he is an active member of a living nation (*umma ḥayya*), being happy when it is happy and being unhappy when it is unhappy. He woke up from his sleep of indifference and tirelessly embarked on the welfare of his nation (*maṣlaḥat ummatihi*). And he saw that there is no path to his happiness except that of unity (*ittiḥād*), and that unity will not be realized except through fraternity (*ikhāʾ*) and equality (*musāwā*). So the communities of the nation and its religions (*milal al-umma wa-adyānuhā*) came together as brothers, and its peoples and ethnic groups (*shuʿūbuhā wa-ʿanāṣiruhā*) became equal [...] and all were convinced that they cannot dispense of the others in their societal life (*ḥayātihi al-ijtimāʿiyya*) and their national felicity (*saʿādatihi al-qawmiyya*) [...]. On this day, the constitution was proclaimed. It determined that the people (*umma*) shall obtain its liberty (*ḥurriyatihā*); it bestowed on it the blessing of its independence and accorded its members (*afrādihā*) the right of their opinion being heeded in administering the affairs of their society (*idārat shuʾūn majmūʿihā*). This blessing is considered a solid basis for the happiness of its [i.e., the *umma*'s] future [...]. Investigation proves and history teaches us that those peoples (*umam*) which are deprived of this blessing do not have a proper social association (*ijtimāʿ ḥaqīqī*) and no real happiness. [...] So it is no wonder that the whole Ottoman nation (*jamīʿ al-umma al-ʿuthmāniyya*) is greatly

59 Farid Wajdi quoted in Rida, Rashid. 1933. "al-Matbuʿat al-Munkira fi al-Din." *al-Manar* 33/7: 513–535, here 523.
60 Al-Banna, Hasan. 1940. "al-Mar'a al-Muslima (2)." *al-Manar* 35/10: 765–773, here 773.
61 Al-Hafiz, Ismaʿil Efendi. 1909. "Khutba li-ʿAyd al-Dustur." *al-Manar* 12/8: 547–551.

celebrating this happy day [...], and it is no wonder that the minds are stretching out in order to acquaint themselves with the meaning of this blessing and its relation to society (*al-hay'a al-ijtimāʿiyya*)."[62]

Those investigating this blessing of a people's liberty are divided in opinion, Hafiz observes, and he further circumscribes his understanding of *umma* along the way: some scholars consider this blessing not as a natural right (*ḥaqq ṭabīʿī*) of a people (*umma*), but as a societal condition (*ḥāla ijtimāʿiyya*) determined by the stage of the people's development. Contrary to this, "the people of understanding," with whom Hafiz sides, maintain that "the rule of the people by and for itself is a natural right, which is accorded to it the day it may rightfully be designated by the term *umma*."[63] After all, if human beings by nature have free will, so does the social collectivity of the *umma*. For "insofar as the *umma* is tantamount to the totality of people (*jumlat al-afrād*) firmly integrated (*mujtamiʿa*) by bonds (*rawābiṭ*) of shared interests (*al-maṣāliḥ al-mushtaraka*) and of general distinguishing characteristics (*al-ṣifāt al-shāmila*), for them collectively (*majmūʿihim*) must be established the same right as has been established for each single one of them."[64] Hafiz designates an *umma* thus integrated and having this natural right as an *umma mujtamiʿa*, whose members attend to the affairs of their integrated whole – that is, of their society (*shuʾūn mujtamaʿi-him*).[65]

This terminology offers central insights concerning the relation of *umma* and *mujtamaʿ*, which becomes even clearer when we also consider Hafiz's usage of *ijtimāʿ* in the following passage:

"The [required] extent of common sense (*tamyīz*) and maturity in a people (*umma*) is that it [i.e., the *umma*] finds itself at the point prepared for it by social association (*ijtimāʿ*) in its most basic meanings. And when it has reached this stage (*martaba*), it is decreed that it has attained its maturity and is able to administer itself. [However,] every human society (*jamʿiyya bashariyya*) has most certainly attained this stage [by definition]. For as man has been created to live collectively (*mujtamiʿan*), he cannot be disengaged from social association (*al-ijtimāʿ*); and the integrated society (*al-umma al-mujtamīʿa*) can not be disengaged from being entitled to independence by its nature. [...]. The people's nat-

62 Ibid., 547 f.
63 Ibid., 548 f.
64 Ibid., 549.
65 Ibid., 549.

ural attainment and realization of its liberty is not conditional upon it having reached the degree of the advanced peoples concerning its social integration (*ijtimāʿihā*)."[66]

After all, Hafiz emphasizes, peoples may well advance in their means of social association (*madārij ijtimāʿihā*), and a society's (*hayʾa ijtimāʿiyya*) attainment of liberty is the *first* step in this advancement; in fact, the liberty of a society (*umma*) is the *principle* of its societal life (*mabdaʾ ḥayātihā al-ijtimāʿiyya*).[67]

While we note in passing that *umma* and *al-hayʾa al-ijtimāʿiyya* are again employed synonymously, this passage clearly shows the normative force of human beings' allegedly natural social association and integration (*ijtimāʿ*). This assertion leads to a claim for the liberty and independence of society – that is, of the people. Above all, *umma* also expresses the meaning of *mujtamaʿ*, insofar as *al-umma* (*al-mujtamiʿa*) is that social collectivity in which human beings' natural tendency toward social association is realized – which reminds us of Rida's explaination of the meaning of *al-shaʿb* as *al-mujtamaʿ* and *al-umma al-mutamaddina*.

Combining the insights gathered from Hafiz's article and the previous discussion, *mujtamaʿ*, while it can be used in a generic sense, mirrors the normativity and double sense of 'society' in that it refers both to a firmly integrated and ordered social collectivity, with common bonds and interests, and to the order of that collectivity. The following section attends to the commonalities and differences between *mujtamaʿ* and the term it supposedly came to replace.

3 *Mujtamaʿ* and *al-Hayʾa al-Ijtimāʿiyya*

3.1 *Mujtamaʿ* and *al-Hayʾa al-Ijtimāʿiyya* in *al-Manar*

Most fundamentally, and somewhat surprisingly, the usage of *mujtamaʿ* in the sense of 'society' does not increase over the years of *al-Manar*'s publication, and that of *al-hayʾa al-ijtimāʿiyya* decreases only slightly, at least in our Islamic journal itself.[68] That is to say, *mujtamaʿ* did not gradually replace *al-hayʾa al-ijtimāʿiyya* as the preferred term for conceptualizing society in *al-Manar*. Rather, both terms had been available to the journal's authors, and while *mujtamaʿ*

66 Ibid., 550.
67 Ibid., 550 f.
68 See appendix, table 2.

was somewhat more established and more frequently used, neither of them was the term preferred by the authors who wrote regularly for the journal. The rather small empirical basis notwithstanding, some noteworthy differences between *mujtamaʿ* and *al-hayʾa al-ijtimāʿiyya* may be discerned.

First of all, however, it ought to be stressed that both terms could well be used synonymously – which is hardly surprising, given that no one term was yet established for conceptualizing society. Both terms appear synonymously in the two earliest usages of *mujtamaʿ*, mentioned above,[69] as well as in an above-mentioned article by Rida from the first volume of *al-Manar*, in which he alternates between *al-hayʾa al-ijtimāʿiyya*, *umma*, and *mujtamaʿ* to conceptualize society.[70] Some further examples from later volumes of *al-Manar* substantiate the continuing possibility of using *al-hayʾa al-ijtimāʿiyya* and *mujtamaʿ* synonymously. In an article from 1913, Amir Ali conceptualizes modern society, which abandoned polygyny, both as *al-hayʾa al-ijtimāʿiyya al-ḥadītha* and as *al-mujtamaʿ al-ḥadīth*.[71] In an article from 1925, Rashid Rida first speaks of persons as "beneficial members of society" (*al-hayʾa al-ijtimāʿiyya*)[72] and then of society (*mujtamaʿ*) benefitting from a certain group of people.[73] And even in the last volume of *al-Manar*, Husayn al-Harawi, in his series of articles on "The Orientalists and Islam," uses both *al-hayʾa al-ijtimāʿiyya* and *mujtamaʿ* to refer to the social collectivity of the Arabs or Easterners and to their social order.[74]

As a first difference, an organic understanding of society conceived of as a social body is more characteristic of *al-hayʾa al-ijtimāʿiyya* than of *mujtamaʿ*. Only four instances in *al-Manar* mention a body of society conceptualized as *mujtamaʿ*. In three occurences, this is Islamic society: in volume two, Rida speaks of nationalism as a threat dissolving the "body of Islamic society" (*jism al-mujtamaʿ al-islāmī*);[75] the same year, an anonymous author from Damascus, who could well be Rafiq al-ʿAzm,[76] observes that "the word of reform (*iṣlāḥ*)

69 See above: chapter 8 section 2.1.

70 See above: chapter 7 section 2.

71 ʿAli, "al-Marʾa," esp. 935, 939.

72 Rida, "Madi al-Azhar," 124.

73 Ibid., 125.

74 Al-Harawi, Husayn. 1936. "al-Mustashriqun wa-l-Islam." *al-Manar* 35/4: 249–260, 267–279, 280–289, here 253, 258, 282, 284.

75 Rida, Rashid. 1900. "al-Hayra wa-l-Ghumma wa-Munashuʾhuma fi al-Umma." *al-Manar* 2/48: 753–758, here 757.

76 Not only is he from Damascus, but he also wrote an article with the same title, "al-Islah al-Islami," that appeared a few pages later.

is reverberating in the body of Islamic society (*hayʾat al-mujtamaʿ al-islāmī*);"[77] and Shakib Arslan, in an article that forms part of his famous book on the reasons for Muslim decline,[78] considers lazy Muslims without occupation to be nothing but "severed members of the body of Islamic society" (*jism al-mujtamaʿ al-islāmī*).[79] As the fourth and last instance, in 1921, Rashid Rida quotes the Lebanese female author, intellectual, and women's rights activist ʿAnbarat Salam (1897–1986) as asserting that a person earning his or her own livelihood proves to be "a living human being (*insān ḥayy*) in the body of human society (*jism al-mujtamaʿ al-basharī*)."[80] Not only was *mujtamaʿ* rarely used to speak explicitly of a 'body of society,' but the related images of physical parts of society and of societal illnesses and cures are also almost absent.[81] Moreover, human society conceptualized as *mujtamaʿ* was almost never envisioned in analogy to nature or animal societies,[82] in contrast to the case of *al-hayʾa al-ijtimāʿiyya*.

In turn, *mujtamaʿ* – more often than *al-hayʾa al-ijtimāʿiyya* – explicitly referred to societal order. This order was often addressed as being in need of reform (*iṣlāḥ*). Other than a physically envisioned social body, which ought to be *cured*, an order in need of *reform* conveys a more abstract understanding of society. (This does not devalue the above-discerned notions of order instilled into *al-hayʾa al-ijtimāʿiyya* or the possibility of *mujtamaʿ* also referring to social collectivities in a generic, supposedly non-normative sense.) The instances in which an order of *mujtamaʿ* was terminologically explicated as *niẓām* (etc.) are too many to enumerate here, whence they are included in the analysis of specific aspects and requirements of order. Aspects of order more prominently adduced for *mujtamaʿ* than for *al-hayʾa al-ijtimāʿiyya* are those of religion, politics, and, especially, law – as will be shown in section 4 of this chapter, where we will also reencounter the domain of morals, which was central to both *al-hayʾa al-ijtimāʿiyya* and *mujtamaʿ*.

Here, I shall briefly mention the aspects of work, women, and education, which were also addressed via both concepts but are of less interest concerning

---

77 Ahad Afadil al-Kuttab fi Dimashq al-Sham [a distinguished autor from Damascus]. 1899. "al-Islah al-Islami." *al-Manar* 2/5: 65–72, here 65.

78 See above: 144.

79 Arslan, "Limadha," *al-Manar* 31/7: 534.

80 ʿAnbarat Salam quoted in Rida, "al-Rihla al-Suriyya," 394.

81 An exception is: Esquiros, "Amil," *al-Manar* 2/42: 670; original: idem., *L'Émile*, 50.

82 The only article that uses *mujtamaʿ* to conceive of human society in analogy to animal societies was written by a German general (von Bernhardi quoted in Jaridat al-Afkar al-ʿArabiyya, "al-Haqq"). This article, which very much subscribes to the premises of social Darwinism, will be further discussed below (see below: 277 f.).

the normative dimensions of *mujtama'*. As education was crucial for almost all reformists of the nineteenth and twentieth centuries,[83] it is trivial to observe that its social importance was stressed via all terms conceptualizing society. Here, it suffices to mention those instances where *mujtama'* is explicitly related to education in footnotes.[84] The same goes for the role of women in society – an important social question which, however, *in al-Manar*, was rarely discussed by employing *mujtama'*.[85] Rashid Rida is the one author who refers most often to the importance of work for society conceptualized as *mujtama'*.[86] The required division of labor and the working-together of different groups or parts of society were, however, addressed more prominently for *al-hay'a al-ijtimā'iyya* than for *mujtama'*.[87]

In a somewhat ideal-typical manner, the major difference between the two concepts can be summarized as follows: *al-hay'a al-ijtimā'iyya in al-Manar* conveyed the normative conception of society as a social body, whereas *mujtama'* was used as a seemingly descriptive term for social collectivities, but equally referred to a more abstract order of society. These two senses combined explain why *mujtama'* lent itself more readily to designating particular societies – that is, entities onto which a religion and a state were mapped. Before the following section works out the crucial domains related to society conceptualized as *mujtama'* in *al-Manar*, I wish to point out one noteworthy use of both *mujtama'* and *al-hay'a al-ijtimā'iyya* beyond our Islamic journal, namely in Niqula Haddad's pioneering, two-volume book on sociology from 1924/1925.[88]

---

83 See above: chapter 4 section 2.2.

84 Rida, Rashid. 1906. "al-'Aql wa-l-Qalb wa-l-Din." *al-Manar* 9/3: 186–195, here 188; Arslan, Shakib. 1928. "Azimat Kitab al-Salat fi Injlitira." *al-Manar* 29/3: 201–214, here 201; Muhammad Amin quoted in Rida, Salih Mukhlis. 1913. "Taqriz al-Matbu'at al-Jadida." *al-Manar* 17/1: 63–67, here 65. The translation of Esquiros's *Émile* once stresses the importance of education for society, and once the role of society as an educator: Esquiros, "Amil," *al-Manar* 3/11: 255 [original: idem., *L'Émile*, 117]; idem., "Amil," *al-Manar* 2/43: 682.

85 Rida, "Ayyuha," 44; Esquiros, "Amil," *al-Manar* 2/42: 666f. (original: idem., *L'Émile*, 46); Rida, "Nida'," *al-Manar* 32/8: 620; 'Abdallah 'Afifi quoted in Rida, "Thawrat al-Mar'a," 464.

86 Rida, Rashid. 1907. "Sunan al-Ijtima' fi al-Hakimin wa-l-Mahkumin la-Hum wa-Jaza'uhum." *al-Manar* 10/2: 107–111, here 108; idem., "Khitab Sahib al-Manar," 16; idem. 1925. "Madi al-Azhar wa-Hadiruhu wa-Mustaqbaluhu (3)." *al-Manar* 26/1: 65–72, here 65f.; idem. 1932. "al-Munazara bayna Ahl al-Sunna wa-l-Shi'a." *al-Manar* 32/2: 145–160, here 148.

87 An exception is: Rida, "Sunan al-Ijtima'," 108f.

88 Al-Haddad, Niqula. 1924–1925. *'Ilm al-Ijtima': Hayat al-Hay'a al-Ijtima'iyya wa-Tatawwuruha.* 2 vols. Cairo: al-Matba'a al-'Asriyya. In his three articles on (Spencer's) sociology, Birbari also employed *mujtama'* and *al-hay'a al-ijtimā'iyya*, albeit much less prominently (e.g., Birbari, "al-Susiyulujiyya," 21/8: 576, 578). Birbari also used *umma* to designate the social collectivity resulting from humans associating (*ijtama'a*) and requiring an order (*niẓām*) (ibid., 577).

3.2 *Mujtamaʿ* and *al-Hayʾa al-Ijtimāʿiyya* in Niqula Haddad's Book on Sociology

Niqula Haddad (1870–1954), whom I already mentioned as a protagonist of Arab socialism,[89] came from an Orthodox family and graduated from the American Protestant College in Beirut.[90] Haddad moved to Cairo in 1900, where he married Ruza Antun, the sister of none other than Farah Antun, whom he also followed to America. There he collaborated with Antun and his sister on their journal *al-Sayyidat wa-l-Banat* (*Women and Girls*), which the Haddad couple revived in Alexandria in the 1920s under the name *al-Sayyidat* (later: *al-Sayyidat wa-l-Rijal*, translated as *Women and Men*).[91] During his lifetime, Niqula Haddad was best known as a novelist, and between 1948 and 1950, he occupied an important position in Egypt's literary scene as the editor of *al-Muqtataf*.[92] His work *al-Ishtirakiyya* from 1920[93] was the first full-fledged elaboration of socialism in Arabic, and Haddad's ideas on socialism were seemingly more influential among his contemporaries than those of Farah Antun or Shibli Shumayyil.[94] His book *ʿIlm al-Ijtimaʿ* (*Sociology*), published in two volumes in 1924/1925 and numbering no less than 694 pages, seems hardly known today, but at the time of publication was widely received by the Egyptian public. An appendix to the book lists endorsements by eighteen journals and newspapers, mainly by secular and liberal publications; but also Rashid Rida, somewhat belatedly in 1928, recommended this book by "his friend" Haddad in *al-Manar*.[95]

According to Haddad, who self-confidently presents his work as the first Arabic book on sociology,[96] this science was completely unknown to Arabs before the translation of works by Le Bon,[97] and he stresses that, contrary to what many believe, Ibn Khaldun was no sociological thinker, for he merely described the social and political conditions of his times and did not discern universal principles or laws on which a proper science could be based.[98] Haddad himself departs from the allegedly natural principle of association as operative in all

89 See above: 124fn162, 195.
90 Reid, "The Syrians," 185.
91 Ibid., 186.
92 Ibid., 186. For the more recent reception of Haddad in Arabic, see: Salim, Salma Mirshaq. 2013. *Niqula al-Haddad: al-Adib al-ʿAlim*. Beirut: Dar al-Jadid.
93 Al Haddad, Niqula. 2002 [1920]. *al-Ishtirakiyya*. n.g.: Dar al-Mada [?] li-l-Thaqafa wa-l-Nashr.
94 Reid, "The Syrians," 188.
95 Rida, Rashid. 1928. "Taqriz al-Matbuʿat al-Haditha." *al-Manar* 29/4: 317–320, here 318 f.
96 Al-Haddad, *ʿIlm*, vol. 1: 4.
97 Ibid., vol. 1: 3.
98 Ibid., vol. 1: 4.

groups (sg. *jamāʿa*) of elements and living organisms, for which he coins the term *ijtimāʿiyya.*[99] The effect of *ijtimāʿiyya* results from a *jamāʿa* being constituted by the similarity (*tamāthul*) of its parts, whence a house and a tree next to each other do not form a *jamāʿa*, but a group of trees does, as do human beings living in one place (*balad*, also: country).[100] With regard to the social association (*ijtimāʿ*) of human beings, with which sociology is concerned, a *jamāʿa*, however, depends not only on common characteristics, but also on shared interests. The principle of association (*ijtimāʿiyya*) in a group (*jamāʿa*) is thus based on similarity (*tamāthul*) and collaboration (*ishtirāk*).[101] The main difference to the way in which animals associate consists in humans doing so rationally, being aware of their social nature, and knowing that collectivism (*ijtimāʿiyya*) is preferable to individualism (*infirādiyya*).[102] The connection between the allegedly natural principle of collectivism and Haddad's socialist convictions is rather obvious here: Haddad – who helped establish the Arabic term for socialism, *ishtirākiyya*, by writing a book with that title in 1920 – seems to have regarded this political program as conforming to the natural principle of collectivism. The detailled connection between the social principles and laws Haddad formulates and his political convictions, as well as his overall conception of sociology and his reception of European thinkers, would merit a detailed analysis in a separate study.

Our interest here lies in the relation between *mujtamaʿ* and *al-hay'a al-ijtimāʿiyya*, both of which Haddad employs quite prominently. Indeed, the subtitle of his book on sociology reads: *Hayat al-Hay'a al-Ijtimaʿiyya wa-Tatawwuruha* (*The Life of Society and Its Development*). The term *mujtamaʿ*, however, is more central to Haddad's analysis. On its title page, the first volume – dedicated to the life of society (*ḥayāt al-hay'a al-ijtimāʿiyya*) – is advertised as "studying the mode of the formation of society (*takawwun al-mujtamaʿ*) and its stages (*aṭwār*)," and the second volume, concerned with the development of society (*taṭawwur al-hay'a al-ijtimāʿiyya*), "studies the corporality of society (*jismāniyyat al-mujtamaʿ*) and the similarity of its orders (*anẓima*) to the apparatuses (*ajhiza*) of the living body." More prominently than the authors in *al-Manar*, Haddad uses *mujtamaʿ* to convey an organic understanding of society. The importance of *mujtamaʿ* in his analysis is also demonstrated in the fact that the term, contrary to

---

99 Ibid., vol. 1: 10f.

100 Ibid., vol. 1: 12.

101 Ibid., vol. 1: 12f.

102 Ibid., vol. 1: 17. In his work on socialism, Haddad contrasts *ishtirākiyya* (socialism) with *ifrādiyya* (individualism) (Haddad, *Ishtirakiyya*, 14). The preface to the reprint edition from 2002 explains that what Haddad termed *ifrādiyya* today is called *ra'smāliyya* (capitalism) (ibid., 9).

al-hayʾa al-ijtimāʿiyya, appears in several titles of (sub-)chapters and is listed with several sub-entries in the indices to both volumes.

As a basic insight, the fact that *al-hayʾa al-ijtimāʿiyya* and *mujtama*ʿ were used on the book's title page shows that both terms were firmly established among the literate Arabic public. Moreover, the author (or his publisher) seemingly regarded them as helpful for marketing the book. Placing *al-hayʾa al-ijtimāʿiyya* in the book's sub-title may be taken as further evidence for the term having been more firmly established as meaning 'society,' whereas *mujtama*ʿ, as we have seen,[103] conveyed a range of meanings. While *al-hayʾa al-ijtimāʿiyya* and *mujtama*ʿ are to some extent used interchangeably in this work, Haddad tends to use *mujtama*ʿ to foreground an order of society, wheres *al-hayʾa al-ijtimāʿiyya* predominantly refers to the group of people forming a society. This transpires not least from his usage of *mujtama*ʿ in chapter titles, such as "the structure of society" (*bunyat al-mujtama*ʿ)[104] or "the order of society" (*niẓām al-mujtama*ʿ).[105] While Haddad extensively uses *al-hayʾa al-ijtimāʿiyya* and especially *mujtama*ʿ to conceptualize human social collectivities and their order, this secular Christian author notably does not employ the term *umma* to this end.[106]

4 Crucial Aspects of *Mujtama*ʿ

4.1 *Mujtama*ʿ and Politics

The question that interests us here is whether *mujtama*ʿ was used to convey an autonomous sphere of society distinct from the state. After all, this distinction is characteristic of the modern idea of society, and *mujtama*ʿ was arguably coined to express that idea. In chapter 4, we have seen that, in Egypt at the turn to the twentieth century, society and the state can meaningfully be identified both as historical actors and as objects of reform. Moreover, the previous chapter pointed out Rafiq al-ʿAzm's conceptualization of the pairing of society and the state as *umma* and *dawla*.[107] In hindsight, the conceptual Arabic pair conveying the distinction between society and the state today – *mujtama*ʿ and *dawla* – is often

103 See above: chapter 8 section 1.
104 Al-Haddad, *ʿIlm*, vol. 1: 20.
105 Ibid., vol. 1: 65.
106 The few instances of *umma* I came across in this work refer to 'the nation' or 'the people' in relation to the government.
107 See above: 217, 219.

projected back onto the period under consideration here.[108] However, this conceptual pair is not yet to be found in *al-Manar.* Some instances in *al-Manar* do stress *mujtamaʿ*'s need for a ruler or address the relation between *mujtamaʿ* and the government. These understandings are significantly less distinctive than the conceptual pairing of society and the state, *mujtamaʿ* and *dawla*, but may have contributed to the evolution of that pair.

First and foremost, a decree by the Sharif of Mecca, quoted in 1918, formulates the relation between society (*mujtamaʿ*) and the government (*ḥukūma*): "Verily," the sharif, who just appointed new ministers, addresses his prime minster ʿAbd Allah Siraj,

"the interests of the subjects (*raʿāyā*), the order of the affairs of society (*intiẓām shuʾūn al-mujtamaʿ*), and the fulfillment of the means for obtaining civilization (*tawaffur asbāb al-ʿumrān*) inevitably require councils (*dawāwīn*), among which must be distributed the handling of the government, including what this contains of general and particular interests, and through which [i.e., these councils] is instituted (*yataʿawwan*) the foundation of the functions (*waẓāʾif*) on which accountability (*masʾūliyya*) and the formation of a government (*takwīn ḥukūma*) for our country (*bilādinā*) is built."[109]

The ministers appointed by the Sharif, whom he lists subsequently, thus have to fulfill the function of government for society.

Rashid Rida addresses the relation between *mujtamaʿ* and politics only in the basic sense of a society's natural requirement for rulers, due to conflict being equally natural. He begins his article "The Laws of Social Association (Sunan al-Ijtimāʿ) Concerning the Rulers and the Ruled and their Recompense" as follows:

"The nature of social association (*ṭabīʿat al-ijtimāʿ*) decrees the existence of rulers (*ḥukkām*), in the same manner as it decreed the existence of strife and controversy. [...] Rule (*ḥukm*) forms part of the people's necessities. And it is carried out by some of them in representation of the others. Thus, it is like the other necessities of sciences, professions, and occupations, such as agriculture, industry, and trade. Whoever is attending to one of these branches is sparing society (*muj-*

---

108 For example: Zajm, Zayn al-ʿAbidin Shams al-Din. 2007. *al-Dawla wa-l-Mujtamaʿ fi Misr fi al-Qarn al-Tasiʿ ʿAshar* [*State and Society in Nineteenth-Century Egypt*]. Cairo: Dar al-Kutub.
109 Sharif Mecca wa-Amiruha Husayn quoted in Jaridat al-Qibla quoted in Rida, Rashid. 1918. "al-Hala al-Siyasiyya fi al-Hijaz fi Awakhir Sanna 1334." *al-Manar* 20/6: 278–288, here 279.

tamaʿ) the trouble of attending to it [...]. And the rulers are like the other performers [of one duty], each group (*ṣinf*) serving the totality of groups (*majmūʿ al-aṣnāf*), which are called a people (*shaʿb*) or a nation (*umma*)."[110]

Concerning Rida's employment of *mujtamaʿ* in the foregoing quote, one may ask whether *mujtamaʿ* does not simply connote 'the collectivity' of a group of people, whereas the idea of 'the people' or the whole 'nation' is conveyed by *shaʿb* and *umma*. Yes, indeed, but this is precisely the point. After all, the question that interests us here is not how Rida related the state and society, but whether he employed *mujtamaʿ* to that end – which, it turns out, he did not. However, Rida elsewhere emphasizes that the *mujtamaʿ* requires laws to be implemented by the ruler, but also to check him. For Rida, as for other Islamic reformists, these laws of society ought to be religiously grounded, whence we will come to the aspect of law after discussing the relation between *mujtamaʿ* and religion.

While there are no other pertinent uses of *mujtamaʿ* to conceive of society in relation to the state or even the government, the view of strife and competition as natural to human society conceptualized as *mujtamaʿ* is most clearly expressed by the German general Friedrich von Bernhardi (1849–1930). The Brazilian newspaper *Jaridat al-Afkar* translated an excerpt from the first volume of von Bernhardi's work *On War of Today*,[111] along with a discussion of that work by the English periodical *Nineteenth Century*. The editors of *Jaridat al-Afkar*, which seemingly catered to the Syro-Lebanese community in South-America, present this article in its subtitle as a "philosophical study on the occasion of the present war, or: a necessary lesson for us Syrians in particular, and for Easterners in general." At the very beginning of the passage translated, von Bernhardi asserts, adhering to the principles of social Darwinism, that "the struggle for survival is the first law (*al-nāmūs al-ūlā*), from which there is no escaping; not only in human society (*al-mujtamaʿ al-insānī*), but also in the whole world of animals. According to this law, it is impossible to achieve success or progress (*irtiqāʾ*), unless the weak member of society (*mujtamaʿ*) is annihilated. The weak, then, must perish and vanish."[112] However, von Bernhardi adds, there is a difference between human and animal societies: unlike animals, humans are not only concerned for their own survival and interests, but also for that of the nation (*umma*) to which they belong. Here we cannot follow further the general's elaboration of that point, although the translation goes on to speak in interesting terms of

110 Rida, "Sunan al-Ijtimaʿ," 107.
111 Von Bernhardi, Friedrich. 1912. *Vom heutigen Kriege*; vol. 1: *Grundlagen und Elemente des heutigen Krieges;* vol. 2: *Kampf und Kriegführung*. Berlin: E.S. Mittler & Sohn.
112 Jaridat al-Afkar al-ʿArabiyya, "al-Haqq," 142.

the *umma* as an ordered whole (*majmūʿ muntaẓam*)[113] and of the ordering of society (*tanẓīm umma*) only being possible if its members rally under the banner of their shared interests (*al-maṣlaḥa al-mushtaraka*).[114] Suffice it to say that, concerning the comportment between nations, von Bernhardi deems war to be a "necessary matter of human society" (*al-mujtamaʿ al-insānī*).[115]

No other article in *al-Manar* so clearly formulates strife as natural to *mujtamaʿ*. In the translation of Esquiros's *Émile*, we merely read that "human society is a giant race course,"[116] and that "every member of the society in which our father destined us to live in is constantly driven to dispute and struggle in the arena of life."[117] And an otherwise unknown author quoted by Rida maintains that disagreement, which is an unchangeable given among human beings, is beneficial for society (*mujtamaʿ*).[118] Other instances from *al-Manar* that stress the naturalness of social strife without employing *mujtamaʿ* could be added.[119] At least equally often, however, the journal's authors foreground not conflict, but rather cooperation as natural to human beings' social association.[120]

To conclude, not only is the conceptual pairing of *mujtamaʿ* and *dawla* in the sense of 'society and the state' absent *in al-Manar*, but *mujtamaʿ* was also rarely used in relation to politics, or even to stress human strife as natural to society – an assertion which may give way to demanding a strong ruler/government/state to keep tensions down.

4.2 *Mujtamaʿ* and Religion

If it is a rather trivial fact that the Islamic reformists upheld the relevance of religion in modernity, not least with regard to social and political questions,[121] the point that interests us here is in which senses *mujtamaʿ* was related to religion in

---

113 Ibid., 142.

114 Ibid., 143.

115 Ibid., 145.

116 Esquiros, "Amil," *al-Manar* 2/43: 682 (original: idem., *L'Émile*, 55).

117 Idem. 1900. "al-Bab al-Thani (al-Walad) min Kitab Amil al-Qarn al-Tasiʿ ʿAshar." *al-Manar* 3/18: 416–422 (original: idem., *L'Émile*, 132).

118 Rida, Rashid. 1912. "Haflat al-Arbaʿin li-Taʾbin al-Marhum al-Sayyid Husayn Wasfi Rida." *al-Manar* 15/6: 466–480, here 467.

119 Rida repeatedly named war as a societal law (*sunnat al-ijtimāʿ*, *sunnat allāh*) (see below: 378fn187).

120 A central meaning of *ijtimāʿ* itself is that of cooperation and concurrence (see below: chapter 10 section 1.1).

121 See above: chapters 4 section 3.2, 5 sections 3 and 4, and 7 section 2.

al-Manar and whether it was used to conceptualize an order of society as distinct from religion. After all, a crucial normative dimension of the concept of 'society' has been to express the modern understanding of a self-sufficient, immanent social order, distinct from religion.[122] The examples grouped here address first the relation between *mujtama*ʿ and religion in general, and then between *mujtama*ʿ and Islam in particular. These examples tentatively suggest that the sense of *mujtama*ʿ as a social order to which religion is related becomes more pronounced in the 1920s. Prior to this, a range of authors, including Rashid Rida in the first volume of *al-Manar*, stressed the need for religious and Islamic teachings or bonds for society conceptualized as *mujtama*ʿ. Overall, however, there is hardly an abundance of instances in which *mujtama*ʿ is used to address the relation of religion and society.

The few instances that explicitly uphold religious teachings or bonds as beneficial or necessary for *mujtama*ʿ tend to do so in comparison with non-religious bonds or teachings. First, however, let me briefly mention two instances that do not include such a comparison: in 1903, an anonymous author remarks in passing that "human society (*al-mujtama*ʿ *al-insānī*) is based on a godly law (*nāmūs rabbānī*)."[123] And in 1912, Salih Mukhlis Rida regards the homeland as the body of society and religion as its spirit (*al-dīn wa-l-waṭan humā ka-l-rūḥ wa-l-jism fī kiyān al-mujtama*ʿ).[124] An article from 1910, originally published in *al-Muqtataf*, highlights the positive contributions of socialism (*al-ishtirākiyya*) but reminds those working toward the reform of society (*iṣlāḥ ḥāl al-mujtama*ʿ) that the course of civilization (*sayr al-*ʿ*umrān*) did not stop at socialism. The author mentions that some people benefit society by spreading moral principles (*al-mabādi*ʾ *al-adabiyya*) and others by spreading religious principles (*al-mabādi*ʾ *al-dīniyya*).[125] More forcefully, in 1924, the Shaykh al-Azhar warns that communism (*al-bulshifiyya*) destroys the order of human society (*niẓām al-mujtama*ʿ *al-insānī*).[126] In 1926, his successor as Shaykh al-Azhar, al-Maraghi, stresses that even political campaigns for reform have been giving themselves a religious flavor; this is because "the life of societies (*al-mujtama*ʿ*āt*) does not lend itself to any kind of reform (*iṣlāḥ*) that does not have the touch of a religious appearance (*ṣubigha bi-ṣibgha dīniyya*) whose basis is belief (*īmān*)."[127] In the case of Egypt,

---

122 See above: chapters 2 section 3, 3 section 2.

123 ʿAlim ʿAmil wa-Katib Fadil [an active scholar and a noble writer], "Ra'y," 729.

124 Rida, Salih Mukhlis. 1912. "al-Taqriz wa-l-Intiqad." *al-Manar* 15/4: 305–312, here 306.

125 Anonymous author from *al-Muqtataf* quoted in Rida, "al-Ishtirakiyya," 915.

126 Shaykh al-Azhar quoted in Rida, "Hukm Hay'a," 381.

127 Al-Maraghi, Muhammad Mustafa. 1928. "Islah al-Azhar al-Sharif." *al-Manar* 29/5: 325–345, here 327.

this can arguably only be Islam, since "the Egyptian nation is a nation whose religion is Islam."[128] Rafiq al-ʿAzm compares religious and ethnic bonds in society in the above-mentioned excerpt from his treatise *al-Jamiʿa al-Islamiyya wa-Uruba* (*Pan-Islamism and Europe*). He states that the goal of these bonds is to preserve a certain balance of powers between human societies (*mujtamaʿāt*).[129] In his opinion, the then-recent phenomenon of Pan-Islamism – that is, Muslims uniting in the name of religion (*dīn*) – only fulfills what is necessary for societies, namely preventing sedition and defending society against enemies.[130] Here, al-ʿAzm offers a pragmatic, almost functionalist view of religion from the perspective of societal requirements.

Concerning the relation between Islamic teachings or bonds and *mujtamaʿ*, in the second volume of *al-Manar*, Rashid Rida stresses the Islamic principles underlying the progress or the order of *mujtamaʿ*. In 1899, he names as one basis of the Islamic religion "the laws of existence (*sunan al-kawn*) and the principles of social association and civilization (*nawāmīs al-ijtimāʿ wa-l-ʿumrān*), through which are known the reasons for the progress (*taraqqī*) and decline (*tadallī*) of human society (*al-mujtamaʿ al-insānī*)."[131] Rida asserts that the Qurʾan had already pointed to these laws, which contemporary philosophers call "natural principles" (*al-nawāmīs al-ṭabīʿiyya*),[132] and that, moreover, European civilization had adopted certain principles from Islam.[133] This assertion serves the overall argument of his article – namely, that there is no life possible or necessary for the community of Muslims except the spirit (*rūḥ*) of the Qurʾan.

In a similar vein, but more explicitly referring to principles of social order, in the last volume of *al-Manar*, the Shaykh of al-Azhar emphasizes that "Islam laid down (*rasama*) the principles of social systems (*uṣūl al-nuẓum al-ijtimāʿiyya*) and the principles of laws (*uṣūl al-qawānīn*), whose bases are all for the good of mankind (*khayr al-bashar*) and for the happiness of human society (*saʿādat al-mujtamaʿ al-insānī*)."[134] Connecting to the reigning paradigms of progress and civilization, in these two examples, Rida and the Shaykh al-Azhar most clearly formulate (Islamic) principles for the order of society.

Less pertinent are several statements in the *Tafsir*, where Rida states as one goal of Islamic teachings the reform or right state of *mujtamaʿ*, and where *muj-*

128 Ibid., 326.
129 Al-ʿAzm "al-Jamiʿa," 589.
130 Ibid., 589, 590, 592.
131 Rida, "al-Hayat al-Milliya," 309.
132 Ibid., 309.
133 Ibid., 308.
134 Muhammad Mustafa al-Maraghi quoted in Rida, "Khitab al-Shaykh al-Akbar," 43.

tamaʿ refers more vaguely to the social collectivity of human beings or Muslims. He defines Islam as "a religion whose goal is (*dīn gharaḍuhu*) the refinement of persons (*tahdhīb al-nufūs*) and the reform of the condition of society (*islāḥ ḥāl al-mujtamaʿ*)."[135] As an example, he names the prohibition of interest rates and the command to give alms as beneficial for the state of human social collectivity (*ḥāl mujtamaʿikum*) in this world and as entailing recompense in the other world.[136] Later in the *Tafsir*, Rida again stresses in a general manner that Muhammad "called you to what revives you in this world (*al-dunyā*) through unity of your forces (*jamʿ kalimatikum*) and reform of you as individuals and as society (*iṣlāḥ afrādikum wa-mujtamaʿikum*)."[137] In the same vein, he maintains that God sent the Qur'an to guide human beings to "the perfection of their innate disposition, the cleansing of their souls, and the removal of causes of corruption from their social order (*iṣlāḥ mujtamaʿihim min al-mafāsid*); causes which had been common to all of their societies (*jamīʿ umamihim*)."[138] Along with these usages of *mujtamaʿ*, we may also include an article from the fourth volume of *al-Manar*, in which Rida explains the term *bayḍa* (substance, essence) as being "the property (*ḥawza*) of a thing, and the root of a people (*qawm*) and their society (*mujtamaʿihim*) and their clan (*ʿashīratihim*). And it is said that the essence of the community (*jamāʿa*) of Muslims is Islam."[139]

The instances of other authors relating Islamic bonds or teachings to *mujtamaʿ* can be summarized quickly. In an article from 1906, Muhammad Tawfiq Sidqi, *al-Manar*'s "most prolific polemicist,"[140] names zakat as one Qur'anic prescription that is beneficial for human society (*al-mujtamaʿ al-insānī*). He takes this to illustrate the fact that the Islamic religion does not lack anything that Westerners (*gharbiyūn*) rejoice in.[141] Eight years later, Sidqi depicts the teachings of the Qur'an as more beneficial for society than those of Jesus.[142] Sidqi's comparisons illustrate quite well the modern demand that religions should answer societal questions.[143] Husayn al-Harawi, in a series of articles on "Islam and

---

135 Rida, Tafsir, vol. 4: 105.

136 Ibid., vol. 4: 107.

137 Ibid., vol. 9: 380.

138 Ibid., vol. 11: 160.

139 Idem. 1902. "al-Umara' wa-l-Hukkam Bala' al-Umma bihim." *al-Manar* 4/21: 809–813, here 810.

140 Ryad, *Islamic*, 243; see above: 143 f.

141 Sidqi, "al-Din," *al-Manar* 8/19: 735.

142 Idem. "Nazra," *al-Manar* 16/9: 692, *al-Manar* 16/10: 784.

143 One here could add the statement by an anonymous author in the last volume of *al-Manar*: in a talk translated from the English, he states that "Islam is the best and most adequate of re-

the Orientalists" ("Al-Islam wa-l-Mustashriqun"), published in the last volume of *al-Manar*, applies *mujtamaʿ* to the founding times of Islam. According to al-Harawi, the fundamental basis (*al-qāʿida al-asāsiyya*) of the society (*mujtamaʿ*) in which the prophet Muhammad lived was pagan cults and pre-Islamic religions.[144] He stresses Muhammad's insight that the only means to reform society (*wasīla li-iṣlāḥ al-mujtamaʿ*) was to fight superstitions and false beliefs.[145] For the Islamic world (*al-ʿālam al-islāmī*) today, Hasan al-Banna, also in the last volume of *al-Manar*, regards it is a duty to value God's grace by establishing the system of pure Islam (*niẓām al-islām al-ḥanīf*) and its program for the reform of society (*manāhijihi fī iṣlāḥ al-mujtamaʿ*).[146]

Instances that explicitly speak of an 'Islamic society' or an 'Islamic social order' (*al-mujtamaʿ al-islāmī*) will be analyzed in the next section. Two major mediators between religion and society were (religious) morals and (religious) law, and their relation to *mujtamaʿ* is dealt with in the following two subsections.

4.3 *Mujtamaʿ* and (Religious) Morals

In the very first volume of *al-Manar*, Rashid Rida stresses the importance of morals for society, partially conceptualized as *mujtamaʿ*. In his above-mentioned article elucidating that "the felicity of the *umma* rests on moral refinement (*tahdhīb*),"[147] Rida conceptualizes the overall social collectivity almost exclusively as *umma*. The alleged centrality of (religious) morals is perhaps most fundamentally demonstrated in the following hadith, as adduced by Rida: "Every structure (*bunyān*) has a foundation, and the foundation of Islam is: the perfection of the human character (*ḥusn al-khalq*)."[148] Throughout this article, Rida himself stresses the fundamental importance of morals for religious and worldly, individual and societal matters. In addition to his initial remark that this article addresses the *mujtamaʿ* (whole collectivity) of this *umma*,[149] Rida employs the concept of *mujtamaʿ* once more – this time referring to human society at

ligions, since it came for the sake of the benefit and comfort of human society (*maṣlaḥat al-mujtamaʿ al-basharī wa-rafāhiyyatihi*)" (Khalid Shildrik quoted in Rida, "al-Mawlid al-Nabawi," 550).

144 Al-Harawi, "al-Mustashriqun," 270.

145 Idem., "al-Mustashriqun," 282 (different article from the same series in the same number).

146 Al-Banna, Hasan. 1940. "Mawqif al-ʿAlam al-Islami al-Siyasi al-Yawm," *al-Manar* 35/10: 747–750, here 750.

147 See above: 264.

148 Rida, "Tabsira," 72.

149 Ibid., 69.

large: the one who has understood the link between morals (*akhlāq*) and deeds (*a'māl*) becomes aware of the great extent to which morals influence human society (*al-mujtama' al-insānī*).[150] Referring to this article later that year, Rida elaborates on slander as one reprehensible attribute (*khilla madhmūma*). He stresses the role of slander "in the corruption (*ifsād*) of human society (*al-mujtama' al-insānī*) and its prevention of true civilization (*al-madaniyya al-ṣaḥīḥa*), which is the felicity of peoples (*umam*)."[151] Slander gives birth to seditions (*fitan*) and is tearing apart the social bonds (*al-rawābiṭ al-ijtimā'iyya*),[152] Rida warns.

Twice more, Rida stresses the general need of the social collectivity and the social order conceptualized as *mujtama'* for (religious) morals. In volume four, he asserts that human beings are in need of godly guidance in order to attain "moral refinement (*tahdhīb*) by which is set right the condition (*ḥāl*) of individuals (*afrād*) and of society (*mujtama'*)."[153] And in volume ten, Rida (again) refutes the alleged opinion of some European philosophers and Europeanized Egyptians that one may dispense with religion in upbringing and education.[154] It was in paraphrasing this opinion that Rida most extensively employed the concept of *al-hay'a al-ijtimā'iyya*, as we have seen above.[155] Here, he uses *mujtama'* to restate his argument that a person will hardly abstain from harmful deeds only because they are harmful for society (*mujtama'*), but that religious morals are required to that end.[156]

As one other concrete example of behavior harmful for human society (*al-mujtama' al-insānī*), Rida mentions married men having unlawful children. This example, taken from the newspaper *Lagos Weekly Record*, which itself took the article from a London newspaper, is quoted three times in *al-Manar*.[157]

The instances in which other authors in *al-Manar* relate (religious) morals to society conceptualized as *mujtama'* stem from the second half of the 1920s and the 1930s, even though the concept was already used self-evidently to that end by Rida in the first volume of his journal, and even in *al-'Urwa al-Wuthqa* in 1884.[158] In 1926, Mahatma Gandhi is translated as saying that the first duty of

150 Ibid., 75.
151 Idem.,"al-Namima," 236.
152 Ibid, 236.
153 Idem. 1901. "al-Dars 30: Waza'if al-Rusul 'alayhim al-Salat wa-Salam." *al-Manar* 4/16: 615–619.
154 Idem. 1907. "al-Ta'lim al-Dini." *al-Manar* 10/2: 123–128, here 123–124.
155 See above: chapter 7 section 2.
156 Ibid., 124.
157 Idem., *Tafsir*, vol. 4: 294; idem., "al-Rijal," 486; idem. "Nida'," *al-Manar* 32/5: 396.
158 See above: chapter 8 section 2.1.

human beings is to "educate their children in a way that makes them righteous and truthful and an ornament to the society (*mujtama*ʿ) in which they live."[159] Here, *mujtama*ʿ in a generic sense refers to a social group, rather than to society imbued with a normative sense of order – in contrast to the following example: in 1930, an otherwise unknown author mentions that when spiritual weakness (*al-ḍaʿf al-rūḥī*) appears and becomes operative in society (*mujtama*ʿ), it inevitably entails moral and ethical weakness (*al-ḍaʿf al-khalqī wa-l-adabī*).[160]

More extensively, in 1928, the Alexandrian teacher Muhammad ʿArafat urges the religious scholars of al-Azhar to engage in society, not least by spreading moral teachings for the good of the social order. In his article on "The True Reform and the Duty of al-Azhar," ʿArafat departs from the premise that "the Egyptian nation (*umma*) like the other nations of the East, is a religious collectivity (*jamāʿa dīniyya*), integrated and united by religion, on which rest its morals and its culture (*ḥaḍāra*)."[161] According to ʿArafat, the men of religion (*rijāl al-dīn*) ought to be responsible for the moral life of Egypt. Their task is to

"spread among the people (*umma*) strength of will (*quwat al-irāda*), soundness of determination (*ṣiḥḥat al-ʿazm*), love of the homeland (*ḥubb al-waṭan*), affection (*īthār*), cooperation (*taʿāwun*), solidarity (*taḍāmun*) and the understanding that they as Egyptians are like a spiritual person (*shakhṣ maʿnawī*), every member working for the interest of the social collectivity (*mujtama*ʿ), and the pain of one member being a pain of the whole society (*mujtama*ʿ) [...]. In the Azharites will be implanted the love of humanity and of society (*mujtama*ʿ), and the [eagnerness to] sacrifice (*taḍḥiyya*) themselves for the felicity of society (*mujtama*ʿ), and [to] the dissemination of virtue in it [i.e., society] and [to] cleansing it of vices."[162]

Here, for once, *mujtama*ʿ designates the social collectivity, conceived of in analogy to the body – something that is rare *in al-Manar.*[163] *Mujtama*ʿ is also imbued with a sense of order, insofar as ʿArafat calls upon Azharites to engage in and for the whole of society and to contribute moral virtues to the order of society – a

159 Ghandi, Mahatma. 1926. "al-Sihha." *al-Manar* 27/8: 604–609, here 609.

160 Nuwayhad, ʿAjaj. 1929. "Hal hadha al-Nahda Khadiʿa li-Sultan al-ʿIlm?." *al-Manar* 30/3: 193–211, here 200.

161 ʿArafa, Muhammad. 1928. "al-Islah al-Haqiqi wa-l-Wajib li-l-Azhar." *al-Manar* 28/10: 758–765, here 758.

162 Ibid., 764.

163 See above: chapter 8 section 3.1.

call which is repeated by leading shaykhs of al-Azhar in the last volume of *al-Manar.*[164]

Also in that last volume, the correspondent for *al-Ahram* in the United States, who quotes a Los Angeles judge worried about the harmful societal effects of increasing divorce rates, alternates in his translation between *al-hayʾa al-ijtimāʿiyya* and *mujtamaʿ*. Both concepts are paired with religion, and both designate a social collectivity and convey a sense of societal order. It seems, however, that this sense of order is more heavily foregrounded in the use of *mujtamaʿ*. Divorce has become an almost trivial act, the judge remarks, despite its contradicting what religions decreed and what the laws of society (*qawānīn al-hayʾa al-ijtimāʿiyya*) made obligatory.[165] He has no doubt that "those incentives (*bawāʿith*) coming upon our civilization (*tamaddun*) in this time" – by which he seemingly means new social practices and mores made possible by increasing liberty –

"work toward the demolition of the pillars of religious balance (*al-tawāzun al-dīnī*) and the deformation of the morals of society (*ādāb al-mujtamaʿ*); and [these incentives] open the paths to human nature (*al-ṭabīʿa al-bashariyya*) which leans toward evil when it oversteps proper bounds (*fī ṭughyānihā*), and they will go to extremes in this without the impediment of religion and the deterrent of the law. So the judge to whom are presented these evil deeds in different cases only sees one useful remedy, namely the resort of society (*al-hayʾa al-ijtimāʿiyya*) to religion, knowledge, and moral refinement (*tahdhīb*), while removing those strange contemporary public developments that have led to the destruction of marital life and the corruption of the morals of the youth."[166]

In his comment on this article, Rashid Rida remarks that religion in the United States[167] no longer serves as a social and moral system (*niẓām ijtimāʿī adabī*), and that now Islam remains the only remedy for all the vices of Western civilization (*al-ḥaḍāra al-gharbiyya*).[168]

---

164 Al-Maraghi, Muhammad Mustafa et al. 1935. "Haflat al-Azhar bi-Shaykhihi al-Ustadh al-Akbar al-Shaykh Muhammad Mustafa al-Maraghi." *al-Manar* 35/2: 136–144, esp. 138, 144.
165 Ben Lindsay quoted by Murasil al-Ahram fi Amrika. 1935. "Tafaqum Sharr al-Talaq fi Amrika." *al-Manar* 35/1: 78–79, here 78.
166 Ibid., 78.
167 Rida here only speaks of "them." In light of what follows, this could also refer to the West more broadly. Still, he seems to have in mind the US-American context here.
168 Ibid., 79.

Overall, while *mujtamaʿ* was more often used in the second half of *al-Manar*'s life span to convey a social order in need of morals, it was not at all exclusively established in this sense, as the continuing, related usage of *al-hay'a al-ijtimāʿiyya* in the last example also demonstrates. While this last example also touched upon the importance of law for society, the following subsection more comprehensively analyzes those instances in *al-Manar* in which law is related to *mujtamaʿ*.

4.4 *Mujtamaʿ* and (Religious) Law

In the late nineteenth and early twentieth centuries, legal reform was a hotly debated topic in Egypt. The codification and rationalization of laws was considered a major requirement for modernization and socio-political order in Arab and European countries alike. The hegemony of European ideas and institutional arrangements, which were regarded as epitomizing modernity, also manifested itself in the field of law. While attempts at political centralization and legal codification had been undertaken prior to colonial times, European legal codes came to serve as a blueprint for future reforms.[169] European standards played an even greater role in countries under factual colonial administration. In Egypt in the 1870s, there were three types of courts: government courts, shariʿa courts, and courts especially for cases involving a European party. Modern reformists, among them Muhammad ʿAbduh, called for centralizing legislation under governmental auspices, codifying laws, and standardizing legal verdicts.[170] One major aspect of legal reforms was the negotiation of boundaries between the competencies of shariʿa and government courts. In basically all (post-)colonial Islamic countries, the fields of competency of shariʿa law were increasingly limited, leaving largely only the field of family law. The life span of *al-Manar* was thus a crucial period for negotiating the relevance and validity of religious and secular laws and for drawing the institutional boundaries between the two. All the examples from *al-Manar* that relate law to *mujtamaʿ* stress the validity of Islamic laws for society, and most of them explicitly regard Islamic laws as superior to positive laws.

Rashid Rida's overall argument for the validity and relevance of Islam in worldly and societal affairs is well known; with regard to law, he thrice expli-

169 See above: chapter 4 section 1.2.

170 See: ʿAbduh, Muhammad. 2002. "Laws Should Change in Accordance with the Conditions of Nations *and* The Theology of Unity." In *Modernist Islam, 1840–1940: A Sourcebook* ed. by Charles Kurzman: 50–60. Oxford/New York: Oxford University Press, here 50–54.

cates this by employing *mujtama'*. Rida already stresses the alleged superiority of Islamic laws concerning the order of society (*niẓām al-mujtama'*) in a brief answer to a reader in 1902. It is not insignificant that the central terms stem from the anonymous reader and are picked up by Rida. In answer to the question posed to him, he writes that Islamic legal rulings (*al-aḥkām al-fiqhiyya*) are more suitable (*aṣlaḥ*) for the order of society (*niẓām al-mujtama'*) than positive laws (*al-qawānīn al-waḍ'iyya*).[171] Rida might not have all societies in mind here, since he goes on to speak of Islamic laws as more suitable "for our society" (*li-mujtama'inā*).[172] In volume four of *al-Manar*, Rida explains the reason why the prophets laid down punishments and laws regarding social relations (*al-'uqūbāt wa-aḥkām al-mu'āmalāt*) as follows:

"Man was created weakly, and he advanced gradually. And insofar as societies (*mujtama'āt*) are composed of households (*buyūt*), peoples (*shu'ūb*), and tribes (*qabā'il*), they necessitate an impediment (*wāzi'*) and a ruler (*musayṭir*) who prevents the injustice (*baghy*) and enmity produced by controversies over societal interests and benefits (*al-maṣāliḥ wa-l-manāfi' al-ijtimā'iyya*) and who punishes those overcome by personal desires (*shahawāt*) to inflict harm on themselves and on the people (*al-nās*). Therefore, the people chose judges and rulers from among the worldly and religious leaders (*ru'asā' al-dīn wa-l-dunyā*)."[173]

Moreover, in the *Tafsir*, Rida mentions that the regulations (*aḥkām*) of the revelation (*shar'*) of God are built upon "the interests (*maṣāliḥ*) of the people (*nās*), and the reform of them as individuals and as society (*iṣlāḥ afrādihim wa-mujtama'ihim*) in the affairs of their religion and their world (*umūr dīnihim wa-dunyāhum*)."[174]

Rafiq al-'Azm, in the first volume of *al-Manar*, elaborates on the role of the government in protecting the order of society via laws. In his article inquiring into "Who is Responsible? The Government or the People?," al-'Azm defines the role of the government concerning the natural and positive laws of social association:

"It has been determined that the basis of social association (*ijtimā'*) in this human existence (*al-wujūd al-basharī*) and the anchor of hope of including the

171 Rida, "As'ila Diniyya," 224.
172 Ibid., 224.
173 Idem. 1901. "Tatimmat al-Dars 30 min Waza'if al-Rusul 'alayhim al-Salam." *al-Manar* 4/18: 688–692, here 688.
174 Idem., *Tafsir*, vol. 10: 362.

working hands, is the government (*ḥukūma*), which has the special task of watching over the governed body (*al-hay'a al-maḥkūma*), and of undertaking the enforcement of the natural and positive laws of social association (*qawānīn al-ijtimāʿ al-ṭabīʿiyya wa-l-waḍʿiyya*). By the first I mean: the customs and morals, which gradually advance from the cradle of a people (*umma*) and progress with the progress of time [...]. And by the second: the laws of legislation (*qawānīn al-tashrīʿ*), which ensure the continuation of the course (*sayr*) of the order of worldly social relations (*al-muʿāmalāt al-dunyawiyya*) in the manner of justice and determine the life of societies (*ḥayāt al-mujtamaʿāt*) and the thriving of states (*ʿumrān al-mamālik*) in every time and place."[175]

Some ten years later, in a speech he gave in front of law students in Cairo, al-ʿAzm compares religious and non-religious bases of legislation. His speech on "Jurisdiction (Qada') of a Single Person (Fard) and of a Group (Jamaʿa) in Islam" begins by stressing the fundamental role of law for the order of society, conceptualized both as *mujtamaʿ* and as *al-hay'a al-ijtimāʿiyya:* "The guarantor of justice, the anchor of tranquility and happiness in every society (*mujtamaʿ*) is the law (*al-qānūn aw al-sharīʿa*), by which rights are protected, oppressors are deterred, and criminals are punished who venture upon the sacrilege of tranquility and security in the social body (*al-hay'a al-ijtimāʿiyya*). And these laws (*qawānīn*) are either of positive or of religious kind (*waḍʿiyya aw sharʿiyya*)."[176] This distinction was already made by Ibn Khaldun (d. 1406), al-ʿAzm recalls, and maintains that the Islamic law is a religious law, insofar as it is based on the Qur'an and the Sunna. From these bases, however, the branches of the law and concrete rulings were developed historically.[177] Not least due to the complexity of law-making, the power of jurisdiction (*qaḍā'*) ought to be vested in the hands of a group (*jamāʿa*), not a sole individual (*fard*). This jurisdiction by a group also ensures that the laws consider that which is most beneficial (*aṣlaḥ*) for the whole group (*jamāʿa*). In fact, al-ʿAzm stresses, "one of the most important bases of Islamic law (*al-sharʿ al-islāmī*) is to take into consideration what is most beneficial (*al-aṣlaḥ*). By it [i.e., this basis] forbidden and harmful acts are warded off and averted from society (*mujtamaʿ*)."[178] According to al-ʿAzm, the principle of common interest (*maṣlaḥa*) must also be considered in matters con-

---

175 Al-ʿAzm, Rafiq. 1899. "Man al-Mas'ul al-Hukuma am al-Shaʿb?." *al-Manar* 1/45: 866–872, here 866f.
176 Idem. 1910. "Qada' al-Fard wa-Qada' al-Jamaʿa fi al-Islam." *al-Manar* 13/1: 33–49, here 33.
177 Ibid., 33–37.
178 Ibid., 37.

cerning which there exists a clear text in the Qur'an or the Sunna.[179] As Islamic law is built on the very basis of warding off what is harmful and ensuring what is beneficial, it is suitable for all times and places, including the present age, with its demands of modern civilization (*al-madaniyya al-ḥadītha*) and the progress of societies (*taraqqī al-mujtamaʿāt*).[180]

The authors of the following four examples from the late 1920s and 1930 also uphold the salience of Islamic law for contemporary society.

In 1924, Muhammad Bahjat al-Bitar, who edited two issues of *al-Manar* in 1936, defends Islamic punishments for murder, adultery, and theft. These punishments aim at the betterment (*iṣlāḥ*) of the individual (*fard*) and the protection of the group (*majmūʿ*), and as such, they entail a benefit for society (*mujtamaʿ*), he maintains; he deems it truly strange to consider them a burden on society, especially since the materialist nations (*al-umam al-māddiyya*), which call for justice and reform, are responsible for the killing of peoples and the corruption of the order of the family and the whole of society (*mujtamaʿ*).[181]

A year later, Abu al-ʿUyun, inspector of al-Azhar and the religious institutes, wrote to ministers of the Egyptian government, urging them to abolish prostitution. He recalls a previous letter in which he had demanded the abolition of prostitution out of respect for religion and homeland (*waṭan*), and in accordance with the civilized states (*al-mamālik al-mutamaddina*), such as America, England, or Germany.[182] In this second letter, he adds several arguments and reasons, of which only the first must concern us. Abu al-ʿUyun reminds the minsters that "the constitution of the Egyptian state declares Islam to be the official religion of the state," and that this has to have an effect on the public affairs of the state. Concerning the matter at hand, al-ʿUyun adduces that "Islam prohibits adultery, and its legislation (*tashrīʿ*) and order (*tanẓīm*) decree the stoning and flogging of the adulterers. And this truly was a compassion and a mercy of Islam upon human society (*al-mujtamaʿ al-insānī*)."[183]

In 1930, the president of the Society of Muslim Youth, ʿAbd al-Hamid Saʿid, stresses that certain areas of legislation are central to Islam, which is why they absolutely must remain in place. Saʿid responds to a French decree that changed the law for Muslim Berbers from Islamic to Berber customary law and argued

---

179 Ibid., 37, 38.

180 Ibid., 41.

181 Al-Bitar, Muhammad Bahjat. 1926. "Kitab al-Mujaz fi al-Ijtimaʿ." *al-Manar* 27/4: 295–306, here 305.

182 Abu al-ʿAyun, "Muharabat," 233.

183 Ibid., 233.

that this would not affect the Islamic creed.[184] Such a statement can only come from someone who has not understood Islam or thinks that the Muslims do not understand it, Saʿid maintains. After all,

"the most peculiar characteristic (*akhaṣṣ khaṣāʾiṣ*) of Islam regarding the social life (*al-ḥayāt al-ijtimāʿiyya*) of the individual (*fard*) and the collective (*majmūʿ*) are its laws (*aḥkām*) concerning inheritance and personal status. And its order (*niẓām*) in this is the only order of all the civil and social orders of Islam (*nuẓum al-islām al-madaniyya wa-l-ijtimāʿiyya*) that still remains in place today, which is why its cessation in any Islamic corner of the earth or region would amount to the extinction from the heart of the individual and from between the people of what there remains of Islam in society (*mujtamaʿ*) and the household."[185]

Finally, in 1931, a teacher from al-Azhar refutes the view that the shariʿa brought by Muhammad has to give way in the face of the order of modern materialist society (*niẓām al-mujtamaʿ al-māddī al-ḥāḍir*).[186]

It is an article from 1928 – first published in the mouthpiece of the Liberal Constitutionalist Party, *al-Siyasa*, which Rida depicted as areligious[187] – that by far most prominently employs *mujtamaʿ* to conceptualize the order of society.[188] This article uses *mujtamaʿ* more often than any other article – namely 14 times. Still more significantly, it is the only article to include *mujtamaʿ* in its subtitle, which reads: "Society for its order cannot do without penal legislation" (*al-mujtamaʿ lā budda li-niẓāmihi min tashrīʿ al-ʿuqūbāt*). Its author, the Alexandrian teacher Hamid Mahmud Muhaysin, refutes the opinion that Islamic laws aim at revenge and are therefore outdated. This opinion had been voiced in a previous article published in *al-Siyasa*, which identified four stages of legal development.[189] Muhaysin stresses that Islamic laws aim not at revenge, but at the betterment of the individual and the reform of society.[190] Premised upon the re-

184 Saʿid, ʿAbd al-Hamid. 1930. "Nidaʾ ila Muluk al-Islam wa-Shuʿubihi Jamiʿan." *al-Manar* 31/3: 205–218, here 216.
185 Ibid., 217.
186 Al-Zankluni, ʿAli Surur. 1931. "Naskh al-Shariʿa al-Muhammadiyya li-Ma Qabluha wa-Baʿthat Muhammad Khatim al-Nabiyin li-l-Nas Ajmaʿin." *al-Manar* 31/8: 608–618, here 616.
187 See above: 258fn30.
188 Muhaysin, Hamid Mahmud. 1928. "al-ʿUquba fi al-Islam laysat Taqriran li-Nazariyya al-Intiqam." *al-Manar* 29/4: 299–308.
189 Ibid., 299.
190 Ibid., esp. 302, 304, 307.

quirements of social life, Islamic law is thus explicitly validated as guaranteeing the order of society (*niẓām al-mujtamaʿ*).[191]

By far the most prominent and explicit usage of *mujtamaʿ* to convey an order of society (in need of laws) is thus to be found in a liberal-nationalist newspaper in the late 1920s. Rashid Rida notably picked up the concept of *niẓām al-mujtamaʿ* only in response to a reader who had used these terms. As with the fields of politics, religion, and morals – addressed in the previous subsections – we thus conclude that *mujtamaʿ* was considered useful for conceptualizing society and social order, but was hardly used in these senses by the regular contributors to *al-Manar*. Despite a small empirical basis, the field of law seems to be the one field in which *mujtamaʿ* was more prominently used than *al-hay'a al-ijtimāʿiyya* – an insight that supports the hypothesis that *mujtamaʿ* was coined to convey a notion of abstract social order.

The following section analyzes usages of *mujtamaʿ* to designate a particular society or social order. In my above analysis of particular usages of *al-hay'a al-ijtimāʿiyya*, I stated the significance of these particular usages as conveying the modern concept of society onto which state and religion can be mapped.[192] As with the particular usages of *al-hay'a al-ijtimāʿiyya*, the authorship of these particular usages of *mujtamaʿ* is highly interesting, since it indicates the channels through which *mujtamaʿ* eventually became established as the concept for 'society.'

5 Particular Societies and Social Orders

5.1 Modern Society, Development, and Progress

> "[Friends of progress,] let it be acknowledged, Christianity is more successful than you, in reconciling the interests of human society with the eternal interests of the individual."
> – Abbé Martinet, 1850[193]

191 Ibid., 299, 303, 304, 307.

192 See above: chapter 7 section 4.

193 Abbé Martinet, [Antoine]. 1850. *Religion in Society or The Solution of Great Problems: Placed within the Reach of Every Mind*; translated from the French of the Abbé Martinet; with an introduction by John Hughes. New York: D. & J. Sadler, vol. 1: 65.

The idea of a specifically modern social order is most clearly expressed in Amir ʿAli's above-mentioned debate on polygyny.[194] In 1913, the Indian reformist depicts polygyny as contradicting both the contemporary meaning of the teachings of the Prophet and "modern civil society" (*al-mujtamaʿ al-madanī al-ḥadīth*).[195] He argues that the flexible Qur'anic law of marriage is in agreement with both "the old society" (*al-mujtamaʿ al-qadīm*) and "the present civil society" (*al-mujtamaʿ al-madanī al-ḥāḍir*).[196] Amir ʿAli hopes that soon the majority will see that polygyny might have been appropriate once, but that in accordance with the development of society today, monogamy is more appropriate. He reminds his readers that, also in Europe, only the new society (*al-mujtamaʿ al-jadīd*) came to abandon polygyny.[197] While *mujtamaʿ* is used six times in this article to conceptualize society, modern society is once conceptualized as *al-hay'a al-ijtimāʿiyya al-ḥadītha*.[198] One could not express the sense of a particular modern social order more clearly than Amir ʿAli does. Significantly, he wrote this article in English; Ahmad Efendi Najib translated it for *al-Mu'ayyad*, Cairo's leading newspaper, where it first appeared.

In his comment on this article, Rashid Rida only picks up *al-hay'a al-ijtimāʿiyya*. Referring to an earlier article of his on the topic of polygyny,[199] he argues that polygyny contradicts humankind's innate disposition and the divine law (*sharʿ*), but that it is beneficial for women and society when there is a shortage of men, such as in times of war, as had been the case in the first Islamic centuries.[200] While Rida shares ʿAli's view of polygyny as appropriate only under certain socio-economic circumstances, he does not premise his argument as strongly on the requirements of a specific modern social order, and consequently does not rule out the possibility of polygyny in his time as strictly as does ʿAli.

The only other usage of *al-mujtamaʿ al-ḥadīth* is to be found in the translation of Esquiros's *Émile*,[201] in which the idea of the development or progress of *mujtamaʿ* also occurs frequently. Mention is made of the different ages (*aʿmār*) of human societies (*mujtamaʿāt*);[202] of the distance of our contemporary societies

194 See above: 214.
195 ʿAli, "al-Mar'a," 936.
196 Ibid., 938.
197 Ibid., 939
198 Ibid., 935.
199 Rida, Rashid. 1910. "As'ila min Baris." *al-Manar* 13/10: 741–748, here 744–748.
200 Rida in ʿAli, "al-Mar'a," 940 f.
201 Esquiros, "Amil." *al-Manar* 2/42: 669; original: idem., *L'Émile*, 49.
202 Idem., "Amil," *al-Manar* 2/38: 602; original: idem., *L'Émile*, 32.

(*mujtamaʿātinā*) from the natural state;[203] of the first human societies (*mujtamaʿāt al-insān al-ūlā*);[204] and of the authentic societies (*al-mujtamaʿāt al-qawīma*).[205] Esquiros also refers to the provisional, man-made arrangements of social life, writing that "the relation of the methods of instruction (*ṭuruq al-taʿlīm*) to education (*al-tarbiya*) is like the relation of rules (*awḍāʾ*) and laws (*qawānīn*)[206] to society (*mujtamaʿ*): they are suitable only for a temporary need (*ḥāja waqtiyya*) of the intellect (*ʿaql*) and thus must all be considered temporary themselves."[207]

A similar statement is to be found in the translation of a letter from the Russian Muslim leader Rida' al-Din bin Fakhr al-Din to the government concerning the legal and political demands of Russian Muslims. Fakhr al-Din asserts that lawmakers have to take into account the customs (*ʿādāt*) and the social condition (*ḥāla ijtimāʿiyya*) of people. The fact that these are constantly changing requires the adaptation of laws. This is why "the European states (*duwal*) renew and modify their laws (*qawānīn*) at least every quarter of a century, something which is absolutely necessary in the movement (*sayr*) of human society (*al-mujtamaʿ al-basharī*)."[208] In the translation of the *Émile*, moreoever, we even read that "man forms his society by his own powers" (*yuʾallif mujtamaʿahu bi-quwāhi al-dhātiyya*).[209]

The authors in *al-Manar* who originally wrote in Arabic do not stress the autonomy of human beings to shape thier society so explicitly, but in some scattered instances, they do relate *mujtamaʿ* to the reigning paradigm of development and progress. In 1926, Rashid Rida published an undated paper by ʿAbduh, mentioning that the manner of social association (*ijtimāʿ*) advances with the growth of societies (*mujtamaʿāt*).[210] With the above-mentioned exception of Rafiq al-ʿAzm, who stressed that Islamic law conforms to the progress of societies (*taraqqī al-mujtamaʿāt*),[211] the other instances all stem from the

203 Idem., "Amil," *al-Manar* 3/15: 351; original: idem., *L'Émile*, 126.
204 Idem., "Amil," *al-Manar* 4/17: 660; original: idem., *L'Émile*, 216.
205 Idem., "Amil," *al-Manar* 4/23: 910; original: idem., *L'Émile*, 240.
206 The original has *institutions* instead of 'rules and laws.'
207 Idem. "Amil," *al-Manar* 4/17: 668; original: idem., *L'Émile*, 226.
208 Bin Fakhr al-Din, "Matalib," *al-Manar* 10/6: 446. In the first part of that article, bin Fakhr al-Din stresses the need for Islamic legal scholars and rulers to be more numerous and more skillful with every step that society (*mujtamaʿ*) advances (idem. 1907. "Matalib Muslimi Rusya min Dawlatihim; transl. Musa ʿAbdallah al-Qazani." *al-Manar* 10/5: 367–377, here 371).
209 Esquiros, "Amil," *al-Manar* 9/8: 627; original: idem., *L'Émile*, 407 (the original does not have *société*).
210 Muhammad ʿAbduh quoted in Rida, "Tarbiyat Umaraʾ," 601, 602.
211 See above: 289fn180.

mid-1930s, and all – supposedly coincidentally – are found in articles responding to or dealing with Rashid Rida. In 1934, a certain ʿAbd al-ʿAziz al-Bishri, reviewing Rida's book *The Muhammadan Revelation*, speaks of the progress (*ruqī*) and maturity (*bulūgh*) of human society (*al-mujtamaʿ al-insānī*).[212] A eulogy on Rida a year after his death focuses on his School for Proselytization and Guidance (Dar al-Daʿwa wa-l-Irshad) and mentions that society (*mujtamaʿ*) today is different from what it was yesterday, when pupils needed to apply to leave the school for Cairo.[213] And in the same issue from 1936, the Shaykh of al-Azhar lauds Rida's knowledge of "the conditions of society (*aḥwāl al-mujtamaʿ*) and [of] the stages (*adwār*) that Islamic history (*al-tārīkh al-islāmī*) went through."[214] Rida himself only mentions the stages of *mujtamaʿ* when quoting the title page of Haddad's book on sociology.[215]

ʿAbd al-Hamid al-Zahrawi is the one author who most explicitly contrasts contemporary and previous societies. In his above-mentioned series of articles entitled "Khadija Umm al-Muʾminin," which was later published as a book,[216] he uses *mujtamaʿ* fifteen times over four articles. Al-Zahrawi not only applies the term to the time of Khadija, Muhammad's first wife, but also compares contemporary societies to that society:

"[T]oday we cannot imagine a civilized society (*mujtamaʿ ḥaḍarī*) without a commanding ruler and protecting soldiers, with farmers, workers, and traders guaranteeing the livelihood. While the reader saw that the society (*mujtamaʿ*) of Khadija existed without having a ruler or soldiers, we should not reason from the fact that it could do without the rule of a commander that it could also do without agriculture, industry, and trade. For there is no foundation for a people (*qawm*) without these three."[217]

Here, al-Zahrawi singles out the specifics of contemporary societies, but also defines universal features. As a sidenote, the foregoing quote reminds us of a passage from *A quoi tient la superiorité des Anglo-Saxons*, in which Demolins maintains that "[u]ne société peut, à la rigueur, vivre sans avocats, sans journalistes,

212 ʿAbd al-ʿAziz al-Bishri quoted in Rida, "Taqariz Kitab al-Wahy," 777.
213 Al-Battal, ʿAbd al-Samiʿ. 1936. "Faqid al-Islam al-Sayyid Muhammad Rashid Rida wa-Madrasat Dar al-Daʿwa wa-l-Irshad." *al-Manar* 35/3: 195–200, here 197.
214 Al-Maraghi, "Khutbat al-Ustadh," 187.
215 Rida, "Taqriz," *al-Manar* 29/4: 318 f.; see above: 273fn95, 274.
216 See above: 144fn45.
217 Al-Zahrawi, ʿAbd al-Hamid. 1908. "[Khadija Umm al-Muʾminin:] al-Fasl al-Sabiʿ [wa-l-Thamin wa-l-Tasiʿ]." *al-Manar* 11/5: 383–451, here 393.

sans avoués, sans médecins, sans fonctionnaires, mais elle ne peut vivre sans les agriculteurs, […] sans les fabricants […]; sans les commerçants."[218] Ahmad Fathi Zaghlul, who translated Demolins's work into Arabic, here rendered *société* as *umma*.[219] For the same statement, al-Zahrawi chose *qawm*, which tended to be used as a generic term for a group of people.[220] This generic sense seems intended here by *société*, *umma*, and *qawm* alike, while *mujtamaʿ* in the foregoing quote from al-Zahrawi clearly conveys a normative sense of social order.

In another article, al-Zahrawi likens the makeup of Khadija's society to contemporary concepts when he states that Khadija's society was republican (*jumhūriyyan*) in today's terms.[221] Another author who projects the concept of *mujtamaʿ* back onto pre- and early Islamic times is Husayn al-Harawi, who – in his series on "Islam and the Orientalists," published in the last volume of *al-Manar* – speaks of the *mujtamaʿ* of the Arab tribes before Islam[222] and of the *mujtamaʿ* in which Muhammad lived.[223]

5.2 Particular Societies

The authorship of those instances in which *mujtamaʿ* is used to designate a particular social collectivity or order is most remarkable. The concept of 'Arab society' first crops up in 1919, in a translation of excerpts from Gustave Le Bon's *Psychologie politique*. Le Bon refutes the argument that polygyny is a primary cause of the backwardness of Arab society (*al-mujtamaʿ al-ʿarabī*).[224] The same passage, translated slightly differently, reappears in 1930.[225] Other than Le Bon's translator, the sole author referring to an Arab society or Arab societies in the plural (*al-mujtamaʿāt al-ʿarabiyya*) is Muhammad ʿAbdallah ʿAnan.

In an article from 1928, ʿAnan also speaks of "Turkish society" (*al-mujtamaʿ al-turkī*), "European society" (*al-mujtamaʿ al-ūrūbī*), "Western societies" (*al-muj-*

---

218 Demolins, *A quoi*, 223.

219 Idem., *Sirr*, 181.

220 See above: chapter 7 section 5.

221 Al-Zahrawi, ʿAbd al-Hamid. 1908. "[Khadija Umm al-Muʾminin:] al-Fasl al-Awwal [wa-l-Thani wa-l-Thalith]." *al-Manar* 11/2: 145–160, here 151.

222 Al-Harawi, "al-Mustashriqun," 253.

223 Idem., "al-Mustashriqun," 270 (a different article in the same series in the same number of *al-Manar*).

224 Le Bon, Gustave. 1920. "Namudhaj min Kitab al-Falsafa al-Siyasiyya; transl. ʿAbd al-Basit Efendi Fath Allah al-Bayruni." *al-Manar* 21/7: 345–353, here 353; original: idem. 1912. *La Psychologie politique et la Défense sociale*. Paris: Ernest Flammarion, 235–237.

225 Rida, "Nidaʾ," *al-Manar* 32/5: 400.

tamaʿāt al-gharbiyya), and "Islamic society" (*al-mujtamaʿ al-islāmī*).[226] Criticizing the change from Arabic to Latin letters under Kemal Atatürk, he denies that Turkish society had a specific civilization or culture of its own (*madaniyya aw thaqāfa khāṣṣa*).[227] In another article, a biography of Amir ʿAli, ʿAnan depicts the recently deceased ʿAli as the first Muslim able to present a complete and correct picture of the ancient Islamic society, its civilization, and its history to the West.[228] Even more significant than the concrete characteristics ʿAnan ascribes to *mujtamaʿ* is the fact that both of his articles first appeared in *al-Siyasa*. Moreover, it is certainly no coincidence that it was ʿAnan who translated the doctoral thesis of Taha Husayn (1899–1973) from French into Arabic.[229] The term *société* appears on every second page of this thesis, which was written under the supervision of Émile Durkheim, a founding father of sociology. ʿAnan translates *société* as *mujtamaʿ* whenever it refers to society as an abstract entity (which is mostly the case). Yet he prefers the Arabic term *jamāʿa* when *société* refers to a specific societal sub-group or organization.[230] This suggests that *mujtamaʿ* had already firmly acquired the distinct meaning of the modern concept of 'society' within those circles that were receiving European social thought in the first two decades of the twentieth century.

Of those particular societies conceptualized by ʿAnan as *mujtamaʿ*, 'European society' is mentioned only once more – by an anonymous author in 1916, most probably writing from England[231] – and Rafiq al-ʿAzm is the only other author who mentions 'Eastern society,' and this in 1898.[232] With the sole exception of al-ʿAzm, the authors who wrote regularly for *al-Manar*, and most prominently again al-ʿAzm, only refer to one particular society by name – that is, 'Islamic society' (*al-mujtamaʿ al-islāmī*).

In two of its eighteen occurrences, *al-mujtamaʿ al-islāmī* denotes an association[233] or an assembly[234] rather than society; yet, as early as 1899, Rida twice

---

226 ʿAbdallah ʿAnan quoted in al-Rafiʿi, Mustafa Sadiq. 1928. "Khatar Hujum al-Kamaliyin ʿala al-Islam." *al-Manar* 29/6: 456–463, here 461 f.

227 Ibid., 462.

228 ʿAbdallah ʿAnan quoted in Rida, Rashid. 1928. "Wifat Sayyid Amir ʿAli." *al-Manar* 29/5: 352–357, here 352, 354, 355.

229 Husayn, *La philosophie*; idem. 1925. *Falsafat Ibn Khaldun al-Ijtimaʿiyya: Tahlil wa-Naqd*; transl. Muhammad ʿAbdallah ʿAnan. Cairo: Matbaʿat al-Iʿtimad.

230 For example idem., *La philosophie*, 58–59; idem., *Falsafat*, 68–69.

231 Muslim Ghayr Mutafarnij (a non-Europeanized Muslim) quoted in Rida, Rashid. 1915. "al-Islam fi Injiltirra." *al-Manar* 18/1: 73–79, here 77.

232 Al-ʿAzm, "Man al-Masʾul," 867.

233 Fadil Hindi [a distinguished man from India]. 1899. "Mustaqbal al-Islam." *al-Manar* 1/41: 805–812, here 806.

uses *al-mujtamaʿ al-islāmī* in the sense of 'Islamic society.' He stresses that, in its heyday, Islam had replaced fear with security; "therefore the Islamic society did not know any scarcity."[235] I have already mentioned the two articles that use *mujtamaʿ* to denote the body (*jism*) of Islamic society.[236] In a supposed sequel to the only usage of *hay'at al-mujtamaʿ al-islāmī*, al-ʿAzm discusses the conception of rulers and law in an envisioned order of the great Islamic society (*niẓām al-mujtamaʿ al-islāmī al-ʿaẓīm*).[237] Chronologically, the next instance also stems from al-ʿAzm, but has not been mentioned yet: in 1910, he criticizes the Persian mode of governance, particularly the doctrine (*maqāla*) of the Shiʿite Imamate, which arguably entails many unlawful innovations that are harmful for Islamic society (*al-mujtamaʿ al-islāmī*).[238] And in an article on "The Islamic Government" – published in 1926, a year after his death – it is again al-ʿAzm who stresses that obedience to a just caliph is obligatory, since his just governance benefits Islamic society (*al-mujtamaʿ al-islāmī*).[239]

The next four instances mention *al-mujtamaʿ al-islāmī* only in passing; two of them originate with Europeans, one is written by Shakib Arslan, and one by an Azhari scholar. In 1905, the Azhari scholar observes different opinions concerning the purpose of religious learning, one of them being the creation of an ordered group of ʿulama' within *al-mujtamaʿ al-islāmī*.[240] The Italian orientalist Insabato,[241] paraphrased in 1920 by the Tunisian journal *al-Fajr* and reprinted in *al-Manar* in 1921, regards the anticipated awakening (*inhāḍ*) of *al-mujtamaʿ al-islāmī* as beneficial for European nations as well.[242] Lord Headley, a British convert to Islam, stresses the calmness with which *al-mujtamaʿ al-islāmī* meets Christian campaigns.[243] And Shakib Arslan, in an excerpt from his famous book on the reasons for Muslim decline, argues that nothing that benefits *al-muj-*

---

234 Rida, "Fransa," 155.

235 Idem. 1899. "al-ʿIzz wa-l-Dhull." *al-Manar* 2/13: 193–199, here 196.

236 See above: 270 f.

237 See above: 216.

238 Al-ʿAzm, Rafiq. 1910. "Asbab Suqut al-Dawla al-Ummawiyya." *al-Manar* 12/12: 933–947, here 935.

239 Idem. 1926. "al-Hukuma al-Islamiyya." *al-Manar* 26/7: 512–522, here 514.

240 ʿAlim Azhari [A scholar from al-Azhar]. 1905. "Ra'y ʿAlim Azhari fi al-ʿUlama' [2]." *al-Manar* 8/3: 110–114, here 110.

241 On Insabato, see Ellis, Marie-Therese Cecilia. 2007. *Empire or Umma. Writing Beyond the Nation in Moroccan Periodicals.* Dissertation, University of California, Berkeley, 176.

242 Majallat al-Fajr al-Tunisiyya. 1921. "al-Islam wa-Siyasat al-Hulafa'." *al-Manar* 22/9: 649–652, here 652.

243 Rahmat Allah Faruq (Lord Headley), "Yaftarun," 345.

tamaʿ al-islāmī can possibly oppose religion (*dīn*), since religion is based on the felicity of humankind (*isʿād al-ʿibād*).[244]

In 1939 – in a terminologically highly interesting article on "The Development (Tatawwur) of Islam," reprinted from a Lebanese journal – an anonymous author uses *mujtamaʿ* to refer to the whole structure of Islamic society, which he divides into various segments. Referencing several European sources, the author depicts the development of Islam based on the premise of a spirit of Islam (*rūḥ al-islām*), which manifests itself in culture. To conceptualize the idea of culture, next to *ḥaḍāra*, he also uses the more recent term *thaqāfa*.[245] While it is noteworthy that participation in a culturalist paradigm also manifests itself terminologically here, the argument of this article itself is also well known in the works of ʿAbduh and Rida. The anonymous author argues that, after the former superiority of Arab over European or Christian culture (*thaqāfa*) in the Middle Ages, ignoring Islamic teachings led to the corruption of *al-mujtamaʿ al-islāmī*.[246] Nevertheless, the author deems it a mistake that the cultivated men (*muthaqqifūn*) among Muslims and the elevated strata (*al-ṭabaqāt al-rafīʿa*) of *al-mujtamaʿ al-islāmī* have distanced themselves from religion in his time.[247]

We come closest to a definition of an Islamic social order in the very last issue of *al-Manar*, in which Hasan al-Banna addresses the relation of men and women. He stresses that, since Islam regards the mingling of men and women outside of marriage as dangerous, "the Islamic society is a segregated, not a joint society" (*inna al-mujtamaʿ al-islāmī mujtamaʿ infirādī/fardī lā mujtamaʿ mushtarak/zawjī*).[248] The fact that – immediately after the second, terminologically slightly different occurrence of this definition – al-Banna uses *mujtamaʿ* to mean gatherings or places of assembly testifies again to the term's multiple meanings. If al-Banna here spells out one aspect of an envisioned future Islamic order, he also conservatively harks back to the arrangement of Egyptian society three decades earlier; after all, "[a]t the beginning of the twentieth century male and female society were no less segregated from one another than at the beginning of the nineteenth. Urban women did not unveil or emerge from their seclu-

244 Arslan, "Limadha [3]" *al-Manar* 31/7: 538, see also 534.

245 The term *thaqāfa* in *al-Manar* first appears in volume 26, and from then on is present in every volume (see appendix, table 10).

246 Adib Ghayr Maʿruf [an unknown writer]. 1939. "Tatawwur al-Islam." *al-Manar* 35/5: 49–60 [page 49 occurs twice in this volume; this is the second occurrence], here 50.

247 Ibid., 59.

248 Al-Banna, "al-Marʾa," 767, 768. The phrase occurs twice, with the indicated alteration of terms.

sion before the First World War."[249] This example illustrates that the vision of a distinct Islamic social order was fueled both by theoretically engaging secular visions of society and by empirically observing changes of societal behavior and norms.

Overall, the usages of *mujtama'* to designate particular societies clearly suggest familiarity with European thought and with the modern concept of 'society' or *société* to be a major impetus for promoting *mujtama'* as the Arabic equivalent to 'society' in its modern meaning. The concluding section will discuss this finding, along with the other main insights of this chapter.

6 Conclusion: The Establishment and Normative Connotations of *Mujtama'*

Since the analysis of the concept of *mujtama'* in this chapter's was based on 358 rather scattered instances of the term in *al-Manar* and thus does not qualify as a conceptual history in the narrow sense, it might be worthwhile to quickly recall (a) our previous knowledge about the evolution of *mujtama'* and the purpose of the analysis in this chapter in the overarching aim of this study before (b) summarizing and interpreting this chapter's findings and explicating (c) their implications for the subsequent course of this study.

(a) Previous knowledge about the conceptual evolution of *mujtama'* amounted to little more than educated guesswork. As shown in chapter 6 section 2, some authors estimated that *mujtama'* became established to mean 'society' in the 1930s or 1940s, while one author dated the term's establishment back to the middle of the nineteenth century. Preliminary hypotheses put forward in secondary sources included that *mujtama'* became established specifically to render the modern concept of 'society' and that it came to replace *al-hay'a al-ijtimā'iyya*, which had been the dominant term for conceptualizing society until the 1930s.

The primary interest of this study lies not in a conceptual history of *mujtama'* as such; that would obviously require a much broader empirical basis – chronologically, geographically, and in terms of genres. Rather, this study inquires into whether the Islamic reformists who wrote for *al-Manar* operated using Arabic equivalents to the concept of 'society,' which is constitutive of the modern self-understanding. It was in pursuit of this overarching aim that I comprehensively analyzed *mujtama'* in *al-Manar*, together with the other (sup-

249 Baer, "Social," 135 f.

posedly) most pertinent Arabic term for 'society' in the period under consideration, *al-hay'a al-ijtimāʿiyya.*

(b) My small empirical basis notwithstanding, the analysis of *mujtamaʿ* in this chapter produced some rather indisputable results concerning the term's semantic range, its establishment, and its authorship. Throughout the life span of *al-Manar*, the dominant meaning of *mujtamaʿ* was 'society,' as the overall social sphere or collectivity, as I demonstrated in distinction from a number of related meanings (see section 1). This dominant meaning of 'society,' imbued with a sense of order, was already self-evident to all the authors who used it in the first volume of *al-Manar* (see section 2). Nevertheless, *mujtamaʿ* was hardly a ubiquitous term in our Islamic journal – in particular, Rashid Rida, the editor of the journal, only rarely used the term to mean 'society,' a fact that will be further discussed below. The reluctant usage of *mujtamaʿ* by most of *al-Manar*'s regular contributors and its disproportionate usage by somewhat secular authors familiar with European thought shows certain parallels to the usage of *al-hay'a al-ijtimāʿiyya* among the authors in *al-Manar.*

The usage of *mujtamaʿ* and *al-hay'a al-ijtimāʿiyya* in *al-Manar* points to a number of commonalities and differences between the two concepts, even though my suggestions here are of a more tentative nature than the findings mentioned in the previous paragraph. While *mujtamaʿ* was already used more frequently than *al-hay'a al-ijtimāʿiyya* in the first volume of *al-Manar*, both terms could be used to address similar aspects of society (see section 3). Slightly more often than *al-hay'a al-ijtimāʿiyya* (see chapter 7 sections 3.2 and 3.3), *mujtamaʿ* was related to religion and politics (see this chapter sections 4.1 and 4.2). These few instances, however, hardly merit the conclusion that *mujtamaʿ* conveyed an order of society clearly distinct from religion and the state – a distinction that was central to the evolution of 'society' (see chapter 2 sections 2 and 3). Remarkably, societal laws (see chapter 2 section 4) were not discussed at all in relation to either *al-hay'a al-ijtimāʿiyya* or *mujtamaʿ*. As the most significant difference from the use of *al-hay'a al-ijtimāʿiyya, mujtamaʿ* was rarely used to convey an organic understanding of society, but was in turn more often related to the sphere of law as a necessary regulator of society. This seems to support the hypothesis that *mujtamaʿ* – more clearly than *al-hay'a al-ijtimāʿiyya* – conveyed an abstract notion of social order. And if *mujtamaʿ* was used both in a clearly normative sense, as referring to a societal order, and in a *seemingly* descriptive sense, to refer to social collectivities, in the latter usages it also tended to convey the normative ideal of a firmly integrated social collectivity.

The identity of the authors who employed *mujtamaʿ* in *al-Manar* alerts us to potential additional normative connotations of the term. Most remarkably, the usages of *mujtamaʿ* to designate particular societies (see this chapter section

5) suggest that familiarity with European thought and with the modern concept of 'society' or *société* were a major impetus for promoting *mujtamaʿ* as the Arabic equivalent to the modern concept of 'society' in its double meaning – that is, firstly, as referring to a particular collectivity of people living in one political space, which was hegemonically imagined and instituted as a nation-state; and secondly, as referring to this collectivity's societal order. Several terms were used to conceptualize the collectivity interacting in societal life, with 'nation,' 'people,' and 'community' as major rivals to 'society,' and *umma*, *shaʿb*, and *jamāʿa* as rivals to *mujtamaʿ*. These rival concepts foreground different aspects. In some cases in which *mujtamaʿ* refers to a social collectivity rather than to a social order, one may indeed translate *mujtamaʿ* as 'the people' or 'community.'[250] More importantly, as with the term 'society,' when *mujtamaʿ* is used to denote particular societies, the two senses of a socio-political collectivity and a social order are collapsed into each other.

The fact that the authors who employed these particular usages – combined with the fact that most of the regular contributors to *al-Manar*, particularly the editor of the journal, Rashid Rida – rarely used *mujtamaʿ* to designate a particular society yields three potential and related implications: (1) *mujtamaʿ* was associated with a socio-political collectivity that was constituted by common ethnic bonds and delineated by the legal-political realm of the nation-state. Rida validated the religiously connoted collectivity of the *umma* over against ethnic ties and national delineations. This raises the question of whether Rida, who did employ *mujtamaʿ* to refer to the social order of the *umma*, might have alternatively collapsed the two senses of socio-political collectivity and societal order into *umma*. (2) *Mujtamaʿ* may have held secular connotations of societies autonomously constructed by human beings. In English, the normative core of 'society' as voluntary purposeful association was maintained when the concept was applied to increasingly larger entities.[251] Rida accounts for 81 percent of the cases in which *mujtamaʿ* refers to a – voluntary and purposeful – gathering, but he was reluctant to widen the applicability of that concept. This was possibly because he valued man-made – and as such, secular – associations on a smaller

---

250 If, however, one decidedly prefers to render *mujtamaʿ* as 'community' instead of 'society,' this presupposes that 'society' only expresses the now-hegemonic (modern) concept, to which (traditional) 'community' stands in marked contrast. And if one were to understand *mujtamaʿ* as 'community' thus defined, one would need to answer the question of which term then expresses the contrasting concept of 'society.' Also in European languages at the time, 'society' and 'community' could largely be used interchangeably (see: Riedel, "Gesellschaft, Gemeinschaft," esp. 859).

251 See above: chapter 2 section 1.2.

scale, but considered the overarching society (*umma*) to be divinely instituted. (3) *Mujtamaʿ* may validate society and social order as the result of human beings' natural tendency toward social association (*ijtimāʿ*). In the case of 'society,' the alleged natural tendency of human beings to socialize could be grounded in nature alone or in God and revelation.[252] Before *mujtamaʿ* became firmly established as the Arabic term for 'society,' a religious perspective that considers human nature as divinely created may have validated alternative concepts of socio-political order – such as *umma* – as the result of human beings' natural but divinely instituted tendency toward social association.

(c) Within the confines of this study, I cannot pursue the task of discerning in greater detail the channels through which *mujtamaʿ* became established in the modern meaning of 'society'; nevertheless, the foregoing implications suggest two lines of inquiry that are taken up in the following two chapters, respectively: firstly, concerning the normative connotations and underpinnings of *mujtamaʿ*, and secondly, concerning the question of alternative terms.

The following chapter pursues the first line of inquiry by attending to selected writings by Rafiq al-ʿAzm, the one regular contributor to *al-Manar* who by far most prominently used *mujtamaʿ* to mean 'society.' I thus investigate his socio-political views, which presumably underlie his use of *mujtamaʿ*, and the epistemic premises from which he derives his understanding of society and social order. It turns out that, if it is constitutive of Islamic reformism to integrate a religious and a societal perspective, al-ʿAzm accounts for the most elaborate societal perspective within the mouthpiece of Islamic reformism – *al-Manar.*

The subsequent chapter then poses the question of alternative terms based on the writings of Rashid Rida. After all, Rida's remarkably reluctant usage of *mujtamaʿ* to mean 'society' allows for only two possible interpretations: either Rida did not share the modern idea of society, or he mainly conceptualized it with terms other than *mujtamaʿ*. If my analysis so far has already shown that Rida used *umma* to expres notions of society that others conceptualized as *mujtamaʿ* and as *al-hayʾa al-ijtimāʿiyya*, chapter 10 will tackle the question of alternative terms from another angle – namely, by focusing on Rida's views on social association (*ijtimāʿ*) and his engagement with soci(et)al (*ijtimāʿī*) laws, topics, and questions.

Since Rashid Rida's œuvre and his main views are rather well known, chapter 10 is mainly concerned with his terminological usage, whereas chapter 9 focuses on socio-political views and epistemic premises as discernible from selected writings by Rafiq al-ʿAzm, whose work has hitherto hardly been studied.

252 See above: chapter 2 section 3.

Chapter 9
Rafiq al-ʿAzm: Islamic Reformist, Secular Historian, and Sociological Thinker

1 The Life and Works of Rafiq al-ʿAzm (1865–1925)

In the previous two chapters, several articles by Rafiq al-ʿAzm have been addressed – more or less extensively – concerning their use of *al-hay'a al-ijtimāʿiyya* and, especially, of *mujtamaʿ*. Al-ʿAzm stands out among the regular contributors to *al-Manar*, and not only concerning his usage of *mujtamaʿ*. More fundamentally, he contributed a secular societal perspective to the discourse of *al-Manar*. To a certain degree, integrating such a perspective is characteristic of Islamic reformists at large. Within *al-Manar*, however, al-ʿAzm goes furthest in elaborating this societal perspective and spelling out its secular consequences. In a sense, he can even be considered a secular interlocutor for major Islamic reformists such as Rashid Rida. It is ultimately due to the remarkable perspective which al-ʿAzm brings to Islamic reformism that a separate chapter of this book is dedicated to him.

Rafiq al-ʿAzm, whom Rida revered as a sociological and historiographical writer,[1] was not only a regular contributor to *al-Manar*,[2] but also a very prolific

---

1 In his biography of al-ʿAzm, Rida characterizes his friend as a "historiographical scholar (*al-ʿālim al-mu'arrikh*), sociological writer (*al-kātib al-ijtimāʿī*), and political activist (*al-ʿāmil al-siyāsī*)" (Rida, "Rafiq al-ʿAzm," 288). Al-ʿAzm was presented in a similar vein in previous articles he published in *al-Manar* – for example, as "known for his historiographical and sociological studies (*mabāḥithihi al-tārīkhiyya wa-l-ijtimāʿiyya*) (Rashid Rida [presumably] in al-ʿAzm, "al-Jamiʿa," 589).

2 Articles by al-ʿAzm, other than those already dealt with in the previous chapters, include: al-ʿAzm, Rafiq. 1900. "Iqtirah ʿala al-Sadat al-ʿUlama' fi Taqwim Iʿwijaj al-Wuʿʿaz wa-l-Khutaba'." *al-Manar* 2/44: 689–695 (on the role of Muslim preachers); idem. 1904. "Kalima Thaniyya fi Ahl al-Dhimma." *al-Manar* 7/1: 11–17 (an excerpt from *Ashhar al-Mashahir*, introduced by Rida); idem. 1909. "al-Inqilab al-Maymun wa-Athr al-Sultan ʿAbd al-Hamid fi al-Dawla wa-Muqawimatuhu li-l-Dustur (Istidrak ʿala al-Manar)." *al-Manar* 12/5: 340–349 (refuting the views of an Indian writer and an Indian newspaper on the Turkish Revolution and the role of Sultan ʿAbd al-Hamid); Rafiq al-ʿAzm quoted in Rida, Husayn Wasfi. 1910. "al-Akhbar wa-l-Ara' (Dars ʿala Kitab al-Daris fi al-Madaris)." *al-Manar* 13/9: 697–709, here 697–706. This last article is a lecture on the importance of Islamic history for contemporary social life, namely in the field of education. Al-ʿAzm discusses and quotes extensively from a book by the historian Muhammad bin Muhy al-Din al-Naʿim. Pointing out a number of schools founded through individual efforts, al-ʿAzm argues that the individual work of persons (*ʿamal al-ashkhāṣ al-munfaridīn*) has the same impact on society (*al-hay'a al-ijtimāʿiyya*) as their collective work (*ʿamaluhum mujtamiʿīn*) (ibid., 704).

https://doi.org/10.1515/9783110545845-010

Fig. 1. Rafiq al-ʿAzm, undated. Source: al-ʿAzm, *Majmuʿat*, vol. 1:5.

author in general. For my analysis of his socio-political views and epistemic premises, I have selected two of his works, in addition to a debate he held in *al-Manar* with the Indian reformist al-Yafiʿi.[3] The works in question are his *Les-*

3 Idem., "Hadha Awan;" al-Yafiʿi, "Asbab;" al-ʿAzm, "Daʿf;" al-Yafiʿi, "Shakl."

sons Containing Wisdom for Islamic Youth[4] and *Alerting Intellects to the Demands of Societal Life and Islam*[5], both published in 1900. These pertinent writings by al-ʿAzm will be presented and analyzed in the following sections. In this section, I briefly mention al-ʿAzm's other writings, along with existing studies on them, before sketching his biography.

Al-ʿAzm's best-known work is his history of Islamic political and military leaders, *Ashhar Mashahir al-Islam fi al-Hurub wa-l-Siyasa*, originally published between 1903 and 1908.[6] Other works not included in my analysis here, but which are worth mentioning nevertheless, are the following: in 1886, al-ʿAzm had already written his *Book on the Elucidation of Civilization (Tamaddun) and of the Causes of Culture (ʿUmran)*.[7] In the first part of this 80-page book, al-ʿAzm stresses humankind's innate disposition toward progress, the importance of education, and the value of culture. He then elaborates on sciences and knowledge and the importance of patriotism, liberty, and justice.[8] In 1910, *al-Manar*'s press released a selection of al-ʿAzm's historiographical lectures,[9] and in 1912, the Islamic Press in Cairo published his *Treatise Elucidating the Manner of the Spread of Religions.*[10] This treatise ultimately amounts to an Islamic sociology of religion, as I have shown elsewhere.[11] Finally, in 1925, the year of his death, *al-Manar*'s press released a two-volume selection of al-ʿAzm's works, some of which were previously unpublished.[12] These works were collected by Ra-

---

4 Al-ʿAzm, Rafiq. 1317 h [1899/1900]. *al-Durus al-Hikamiyya li-l-Nashiʾa al-Islamiyya.* Cairo: Matbaʿat al-Muʾayyad wa-l-Adab.

5 Idem. 1900. *Tanbih al-Afham ila Matalib al-Hayat al-Ijtimaʿiyya wa-l-Islam.* Cairo: Matbaʿat al-Mawsuʿat.

6 The earliest edition available seems to be: Idem. 1327 h. [1909]. *Ashhar Mashahir al-Islam fi al-Harb wa-l-Siyasa.* Cairo: Matbaʿa Hindiyya.

7 Idem. 1304 h [1886/1887]. *Kitab al-Bayan fi al-Tamaddun wa-Asbab al-ʿUmran.* Cairo: al-Matbaʿa al-Iʿlamiyya; re-edition: idem. 2012. *al-Bayyan fi al-Tamaddun wa-Asbab al-ʿUmran;* ed. ʿAbd al-Rahman Hilali. Alexandria/Beirut/Cairo: Maktabat al-Iskandriyya/Dar al-Kitab al-Lubnani/Dar al-Kitab al-Misri.

8 Pellitteri, Antonino. 1998. *Islam e riforma: l'ambito arabo-ottomano e l'opera di Rafīq bey al-ʿAẓm intellettuale damasceno riformatore (1865–1925).* Palermo: n.g., 104f.

9 Al-ʿAzm, Rafiq. 1910. *al-Khutab al-Taʾrikhiyya.* Cairo: Matbaʿat al-Manar.

10 Idem. 1912. *Risala fi Bayan Kayfiyyat Intishar al-Adyan.* Cairo: Matbaʿat al-Islam.

11 For this, see my forthcoming article on al-ʿAzm in the journal *Historical Social Research*, special issue on Muslim Secularities.

12 Idem. 1344 h [1925]. *Majmuʿat Athar Rafiq Bik al-ʿAzm; vol. 1: Kitab al-Sawanih al-Fikriyya fi al-Mabahith al-ʿIlmiyya; Kitab Tarikh al-Siyasa al-Islamiyya; al-Jamiʿa al-ʿUthmaniyya wa-l-ʿAsabiyya al-Turkiyya aw al-Taʾlif bayna al-Turk wa-l-ʿArab; vol. 2: Khutab Rafiq Bik al-ʿAzm al-Tarikihiyya; Rasaʾil Rafiq Bik al-ʿAzm; al-Jamiʿa al-Islamiyya wa-Uruba*; ed. by ʿUthman al-ʿAzm, with a biography by Rashid Rida. Cairo: Matbaʿat al-Manar.

fiq's elder brother ʿUthman, who – in his introduction – mentions the assistance of Rafiq's "dearest and most faithful friend," Rashid Rida,[13] whose extensive biography of al-ʿAzm also opens the first volume.[14]

Overall, Rafiq al-ʿAzm's works have been astonishingly sparsely received, both in Arabic and in European languages. Werner Ende provided what is the still most substantial analysis of al-ʿAzm's socio-political views, and especially his historiographical approach, in his study on twentieth-century Arab views of the Umayyads in Islamic constructions of the nation.[15] In the following section, I will refer to Ende's insights, inasmuch as these are relevant for my research questions. In his overview of early modern Arab political movements, Eliezer Tauber presents the political activities of al-ʿAzm.[16] In a monograph dedicated to al-ʿAzm,[17] Antonino Pelliterri broadly characterizes al-ʿAzm as a member of the Islamic reform movement and briefly touches upon his ties with other Damascene reformists. He then sketches al-ʿAzm's life, gives very brief summaries of his works, and – in a quite unsystematic manner – compiles statements by al-ʿAzm that he deems relevant. Thus, unfortunately, this 180-page book – the only one in any European language fully dedicated to al-ʿAzm – lacks an analytical perspective and does not provide substantial insights concerning al-ʿAzm's socio-political views.

The most extensive study on al-ʿAzm was written in Arabic by Basam al-Batush in 2007[18] and is also the only relevant study in Arabic.[19] Interestingly for my question, al-Batush foregrounds the importance of al-ʿAzm as "one of the first modern Arab thinkers who attended to the social question (*al-masʾala al-ijtimāʿiyya*)."[20] This statement opens the first thematic chapter of al-Batush's work, which is dedicated to the social, educational, and political thought of al-ʿAzm.[21] The subsequent chapter situates al-ʿAzm among the intellectual and

---

13 Ibid., 3.

14 Ibid., bāʾ–lām; also published as: Rida, "Rafiq al-ʿAzm."

15 Ende, *Arabische*, esp. 32–42, 55–59.

16 Tauber, *The Emergence* (see therein the index, page 392 for mention of al-ʿAzm).

17 Pellitteri, *Islam*.

18 Al-Batush, *Rafiq al-ʿAzm*. A less substantial, but also useful overview of al-ʿAzm's life and works, including some of his central viewpoints, is ʿAbd al-Rahman al-Hilali's introduction to the reprint edition of the *Elucidation of Civilization* (al-ʿAzm, *al-Bayan*, 13–44).

19 Cf. the very tendentious portrayal of al-ʿAzm on a website run by the Muslim Brotherhood: al-ʿAntabali, Ashraf ʿAyd. n.g. "Rafiq al-ʿAzm: Rajul al-Islah al-Siyasi wa-l-Fikri." In *Ikhwanwiki*. http://www.ikhwanwiki.com/index.php?title=رفيق_العظم.#.D8.A3.D9.88.D9.84.D8.A7_:_.D8.A7.D9.84.D9.85.D9.82.D8.AF.D9.85.D8.A9 (accessed July 19, 2017).

20 Al-Batush, *Rafiq al-ʿAzm*, 35, also 212.

21 Ibid., 33–74.

political trends of his time,[22] and the following three chapters deal with al-ʿAzm's political views and activities concerning the Arab, the Syrian, and the Palestinian questions. Even though al-Batush occasionally inserts his own normative stance,[23] overall his study is a very solid and useful one, whence I will partially rely on al-Batush's insights from the first two thematic chapters to show that al-ʿAzm ideal-typically belongs to the trend of Islamic reformism and to depict some of his socio-political views. Preceding the book's thematic chapters, al-Batush offers the most comprehensive biography of al-ʿAzm. He extensively and somewhat uncritically relies on Rashid Rida's biography of his collaborator,[24] but he also considers additional sources. Hence, the following sketch of al-ʿAzm's life is largely based on al-Batush's work, relying on Tauber's study for an overview of al-ʿAzm's political activities.

Rafiq al-ʿAzm was born into a high-ranking family in Damascus in 1865. Members of the al-ʿAzm family had been governors of Ottoman Syrian provinces between 1724 and 1808 and continued to occupy administrative positions in Damascus until after Syrian independence from the Ottoman Empire in 1918, and even during the subsequent French occupation.[25] His father, Mahmud al-ʿAzm (d. 1874), belonged to the Sufi order of the Shadhiliyya and himself wrote works of mystical poetry.[26] When choosing a school for Rafiq, Mahmud al-ʿAzm, who had not received a formal education himself, opted against a government school. This was possibly – as al-Batush hypothesizes, following Rida – because he did not want Rafiq to join children from poorer families attending these schools with the aim of subsequently becoming government employees. Mahmud al-ʿAzm also decided against a local Arab school and instead sent his seven-year-old son to a Roman Catholic school, where he was also meant to learn French.[27] However, with the death of his father the following year, Rafiq al-ʿAzm left the Catholic school and subsequently received his education, in both Turkish and Arabic, from semi-institutional learning circles (sg. *ḥalqa ʿilmiyya*) in Damascus.[28] While some of the leaders whose circles al-ʿAzm's frequented explicitly designated themselves as 'salafis' and were "considerably

22 Ibid., 75 – 106.
23 See, for example, concerning Western foreign policy: ibid., 94.
24 Rida, "Rafiq al-ʿAzm."
25 Batush, *Rafiq al-ʿAzm*, 17 f.
26 Ibid., 16.
27 In his later years, al-ʿAzm supposedly did acquaint himself with French, to a rather limited extent (ibid., 23).
28 Ibid., 20.

more conservative than ʻAbduh and al-Afghani,"[29] in one of these circles, al-ʻAzm also studied the writings of Muhammad ʻAbduh,[30] whose ideas he defended.[31]

One of many Syrian emigrants to Egypt,[32] Rafiq al-ʻAzm settled in Cairo in 1894,[33] where he joined the circle of Muhammad ʻAbduh and became a close collaborator and friend of Rashid Rida. In addition to *al-Manar*, al-ʻAzm also contributed to the journals *al-Muqtataf* and *al-Hilal* and published in a range of newspapers, namely *al-Ahram*, *al-Muqattam*, *al-Mu'ayyad*, *al-Liwa'*, *al-Mufid*, *al-Ittihad al-ʻUthmani*, *al-Muqtabas*, and *al-Huda*.[34] Nevertheless, his affiliation with *al-Manar* appears to have been especially strong. This is certainly true of al-ʻAzm's relation with Rida, as demonstrated by their collaboration in political societies: in 1907, they founded the Society of the Ottoman Council (Jamʻiyyat al-Shura al-ʻUthmaniyya), with Rida as president and al-ʻAzm as treasurer.[35] This Ottoman-oriented society intended to counter the increasing dominance of nationalist Turks and included members of different ethnicities and of both Christian and Muslim backgrounds.

Rida also belonged to the very small inner circle[36] of the influential Ottoman Party for Administrative Decentralization (Hizb al-Lamarkaziya al-Idariya al-ʻUthmani), founded in 1912 and presided over by Rafiq al-ʻAzm.[37] Other noteworthy members of this party were Shibli Shumayyil; ʻAbd al-Hamid al-Zahrawi; Rashid Rida's brother, Salih Mukhlis Rida; Rafiq al-ʻAzm's brother, ʻUthman; and their cousin, Haqqi al-ʻAzm. This 'party' was in fact a political society, too, and it included both Christian and Muslim Syrians. While the society's overall aim was a strong Syria, opinions differed – both between members and over time – as to the desirable degree of autonomy from the Ottoman Empire, the use of revolutionary means, and the appropriate stance toward English and French politics.[38] Rashid Rida and Rafiq al-ʻAzm notably held different attitudes

---

29 Griffel, "What," 203. The protagonists named by Griffel here are stated as leaders of circles attended by al-ʻAzm in Tauber, *The Emergence*, 43f.

30 Batush, *Rafiq al-ʻAzm*, 22.

31 Ibid., 23.

32 See above: chapter 4 section 3.1.

33 Ibid., 25.

34 Ibid., 26.

35 Tauber, *The Emergence*, 51–53.

36 Ibid., 324.

37 Ibid., 121–134.

38 Ibid., 128, 237, 277.

toward European powers.[39] On the eve of the First World War, al-ʿAzm envisioned a positive role for French advisers in Syria and Lebanon, while Rida, based on his experience of British colonial power, denounced this demand for foreign advisers.[40]

Al-Batush helpfully distinguishes the following layers and foci of political sentiments and identity during al-ʿAzm's life: (1) Pan-Islamism, (2) Ottomanism, (3) ethnic nationalism (*qawmiyya, jinsiyya*), and (3) ethnic-geographic nationalism (*waṭaniyya*). Al-ʿAzm did (1) regard Muslims uniting based on religion as a natural phenomenon and defended the Pan-Islamic movement,[41] but he also thought that Pan-Islamism was a political concept that did not manifest itself in the heterogeneous reality of Muslim peoples.[42] As such, he also qualified European fears of and attacks against Pan-Islamism as politically motivated.[43] Al-ʿAzm's political activities, as mentioned in the previous paragraph, already testify to his (2) Ottomanist convictions and his aim to preserve the integrity of the empire.[44] When the disintegration of the Ottoman Empire and the dominance of Turkish nationalists became obvious, al-ʿAzm (3) increasingly focused on ethnic ties and stressed the connection between Arabism and Islam.[45] In yet another twist, he then (4) foregrounded the ties of the Syrian people, adopting the prominent nineteenth-century slogan that "homeland is part of belief" (*al-waṭan min al-īmān*).[46] If al-ʿAzm thus maintained multiple layers of belonging, over the course of his life, he shifted his focus from Islamic unity (*al-ittiḥād al-islāmī*) and then the Ottoman bond (*al-rābiṭa al-ʿuthmāniyya*) to Arab independence (*al-istiqlāl al-ʿarabī*) and eventually to the unity and independence of his Syrian homeland (*waḥdat al-waṭan al-sūrī wa-istiqlāluhu*).[47] During all of these phases of his political convictions, Rafiq al-ʿAzm advocated gradual reform and opposed revolutionary means.[48] While he declined the positions in the Syrian government that were offered to him, this was also due to his bad health, which further deteriorated in the years preceding his death in 1925.[49]

---

39 Here, we must not dwell on their differences concerning strategic decisions or evaluations of individual persons (see ibid., 129, 208).
40 Ibid., 268 f.
41 Al-Batush, *Rafiq al-ʿAzm*, 90 f.
42 Ibid., 92 f.
43 Ibid., 93.
44 Ibid., 95–99.
45 Ibid., 99–102.
46 Ibid., 102 ff.
47 Ibid., 211.
48 Ibid., 30, 51, 210; Tauber, *The Emergence*, 237.
49 Al-Batush, *Rafiq al-ʿAzm*, 30 f.

The following section first substantiates the designation of al-'Azm as part of the ideal-tpyical trend of Islamic reformism and then highlights his secularist Islamic view concerning the relation of religion and politics.

2 A Secular(ist) Islamic Intellectual

Following the threefold scheme of Islamic intellectual trends in modernity, which remains useful for a first ideal-typical orientation in a complex intellectual landscape,[50] Rafiq al-'Azm belongs to the trend of Islamic reformism. This is tentatively indicated by his regular contributions to *al-Manar*, the mouthpiece of Islamic reformism, and his close collaboration with Rashid Rida. As mentioned before, the Islamic reformists did share certain attitudes, interests, and views with non-Muslim intellectuals. In fact, Eliezer Tauber – who summarized al-'Azm's activities in political societies, which also included Christian members – points out a commonality between al-'Azm and the Syrio-Lebanese Christian Butrus al-Bustani: both advocated a *partial* opening to and adoption of European inventions and ideas.[51] Concerning the Islamic framing and elaboration of this attitude, al-'Azm shares the broadest characteristics of Islamic reformists, not least focusing on the alleged essence of Islam to fulfill the requirements of the modern age.

Al-Batush substantiates this idealtypical characterization of al-'Azm as an Islamic reformist by situating him among the other intellectual trends of his time. He names al-'Azm in a line with al-Afghani, 'Abduh, Tahir al-Jaza'iri (d. 1920), and Rida as a protagonist of the Islamic reformist trend, which aimed at combining past and present, Islamic shari'a and Western progress.[52] As such, al-'Azm was critical of both those *mutafarnijūn* who allegedly advocated full Westernization[53] and those *muqallidūn* who allegedly wholeheartedly opposed reform.[54] If al-'Azm advocated a selective adoption of the West, in the same conciliatory manner, he stressed that not all men or scholars of religion (*rijāl/ 'ulamā' al-dīn*) are stubborn traditionalists, but that some of them exhibit great efforts toward the reform of religion,[55] which he regarded as a necessary

50 For a critical discussion of that scheme, see above: chapter 5 section 3.

51 Tauber, *The Emergence*, 268f. On al-Bustani, see above: chapter 6 section 3.

52 Al-Batush, *Rafiq al-'Azm*, 78.

53 Ibid., 77–83.

54 Ibid., 84–87.

55 Ibid., 84.

means to worldly reform.[56] Indeed, the most fundamental characteristic of al-ʿAzm's thought, according to al-Batush, was moderation (*iʿtidāl*) and the advocacy of a middle position (*wasaṭiyya*) between alleged extremes.[57]

The secular views of this Islamic intellectual manifest themselves in his historiographical writings; 'secular' is used here in the sense which I suggested was most fundamental at the outset of this study – namely, as postulating and relying on autonomous, inner-worldly causes. Werner Ende showed that al-ʿAzm demanded and worked toward "the emancipation of historiography from theology."[58] Like al-ʿAzm, the Christian intellectual Jurji Zaidan[59] also demanded that the historian look at history from "a civilizational, not a religious viewpoint" (*min al-wijha al-ʿumrāniyya lā min al-wijha al-dīniyya*).[60] Differences in their historiographical presentations notwithstanding, Ende characterizes both al-ʿAzm and Zaydan as "secularists."[61] We should add that the fact that al-ʿAzm epistemologically validated immanent over transcendent causes did not necessarily mean that he was perceived as a secular actor by his contemporaries. Thus, the famous Muslim intellectual Taha Husayn, who had written his PhD thesis under the supervision of Émile Durkheim,[62] criticized al-ʿAzm for his lack of historical criticism[63] and his "veneration of the religious."[64] In any case, in his historiographical writings, al-ʿAzm stressed political over religious factors along with secular causes. He argued that the division of Muslims over the succession of Muhammad was due to political interests only, and criticized Shiʿites for turning this political question into a religious one.[65] Al-ʿAzm also adduces Islamic history in his argument supporting the separation of religion and politics in contemporary Muslim societies, as is most explicitly the case in his debate with the Indian reformist al-Yafiʿi.

This debate, which was held in volume eight of *al-Manar* and to which we now turn, shows al-ʿAzm's pioneering Islamic secularist views; here, I use 'secularist' in the sense of demanding a separation of religion and politics. As al-ʿAzm

56 Ibid., 87.
57 Ibid., 83.
58 Ende, *Arabische*, 36, 37; transl. F.Z.
59 See above: chapter 2 section 4.1.
60 Ende, *Arabische*, 41.
61 Ibid., 41. While al-ʿAzm and Zaydan debated mainly over historiographical details, Rida more forcefully attacked Zaydan's work on Islamic history (see above: 133).
62 See above: 66, 296.
63 Ende, *Arabische*, 59.
64 Ibid., 57.
65 Ibid., 34 f.

sharpened his argument over the course of this debate, I will first summarize the individual articles before turning to an interpretation of al-ʿAzm's secular stance and its implications.

It was in *al-Manar* in 1904 that al-ʿAzm gave his answer to an eminent question of the time – namely, the question of why Muslims are supposedly behind other peoples and how the defects in their social life may be rectified.[66] This two-part article is entitled "This is the Time of Warning" ("Hadha Awan al-ʿIbar"). As the title is not vocalized, the Arabic reader may, in addition to *ʿibar* (warning), also read *ʿabr*, meaning 'crossing' or 'passage.' While the sense of 'warning' is dominant throughout the article, al-ʿAzm might have had this double-meaning in mind when titling his article. After all, it is a common trope of Islamic reformists to characterize the present moment as a crossroads, and this in two senses: one needs to look back to the past in order to envision the future, and one needs to decide which way to march forward – especially whether to follow the European (or Western) path, or whether to try to progress on one's own (yet-to-be-constructed) path. The question of Muslim backwardness, of "what went wrong"[67] in Islamic history, is thus intrinsically connected to the question of what went right in the history of the advanced nations (*al-umam al-mutamaddina*), which epitomize civilization and modernity.[68]

To al-ʿAzm, the strength of the advanced nations ruling the world is based on their just political orders, which again rest on their civilization, which has been erected upon science and knowledge.[69] He thus regards scientific innovations and the acquisition of knowledge as the underlying cause of material and political strength and maintains that since in his time, unlike in previous times, countries and peoples are strongly connected, Muslims lack any excuse for not accessing and benefitting from the knowledge available in other regions.[70] Despite its connectedness, al-ʿAzm depicts humanity as consisting of

66 Al-ʿAzm, "Hadha Awan."

67 Lewis, Bernard. 2003. *What Went Wrong? Western Impact and Middle Eastern Response*. London: Phoenix. As mentioned in chapter 3 section 4, Islamic reformists tend to share the orientalists' view of certain defects in Islamic history – of something having gone wrong.

68 Which peoples or nations were considered to epitomize modernity varied between thinkers and over time. In the nineteenth and early twentieth centuries, and especially in the colonial context of Arab countries, this was mainly England and France. Obviously, the United States took over that position in later decades. In the first two decades of the twentieth century, Islamic reformists also adduced Japan as an example of an advanced nation, especially after its victory over Russia in 1905.

69 Al-ʿAzm, "Hadha Awan," *al-Manar* 7/7: 269 f.

70 Ibid., 269 f.

three main groups: Muslims, Christians, and "pagans" (*wathniyūn*).[71] Al-ʿAzm ends the first part of his article with the pseudo-empirical observation that the "pagan" nation of Japan quickly caught up with the advanced Christian nations, while Muslims remain backward and are dominated by others.[72]

In the second part, after some testimonies to that backwardness by Muslim authors,[73] al-ʿAzm ventures to name the *Islamic* government as the central cause of both the bad socio-political conditions Muslims find themselves in and their lack of civilization. He mainly illustrates this point with regard to the Ottoman Empire, which, to him, is still the most advanced of all Muslim countries (*mamālik*, sg. *mamlaka*).[74] Unlike other Islamic countries, the Ottoman Empire actually shares in the benefits of civilization and order, al-ʿAzm maintains.[75] In particular, it possesses good "military schools (*al-madāris al-ḥarbiyya*) that would have created for this state (*dawla*) an ordered military (*jaysh munaẓamma*) in its most advanced form, if it had not been afflicted by the weakness of politics (*siyāsa*) and financial resources (*māl*), and indeed by the weakness of the basis (*asās*) of the government, because it is an Islamic government (*ḥukūma islāmiyya*)."[76] Al-ʿAzm makes this remarkable statement – blaming the Islamic nature of government in the Islamic journal *al-Manar* – in quite a self-evident manner, and proceeds to give additional examples of Muslim backwardness from different countries,[77] before coming back to the question of what actually prevents Muslim progress.

Having briefly refuted those who maintain that Muslim backwardness is due to a difference in character or ability, al-ʿAzm elaborates on why those who regard the Islamic religion as a major obstacle to progress are also mistaken.[78] His basic premise is that God, through the means of his religions, only wants the best for humankind.[79] Islam was intentionally sent to the beduin Arabs, who "did not possess anything of [the knowledge of] the laws of social association (*qawānīn al-ijtimāʿ*), of the order of the advanced governments (*niẓām al-ḥukūmāt al-rāqqiyya*), and of the civilized peoples (*al-shuʿūb al-mutamaddina*)."[80] Due to their simplicity, these beduin Arabs mixed religion (*dīn*) with every aspect

71 Ibid., 270.
72 Ibid., 271.
73 Idem., "Hadha Awan," *al-Manar* 7/8: 304 f.
74 Ibid., 305, 306.
75 Ibid., 305.
76 Ibid., 306.
77 Ibid., 306 f.
78 ibid, 307 f.
79 Ibid., 308.
80 Ibid., 308.

of worldly life (*al-ḥayāt al-dunyawiyya*) – especially the political life of peoples (*ḥayāt al-umam al-siyāsiyya*). Contrary to the customs of these simple Arab people, the prophet Muhammad distinguished between religious and worldly matters,[81] conveying the insight that, "in affairs of the world (*dunyā*), the authority lies with the public interest (*maṣlaḥa*) and reason (*ʿaql*), and this is one side, whereas religion (*dīn*) is another side."[82]

However, al-ʿAzm attests, the pre-Islamic practice of infusing religion into the worldly matters of the collectivity (*umūr al-umma al-dunyawiyya*) and into its societal interests (*maṣāliḥuhā al-ijtimāʿīyya*) persisted, and it was especially the connection of religion and politics (*siyāsa*) that has produced the misfortune of Muslims until today.[83] After all, the existence of peoples (*umam*) depends on governments (*ḥukūmāt*), "and if the government does not have legal bonds which are appropriate for all times and peoples and which evolve with the progress (*taraqqī*) of societies (*umam*), then they can give no life to the people."[84] The early Arab Muslims had failed to lay down the principles of governments (*uṣūl al-ḥukūmāt*) in a constitutional manner (*ṣibgha dustūriyya*). In turn, by having done so, the Romans approached the presently successful type of a republican or moderate (*muʿtadila*) government.[85] Since the Arabs did not have an ordered government, which would also imply its being separated from religion, the first political strife between Muslims over the succession of Muhammad was of a religious nature.[86] As an outcome, the caliphs came to monopolize all governmental affairs, and Islamic society (*umma*) forgot to contemplate its actual political interests (*maṣlaḥatuhā al-siyāsiyya*).[87]

In al-ʿAzm's opinion – and he suggests that belief is a matter of private conscience alone – the religious tainting of Islamic politics and the concomitant corruption of both religion and politics became worse still under Iranian influence.[88] Scholars of religion justified the religious lineage and legitimacy of rulers, who came to govern based on their alleged piety (*taʿabbud*). Piety, however, ought to be merely a matter of conscience (*amr wijdānī*), as is respected by

---

81 Ibid., 308.
82 Ibid., 309.
83 Ibid., 309.
84 Ibid., 309.
85 Ibid., 310.
86 Ibid., 309 f.
87 Ibid., 310.
88 Ibid., 310. Al-ʿAzm's article was translated into Farsi (Rashid Rida [presumably] in al-Yafiʿi, "Asbab," *al-Manar* 7/14: 540).

democratic governments (*al-ḥukūmāt al-dīmuqrāṭiyya*) today.[89] Muslims, in turn, have become accustomed to despotic rule and stagnation, and have even become hostile to those exceptional rulers who attempt to reform social affairs (*shu'ūn ijtimā'iyya*).[90] If things have gotten worse over the course of Islamic history, the root of the problem – according to al-ʿAzm – remains the early beduin Arab's mixing of religion and politics, which is also evidenced by the fact that contemporary Beduins are still the least advanced of all Muslim peoples.[91]

In the name of the true Islamic religion, al-ʿAzm calls upon his fellow Muslims at the end of his article to pay heed to the bases of the advanced nations today and to work toward that type of government that is appropriate for the present age – namely, a democratic government (*ḥukūma dīmuqrāṭiyya*).[92] After all, unlike animal life, human life progresses constantly, and one ought to emulate those who are moving fastest (*al-musriʿūn*) – as long as this does not contradict religion, al-ʿAzm maintains, adding that religion cannot possibly prevent or oppose what would contribute to the progress of Muslims.

The reaction to al-ʿAzm's article by the Indian reformist Salih bin ʿAli al-Yafiʿi appeared in *al-Manar* three months later under the title "The Reasons for Muslims' Weakness and Its Remedy."[93] Al-Yafiʿi pays respect to al-ʿAzm for attending to this important question and quite faithfully summarizes his main arguments. He focuses on al-ʿAzm's two central arguments: that Muslim weakness is due to "the Arabs infusing religion into all aspects of the worldly affairs of life (*umūr al-ḥayāt al-dunyawiyya*) and especially the political life of peoples (*ḥayāt al-umam al-siyāsiyya*)"; and that, "if the Arabs at the beginning of the matter [of instituting a government] had put religion on one side (*jānib*) and societal politics (*al-siyāsa al-ijtimāʿiyya*) on another, and had followed the civilized peoples (*al-umam al-mutamaddina*) of the time, like the Romans, then the Islamic community (*al-umma al-islāmiyya*) would not have declined in the manner it did." Overall then, according to al-Yafiʿi, al-ʿAzm suggests that there is "no deliverance [from the present state of weakness], except when Muslims come together (*yajtamiʿ*) and [agree to] put religion on one side and the administration of power (*siyāsat al-mulk*) on another."[94]

---

89 Al-ʿAzm, "Hadha Awan," *al-Manar* 7/8: 310 f.
90 Ibid., 311.
91 Ibid., 311.
92 Ibid., 312.
93 Al-Yafiʿi, "Asbab."
94 Idem., "Asbab," *al-Manar* 7/14: 541.

Al-Yafiʿi blames a different historical development for the deplorable present state of affairs – namely, the alleged fact that Muslims did not respect and pay heed to their religion, both in their personal affairs and in their socio-political life (*ḥayātuhum al-ijtimāʿiyya al-siyāsiyya*).[95] According to al-Yafiʿi, this led to the disaster of illegitimate persons taking over the caliphate, which he regards as the most significant single factor in Muslim decline.[96] As another factor, al-Yafiʿi adduces strife and conflicts between Muslims,[97] something he also deems to be in clear opposition to the Islamic religion. According to al-Yafiʿi, both factors are the result of deviating from the true principles of the shariʿa, as embodied in the Qurʾan and the Sunna, and as exemplified by the first generation of Muslims and the Rightly Guided Caliphs. The neglect of these principles, in the first instance by the rulers, led to the introduction of unlawful innovations (*bidaʿ*, sg. *bidʿa*) and the uncritical imitation of accumulated traditions (*taqlīd*).[98] Having neglected rational inquiry themselves, some Muslims in modernity turned to Western education, a turn which furthered the dissolution of societal bonds (*al-rawābiṭ al-ijtimāʿiyya*).[99] To al-Yafiʿi, then, the root cause of the present state of weakness and division consists in something which al-ʿAzm allegedly did not address – namely, in deviation from the true teachings of the Islamic religion and the shariʿa, especially concerning power (*mulk*) and the life of societies (*ḥayāt al-umam*).[100]

Al-Yafiʿi also counters al-ʿAzm's consideration that Islamic history would have taken a better turn had the early Muslims followed the Romans' principles of legal-political order – after all, he maintains, the Islamic principles were actually more advanced than the Roman ones,[101] and in fact underlie the modern European socio-political order.[102] Al-Yafiʿi thus shares in the well-known reformist argument that modern European progress, civilization, and power stems from Europeans having appropriated Arab-Islamic knowledge and principles, a process he dates back to the Crusades.[103] Adding a logical argument to this historical one, at the end of the first part of the article, al-Yafʿi maintains that one may not, as al-ʿAzm did, deduce from the fact that Muhammad or the Rightly Guided Ca-

95 Ibid., 542.
96 Ibid., 542f.
97 Ibid., 543.
98 Ibid., 546.
99 Ibid., 547f.
100 Ibid., 548.
101 Ibid., 548.
102 Ibid., 549.
103 Ibid., 549f.

liphs did not elaborate on social and political teachings (*al-taʿālīm al-siyāsiyya wa-l-ijtimāʿiyya*) the idea that the Islamic religion does not address these fields.[104]

Having laid out the alleged reasons for Muslim weakness, in the second part of the article, al-Yafiʿi suggests solutions – all of which branch out, unsurprisingly, from his central assertion that the Islamic religion contains the most perfect principles and teachings, also concerning questions of political order. The belief that Islam is the most perfect (*akmal*) and most just (*aʿdal*) of all religions implies for al-Yafiʿi that its politics (*siyāsatuhu*) is also the most just of all politics.[105] The crucial principles of Islamic politics are those of consultation and election, al-Yafiʿi argues, and he views these principles as having been realized by Muhammad and his first successors in a way analogous to the political practices of modern Western peoples.[106] He stresses that Islam commands consultation (*shūrā*) and independent legal investigation (*ijtihād*) in all cases for which there is no clear statement in the Qur'an and the Sunna. Therefore, the separation of religion and politics is, in contrast to al-ʿAzm's claims, not necessary for realizing the benefits of consultation.[107] Based on his conviction that the political order and unity of Muslims ought to be based on religion, al-Yafiʿi ends his article by suggesting the creation of an Islamic assembly of consultation (*majlis al-shūrā*), with its possible headquarters in Egypt, and with branches in different Islamic countries.[108]

While the fundamental similarities between al-Yafīʿi's and al-ʿAzm's understanding of religion will be addressed below, here one may already ask to what extent al-Yafiʿi clothed secular principles in a religious discourse in order to convince the masses and to ensure unity against perceived external threats. After all, as a reason for his suggested solution, he argues that Muslims have always responded well to the calls of their religion,[109] and he stresses that those Muslims who doubt the adequacy of the Islamic religion or shariʿa for answering contemporary questions are serving their enemies – that is, the European invaders of Muslim countries.[110]

104 Ibid., 550.
105 Idem., "Asbab," *al-Manar* 7/15: 581.
106 Ibid., 581 ff.
107 Ibid., 584.
108 Ibid., 586 ff.
109 Ibid., 581; see also his subsequent response to al-ʿAzm: idem., "Shakl," 910.
110 Idem., "Asbab," *al-Manar* 7/15: 585.

In response to al-Yafiʿi, Rafiq al-ʿAzm elaborates on why he considers the "mixing of politics with religion" (*mazj al-siyāsa bi-l-dīn*) to be the root cause of Muslim weakness. The exact wording of the article's title, "The Weakness of Muslims is Due to the Mixing of Politics with Religion"[111] seems to be taken from Rida's summary of al-Yafiʿi's critique of al-ʿAzm.[112] In that summary, Rida terminologically pinpointed the argument al-ʿAzm had made in his first article. Here, I will not summarize all the points in which al-ʿAzm found that al-Yafiʿi had misunderstood him, but rather focus on those aspects that add to or sharpen the views he laid out in the first article.

Al-ʿAzm begins his response by opposing two contemporaneous types of government: absolute and democratic. He lays the central blame for Muslim misery on the oppression (*istibdād*) of absolute governments (*al-ḥukūmāt al-muṭlaqa*) and repeats his historical argument that Islamic governments only evolved into this type of absolute government, rather than into the counter-type of democratic government (*al-ḥukūmāt al-dīmuqrāṭiyya*), due to the mixture of religion and politics.[113]

Al-ʿAzm stresses that his statement that "politics are distinct from religion" (*al-siyāsa ghayr al-dīn*) must not be misunderstood as calling "Muslims to abandon their religion or [as having asserted] that Islam is not suitable for the progress of society (*taraqqī al-umma*)."[114] He agrees with al-Yafiʿi that despotism would not have befallen the Islamic umma if the caliphs had adhered to the shariʿa. However, al-ʿAzm maintains, what really matters are the principles on which a state is built – above all, justice and the control of the government by the people. In the present, he argues, this basis is a constitution (*al-niẓām al-asāsī*), upon which democratic states and parliamentary governments are built. Pointing to the success of pagan Japan, al-ʿAzm refutes al-Yafiʿi's claim that political life is only sustainable when imbued by religion. However, al-ʿAzm stresses, this does not mean that religion ought to be given up completely. "By separating politics from religion (*faṣl al-siyāsa ʿan al-dīn*), I did not mean or intend to abandon the rules of religion and its teachings (*aḥkām al-dīn wa-taʿālīmahu*), but rather that the constitutions of states (*al-niẓāmāt al-asāsiyya li-l-duwal*) follow the public interest (*al-maṣlaḥa*), which is dependent upon rational investigation (*manūṭa bi-l-ijtihād*) and not an inseparable part of religion."[115]

111 Al-ʿAzm, "Daʿf."

112 Rashid Rida in al-Yafiʿi, "Asbab," *al-Manar* 7/14: 540.

113 Al-ʿAzm, "Daʿf," 660 f.

114 Ibid., 661.

115 Ibid., 663.

To substantiate this point historically – a point which he considers a truth established by both reason (*ʿaql*) and revelation (*sharʿ*) – al-ʿAzm summarizes the argument of his main historiographical work, *Ashhar al-Mashahir*, that the Prophet primarily conveyed a religious message, whereas the main tasks of his successors were of a worldly nature. Muhammad, like the prophets before him, brought a shariʿa. The successors of the Prophet were required to ensure the continuation of the worldly aspects of the shariʿa, which consist of rules ensuring security and rights. Concerning the religious task of laying down the bases (*uṣūl*) of the shariʿa, the Prophet did not have a successor. While Abu Bakr is a slight exception to this, since he was to lead Muslims in prayer, he also primarily acted as the leader of the first state (*dawla*) in Islam. As such, he was entrusted with implementing the worldly aspects of the shariʿa for a people that had gathered on a religious basis. It must be noted, al-ʿAzm stresses, that "the state is distinct from religion" (*al-dawla ghayr al-dīn*), and that there is no statement in the Islamic sources determining the basis of the state. Since the revelation (*sharʿ*) does not prescribe the form of government, it is up to Muslims to decide on the best form – which, for al-ʿAzm, is clearly that of a representative government (*al-ḥukūma al-niyābiyya*).[116]

In addition to this historical argument, al-ʿAzm adduces three other arguments. First, he draws on the well-known distinction between *ʿibādāt* and *muʿāmālat*, between religious and worldly matters. He conceives of this distinction in a manner that accords worldly matters great scope and freedom. The section of the revelation (*sharʿ*) pertaining to this world (*dunyā*), according to al-ʿAzm, comprises the communal interests of the nation (*maṣāliḥ al-umma al-ijtimāʿiyya*). It therefore makes no sense to him to consider politics or the state as religious matters, in which no rational inquiry (*ijtihād*) is allowed.[117] Second, as the early Muslims had no experience in ordered politics, they could offer no good advice to the Prophet in this matter.[118] Third, if politics and religion were inseparable, one could hardly explain the oppressive nature of Islamic rulers after the first three caliphs,[119] given that religion only desires the felicity of humankind.[120]

For al-ʿAzm, the combination of these arguments proves "that politics is different from religion (*al-siyāsa ghayr al-dīn*), that the foundation of the state (*taʾsīs al-dawla*) depends on the public interest (*maṣlaḥa*), which is determined

116 Ibid., 664.
117 Ibid., 664 f.
118 Ibid., 665.
119 In *Ashhar al-Mashahir*, al-ʿAzm evaluated the first three caliphs as representing a constitutional government; see: al-Batush, *Rafiq al-ʿAzm*, 58 ff.
120 Al-ʿAzm, "Daʿf," 665.

by the need (*ḥāja*) of Muslims, and that the companions of the Prophet (may God be content with them) did not manage to unite the political forces of the community (*kalimat al-umma al-siyāsiyya*) in such a way as the Prophet (peace be upon him) united its religious forces (*kalimatahā al-dīniyya*), because they failed to found the state on the basis of firm representative rule (*al-ḥukm al-niyābī*), by which the interests of the peoples (*shuʿūb*) are united, irrespective of their religious or political affiliation (*al-mashārib wa-l-aḥzāb*)."[121]

Since the principle of consultation (*shūrā*) is arguably beneficial for all peoples and endorsed by God himself, al-ʿAzm cannot understand why al-Yafiʿi criticized him for deploring the fact that the early caliphs did not adopt Roman legal-political principles – which, at the time, best embodied this universal principle of consultation. Whereas despotism became prevalent and even customary among Muslim peoples, the Western peoples who adhered to the principle of consultation progressed.[122] Calling on Muslims to adopt a democratic form of government embodied by the advanced nations is not to betray Muslims to foreign powers or to work against religion, al-ʿAzm insists, but rather to follow up on the indisputable fact attested to by God, the angels, and the Prophet – namely, that "Islam is most conducive of what is good and the greatest guide to the felicity of peoples (*umam*), irrespective of their creed."[123]

In a brief comment on this article, Rashid Rida notes that the readers of *al-Manar* know the journal's stance on this question well: as the Qurʾan laid down the basis of consultation (*asās al-shūrā*) but left the details of government to rational investigations, "politics from one perspective (*min jiha*) is religious (*dīniyya*), and from another is subject to rational investigation (*ijtihādiyya*)."[124]

The last contribution to this debate is another, rather conciliatory, response by al-Yafiʿi, entitled "The Form of Government in Islam,"[125] in which – many repetitive points aside – he elaborates on the fact that he shares al-ʿAzm's preference for a consultative, representative authority (*sulṭa shūriyya niyābiyya*),[126] but justifies this preference more strongly with Islamic sources. Al-Yafiʿi reiterates his main argument that the Islamic sources also address the question of political order, adding that the Rightly Guided Caliphs did not institutionalize a consultative government because they were occupied with preserving and spreading

121 Ibid., 665.
122 Ibid., 666 f.
123 Ibid., 667.
124 Ibid., 667.
125 Al-Yafiʿi, "Shakl."
126 Ibid., 901.

the Islamic religion.[127] Al-Yafi'i distinguishes three possible types of public authority (*al-sulṭa al-ʿāmma*): republican representative (*jumhūriyya niyābiyya*), constrained personal (*shakhṣiyya muqayyada*), and absolute personal (*shakhṣiyya muṭlaqa*).[128] He stresses that revelation (*sharʿ*) and reason (*ʿaql*) clearly prohibit the last type.[129] As arguably transpires from the Qur'an and the Sunna – which, according to al-Yafi'i, are not silent on the matter at all – either one of the first two types is possible or even preferable, depending on the circumstances.[130] According to the demands of the time, the Rightly Guided Caliphs represented a constrained personal authority, with the constraint consisting in consultation (*shūrā*).[131] Al-Yafi'i adduces several hadiths and Qur'anic verses that allegedly attest to the permissibility of a republican representative government as well.[132] While both religious law and reason contain insights concerning political life, al-Yafi'i is convinced that religion is the strongest basis for unity and cooperation, and that the political life of a supposedly pagan people – such as the Japanese – in the end also rests on a religious basis.[133] As al-Yafi'i deems the neglect of religious teachings to be the root cause of Muslims' weakness, it follows that he blames the 'ulama' for not preventing and even perpetuating corrupted teachings.[134] Fortunately, under the leadership of Muhammad 'Abduh, there have recently been attempts at reform (*iṣlāḥ*), al-Yafi'i points out; finally, he thanks Rafiq al-'Azm – whose statement about the separation of religion and politics had previously misled him into doubting al-'Azm's convictions – for his sincere investigation into such an important matter.[135]

At least as enlightening as al-Yafi'i's elaboration on his views is Rashid Rida's comment on this last article, in which he characterizes the debate between al-'Azm and al-Yafi'i as that between a contemporary viewpoint, distinguishing between religion and politics, and a classical Islamic viewpoint, which does not make this distinction. Rida stresses that al-'Azm's initiative was motivated by – and ought to be seen in the context of – recent attacks on Islam by foreigners, especially regarding its allegedly despotic form of government. Some 'ulama'

127 Ibid., 902.
128 Ibid., 903.
129 Ibid., 903 f.
130 Ibid., 904 f.
131 Ibid., 904.
132 Ibid., 906 f.
133 Ibid., 910.
134 Ibid., 911.
135 Ibid., 911 f.

have indeed been supporting such a government and have even made the masses believe that disobedience to any ruler amounts to unbelief. This also became possible, Rida suggests, on the premise that the shariʿa is silent on the matter, and thus does not constrain the political ruler. Rafiq al-ʿAzm – who, according to Rida, confronted these advocates of a despotic government and of blind obedience toward it – understands religion as the aspects of piety and worship (*al-qism al-taʿabbudī*) which are exclusively and comprehensively addressed by clear texts in the Qurʾan and the Sunna, and he considers the shariʿa as addressing the issue of government by foregrounding the principle of rational investigation (*li-l-ḥukūma aṣlan ijtihādiyyan fī al-sharīʿa*). Rida then contrasts al-ʿAzm's viewpoint with that of al-Yafiʿi: "His [i.e., al-ʿAzm's] argument (*kalām*) of leaving religion on one side [and politics on another] thus rests on (*mubnī ʿalā*) the difference (*farq*) between the purely religious section (*al-qism al-dīnī al-mahḍ*) and the purely worldly section (*al-qism al-dunyawī al-mahḍ*) of the shariʿa; and that is a recent usage (*iṣṭilāḥ ʿaṣrī*). Al-Yafiʿi's argument [in turn] rests on the [premise of] inseparability (*ʿidm al-tafriqa*); and that is the old Islamic usage (*al-iṣṭilāḥ al-islāmī al-qadīm*)."[136]

Rida stresses that he opened the pages of *al-Manar* to this debate in order to reveal the truth in this eminent question of governance. He points to a collection of hadiths concerning the matter, which he had published previously, and remarks that al-Yafiʿi has aptly revealed the root of the question, even though some of his arguments leave room for further debate.[137] Thus Rida does not clearly side with either of the two opponents, but tries to steer a middle course between two Islamic reformists, who already claim to represent a middle course themselves.

Instead of trying to pinpoint an Islamic reformist's view as either 'secular' or 'religious,' I take the foregoing debate as testimony to the permeability of the religious and the secular. Since they were already distinguished – also within an Islamic discourse – but not locked in firm opposition, this allowed Muslim intellectuals to rather easily shift between religious and secular perspectives.

One common aim shared by al-ʿAzm and al-Yafiʿi, and by Islamic reformists in general, was to disentangle an alleged core of religion from its historical manifestations and accumulated traditions. This basically amounts to the distinction between a supra-temporal, transcendent religious sphere and its contingent manifestations and other immanent spheres. However, transcendent religion

136 Ibid., 912.
137 Ibid., 912.

can become reentangled with history and politics when its supra-temporal teachings are posited as relevant for contingent historical and political affairs. Different thinkers may conceive of the scope of this transcendent religious realm quite differently – infusing it with politically relevant aspects, or not. Moreover, the relation between transcendent religion and immanent political life may also be understood quite differently. One may even question – in general, and not only pertaining to Islamic discourses – the extent to which the distinction between immanence and transcendence can be maintained. The combination of these considerations shows that there is a thin line – or rather, an underlying connection – between religious and secular Islamic viewpoints concerning the relation of religion and politics.

The distinction between a religious and a secular realm was demonstrated in Rafiq al-ʿAzm's updating of the distinction between religion and world (*dīn wa-dunyā*) to distinguish between religion and politics (*dīn wa-siyāsa*), thus allowing for the possibility of a non-religious foundation of politics. The unproblematic shift between a religious and a secular perspective within an Islamic discourse was most evident in the above handling of the concept of *shūrā*. This principle of consultation identified in the Qurʾan and the Sunna may either be taken to demand autonomous, rational investigation in matters of politics, or it may be used as a starting point for formulating an allegedly timeless, Islamic theory of political order. Whereas those opposed to disentangling religion and politics may discredit the first position as secular, its proponents often try to ground their views in Islamic sources. Hence, one can easily discern secular premises in the second position advocating an Islamic political order. The foregoing debate thus nicely illustrates that, once religion and politics or religion and the secular are distinguished, intellectuals may envision different and varying degrees and modes of their separation or connection. Muslim intellectuals can shift rather easily between a religious and a secular perspective within an Islamic discourse and – depending on their socio-political and intellectual contexts, their audience, and their aims – can tighten or loosen the connection between religion and politics or religion and the secular.

Indeed, four years earlier, Rafiq al-ʿAzm had foregrounded basic Islamic principles of government, as we shall see in the following section. And in an article on "The Islamic Government," published posthumously in 1926,[138] he tightened the connection between religion and politics. There, al-ʿAzm defines the ca-

---

138 Al-ʿAzm, "al-Hukuma." This article is part of the introduction to al-ʿAzm's work *Tarikh al-Siyasa al-Islamiyya*, of which, in fact, he only completed the introduction. It was also published in idem., *Majmuʿat.*

liphate or imamate as "general leadership (*riʾāsa ʿāmma*) in religion and the world, upon whose possessor has come the succession (*khilāfa*) of prophethood concerning the guardianship of religion (*ḥirāsat al-dīn*) and the governance of the world (*siyāsat al-dunyā*)."[139]

Here, we can only speculate as to why al-ʿAzm strengthened the connection between religion and politics in this undated article. He may possibly have followed al-Yafiʿi's conviction that religion is the best means of convincing the masses. Assuming that this incomplete article was written in the 1920s, the looming dissolution of the caliphate as a symbol of Muslim unity may have played a role. There was also a general trend in the 1920s and 1930s of somewhat secular-liberal Muslim authors, in Egypt and beyond, turning to Islam and expanding the scope of religion. In any case, I lack the space here to comprehensively work out al-ʿAzm's views concerning political order and its relation to religion, let alone the possible shifts his views underwent in this regard.[140] What is significant for the interests of this study in Arabic concepts of 'society' and their potential normative connotations is that the one regular contributor to *al-Manar* who by far most prominently used *mujtamaʿ* to convey the modern idea of society had already formulated a secularist Islamic position advocating the separation of religion and politics at the beginning of the twentieth century.

Indeed, in his articles from 1904 analyzed above, Rafiq al-ʿAzm advanced central arguments for an Islamic foundation of political secularism – which, twenty years later, ʿAli ʿAbd al-Raziq elaborated in his much-discussed book *Islam and the Foundations of Power*, which is commonly considered to be the first Islamic argument for secularism.[141] ʿAbd al-Raziq not only elaborated this secularist viewpoint more fully, but – in comparison with al-ʿAzm's primarily historiographical and sociological approach – also argued more strongly based on theological premises and by employing Qurʾanic verses and hadiths. However, both al-ʿAzm and ʿAbd al-Raziq maintain that the Prophet essentially conveyed a religious message, whereas his successors were political rulers. Moreover, both consider the mixture of religion and politics as the root cause of contemporary Muslim weakness and argue for the adoption of a democratic government. The similarities between al-ʿAzm's and ʿAbd al-Raziq's arguments were also apparent to Basim al-Batush, who finds that our Islamic historian still retained a certain connection between religion and politics in Islam, whereas the Azhari theologian

139 Idem., "al-Hukuma," 513.

140 Al-Batush also refers to divergent statements by al-ʿAzm concerning the relation of religion and politics. However, he offers no interpretation of or explanation for this divergence (al-Batush, *Rafiq al-ʿAzm*, 65–68).

141 See above: 135f., 172f.

completely denied such a connection.[142] One could again object that ʿAbd al-Raziq viewed Muhammad as a political leader, too, but considered his political activities as mere means for spreading religion. ʿAbd al-Raziq also more specifically argued against the obligatory nature of the caliphate, because the institution had been abandoned a year before he published his work, and prominent activists and intellectuals – not least Rashid Rida – demanded its resurrection. In this context, ʿAbd al-Raziq did not deny the social or economic relevance of Islamic teachings, but more specifically argued against their political relevance. The spheres of society, politics, and economics were not yet as clearly distinguished in al-ʿAzm's writings, although he also tended to argue against the political relevance of Islamic teachings, but in favor of their societal relevance – as we will see in the following two sections.

3 *Al-Durus al-Hikamiyya:* An Anthropological and Sociological Argument for Society, Religion, and Government

This book, published in 1900, is based on lessons Rafiq al-ʿAzm gave to students of the Ottoman School (al-Madrasa al-ʿUthmaniyya) in Cairo. For al-Batush, these lectures prove al-ʿAzm's focus on education as a means of reform and his efforts in this regard.[143] In his biography of al-ʿAzm, Rashid Rida writes that "as a recommendation of this work it suffices to mention that [Muhammad ʿAbduh] decided to teach it in the schools of the Islamic Benevolent Society."[144] The seventh of these lessons, arguing for the necessity of religion for society, was reprinted in *al-Manar.*[145] Ten years after the original publication,[146] a reprint of the book was published in Damascus.[147] In a revised edition published by the Saudi Arabian Ministry of Education in 1988,[148] the editor not only updated

142 Al-Batush, *Rafiq al-ʿAzm*, 68 f.

143 Ibid., 51.

144 Rida, "Rafiq al-ʿAzm," 297.

145 Al-ʿAzm, Rafiq. 1899. "Kitab al-Durus al-Hikmiyya li-l-Nashiʾa al-Islamiyya." *al-Manar* 2/15: 225–227.

146 Idem., *al-Durus* [1899/1900].

147 Idem. 1328 h [1911/1912]. *al-Durus al-Hikamiyya li-l-Nashiʾa al-Islamiyya.* Damascus: al-Matbaʿa al-Wataniyya.

148 Idem. 1988. *al-Durus al-Hikamiyya li-l-Nashiʾa al-Islamiyya*; ed. Mahmud Radawi. al-Saʿudiyya: Jamiʿat al-Imam Muhammad Bin Saʿud al-Islamiyya/Idarat al-Thaqafa wa-l-Nashr.

some of the terms,[149] but also significantly altered certain statements by al-ʿAzm – apparently not least in order to replace immanent with transcendent premises[150] and to suppress democratic sentiments[151]. Below, I refer to some of the differences between this revised edition and the original edition from 1900, which forms the basis of my analysis.

In the preface, al-ʿAzm states that the goal of his lessons was to elucidate the true teachings of the Islamic religion, which he approaches from a rather clearly utilitarian perspective that analyzes religion based on the requirements of society. Al-ʿAzm begins by referring to some central arguments he made in *al-Muʾayyad* and *al-Manar* concerning the requirement for and means of social reform, among them the acquisition of practical knowledge, the institution of rights, and the principle of mutual solidarity (*al-takāful al-ʿāmm*).[152] Al-ʿAzm then explains that he chose (*ikhtartu*) the means of religion (*ṭarīq al-dīn*) for reform,

> "because on it was erected the Islamic glory (*al-majd al-islāmī*) and its civilization (*madaniyyatuhu*); on it were founded the pillars (*daʿāʾim*) of the great states in Islam (*al-duwal al-ʿaẓīma fī al-islām*); and on it the Islamic nation (*al-umma al-islāmiyya*) spread into the cultured corners of the earth (*manāḥī al-ʿumrān*). So [the Islamic nation's] weakness and strength correspond to the weakness and strength of its religion, and this in contrast to the other societies (*al-umam al-ukhrā*) which were erected with respect to something other than religion (*min jiha ghayr jihat al-dīn*)."[153]

One may remark here that European intellectuals also could and did stress the religious basis of civilization; more significant, however, is the way in which al-ʿAzm conceives of religion here.

For him, the Islamic religion has and shall again serve as the basis of Islamic society and civilization, because "the Islamic shariʿa set forth the bases of those excellent qualities (*uṣūl al-faḍāʾil*) on which depends the progress of Islamic so-

149 As is explicated in the preface: ibid., 6.

150 Compare, for example, page 10 in the original with page 13 in the Saudi Arabian revised edition.

151 Compare, for example, page 27 in the original with page 35 in the Saudi Arabian revised edition.

152 Al-ʿAzm, *al-Durus* [1327 h.], 3 ff.; for an article in which al-ʿAzm centrally employs the concept of *al-takāful al-ʿāmm*, see above: 215–220. The concept also figures prominently in al-ʿAzm, *Tanbih*, which will be presented in the following section.

153 Al-ʿAzm, *al-Durus* [1327 h.], 5.

ciety (*taraqqī al-mujtama' al-islāmī*), especially the appeal to reason (*'aql*) and the incitement to work (*'amal*), liberty (*ḥurriyya*), and knowledge (*'ilm*), among others."[154] Other peoples could only achieve these qualities through force, al-'Azm maintains. Here, he is seemingly referring to European societies allegedly having had to fight for these assets against the obstruction of Christian religion. Since, for al-'Azm, intellectual and political freedom were instituted by the Islamic religion and shari'a, Muslim youth ought to be taught the true Islamic teachings, which are the most promising means for societal reform. For al-'Azm, religion was mainly about society, and Islamic teachings were mainly societal teachings – keeping in mind that, in the intellectual setting in which al-'Azm operated, religion and the secular, a religious and a societal perspective, were distinguished but not locked in firm opposition. While al-'Azm most clearly constructs Islam as (a principle of) social order in *Tanbih al-Afham*, which will be presented in the following section, in *al-Durus al-Hikamiyya* – in a certain sense – he lays the basis for this construction by according epistemological primacy to human society.

The centrality of society – for the realization of which religion and the state are means – is already apparent in the structure of *al-Durus al-Hikamiyya*, which consists of three parts, each dealing with different aspects of social association and human society (*al-ijtimā'*): its foundations (*mabādi*), its bonds (*rawābiṭ*), and its constituents (*muqawwimāt*). The following overview of the individual chapters helps us understand al-'Azm's line of argument and the premises upon which he bases his exhortation to acquire knowledge and to put it to practical use for the sake of society and the nation.

In the first part, comprising four chapters or "lessons," al-'Azm starts from the anthropological premise that human beings were created to be physically weaker than the animals (1) and were therefore endowed with the capacity for reason (2) and a social nature (3). He then suggests (4) that human beings are perfected by accepting the teachings of revealed religion, both for themselves and as the basis for their society.

The second part, which is divided into seven lessons, addresses the bonds of society: al-'Azm elaborates on the need for religion (5), the unity it creates (6), and the obligatory knowledge of it (7). He then turns to society's need for a government (8), which is addressed in the Islamic sources (9). A crucial quality of society and the government is that of justice (*'adl*), as is also attested by Islamic sources (10), and al-'Azm names equal treatment under the law and godly rulings as the first level of justice (11).

---

154 Ibid., 5.

Based on the religiously supported anthropological and sociological premises and arguments of the first two parts, in the third and longest part, al-ʿAzm develops sixteen lessons on the assets and constituents of (modern) society, as he envisions it. For him, the second level of justice consists of liberty (*ḥurriyya*) and legal equality between all members of society, irrespective of religious affiliation (12). Al-ʿAzm further defines liberty (13), and compares Islamic and Western conceptions of it (14), before attending to the third level of justice, which amounts to fairness and equality not only before the law, but also in social interactions (15). The following lessons are then dedicated to specific virtues and vices of social behavior, namely hypocrisy (16), treachery and falsification (17), endurance and patience (18), and self-confidence (19, 20). Al-ʿAzm subsequently elaborates on the need to acquire knowledge (21) and the need for knowledge to manifest itself in practice (22). In order to be put to good use, intellectual education and knowledge must be complemented with moral education (23) and the cultivation of morals and virtues (24). For al-ʿAzm, attachment to the homeland (*waṭan*) is a foremost virtue and a part of belief (25). Relatedly, attachment to one's fellow citizens is necessary to ensure cooperation and unity and to thereby achieve societal progress and national strength (26). In the conclusion, al-ʿAzm calls on Muslims to actively contribute their individual efforts to the life of society and the strength of the nation.

Al-ʿAzm's aim and line of argument becomes quite apparent here: the construction of a proper society and the individual's contribution to a strong nation hinges on knowledge, moral virtues, and political rights, the necessary acquisition and implementation of which follow from the creation of humankind as physically weak but rational beings in need of social association. Based on this anthropological and sociological premise, al-ʿAzm upholds the necessity for religion and government, as we have seen in the above summary of his preface. I shall now refine this reading of al-ʿAzm as representing a societal perspective on religion and the state by demonstrating (a) which socio-political collectivity he addressed, (b) where the Qurʾan or God enter into his argumentation, (c) how he actually conceives of *dīn*, (d) how he argues for the necessity of a government, (e) which Islamic principles of government he highlights, and (f) how he contrasts Islamic and Western conceptions of liberty.

(a) While al-ʿAzm presents this book in its title as lessons for "Islamic youth"[155] and repeatedly addresses "the Islamic umma" as a whole, Muslims still ought to realize their actual social and political order in their respective homelands (*waṭan*), and this together with their non-Muslim compatriots. In

155 In his conclusion, he calls upon the "Eastern youth (*al-shabība al-sharqiyya*)" (ibid., 90).

line with the credo that "homeland is part of belief" (*al-waṭan min al-īmān*), al-'Azm displays an affinity for both his religious community (*milla*) and his homeland.[156] He does not even see the need to address a possible contradiction between the two, as later proponents of a supra-national Islamic political order would do. (Substantial passages in which al-ʿAzm stresses the love for one's homeland have been cut from the revised edition published in 1988.[157]) For al-'Azm, both religious and patriotic sentiments may instill the desired unity and active cooperation between members of society.[158] Moreover, he stresses absolute legal equality and the need for cooperation between Muslim and non-Muslim members of one country (*abnāʾ al-waṭan al-wāḥid*).[159] And while al-ʿAzm nowhere addresses the possibility of Muslims being excluded from the community of believers on theological grounds, citing a hadith condemning corruption,[160] he does consider this possibility for those who deviate from the necessary course in societal transactions.

(b) As with the above-mentioned hadith, al-ʿAzm also cites Qurʾanic verses, which stand at the beginning of every lesson and are occasionally inserted throughout, either to illustrate arguments he had already made or to provide a starting point for societal arguments, which then markedly depart from this starting point. Take the following example from lesson 22, on the need for knowledge to entail action and the need for both to be balanced in nations and societies:

"Know that knowledge is the balance (*mīzān*) by which the forces of the peoples competing (*al-shuʿūb al-mutanāziʿa*) in the arena of civilizational life (*miḍmār al-ḥayāt al-madaniyya*) are leveled, as long as the practice of knowledge (*al-ʿamal bi-hi*) is also reciprocal (*mutabādal*) between the two competitors (*al-mutanāziʿayn*). Whenever one of them suspends its duty [to put knowledge to practice] and the other continues it, the second necessarily surpasses the first, contests its survival (*nāzaʿahu al-biqāʾ*),[161] and conquers it. Thus the reminder was sent in the word of God: "Indeed, We send forth Our apostles with all evidence of truth; and through them We bestowed revelation from on high, and [thus gave you] a balance (*mīzān*), so that men might behave with equity (*qisṭ*)."[162] This

156 Ibid., 8.

157 Compare pages 83 ff. in the original with pages 104 ff. in the Saudi Arabian revised edition.

158 Most pertinently: al-ʿAzm, *al-Durus* [1327 h.], 81, 86 f.

159 Ibid., 38, see also 39.

160 Ibid., 51.

161 This wording refers to the Darwinist "struggle for existence (*tanāzuʿ al-biqāʾ*)," mentioned also at the very end of this quotation.

162 Parts of Qurʾan 57:25; translation based on Asad, *The Message*.

means that [He has sent them] with justice preventing (*al-ʿadl al-māniʿ*) the struggle between people (*al-nās*), which leads to the weakness of societies (*al-mujtamaʿāt*) and to their perdition (*fanāʾ*). And whenever the people practice fairness (*qisṭ*) by laying all deeds on the scale of the revealed law (*sharʿ*), which is tantamount to the Book guiding the knowledge of human beings' worldly and otherworldly interests (*maṣāliḥ al-insān al-dunyawiyya wa-l-ukhrawiyya*), and when the people practice fairness and counter-balance each other on the scale of works in the interests of their societal life (*maṣāliḥ ḥayātihim al-ijtimāʿiyya*), then every group (*farīq*) of them is safe from the dangers pertaining to the struggle of existence (*tanāzuʿ al-biqāʾ*)."[163]

While the equation of revealed law and religion with human beings' worldly and otherworldly interests will be further examined as aspect of (c), here we note that al-ʿAzm uses a Qurʾanic verse in a purely illustrative manner to support his argument for just and balanced dealings between nations and societies. Clearly, he is thinking of the dominant European nations, and he calls upon his fellow Muslims and compatriots to actively contribute to the strength of their societies and nations so as to balance out the strength of the Europeans. Concerning questions of social and political order, for al-ʿAzm, the Qurʾan functions as a rather abstract guide and a resource for supporting his anthropological and sociological premises or his historical and empirical arguments, and it does not provide a particular socio-political order.[164]

Furthermore, in al-ʿAzm's depiction, God is shifted into the background of inner-worldly events. Al-ʿAzm does mention that it was He who united the peoples;[165] however, this must be read as stressing the societal value of revelation over against claims to the contrary. And when he maintains that human beings were guided by godly revelations (*al-sharāʾiʿ al-ilāhiyya*) to discern the secrets of creation,[166] it is important to note that these revelations are basically equated with calls to employ reason, based on al-ʿAzm's use of premises and arguments. Human beings, whom God endowed with reason, have, with the progress of time and reason, increasingly been able to autonomously discern inner-worldly laws. Significantly, al-ʿAzm attributes this progress to the course of immanent history,

163 Al-ʿAzm, *al-Durus* [1327 h.], 73f.
164 Where al-ʿAzm spoke of the Qurʾan as the guide (*murshid*) of the umma, the Saudi Arabian revised edition notably replaces *murshid* with *dustūr* (constitution). Compare page 67 in the original with page 87 in the revised edition.
165 Al-ʿAzm, *al-Durus* [1327 h.], 20.
166 Ibid., 16.

rather than to continuous godly interventions.[167] However, God did send prophets as a reminder, since human beings sometimes forgot to properly employ the reason God bestowed on them.[168] The prophets always addressed a people according to their readiness, which progressed with time, so that Muhammad – as the last prophet – came to address humankind in purely rational terms, guiding them in the discernment of the natural laws of existence.[169] Al-ʿAzm clearly shares an evolutionist view of religion and the understanding of Islam as the religion of reason,[170] as most prominently formulated in ʿAbduh's *Risalat al-Tawhid.* God, in al-ʿAzm's view, created the world with its autonomous, stable laws and bestowed reason on human beings, who subsequently ought to rationally discern these inner-worldly laws and act accordingly, also in the construction of their social and political orders.

(c) While al-ʿAzm upholds the need for godly revelations (*sharāʾiʿ*) based on his view of revelation as a call to employ reason, he maintains society's need for religion (*dīn*) based on his view that religion constitutes social solidarity and is basically tantamount to public interest. In the background of al-ʿAzm's assertions, one hears echoes of secularist views of religion as an obstacle to the proper functioning and progress of society. Al-ʿAzm asserts that "the need of mankind for religion is like the need of the body for food," and that religion has been "the educator (*murabbī*) of man and the guide of peoples (*umam*) to the ways of civilization (*ṭuruq al-madaniyya*), and this since the formation of human collectivities (*jamʿiyyāt al-bashar*)."[171] Significantly, the positive value and function of religion is not due to its representing otherworldly insights otherwise unattainable by human beings. On the contrary, in a circular argument, al-ʿAzm, basically equates religion with humankind's social interests: religion is the primary bond (*rābiṭa*) of social association (*ijtimāʿ*), he writes, "because it is the basis (*asās*) of welfare (*al-khayr*), which rests on the public interest (*al-maṣlaḥa al-ʿāmma*)."[172] For al-ʿAzm, the benefits of revealed laws (*sharāʾiʿ*) consequently result from their mirroring the interests of humankind (*maṣāliḥ*

---

167 The Saudi Arabian revised edition tellingly replaces "time and reason" with "God and prophets" (compare page 10 in the original with page 12f. in the revised edition).

168 Al-ʿAzm, *al-Durus* [1327 h.], 62f.

169 Ibid., 63, 20f.

170 While the definition of Islam as *dīn al-ʿaql* is present in other writings by al-ʿAzm but absent in *al-Durus*, here, too, this understanding is clearly given, and Islam is even equated with intellectual liberty, as shown below.

171 Ibid., 17.

172 Ibid., 17.

al-bashar).[173] For al-ʿAzm, society's need for religion is demonstrated precisely in the alleged fact that peoples without a revealed religion, or those who have abandoned it, have had to invent a positive religion (*dīn waḍʿī*).[174] The possible substitution of man-made religion in place of revealed religion shows al-ʿAzm's functionalist view of religion from a societal perspective.

While Islam is the true religion in al-ʿAzm's view, he does not address belief in the one true God as ensuring otherworldly salvation, but rather as ensuring inner-worldly social solidarity. Nevertheless, there is a difference between al-ʿAzm's view and a purely sociological, Durkheimian perspective on religion – although possibly only in terms of emphasis. Al-ʿAzm does not suggest that human beings have produced religion for the sake of social solidarity, but rather that the real existing God himself has instituted the community of believers and has, via his revealed religion, effected social solidarity. Al-ʿAzm stresses the need to preserve this solidarity, since it is a requirement for social order and political strength. With this aim in mind, he highlights obedience (*ṭāʿa*) to God, his Prophet, and the rulers (*ulū al-amr*) as the one aspect of "obligatory knowledge of religion."[175] This stress on obedience does not contradict al-ʿAzm's societal and somewhat secular take on religion: the God to be obeyed is a just God, Muhammad did bring a rational message, and the rulers are bound by the just and rational religious laws, which mirror social interests.

(d) Before elucidating this last aspect as part of al-ʿAzm's conception of an Islamic government, it helps to briefly note that, as with religion, al-ʿAzm argues for the necessity of a government based on the requirements of society. After lessons five through seven established society's need for religion, the eighth lesson on "the necessity of government for social association (*ijtimāʿ*)" begins as follows: "Since you now have learnt the requirement (*luzūm*) of society (*ijtimāʿ*) for religion, you must also learn that power (*mulk*) is equally a requirement of religion and society (*al-dīn wa-l-ijtimāʿ*). For this reason it is mentioned in the hadith of the Prophet: 'Islam and power (*sulṭān*) are like twins.' And this in accordance with what has been explained before, namely that the interests of mankind (*maṣāliḥ al-bashar*) can only be realized in society (*ijtimāʿ*)."[176] As stated under (b) above, the hadith here serves to illustrate an argument al-ʿAzm makes based on assumptions about the nature of human society. His assumption is that strife and competition (*munāzaʿāt*) naturally occur in human society.[177]

173 Ibid., 18.
174 Ibid., 17, 19.
175 Ibid., 22ff.
176 Ibid., 25.
177 Ibid., 25.

This contains the danger of the strong eating the weak, which produces an imbalance in the order of societies (*niẓām al-mujtamaʿāt*), leading to their corruption and destruction.[178] In order to maintain social balance, the natural rivalries within society have to be controlled by a power that implements just laws.

Therefore, when God revealed his just laws, which mirrored human interests, he also tasked prophets, Muhammad's successors (*khulafāʾ*), and the leaders of the community (*aʾima*) with protecting and implementing these laws – today, this task is to be fulfilled by the government:

"governments (*ḥukūmāt*) are necessary (*ḍarūriyya*) for mankind, and there is no sustenance for a society (*qiwām li-umma*) or life for a people (*ḥayāt li-shaʿb*) except through a government or ruler (*sulṭān*). The government's concern is to protect the laws (*al-sharāʾiʿ wa-l-qawānīn*) and to apply them so as to regulate (*tartīb*) the livelihood of the people (*maʿīshat al-shaʿb*) and the order of society (*niẓām al-umma*); and [its concern is] to consider all other interests (*sāʾir al-maṣāliḥ*) which entail good for the governed body (*al-hayʾa al-maḥkūma*) and keep evil away from it."[179]

Next to regulating the internal affairs of society, the government is also responsible for relations with neighboring nations.[180] As the best form of government, al-ʿAzm here names the moderate constitutional type (*al-nawʿ al-dustūrī al-muʿtadil*), representing a middle way between the extremes of an absolute (*al-istibdādī al-muṭlaq*) and a republican (*jumhūrī*) government.[181]

(e) For al-ʿAzm, legislation is the essential means by which the ideal government ensures justice and liberty – the very principles established by Islam in this regard. Al-ʿAzm defines the government as a group (*jamāʿa*) from among the people (*al-shaʿb*) who do not differ from the rest of the people, except in their role as the custodians (*qawwām*) of godly or man-made law (*al-sharīʿa aw al-qānūn*).[182] Al-ʿAzm stresses the need for laws to be just, whether they are conceived of as religious or as positive laws. Notice his shifting terminology in the following statement: "The governors must comply with revelation (*sharʿ*), as this enables them to implement the commands of the religious law (*sharīʿa*) and to control the order of society (*tanẓīm niẓām al-umma*) by stopping individuals from vying with each other (*al-nufūs al-mutaghāliba*) through the limits set

178 Ibid., 26.
179 Ibid., 26 f.
180 Ibid., 27.
181 Ibid., 27.
182 Ibid., 28.

by the law (*ḥadd al-qānūn*), which [i.e., the *qānūn*] is the bulwark (*siyāj*) of societies (*mujtamaʿāt*) and the anchor of the social peace (*rāḥa*) of peoples (*shuʿūb*)."[183] One may discern a possible distinction between the shariʿa as the underlying principles and the *qānūn* as the concrete implementation of these principles. Al-ʿAzm might thereby safeguard the basic principles of justice and liberty by relegating them to the timeless realm of the shariʿa revealed by God: since history has shown, and the laws of social association (*sunan al-ijtimāʿ*) have determined, that absolute rule is destructive for societies, Islam has firmly established the principles of justice (*ʿadl*), intellectual independence (*al-istiqlāl al-ʿaqlī*), and freedom of conscience (*ḥurriyyat al-ḍamāʾir*) in its shariʿa.[184]

Al-ʿAzm illustrates the fundamental dimension of the principle of justice – as embodied by and even equated with Islam – when he depicts the peoples prior to the advent of Islam as in the grips of "the satan of absolute rule" (*shayṭān al-istibdād*).[185] Muhammad brought a shariʿa that established absolute equality between human beings, except in degree of piety, and gave reason its proper right to absolute independence (*al-istiqlāl al-muṭlaq*).[186] Thus the spirit of justice was instituted – a spirit which is suggested to equal the spirit of Islam, and which is fundamental to the workings of society and the strength of the nation:

"States (*duwal*) were not erected, the shelters of cultured life (*ẓilāl al-ʿumrān*) did not extend, the forces of the peoples (*shuʿūb*) were not united, and the bonds of society (*ʿurā al-ijtimāʿ*) were not consolidated, except through justice. Therefore, justice (*ʿadl*) is the spirit (*rūḥ*) and societies (*umam*) are the body (*juthmān*), and whenever this spirit departs that body, it is dissolved and its parts are diffused in the open space (*taṭayyarat fī al-faḍāʾ*), and its name is effaced from the world of human society (*ʿālam al-ijtimāʿ*)."[187]

The strength of the states of Islam (*duwal al-islām*) thus resulted from unity and obedience to just rulers, who complied with and ensured the principle of justice, as established by the Islamic shariʿa.[188] To prevent manipulation of the laws (by the rulers), the Qurʾan moreover decreed the principle of mutual solidarity (*al-ta-*

183 Ibid., 28.
184 Ibid., 29f.
185 Ibid., 31.
186 Ibid., 32.
187 Ibid., 34.
188 Ibid., 35f.

kāful al-ʿāmm). "This," al-ʿAzm maintains, "is Islam, and this is the right religion (*al-dīn al-qayyim*) which God decreed (*sharaʿahu*) for the people."[189]

(f) While al-ʿAzm basically equates Islam as "the right religion" with the principle of mutual solidarity – the implementation of which he considers crucial for the functioning of society – he also validates as Islamic a certain view of the natural and thus universal right to liberty (*ḥurriyya*), and he contrasts this view with the alleged Western understanding. Al-ʿAzm defines *ḥurriyya* as "independence of reason (*istiqlāl al-ʿaql*) and liberty of man (*inṭilāq al-insān*) from the chains of absolute subjugation."[190] Relatedly, he distinguishes between public and personal liberty (*al-ḥurriyya al-ʿumūmiyya/al-shakhṣiyya*). The first concerns the rights of the people with respect to the government. He considers these rights a prerequisite for progress and civilization and suggests that they were realized in early Islam and are now realized in Europe.[191] As concrete examples of personal liberty, al-ʿAzm names three of the six *maqāṣid* of classical Islamic legal theory[192] – namely, the protection of a person's life (*nafs*), of honor (*ʿirḍ*), and of property (*māl*). He notably adds to these man's (*al-insān*) "other personal rights which the nature of human society (*ṭabīʿat al-ijtimāʿ*) granted (*yakhūluhu*) to him in view of his being a working member in it [i.e., in human society]."[193] In this age, however, some Western proponents of a new understanding of liberty (*al-ḥurriyya al-jadīda*) have extended this natural right in a way that contradicts the balance (*al-ʿadl*) in the Islamic conception of liberty (*al-ḥurriyya al-islāmiyya*).[194] In contrast to Islam's measured and just application of liberty, the mistaken Western understanding of liberty – according to al-ʿAzm – facilitates the spread of moral vices[195] and excessive political protest,[196] and at the same time produces inequality between the members of a society and between different peoples.

Liberty is the one socio-political concept concerning which al-ʿAzm compares Islamic and Western understandings in *al-Durus*. His ideal Islamic conception of liberty is closely related (and somewhat subordinated) to the primary concept of *ʿadl*, which refers to both legal and socio-political justice, balance, and

189 Ibid., 36.

190 Ibid., 43.

191 Ibid., 40 f.

192 See above: 171. Honor is a sixth goal added by some theorists, while most only name five goals.

193 Al-ʿAzm, *al-Durus* [1327 h.], 41.

194 Ibid., 41.

195 Ibid., 41 f.

196 Ibid., 44.

equity and connotes a reasonable and measured course. The principle of *ʿadl* also reigns supreme when it comes to societal behavior, dealings, and affairs (*muʿāmalāt*), which al-ʿAzm addresses in lessons fifteen through twenty-four. These lessons can be read in part as advancing an Islamic conception of social order, insofar as al-ʿAzm connects Islamically grounded moral virtues – such as trust or honesty – to the proper arrangement and strength of society or civil life.[197]

More overtly than in *al-Durus al-Hikamiyya*, however, in *Tanbih al-Afham* al-ʿAzm constructs Islam as response to contemporary questions of society and social order and compares his Islamic construction with European responses to these questions.

4 *Tanbih al-Afham:* Islam as (a Solution to the Problem of) Social Order

The book *Tanbih al-Afham ila Matalib al-Hayat al-Ijtimaʿiyya wa-l-Islam* (*Alerting Intellects to the Demands of Societal Life and Islam*)[198] originated from five articles Rafiq al-ʿAzm published in the journal *al-Mawsuʿat*,[199] which appeared in Cairo between 1898 and 1901.[200] To these articles, which had "elucidated some characteristics of this religion that were the reason for the advancement of Muslims,"[201] al-ʿAzm added another four "articles" investigating the reasons for the alleged subsequent decline of Islamic civilization and society. Foremost among these reasons, which we must not dwell on again here,[202] are political and subsequently religious strife;[203] the imbrication of religious leaders and political

197 For example: ibid., 48, 50.

198 Idem., *Tanbih*.

199 Those articles were entitled "Matalib al-Hayat al-Ijtimaʿiyya wa-l-Islam" (ibid., 2). Pellitteri gives the following page numbers: *al-Mawsuʿat* (1899–1900) 2/6: 161–166, 2/7: 193–198, 2/8: 225–232, 2/12: 353–357 (Pellitteri, *Islam*, 105).

200 This time span is given by: https://www.zmo.de/jaraid/ (accessed March 22, 2016), which names as owners and editors Ahmad Hafiz ʿAwad and Mahmud Abu al-Nasr. Another source, which depicts *al-Mawsuʿat* as a "scientific journal (*majalla ʿilmiyya*)," adds the name of the Egyptian nationalist leader Muhammad Farid (1868–1919) to its founders (al-Saʿid, Rifʿat. 2003. *al-Zuʿamat al-Siyasiyya al-Misriyya*. Cairo: Akhbar al-Yawm, 32).

201 Al-ʿAzm, *Tanbih*, 2.

202 Negligible nuances aside, al-ʿAzm's sketch of Islamic history here conforms with the one presented in chapter 9 section 2.

203 Ibid., esp. 42, 57.

rule;[204] the introduction of harmful innovations (*bidaʿ*),[205] blind imitation (*taqlīd*), and stagnation (*jumūd*);[206] and the neglect and corruption of Islamic morals and teachings in general.[207] In order to remedy their present misery and bring back their previous strength, Muslims ought to recall the true teachings and principles of the Islamic religion, which al-ʿAzm here – even more strongly than in *al-Durus al-Hikamiyya* – equates with reason, justice, moderation, and human interests.

Moreover, al-ʿAzm clearly distinguishes between a worldly and an otherworldly,[208] a societal and a spiritual dimension of Islam. While he calls upon the ʿulamaʾ to once again take up their duty of *ijtihād* and to reform religious teachings,[209] al-ʿAzm himself is interested in the worldly and societal teachings discernible from Islamic sources, which he refers to selectively to support his aim of solving the modern problem of social order. It thus transpires, I argue, that al-ʿAzm considers personal faith in the true God as constituent for Islamic social collectivities but relegates the religious teachings of Islam to the ʿulamaʾ, while he himself approaches the Qur'an as a text about society and reconstructs Islam as a socio-economic order.

Rashid Rida announced the book, of which a Turkish translation appeared in 1906,[210] in volume four of *al-Manar*, positing that the book's title already demonstrates the eminence of its subject and the benefits of this study, especially for those interested in Islamic civilization (*al-madaniyya al-islāmiyya*) and its relation to Western civilization (*al-madaniyya al-gharbiyya*).[211] Rida's framing illustrates the close connection between questions of social order and civilization at that time: here, in fact, *madaniyya* could well be rendered as 'civil order' instead of 'civilization.' Rafiq al-ʿAzm himself also connects his arguments to the reigning paradigm of civilization. However, the starting point and overarching problem of this book is clearly "the social question" (*al-masʾala al-ijtimāʿiyya*), under which he subsumes discussions of the Islamic religion and civilization. While Muslim intellectuals had already turned to social topics earlier in the util-

204 Ibid., esp. 58.
205 Ibid., esp. 37, 44 f., 57, 64.
206 Ibid,, esp. 44 f., 58.
207 Ibid., esp. 41–57.
208 Ibid., esp. 56, 66 f.
209 Ibid., esp. 34, 65, 67 f., 71 f.
210 Idem. 1324 h [1906]. *Qıwam-i Islam: Tanbih al-Afham ila Matalib al-Hayat al-Ijtimaʿiyya wa-l-Islam*; transl. Izmirli Hocazade Mehmed Ubeydallah. Cairo: n.g.
211 Rida, Rashid. 1901. "al-Hadaya wa-l-Taqariz." *al-Manar* 4/3: 105–108, here 107.

itarian age of progress, Rafiq al-ʿAzm might have been the first to explicitly formulate an Islamic response to "the social question."

The social question primarily concerned the proper societal distribution of work and economic resources and, according to al-ʿAzm, manifested itself most forcefully in European societies, due to their being the most advanced and thus most resourceful and complex societies. Following the anthropological and evolutionist premises he established in *al-Durus al-Hikamiyya*, al-ʿAzm asserts that, in the beginning, the means of livelihood (*maʿīsha*) were very basic, in accordance with the basic state of social association (*ijtimāʿ*). With the advancement of society (*ijtimāʿ*) and civilization (*madaniyya*), societal needs (*al-ḥājāt al-ijtimāʿiyya*) necessarily increased.[212] This is problematic insofar as different social groups (*ṭabaqāt al-nās*) disagree about how to arrange and satisfy these needs and are thus unable to attain the goal of social life – that is, felicity. Due to their weak position in society (*al-hayʾa al-ijtimāʿiyya*), it is especially the poor factions of society (*al-ṭabaqāt al-nāzila*)[213] that have to suffer. Their misery, however, amounts to the derangement (*tashwīsh*) of the overall order of society (*niẓām al-ijtimāʿ*). This vexed problem (*ʿuqda*) manifests itself in Europe in his time, and the scholars of civilization (*ʿulamāʾ al-ʿumrān*) have been addressing it as "the social question (*al-masʾala al-ijtimāʿiyya*) or the question of the workers' misery (*masʾalat shaqāʾ al-ʿummāl*)."[214] Al-ʿAzm explains that what these scholars and contemporary philosophers have been calling "the social question," he addresses as "the demands (*maṭālib*) of societal life (*al-ḥayāt al-ijtimāʿiyya*)."[215]

According to al-ʿAzm, European societies fail to satisfy these demands because their rival schools of thought all focus on only one of the problems of societal life, to the exclusion of the others. To the socialists (*al-ishtirākiyūn*), the problem consists in the rich absorbing all property and wealth (*māl, tharwa*). To solve this problem, they suggest that the government should distribute wealth equally among the people.[216] While the socialists aim to gain government power by first convincing the majority of the people, the anarchists (*al-fawḍiyūn*), who share the socialists' basic doctrines, favor revolutionary means. Nihilists (*al-ʿadamiyūn*), as another group briefly mentioned, think that the felicity of the whole (*saʿādat al-kull*) lies in the negation of the whole (*ʿadam al-kull*). The re-

---

212 Al-ʿAzm, *Tanbih*, 3.
213 Al-Batush explains that by "*al-ṭabaqa al-nāzila*" al-ʿAzm meant "the poor societal groups (*al-fiʾāt al-ijtimāʿiyya al-faqīra*)" (al-Batush, *Rafiq al-ʿAzm*, 39fn*).
214 Al-ʿAzm, *Tanbih*, 4.
215 Ibid., 7.
216 Ibid., 5, 8.

ligionists (*al-dīniyūn*), in turn, consider moral education essential for mutual affection and the elimination of personal desires. Finally, the liberalists – namely, those advocating the principle of personal independence (*mabdaʾ al-istiqlāl al-dhātī*) – stress that individuals must rely exclusively upon themselves and will attain felicity through the well-earned fruits of their hard work.[217] Al-ʿAzm takes this plurality of approaches as proof of the confusion at which the civilized world has arrived, and of its inability to harmonize the various demands of societal life in a just manner.[218]

Based on this pseudo-empirical diagnosis, the book's main argument – which is repeated time and again – is that it was Islam which had perfectly harmonized these various demands and which, already 1300 years ago, had combined the insights of the different European schools in a just, moderate, and reasonable manner.[219] Thus, in the same year that al-ʿAzm denied that Islam originally contained a political order, he validated the Islamic sources as containing a societal order.

While al-ʿAzm does not further concern himself with anarchists and nihilists, he refutes the "religionists'" – that is, certain Christians' – conception of religious education. Still more fundamentally, he engages with the supposed doctrines of socialists and liberalists. The remainder of this section shows (a) that al-ʿAzm positions Islam as a middle way between socialism and individualism; (b) the premises on which he constructs Islam as a principle of social order; (c) that he separates the spiritual from the societal teachings of Islam and connects religion to society (only) through a religious ethics of work; and (d) finally suggests that, in confronting Islam with European conceptions, he is actually confronting an ideal, universal, and timeless principle with its contemporary manifestation.

(a) Pursuing his aim of showing that Islam harmonizes the demands put forward by the separate European schools of thought, al-ʿAzm first engages with the demands of the socialists, whom he deems – following the translation of Demolins's *A quoi tient la superiorité*[220] – the dominant school in Europe at the time.[221] He argues that Islam remedies the misery of the poor in the way the socialists aspire to, but does so without restricting the independence of work.[222] In Islam, part of one's wealth is for one's personal disposal, whereas another part

217 Ibid., 5.
218 Ibid., 6.
219 See especially: ibid., 6f., 23f., 36f., 37f., 56.
220 Demolins, *A quoi*; idem., *Sirr*; see above: 128f.
221 Al-ʿAzm, *Tanbih*, 5, 7.
222 Ibid., 8.

belongs to the community.[223] Islam acknowledges that personal efforts need to be rewarded so as to incite people to work in the first place. In this, Islam – in contrast to socialism – pays heed to the natural laws of human society (*nawāmīs al-ijtimāʿ al-ṭabīʿiyya*).[224] Having dealt with the socialists in his first article, in his second article, al-ʿAzm engages European liberalists, whom he circumscribes as "those advocating the principle of personal independence" (*mabdaʾ al-istiqlāl al-dhātī*).[225]

According to al-ʿAzm, while the socialists do not acknowledge personal efforts at all, the liberalists stand at the other extreme – they do not respect the need for society and social solidarity at all. Al-ʿAzm asserts that Islam clearly calls for the independence of thought and will (*istiqlāl al-fikr wa-l-irāda*) and that it incites personal ambitions (*al-himma al-dhātiyya*).[226] This importance of the subject's independence and autonomy has only recently become apparent to some Europeans, al-ʿAzm maintains, referring namely – and almost certainly with Demolins's *Sirr al-Taqaddum al-Inkliz al-Saksuniyin* in mind – to the Anglo-Saxon school that wanted to base education on the principle of personal independence (*al-istiqlāl al-shakhṣī*).[227] This school, however, allegedly focuses too much on the subject's liberty, which leads to the brutal domination of the strong over the weak. In contrast, Islam ensures justice (*ʿadl*) by harmoniously combining the principle of independence (*mabdaʾ al-istiqlāl*) with that of cooperation and sharing (*mabdaʾ al-ishtirāk*).[228]

In a remarkably dense passage at the beginning of the third article, al-ʿAzm once again adduces human beings' social nature in order to refute the demands of liberalism, but in slightly different words, he stresses Islam's combination of the principles of individualism and socialism, and then transitions to his subsequent elaboration of Islam as a social order:

"There is no need for us to elaborate in this article on the established fact that man is a civil being by nature (*madanī bi-l-ṭabʿ*), which means, he is in need of cooperation (*taʿāwun*) and social association (*ijtimāʿ*); for this is proven by the naturalness of social association itself (*bi-bidāhat al-ijtimāʿ nafsihi*). And [there is no need for us] to refute the doctrine (*madhhab*) of excessive personal liberty (*al-ḥurriyya al-shakhṣiyya*) of those Europeans who insist upon independence of

223 Ibid., 9.
224 Ibid., 12
225 Ibid., 12.
226 Ibid., 15.
227 Ibid., 17.
228 Ibid., 17.

the subject (*al-istiqlāl al-dhātī*) in the sense of considering man a socio-political entity unto himself (*al-insān umma fī nafsihi*), not belonging to a [larger] social collectivity (*lā umma la-hu*) all [members] of which rely upon each other (*yatakāfil wa-ayyuhā*) for acquiring the benefits of social life (*manāfiʿ al-ḥayāt al-ijtimāʿiyya*) and repulsing the harms of animal-like solitariness (*al-waḥda al-ḥayawāniyya*); for this is refuted by his nature. Rather, we want to elucidate the meaning of society (*ijtimāʿ*) in Islam, insofar it is a [principle of] social association (*min ḥaythu kawnuhu ijtimāʿan*) according to which man is an independent entity unto himself (*umma mustaqilla fī nafsihi*) when one looks at his specificity (*bi-l-naẓr al-akhaṣṣ*), whereas in a broader view (*bi-l-naẓr al-aʿamm*)[229] the members of one community (*abnāʾ al-milla al-wāḥida*) are a society jointly guaranteeing (*umma mutakāfila*) its interests (*maṣāliḥahā*)."[230]

Still more remarkable than al-ʿAzm adducing human nature to refute the allegedly extreme demands of socialists and liberalists and to confirm the Islamic view of social order, is that he explicates his interest in Islam as concerns its being a principle of social association (*min ḥaythu kawnuhu ijtimāʿan*).

(b) In al-ʿAzm's depiction of the first Muslims' social association, Islam represents, I would suggest, the principle of a society made up of individuals over against the principle of community represented by *ʿaṣabiyya* – that is here, tribal solidarity. According to al-ʿAzm, Islam replaced the existing, contradictory loyalties with a single element – namely, Islam itself – and thus created "one society (*umma wāḥida*) which mutually vouches for (*tatakāfil*) its public interests (*maṣāliḥihā al-ʿāmma*), and all of whose individuals (*kull fard minhā*) can independently dispose of the fruits of their personal work (*ʿamalihi al-khāṣṣ*)."[231] It is their common belief (*īmān*) that incites Muslims to socialize in the proper way, creating common brotherhood (*al-ulfa al-ʿumūmiyya*) between them. Al-Batush updates al-ʿAzm's wording in an interesting way when he interprets *al-ulfa al-ʿumūmiyya* as meaning *waḥdat al-mujtamaʿ* (the unity of society).[232]

But al-ʿAzm himself also clearly elaborates the brotherhood of believers as a principle of modern society when he says that its realization rests upon three conditions, which represent the principle of mutual solidarity (*takāful*) in Islam: first, cooperation (*taʿāwūn*) on what is righteous (*birr*) and abstention

229 Translation in conjunction with the following bullet point in the article's list of contents: "*al-muslim mustaqillan fī khuṣūṣiyyātihi mujtamiʿan maʿ ikhwānihi fī ʿumūmiyyāt mujtamaʿihim*" (ibid., 18).
230 Ibid., 19.
231 Ibid., 20.
232 Al-Batush, *Rafiq al-ʿAzm*, 49.

from evil (*shirr*), which amounts to justice in social interactions (*muʿāmalāt*);[233] second, jointly guaranteeing the implementation of the laws (*sharāʾiʿ*) of Islam, mainly as a means to ensure unity;[234] third, complete freedom of conscience (*iṭlāq ḥurriyyat al-ḍamāʾir*) and independence of thought (*istiqlāl al-afkār*).[235] Al-ʿAzm argues that two things are achieved by a people thus united by fraternity in belief (*ahl ukhūwat al-īmān*): "[firstly,] intellectual independence (*al-istiqlāl al-ʿaqlī*), so that every individual (*fard*) of them is a nation unto himself (*umma fī nafsihi*), acting in moderation (*qisṭ*) (that is, justness [*ʿadl*]) [...;] and [secondly,] mutual solidarity (*takāful*) between all of them, so that they all are one nation (*umma wāḥida*) pursuing the interests of its society (*maṣāliḥ mujtamaʿihā*) by pursuing the ways of revelation (*sharʿ*) and justness (*ʿadl*)."[236] Clearly then, al-ʿAzm here validates belief in God not as a prerequisite for otherworldly felicity, but exclusively as a means to inner-worldly solidarity between the individuals of one nation in the interests of its social order.

Crucial for the sustenance of social order and the unity of society is the application of the godly Islamic shariʿa, which – in al-ʿAzm's conception here, even more clearly than in *al-Durus al-Hikamiyya* – is tantamount to the application of reason in pursuit of public interests. According to al-ʿAzm, it was Islam that "altered (*qalaba*) the foundations of the states (*awḍāʿ al-duwal*) and disseminated (*baththa*) the spirit of societal life (*rūḥ al-ḥayāt al-ijtimāʿiyya*) among the peoples of the earth (*umam al-arḍ*)."[237] The quick spread of Islam is adduced as testimony to its godly origins.[238] This should not necessarily be taken at face value, however, as I will argue below. Nevertheless, if one does so, then it becomes especially significant that al-ʿAzm conceives of Islam and its law as mirroring the primary principles of rationality and human interests. When Islam spread, al-ʿAzm maintains,

"it made all the peoples (*umam*) that submitted to it into one nation (*umma wāḥida*) pursuing a single goal, enjoying the same rights (*ḥuqūq wāḥida*), and speaking the same language, since they were integrated by one basic principle (*qānūn wāḥid*) that God gave (*sharaʿa*) to humankind. It is absolutely unthinkable that laws drawn up by mankind (*sharāʾiʿ al-bashar*) would approximate [this godly law and its effects] or that human societies (*mujtamaʿāt al-insān*) would be

233 Al-ʿAzm, *Tanbih*, 20 f.
234 Ibid., 21.
235 Ibid., 22.
236 Ibid., 22.
237 Ibid., 32.
238 Ibid., 32 f.

set right by means other than it (*bi-ghayrihi*); this is because the goals (*maqāṣid*) of the Islamic law (*al-sharʿ al-islāmī*) without exception (*kulluhā*) are oriented toward the benefits of humankind, the life of civilization (*madaniyya*), and culture (*ʿumrān*)."[239]

It is the duty of human beings, al-ʿAzm stresses, to derive rules for social and political life from the principles of the shariʿa, in accordance with the progress of time and society.[240]

As mentioned above, al-ʿAzm delegates the procedure of deriving such rules entirely to religious leaders and scholars, and he himself validates the shariʿa as representing broad principles of socio-political order – such as justice and equality – whose preservation necessitates (and here we once again encounter a central concept of al-ʿAzm's socio-political thought) common solidarity (*al-takāful al-ʿāmm*). To most Islamic reformists, including al-ʿAzm, it was the first generations of Muslims (*al-ṣaḥāba wa-l-tābiʿūn*) who were most familiar with the truth of Islam and who instituted the shariʿa in practice. Based on that assertion, different aspects may be highlighted as exemplary knowledge and practice. Al-ʿAzm foregrounds the idea that the first Muslims "made the peoples of the earth (*umam al-arḍ*) submit to their power by [the attractiveness of] the basic principle of justice and equality (*qānūn al-ʿadl wa-l-musāwā*) concerning all rights (*ḥuqūq*) which are shared by the members of one society (*abnāʾ al-mujtamaʿ al-wāḥid*)."[241] As al-Batush has shown, al-ʿAzm was one of the first Arab intellectuals to elaborate the concept of common social solidarity (*al-takāful al-ʿāmm/al-ijtimāʿī*).[242] The common, solidary collaboration of society to protect the shariʿa – which, in al-ʿAzm's conception, is tantamount to justice, equality, and human interests – in conjunction with his validation of individual efforts and rewards, can be considered the core of his Islamic response to the problem of society.

(c) It is in his engagement with the European 'religionists' (*dīniyūn*) that al-ʿAzm addresses the spiritual dimension of the Islamic religion, which he notably separates quite clearly from its societal dimension, envisioning religious ethics as a mediator between the two. It was on the above-mentioned bases that Islamic peoples had ascended the ladder of civilization (*madaniyya*) and had come to enjoy the goodness of social life (*al-ḥayāt al-ijtimāʿiyya*), as al-ʿAzm maintains;

239 Ibid., 33.
240 Ibid., 34.
241 Ibid., 56.
242 Al-Batush, *Rafiq al-ʿAzm*, 48ff.

he adds, implicitly in view of the presumed subsequent decline of Islam, that civilization requires a shield to protect societies (*mujtamaʿāt*).[243] According to him, this shield consists of rightful laws (*al-qawānīn al-sharʿiyya*) – which have been addressed in the previous two paragraphs – and of spiritual education (*al-tarbiya al-rūḥiyya*).[244] The European religionists, who advocate moral and spiritual education as essential for society, do not do so on a rational basis, al-ʿAzm argues. Their opponents then wrongly extend their criticism of this position – which is, in the first place, understandable – to all religions, including "the Islamic religion, which is the religion of human beings' innate disposition and reason (*dīn al-fiṭra wa-l-ʿaql*) that combines the demands of societal life (*maṭālib al-ḥayāt al-ijtimāʿiyya*)."[245]

As such, Islam also set forth the principles of spiritual education (*uṣūl al-tarbiya al-rūḥiyya*) – not in a manner that makes them in themselves liable "to accomplish the other civilizational demands of human society (*ḥājāt al-ijtimāʿiyya al-madaniyya*), as the party advocating the moral influence (*al-muʾaththir al-adabī*) in Europe has it, but rather so that they are a shield (*siyāj*) for the other demands of human society (*ijtimāʿ*) that Islam has established."[246] Al-ʿAzm identifies the central aim of the spiritual teachings of Islam as making human hearts actively aspire to good and just deeds.[247] Far from containing concrete norms of behavior, in al-ʿAzm's conception, Islam's spiritual teachings basically consist in an ethical call to active, reasonable, moderate, and just social behavior.[248] Allegedly in contrast to the European proponents of spiritual and ethical teachings, Islam's spiritual teachings – similarly to its societal teachings, according to al-ʿAzm – conform to human beings' innate disposition and reason; as such, Islam's spiritual teachings acknowledge what the Europeans neglect – namely, the human need to work,[249] to be an active member of society.

(d) In *Tanbih al-Afham*, Rafiq al-ʿAzm does not so much transform Islamic religious discourse to meet the societal requirements of the utilitarian age of progress,[250] but rather, I would argue, reconstructs Islam *as* society – that is, as a principle of social order. Since he does so in overt engagement with Euro-

243 Al-ʿAzm, *Tanbih*, 25.
244 Ibid., 26.
245 Ibid., 26.
246 Ibid., 26 f.
247 Ibid., 27.
248 Ibid., 27–30.
249 Ibid., 30 f.
250 For this reaction of religious discourse to secular societal requirements, see above: chapters 2 section 3 and 4 section 3.2.

pean schools of thought, one may in hindsight detect the kernels of an opposition between Islamic and European socio-political orders, or even between Islam and the West. However, in view of both the tenor of this text and al-ʿAzm's broader socio-political views, I would like to suggest another reading – namely, that Islam represents universal, timeless, and metaphysical principles, which find their particularized, contingent, and immanent embodiment in the different European schools of thought.

This interpretation is related to a number of tropes known from the work of Islamic reformists in general, not least their strategy of incorporating secular premises associated with Europe into an Islamic discourse. Al-ʿAzm also shares the definition of Islam as *dīn al-ʿaql* and *dīn al-fiṭra*, as we have seen, and distinguishes this ideal religion from its historical manifestations and the current practices of Muslims.[251] As a metaphysical principle, the Islamic religion – and notably also the Islamic shariʿa, in al-ʿAzm's conception – represent and are tantamount to rationality, human interests, justice, and solidarity. If al-ʿAzm, as a secular historian, claims that the quick and unprecedented spread of Islam testifies to its not having been the work of human beings alone,[252] he hardly assumes direct divine interventions into immanent history, but rather adduces this alleged fact in order to validate a metaphysical principle. This principle also partly manifests itself in contemporary European civilization, which – according to al-ʿAzm – significantly rests upon Islam and the Islamic shariʿa. However, the Europeans have allegedly neglected the most important political teaching of Islam – namely, that of absolute equality between a conqueror and a conquered people.[253] In a colonial context, al-ʿAzm, who also criticized the internal oppression perpetrated by despotic governments, thus voices his demands by appealing to Islam as a universal principle of socio-political equality and justice. While he repeatedly mentions that Islam guides human beings to both inner-worldly and otherworldly felicity, he is exclusively interested in the first dimension and quite clearly separates societal from spiritual teachings in Islam. Thus al-ʿAzm constructs Islam as an overarching, timeless, and supreme principle of society and social order, which perfectly integrates all the particularized, contingent, and inferior insights manifest in European civilization.

251 Al-ʿAzm, *Tanbih*, 11, 23.
252 Ibid., 31 f.
253 Ibid., 35.

5 Conclusion: Islam, Religion, Secularity, and Concepts of Society

Having ventured quite far into the interpretation of Rafiq al-ʿAzm's views on society, religion, and politics, it might be worth recalling that it was his remarkable usage of *mujtamaʿ* in *al-Manar* that had alerted me to his writings in the first place. Al-ʿAzm was the one regular contributor to our Islamic journal who used *mujtamaʿ* most prominently to conceptualize modern society. Other pertinent usages stemmed mainly from translations of French or English texts and from articles previously published in *al-Siyasa*. This finding indicated not only important channels through which *mujtamaʿ* became established in its modern meaning of 'society,' but also suggested secular connotations of the concept. Investigating al-ʿAzm's socio-political views in the first place was intended to test the hypothesis of the secular connotations of *mujtamaʿ*.

It ought to be clear by now that my analysis of selected writings by al-ʿAzm does not claim to have fully discerned his views in this regard. I could only hint at certain developments in al-ʿAzm's views over time,[254] without further pursuing that line of inquiry. Nevertheless, the two works from 1900 – which, in addition to a pertinent debate in *al-Manar* from 1904, I have selected for my analysis – provide more than mere a snapshot of his views at that time. Published shortly after the foundation of *al-Manar*, these works share the basic epistemology of modernity – namely, an immanent, secular perspective on the world. Moreover, these works attest to the possibility that this modern perspective could be elaborated in an Islamic discourse, which offers participants the continuous choice of whether or not to connect, in different degrees and forms, the immanent frame to a transcendent realm.

While this point could also be made based on writings of other Islamic reformists, characteristic for whom is the integration of secular premises and arguments into an Islamic discourse, Rafiq al-ʿAzm stands out for his clearly secular and societal perspective on religion, which not only connects Islam and social order, but constructs Islam – in one of its two dimensions – *as* a social order. Al-ʿAzm is not interested in a reform of Islamic religious teachings, but rather constructs a peculiar societal understanding of Islam. His take on Islam, to be clear, does not at all diminish his belief in God, in Muhammad as his last prophet, and in the Qurʾan as the word of God. This common belief of Muslims is, for him, what also constitutes the group of people who form an Islamic polity. However, when it comes to the organization of that polity, to its social and political

254 See above: chapter 9 sections 1 and 2.

order, religious belief retreats into the background and is, as a matter of conscience (*amr wijdānī*), relegated to the private realm.

On another level, to overtly deny the relevance of religion or Islam in Arabic public debates of the late nineteenth and early twentieth centuries would have meant placing oneself at the very margins of public discourse, which amounts to not bringing one's arguments across at all. In this regard, the debate between al-ʿAzm and al-Yafiʿi can be read as testing the limits of accepted public discourse. The fact that not only al-ʿAzm, but also Islamic reformists in general addressed both religion and society as *islām*, *dīn*, and *sharīʿa* sometimes makes it hard to distinguish the two spheres within their discourse. One must also take care not to project a later secularist distinction onto reformist writings from the turn to the twentieth century. However, it is precisely in this regard that al-ʿAzm's writings are enlightening, as he distinguishes between the spheres of religion, politics, and society more clearly than others. (Again, this does not mean that he fully separated them, but it might be worth recalling here, that this call for full separation has now been identified as a particular secularist perspective within a range of secular views in modernity, including religious ones.) As we have seen, al-ʿAzm accords greater relevance to Islamic teachings for the social than for the political order – or, better put, he formulates Islam as an order of society rather than the state.[255]

Concerning *mujtamaʿ*, this chapter's findings further substantiate the hypothesis that the term did have secular connotations and was established in order to conceptualize the modern idea of society. After all, Rafiq al-ʿAzm can be designated as an early secularist Islamic reformist and intellectual who explicitly engaged European responses to "the social question" and thus the modern problem of social order. It is worth noting that al-ʿAzm – who supposedly spoke only a little French, in addition to to Arabic and Turkish – rarely refers to European works in his writings. The only explicit references I have come across are translations of two historiographical works which allegedly support his depiction of Islam.[256] What seems obvious, albeit not explicated, is al-ʿAzm's familiarity with the translation of Demolins's famous work *A quoi tient la superiorité des Anglo-Saxons*.[257] In al-ʿAzm's works, one might well detect further appropriations of or analogies to European writings. After all, it is clear that

255 Also Muhammad ʿAbduh and other leading Islamic reformists who wrote for *al-Manar* focused primarily on society, not the state (see Kerr, *Islamic Reform*, 151 f.; Haddad, "The Manarists," esp. 57; above: chapter 5 section 4).

256 Al-ʿAzm, *Tanbih*, 23fn1, 35fn1.

257 Ibid., 17; Demolins, *A quoi*; idem., *Sirr*.

al-ʿAzm shares hegemonic modern anthropological, historiographical, and sociological premises. Overtly, however, he elaborates these modern premises by validating concepts from an Islamic discourse – most notably that of *al-takāful al-ʿāmm*. And while al-ʿAzm makes only marginal use of *al-hay'a al-ijtimāʿiyya*,[258] he also uses *umma*, in addition to *mujtamaʿ*, to conceptualize the modern idea of society – or, put otherwise, he instills the concept of *umma* with notions of 'society.'

Al-ʿAzm's usage of these terms confirms three other findings of the previous two chapters: firstly, a plurality of Arabic terms was used to expressing notions of 'society,' with *umma* a major rival to *mujtamaʿ*, a term that was not yet widespread but already firmly established in meaning. Secondly, *umma* was a more generic term than *mujtamaʿ*, which was more clearly imbued with a sense of order, especially when the two terms were related to each other, as when an author refers to a certain *umma*'s *mujtamaʿ* in the sense of the social order of a particular collectivity.[259] Thirdly, *mujtamaʿ* often conveys not so much the idea of an abstract order of society as the – equally normative – idea of an integrated collectivity.[260] The analysis in this chapter adds to these findings the idea that *mujtamaʿ* may also designate social collectivities in a more generic sense. As such, *mujtamaʿ* shifted between the not yet clearly distinguished meanings of 'nation,' 'society,' or 'community,' but seldom of 'the people,' while always retaining its normative, core meaning of an integrated collectivity or order.

There is a strong link between that normative core of *mujtamaʿ*, as was most clearly visible in *Tanbih al-Afham*, and the normative connotations of *ijtimāʿ*, which – in the sense of 'social association' and 'human society' – formed the starting point and guiding thread for *al-Durus al-Hikamiyya*. It was based on the allegedly natural need for human beings to socialize that al-ʿAzm developed his arguments for religion and government. The seemingly natural act of socializing becomes normative when al-ʿAzm purports claims as to which form of religion or government is appropriate for human beings' social association. The act of socializing is thereby developed into an order of society. This is terminologically explicated in the concept of *niẓām al-ijtimāʿ* (the order of society).[261] Other meanings of *ijtimāʿ* include 'cooperation,' 'unity,' 'coherence,' and 'concord,' which significantly play into *ijtimāʿ* in the sense of society as well as into the sense of *mujtamaʿ*.

---

258 The only instances in the writings analyzed here are: al-ʿAzm, *al-Durus* [1327 h.], 69; idem., *Tanbih*, 4, 8, 26.

259 For example: ibid., 22.

260 For example: ibid., 39, 41, 42; idem., *al-Durus* [1327 h.], 20.

261 For example: ibid., 53.

I shall further establish the semantic range of *ijtimāʿ* at the beginning of the following chapter, which discerns Rashid Rida's conceptualizations of society based on his usage of *ijtimāʿ* in the sense of 'social association' and 'human society' and his usage of *ijtimāʿī* in the sense of 'the social.'

Chapter 10
Social Association Reified: *Ijtimāʿ*, *Ijtimāʿī*, and *Umma* in Articles by Rashid Rida

1 *Ijtimāʿ* and *Ijtimāʿī(ya)*: Ubiquity, Semantic Range, and Positive Connotation

1.1 Social Association, Society, Concurrence, Unity – The Semantic Range and Normativity of *Ijtimāʿ*

> "An animal so massive that the image of it has not crossed the imagination of any of the Ancients has only now been discovered by the modern philosophers. ... We are not speaking figuratively or in riddles. That such an animal exists is quite certain, if we are to believe the modern philosophers. You will ask us: 'And what is this strange animal?' The answer is 'Society' (*al-ijtimāʿ al-insānī*, literally the 'human collective')."
> – *al-Muqtataf*, 1885[1]

In this study, we first encountered *ijtimāʿ* as part of the most famous subtitle of *al-Manar:* "a monthly journal exploring the philosophy of religion and the affairs of social association and civilization" (*majalla shahriyya tabḥuth fī falsafat al-dīn wa-shuʾūn al-ijtimāʿ wa-l-ʿumrān*).[2] The fact that *al-Manar* and a host of other journals were advertised as addressing *ijtimāʿ* already shows the contemporaneous relevance and positive connotation of the term. Together with *ijtimāʿī(ya)*, the adjective derived from it – which was also included in several subtitles of *al-Manar* and other journals – the prominent placement of *ijtimāʿ* heightened the expectation that one could discern an Arabic concept of 'society' in *al-Manar.* Chapters 7 and 8 have comprehensively analyzed the two most pertinent candidates in that regard – namely, *al-hayʾa al-ijtimāʿiyya* and *mujtamaʿ*. As chapter 6 has shown, *ijtimāʿ* itself was supposedly not as pertinent: in his dictionary from 1860, Kazimirski rendered the term as "réunion, état de ce qui est réuni, vie sociale," and in 1881, Dozy only gave "conjonction, rencontre apparente des astres, incorporation."[3] According to Khuri-Makdisi, *ijtimāʿ* mainly oc-

1 Quoted from: ElShakry, *Reading*, 82; transliteration corrected and adjusted. As will become clear in this subsection, I prefer to translate *ijtimāʿ* as 'social association,' since it can hardly be reified.

2 See above: chapter 5 section 2.

3 See above: 190 f.

https://doi.org/10.1515/9783110545845-011

curred as part of the composite *al-hayʾa al-ijtimāʿiyya* until the 1890s, and then increasingly stood alone to conceptualize the social.[4]

My finding that *al-hayʾa al-ijtimāʿiyya* and *mujtamaʿ* were established in the sense of society but were not as pertinent as expected brings us back to *ijtimāʿ* as a less specific term which, however, points to alternative conceptualizations of society. In the first three chapters of part C, we have already seen how claims about social order were derived from human beings' allegedly natural inclination to social association (*ijtimāʿ*) and that the reified society resulting from this natural association may be conceptualized as *mujtamaʿ* or *al-hayʾa al-ijtimāʿiyya*, but also as *umma*. Moreover, societal (*ijtimāʿī[ya]*) laws and topics may be applied and discussed with regard to different social collectivities. Building on these considerations, this chapter takes its starting point from *ijtimāʿ* and *ijtimāʿī(ya)* to identify conceptualizations of society in the writings of Rashid Rida.

The combined findings and arguments of this chapter eventually lead to the main argument of this study: Rida, along with other Islamic reformists, used *umma* to express his vision of a society that results from human beings' natural but divinely ordained need for social association; that functions according to largely autonomous societal laws, which are the laws of God; and that requires the guidance of a societal religion to attain perfection. This is modernity in Islamic tradition.

To return to this chapter's starting point, the semantic range of *ijtimāʿ* is considerably greater than that of *al-hayʾa al-ijtimāʿiyya* (which in all cases referred to society as the overall social sphere) and *mujtamaʿ* (which did so in its most prominent strands of meaning, but could also refer to smaller human and non-human collectivities. Since, moreover, *mujtamaʿ* is derived from the same verb as *ijtimāʿ*, and the adjective *al-ijtimāʿī(ya)*, which attributes *al-hayʾa*, is supposedly derived from *ijtimāʿ* itself, the semantic range of *ijtimāʿ* also confirms certain connotations of *al-hayʾa al-ijtimāʿiyya* and *mujtamaʿ*, which were visible in a few but certainly not all usages of these two terms. In fact, in one strand of its meaning, *ijtimāʿ* itself designates 'society' – in a different sense, however, than *al-hayʾa al-ijtimāʿiyya*, *mujtamaʿ* or *umma*, as I will show below.

First, however, I offer a brief overview of the term's other meanings, some of which are highly informative for the normativity of its meaning 'society.' I have discerned these meanings based on the 2,722 occurrences of *ijtimāʿ* in *al-Manar*.

4 See above: 14.

In view of the ubiquity of *ijtimāʿ*, it is neither feasible[5] nor relevant[6] to identify the authors of all the instances of the term. It is safe and sufficient to say that *ijtimāʿ*, unlike *al-hay'a al-ijtimāʿiyya* or *mujtamaʿ*, was used in all of its meanings by all the authors who wrote for *al-Manar*. It also proved impractical to group the instances of *ijtimāʿ* into different categories of meaning (even without identifying the authorship), since the term's different meanings very often overlap, as we will see in the following discussion.

The basic commonality underlying the different meanings of *ijtimāʿ* is discernible from its root *j-m-ʿ*, whose core meaning is 'to gather,' 'collect,' 'combine,' or 'unite.' *Ijtimāʿ* is the verbal noun of the eighth stem of *j-m-ʿ*, *ijtamaʿa*, whose range of meanings comprises: 'to come together,' 'to gather,' 'to meet,' 'to fuse,' 'to join,' 'to unite,' and 'to concur.' In many usages of *ijtamaʿa*, the term oscillates between these meanings. This is also the case with *ijtimāʿ*, which, as the verbal noun derived from *ijtamaʿ*, may designate the aforementioned actions as well as their outcomes. The last aspect is obvious in one dominant strand of meaning of *ijtimāʿ*, both in *al-Manar* and until the present day – namely, the reference to a meeting of people. I may add briefly that, like *mujtamaʿ*, *ijtimāʿ* could also refer to an assembly of certain things.[7] Concerning persons, *ijtimāʿ* may refer to the unification of husband and wife[8] (as did *mujtamaʿ* in a few cases) or to the coming-together and connection of two persons. Much more often, however, *ijtimāʿ* refers to the meeting of at least several persons, if not a larger group of people. The other meanings of *ijtamaʿa* play into its reference to a meeting, since people usually meet for a common purpose, not least to create unity or to achieve concurrence on a certain matter. Moreover, claims to freedom of assembly – and thus potentially to a social sphere autonomous from the state – point to the political relevance of gatherings.[9] Thus, even in its seemingly de-

5 After all, based on the search results in the electronic version of *al-Manar*, this procedure necessitates identifying the article in which an instance occurs in the printed version and reading that article at least carefully enough so as to establish whether the passage which includes the search term was written by the author of the article themself, or whether they quoted someone else.

6 Whereas for the sparsely used terms *al-hay'a al-ijtimāʿiyya* and *mujtamaʿ*, authorship mattered greatly, *ijtimāʿ* was readily used by all the authors who wrote for *al-Manar* without distinction, and its ubiquity beyond *al-Manar* can also easily be discerned from a glance at some of its rival journals.

7 Such as the combination of letters (Rida, *Tafsir*, vol. 1: 135), clouds (ibid., vol. 1: 145) or attributes (ibid., vol. 7: 338).

8 For example: ibid., vol. 5: 61.

9 See, for example: idem. 1912. "Khatimat al-Maqalat: Shujun wa-Muhawarat (10)." *al-Manar* 15/1: 48–55, here 51, 53; idem. 1922. "al-Rihla al-Suriyya al-Thaniyya (10)." *al-Manar* 23/4: 313–317,

scriptive reference to a meeting, *ijtimāʿ* carries positive normative connotations of unifying and concurring.[10]

In volume one, Rida praises the spirit of social association, even when people initially concur on something invalid. Other than Egyptians, he claims, Indians and Indonesians

> "did not possess the spirit of social association (*rūḥ al-ijtimāʿ*) through which their thoughts (*afkār*) come together in one atmosphere (*jaww*). Truly, the coming-together of thoughts in one atmosphere is beneficial even when its air is foul (*fāsid*), because division (*tafarruq*) does not entail anything but evil, whereas concurrence (*ijtimāʿ*), even around falsehood (*al-bāṭil*) and error, is the foundation of unity (*mabdaʾ al-waḥda*), due to it [at some point] being replaced by concurrence around truth (*al-ḥaqq*) and rightness. Egyptians recently have already attained the principle of social association (*ijtimāʿ*) in the name of the nation and the homeland (*bi-ism al-umma wa-l-waṭan*) [...]. Egyptians furthermore have societal gatherings (*ijtimāʿāt*) unlike the other two [peoples]."[11]

Rida here validates the spirit of social association, which manifests itself in a general sense of national concurrence and individual gatherings alike, as a condition for unity.

The normative sense of *ijtimāʿ* as stressing unity, concurrence, coherence, or cooperation indeed becomes most clear when we examine the synonymous[12] and antonymous terms frequently related to *ijtimāʿ*. A most pertinent example in this regard is Muhyi al-Din Azad's above-mentioned book on the *Islamic Ca-*

---

here 314; idem. 1930. "Israr Fransa ʿala Ikhraj al-Barbar min al-Islam." *al-Manar* 31/4: 309–317, here 309 f., 311.

10 In their primary usage, it seems that all the words derived from the root *j-m-ʿ* are more or less positively connoted. However, once established, one may of course play out one word from that root against another, such as *jamāʿa* against *mujtamaʿ*. It is worth inquiring into whether the early Arabic term for 'socialism,' *ijtimāʿiyya*, which was rather quickly superseded by *ishtirākiyya*, was also coined in a positive sense by proponents of socialism. The owners of *al-Hilal* presented Niqula Haddad, whom they asked to write a book on socialism, as *al-kātib al-ijtimāʿī* (Haddad, *al-Ishtirakiyya*, 11). Rida once uses *ijtimāʿīyūn* to designate socialists (Rida, *Tafsir*, vol. 11: 22) and once uses *ijtimāʿī* in critical reference to communism (Rashid Rida commenting upon Arslan, Shakib. 1929. "Madha Yuqal ʿan al-Islam fi Uruba (2)." *al-Manar* 30/1: 211–224, here 216fn3). The designation of thinkers as *kātib ijtimāʿī* etc. in *al-Manar* was exlusively positively connoted (see chapter 10 section 2.1).

11 Rida, Rashid. 1899. "Hayat al-Islam fi Misr." *al-Manar* 2/9: 161–166, here 162; see also: idem., *Tafsir*, vol. 4: 116 f.

12 'Synonymous usage' does not connote complete equivalence, but rather substantial overlap in meaning.

liphate. Azad characterizes his times as "the age of coherence and concord" (*ʿahd al-ijtimāʿ wa-l-iʾtilāf*), giving *tashattut* and *intishār* as antagonizing concepts. Moreover, he contrasts Islam, which rests on this principle of concord (*jamāʿa*), with the pre-Islamic age (*jāhiliyya*), which embodies the principle of division (*firqa*).[13] In numerous other examples, *ijtimāʿ* is used synonymously with *iʾtilāf* (concord, harmony),[14] *ittifāq* (agreement),[15] and especially *ittiḥād* (unity)[16] and *taʿāwun* (cooperation);[17] it is contrasted with division, scattering, and dispersal (*iftirāq*,[18] *tafarruq*,[19] *tafrīq*[20]). In several cases, the meanings of *ijtimāʿ* as a stand-alone term oscillate between that of 'unity,' 'coherence,' 'concord,' 'cooperation,' and 'society,' in the sense of social association – for example, when Rida posits that Islam is the "religion of humankind's innate disposition and of *ijtimāʿ*."[21]

Constructing one's society in the sense of an integrated social body and a functioning social order was considered conditional upon unity, concord, and coherence, whether society was conceptualized as *al-hayʾa al-ijtimāʿiyya*, as *mujtamaʿ*, or as *umma*. This reminds us of French authors in the seventeenth and eighteenth centuries, who claimed that "les sauvages vivent avec peu de société."[22] The aforementioned senses of *ijtimāʿ* clearly play into the normativity of *al-hayʾa al-ijtimāʿiyya* and, especially, *mujtamaʿ*. After all, at the turn to the twen-

13 See above: chapter 7 section 4.3.

14 For example: Rida, *Tafsir*, vol. 4: 74.

15 For example: idem., 1904. "Bab al-Suʾal wa-l-Fatwa." *al-Manar* 6/22: 857–862, here 862.

16 For example: idem., *Tafsir*, vol. 1: 105, vol. 2: 14, vol. 4: 39; Rashid Rida in al-Fawiki, N. 1899. "al-Gharb al-Aqsa, Hal Yumkin Istirjaʿ Majd al-Sharq bi-Quwat al-Islam?." *al-Manar* 1/40: 794–801, here 800; Rashid Rida and Isʿaf al-Nashashibi signing for Lajnat al-Daʿwa wa-l-Irshad li-l-Muʾtamar al-Islami al-ʿAmm in Rida, Rashid. 1932. "al-Muʾtamar al-Islami al-ʿAmm fi Bayt al-Muqaddas (2)." *al-Manar* 32/3: 193–208, here 208.

17 For example: Rida, *Tafsir*, vol. 3: 223, vol. 4: 23, vol. 5: 111, vol. 6: 83, vol. 11: 302; idem. 1905. "Athar ʿIlmiyya Adabiyya." *al-Manar* 8/11: 434–440, here 436; idem. 1910. "Quwat al-Ijtimaʿ wa-l-Taʿawun." *al-Manar* 13/5: 345–348.

18 For example: idem., *Tafsir*, vol. 2: 14, 50.

19 For example: idem. 1898. "al-Juyush al-Gharbiyya al-Maʿnawiyya." *al-Manar* 1/12: 299–308, here 300; idem. 1904. "Bab al-Suʾal wa-l-Fatwa." *al-Manar* 7/12: 457–474, here 473; idem. 1913. "Laʾihat al-Islah li-Wilayat al-Bayrut." *al-Manar* 16/4: 275–280; idem. 1923. "Khitab Maftuh min Ruh al-Islam wa-l-Jamiʿa al-ʿArabiyya ila al-Shaʿb al-Inklizi wa-l-Hukuma al-Britaniyya." *al-Manar* 24/6: 441–448, here 441.

20 For example: idem., *Tafsir*, vol. 4: 17; idem. 1900. "Madaniyyat al-ʿArab." *al-Manar* 3/13: 289–294, here 293.

21 Rashid Rida in Wajdi, "Kayfa," 667. More examples of the relation between religion and society in Rida's writings will be given in chapter 10 section 3.

22 Baker, "Enlightenment," 87; Branca-Rosoff and Guilhaumou, "De 'société'," 52.

tieth century, *mujtamaʿ* – as the passive participle of *ijtamaʿa* – is not primarily the place in which something is collected, as a nineteenth-century dictionary suggested,[23] but also a firmly integrated and thus ordered society, as we have seen in several of the examples above. Again, this ideal of an ordered society – which, under the reigning paradigm of progress, contributed to the strength of the nation – could also be conceptualized as *umma*. Rida makes this quite clear in the first volume of *al-Manar* when he twice writes that "society (*al-umma*) comes into existence (*tatakawwan*) by concurring on the beneficial (*bi-l-ijtimāʿ ʿalā l-intifāʿ*) and uniting to obtain what is desired (*al-ittiḥād ʿalā nayl al-murād*)."[24]

In contrast to *al-hayʾa al-ijtimāʿiyya*, *mujtamaʿ*, and especially *umma*, *ijtimāʿ* in *al-Manar* is almost never used to refer to a particular society – that is, to an entity in which social association is reified.[25] Of the 44 usages of *ijtimāʿ* in the plural, 37 clearly refer to specific meetings or gatherings,[26] and two convey the idea of overall human society.[27] No more than six out of the 2,722 occurrences of *ijtimāʿ* in *al-Manar* are attributed so as to refer to a particular society by name. Twice this is 'Eastern society' (*al-ijtimāʿ al-sharqī*), once mentioned by Rafiq al-ʿAzm[28] and once by Shakib Arslan,[29] who also speaks of

---

23 Lane, *An Arabic-English*, 459.

24 Rida, Rashid. 1898. "Sayhat Haqq." *al-Manar* 1/13: 217–225, here 220; idem. 1898. "Mashruʿ Sikkat Hadid bayna Bur Saʿid wa-l-Basra." *al-Manar* 1/18: 318–331, here 328.

25 See appendix, table 4c.

26 For example: Idem. 1899. "Wamid Lamʿ fi Zalimat Bidaʿ." *al-Manar* 1/42: 828–829, here 829; ʿAbduh, Muhammad. 1902. "al-Idtihad fi al-Nasraniyya wa-l-Islam." *al-Manar* 5/11: 401–434, here 429; Rida, "Bahth fi al-Muʾtamar," 682; idem. 1920. "Istiqlal Suriyya wa-l-ʿIraq." *al-Manar* 21/8: 434–447, here 435; Rashid Rida in Arslan, Shakib. 1927. "al-Ziyy al-Islami wa-l-Shaʿaʾir al-Islamiyya wa-l-Alqab al-ʿArabiyya ʿind Khawass Amrika." *al-Manar* 28/6: 450–454, here 450; Rida, Rashid. 1933. "al-ʿIbra bi-Sirat al-Malik Faysal (3)." *al-Manar* 33/8: 631–634, here 632.

27 Al-Zahrawi, "Nizam," *al-Manar* 6/19: 752; Muhammad ʿAbduh quoted in Rida, "Tarbiyat ʿUmara," 602. The following five instances refer not to individual gatherings, but to human social associations in a general sense, without conveying the idea of an overall society. Four of these articles are notably written by al-Afghani, if we attribute the articles from *al-ʿUrwa al-Wuthqa* to him: al-Afghani, Jamal al-Din. 1900. "al-Hukuma al-Istibdadiyya [2]." *al-Manar* 3/26: 601–607, here 602; al-ʿUrwa al-Wuthqa. 1906. "Madi al-Umma wa-Hadiruha wa-ʿAlaj ʿIlaliha." *al-Manar* 9/9: 664–672, here 671; al-ʿUrwa al-Wuthqa quoted by Rashid Rida in ʿAbd al-Raziq, Mustafa. 1923. "Dhikra Rinan fi al-Jamiʿa al-Misriyya." *al-Manar* 24/5: 385–393, here 388; al-Afghani, Jamal al-Din. 1922. "al-ʿIlla al-Haqiqiyya li-Saʿadat al-Insan." *al-Manar* 23/1: 37–45, here 37 (identical with the foregoing); Rida, Rashid. 1927. "al-Matbuʿat al-Haditha (Miftah al-Khataba wa-l-Waʿz)." *al-Manar* 28/5: 397–400, here 399.

28 Al-ʿAzm, "Asbab," 946.

29 Arslan, Shakib. 1925. "al-Sufur wa-l-Hijab." *al-Manar* 26/4: 300–307, here 301.

'American society' (*al-ijtimāʿ al-amīrikī*).[30] Twice we also find 'Islamic society' (*al-ijtimāʿ al-islāmī*): *al-Muʾayyad* depicts articles by Muhammad ʿAbduh as studies on *al-ijtimāʿ al-islāmī*,[31] and Rida writes that Islamic newspapers have been dedicated to "the question of *al-ijtimāʿ al-islāmī*."[32] In both cases, *ijtimāʿ* refers as much to 'unity' as to 'society,' or possibly to a certain way or principle of social association. The latter meaning is clearly intended when Muhammad ʿAbduh addresses *al-ijtimāʿ al-ʿarabī*. In an article that repeatedly conceptualizes society as *mujtamaʿ*, ʿAbduh uses this composite as shorthand for "the Arab's state of social association before [the coming of] Islam" (*ḥālat al-ijtimāʿ allatī kānat ʿalayhā al-ʿarab qurb al-islām*).[33] This reference to a certain way of social association, rather than to a reified society, is even clearer in his mentioning of "the Beduin *ijtimāʿ*,"[34] which I did not include in our list of particular usages of the term. While *ijtimāʿ* was rarely used to refer to a particular social collectivity, the term was repeatedly attributed to refer to human society in general. The attributes *insānī* and *basharī* (human), which occur 120 and 23 times respectively, explicitly convey the basic idea of humans as social beings who, by nature, aspire to social association and the formation of groups.

This idea was already expressed by pre-modern thinkers, most famously by Ibn Khaldun. In his *Muqaddima*, he asserted that "human social association (*al-ijtimāʿ al-insānī*) is a necessity, something which the philosophers expressed by saying 'human beings are civil by nature (*al-insān madanī bi-l-ṭabʿ*)'; that is to say that they cannot do without social association (*ijtimāʿ*), which in their parlance they express as town (*madīna*), and which also is tantamount to the meaning of culture (*ʿumrān*)."[35] Since *ijtimāʿ* here refers to human beings' natural impetus to socialize rather than to a reified society, "experts on Ibn Khaldun have translated [*ijtimāʿ*] as sociability rather than society."[36] We also note that in the concept of humans as civil beings (*madanī bi-l-ṭabʿ*), the social and the political are not yet distinguished, which is analogous to the conceptual history of 'the civil.'[37] The meanings of *ijtimāʿ* as 'meeting,'[38] 'unification,'[39] or 'concurrence'[40]

---

30 Idem., "al-Ziyy," 453.

31 Al-Muʾayyad quoted in Rida, "Athar ʿIlmiyya," *al-Manar* 10/5: 392.

32 Rida, Rashid. 1899. "al-Jamiʿa al-Islamiyya wa-Araʾ Kuttab al-Jaraʾid fiha." *al-Manar* 2/22: 337–345, here 342.

33 Muhammad ʿAbduh quoted in Rida, "Tarbiyat Umaraʾ," 602.

34 Rida, *Tafsir*, vol. 12: 159.

35 Ibn Khaldun, ʿAbd al-Rahman. 2005. *al-Muqaddima*; ed. ʿAbd al-Salam al-Shaddadi. Casablanca: Bayt al-Funun wa-l-ʿUlum wa-l-Adab, vol. 1: 67.

36 Khuri-Makdisi, "The Conceptualization," 96.

37 See above: chapter 2 section 2.

38 For example: Rida, *Tafsir*, vol. 4: 218.

and its reference to social association and organization on various levels, most notably the town,[41] in addition to the fundamental sense of *ijtimāʿ* as natural sociability, are also not peculiarly modern.

In *al-Manar*, the basic sense of human beings as social creatures becomes most obvious in analogies to social animals. Rida's basic premise is that "man is a collective being by nature (*madanī bi-l-ṭabʿ*), leaning toward social association (*ijtimāʿ*) by his innate disposition (*fiṭra*),"[42] and that the "nature of human society (*ṭabīʿat al-ijtimāʿ al-basharī*) is like the nature of all living beings."[43] The necessity for social association (*ijtimāʿ*) and cooperation (*taʿāwun*) is common to human beings and societal animals, for which Rida repeatedly adduces bees and ants as primary examples.[44] Humans, however, differ from animals in that their social association (*ijtimāʿ*) takes place in increasingly large and complex societies, as Rida points out; he then proceeds to posit Islam as the most comprehensive and thus most appropriate bond for social association/society (*ijtimāʿ*) in contemporary large, diverse, and complex societies/nations (*umam*).[45]

As in this example, in *al-Manar* more generally, the meaning of *ijtimāʿ* repeatedly oscillates between the act of socializing and concurring and the resulting state of society – that is, of an integrated social collectivity. *Ijtimāʿ* most clearly refers to such a collectivity[46] when it is contrasted with *afrād* (individuals)[47] or with a singular person (*shakhṣ*).[48] When speaking of *ḥāl al-ijtimāʿ*, the authors refer to the state of or resulting from social association.[49] *Ijtimāʿ* can be used as shorthand for this state of social association, as well as for societal

39 In the *Tafsir*, Rida quotes al-Tabari (839–923) as using the standard expression "unification of forces (*ijtimāʿ al-kalima*) (ibid., vol. 4: 74).

40 Ibn Taymiyya, Taqi al-Din Ahmad. 1907. "Khilaf al-Umma fi-l-ʿIbadat wa-Madhhab Ahl al-Sunna wa-l-Jamaʿa." *al-Manar* 10/4: 265–279, here 265 ff.

41 For examples, see Nassar, *Mafhum*, esp. 33–41 (mainly on al-Farabi).

42 Rida, Rashid. 1899. "al-Jinsiyya wa-l-Din al-Islami." *al-Manar* 2/21: 321–327, here 321.

43 Idem. 1899. "Falsafat al-Harb al-Hadira." *al-Manar* 2/32: 497–502, here 498 f.

44 This analogy is used in: idem., *Tafsir*, vol. 10: 271, vol. 11: 235; idem. 1912. "As'ila min al-Quqas." *al-Manar* 15/11: 826–832, here 829; idem. 1934. "Shahr Ramadan: Mawsim al-ʿIbada al-Ruhiyya al-Badaniyya al-Ijtimaʿiyya." *al-Manar* 34/6: 473–474, here 473.

45 Idem. 1905. "Rawabit al-Jinsiyya wa-l-Hayat al-Milliya wa-Falsafat al-Ijtimaʿ al-Bashari." *al-Manar* 8/20: 784–791; see also: idem., "al-Jinsiyya wa-l-Din."

46 Other examples include: idem. 1900. "Hikam al-Falasifa wa-Nawadiruhum." *al-Manar* 3/14: 326–327, here 327; idem., "al-As'ila," *al-Manar* 6/23: 907 (potentially as a short form of *al-hay'a al-ijtimāʿiyya* used earlier in the text; this usage would be an exception).

47 For example: idem., *Tafsir*, vol. 2: 25, 26.

48 ʿAbduh, Muhammad. 1898. "Wazifat al-Rusul (ʿAlayhim al-Salam) (Min Risalat al-Tawhid)." *al-Manar* 1/16: 286–294, here 291.

49 See, for example: Rida, *Tafsir*, vol. 5: 29, 48, 265 (the last instance again in contrast to *afrād*).

life (*al-ḥayāt al-ijtimāʿiyya*) or the affairs of society (*shuʾūn al-ijtimāʿ*). In its double reference to both a process and its outcome, *ijtimāʿ* reminds us of 'civilization' and its Arabic equivalents, *tamaddun* and *madaniyya*.[50] In fact, *ijtimāʿ* could be used synonymously with *madaniyya*,[51] and the advancement of *ijtimāʿ*, which is repeatedly addressed in *al-Manar*, refers to the advancement of societal affairs and societal integration.[52] Like *mujtamaʿ* and 'society,' *ijtimāʿ* can designate a wide range of social associations, including the family.[53] The largest collectivity formed through *ijtimāʿ* is that of the *umma*.[54] While *ijtimāʿ*, in designating a social collectivity, could well be translated as 'society,' in most cases I prefer to render it as 'social association,' so as to foreground the fact that *ijtimāʿ* – unlike *umma*, *mujtamaʿ*, or *shaʿb* – was not used to designate particular, reified social collectivities, and also to underline *ijtimāʿ*'s double reference to a process and its outcome.

While *ijtimāʿ* was not used to conceptualize the most modern idea of particular societies, the authors in *al-Manar* repeatedly derived claims about socio-political order from its pre-modern reference to human beings' allegedly natural tendency toward social association, as is most clearly visible in the composite *niẓām al-ijtimāʿ*. In 1898, Rida already stresses that the order of society (*niẓām al-ijtimāʿ*) requires two powers for its completion: "the power of religion (*sulṭat al-dīn*) and the power of politics (*sulṭat al-siyāsa*), or as the men of this age (*ahl hadhā al-ʿaṣr*) say, the spiritual power (*al-sulṭa al-rūḥiyya*) and the temporal power (*al-sulṭa al-zamaniyya*)."[55] Since *mujtamaʿ* and *al-hayʾa al-ijtimāʿiyya*

---

50 The early Arabic term for 'civilization,' *tamaddun*, very much conveyed the idea of civilization as a process, whereas its successor, *madaniyya*, more heavily emphasizes the result of this process.

51 In volume one of *al-Manar*, Rida states: "*ijtimāʿ* contains undeniable material and moral benefits. In fact, *madaniyya* is nothing other than *ijtimāʿ* for the sake of acquainting and cooperating with each other in works beneficial for society (*umma*)" (Rida, "Munkarat," 98). Another pertinent example is: idem. 1900. "al-Dunya wa-l-Akhira (2)." *al-Manar* 3/7: 145–151, here 149fn1.

52 For example: idem., *Tafsir*, vol. 2: 335, vol. 6: 263; idem. 1902. "Bab al-ʿAqaʾid min al-Amali al-Diniyya." *al-Manar* 5/7: 245–252, here 251; idem., "al-Sultatan," 841.

53 For example: idem. 1930. "Musawat al-Marʾa li-l-Rajul fi al-Huquq wa-l-Wajibat: al-Radd al-Tafsili fi Mawduʿ al-Munazara (7)." *al-Manar* 30/9: 690–709, here 698.

54 For an explicit example: idem. 1909. "al-Jinsiyyat al-ʿUthmaniyya wa-l-Lughatan al-ʿArabiyya wa-l-Turkiyya." *al-Manar* 12/7: 501–512, here 502; see also: idem., "al-Sultatan," 857.

55 Idem., "Sultat Mashyakhat," 404. Rida quotes this central statement in: idem. 1898. "al-Khilafa wa-l-Khulafaʾ (1)." *al-Manar* 1/33: 628–633, here 629. For a longer passage from the original article, see above: 262f.

were related to religion or the state in only a few occurrences, we may suppose that the sense of 'society' as a social order distinct from religion and the state was rather expressed by *ijtimāʿ*. Then again, *niẓām al-ijtimāʿ* in itself refers less to the order of one particular society[56] than to the proper order of human beings' social association in general, or on different levels – such as when Rida defines good works (*ṣāliḥāt*) as that which rectifies the souls of individuals (*anfus al-afrād*) and the order of social association (*niẓām al-ijtimāʿ*) in families (*buyūt*), society (*umma*), and the state (*dawla*).[57]

Overall then, the normativity of *ijtimāʿ* is twofold. Firstly, the term conveys the ideas of unity and concurrence, which are necessary to realizing an integrated society (*mujtamaʿ*, *umma*). Secondly, *ijtimāʿ* in *al-Manar* was used to derive claims from the fact of being a social collectivity, which again results from human beings' natural need for social association. It seems, then, that *ijtimāʿ* conveyed that idea of society which was chronologically prior to and an epistemic prerequisite for the subsequent and most modern understanding of 'society' as a reified entity onto which state and religion could be mapped, and which, in Arabic, eventually came to be hegemonically conceptualized as *mujtamaʿ*.

Below I will inquire into how far *ijtimāʿ* conceptualized an understanding of social association as distinct from religion and as operating according to autonomous laws.[58] First, however, the following subsection attends to the adjective *ijtimāʿī(ya)*, showing the centrality of societal issues and reforms in *al-Manar*.

1.2 Societal Aspects and Social Reform: *Ijtimāʿī(ya)* in *al-Manar*

As mentioned above, many Arabic journalists in the early twentieth century, who regarded themselves as spokespersons for the nation and society, advertised their journal as a *majalla ijtimāʿiyya* – that is, as dealing with societal issues. In the subtitles of half of all the volumes of *al-Manar*, Rida positioned his journal as a "monthly journal examining the philosophy of religion and the affairs of social association and civilization" (*majalla shahriyya tabḥuth fī falsafat al-dīn wa-shuʾūn al-ijtimāʿ wa-l-ʿumrān*). The fact that *ijtimāʿ* and *ijtimāʿī*[59] are absent from

---

56 When Rida distinguishes between the beduin and the civil order of society (*niẓām al-ijtimāʿ al-badawī wa-l-madanī*), he designates certain types of social order rather than particular societies (idem., *Tafsir*, vol. 10: 125).

57 Ibid., vol. 11: 415.

58 See sections 2 and 3 of this chapter. The distinction of 'the social' from 'the political' is not in much need of discussion, and thus will be addressed only briefly in the following section.

59 For the sake of reader-friendliness, from hereon I will only use the shorter male adjective.

the subtitles of the other half of the volumes does not diminish the prominence of societal questions in these volumes. In *al-Manar*, *ijtimāʿī* was rather firmly established for conceptualizing 'the social,' but it was not without its competing terms.

I shall thus briefly justify my identification of social knowledge, laws, and issues in *al-Manar* solely via the term *ijtimāʿī*. In his French-Arabic dictionary from 1913, Belot still gives for *social* the Arabic circumscription *khāṣṣ wa-mukhtaṣṣ bi-l-ulfa aw bi-l-jamāʿa* (*relatif à la société*), adding the stand-alone adjective *ulfī*.[60] However, the general problem of dictionaries registering terminological changes has been mentioned above. In this specific case, Belot might have largely reproduced the entry on *social* he found in Bocthor's dictionary from 1828, which notes for the French adjective *social* the circumscription *yakhuṣṣ jamāʿat al-nās* (*qui concerne la société*).[61] In *al-Manar*, the main other terms used to address social relations and issues are, somewhat vaguely, *dunyawī* (usually: 'worldly'), and, slightly more specifically, *qawmī* (usually: 'national') and *madanī* (usually: 'civil'). However, my foremost interest lies in the authors themselves delineating 'the social' by designating it with a specific term. This specificity is only to be expected from *ijtimāʿī*, whose 2,170 occurrences in *al-Manar* are moreover more than sufficient for identifying social laws, knowledge, and issues.

If the advertising of journals as *ijtimāʿī* already indicated the term's positive connotations and contemporary relevance, this becomes even more obvious in Rida's foregrounding of societal transformations, societal knowledge, and societal works, especially in the first decade of the twentieth century. According to Rida, who qualifies the very expression 'social condition' (*al-ḥāl al-ijtimāʿiyya*) as contemporary,[62] the Islamic or Arab society, which is still in the stage of childhood,[63] is currently moving from one social condition or stage (*ḥāl ijtimāʿiyya*) to another.[64] Rida tries to motivate his readers to acquire societal knowledge, to sense the importance of societal life, and to undertake societal works. He does so either by pointing to positive efforts among Muslims or Arabs in this regard or by deploring the lack of such efforts.[65] A primary social question or issue

---

60 Belot, *Dictionnaire*, 1404.

61 Bocthor, *Dictionnaire*, 324.

62 Rida, *Tafsir*, vol. 4: 31.

63 Idem. 1900. "Istimaha wa-Tahni'a." *al-Manar* 3/4: 96; idem., "al-Hayra," 754.

64 Idem. 1908. "Taqriz al-Matbu'at al-Jadida." *al-Manar* 11/7: 528–539, here 538. Rida is here referring to Demolins, *Sirr* and Esquiros, *Amil*.

65 See for example: Rida, Rashid. 1902. "Hurriyyat al-Jara'id wa-l-Shuʿur al-ʿAmm bi-l-Fadila fi Misr." *al-Manar* 5/1: 38–40, here 39; idem. 1904. "al-Ihtifal li-Tadhkar Ta'sis al-Dawla al-ʿAliyya." *al-Manar* 6/22: 875–880, here 876; idem. 1906. "Muslimu al-Sin wa-l-Islam fi al-Yaban." *al-Manar*

which Rida explicitly designates as such – that is, as a *masʾala ijtimāʿiyya* or *shaʾn ijtimāʿī* – is the woman question.[66] Among other topics which Rida characterizes as *ijtimāʿī* are education and interaction between confessional communities.[67] In analogy to the noun *ijtimāʿ*, from which it is derived, *ijtimāʿī* could also rather vaguely denote collective issues, as distinct from personal ones,[68] and could also refer to social associations on various scales, beginning with the married couple and the family or household.[69] Most relevant for our purposes, *ijtimāʿī* could refer to the whole society,[70] sometimes even bordering on the meaning of 'national,' and always conveying a positive sense of connection and integration.

It is primarily the level of the whole society Rida has in mind when, in 1902, he positions journalists as authorities for the modern problématique of societal life:

"[T]he subscribers to newspapers and journals (*al-jarāʾid*) are the leading personalities of the nation (*khawāṣṣ al-umma*) concerning thinking and knowledge (*al-fikr wa-l-ʿilm*), or those equaling (*al-mutashābihūn*) the leading persons; for by knowledge I mean the knowledge of societal life (*ʿilm al-ḥayāt al-ijtimāʿiyya*) and what is related to it, and this is the highest of all types of knowledge (*aʿlā al-ʿulūm*). And the owners of newspapers and journals (*aṣḥāb al-jarāʾid*) who aim at the progress of the nation (*tarqiyat al-umma*) in its collective life (*ḥayātihā al-ijtimāʿiyya*) are the persons most knowledgeable about the condition of society (*ḥāl al-umma*) and the level of its intellectual progress therein (*darajat taraqqī al-fikr fīhā*) and the strength or weakness of its life [i.e., the life of society] among its individuals (*fī afrādihā*)."[71]

8/22: 879–880, here 879, 880; Rashid Rida commenting upon M. N. 1915. "Hal al-Muslimin al-Yawm wa-Jamaʿat al-Daʿwa wa-l-Irshad." *al-Manar* 18/10: 793–799, here 799.

66 See for example: Rida, *Tafsir*, vol. 4: 287; idem., "al-Rijal," 483; idem., "al-Hadaya," *al-Manar* 5/14: 515; idem. 1911. "Taqriz al-Matbuʿat al-Jadida." *al-Manar* 14/1: 71–74, here 71.

67 See, for example: idem. 1899. "Athar ʿIlmiyya Adabiyya." *al-Manar* 2/8: 123–125, here 125; idem. 1921. "al-Rihla al-Suriyya al-Thaniyya (6)." *al-Manar* 22/8: 617–623.

68 For example: idem., *Tafsir*, vol. 3: 113, vol. 6: 263, vol. 8: 173, 408.

69 For example: ibid., vol. 2: 300 f.

70 For example: idem. 1932. "al-Muʾtamar al-Islami al-ʿAmm fi Bayt al-Muqaddas (3)." *al-Manar* 32/4: 284–292, here 286 (*al-aʿmāl al-nāfiʿa min shakhṣiyya wa-manziliyya wa-ijtimāʿiyya*). Salih Mukhlis Rida once explains *ijtimāʿī* as *qawmī* (national) in distinction from the level of the household (Rida, Salih Mukhlis, "al-Taqriz," *al-Manar* 15/4: 308).

71 Rida, Rashid. 1902. "Mutill Qiraʾ al-Jaraʾid." *al-Manar* 4/23: 919–920, here 919 f. A few issues prior to this, Rida characterized papers as "social schools (*madāris ijtimāʿiyya*)" and their own-

According to Rida, the first person to write about the societal conditions of Muslims (*aḥwāl al-muslimīn al-ijtimāʿiyya*) was al-Afghani.[72] With *al-Manar*, Rida claims to follow up on the societal teachings of *al-ʿUrwa al-Wuthqa*,[73] the short-lived paper founded by al-Afghani and ʿAbduh, which Rida says motivated him to become a journalist.[74]

In the Islamic journal *al-Manar*, the goal of social reform – to which many journalists dedicated themselves – was mostly put forward in conjunction with religious reform. Rida repeatedly formulates the goal of *al-Manar* as *al-iṣlāḥ al-dīnī wa-l-ijtimāʿī* (religious and societal reform)[75] and presents the journal or its articles as dealing with these two aspects.[76] An interesting variation on this is the substitution of 'philosophical' for 'religious,'[77] recalling the fact that *al-Manar*'s most famous subtitle also reads *falsafat al-dīn* (the philosophy

---

ers and writers as directors of these schools (idem. 1901. "al-Akhbar al-Tarikhiyya." *al-Manar* 4/18: 714–720, here 719 f.).

72 Idem., "al-Jamiʿa al-Islamiyya," 337.

73 Ibid., 342; see also: idem. 1899. "al-Islah al-Islami fi al-Jaraʾid." *al-Manar* 1/49: 949–956, here 949.

74 See above: 139.

75 For example: idem. [1907]. "Muqaddimat al-Tabʿa al-Thaniyya li-l-Mujallad al-Awwal min al-Manar." *al-Manar* 1/1–8, here 1 (this introduction, which was added to the reprint of the first volume, quotes these goals of reform from the original introduction); idem. 1905. "Khatimat al-Sanna al-Sabiʿa." *al-Manar* 7/24: 954–960, here 954; idem. 1919. "al-Shaykh Muhammad Kamil al-Rafiʿi (3)." *al-Manar* 21/6: 325–327, here 325; idem. 1932. "al-Malik Faysal al-Husayni al-Hashimi." *al-Manar* 33/5: 387–390, here 389. Rida said he would only publish biographies of figures with merits in societal or religious reform (idem.,"Tarjamat al-Tabib," 485). Rida exemplifies the ubiquitous meaning of *ijtimāʿ* as unity and concurrence, when he writes that "*al-Manar* is a paper for all Muslims [...], calling them to *al-ijtimāʿ* based on what they agree upon" (idem. 1911. "Fatihat al-Mujallad al-Rabiʿ ʿAshar." *al-Manar* 14/1: 1–8, here 8).

76 For example: idem. 1925. "Min ʿAdhiri." *al-Manar* 26/4: 307–318, here 311. Readers and commentators also praised *al-Manar* for attending to religious and societal issues, or to religion and society (for example: Saʾih Muhibb li-l-Manar, "Siraliyun," 757; a reader from Sudan quoted in Rida, Rashid. 1909. "al-Qadaʾ wa-l-Qadr." *al-Manar* 12/3: 189–200, here 89 f.; al-Liban, Mustafa Ahmad al-Rifaʿi. 1935. "Zuhur al-Manar wa-Dalalatuhu." *al-Manar* 35/1: 77–79, here 79). One reader critically remarked that *al-Manar* is giving less attention to the affairs of society than promised (Ahmad Zaki Abu Shadi quoted in Rida, Rashid. 1916. "al-Intiqad ʿala al-Manar." *al-Manar* 19/4: 190–192, here 190 f.); but compare his letter to one published later in the same year: Abu Shadi, Ahmad Zaki. 1917. "Taʾthir al-Sihafa fi Akhlaq al-Umma." *al-Manar* 19/8: 507–509.

77 Rida, "Muqaddimat al-Tabʿa al-Thaniyya," 8; idem., "Rawabit al-Jinsiyya," 784; idem., "Khatimat al-Sanna al-Sabiʿa," 960. Articles could also be "social and philosophical" (idem. 1913. "ʿIbar al-Harb al-Balqaniyya wa-Khatar al-Masʾala al-Sharqiyya." *al-Manar* 16/1: 54–63, here 60). And, writing to Lord Cromer, Rida presented himself as the "owner of an Islamic journal, defending religion (*dīn*) and investigating its philosophy" (idem., "al-Jamiʿa al-Islamiyya," 231).

of religion). Other variations on the conceptual pair *dīnī–ijtimāʿī* are the replacement of *dīnī* with *rūḥī* (spiritual)[78] or, less often, *maʿnāwī* (spiritual/mental)[79] and the replacement of *ijtimāʿī* with *madanī* (civil).[80] The ethical (*adabī/akhlāqī*) is repeatedly introduced as a mediating sphere between religion and society.[81] *Ijtimāʿī* could also be addressed as an aspect of religion itself,[82] and the religious as an aspect of the social,[83] further testifying to the possibility that terms could shift position in relation to other terms. Nevertheless, Rida conceived not only of particular societal reasons,[84] but also of a societal perspective,[85] not least in distinction from a religious perspective.[86] Relatedly, and although he occasionally also validated scholars of religion in their knowledge of societal affairs,[87] Rida singled out societal writers or philosophers in an exclusively positive manner, as will be shown in the following subsection (2.1). Clearly then, Rida distinguished between religious and societal aspects, reasons, perspectives, and actors.

In fact, Rida's own Islamic discourse can be characterized as shifting between a religious and a societal perspective, thereby integrating both perspectives. The following statements by Rida and contemporaneous observers support

---

78 Often, this is in the context of addressing spiritual and social defects or diseases (for example: idem. 1899. "Khitab Waʿzi li-l-Insan." *al-Manar* 2/1: 1–12, here 3; idem. 1900. "Athar ʿIlmiyya Adabiyya." *al-Manar* 3/3: 64–72, here 67; idem., "al-Rihla al-Urubiyya," *al-Manar* 23/4: 309; idem. 1933. "ʿIsmat al-Anbiyaʾ." *al-Manar* 33/8: 609–614, here 614). For *rūḥī* complementing *ijtimāʿī* concerning the aspired reform, see: idem., *Tafsir*, vol. 8: 94.

79 For example: ibid., vol. 7: 197; idem. 1915. "Fasl fi Hikam Shahadat Ghayr al-Muslimin ʿala al-Muslimin." *al-Manar* 18/8: 575–583, here 583.

80 Where *ijtimāʿī* refers to collective life more vaguely, it may itself be distinguished into *dīnī* (religious) and *madanī* (civil) (for example: idem. 1900. "Khatimat al-Sanna al-Thaniyya li-l-Manar." *al-Manar* 2/48: 767–768, here 768).

81 In chapter 10 section 3, I suggest that Rida conceived of ethics as a mediator between religion and society.

82 For example, distinguishing between the social (*ijtimāʿī*) and spiritual (*rūḥī*) aspects of religion (*dīn*): idem. 1899. "al-Shariʿa wa-l-Tabiʿa wa-l-Haqq wa-l-Batil." *al-Manar* 2/41: 641–648, here 645.

83 For example: idem., *Tafsir*, vol. 10: 123.

84 For example: idem. 1904. "al-Suʾal wa-l-Fatwa: Taʿaddud al-Zawjat." *al-Manar* 7/6: 231–240, here 232; idem., "Bahth fi al-Muʾtamar," 676.

85 For example: idem. 1904. "Taʾthir al-Jaraʾid wa-Haluha fi Misr." *al-Manar* 7/10: 399–400, here 400; idem. 1911. "Taqrir al-Lajna al-Tahdiriyya li-l-Muʾtamar al-Misri." *al-Manar* 14/6: 449–457, here 451.

86 For example: idem. 1907. "al-Muʾtamar al-Islami." *al-Manar* 11/3: 181–184, here 184; idem., "al-Khilafa," *al-Manar* 24/5: 364; idem. 1927. "al-Murad bi-l-Taʿn fi al-Din – wa-Kawn Mukhalafat al-Qurʾan Kufran." *al-Manar* 28/8: 578–583, here 583; idem., *Tafsir*, vol. 4: 56, vol. 10: 273.

87 For example: idem. 1907. "ʿUlamaʾ Tunis wa-Misr wa-Jamiʿ al-Zaytuna wa-l-Azhar." *al-Manar* 10/1: 71–80, here 73.

this characterization. In 1899, Rida himself wrote that he partially agrees both with Muslims who assert that religion is the only means to progress and with experts on *ijtimāʿ* who blame religion for Muslims' weakness.[88] Furthermore, while Rida characterized Islamic reformists (*muṣliḥūn*) as criticizing both Westernized and traditionalist Muslims (*mutafarnijūn, muqallidūn*), he depicted reformism less as a middle way between Islam and the West and more as the desire to reform the societal conditions of Muslims (*ḥāl al-muslimīn al-ijtimāʿiyya*) while preserving religion.[89] To this end, the party of the middle way ought to turn on "one side to order (*niẓām*) and civilization (*madaniyya*), and [on] one to religion."[90] Furthermore, Lord Cromer, whose depiction of Islamic reformism as a middle way Rida drew upon, said that Muhammad ʿAbduh had created a "moderate party combining the principles of Islam and of civilization (*madaniyya*)."[91] And in 1913, the editor of a French journal published in Cairo attested that Rida had "elevated his journal to the highest position, which it rightfully occupies, between the world of societal thought (*al-ʿālam al-fikrī al-ijtimāʿī*) and the world of Islamic religious thought (*al-ʿālam al-dīnī al-islāmī*)."[92]

While the characterization I suggest here somewhat resembles the common depiction of Islamic reformism as a middle way between (traditional) Islam and the (modern) West, it foregrounds the fact that the West was not the exclusive originator and proprietor of modernity, but rather epitomized modernity, civilization, and societal knowledge. Rida shared the view of the West as contemporaneously embodying the principles of society, but ultimately regarded these principles as universal, and thus as expressible from within an Islamic discourse as well.[93] Moreover, Rida keeps shifting perspective from the religious to the social and back: he posits religion as a requirement of society (since humankind's social nature is created by God) and argues for proper social association, as required by religion. Rida's integration of religious and societal reasons and perspectives thus seems a more adequate depiction of his Islamic discourse than the idea that he combined (Islamic) tradition and (Western) modernity.

---

88 Idem., "al-Shariʿa wa-l-Tabiʿa," 646.

89 Idem., "al-Shaykh Muhammad ʿAbduh," 282.

90 Ibid., 286.

91 Idem., "al-Radd ʿala al-Lurd," 205.

92 Al-Majalla al-Misriyya al-Fransiyya quoted in Rida, Rashid. 1913. "al-Majalla al-Misriyya al-Fransiyya wa-Ra'yuha fi al-Manar." *al-Manar* 16/8: 619.

93 See the following section.

In any case, to the two constitutive categories of the religious and the social (or religion and society)[94] in *al-Manar* is often added a third – namely, the political.[95] In 1908, Rida interestingly quotes from the journal's first volume that the aim of *al-Manar* was religious and social reform (*al-iṣlāḥ al-dīnī wa-l-ijtimāʿī*) and adds that it was ʿAbduh who had made him delete the third goal – political reform (*al-iṣlāḥ al-siyāsī*).[96] In this threefold scheme, *ijtimāʿī* was more frequently replaced with *madanī* than in the basic distinction between religion and society.[97] The two other main aspects or spheres that are sometimes additionally distinguished from the religious, the societal, and the political are the economic (*iqtiṣādī*)[98] and the military (*ḥarbī/ʿaskarī*).[99] While it would be worthwhile to investigate the conceptual evolution of the economic and its relation to the societal

94 While Rida directly relates religion (*dīn*) to social association (*ijtimāʿ*) less often than he addresses religious aspects in relation to societal ones, he adduces these two central categories in the subtitle of *al-Manar* (*...falsafat al-dīn wa-shuʾūn al-ijtimāʿ...*). He uses this pair again in a book review from 1904 (Rida, Rashid. 1904. "al-Taqriz." *al-Manar* 6/21: 838–840, here 838). And in 1914, for example, he entitled a section of an article: "the harms of Europeanized [Muslims or Arabs] (*mutafarnijīn*) concerning the matter of religion and society (*amr al-dīn wa-l-ijtimāʿ*)" (idem. 1914. "al-Akhbar wa-l-Araʾ." *al-Manar* 17/2: 153–160, here 156). Rida refers to this in: idem., *Tafsir*, vol. 9: 273.

95 For example: idem. 1902. "Masir al-Anam wa-Masir al-Islam." *al-Manar* 5/18: 681–693, here 681; idem. 1902. "Khatimat al-Sanna al-Rabiʿa." *al-Manar* 4/24: 959–960, here 960; idem. 1905. "Athar ʿIlmiyya Adabiyya." *al-Manar* 8/7: 272–275, here 275; idem. 1909. "al-Hurriya wa-Istiqlal al-Fikr." *al-Manar* 12/2: 113–117, here 114; idem. 1912. "Taqriz al-Matbuʿat al-Jadida." *al-Manar* 15/12: 945–953, here 951; idem. 1914. "Muhadarat al-Duktur Kristiyan Snuk Hurghrunj al-Hulandi fi al-Islam wa-Mustaqbal al-Muslimin." *al-Manar* 17/4: 268–272, here 270; idem. 1919. "al-Tatawwur al-Siyasi wa-l-Dini wa-l-Ijtimaʿi bi-Misr." *al-Manar* 21/5: 274–277; Rashid Rida commenting upon Arslan, "Azimat," 201fn*; Rida, "al-Tajdid," *al-Manar* 32/3: 227; idem. 1933. "al-Malik Faysal: al-ʿIbra bi-Hayatihi wa-Wifatihi." *al-Manar* 33/6: 457–461, here 457.

96 Idem. 1909. "Fatihat al-Sanna al-Thaniyya ʿAshara." *al-Manar* 12/1: 1–15, here 2. Rida nevertheless portrayed himself, and was regarded by others, as continuing the path of al-Afghani and ʿAbduh concerning *al-iṣlāḥ al-dīni wa-l-ijtimāʿī wa-l-siyāsī* (idem., "al-Inqilab," 554 f.; Amin, ʿAbdallah. 1935. "Naʿi Faqid al-Islam wa-l-Muslimin al-Sayyid al-Imam Muhammad Rashid Rida Munshiʾ al-Manar." *al-Manar* 35/2: 153–161, here 155).

97 For example: Rida, "al-Muʾtamar," *al-Manar* 32/2: 114.

98 For example: idem., "al-Marʾa al-Jadida," 28; idem., "Bahth fi al-Muʾtmar," 676; idem., "al-Akhbar wa-l-Araʾ," *al-Manar* 17/2: 158; idem. 1928. "al-Hukumat al-Ladiniyya li-l-Shuʿub al-Islamiyya al-Aʿjimiyya wa-ʿAwaqibuha fi al-Turk wa-l-Fars wa-l-Afghan." *al-Manar* 29/8: 635–636, here 636; idem. 1935. "al-Tarbiya al-Islamiyya wa-l-Taʿlim al-Islami." *al-Manar* 34/7: 544–548, here 544.

99 For example: idem., *Tafsir*, vol. 6: 81; idem. 1921. "Asʾila Maghribiyya min ʿAsimat al-Bilad al-Isbaniyya." *al-Manar* 22/6: 429–442, here 435.

in Rida's writings,[100] what matters to us here, in view of the pre-configured understanding of 'society,' is that Rida conceptually distinguished social from religious and political aspects of life.

The fact that Rida shared the modern distinction between the social and the political is not in much need of elaboration. Since Rida and other Islamic reformists are known to have aimed primarily at the reform of society rather than the state,[101] they clearly perceived a pre-political social association. In this regard, it is worth considering the differentiation of the pre-modern concept *madanī* into *ijtimāʿī* and *siyāsī*[102] – at least, I am unaware of any pre-modern usages of the adjective *ijtimāʿī*. Moreover, Rida not only shares the threefold scheme of the religious, the social, and the political, as shown in the previous paragraph, but also frequently distinguishes social (*ijtimāʿī*) from political (*siyāsī*) matters[103] or reforms[104]. However, in cases where *ijtimāʿī* refers more vaguely to 'the collective,' it often comprises both the social and the political. The political can also be present in *ijtimāʿī* as an extension of the social – from which, after all, political claims were derived. Thus, *ijtimāʿī* can refer either to the social in distinction from the political or to the socio-political.

Keeping this in mind, the following two sections attend to the other two crucial aspects of our pre-configured concept of 'society.'[105] Recalling that it was the

---

100 The term *iqtiṣād*, including the adjective *iqtiṣādī(ya)*, occurs 829 times in *al-Manar.* It is present from the first volume onward and does not notably increase over the journal's life span. Only 35 out of the 829 occurrences are in the *Tafsir.* A related term denoting (much less specifically) the economic sphere is *mālī(ya).*

101 See, for example: Haddad, "The Manarists." In volume two of *al-Manar*, Rida explains that "the direction (*wijha*) of *al-Manar* in calling for the Islamic reform (*al-iṣlāḥ al-islāmī*) is the Islamic society (*al-umma al-islāmiyya*), without its government (*dūn ḥukūmatihā*)" (Rida Rashid. 1899. "Tahrif al-Kalam ʿan Mawadiʿihi: Radd ʿala Muslim Hurr al-Afkar." *al-Manar* 2/25: 385–391, here 386).

102 On the background of this differentiation, Rida posits human social association (*ijtimāʿ*) to be political by nature (*madanī bi-ṭabʿ*). Here, he notably conceives of social association – which, according to him, requires both a spiritual and a worldly authority – within the modern threefold scheme of society, religion, and state (idem., "al-ʿIzz," 194).

103 For example: idem. 1905. "al-Akhbar wa-l-Araʾ." *al-Manar* 7/21: 833–840, here 835; Rashid Rida commenting upon al-Kawakibi, ʿAbd al-Rahman. 1906. "Tijarat al-Raqiq wa-Ahkamuhu fi al-Islam." *al-Manar* 8/22: 854–861, here 861; Rida, Rashid. 1907. "Bab al-Intiqad ʿala al-Manar." *al-Manar* 10/2: 160; idem. 1911. "Fatawa al-Manar." *al-Manar* 14/3: 178–190, here 180; idem., "al-Rihla al-Urubiyya," *al-Manar* 23/8: 638; idem., "al-Ladiniyun," 499 f.

104 For example: idem. 1903. "Raʾy fi Islah al-Muslimin aw Raʾyan." *al-Manar* 5/24: 921–930, here 926; idem., "Mulakhkhas Sirat," *al-Manar* 8/10: 400; idem., "al-Sayyid ʿAbd al-Hamid al-Zahrawi," 170.

105 See above: chapter 2 sections 3 and 4.

discipline of sociology that institutionally expressed and then solidified the understanding of society and its laws as autonomous, the following section (2) analyzes the place and role of sociology and societal laws in Rida's writings. The subsequent section (3) will then explore how Rida related the social (*ijtimāʿī*) to the religious (*dīnī*) and to *islām*.

2 Sociology and Soci(et)al Laws: Grounding the Social in Nature and God

2.1 Sociology and Societal Thinkers: Rida's Positive but Vague Reception

It is a remarkable statistical fact that Rida, who avoided the supposedly pertinent terms for 'society' – *al-hayʾa al-ijtimāʿiyya* and *mujtamaʿ* – accounts for a total of 103 of the overall 132 occurrences of *ʿilm al-ijtimāʿ* (sociology) in *al-Manar.*[106] This subsection shows that Rida very much stressed the need for *ʿilm al-ijtimāʿ* and referred to its practitioners in an exclusively positive vein. However, he did not engage with sociological thought in depth. Two aspects worth addressing are the extent to which Rida shared the understanding of sociology as peculiarly modern, and whether he conceived of sociology as a distinct discipline.

In the first volumes of *al-Manar*, Rida already explains *ʿilm al-ijtimāʿ al-basharī* as meaning *al-susiyūlūjiyya* (sociology),[107] and distinguishes *ʿilm al-ijtimāʿ* from history (*ʿilm al-tārīkh*) and even from its neighboring discipline, political economics (*ʿilm al-iqtiṣād al-siyāsī*).[108] In a manner typical of Islamic reformists, he considers these branches of knowledge equally important as knowledge about religion, morals, Islamic law, or the Arabic language.[109] We here recall the context of new secular educational institutions undoing the former monopoloy of religious institutions.[110] The strength of European nations also rested on their knowledge of *ʿilm al-ijtimāʿ*,[111] Rida maintains, and he consequently attrib-

---

106 35 instances of *ʿilm al-ijtimāʿ* are found in the *Tafsir.* Of the ten instances in the verses commented upon by ʿAbduh, I have attributed only those four instances to Rida in which he clearly marks himself as the author. He may well have written additional instances of these examples.
107 Rida, Rashid. 1901. "al-Muhawarat bayna al-Muslih wa-l-Muqallid (4)." *al-Manar* 3/32: 795–804, here 804.
108 Idem., "Ma La Budda," 572.
109 Ibid., 572; idem., "al-Kutub al-ʿArabiyya," 51; idem. 1900. "al-ʿIlm wa-l-Jahl." *al-Manar* 3/24: 553–557, here 555f.
110 See above: 110.
111 Rida, Rashid. 1911. "al-Muslimun wa-l-Qubt (1)." *al-Manar* 14/2: 108–114, here 109.

utes Muslim weakness in part to their ignorance of this science.[112] Rida repeatedly adduces knowledge about the social and about the characteristics of society (*umma*) as the decisive criterion in socio-political debates,[113] without entering into sociological arguments proper or even justifying the validity of *ʿilm al-ijtimāʿ* in the first place. Rida further elevates *ʿilm al-ijtimāʿ* by stressing that only the most intelligent among those studying history (*ʿilm al-tārīkh*) and ethics (*ʿilm al-akhlāq*) are capable of discerning the bases of *ʿilm al-ijtimāʿ*.[114]

In fact, Rida repeatedly identifies history and the modern historiographical method as the foundation of *ʿilm al-ijtimāʿ*,[115] whence it comes as no surprise that he praises the fourteenth-century Arab philosopher and historian Ibn Khaldun as "the founder of sociology" (*muʾassis ʿilm al-ijtimāʿ*).[116] This is also not surprising given that Ibn Khaldun was more widely and is still today considered an early sociologist by Muslim and non-Muslim scholars alike.[117] In *al-Manar*, Ibn Khaldun is implicitly or explicitly referred to by several authors.[118] Remarkably, however, with one exception,[119] Rida is the sole contributor to *al-Manar* who explicitly adduces Ibn Khaldun as a 'sociologist' or 'social philosopher.'[120] Accord-

---

112 Implicitly: ibid.: 109; explicitly: idem. 1911. "Radd al-Manar." *al-Manar* 14/10: 770 – 781, here 771.

113 For example: idem., *Tafsir*, vol. 5: 7; idem. 1910. "al-Tarbiya al-Qawima wa-l-Siyasa al-Hikmiyya: al-Thiqqa wa-l-Zinna." *al-Manar* 13/8: 591–597, here 597; idem., "al-Tarbiya wa-Wijh," 572 f.

114 Idem., *Tafsir*, vol. 4: 33.

115 For example: Rashid Rida commenting upon ʿAbduh, Muhammad. 1899. "al-Quwa wa-l-Qanun." *al-Manar* 1/48: 917–923, here 922 f.; idem., "al-Muhawarat," *al-Manar* 3/32: 804; idem. 1925. "al-Matbuʿat al-Jadida." *al-Manar* 25/10: 797–799, here 797 f.; idem, *Tafsir*, vol. 1: 235 (here naming sociologists as a sub-group of historians). Elsewhere, Rida posits history as a branch of *ʿilm al-ijtimāʿ* (idem., "Kitab Misr," 107); as did ʿAbduh once (Muhammad ʿAbduh quoted in Rida, Rashid. 1922. "al-Ihtifal bi-Dhikra al-Ustadh al-Imam (2)." *al-Manar* 23/8: 593 – 611, here 596).

116 Idem. 1928. "Rihlat Jalalat Malik al-Afghan (Aman Allah Khan)." *al-Manar* 28/10: 782–787, here 785.

117 See above: 66.

118 Most substantially in: al-Bitar, "Kitab," *al-Manar* 27/4: 296.

119 Al-Nashashibi, Isʿaf. 1927. "al-ʿArabiyya wa-Shaʿiruha al-Akbar Ahmad Shuqi Bek." *al-Manar* 28/3: 213 – 224, here 219 (*wāḍiʿ ʿilm al-ijtimāʿ*).

120 Rida, *Tafsir*, vol. 5: 227, vol. 9: 400; idem. 1905. "Taqrir Mashyakhat ʿUlamaʾ al-Iskandriyya: al-Ihsaʾ al-ʿAmm." *al-Manar* 8/21: 820 – 832, here 828; idem. 1912. "al-Khutba al-Raʾisiyya fi Nadwat al-ʿUlamaʾ bi-Lukunuhuʾ [Lucknow] al-Hind li-Sahib al-Manar (1)." *al-Manar* 15/5: 331– 341, here 339; idem. 1914. "al-Taʿrif bi-Kitab al-Iʿtisam." *al-Manar* 17/10: 745 – 749, here 746; idem. 1923. "al-Khilafa al-Islamiyya (6)." *al-Manar* 24/5: 345 – 365, here 357; idem. 1929. "al-Jamʿ bayna Masʾalat al-Dhikran wa-l-Inath fi al-Madaris wa-Masʾalat al-Tajdid wa-l-Tajaddud." *al-Manar* 30/2: 115 – 127, here 120.

ing to Rida, the famous *Muqaddima* of Ibn Khaldun was the sole Arabic book on sociology available to Azhari students around the turn to the twentieth century.[121] No knowledgeable person would contest the place of the *Muqaddima* in the philosophy of history and sociology (*falsafat al-tārīkh wa-ʿilm al-ijtimāʿ*),[122] Rida contends, and he recommends this work as an entry point into the discipline of sociology.[123] In fact, the *Muqaddima* provided the basis upon which Europeans expanded the sciences of civilization, politics, and society (*ʿulūm al-ʿumrān wa-l-siyāsa wa-l-ijtimāʿ*), Rida claims.[124] He further suggests the distinctiveness of contemporary sociology when he mentions that Ibn Khaldun's "philosophy of history and science of the social and of civilization" (*ʿilm al-ijtimāʿ wa-l-ʿumrān*)" was the best work at the time, but that the social sciences have progressed since.[125]

There are only a very few references to contemporaneous Arabic works on sociology in *al-Manar*, something which can only partially be explained by the fact that there were plainly few such works. Rida points out that Muhammad ʿAbduh complemented the foundation laid by Ibn Khaldun[126] and not only taught the *Muqaddima* to his students, but also composed a work on the philosophy of society and history himself, in which he partly criticized Ibn Khaldun.[127] Rida offered subscriptions to the Beirutian *Journal of Social Sciences* (*Majallat al-ʿUlum al-Ijtimaʿiyya*)[128] via the office of *al-Manar*.[129] In his own journal, however, he accorded merely a few lines to Niqula Haddad's pioneering two-volume work on *ʿIlm al-Ijtimaʿ*.[130] The only article in *al-Manar* fully dedicated to sociology was written in 1926 by Muhammad Bahjat al-Bitar, who discussed a book by the Damascene scholar, ʿArif al-Nakdi (1887–1975).[131] The department of sociology estab-

---

121 Idem., *Tafsir*, vol. 4: 33. This volume of the *Tafsir* is based on volumes 10–13 of *al-Manar* (1907–1911). Rida here refers back to lessons ʿAbduh gave at al-Azhar; see also: idem., "al-Marʾa," *al-Manar* 4/1: 28.

122 Idem. 1904. "al-Taqriz." *al-Manar* 7/15: 596–600, here 596.

123 Idem., "al-Muhawarat," *al-Manar* 3/32: 804.

124 Idem. 1902. "al-Hadaya wa-l-Taqariz." *al-Manar* 4/21: 836–840, here 836.

125 Idem., *Tafsir*, vol. 5: 234.

126 Idem. 1931. "Ilhad fi al-Qurʾan wa-Din Jadid bayna al-Batiniyya wa-l-Islam [4]: al-Sunan al-Kawniyya al-Ijtimaʿiyya wa-Nizam al-Kawn." *al-Manar* 32/1: 33–48, here 42.

127 Idem., "Tatimmat Mulakhkhas;" 403 f.; idem. 1905. "Tatimmat Sirat al-Ustadh al-Imam." *al-Manar* 8/13: 487–495, here 492.

128 For a brief presentation of the journal, see: Rida, Salih Mukhlis, "Taqriz," *al-Manar* 17/1: 67.

129 Maktabat al-Manar. 1914. *Fihris Maktabat al-Manar li-Ashabiha Rida wa-Khatib wa-Qatalan*. Cairo: Matbaʿat al-Manar, 155.

130 See above: 273.

131 Al-Bitar, "Kitab," *al-Manar* 27/4; idem., "Kitab al-Mujaz fi al-Ijtimaʿ." *al-Manar* 27/5: 354–362.

lished at Cairo University at the same time is not mentioned at all in *al-Manar.*[132] While this scarcity of references to contemporaneous sociology in Arabic already points to the possibility that Rida more loosely infused sociological knowledge into other discourses (see the following subsection), a look at those actors whom Rida designated as social philosophers or as knowledgable about society confirms a certain distinctiveness of the societal perspective.

Whenever Rida characterizes someone as an *ʿālim ijtimāʿī* (sociologist, also more broadly: someone knowledgeable about society), this is done in the most respectful and positive sense. This is best demonstrated in Rida's discussion of the underlying reason for the progress of society (*umma*). Rida first paraphrases the opinions of four groups: intellectuals (*ʿuqalāʾ*), those dealing with politics (*al-mushtaghilūn bi-l-siyāsa*), scholars of education (*ʿulamāʾ al-tarbiya*), and economists (*ʿulamāʾ al-iqtiṣād*). The different reasons these groups bring forward are all refuted by *al-ʿālim al-ijtimāʿī*, who himself adduces the formation of associations (*jamʿiyyāt*) and corporations (*sharikāt*) as central for the advancement of society (*umma*).[133] Rida suggests some distinctiveness in the designation of *ʿālim ijtimāʿī* when he corrects one of his contributors, who uses the wording *ʿuqalāʾ al-ijtimāʿ* to *ʿulamāʾ al-ijtimāʿ*.[134] However, he himself repeatedly uses it in a loose sense to positively characterize persons knowledgable about communal affairs. Thus, for example, he designates Bismarck as "the most famous of political leaders (*zuʿāmāʾ al-siyāsa*) and of those knowledgeable about society (*ʿulamāʾ al-ijtimāʿ*)."[135]

Concerning contemporary Arab thinkers, Rida more often speaks of 'societal writers' or 'social philosophers' than of *ʿulamāʾ al-ijtimāʿ*, again in an exclusively positive manner, suggesting a particular societal perspective. He foregrounds the particularity of this perspective when he explains that ʿAbd al-Rahman al-Kawakibi is "from among the scholars of society and politics (*ʿulamāʾ al-ijtimāʿ wa-l-siyāsa*), not from among the scholars of religion (*ʿulamāʾ al-dīn*)."[136] Elsewhere, Rida characterizes al-Kawakibi as a sociological scholar (*ʿālim ijtimāʿī*)[137] or as a philosopher of society (*ḥakīm al-ijtimāʿ*)[138]. Qasim Amin is the only other contem-

---

132 At least not by employing the term *ijtimāʿ*.

133 Rida, "Manafiʿ," *al-Manar* 10/5: 340 – 344.

134 Idem. 1914. "Namudhaj min Inshaʾ Talabat Dar al-Daʿwa wa-l-Irshad." *al-Manar* 17/7: 545 – 555, here 547fn3.

135 Idem., "al-ʿAql," 190.

136 Idem. 1913. "Fatawa al-Manar." *al-Manar* 16/9: 675 – 688, here 687.

137 Idem., "Khatimat al-Sanna al-Rabiʿa," 959.

138 Idem. 1902. "Masab ʿAzim bi-Wifat ʿAlim Hakim." *al-Manar* 5/6: 237 – 240, here 237; idem., "al-Muʾtamar al-Islami," *al-Manar* 32/2: 114.

porary Arab thinker whom Rida designates as *ʿālim ijtimāʿī* – or rather, as "from among the scholars of rights (*ḥuqūq*), morals (*akhlāq*), society (*ijtimāʿ*), and rational philosophy (*al-falsafa al-ʿaqliyya*)."[139] Moreover, Rida reveres Amin as having belonged to "the societal reformists" (*al-muṣliḥūn al-ijtimāʿīyūn*).[140] Such 'societal reformists' are mentioned only once more, by Lord Cromer.[141] Rida further characterizes Jamal al-Din al-Afghani as a "social and political philosopher" (*al-ḥakīm al-ijtimāʿī al-siyāsī*).[142] As 'societal philosophers,' he also designates Shibli Shumayyil (*al-ḥakīm al-ijtimāʿī*)[143] and ʿAbd al-Hamid al-Zahrawi (*min al-falāsifa al-ijtimāʿiyīn*)[144]. On two other occasions, Rida characterizes al-Zahrawi as a "societal writer" (*al-kātib al-ijtimāʿī*).[145] The only other author Rida thus characterizes repeatedly – other than, as mentioned above, Rafiq al-ʿAzm[146] – is Farid Wajdi.[147] Overall then, the designation of someone as a 'social philosopher' or 'societal writer' was a distinction Rida accorded to only a few Arab writers – those who specialized in questions of socio-political order and societal life.

---

139 Idem. 1908. "Masab Misr bi-Qasim Bek Amin." *al-Manar* 11/3: 226–229, here 226.

140 Ibid., 229.

141 Lord Cromer quoted in Rida, Rashid 1905. "al-Hayat al-Zawjiyya (3)." *al-Manar* 8/5: 182–190, here 184.

142 Rashid Rida commenting upon al-Afghani, Jamal al-Din. 1924. "al-Maqalat al-Jamaliyya (2): al-Sharq wa-l-Sharqiyun." *al-Manar* 25/8: 593–621, here 598.

143 Rida, "al-Duktur," 625.

144 Idem., "al-Sayyid ʿAbd al-Hamid al-Zahrawi," 169.

145 Rashid Rida in al-Zahrawi, ʿAbd al-Hamid. 1906. "Kayfa yakun al-Naqd? Kalam fi 'Kitab al-Taʿlim wa-l-Irshad' wa-Masaʾil Shatta." *al-Manar* 9/10: 788–795, here 795; Rida, Rashid. 1908. "Tarikh al-ʿArab wa-l-Islam fi Silk al-Qisas wa-l-Riwayat." *al-Manar* 11/1: 64.

146 See above: 303fn1.

147 Idem. 1933. "Taqriz al-Matbuʿat al-Jadida." *al-Manar* 33/2: 141–150, here 145; idem. 1933. "Daʾirat al-Maʿarif al-Islamiyya." *al-Manar* 33/6: 474–478, here 475; idem., "al-Matbuʿat al-Munkara," 534. For Wajdi's own understanding of *ʿilm al-ijtimāʿ*, see: Wajdi, Muhammad Farid. 1971. *Daʾirat Maʿarif al-Qarn al-ʿAshrin*. Beirut: Dar al-Fikr, vol. 3: 149–162. Once each, Rida characterizes as *al-kātib al-ijtimāʿī* Ahmad Faris (Rida, Rashid. 1915. "Sufur al-Nisaʾ wa-Ikhtilatuhunna bi-l-Rijal wa-Fawda al-Adab bi-Misr." *al-Manar* 18/3: 227–233, here 228), Muhammad Ahmad Jad (idem., "Taqriz," *al-Manar* 33/2: 141), and the priest Anistas al-Karmali (idem. 1915. "Taqriz al-Matbuʿat al-Jadida." *al-Manar* 18/4: 315–320, here 319). He twice introduces the poet Hafiz Ibrahim as *shāʿir ijtimāʿī*, possibly referring to his popularity (idem. 1932. "Muhammad Hafiz Bak Ibrahim Shaʿir Misr al-Ijtimaʿi." *al-Manar* 32/8: 625–630; idem. 1932. "Ahmad Shawqi Bek Amir al-Shuʿaraʾ." *al-Manar* 32/9: 719–720, here 719) and calls Talʿat Harb, the founder of the Bank of Egypt, an *ustādh ijtimāʿī iqtiṣādī* (idem., "al-Jamʿ," 128). The only other two mentions of a 'societal writer' are when Rashid Rida's brother Salih Mukhlis thus designates Ahmad Shaʾit (Rida, Salih Mukhlis, "al-Taqriz," *al-Manar* 5/4: 311) and Jubran Khalil Jubran (idem. 1920. "Taqriz al-Matbuʿat al-Jadida." *al-Manar* 21/7: 389–391, here 389).

The European sociological thinkers or social philosophers whom Rida explicitly thus designated are mainly those figures whose reception by Islamic reformists such as ʿAbduh and Rida was already known[148] – above all, Gustave Le Bon and Herbert Spencer. Rida praises Spencer as the greatest or "the shaykh" of European social philosophers,[149] or of social philosophers of that age,[150] and calls him "the founder of sociology" (*muʾassis ʿilm al-ijtimāʿ*).[151] While Rida does not engage in any depth with Spencer's ideas, he adduces Spencer in his argument that materialist ideas are morally harmful[152] and that civilization (*madaniyya*) and society (*umma*) necessarily ought to rest on religion.[153] More than twenty times, Rida refers to the 'social (and historical) philosopher' Gustave Le Bon.[154] Similarly to his treatment of Spencer, Rida mentions arguments by Le Bon only briefly to support his own viewpoints, mainly concerning the need for education and morals and the development of Arab history. Nor does Rida further engage with the thought of Edmond Demolins – whom, when presenting the Arabic translations of two of his works,[155] Rida reveres as a "sociologist" (*al-ʿālim al-ijtimāʿī*)[156] and as versed in the "science of society" (*fann al-ijtimāʿ*).[157] Rida seems to have been familiar with Benjamin Kidd's book *Social*

148 See above: 128 ff.

149 Rida, *Tafsir*, vol. 1: 186; idem., "al-Mutafarnijun," 341; idem. 1903. "al-Ihtifal bi-Tadhkar ʿId al-Julus al-Sultani." *al-Manar* 6/12: 486 – 490, here 487; idem. 1929. "Thawrat Filastin – Asbabuha wa-Nataʾijuha: Haqiqat fi Bayan Hal al-Yahud wa-l-Inkliz wa-l-ʿArab wa-l-Raʾy fi Mustaqbal al-ʿArab wa-l-Sharq." *al-Manar* 30/6: 450 – 468, here 453 (without explicating Spencer's name, thus taking his standing for a given); see also: idem. 1907. "al-Haw wa-l-Huda aw al-Ladhdha wa-l-Manfaʿa." *al-Manar* 10/2: 104 – 107, here 106.

150 Idem., *Tafsir*, vol. 4: 351, vol. 11: 299.

151 Idem., "Fatihat al-Kitab al-Khilafa," 463.

152 Idem., "Thawrat Filastin," 453.

153 Idem., *Tafsir*, vol. 4: 351.

154 For example: ibid., vol. 6: 39, vol. 10: 32, 312, vol. 11: 172; idem., "al-Jinsiyyat," 505; idem. 1912. "al-Jihad aw al-Qital fi al-Islam." *al-Manar* 16/1: 25 – 28, here 28; idem. 1917. "Taqriz al-Matbuʿat al-Jadida." *al-Manar* 19/9: 574 – 576, here 574; idem. 1921. "al-Haqaʾiq al-Jaliyya fi al-Masʾala al-ʿArabiyya." *al-Manar* 22/6: 442 – 479, here 475; idem. 1922. "al-Rihla al-Urubiyya (7)." *al-Manar* 23/9: 696 – 702, here 698; idem. 1923. "al-Khilafa al-Islamiyya (3)." *al-Manar* 24/2: 98 – 120, here 117; idem. 1925. "al-Ighraʾ bayna al-Nasara wa-l-Muslimin." *al-Manar* 25/9: 709 – 713, here 709; idem. 1926. "al-Thawra al-Suriyya wa-l-Hukuma al-Fransiyya wa-l-Intizaʿ bayna al-Sharq wa-l-Gharb." *al-Manar* 26/8: 585 – 594, here 589; idem., "Taqriz," *al-Manar* 29/4: 317; idem., "Thawrat Filastin," 457. For Arabic translations of Le Bon, see above: 128.

155 For these translations, see above: 128 f. The most extensive discussion of Demolins in *al-Manar* is: al-Dimashqi, "al-Istiqlal."

156 Rida, Rashid. 1901. "al-Hadaya wa-l-Taqariz." *al-Manar* 4/16: 629 – 634, here 630.

157 Idem., "Athar ʿIlmiyya," *al-Manar* 2/18: 282.

Evolution, published in 1894 and translated into Arabic in 1913,[158] since he refers to specific page numbers of that work.[159] Only once more does Rida characterize European thinkers as 'social philosophers or historians.'[160] Still, with only two exceptions,[161] Rida is the only contributor to *al-Manar* who explicitly designates any European thinker as a 'societal writer' or a 'social philosopher,' and this in an exclusively positive sense.

Combining the findings of this subsection – namely, Rida's exclusively positive but equally vague reception of sociological thinking – leaves us with the question of where and with which concepts Rida then addressed sociological thought. The following subsection shows that Rida validated the Qur'an as a text about sociological thought and societal laws, while the subsequent section (3) will establish that he conceptualized the object of sociological inquiry and the locus of societal laws as *umma*.

2.2 Sociology and the Qur'an, Societal and Godly Laws: An Open Spin on the Immanent Frame

In the previous subsection, we have seen that Rida conceives of *'ilm al-ijtimāʿ* as a contemporary science, with roots in historiography and distinct from the religious production of knowledge. In general, Rida positioned Islam as the religion of reason (*dīn al-ʿaql*), conforming to and inciting the quest for useful contemporary knowledge. Along these lines, he equates ignorance of the Qur'an, taken to be the alleged essence of the ideal Islamic religion, with ignorance of *'ilm al-ijtimāʿ*. Rida even reads the Qur'an as partly a sociological text, equating some of its statements with those of *'ilm al-ijtimāʿ*. The overall picture that emerges is that Rida shared the modern understanding of stable and autonomous natural and social laws. Based on these laws, it is up to human beings to construct their society (*umma*). To varying degrees, Rida foregrounds the idea that it was God who instituted societal laws and asserts the need for religious guidance in respecting these laws when constructing one's society. This amounts to an open spin on the immanent frame.

---

158 See: Rida, Salih Mukhlis, "Taqriz," *al-Manar* 17/1: 66.

159 Rida, *Tafsir*, vol. 10: 33.

160 Idem. 1926. "Jamʿiyyat Tajdid al-Ilhad wa-l-Zandaqa wa-l-Ibahat al-Mutlaqa." *al-Manar* 27/5: 387–398, here 398.

161 Rida, Salih Mukhlis. 1912. "al-Taqariz." *al-Manar* 15/9: 703–716, here 712; ʿAbd al-Raziq, "Dhikra," 303.

Rida asserts that contemporaneous sociological knowledge – of which little is produced in Arabic, as he said himself – is already to be found in the Qurʾan. Therefore, only non-Muslim Easterners might be excused for their pessimism concerning the science of human society (*ʿilm al-ijtimāʿ al-basharī*), as Rida maintains in volume two of *al-Manar*.[162] Two decades later, responding to the argument made by an intellectual he met in Geneva that "the law of social association (*sunnat al-ijtimāʿ*) in all societies (*umam*) is one and the same and unchangeable," Rida argues that "we are certain (*naʿtaqid*) of that [, too]; those of us who are familiar with *ʿilm al-ijtimāʿ*, and those who are not, because it is written down (*manṣūṣ*) in the Qurʾan."[163] Rida maintains that religion, properly understood, is not the problem, but the solution – concerning sociology as well as other fields of knowledge:

"those who say that the religion of Islam (*dīn al-islām*) is the reason for the ignorance of Muslims and their weakness, and that there is no life for us except by adopting (*iqtibās*) the science of society and of the ways of civilization (*ʿilm al-ijtimāʿ wa-sunan al-ʿumrān*) from the non-Islamic peoples (*umam*) which have conquered us by these sciences, and [by adopting] the arts and crafts (*al-funūn wa-l-ṣināʿāt*) which support [these sciences]; those [who say that] are most ignorant of Islam, for the book of Islam is the first guide towards the ways of society and civilization (*sunan al-ijtimāʿ wa-l-ʿumrān*)."[164]

In fact, the Qurʾan established what European *ʿilm al-ijtimāʿ* has discovered only recently, Rida maintains,[165] whence Muslims are only reclaiming their own by orienting themselves toward the sociological inquiry presently spearheaded by Europeans.

While these arguments are obviously apologetic, one should take into account that Rida not only consciously refers to an ideal Islam – the contrasting of which with the present state of Muslims and the dominant understanding of Islam is central to Islamic reformism – but moreover himself explicates the contemporaneity and peculiarity of his reading of the Qurʾan as partly a sociological text. In every age, people only take from religion "what conforms to their readiness and social conditions,"[166] Rida asserts, and he advertises the *Tafsir al-Manar* as the only commentary elucidating the Qurʾan's societal teach-

---

162 Rida, Rashid. 1899. "al-Iʿtimad ʿala al-Nafs." *al-Manar* 2/9: 129–133, here 133.
163 Idem. 1922. "al-Rihla al-Urubiyya [6]." *al-Manar* 23/8: 635–640, here 639.
164 Idem., *Tafsir*, vol. 9: 481 f.
165 Idem. "Bab al-Asʾila," *al-Manar* 4/13: 496.
166 Ibid., 496.

ings.[167] He thinks that contemporary social sciences have expanded not only on Ibn Khaldun, as mentioned in the previous subsection, but also on the allegedly timeless truth established by the Qur'an.

According to Rida, the Qur'an was sent to a people farthest remote from knowledge about society.[168] Knowledge and sciences have progressed since, and it is up to human beings to discover, elaborate, and expand upon the basic principles the Qur'an set forth.[169] This argument is very close to a reformist approach to Islamic law, which distinguishes between timeless, godly principles and their contingent, human elaboration – and Rida himself draws an analogy between scholars of law and of society in this regard.[170] According to Rida, then, the Qur'an, which conforms to all sound sociological laws, does not contain these laws in detail, but rather guides human beings to them by establishing basic principles and inciting human reason to empirical and historiographical investigation.

Here, the self-conscious strategy of Islamic reformists to promote contemporary knowledge deemed necessary for the functioning of society and the strength of the nation by claiming it as authentically one's own becomes very obvious. Rida considered Europeans' knowledge of *'ilm al-ijtimā'* as a source for the proper functioning of their societies and the strength of their nations, and he regarded Muslims' ignorance of this science as a major reason for their decline. He stresses that *'ilm al-ijtimā'* is necessary for realizing public interests (*al-maṣāliḥ al-'āmma*) and unity (*ittiḥād*) but won't have an effect as long as it is considered contradictory to religion.[171] Rida considers sociology a recent science and distin-

---

167 Idem., *Tafsir*, vol. 1: 10, vol. 12: 204; see also idem., "Athar," *al-Manar* 3/3: 67 f. (on 'Abduh's lessons on which the *Tafsir al-Manar* is based). Its readers also appreciated the *Tafsir al-Manar* for addressing societal issues; for example: al-Dirdiri, Yahyi Ahmad. 1932. "Hadiyat al-Qur'an." *al-Manar* 32/2: 102–109, here 104 (approvingly quoting Rida's depiction of his *Tafsir*); Abu Rayya, Mahmud. 1934. "Kalima Khalisa li-Wijh Allah." *al-Manar* 34/3: 212–215, here 213; al-Liban, Mustafa Ahmad al-Rifa'i. 1934. "Tafsir al-Manar li-'Alamat al-Dahr wa-Muslih al-'Asr."*al-Manar* 34/4: 284–289, here 286. Qur'anic teachings on society was also a class at the Dar al-Da'wa wa-l-Irshad, as was *'ilm (sunan) al-ijtimā'* (Rida, Rashid. 1911. "al-'Ulum wa-l-Funun allati Tudarras fi Dar al-Da'wa wa-l-Irshad." *al-Manar* 14/11: 801–821, here 803, 814 f.). There also was an exam on the laws of society (*sunan al-ijtimā'*) (idem. 1911. "Nizam Madrasat Dar al-Da'wa wa-l-Irshad." *al-Manar* 14/10: 785–800, here 799).

168 Idem. 1899. "Khawariq al-'Adat wa-l-Khilaf fi al-Karamat." *al-Manar* 2/27: 417–422, here 417.

169 Van Nispen Tot Sevenaer, *Activité*, 138 f.; Rida, Rashid. 1907. "Fatihat al-Sanna al-'Ashira." *al-Manar* 10/1: 1–9, here 6 f.

170 Rida, "al-Hayat al-Milliya," 308 f.

171 Idem. 1910. "al-Ittihad al-Shamil wa-l-Ta'lim al-Shamil: Ayyahuma Yatawaqqif 'ala al-Akhar." *al-Manar* 13/4: 260–264, here 263. Shakib Arslan tries to overcome skepticism of the so-

guishes between religious and societal knowledge. However, he strategically validates modern sociological approaches by portraying them as religious and defies neglect of societal teachings as ignorance of religion: "in this age, we see non-Muslims knowing more than Muslims about those societal laws (*al-sunan al-ijtimāʿiyya*) to which the Qur'an guided us;"[172] furthermore, Muslim weakness is the result of ignoring not European sociology specifically, but rather the Qur'an and "the ways of God concerning social association" (*sunan allāh fī al-ijtimāʿ*).[173]

Rida's shifting terminology from *ʿilm al-ijtimāʿ* and *al-sunan al-ijtimāʿiyya* to *sunan allāh* (*fī al-ijtimāʿ*) forms part of his overall reformist strategy, which can be read both as a validation of secular knowledge and as its subsumption under religion. One aspect which is of particular interest to our terminological inquiry becomes especially apparent here – namely, the inscription of modern ideas onto traditional concepts and the equation of terms from classical Islamic discourse with contemporaneous expressions. Indeed, Rida continuously uses *sunan allāh* (*fī al-ijtimāʿ*) synonymously with *sunnat al-ijtimāʿ* or *al-sunan al-ijtimāʿiyya* – which, like *ʿilm al-ijtimāʿ*, he qualifies as a recent expression.[174] This is a primary example illustrating that research on Arabic conceptualizations of modern ideas should not only look at recent terms, such as *sunnat al-ijtimāʿ* or *mujtamaʿ*, but also at terms from classical Islamic discourse, such as *sunnat allāh* or *umma*.

Rida deliberately used shifting terminology, I argue, first to universalize and subsequently to appropriate modern sociological insights and societal laws and, relatedly, to connect immanent social laws to a transcendent realm. We recall that in Europe, the modern idea of society could be based on nature alone or on a providential God, who increasingly receded into the background.[175]

Rida clearly equates the nature of society with divine providence: "if I say that this thing is determined by the nature of human society (*ṭabīʿat al-ijtimāʿ al-insānī*), this is the same as when I say it is determined by the innate disposition of [i.e., laid down by] God (*fiṭrat allāh*) on which were created all people

---

cial sciences by plainly asserting that "every science (*ʿilm*) that benefits human society (*al-ijtimāʿ al-basharī*) is a religious science" (Arslan, "Limadha," *al-Manar* 31/7: 539).

172 Rida, *Tafsir*, vol. 9: 16; idem., "al-Haqq," 55 f. The English are closest to respecting the laws of society (*sunan al-ijtimāʿ*), Rida says elsewhere (idem., "Thawrat Filastin," 451).

173 Idem., *Tafsir*, vol. 9: 554.

174 Ibid., vol. 8: 219.

175 See above: chapter 2 section 3.

without distinction."[176] Similarly, what in this age is called the "science of society and of natural laws" (*ʿilm al-ijtimāʿ wa-ʿilm nawāmīs al-ṭabīʿa*), according to Rida, is tantamount to knowledge about "His ways in His creation" (*sunanihi fī khalqihi*);[177] or, slightly modified: what today is called 'sociology' (*ʿilm al-ijtimāʿ*) is a recent expression for "God's ways in the common affairs of mankind" (*sunan allāh fī shuʾūn al-bashar al-ʿāmma*);[178] and again: "the ways of God Most High concerning social association (*ijtimāʿ*) and civilization (*ʿumrān*) and the affairs of societies (*shuʾūn al-umam*), what in the usage of our age is termed *ʿilm al-ijtimāʿ*."[179] Rendering *sunnat al-ijtimāʿ* as *sunnat allāh* infuses both modern ideas into a traditional concept and, at the same time, blurs their modern specificity – the analogy to *mujtamaʿ* and *umma* is obvious.

Before discussing the modernity of Rida's understanding of sociological laws – conceptualized as *sunan allāh* or *sunan al-ijtimāʿ*, with a few variations[180] – I should mention the main aspects concerning which Rida validated sociological laws. Commentary on the Qur'an is the genre in which Rida most substantially elaborated his understanding of societal laws. As mentioned above,[181] van Nispen tot Sevenaer showed that the *Tafsir al-Manar* gave unprecedented prominence to the concept of *sunan allāh*. ʿAbduh and, even more so, Rida used this concept to validate stable natural and societal laws[182] and infused it with modern sociological thought.[183] Rida most explicitly equates Qur'anic verses and modern theory concerning laws of social evolution, including social Darwinism.[184] In addition to social evolution, Rida prominently addresses societal laws concerning the reasons for progress and decline, for the strength and weakness of society, and for the rise and fall of nations.[185] One reason for the decline of society – and thus a main *sunnat allāh* or *sunnat al-ijtimāʿ*, which Rida mentions repeat-

176 Idem. 1898. "Istilahat Kuttab al-ʿAsr." *al-Manar* 1/1: 14–19, here 15; see also: idem. 1908. "Tatimmat al-Khutba al-Ula min Khutabina al-Islamiyya fi al-Diyar al-Suriyya (2)." *al-Manar* 11/10: 737–742, here 738.

177 Idem., "Taqrir Mashyakhat," 831

178 Idem., *Tafsir*, vol. 8: 255; see also: vol. 4: 114.

179 Ibid., vol. 9: 465.

180 Most often: *sunan ijtimāʿiyya*, *sunan allāh fī al-ijtimāʿ*.

181 See above: 173 f.

182 Van Nispen tot Sevenaer, *Activité*, 98, 141.

183 Ibid., 106, 115.

184 Ibid., 87; Rida, *Tafsir*, vol. 2: 393, vol. 8: 5, 29, vol. 9: 550, vol. 12: 157.

185 Van Nispen Tot Sevenaer, *Activité*, 129; see also: Rida, *Tafsir*, vol. 1: 10. For lists of *sunan*, including some of the above and additional ones, see Van Nispen Tot Seveneaer, *Actitivité*, 129–142; Rida, *Tafsir*, vol. 10: 120–124.

edly – is that of oppression.[186] Other laws include those of struggle or war in society[187] and the law of conservatism and renewal.[188] Overall then, the main headings under which Rida discusses and validates societal laws are unity, strength, and the progress of societies and nations.

Rida's modern understanding of these godly, societal laws shows in the fact that he considered them stable and unchangeable, whence human beings could autonomously discern these laws and construct their societies accordingly. Rida stresses that it was God who instituted both social and natural laws, and that He is above these laws.[189] On a most fundamental epistemic level, Rida might perceive God as continuously intervening in societal laws merely by maintaining them and linking them to each other.[190] Still, God very much recedes into the background, since he always maintains and links these laws in the same manner.[191] For Rida, these stable laws do not threaten, but rather affirm God's existence and power: He instituted and maintains these laws, but he nevertheless gave human beings free will and encourages free inquiry. Thus, and quite in contrast to a determinant view,[192] human beings may and shall, through historical and empirical investigation, discern and apply these stable societal laws, both from God's book and from his creation.

Moreover, as these objective and basically secular laws instituted by God apply to believers and non-believers alike,[193] every group of people has the society it deserves, based on its own deeds,[194] and is itself responsible for its own

---

186 Ibid., vol. 6: 49, vol. 9: 73, vol. 11: 257, vol. 12: 158, 203.

187 Van Nispen tot Sevenaer, *Activité*, 135 ff.; See also on war: Rida, Rashid. 1915. "Harb Umam al-Madaniyya La al-Milal al-Diniyya." *al-Manar* 18/10: 746–752, here 749; idem., *Tafsir*, vol. 10: 43, 51, 73, 123, 271; on sedition (as underlying struggle): ibid., vol. 8: 190; idem. 1929. "Muqaddimat Rasa'il al-Sunna wa-l-Shi'a." *al-Manar* 29/9: 671–686, here 671.

188 Idem. 1919. "Bahithat al-Badiyya – Tatimmat Tarjamatiha." *al-Manar* 21/3: 163–168, here 165; idem. 1931. "al-Tajdid wa-l-Tajaddud wa-l-Mujaddidun (2)." *al-Manar* 32/1: 49–60, here 50.

189 Idem., "Ilhad," *al-Manar* 31/9: 683 f.

190 Van Nispen tot Sevenaer, *Activité*, 101.

191 Rida stresses the stability and invariability of natural laws when he says that there have been no miracles since the time of Muhammad, the last prophet (ibid., 74 f.; see also 95 f.; van Leeuwen, "Islamic Reformism"). Concerning societal laws, Rida once mentions their variations between different types of society (Rida, "Ilhad," *al-Manar* 32/1: 42 f.). In regards to the respective types of society, however, these laws again seem to be firm and stable. In general, this is very much the case in Rida's opinion; he stresses that the prophet Muhammad also did not change the laws of society (*sunan al-ijtimāʿ*), for there is no changing the law of God (*sunnat allāh*) (idem., *Tafsir*, vol. 5: 219).

192 Van Nispen tot Sevenaer, *Activité*, 107.

193 Ibid., 125.

194 Ibid., 115 f.

destiny.[195] Viewed in this way, the European nations' present advancement signifies their paying heed to the universal societal laws. That Rida considers God's laws concerning society to be just as natural as those concerning individuals is demonstrated in his occasionally designating them as *sunan al-fiṭra* (the laws of the natural disposition). Overall then, as van Nispen tot Sevenaer succinctly put it, "the laws of God express the structure of action which corresponds to [the *fiṭra*]; and these are the laws which must be respected if man wants to realize 'the *fiṭra* of God' and construct the *umma*, the true human community which is the social dimension of that *fiṭra*."[196] While linked to a transcendent ideal of socio-political order, *umma* here conveys the modern meaning of 'society,' in that it has to be continuously constructed by human individuals based on their own insights.

Fundamentally, Rida thus shared the modern, secular understanding of an immanent frame, but he did not share the modernist, secularist closed spin on the immanent frame as all that there is; instead, he promoted an open reading, linking immanence to transcendence. We recall that the modern idea of society could initially be grounded in nature alone or in God. Once the crucial distinction between immanence and transcendence is operative, each can be related to the other in different ways. Charles Taylor noted in passing that Islam might be the only tradition other than Christianity that perceived of this distinction.[197] According to Taylor's story of secularization, the connection to God was increasingly lost, and the immanent frame came to be understood as fully self-sufficient. Rida offers another particular understanding, surely partly in response to secularist claims. In Rida's view, nature and the social are quite stable and autonomous, but they alone could not provide the ground beneath our feet, whence they themselves have to be regrounded in something beyond – namely, God.[198]

Building on his ontological premise, Rida validates the necessity of religion in regard to societal laws in two additional senses: one concerning the acquisition of knowledge, the other its application. Concerning the first aspect, Rida maintains that knowledge about society cannot dispense with religion. However, it should be remembered that he is referring to a particular ideal of religion,

195 Ibid., 137–141. Islamic reformists in this context often cite Qur'an 13:11 (see Ivanyi, "God's Custom"). An example of Rida using this verse to elucidate the *sunna* in question is: Rida, *Tafsir*, vol. 10: 32.

196 Van Nispen tot Sevenaer, *Activité*. 30; transl. F.Z.

197 Taylor, *A Secular Age*, 781fn19.

198 Van Nispen tot Sevenaer makes a similar point when he says that Rida connected sociology to a religious vision (ibid., 138 f.).

which fundamentally contains the same societal knowledge. Islam, for that matter, is "the religion of God's laws concerning society,"[199] and Rida once even suggests that "knowledge about human society (*ʿilm al-ijtimāʿ al-basharī*) is [identical with] knowledge about the prophets (*ʿilm al-anbiyāʾ*) and the religion of Islam is the most perfect of religions in this regard."[200] The fact that secular Europeans have allegedly realized Islam's truths about society more than Muslims have done illustrates the secular and universal character of these truths. Rida integrates sociological teachings into religious sources for the sake of authenticity and to position religious actors as authorities in societal matters, but he does not derive particular premises or insights from these religious sources.

When it comes to the application of societal knowledge, religion truly provides an additional layer to societal teachings – namely, that of moral guidance. "Knowledge about the laws of social association and civilization (*sunan al-ijtimāʿ wa-l-ʿumrān*)," Rida maintains, "cannot dispense with the guidance of religion (*hidāyat al-dīn*), which prevents human passions and desires from bolting (*tajmaḥ*) to where there are no limits for evil."[201] This argument calls to mind Rida's validation of a society guided by religious morals (*umma*) over against a society based on reason alone (*al-hayʾa al-ijtimāʿiyya*).[202] And indeed, also with regard to societal laws, Rida develops his position by engaging a secular claim to the contrary: "In no previous age," he writes, "had human beings attained more than a tenth of what they arrived at in this age concerning knowledge about what is useful (*al-manāfiʿ*) and what is harmful (*al-maḍārr*), what is beneficial (*al-maṣāliḥ*) and what is corrupting (*al-mafāsid*) in human society (*al-ijtimāʿ al-basharī*) concerning its social interactions (*muʿāmalātihi*) and its morals (*ādābihi*); so that many scholars and thinkers even declared that it is possible to, by means of science (*bi-ʿilm*), dispense with religion in the moral education (*tarbiya*) of the youth."[203] Rida's ideal society (*umma*) functions according to the same universal societal laws as non-religious societies, but it is superior to them due to its firm grounding in God, its religious constituents, and its moral guidance.

For Rida, the field of morals was indeed a crucial link between the religious and the social life of the *umma*, as will be suggested in the following section.

---

199 Van Nispen tot Sevenaer, *Activité*, 127; transl. F.Z.

200 Rida, Rashid. 1901. "Bab al-Asʾila wa-l-Ajwiba al-Diniyya." *al-Manar* 4/13: 493–503, here 496.

201 Rida, *Tafsir*, vol. 9: 18; see also: van Nispen tot Sevenaer, *Activité*, 117 f.

202 See above: chapter 7 section 2.

203 Rida, *Tafsir*, vol. 8: 472.

First, however, the concluding subsection of this section establishes that Rida conceptualized the object of sociology and the locus of societal laws as *umma*.

2.3 *Umma* as the Object of Sociological Inquiry

> "Sociology, for instance, tended to conflate the specific historical form of the European nation-state with the general solution to, as it was often called, the problem of life in common, or the political problématique, which was expressed in the concept 'society'."
> – Wagner, *Modernity*, 10

If it seems obvious today that the object of sociology is 'society,' this has not always been the case. At the beginning of the twentieth century, German sociologists preferred the more conservative notion of *Volk* (the people) in this regard, before shifting to *Gesellschaft*.[204] The Arab socialist Niqula Haddad, in his pioneering 1924 book *Sociology* (*ʿIlm al-Ijtimaʿ*), conceptualized his object of society as *al-hayʾa al-ijtimāʿiyya* and *mujtamaʿ*.[205] Rida again prefers the term *umma* to conceptualize this object of sociological inquiry and the locus of societal laws. It is true that *umma* was often used in a seemingly descriptive sense, as a generic term for a social collectivity, such as when Rida explains that "the meaning of man being a social creature (*khalq ijtimāʿī*) is that he feels that he is part (*ʿuḍw*) of a society (*min umma*)."[206] However, this usage is only seemingly descriptive, due to the normative connotations of *umma*, especially as distinct from *al-hayʾa al-ijtimāʿiyya* and *mujtamaʿ*. In this context, it would be futile to debate whether *umma* should best be rendered as 'people,' 'community,' 'society,' or 'nation.' What matters is that, in the same sense as conservative sociologists validated 'the people' over 'society,' Rida uses *umma* as an equivalent to *mujtamaʿ* and positions the *umma* as the object of sociological inquiry.

This has already been evident in several examples in the previous subsection and shall be further explored here. This subsection resembles a simple collection of examples, since it is interested in terms rather than contents, although some thematic topics may also be discerned.

In 1927, as a particular asset of the ninth volume of his *Tafsir*, Rida highlights the fact that it contains a section on "the ways of God concerning human social association and civilization (*al-ijtimāʿ wa-l-ʿumrān al-basharī*) and the affairs of

204 See above: 52fn66.
205 See above: chapter 8 section 3.2.
206 Rida, "al-Muhawarat," 666 [misprinted as 636].

societies (*shu'ūn al-umam*), or what today is called *'ilm al-ijtimā'*."[207] Shortly after this, writing to the Afghan ruler concerning religious and civil reforms, he stresses the importance of minding "God's ways concerning societies (*sunan allāh fī al-umam*), to which is dedicated *'ilm al-ijtimā'*."[208] In the *Tafsir* itself, Rida defines *'ilm al-ijtimā'* as "that science in which are studied the conditions (*aḥwāl*) of peoples (*umam*) in their beduin state (*badāwatihā*) and their civilized state (*ḥaḍāratihā*), and the reasons for their weakness and strength and for their decline and progress (*taraqqī*)."[209] There are many verses in which God addresses societies (*umam*), Rida suggests, since "the addressing (*al-kalām fī*) of *umam* is tantamount to addressing the characteristics of social association (*ṭabā'i' al-ijtimā'*)."[210] Furthermore, one section of the *Tafsir* is tellingly entitled, "The godly customs (*al-sunan al-ilāhiyya*) concerning individuals and societies (*afrād al-bashar wa-umamihim*); and these [customs] relate to (*tadkhul fī*) psychology (*'ilm al-nafs*) and sociology (*'ilm al-ijtimā'*)."[211]

Rida repeatedly addresses *umma* as a topic of *'ilm al-ijtimā'* in relation to one complementary aspect of modern society – namely, the individual persons (*afrād*) of which society is composed. The scholars of society (*'ulamā' al-ijtimā'*), Rida maintains, have discerned for the *umam* what medical scholars (*'ulamā' al-ṭibb*) have discerned for persons (*ashkhāṣ*).[212] According to Rida, scholars of society (*'ulamā' al-ijtimā'*) moreover unanimously agree that "the felicity of the *umma* depends on the perfection of the moral education (*ḥusn al-tarbiya*) of its individuals (*afrādihā*)."[213] Additionally, "the researchers in the science of social association (*al-bāḥithūn fī 'ilm al-ijtimā'*) and the moral education of peoples (*tarbiyat al-umam*) have determined that the spirit of progress of society (*rūḥ taraqqī al-umma*) consists of the reliance of its individuals (*afrādihā*) upon themselves."[214] And finally, Rida names as "one of the topics of *'ilm al-ijtimā'* that the individuals (*afrād*) and the societies (*umam*) composed

207 Idem. 1927. "al-Juz' al-Tasi' min Tafsir al-Qur'an al-Hakim." *al-Manar* 29/6: 450 – 455, here 455.
208 Idem. 1928. "al-Inqilab al-Madani al-Dini bi Bilad al-Afghan." *al-Manar* 29/7: 549 – 559, here 555.
209 Idem., *Tafsir*, vol. 4: 33.
210 Ibid., vol. 3: 196.
211 Ibid., vol. 10: 120.
212 Idem. 1901. "al-Muhawarat bayna al-Muslih wa-l-Muqallid: al-Ijtihad wa-l-Wahda al-Islamiyya." *al-Manar* 4/6: 205 – 217, here 206.
213 Idem. 1900. "al-Siyam wa-l-Tamaddun." *al-Manar* 2/43: 673 – 678, here 675.
214 Idem. 1900. "Ufkuha Ghariba." *al-Manar* 2/48: 767.

of them (*mu'allafa minhā*) adopt from who mingles with them or is adjacent to them what suits their readiness."[215]

This last example points to another pertinent aspect researched in *'ilm al-ijtimā'* – namely, the rise and decline, the weakness and strength of the *umam.*[216] It is the science of society (*'ilm al-ijtimā'*), Rida writes, which "has proven to us that strength and progress (*taraqqī*) have their laws (*nawāmīs*), and weakness and decline (*tadallī*) have other laws, and that every one society (*kull umma min al-umam*) has its particular qualities (*shu'ūn*) concerning its advancement (*taqaddum*) and backwardness (*ta'akhkhur*), and its rise and decline."[217] Moreover, according to Rida, the scholars of society (*'ulamā' al-ijtimā'*) know that "the conditions and stages of societies (*umam*) can not be changed by imitating another [society] in its laws (*qawānīn*) and outward appearances, due to its contradicting it [i.e., one's own society] in its history, moral upbringing (*tarbiya*) and beliefs (*'aqā'id*)."[218] Rida considers it "a trial for Muslims that every one appeals [for his own arguments] to complete understanding of the science of human society (*'ilm al-ijtimā' al-insānī*) and to knowledge of the reasons of the progress and decline of societies (*umam*)."[219] Some of these "researchers into the conditions of society (*aḥwāl al-umma*) who are truly perceptive of *'ilm al-ijtimā'* think [and correctly so] that a people (*umma*) will not succeed as long as they are subject to blind submission [to the government]."[220] And Rida himself is "convinced, as are all men of reason (*'uqalā'*) who have if only partial knowledge of *'ilm al-ijtimā'*, that the advancement of peoples (*umam*) and their backwardness, their felicity and despair, their being rich or poor, their independence or enslavement by others, all this depends on their education (*tarbiya*)."[221]

While Rida conceptualizes the object of *'ilm al-ijtimā'* exclusively as *umma*, he also applies societal laws mainly to *umma*, but slightly less exclusively so.

---

215 Idem., "Manafi'," *al-Manar* 10/3: 195.

216 In the one article in *al-Manar* that deals most extensively with sociology, Muhammad Bahjat al-Bitar also foregrounds that "'*ilm al-ijtimā'* studies the laws of God Most High concerning the life and death of peoples (*umam*)." Shortly before this, he conceptualizes the object of sociological inquiry differently, stressing the need of societies (*umam*) for "'*ilm al-ijtimā'*, which guides them toward the laws of God Most High concerning existence (*al-wujūd*) and teaches the secrets of the advancement of kingdoms (*mamālik*) and peoples (*shu'ūb*) [...]" (al-Bitar, "Kitab," *al-Manar* 27/4: 295).

217 Rida, "Tahrif," 387. The continuation of this quote can be found in the last paragraph of this section.

218 Idem. 1926. "Ahwal al-'Alam al-Islami." *al-Manar* 27/1: 71–77, here 72.

219 Idem. 1899. "Izalat Shibha." *al-Manar* 2/16: 253–254, here 254.

220 Idem., "al-Hayra," 756.

221 Idem., "al-Kitaban," 282.

One societal law Rida adduces combines the two aforementioned aspects – namely, the rise and fall of societies and the fact that they are composed of individuals: "It is a law of God Most High concerning human social association (*al-ijtimāʿ al-insānī*)," Rida writes, "that societies are mutually solidary (*takūn al-umam mutakāfila*), each individual (*fard*) considering his felicity in relation to the felicity of the other individuals and his misery in relation to their misery. […] And this mutual solidarity in societies (*umam*) is the strongest ladder (*al-miʿrāj al-aʿẓam*) for their ascent (*raqqī*)."[222] Elsewhere, Rida synonymously speaks of "societal laws" (*al-sunan al-ijtimāʿiyya*), laws concerning "the social life of human beings," and "the laws of God Most High concerning societies (*umam*)."[223] Translating into contemporary parlance what al-Ghazali said about different branches of knowledge, Rida describes the social sciences (*al-ʿulūm al-ijtimāʿiyya*) as "elucidating to us the laws of God Most High concerning societies (*umam*)."[224] Rida rarely conceptualizes the social collectivity onto which societal laws apply with terms other than *umma*, such as *shaʿb*[225] or *qawm*[226]. In one singular instance, he addresses societal laws for *al-mujtamaʿ al-insānī:* one of the principles (*qawāʿid*) to which the Qurʾan guided human beings, Rida writes, is "the principle of the laws of existence (*sunan al-kawn*) and the laws of society and civilization (*nawāmīs al-ijtimāʿ wa-l-ʿumrān*) by which are known the reasons for the progress (*taraqqī*) of human society (*al-mujtamaʿ al-insānī*) and its decline."[227]

Rida – and this transitions to the following section, which attends to the relation between religion and society – also adduces sociological insights and societal characteristics concerning Islamic society in particular. "History – which is the source and origin (*mawrid wa-maṣdar*) of *ʿilm al-ijtimāʿ* – has shown us," Rida maintains in 1899, "that the Islamic nation (*al-umma al-islāmiyya*) did not attain this exalted power [it once had] and did not oversee the earth by commanding [right] and forbidding [wrong] from the lofty heights of strength and power, and did not shine over the earth with justice and beneficence from the heaven (*samāʾ*) of science and knowledge, except through its religion, insofar

222 Idem., *Tafsir*, vol. 1: 266. Rida quotes this passage when discussing another Qurʾan commentary, which, according to him, stole the few true insights it contains from the *Tafsir al-Manar* (idem. 1930. "Ilhad fi al-Quran wa-Din Jadid bayna al-Batiniyya wa-l-Islam [1]." *al-Manar* 31/9: 673–697, here 687).

223 Idem., "al-Haqq," 55.

224 Idem. 1907. "Hujjat al-Islam Abu Hamid al-Ghazali (3)." *al-Manar* 10/9: 694–705, here 696.

225 For exampe: idem., *Tafsir*, vol. 11: 249.

226 For example: ibid., vol. 12: 197.

227 Idem., "al-Hayat al-Milliyya," 309.

as it combines the two powers [i.e., the religious (*al-dīniyya*) and the political (*al-siyāsiyya*)] in one leader (*ra'īs*) restrained by the just shari'a (*al-sharī'a al-'ādila*)."[228]

And twelve years later, he writes:

"The social and political questions by which the conditions (*aḥwāl*) and dispositions (*ṭabā'i'*) of societies (*umam*) and the reasons for their progress and decline, their life and death, are studied; these are the most elevated and most difficult questions of human sciences (*al-'ulūm al-bashariyya*) in general, especially when their understanding depends on the familiarity of the investigator with the religion of the society (*umma*) whose conditions he is studying, the comprehension of its roots (*fiqh uṣulihā*), and knowledge of its original source (*yanbū'ihi*), as [is the case concerning] the Islamic society (*al-umma al-islāmiyya*)."[229]

3 Islam, Religion, and Society

3.1 Religion as a Natural Requirement of and a Superior Bond for Society

It is a well-established fact – not only based on the last two quotations in the previous section, but also in view of the previous chapters, and even the basic characteristics of Islamic reformism – that Rida foregrounded the religious foundations of the Islamic *umma*, the societal teachings of Islam, and consequently the continuous relevance of religion for socio-political order. Analytically, it is indeed quite convincing to characterize Rida as an opponent of secularism or as an advocate of Islamic society. However, this study is interested in whether the actors to whom the analytical categories of society and religion are applied themselves operated according to these categories.

Consequently, this section explores whether Rida himself conceptually distinguished between the religious and the social. It transpires that he clearly did do so, but argued for the connection of the religious and the social in an overarching Islamic discourse and in the ideal Islamic society, the *umma*. Significantly, the integration of the religious and the social and the postulation of Islam as a societal religion is only possible based on the previous conceptual distinction between the two spheres; and while, in analogy to sociological

228 Idem., "Tahrif," 387.
229 Idem., "Radd al-Manar," 770.

laws expressed as *sunan allāh*, this integration blurs the modern specificity and autonomy of the social, it does not essentially do away with it.

While I am primarily interested in Rida's terminological usage and do not aim to develop a full-fledged analytical model for the relation between religion and society in his writings, I have ordered his pertinent statements systematically according to the basic relation between religion and society they suggest. This subsection shows that Rida postulated religion as (a) a natural requirement of social association and (b) that he considered the Islamic religion in particular as the most comprehensive and thus the most appropriate bond for large contemporary societies.

(a) If, as a basic premise, Rida postulates religion as a natural requirement of human society, he is notably arguing from a societal perspective (which he integrates into religion) and, moreover, in view of claims that human social association was possible without religion. In an article entitled "Doubts Concerning Revelation" from 1904, Rida refers to ʿAbduh having shown that the call (*daʿwa*) of the prophets is "a natural requirement (*ḥāja ṭabīʿiyya*) of the requirements of human society (*ḥājāt al-ijtimāʿ al-basharī*)."[230] Five years later, he counters a sociological view adhering to the now-outdated paradigm of modernization and secularization as the continuous decline of religion:

"many sociologists (*ʿulamāʾ al-ijtimāʿ*) say that mankind as a whole is heading towards increasing unbelief and apostasy year after year, and that this course will end with all societies (*umam*) abstaining from religiosity (*tadayyun*) after some centuries [...]. Others say that it is impossible for mankind to do without religion [...] and that people will continue to differ in religion. Still others maintain that in the future the majority of human beings will inevitably follow a single religion [...]. And I have more than once heard al-Ustadh al-Imam [Muhammad ʿAbduh] saying: "I have believed for twenty years that the religion of the future (*dīn al-mustaqbal*) is Islam, and for this I have both sociological proofs (*adilla ijtimāʿiyya*) and proofs transmitted from religious sources (*adilla naqliyya*)."[231]

And in 1906, Rida asserts: "Religion in its entirety is a natural necessity for mankind (*ḥāja ṭabīʿiyya li-l-bashar*). [...] Religion is one of the great laws of society (*sunna min sunan al-ijtimāʿ al-kubrā*), and it manifests itself in reality (*al-*

---

230 Rida, Rashid. 1904. "Shubha ʿala al-Wahy." *al-Manar* 6/20: 788–792, here 791.

231 Idem. 1909. "Din al-Mustaqbal wa-Hal Yakfur Man la-Hu Raʾy fihi." *al-Manar* 12/2: 93–95, here 94 f.

wāqiʿ) as either true or false, with societal confirmation for its truth (*muʾayyid bi-ḥaqq ijtimāʿī*) being the unity (*waḥda*) of the community (*umma*) in belief and practice and their dominion and power over those competing with it."[232] Rida again refers to Muhammad ʿAbduh in 1930, when he repeats his argument that religion is "a requirement of humankind's innate disposition (*ḥājat al-fiṭra al-bashariyya*) and even a social necessity (*ḍarūra ijtimāʿiyya*)."[233] Prior to this assertion, Rida validates religion as spiritual guidance (*hidāya rūḥiyya*) which is required for the formation of moral beings and as one of the strongest political bonds (*jāmiʿa siyāsiyya*).[234]

Moral guidance and political unification are indeed the two main assets Rida ascribes to religion. It is based on these two assets that religion is validated as a requirement of human nature and social association and as the constituent and guiding principle of society itself. Again, the primacy of social requirements, and thus Rida's societal perspective on religion in this regard, is quite obvious here.[235] Unsurprisingly, Rida particularly endorsed the Islamic religion as the basis for socio-political unity and thus as a principle for society, as I will now illustrate.

(b) Concerning the eminent aim of attaining socio-political unity, Rida positions religious foundations and bonds as superior to ethnic or national ones, and consequently formulates Islam as a principle of social association. In 1899, he had already attacked nationalism (*al-jāmiʿa al-waṭaniyya*) as "a means to dissolve the body of the Islamic society (*jism al-mujtamaʿ al-islāmī*) and to cut off the religious bond (*al-rābiṭa al-dīniyya*), which is the strongest and most noble of all bonds."[236] According to Rida, those spreading "among Muslims the poison of nationalism (*waṭaniyya*) and making it the most sacred (*aqdas*) of social bonds (*al-rawābiṭ al-ijtimāʿiyya*)" aim to weaken the bond between Muslims around the world and to divide the Muslims in one country from their fellow non-Muslims.[237] Rida here refers back to his article "Nationalism and the Islamic Religion" ("Al-Jinsiyya wa-l-Din al-Islami"), published earlier that year, which argues that the Islamic religion is the highest and most all-encompassing basis for

232 Idem., "al-Haqq," 61.
233 Idem., "Munazara fi Musawat," 622.
234 Ibid., 622.
235 As mentioned above (page 166), the modern Islamic reformists somewhat reversed the primacy of religion and the world. I have come across only few instances in which Rida stresses religion's need for concurrence and cooperation, which amounts to prioritizing religion instead of socio-political unity (for example: idem., *Tafsir*, vol. 8: 196).
236 Idem., "al-Hayra," 757.
237 Ibid., 757.

social association (*ijtimāʿ*).[238] In his *Tafsir*, Rida likens Europeans clinging to an ethnic principle of belonging (*jinsiyya ʿaṣabiyya*) to the pre-Islamic time of the *jāhiliyya*.[239] Muhammad brought a unifying religion to replace the divisive tribal solidarity of the jahiliiya, Rida maintains, and he demands that in his time, "we [Muslims should] create (*najʿal*) our social association (*ijtimāʿanā*) and our unity (*waḥdatanā*) based on His book; around it we concur (*najtamiʿ*) and by it we unite (*nattaḥid*)."[240] Rida stresses that clinging (*iʿtiṣām*) to the rope of God is the principle (*aṣl*) that will bring about "concurrence (*ijtimāʿ*) and that unity (*ittiḥād*) which makes the umma become like a single person (*shakḥs wāḥid*)."[241]

Examples abound in which Rida positions Islam as the one religion that calls humankind to unity and concurrence, thus serving as a principle for social association; this is especially the case in the early volumes of *al-Manar*. In the first volume, Rida stresses that the Qur'an, among other things, "instituted the principles of unity (*waḥda*) in creed (*iʿtiqād*) and social association (*ijtimāʿ*)."[242] The following year, we read that "the religion of God is one, and there must be no sedition (*tafarruq*) or controversy (*ikhtilāf*) concerning it; for it was instituted for the felicity of mankind, and felicity lies in concurrence (*ijtimāʿ*) and unity (*tawḥīd*)."[243] The circle of social association (*ijtimāʿ*) increasingly widened with the progress of mankind, Rida goes on, and he asserts that God sent to every people (*qawm*) a messenger "informing [them] about unity (*tawḥīd*) [both of God and as a principle] and calling [them] to what completes the order of social association (*niẓām al-ijtimāʿ*) concerning the refinement of morals and behavior (*al-tahdhīb wa-l-taʾdīb*). [...] When humankind had reached a stage at which all nations and peoples could be connected and united, God sent His last messenger to guide them toward the order of this great society (*niẓām hadhā al-ijtimāʿ al-kabīr*)."[244] Again, a year later – that is, in 1901 – we read that "the social reform (*al-iṣlāḥ al-ijtimāʿī*) brought by Islam consists of bringing about unity of the nations of the earth (*waḥdat umam al-arḍ*) by making them agree in language and religion, and this is what European philosophers in their theories and the strong states [of Europe] have finally also turned to."[245]

---

238 Idem., "al-Jinsiyya wa-l-Din," 321 f.

239 Idem., *Tafsir*, vol. 4: 17.

240 Ibid., vol. 4: 16; see also: idem. 1906. "al-Akhbar wa-l-Araʾ," *al-Manar* 9/8: 636–640, here 637.

241 Idem., *Tafsir*, vol. 4: 39.

242 Idem. 1899. "Ramadan al-Mubarak." *al-Manar* 1/43: 829–831, here 829.

243 Idem. 1899. "Durus Jamʿiyyat Shams al-Islam (3)." *al-Manar* 2/30: 475–479, here 475.

244 Ibid., 475.

245 Idem., "Bab al-Asʾila," *al-Manar* 4/13: 496.

In the *Tafsir*, Rida again uses the term *tawḥīd* not only to designate the absolute unity of God, but also the unity of humankind through belief in Him: "Islam is the religion of absolute unity (*tawḥīd*) and social concurrence (*ijtimāʿ*) and condemns in the strongest terms sedition (*tafrīq*) and controversy (*ikhtilāf*)."[246] Nevertheless, sedition (*tafarruq*) is a law of social association (*sunnat al-ijtimāʿ*), in religion and politics alike.[247] According to Rida, the intention behind strife (*fitna*) in religion being one of God's laws (*sunan allāh*) concerning the order of society (*niẓām al-ijtimāʿ*) is to distinguish true believers from non-believers.[248] For Rida, it is common belief in the one God that may bring an end to socio-political strife and constitute an all-encompassing society.

The gist of Rida's foregoing statements recalls Keith Baker's summary of the reaction to secularist claims about the self-sufficiency of society by a French religious actor, who asserted in 1790 that it was God who, "in giving mankind the need to live in society, has also imposed upon it the obligation of social life. [...] Behind the necessity of society there lies, in this account, the necessity of religion. God, it turns out, is the ultimate founder of society."[249]

3.2 Islam as a Societal Religion

While the foregoing collection of statements attests to the fact that Rida upheld the Islamic religion as a principle for a unified social association – that is, for society – the following statements show (a) that he shares the modern conception of Islam as a 'societal religion' (*dīn ijtimāʿī*), which (b) addresses the order of society and aims at social reform, and which (c) entails religious practices that contain societal value.

(a) The explicit definition of Islam as a *dīn ijtimāʿī* notably includes references to unity as well as to society. It may even refer not to society, but rather to Islam "combining" divergent aspects, such as teachings concerning this world and the next.[250] One also needs to keep in mind the two senses of Islam continuously present in Rida's writings – the ideal, transcendent Islam and its current, immanent manifestations. Implicitly referring to the latter in 1900, when criticiz-

---

246 Idem., *Tafsir*, vol. 7: 119; see also vol. 8: 250.

247 Idem., "Muqaddimat Rasa'il," 671.

248 Idem. 1933. "Muqaddimatuna li-Tasdir Kitab Naqd Mata'in fi al-Qur'an al-Karim." *al-Manar* 33/3: 193–210, here 209.

249 Baker, "Enlightenment," 93.

250 See: Rashid Rida commenting upon al-Afghani, Jamal al-Din. 1906. "Kitaban Siyasiyyan li-Hakim al-Islam al-Sayyid Jamal al-Din al-Afghani." *al-Manar* 10/11: 820–833, here 833.

ing saint festivals for containing more societal harms than benefits, Rida laments that "this poor umma does not have a societal religion (*dīn ijtimāʿī*) as its religion and no civilizational shariʿa (*sharīʿa ʿumrāniyya*) as its shariʿa."[251] The ideal Islam for Rida is manifest in the Qurʾan, the Sunna of the Prophet, and the first generations of Muslims. While Rida claims to return to a pristine Islam, this was a recent construction of Islam as a comprehensive response to contemporary questions, including societal ones.

This holistic image of Islam as combining religion and society was jointly constructed by European orientalists and Islamic reformists, such as Jamal al-Din al-Afghani and Muhammad ʿAbduh.[252] Conceptually, they seem to have drawn upon and updated Islam's reference to religion and the world (*dīn wa-dunyā*) and to this world and the next (*al-dunyā wa-l-ākhira*). In the introduction to the *Tafsir al-Manar*, Rida stresses one of the central assets of the program (*manhaj*) of *al-ʿUrwa al-Wuthqa*, which inspired him to found *al-Manar*, as "elucidating that Islam is the religion of leadership and power (*siyāda wa-sulṭān*), combining the felicity of this world and of the next (*saʿādat al-dunyā wa-saʿādat al-ākhira*), whence it is proven to be a spiritual and societal religion and a political and military one (*muqtaḍā dhalik annahu dīn rūḥānī ijtimāʿī wa-madanī ʿaskarī*)."[253] Rida himself foregrounds the social teachings of Islam, not least in his work *The Muhammadan Revelation* from 1933,[254] a book praised by one reader for showing Islam to be not merely a religion of piety and worship (*dīn taʿabbudī*), but a societal religion (*dīn ijtimāʿī*).[255]

Quotations of European orientalists in *al-Manar* attest to their participation in construing Islam as a societal religion. In 1900, Rida approvingly quotes Van Dyck[256] as confirming that "the principle of reform instituted by Muhammad is the greatest and strongest of all principles, namely unity in creed and in social association (*al-waḥda fī al-iʿtiqād wa-l-ijtimāʿ*)."[257] In an article reprinted from a Turkish paper in 1913, which discusses Thomas Arnold's work *The Preaching of Islam*, we read that "some people claim that Islam is not a societal religion (*dīn*

---

251 Rida, Rashid. 1900. "al-Mawalid wa-l-Muwasim." *al-Manar* 3/21: 501–502, here 502.

252 See above: 169.

253 Rida, *Tafsir*, vol. 1: 10.

254 Idem., *al-Wahy*; idem., *The Muhammadan*; idem., *The Revelation*.

255 Muhammad ʿAli Zubyan al-Kilani quoted in Rida, Rashid. 1934. "Taqariz Kitab al-Wahy al-Muhammadi." *al-Manar* 33/9: 697–710, here 706.

256 In all likelihood – Rida writes that "the famous Van Dyck" has said this to him in person – this is Cornelius Van Dyck (1818–1895), an American missionary who taught at the Syrian Protestant College in Beirut and translated the Bible into Arabic.

257 Rida, Rashid. 1900. "Masʾalat Zayd wa-Zaynab: Idah wa-Khilasa." *al-Manar* 3/29: 714–720 [misprinted as 684–690], here 717 (misprinted as 687).

ijtimāʿī) but professor Arnold disproves this claim."[258] The following year, *al-Manar* reprinted the translation of a speech by the Dutch orientalist Christiaan Snouck Hurgronje from a Syrian paper published in New York, in which he said that "Islam contains laws (*sharāʾiʿ*) related to life in all its states (*aṭwār*), personal and public (*shkahṣiyya wa-ʿumūmiyya*), individual and collective (*fardiyya wa-ijtimāʿiyya*)."[259] And a collection of testimonies by Western scholars concerning Islam, published in 1929, includes the following lines from the introduction of a translation of the Qurʾan: "The guide (*murshid*) of Muslims is the Qurʾan alone; and the Qurʾan is not only a religious book (*kitāb dīnī*) but a book of science and morals (*ādāb*); and it contains an elucidation of the political and social life (*al-ḥayāt al-siyāsiyya wa-l-ijtimāʿiyya*)."[260]

One author who stands out concerning the characterization of Islam as a societal religion is Shibli Shumayyil. In 1909, Rida defends his Christian friend, saying that he had continuously emphasized that "there is no societal religion (*dīn ijtimāʿī*) other than the religion of the Qurʾan." In this way, Rida explains (thus updating the classical conceptual pair *dunyawī* and *ukhrawī*, this-worldly and otherworldly), Shumayyil is appealing to one half of Islam – namely, its worldly half (*al-nuṣf al-dunyawī minhu*).[261] A year earlier, when foregrounding Shumayyil's positive view of the prophet Muhammad, Rida relates his friend's explication that he is approaching the Qurʾan "insofar as it is a societal book not in its being a religious book" (*min ḥaythu huwa kitāb ijtimāʿī lā min ḥaythu huwa kitāb dīnī*).[262] And in his biography of Shumayyil, Rida again foregrounds his friend's conviction that "there exists no societal religion (*dīn ijtimāʿī*) conforming to the civilizational interests of mankind (*maṣāliḥ al-bashar al-madaniyya*), except the religion of the Qurʾan."[263]

(b) Rida had stressed the societal teachings of Islam and the fact that it contains an order of society since the foundation of *al-Manar*, but this emphasis increased markedly from the 1920s onward. Again, this observation is solely based on pertinent instances of *ijtimāʿ* and *ijtimāʿī* used in relation to Islam or religion.

---

258 Saʿid, Muhammad. 1913. "al-Islam wa-Hurriyat al-ʿAqida wa-Kitab al-Daʿwa al-Islamiyya." *al-Manar* 16/12: 929 – 932, here 930.

259 Hurghrunj, Kristiyan Snuk. 1914. "al-Islam Yuqawim Nufudh al-Nasraniyya." *al-Manar* 17/3: 210 – 217, here 212.

260 Al-Dimashqi, Zaki Kiram. 1929. "Shuhadat 'Ulama' al-Gharb al-Munsifin li-l-Islam wa-l-Nabi wa-l-Muslimin (1)." *al-Manar* 30/2: 140 – 144, here 141. Due to the lack of vowels, I could not identify the proper name of the translator, which is given as "*M-n-n-y.*"

261 Rashid Rida commenting upon Qabani, "al-Duktur," 637.

262 Rida, "al-Qurʾan wa-Najah," 10fn1.

263 Rida, "al-Duktur," 627.

As shown in the previous subsection, it was especially in early volumes of *al-Manar* that Rida validated Islamic bonds as constituting a socio-political collectivity. One hypothesis following from this observation is that Rida first validated Islam as constituting and integrating a socio-political collectivity (ideal-typically: 'nation') and then increasingly formulated the social functioning and order of this collectivity (ideal-typically: 'society') in an Islamic framework. At this point, however, I can only offer a collection of pertinent instances demonstrating that Rida conceptually reformulated Islam to address the order of society.

In the first volume of the journal, Rida already praises ʿAbduh's *Theology of Unity*[264] as demonstrating – among other things – that revelation perfects the order of society (*kamālan li-niẓām al-ijtimāʿ*).[265] Four years later, Rida validates the "spiritual and social reform (*al-iṣlāḥ al-rūḥī al-ijtimāʿī*) brought by Muhammad" as having "changed the appearance of the earth (*hayʾat al-arḍ*) and altered the order of human society (*niẓām al-ijtimāʿ al-insānī*) concerning politics, warfare, civil order (*madaniyya*), sciences, and morals (*ādāb*)."[266] Also in two instances from the *Tafsir*, written before the First World War, Rida foregrounds the new order of society (*niẓām al-ijtimāʿ*) instituted by God or Muhammad.[267] And in volume eight of *al-Manar*, he recalls having "elucidated more than once that the beliefs (*ʿaqāʾid*) of Islam are what is elevating the intellect (*mirqāt al-ʿaql*), and that its morals and religious practices (*ādābuhu wa-ʿibādātuhu*) are elevating the soul (*nafs*), and that its laws (*aḥkām*) are elevating society (*ijtimāʿ*)."[268]

In 1920, then, Rida bemoans the fact that most Islamic religious scholars still fall short of "elucidating the societal principles (*al-uṣūl al-ijtimāʿiyya*) and the questions of politics and civilization (*masāʾil al-siyāsa wa-l-ʿumrān*) contained in the Qur'an (*al-kitāb*) and the Sunna."[269] Subsequently in the same article, he explains that what his contemporaries refer to as *ijtimāʿiyya* means that which refers to society (*umma*) and civilization (*ʿumrān*); this is in distinction from rules concerning the individual and the household, respectively.[270] And

264 ʿAbduh, *Risalat*; idem., *The Theology.*
265 Rida, Rashid. 1898. "Risalat al-Tawhid." *al-Manar* 1/13: 231–233, here 232.
266 Idem. 1902. "(al-Dars 36) Muhammad Rasul Allah wa-Khatim al-Nabiyin." *al-Manar* 5/9: 329–338, here 335; see also ibid., 337.
267 Idem., *Tafsir*, vol. 2: 233, vol. 5: 115.
268 Idem. 1905. "Fatawa al-Manar." *al-Manar* 8/4: 150–155, here 154; see also: idem. 1905. "Fatawa al-Manar." *al-Manar* 8/1: 18–24, here 19.
269 Idem. 1920. "ʿAqibat Harb al-Madaniyya al-Urubiyya." *al-Manar* 21/7: 337–344, here 341. This passage is quoted in: idem. 1939. "al-Manar mundhu 'Ishrin Sanna." *al-Manar* 35/6: 450–462, here 457.
270 Idem., "ʿAqibat," 342; quoted in: idem., "al-Manar mundhu," 457 f.

five years later, he asserts that "everyone who is familiar with Islam knows that it is a religion (*dīn*), a political and judiciary legislation (*tashrīʿ siyāsī qaḍāʾī*), and a social order (*niẓām ijtimāʿī*)."[271] Two instances from the *Tafsir*, written in the late 1920s, show that concerning societal affairs, Rida also endorsed the Islamic religion (*dīn*) as the true manifestation of the timeless religion (also: *dīn*) of God, and thus as superior over other religious traditions (*adyān*): European critics of Islam should know, Rida writes, that Islam is "the one solving all the problems of social association (*al-ḥallāl li-jamīʿa mashākil al-ijtimāʿ*) which are ruining civilization (*al-mufsida li-l-ḥaḍāra*), and that it elucidated to them the truth of their religion (*ḥaqīqat dīnihim*)."[272] Moreoever, "no religion (*dīn min al-adyān*) had such a spiritual, rational, material, social, and political impact (*al-taʾthīr al-rūḥī wa-l-ʿaqlī wa-l-māddī wa-l-ijitmāʿī wa-l-siyāsī*), except Islam alone."[273]

In the 1930s, examples of Rida foregrounding the societal teachings of Islam increased, not least in his book *The Muhammadan Revelation*. With no false humility, Rida advertises this book – which, as we have seen above, was also received as proof that Islam was a societal religion[274] – as elucidating "the goals (*maqāṣid*) of the Qurʾan and its sciences (*ʿulūm*) concerning the religious, social, political, financial, and military reform of mankind (*iṣlāḥ al-bashar al-dīnī wa-l-ijtimāʿī wa-l-siyāsī wa-l-mālī wa-l-ḥarbī*)."[275] He claims to have shown in this work that Islam, the religion of the balanced middle, is "the one solving the financial and spiritual problems of society and those [problems] related to the question of women" (*mashākik al-ijtimāʿ al-māliyya wa-l-rūḥiyya wa-l-nisāʾiyya*).[276] In other articles from the 1930s,[277] Rida defines true Islam as consisting, among other things, of "the social order (*al-niẓām al-ijtimāʿī*) which the shariʿa has laid down,"[278] and stresses again that Muhammad's birth was the origin of a new

---

271 Idem. 1925. "al-Din wa-l-Siyasa wa-Malahidat al-Mutafarnjin min al-ʿArab wa-Ghayrihim." *al-Manar* 26/1: 47–59, here 49.
272 Idem., *Tafsir*, vol. 10: 301.
273 Ibid., vol. 10: 339.
274 See above: 390.
275 Idem. 1933. "Majallat al-Manar Sanna 33." *al-Manar* 33/1: 78–79, here 78; basically identical: idem. 1933. "Muqaddimat Kitab al-Wahy al-Muhammadi." *al-Manar* 33/4: 282–289, here 289.
276 Idem. 1934. "Tafnid Iʿtirad Katib Juzwiti ʿala Kitab al-Wahy al-Muhammadi." *al-Manar* 34/2: 147–151, here 151.
277 Additional examples from that decade include: idem. 1933. "Tahaddi al-ʿAlam bi-Taʿalim al-Wahy al-Muhammadi." *al-Manar* 33/2: 102–103, here 102, 103; idem., "al-Natija al-Maqsuda," 105; idem., "Fatihat Kitab al-Manar," 298.
278 Idem. 1931. "Tasdir al-Tarikh." *al-Manar* 32/1: 2–14, here 13.

order of society (*niẓām al-ijtimāʿ*) that helped humankind enter a new stage of development.[279]

(c) While the foregoing examples have addressed the societal teachings of Islam and the social order of this religion in a rather general vein, we now turn to examples of concrete religious practices to which Rida ascribes societal value.

In 1901, Rida distinguishes between individual and societal religious practices: "religion has been decreed (*shurriʿa*) for the felicity of persons individually (*al-afrād fī anfusihā*) and of peoples collectively (*al-shuʿūb fī majmūʿihā*). Therefore, some of its practices (*aʿmāl*) are acts of worship (*ʿibādāt*) related to the purification of individuals (*tahdhīb al-afrād*) and others are religious ceremonies (*shaʿāʾir*) related to society (*ijtimāʿ*), like the hajj, the two holidays [i.e., *ʿīd al-fiṭr* and *ʿīd al-aḍḥā*], the Friday prayer, and congregational prayer. These ceremonies certainly have an astonishing influence on religious and societal life (*al-ḥayat al-milliya wa-l-ijtimāʿiyya*)."[280] Eight years later, Rida adduces this article from 1901 as having shown that "holidays (*aʿyād*) belong to those ceremonies (*shaʿāʾir*) which revive the sentiments of nations (*umam*) in that sense for which the holiday was instituted, whether religious or social (*dīniyyan aw ijtimāʿiyyan*)."[281] In his *Tafsir*, he again mentions holidays (*aʿyād*) and festivities (*mawāsim*) as examples of the social practices of religion (*aʿmāl al-dīn al-ijtimāʿiyya*).[282] Much more often than religious holidays, however, Rida foregrounds the societal value of the four practical pillars of Islam – namely prayer (*ṣalāt*), almsgiving (*zakāt*), fasting (*ṣiyām*), and the pilgrimage to Mecca (*ḥajj*).

Among the social benefits (*al-fawāʾid al-ijtimāʿiyya*) of fasting, Rida writes in his *Tafsir*, is "equality (*musāwā*) of the rich and the poor, the kings and the rabble (*sūqa*), and among [these benefits] is its teaching the community (*umma*) the [proper] order of livelihood (*niẓām al-maʿīsha*), for all Muslims are breaking the fast at the same time."[283] Rida goes on to adduce the benefits of fasting concerning health (*fawāʾid al-ṣiḥḥa*) in addition to its spiritual and devotional benefits (*al-fawāʾid al-rūḥiyya wa-l-taʿabbudiyya*). Not only does he clearly distinguish these dimensions, but he also deems it necessary to stress that the spiritual benefits are the greatest and are an end unto themselves. We find the same threefold distinction in an article from 1925, in which Rida recalls having written "several

---

279 Idem. 1934. "Dhikra al-Mawlid al-Nabawi." *al-Manar* 34/2: 129–139, here 129.

280 Idem. 1901. "al-Shuʿur wa-l-Wijdan wa-Shaʿaʾir al-Umam wa-l-Adyan." *al-Manar* 4/17: 641–647, here 644.

281 Idem. 1909. "al-Ihtifal bi-ʿId al-Dustur al-ʿUthmani." *al-Manar* 12/6: 478–480, here 478.

282 Idem., *Tafsir*, vol. 7: 431; see also: vol. 2: 35, vol. 11: 232.

283 Ibid., vol. 2: 118.

times about the duty of fasting and its wisdoms (*ḥikam*) and [about] its spiritual, physical, and social benefits (*fawāʾidihi al-rūḥiyya wa-l-badaniyya wa-l-ijtimāʿiyya*)."[284]

In 1899, Rida had already adduced the duty of almsgiving in his argument that Islam contains socio-economic teachings superior to those of Europeans, especially socialism. In a way that resembles the arguments of Rafiq al-ʿAzm,[285] Rida maintains that there is no remedy for the social disease (*al-dāʾ al-ijtimāʿī*) presented by socialists and anarchists in Europe other than "the religion of Islam, which prescribes zakat and impels equality."[286] Moreover, he is optimistic that the day will come "when [the Europeans'] societal knowledge (*maʿārifuhum al-ijtimāʿiyya*) will guide them to establish this firm civilizational pillar (*al-rukn al-madanī al-rakīn* [i.e., zakat]) and subsequently the other pillars of Islam."[287] In volumes of the *Tafsir* written around 1930, Rida again validates zakat as "the financial-societal pillar (*al-rukn al-mālī al-ijtimāʿī*) among those pillars of Islam on which rests its public order (*niẓāmuhu al-ʿāmm*)."[288] With its prescription of zakat, Islam is arguably superior to all other religions; for, after all, "money is the supporter or even the foundation of societal and confessional life (*al-ḥayāt al-ijtimāʿiyya wa-l-milliyya*) and the subsistence of its order (*niẓāmihā*)."[289]

Rida, who nowhere elaborates an economic order in any substantial sense, repeatedly portrays zakat as the main social pillar of Islam, in distinction from prayer, which concerns the individual: "Prayer," he writes, "is the firm pillar for the reform of souls (*iṣlāḥ al-nufūs*), and zakat is the firm pillar for the reform of social association (*iṣlāḥ al-ijtimāʿ*), and if it is destroyed, there remains no Islam in the state (*lā islām fī al-dawla*)."[290] And again: "prayer is the support (*ʿimād*) of Islam, and its greatest pillar for personal acts of worship (*al-ʿibādāt al-shakhṣiyya*), and zakat is its greatest pillar on which is built its societal life (*ḥayātuhu al-ijtimāʿiyya*)."[291]

While in these examples Rida qualified prayer as a personal matter, he elsewhere very clearly foregrounds its societal dimension and benefits. Once again

---

284 Idem. 1925. "al-Muftirun fi Ramadan." *al-Manar* 25/10: 743–744, here 743.

285 See above: 339.

286 Idem. 1900. "al-Zakat wa-l-Tamaddun (2)." *al-Manar* 2/46: 722–725, here 723.

287 Ibid., 725.

288 Idem., *Tafsir*, vol. 10: 151.

289 Ibid., vol. 10: 442.

290 Ibid., vol. 2: 348; see also: vol. 1: 304, 347.

291 Rashid Rida commenting upon Abu Zayd, Muhammad ʿAli. 1915. "al-Burhan ʿala Khuruj Tarik al-Salat wa-Maniʿ al-Zakat min al-Iman (3)." *al-Manar* 18/9: 662–672, here 672.

addressing prayer together with almsgiving as the two main pillars of Islam, he writes that prayer is "the religious-spiritual-social bond (*al-rābiṭa al-dīniyya al-rūḥiyya al-ijtimāʿiyya*) between Muslims, and zakat is the financial-political-social bond (*al-rābiṭa al-māliyya al-siyāsiyya al-ijtimāʿiyya*," and that "prayer is the most elevated spiritual and the exemplary social act of worship (*al-ʿibāda al-rūḥiyya al-ʿulyā wa-l-ijtimāʿiyya al-muthlā*) and zakat is the greatest financial and social devotional service (*al-ʿibāda al-māliyya al-ijtimāʿiyya al-kubrā*)."[292] While Rida once advances social equality (*al-musāwā al-ijtimāʿiyya*) between rich and poor as an effect of congregational prayer,[293] he much more often identifies the bringing together and uniting of the believers as a societal benefit of prayer: praying in one mosque, he writes, contributes to one of the societal goals of Islam (*maqāṣid al-islām al-ijtimāʿiyya*), namely "mutual acquaintance (*taʿāruf*), affection (*taʾāluf*), cooperation (*taʿāwun*), and the unity of forces (*jamʿ al-kalima*)."[294] The Friday prayer in particular is a collective act of devotion (*ʿibāda ijtimāʿiyya*) for which association (*ijtimāʿ*) in one place is commanded for all who are obligated to serve the precepts of religion (*jamīʿ al-mukallifīn*).[295] But Muslims are also united when they pray separately, since they all face the direction of Mecca, Rida maintains, and he argues that unity and concurrence (*ijtimāʿ*) of the community of believers (*umma, milla*) is the very reason for God having determined the direction of prayer (*qibla*).[296]

Mutual acquaintance, concurrence, and unity are also the main societal benefits of the pilgrimage, the one religious practice Rida adduces most often in this regard. The hajj, he maintains, "induces in the souls of the community (*nufūs al-umma*) love for mutual acquaintance (*ḥubb al-taʿāruf*) and affection between the different peoples (*shuʿūb*), and it enforces the bond of society (*rābiṭat al-ijtimāʿ*)."[297] Rida sometimes characterizes the hajj as solely a social pillar (*rukn ijtimāʿī*),[298] and at other times additionally names religious or spiritual (*dīnī*,

---

292 Rida, *Tafsir*, vol. 11: 177; see also: vol. 10: 190 f.

293 Idem., "Haqaʾiq," 469.

294 Idem., *Tafsir*, vol. 11: 31.

295 Idem. 1932. "Fatawa al-Manar." *al-Manar* 32/4: 268–279, here 271.

296 Idem., *Tafsir*, vol. 1: 89, 357, vol. 2: 5, 8.

297 Idem. "al-Suʾal," *al-Manar* 7/10: 378.

298 For example: idem., *Tafsir*, vol. 10: 143, 146; Rashid Rida commenting upon ʿImran, Muhammad Basyuni. 1927. "Wujub al-Hajj." *al-Manar* 27/10: 778–781, here 780fn1 (Basyuni uses the same expression on that page); Rida, Rashid. 1929. "Hal al-Muslimin fi al-Sharq wa-l-Janub." *al-Manar* 29/10: 759–764, here 764.

rūḥī)[299] or even bodily (*badanī*/*jasadī*) and financial (*mālī*) benefits.[300] In the first volume of *al-Manar*, he already clearly distinguishes between the religious core of the pilgrimage and its socio-political extension when he writes that this greatest congregation (*aʿẓam ijtimāʿ*) in the world, "in spite of its being religious (*maʿ kawnihi dīnīyan*), contains obvious civil and political benefits (*al-fawāʾid al-madaniyya wa-l-siyāsiyya*)."[301] And the following year, when referring to the unification of Muslims as the secret of the pilgrimage, Rida defines the religion of Islam (*dīn al-islām*) as "the religion of the grand civilization (*al-madaniyya al-kubrā*) and of social association (*ijtimāʿ*)."[302] Rida foregrounds the hajj as a societal pillar of Islam still more frequently from the 1920s onward, a fact that may be attributed to his closer relations with the Saudi rulers, the guardians of Mecca and Medina.[303] The greater political aspect of the hajj, in comparison with the other religious practices dealt with above, is also discernible in the fact that Rida addresses it mainly in sections of *al-Manar* other than the *Tafsir*, and this in marked contrast to the other three practical pillars. Throughout, and whether in view of the Saudi dynasty as the aspirational center of political power or not, the example of the hajj clearly illustrates the normativity of *ijtimāʿ* as social association–concurrence–unity–society.

Both concerning the hajj and elsewhere in this subsection, we have seen that Rida integrates spiritual and societal aspects of religion or religious and societal aspects of Islam, based on their previous conceptual distinction. I will solidify this point in the following subsection.

3.3 The Distinction and Subsequent Connection of Religion and Society

While it has become clear by now that Rida perceived the religious and the social as distinct, albeit not sharply separated categories, this point merits some elab-

299 Idem., "Bab al-Suʾal," *al-Manar* 6/22: 860; idem. 1927. "al-Radd ʿala al-Zaʿim Muhammad ʿAli al-Hindi fi Mawduʿ Malik al-Hijaz wa-Hukumatihi wa-Qawmihi wa-l-Khilafa (1)." *al-Manar* 29/3: 162–180, here 165.
300 Idem., *Tafsir*, vol. 7: 89; idem. 1917. "Rihlat al-Hijaz (4)." *al-Manar* 20/2: 108–126, here 119; idem. "Khitab ʿAmm," 35f.
301 Idem. 1899. "Muluk al-Muslimin wa-l-Tarikh." *al-Manar* 1/48: 929–930, here 930.
302 Idem., "Fransa," 153.
303 In addition to the previous examples from the 1920s, see: idem. 1923. "al-Istiftaʾ fi Malik al-Hijaz." *al-Manar* 24/8: 593–618, here 608; idem. 1923. "Ahwal al-ʿAlam al-Islami." *al-Manar* 24/10: 796–799, here 798; idem. 1928. "Fatihat al-Mujallad al-Tasiʿ al-ʿIshrin min al-Manar." *al-Manar* 29/1: 1–8, here 6; idem. 1932. "Adhan Ibrahim al-Khalil bi-l-Hajj wa-Duʿaʾuhu li-Ahl al-Haram bi-l-Rizq." *al-Manar* 32/3: 217–221, here 217.

oration. The distinction between *dīnī* and *ijtimāʿī*, in its primary sense, is notably a distinction of inner-worldly spheres or aspects. When paired with the social, the religious is an inner-worldly expression of the (connection to the) godly reality beyond this world, that is, 'the transcendent.' When referring to this transcendent reality in itself, *dīn* is notably paired with *dunyā* (this world), rather than with 'the social.' Occasionally, Rida elucidates the more recent distinction between the religious and the social by referring back to the earlier distinction between religion and the world (e.g., *al-ijtimāʿī al-dunyawī*), and since the ideal religion for Rida addresses both the spiritual and the social, he sometimes contrasts *ijtimāʿī* with *rūḥī* as the two dimensions of *dīn*.[304] These cross-references notwithstanding, Rida's conceptual usage suggests that, on one level, it is religion and the world sustaining each other, while on another, it is religion and society. Above all, it helps to distinguish two basic references of the religious (*dīnī*) and of religion (*dīn*): one to the timeless religion of God, and one to its immanent manifestations. What is more, *dīn* can shift its conceptual position in relation to *islām:* it is often equated with *islām*, which is then conceived of as a religion (*dīn al-islām, al-dīn al-islāmī*), but equally often *dīn* forms part of *islām*, which is differentiated into its worldly and religious aspects or its societal and religious aspects.[305] These varying references of *dīn* and *islām* make it harder to analytically discern the distinction between the religious and the social, as does Rida's aim to reconnect both spheres.

Therefore, I will first establish (a) that Rida distinguishes between the two spheres; and then (b) *hypothesize* that he increasingly integrated both spheres, not least in reaction to a purely worldly Islam; and furthermore (c) that he conceived of ethics as a crucial mediator between religion and society.

(a) In 1900, Rida responds to the French historian and politician Gabriel Hanotaux (1853–1944), who claimed that the national bond (*al-rābiṭa al-waṭaniyya*) is more comprehensive and stronger than the religious one, and that it underlies the progress of Europe: "This statement does not apply to the Islamic religion (*al-dīn al-islāmī*), for to the Islamic bond (*al-rābiṭa al-islāmiyya*) there are two sides (*ṭarfān*): a spiritual side (*ṭarf rūḥī*) joining the members of [the Islamic]

---

304 For example: idem. 1902. "A-Yasumuna wa-la Yusilluna wa-hum Muʾminun?." *al-Manar* 5/17: 641–650, here 641.

305 In one article, for example, Rida states as the three fields of Islamic reform the religious, the social, and the political (*al-iṣlāḥ al-islāmī al-dīnī wa-l-ijtimāʿī wa-l-siyāsī*) (idem. 1923. "Lughat al-Islam wa-l-Lugha al-Rasmiyya bayna al-Mamalik al-Islamiyya (1)." *al-Manar* 24/10: 753–765, here 755). Later in the same article, he names as the three aspects of the Islamic religion (*dīn al-islām*), "its spiritual guidance (*hidāyatuhu al-rūḥiyya*), its social bond (*rābiṭatuhu al-ijtimāʿiyya*), and its just and civil government (*ḥukūmatuhu al-ʿādila al-madaniyya*)" (ibid., 764).

religion (*abnāʾ al-dīn*) [...] and a material-social side (*ṭarf māddī ijtimāʿī*) that includes with Muslims all other [religious or ethnic] elements (*ʿanāṣir*), except those at war [with Muslims] with whom there is no contract, making them all equal in rights."[306] Adopting the primary categorical distinction between the spiritual and the socio-political, Rida maintains that the Islamic religion addresses both spheres.

In its comprehensiveness, then, the Islamic religion clearly shares the contemporaneous distinction between the two spheres of the religious-spiritual and the legal-societal, as Rida stresses in 1907, against European claims to the contrary:

"Contemporaneous writers (*kuttāb al-ʿaṣr*) separate religion (*dīn*) and law (*sharīʿa*). By religion they designate belief (*iʿtiqād*), religious practices (*ʿibādāt*), and virtues (*faḍāʾil*), that is, that by which is sought the reform of souls (*iṣlāḥ al-arwāḥ*) and their preparation for felicity in the next world (*al-ākhira*) first and in itself, even if it also benefits felicity in this world (*al-dunyā*). And by law they designate that by which the rulers govern the people (*al-nās*) and arbitrate between them in controversies, that is, the means by which the reform of the political, civil, and criminal conditions of society (*iṣlāḥ aḥwāl al-ijtimāʿ al-siyāsiyya wa-l-madaniyya wa-l-jināʾiyya*) is sought. And it is known that Moses brought religion and law, and the greatest part of what he set forth were worldly regulations (*aḥkām dunyawiyya*); and [it is known] that Jesus brought religion only, and the Jews stuck with the laws of Moses; and [it is known] that that what Muhammad (on him and on both of them [i. e., Moses and Jesus] be blessings and peace) brought combined the two matters. The Europeans [therefore] think that the Muslims do not distinguish between religion and law, because they consider both of them godly (*ilāhī*). Since worldly affairs (*al-umūr al-dunyawiyya*) inevitably differ with time and place, it is [however] impossible to lay down for them a complete law appropriate for the well-being (*maṣlaḥa*) of people in all ages and at all times; in this question no two people with a sound mind disagree. The Europeans [wrongly] think that it is impossible for Muslims to be equal to them in civilization (*madaniyya*), as long as they consider their shariʿa on which their worldly affairs rest as godly and as not allowing for changes."[307]

Referring to the distinction between shariʿa and fiqh – that is, between universal principles and their contingent, human elaboration – Rida argues that Islam

306 Idem. 1900. "Hanutu wa-l-Islah al-Islami." *al-Manar* 3/15: 337–345, here 344.
307 Idem., "al-Jamiʿa al-Islamiyya," *al-Manar* 10/3: 226.

clearly shares the modern distinction between the religious and the other spheres of societal life. He notably does so primarily in engaging European claims to the contrary. The foregoing quotation stems from his article on "Pan-Islamism," in which Rida, partly quoting ʿAbduh, engages the opinions of Hanotaux and Cromer on Islam. In a related discussion, he states that Cromer evaluates Islam both in its status as a religion (*min ḥaythu huwa dīn*) and in its status as a law (*sharīʿa*) and a social order (*niẓām ijtimāʿī*).[308] If Rida foregrounds the distinction between the religious and the social within Islam when engaging European writers, he notably draws on the Islamic discursive tradition to justify and elaborate on that distinction.

In his book *The Islamic Caliphate*,[309] Rida also divides Islam into purely religious or spiritual aspects and those related to society. In the introduction, he defines Islam as:

"a spiritual guidance (*hidāya rūḥiyya*) and a civil social politics (*siyāsa ijtimāʿiyya madaniyya*) by which God perfected the religion of the prophets and the laws of progress (*sunan al-irtiqāʾ*), on which rests the order of human society (*niẓām al-ijtimāʿ al-basharī*). Concerning purely religious guidance (*al-hidāya al-dīniyya al-mahḍa*), this it set forth root and branch [...]. And concerning civil social politics (*al-siyāsa al-ijtimāʿiyya al-madaniyya*), Islam indeed laid down its basis (*asās*) and principles (*qawāʿid*) and prescribed the community (*umma*) to form their opinion and investigate rationally therein, because it [i.e., this politics] differs with the difference of time and place and progresses with the progress of civilization, sciences, and knowledge."[310]

It is true that, for Rida, Islam is both "a spiritual guidance (*hidāya rūḥiyya*) and a socio-political bond (*rābiṭa ijtimāʿiyya siyāsiyya*)."[311] However, the distinction of the spheres of religion and society, according to Rida, is maintainable even when authority over both spheres is combined in one person, contrary to what Christians claim, based on their historical experience:

"[I]t has been of the work of modern civilization (*aʿmāl al-tamaddun al-ḥadīth*) to separate religious and civil power (*al-sulṭa al-dīniyya wa-l-sulṭa al-madaniyya*).

---

308 Idem., "Kitab Misr," 82.

309 Idem., *al-Khilafa*; Laoust, *Le Califat.*

310 Rida, "Fatihat Kitab al-Khilafa," 461f. Muhamamd Bahjat al-Bitar centrally adduces this statement as testimony to Islam's universal validity (al-Bitar, "Kitab," *al-Manar* 27/5: 361).

311 Idem. 1923. "al-Ahkam al-Sharʿiyya al-Mutaʿalliqa bi-l-Khilafa al-Islamiyya." *al-Manar* 24/1: 33–67, here 66.

So to the church was left the right to authority (*sayṭara*) over belief (*iʿtiqād*) and practices, insofar as they concern the interaction (*muʿāmala*) between the servant and his Lord [...]; and the civil authority (*al-sulṭa al-madaniyya*) was granted the right to legislate in the interactions (*muʿāmalāt*) between people and the right of authority over that which preserves the order of their society (*niẓām ijtimāʿihim*) in this world not the next (*fī maʿāshihim lā fī maʿādihim*); and they consider this separation to be the source for their greatest well-being. Based on this, they misconstrue what they charge Islam with, namely that it imposes the combination of these two powers in one person. They think that for Muslims this means that the sultan is the one deciding concerning religion, the one laying down its rules and implementing them. [...] You [however] have learned that there is no religious authority in Islam except the authority of good spiritual counsel (*sulṭat al-mawʿiẓa al-ḥusna*), of invitation to what is good (*al-daʿwa ilā al-khayr*) and deterrence from evil (*al-tanfīr ʿan al-sharr*). And this is an authority that God has granted to the lowest of Muslims so that by it he may admonish [lit.: touch the nose of] the highest one of them; in the same way as He has granted it to the highest one of them so that by it he may reach for the lowest one of them."[312]

Finally, in 1933, Rida formulates the religious and the socio-political as two separate but mutually complementary spheres, necessary for felicity in this world and the next:

"Islam is a spiritual religion (*dīn rūḥānī*) and a socio-political order of the state (*niẓām dawlī ijtimāʿī siyāsī*), and each of its two halves (*jānibayn*) solidifies and completes the other (*muʿazziz li-l-ākhar mukmil la-hu*); and thus its goal is felicity in both realms, this world and the next (*al-dunyā wa-l-ākhira*). The subject matter of the first half is the purification of human souls through proper beliefs, reasonable devotional practices, elevated morals, and noble and beneficial deeds, so as to make them [i.e., the souls] acceptable for the proximity of God Most High in the gardens of the other world. And the subject matter of the order of the state (*al-niẓām al-dawlī*) is to protect, guarantee, and defend this religion (*hadhā al-dīn*) and its adherents and homelands (*awṭān*) by force; and to establish truth, justice, and liberty among its adherents and all others belonging to its state, so as to erect civilization (*ʿumrān*); and to unveil the laws of God and the secrets of His creation based on the progress of the human species. So the devotional-spiritual half of Islam (*al-jānib al-taʿabbudī al-rūḥānī*) completes the civil order

312 Idem., "al-Khilafa," *al-Manar* 24/5: 350.

(*al-niẓām al-madanī*) by igniting the spirit of honesty and truthfulness in it, so that politics is not a mere means for the ambitions and desires of this world and for the strong oppressing the weak; and the civil-political order (*al-niẓām al-madanī al-siyāsī*) supports the devotional side and enables it by making the worshippers free and respected men."[313]

This last quotation shows that, by 1930, Rida had conceptually solidified the distinction between the religious-spiritual and the socio-political aspects of Islam. Rida thus constructed an Islamic discourse to mirror the modern distinction between the religious and the socio-political, sometimes additionally distinguishing between the social and the political.

In this case, however, increasing conceptual distinction is not tantamount to separation; on the contrary, Rida increasingly portrayed a socio-political dimension as indispensable to the Islamic religion as such. This is commonly known as Rida's turn to political Islamism. While it is hardly possible – not least due to Rida's varying statements – to model a systematic process of how this understanding came about, I shall now at least advance one hypothesis in this regard.

(b) Departing from pertinent usages of *ijtimāʿ* and *ijtimāʿī* in relation to *dīn*, *dīnī*, *islām*, and *islāmī*, I suggest that it was not least to counter a purely worldly understanding of Islam – which, notably, was possible – that Rida delineated a political dimension as part of the essence of Islam as a religion.

Following the foregoing quotation from 1933, Rida considers that a Muslim adopting French citizenship first gives up only Islam's political-societal half (*al-jānib al-siyāsī al-ijtimāʿī*), but may still fully adhere to its spiritual half (*al-jānib al-rūḥī*). However, as both halves equally form part of the Islamic religion and are decreed by God, abandoning one side entails abandoning the other.[314] Rida thus integrates two distinct, immanent spheres on the meta-level of transcendent religion. This requires the previous distinction of these spheres and thus differs from Rida's early validation of religion as in itself constituting a superior bond for social association.[315]

While Rida's subsequent statements vary, and he occasionally comes back to this early understanding,[316] he *seems* to increasingly distinguish between the re-

---

313 Idem. 1933. "Mas'alat al-Tajnis al-Fransi." *al-Manar* 33/3: 224–230, here 228f.

314 Ibid., 229.

315 See above: chapter 10 section 3.2.

316 A possible, if not overly obvious, example in this regard is: idem. 1916. "Hikam al-Siyam wa-Jinayat Tarikihi 'ala Anfusihim wa-'ala al-Muslimin wa-l-Islam." *al-Manar* 19/2: 82–88, here 87.

ligious and the purely worldly or socio-political aspects of Islam. In the opening article of volume 13, he refers back to his article on “the political bond of Islam” (*jinsiyyat al-islām*)[317] from 1899. He claims to have shown there that Islam consists of “two social bonds (*rābiṭatayn ijtimāʿiyyatayn*). The first of them is worldly and socio-political (*dunyawiyya ijtimāʿiyya*), connecting all those who live in its realm (*dār*) and who submit to its rule based on the shariʿa of justice, equality, righteousness, and beneficence, however their religions may differ. And the second is spiritual (*rūḥaniyya*), connecting in another fraternity those adopting its creed and morals.”[318] And in 1924, Rida distinguishes three dimensions of Islam – namely its religious bond, (*al-jinsiyya al-dīniyya*), its social and moral bond (*al-jinsiyya al-ijtimāʿiyya al-adabiyya*), and its political bond (*al-jinsiyya al-siyāsiyya*).[319]

What is certain throughout is that Rida opposed those who wanted to turn religion into a solely political identity. In 1903, he argues that Christians allegedly unfairly evaluate the Qur'an and the Islamic religion because they have adopted

“religion as a national identity (*jinsiyya*) and a socio-political bond (*rābiṭa ijtimāʿiyya siyāsiyya*), whence they preserve the confessional doctrines, traditions, and customs which connect them with all the members of their community; for, if they would neglect these [doctrines, etc.], their union (*jāmiʿa*) would dissolve and they would cease to be a nation (*umma*) and a community (*milla*). And they have not looked upon Islam in a just manner that would make them understand its principles, because those Muslims who have also turned religion into a political identity (*jinsiyya*) were hostile towards them in a manner not endorsed by Islam.”[320]

In 1907, he maintains that those who deny the truth of religion and only want to maintain it as a social bond (*rābiṭa ijtimāʿiyya*) equivalent to race (*jins*) or language can only be convinced rationally by foregrounding the socio-political benefits of religion as a political constituent (*jinsiyya*).[321] In a similar vein, in 1929, Rida again distinguishes between unbelieving Muslims who deny religion root

317 This most probably is: idem., “al-Jinsiyya wa-l-Din”

318 Idem. 1910. “Fatihat al-Sanna al-Thalitha ʿAshar.” *al-Manar* 13/1: 3–8, here 5fn1.

319 Idem. 1924. “Tajannus al-Muslim bi-Jinsiyya Tunafi al-Islam.” *al-Manar* 25/1: 21–32, here 31f.

320 Idem. 1903. “Bayan al-Qur'an wa-Balaghatuhu wa-ma Yawhim Ghayr Dhalik.” *al-Manar* 6/12: 461–466, here 463.

321 Idem. 1907. “Tamthil al-Qisas aw al-Tiyatru.” *al-Manar* 10/1: 38–42, here 39ff.

and branch and those who want to retain it as a socio-political bond (*rābiṭa ijtimāʿiyya siyāsiyya*).[322] In his response to Lord Cromer from 1910, Rida had notably denied the existence of a Pan-Islamic movement and said that Muslims' nationalist and political statements have nothing to do with religion, and even contradict it in many regards.[323] While the political context of the last statement in particular obviously needs to be considered, Rida clearly conceived of and negated the possibility of a purely worldly Islam constructed merely for socio-political means.

Conceptually, this is best demonstrated when he posits the novel concept of a religious Islam (*al-islām al-dīnī*) over against an ethnic or customary Islam (*al-islām al-jinsī/al-ʿurfī*). In his comment on an article from 1915, Rida first sketches a religious Islam (*al-islām al-dīnī*), at whose core is belief and submission to the message brought by Muhammad, which inherently leads to fulfilling religious practices. "And there is another Islam (*islām ākhar*), which is tantamount to a political or social identity (*jinsiyya siyāsiyya aw ijtimāʿiyya*) attained by inheritance or by membership in a group of people (*qawm*) called Muslims. And in this Islam knowledge about the doctrines of religious Islam (*ʿaqāʾid al-islām al-dīnī*) is not conditional [...]. Verily, we have seen some unbelievers trying to destroy religious Islam by customary ethnic Islam (*al-islām al-iṣṭilāḥī al-jinsī*)."[324] In a similar vein, in his *Tafsir*, Rida contrasts religious Islam with customary Islam (*al-islām al-ʿurfī*), which merely consists of outward belonging and of a socio-political identity.[325] Rida also once uses – in a seemingly self-evident and overtly derogatory manner – the concept of 'geographical Muslims' (*al-muslimūn al-jiyughrafiyūn*), a designation I have not come across elsewhere.[326] Rida's rejection of a purely outward, customary Islam is related to his general validation of critical rational inquiry (*ijtihād*) over what he portrays as mere blind imitation of tradition (*taqlīd*). More fundamentally, for Rida, the true Islamic religion – of which rational inquiry notably forms a part – is an expression of a timeless supernatural reality, whose core consists of belief in the one God.

Based on this conviction, Rida not only attacks those who allegedly want to turn Islam into a merely socio-political identity, but also denies a proto-secular understanding of Islam as concerned primarily with social and economic order.

---

322 Idem. 1929. "Fatihat al-Sanna al-Thalathin." *al-Manar* 30/1: 1–16, here 4.

323 Idem., "al-Jamiʿa al-Islamiyya," 200; see above: chapter 7 section 4.1.

324 Rashid Rida commenting upon Abu Zayd, "al-Burhan," 772.

325 See: Smith, Jane Idleman, *An Historical*, 196–203; see also: Rida, *Tafsir*, vol. 8: 214.

326 Idem. 1928. "Iqtirah Ibtal al-Awqaf al-Ahliyya wa-Makan al-Din min al-Dawla al-Misriyya fi Qismayha al-Tashriʿi wa-l-Tanfidhi." *al-Manar* 29/1: 75–78, here 77.

In a section of his *Tafsir* written around the year 1930,[327] Rida upholds the societal benefits of zakat, but refutes the understanding of Islam as consisting primarily of social and economic teachings. Before engaging an Italian historian, Rida criticizes an Arabic author, who according to him, says, "following the [erroneous] opinion of some European historians, that Islam was not a purely religious idea (*fikra dīniyya maḥḍan*) but was also an economic and societal matter (*mas'ala iqtiṣādiyya wa-ijtimāʿiyya*), or that this was [even] the primary aim aspired to in itself [by Islam] and that religion was only a means (*wasīla*) to that. And the famous Italian historian Caetani [1869–1935] relates that Islam was not religious (*dīniyyan*) except outwardly (*fī al-ẓāhir*) and that its essence (*jawharahu*) was political and economic (*siyāsiyyan wa-iqtiṣādiyyan*)."[328] Rida attributes this foregrounding of socio-economic aspects to Caetani's alleged communist convictions. He stresses that "the truth is that Islam is the balanced religion (*al-dīn al-wasaṭ*), combining the interests of the spirit and the body (*maṣāliḥ al-rūḥ wa-l-jasad*), for [the sake of] rule in this world (*siyāda fī al-dunyā*) and felicity in the other world (*saʿāda fī al-ākhira*); so it is between financial and worldly Judaism and spiritual and ascetic Christianity."[329]

Above (a) I established that Rida operated with the categorical modern distinction between the religious and the social and constructed a modern understanding of Islam to mirror that distinction. To this I have now added the hypothesis that Rida came to imbue the core of the Islamic religion with a clearly delineated political dimension when he countered not only non-religious nationalist positions, but also a purely worldly understanding of Islam.

The modernity of religio-political Islamism consists precisely in its integration of the modern understanding of a self-sufficient, socio-political realm into an allegedly timeless religious essence. In doing so, religio-political Islamism blurs – but cannot possibly do away with – the distinction between religion and society. Once this distinction is made, religion and society or religious and socio-political order can be related in different ways, and their connection can be loosened or tightened, as we have already seen in the debate between al-ʿAzm and al-Yafiʿi[330]. The trajectory of Rida's writings illustrate, it seems to me, that the point of integration for religion and society may be shifted very far into the transcendent background – namely, to a creator God – or brought into the immanent foreground – namely, in the person of the caliph.

---

327 The eleventh volume of the *Tafsir* is based on articles published in volumes 31 to 33 of *al-Manar* (1929–1933).

328 Rida, *Tafsir*, vol. 11: 22.

329 Ibid., vol. 11: 23.

330 See above: chapter 9 section 2.

I will now suggest that, regardless of how closely Rida connected religion and society, a primary immanent connector between these two spheres was a religious ethics, which should be internalized by the believing individual.

(c) Constitutive for the modern idea of society is that societal order is continuously negotiated and constructed by self-reflective, autonomous individuals. As seen above, Rida – in concert with the vast majority of Arab reformists of the nineteenth and early twentieth centuries – stressed the need for the intellectual and moral education and activity of reflective individuals. The reformists conceived of a mutual dependency and complementarity of the internal order of civilized individuals and the external order of a civilized society.[331] Rida's ideal society – the *umma* – consisted of believing individuals who internalize the moral teachings of religion and enact them for the benefit of society. For Rida, these teachings notably include Islamic legal rulings and, increasingly, political principles. However, even when an institutionalized Islamic government became the goal, believing individuals remained the starting point and the only way of achieving this. Again, space does not allow me to comprehensively discern how Rida relates the fields of religion, ethics, laws, and politics at different stages in his writings. Based on the terminological observation that Rida repeatedly introduces 'the ethical' (*al adabī*) as an intermediary between 'the religious' and 'the social'[332] or replaces 'the religious' with 'the ethical' as complementing 'the social' and 'the political,'[333] I merely want to point out religious ethics as a crucial mediator between transcendent religion and immanent society.

In the first volume of *al-Manar*, Rida very clearly formulates the links between godly reality, individual morals, societal cooperation, unity, and the overarching paradigm of civilization: "Religion is a true godly foundation (*waḍʿ ilahī ḥaqq*), commanding the cleansing of the souls and their purification, urging affection and harmony, and forbidding hostility and controversy; thus it is the one which incites [human beings] to socialize based on cooperation (*bāʿith al-ijtimāʿ ʿalā al-taʿāwun*) and the one which invites reason (*dāʿī al-rashād*) to agreement and unity (*al-ittifāq wa-l-ittiḥād*), combining what is scattered and uniting what

331 See: Noorani, *Culture*, 71.

332 For example: Rida, "al-Shaykh Muhammad Kamil al-Rafiʿi," 326; idem. 1922. "al-Islam wa-l-Nasraniyya." *al-Manar* 23/4: 267–272, here 268; idem. 1931. "al-Tajdid wa-l-Tajaddud wa-l-Mujaddidun." *al-Manar* 31/10: 770–777, here 771; idem., *Tafsir*, vol. 9: 380.

333 For example: idem. 1905. "Mulakhkhas Sirat al-Ustadh al-Imam." *al-Manar* 8/10: 379–400, here 389; idem., "Fasl fi Hikam," 581; idem., "al-Tawr," 496 f.; idem. "al-Tarbiya al-Islamiyya," 544.

is variegated, and this is the principle of civilization (*mabda' al-madaniyya*) or is tantamount to it (*aw huwa hiya*)."[334] Earlier that year, Rida had articulated the basic importance of morals for society in an article "elucidating that the felicity of society (*sa'ādat al-umma*) lies in moral refinement (*tahdhīb*)": the only true and unanimously agreed upon basis for social association (*ijtimā'*), according to him, is to strive for felicity and to deflect harm from oneself and those one is interacting with.[335]

Rida is convinced that only religion can provide the firm basis for the moral refinement of individuals that is necessary for constructing a well-functioning, sustainable society (*umma*). This had already become very clear in his validation of *umma* over against *al-hay'a al-ijtimā'iyya* in this regard.[336] In his *Tafsir*, Rida writes that "curing the illnesses of morals (*amrāḍ al-akhlāq*) and the diseases of society (*adwā' al-ijtimā'*) is more difficult than healing the limbs of persons (*afrād*). And it is firmly known that the Qur'an combines true doctrines of belief (*al-'aqā'id al-ṣaḥīḥa*), elevated morals (*al-ādāb al-'āliyya*), and principles of social and civil legislation (*uṣūl al-tashrī' al-ijtimā'ī wa-l-madanī*)."[337]

What Rida's ideal Islam adds to the universal principles of civilization is precisely the dimensions of belief and of ethical prescriptions. As Rida asserts in 1902:

"The morals (*akhlāq*) to which the Qur'an calls [humankind] are the morals of society (*ijtimā'*), civilization (*'umrān*), power (*'izza*), and rule (*sulṭān*). And the principles of rules (*aḥkām*) and of the political, civil, legal, and military laws (*al-sharā'i' al-siyāsiyya wa-l-madaniyya wa-l-qaḍā'iyya*) in Islam conform to those whose benefit is established among the Western peoples (*al-umam al-gharbiyya*), and they [i.e., these principles] contain what they [i.e., the Westerners] have not arrived at and what they would rely upon if they knew it. The Qur'an contains a healing remedy for every single disease of civilization (*'umrān*) and for every single illness of human society (*al-ijtimā' al-basharī*). Some of these remedies benefit without belief (*īmān*), and others are only realizable through it, such as the remedy of zakat for the diseases of the great social question (*al-mas'ala al-ijtimā'iyya*). As the Most High said: "We bestow though this Qur'an that which is healing for and a grace unto those who believe" [17:82].

334 Idem. 1898. "al-Din wa-l-Madaniyya fi al-Sharq." *al-Manar* 1/14: 242–250, here 242.

335 Idem., "Tabsira," 70.

336 See above: chapter 7 section 2.

337 Rida, *Tafsir*, vol. 1: 182; see also: vol. 6: 107, vol. 11: 238f.

Truly, the perfect civilization (*al-madaniyya al-kāmila*) toward which the advanced peoples (*al-umam al-rāqiyya*) are heading will not be realized except by a religion (*dīn*) combining these principles[338] which we have summarized just now, and some of whose details have already been set forth in *al-Manar*, to which we will add more if time permits."[339]

Thus Rida posits religious morals for society as superior to philosophical ones grounded in nature, because they are firmly rooted in the allegedly timeless and invariable truth of transcendent religion, as revealed by the prophets, and can moreover be understood by all people. Note again the implicit causal chain from belief in God via morals to society in the following passage from 1933:

"If it is said that belief (*īmān*) in the unseen world and in the existence of the Lord are an instinct (*gharīza*) in humankind's innate disposition (*al-fiṭra al-bashariyya*), as you have asserted, or one of its instincts (*ilhām*), which comes to inspire individuals during puberty, and that some reflecting philosophers (*al-ḥukamāʾ al-mufakkirīn*) have advanced in their rational knowledge to the point that they established proofs (*barāhīn*) for the existence of that which necessarily must exist (*wujūd wājib al-wujūd* [i.e., God]), for His intellection (*ʿilm*) and wisdom (*ḥikma*), and for the duty of exalting, thanking, and worshipping Him. And some of them have even determined the continuation of the soul (*nafs*) after death and its remaining in comforting ease (*naʿīm muqīm*) or painful suffering (*ʿadhāb ʿalīm*), and have established for the people (*al-nās*) principles of virtues (*faḍāʾil*) and of legislation (*tashrīʿ*) and morals (*ādāb*) by which humanity (*al-insāniyya*) and the bonds of society (*rawābiṭ al-ijtimāʿ*) are brought into their proper state (*tuṣlaḥ*). Then I say, yes, all of this has a basis established by past history and testified to by the present age. However, there are differences between the guidance of the prophets and the wisdom and knowledge of the philosophers concerning their respective source (*maṣdar*), the trust (*thiqqa*) in its veracity (*ṣiḥḥa*), the submission (*idhʿān*) to its truth (*ḥaqīqa*), and its influence on the souls (*anfus*) of all the groups of people addressed (*jamīʿ ṭabaqāt al-mukhāṭabīn*)."[340]

338 The exact wording is "*al-uṣūl al-inniyya allatī...* ." I could not detect a meaning for the word *inniyya*, which nevertheless certainly does not alter the content in any significant way.
339 Idem. "Masir al-Anam," 691.
340 Idem., "ʿIsmat," 611f.

Here again,[341] Rida draws on the classical distinction between *ʿāmma* and *khāṣṣa*, between the masses, who require religious guidance, and the elite, who – to some extent – are able to arrive at the same insights rationally. He appropriates this classical distinction for his argument, posited from the perspective of societal requirements, that only transcendent religion, not immanent nature alone, can provide the basis for the morals required by society.

Rida's integration of religious and societal premises, requirements, perspectives, and arguments into an Islamic discourse constitutes the modernity of his Islam. He thereby transforms Islam, rather than reforming it into its original state. Rida's middle position is not only one between Islam and the West, but more fundamentally, between religion and society (keeping in mind that Islam epitomized religion, and the West epitomized modern society). He transforms religion from the perspective of societal requirements and also seeks to transform society from the perspective of religious requirements. Rida thereby constructs a modern societal religion.

On an ontological level, this is demonstrated in his open spin on the immanent frame: he basically shares the modern understanding of immanent causal laws but complements them with and connects them to a transcendent level. On the level of socio-political order, he derives normative claims from humankind's alleged societal nature, but stresses that it was God who created humans as social beings. And the morals required for the functioning of social order can only be provided by a societal religion. If *mujtamaʿ* connoted a society and social order derived from human beings' natural tendency toward social association (*ijtimāʿ*) alone, it is against this that Rida posits the *umma* as a society resting on both *ijtimāʿ* and religion.

Rida, the Islamic reformist, thus addressed the societal demands of religion and the religious demands of society, with the aim of making religion societal and society religious. We can compare this with an analoguous statement by the German Rabbi Ludwig Philippson in 1855:

"My especial aim and endeavour have been to remove religion from the ideal station assigned to it, into the position to which it belongs – into life. Religion has so long abandoned society, that it is scarcely a matter of surprise if society has in its turn abandoned religion. The two thus parted must be reunited. Religion must come to understand that it can exercice no true and beneficient influence on the individual, until society collectively shall have become religious. Society must come to comprehend, that it cannot raise itself from its present prostrate condi-

341 See above: 207.

tion, until it shall have realised the principles which were long ago enunciated by religion, but of which the removal of religion from the actual world, its taking refuge exclusively in the celestial 'Hereafter,' have caused the loss for actual life."[342]

The concluding section will substantiate the argument that *umma* expresses central aspects of 'society' by showing that Rida indeed conceived of the *umma*, in one strand of its meanings, as a society to be constructed by individuals via their social association.

4 Conclusion: *Umma* as 'Society'

4.1 Individuals Cooperating to Construct the Integrated Social Body of the *Umma*

Before presenting examples of *umma* expressing crucial aspects of 'society,' I want to reiterate one last time that *umma* was the major but not the exclusive alternative to *mujtamaʿ* and *al-hayʾa al-ijtimāʿiyya* in this regard. During the Arabic saddle period, and in the Islamic-Arabic public of which *al-Manar* formed part, no single term was yet established for conceptualizing society. To that end, Rida, more than the secular historian and societal thinker Rafiq al-ʿAzm, preferred the term *umma*. This was a deliberate choice to semantically confine the concept of 'society' using a classical term from the Islamic tradition and to thereby confine the autonomy of secular society.

While *umma* conveyed a range of meanings, I will single out cases in which *umma* can meaningfully be translated as 'society' because it expressed central aspects of the concept and designated the reified society which results from social association (*ijtimāʿ*). Even here, translating *umma* as 'society' does not mean that Rida shared the hegemonic understanding of 'society.' Rather, this translation foregrounds the fact that Rida shared the modern idea of society and is a certain shortcut that results from 'society' having become the standard term for conceptualizing society. In several of the instances below, *umma* could also be translated as 'the people' (*Volk*), if one keeps in mind that this is a substitute for 'society.' The title of this section, "*Umma* as 'Society'," is thus a short

342 Philippso[n], Ludwig. 1855. *The Development of the Religious Idea in Judaism, Christianity and Mahomedanism, considered in twelve lectures on the history and purport of Judaism, delivered in Magdeburg, 1847, by Dr. Ludwig Philippsohn*; translated from the German with notes by Anna Maria Goldsmid. London: Longman, Brown, Green and Longmans, ix.

version of: "*Umma* Conceptualizing the Idea of Society and, in One Strand of its Meanings, Sharing Crucial Aspects of the Concept of 'Society'."

Rida repeatedly uses *umma* to designate that particularly well-integrated and unified social collectivity of individuals aware of and cooperating for their common interests. To Rida, "the umma is that collectivity (*jamā'a*) whose members are united by one bond or interest (*rābiṭa aw maṣlaḥa wāḥida*) or one order (*niẓām wāḥid*)."[343] While Rida validated social association (*ijtimā'*) as inherently positive, even when people initially concur about something false,[344] truly forming a society requires this sense of belonging and of identification with the whole society. In this vein, in the following year, Rida posits it as "one of the signs of collective life (*al-ḥayāt al-ijtimā'iyya*) of a society (*umma*) that its individuals (*afrād*) care for what is said and written concerning its affairs (*shu'ūnihā*)."[345] Thus, as Rida twice states in the first volume of *al-Manar*, "society (*al-umma*) comes into existence (*tatakawwan*) by concurring on the beneficial (*bi-l-ijtimā' 'alā l-intifā'*) and uniting to obtain what is desired (*al-ittiḥād 'alā nayl al-murād*)."[346]

According to Rida, it is this sense of the societal connectedness and cooperation of individuals that Muslims and Easterners have lost, whence they no longer form a true society and consequently have become weak as a nation. In volume one of *al-Manar*, Rida coined the term *ummiyya* – which is, at least for me, otherwise unknown – to express this necessary sense of connectedness of the whole social collectivity:[347] Whereas a Western individual represents and is even tantamount to the whole collectivity (*al-wāḥid fī nafs al-amr umma*), the Easterners are merely unconnected individuals, Rida bemoans,[348] for "they are a people (*qawm*) who do not understand the meaning of *qawmiyya* (usually: 'nationalism') and *ummiyya*, whence their association (*ijtimā'uhum*) and their sedition (*tafarruquhum*) amounts to the same. That these collectivities (*jumū'*) are not an umma, is quite evident."[349]

---

343 Rida, *Tafsir*, vol. 9: 308.

344 See above: 353.

345 Rida, "Kalima," 369.

346 Idem., "Sayhat," 220; idem., "Mashru'." 328. Quoted already above: 355.

347 *Ummiyya* in its established meaning connotes 'illiteracy' or 'ignorance,' and may also mean 'motherhood.' Here, Rida seemingly did not use it in a pejorative sense, in contrast to *qawmiyya*, but rather as a synonym to it.

348 The reference to the West and the East, respectively, becomes clear from the article's subject matter, even if Rida does not spell it out here.

349 Idem., "al-Juyush," 300.

The following year, Rida again emphasizes that the strength or weakness of a people is not a matter of size, but of social integration and of its members' knowledge of societal affairs – in short, of society. In 1900, it is the lack of these aspects – and not primarily of religious doctrines – that he bemoans in the case of the Islamic umma, which consists of 300 million people or more, but which, according to Rida, merely resembles the idea of a society, as a lion painted on a wall resembles a lion. And is this not, Rida asks rhetorically, because

"the great majority of us only care for themselves and their personal fortunes (*ḥuẓūẓihim al-shakhṣiyya*), just like children do?! Do they understand the meaning of society (*maʿnā al-umma*) and [do they] know the constituents (*muqawwimāt*) on which it is based, the bonds (*rawābiṭ*) which connect it, and the authority (*amr*) with which it agrees and to which it aspires? Do they ponder societal life (*al-ḥayāt al-ijtimāʿiyya*) and that which is subject to it? [...] I say concerning society in its figurative sense (*al-umma al-majāziyya*) what I have said concerning the case (*shaʾn*) of children: it is in the strongest need of guides and educators wise and knowledgable about social illnesses (*al-amrāḍ al-ijtimāʿiyya*) and about their remedies and the way to cure [these illnesses], so that through their guidance comes into existence a true society (*umma ḥaqīqiyya*)."[350]

Rida refers back to these two early articles, especially to the second one, in a series of articles on the "Social Condition of Muslims" from 1916,[351] at the outset of which he asserts the natural need for individuals to form a society (*umma*) and states that Islamic reform is basically tantamount to the aim of bringing about a true society:

"Man is a social creature (*al-insān ʿālam ijtimāʿī*), none of whose individuals (*fard min afrādihi*) and none of its peoples (*shaʿb min shuʿūbihi*) attains the perfection decreed for it except through societal works (*al-aʿmāl al-ijtimāʿiyya*), concerning which the persons of a clan (*afrād al-ʿashīra*) and the members of a country and homeland (*ahl al-balad wa-l-waṭan*) and all other people (*sāʾir al-nās*) cooperate. The extent of this cooperation (*taʿāwun*) depends on how close or distanced they are from social perfection (*al-kamāl al-ijtimāʿī*). So societies

350 Idem. 1900. "Tufuliyyat al-Umma wa-Ma fiha min al-Hayra wa-l-Ghumma." *al-Manar* 2/47: 737–740, here 739 f. The contrast between *majāzī* and *ḥaqīqī* is best known from Sufi traditions, where, to summarize the matter very briefly, it refers to mere worldly love vs. true, godly love.
351 Idem. 1916. "Hal al-Muslimin al-Ijtimaʿiyya." *al-Manar* 19/2: 89–96, 19/4: 244–256, 19/5: 297–306.

exist through individuals and individuals through societies (*al-umam bi-l-afrād wa-l-afrād bi-l-umam*). Salutations to that nation (*hanīʾan li-l-umma*) which attains, through the effort of its individuals (*bi-saʿy afrādihā*), the withering (*ghārib*) of power and dominion and inhales the wind of force and felicity ('and woe to that man who does not have an umma')[352]. Not every big aggregation (*jamʿ kabīr*) may rightfully be called an *umma*, unless we extend the meaning to include a metaphorical sense (*law-lā saʿat al-majāz fī al-kalām*), such as when we say of the images of people (*ṣuwar al-nās*) and their representations (*tamāthīlihim*): 'this is this and that person.' Muslims are a big aggregation (*jamʿ kabīr*) to which is applied the name Islamic umma, in accordance with its outward appearance (*ṣūratihi*) or in consideration of that what [the aggregation] ought to be, even if it does not perform the societal works (*al-aʿmāl al-ijtimāʿiyya*) by which are realized the constituents and the characteristics (*muqawwimāt wa-mushakhkhiṣāt*) of societies (*umam*), and by which are preserved its interests and benefits (*maṣāliḥ wa-manāfiʿ*) [...]. I call Muslims an *umma* [only] in consideration of what I hope its condition will eventually result in. And insofar as this [designation of *umma*] refers to its metaphorical existence (*bi-ʿitibār anna dhalik al-istiʿmāl min majāz al-kawn*) I have explained more than once in these [aforementioned] articles [published previously in *al-Manar*] that the Islamic reform (*al-iṣlāḥ al-islāmī*) can be summarized in the maxim (*yanḥaṣir fī kalima*) of forming the [ideal] society (*takwīn al-umma*), for it is no society in reality (*lā umma fī al-ḥaqīqa*)."[353]

The political dimension of forming a society becomes clearest when Rida relates the umma to rulers and the government. "This age," he exclaims in 1905, "is the age of societies (*umam*), not the age of individuals (*afrād*) and the age of the order of human society (*niẓām al-ijtimāʿ*), not the age of despotism (*istibdād*)."[354] In 1908, during celebrations of the Ottoman parliament, Rida defines *umma* as follows:

"[T]he term (*lafẓ*) *umma* in the usage of the scholars of society and politics (*ʿulamāʾ al-ijtimāʿ wa-l-siyāsa*) applies to that great collective (*al-jamʿ al-ʿaẓīm*) which is composed of different peoples (*shuʿūb mutaʿaddida*) and whose members (*afrād*) are connected with each other by common laws and interests (*qawānīn wa-maṣālīḥ mushtaraka*). Social association (*ijtimāʿ*) is the principle (*aṣl*) by

352 In a footnote, Rida claims this is a phrase by Muhammad ʿAbduh.

353 Ibid., *al-Manar* 19/2: 89.

354 Idem. 1905. "al-Akhbar wa-l-Araʾ (Masʾala Makaduniyya)." *al-Manar* 8/19: 753–760, here 759.

which is realized the meaning of the *umma* composed of groups (*jamʿiyyāt*), some of which are bigger than others. The most basic (*al-adnā*) of them is the family (*usra*), and this is the primary and oldest type of human social association (*ijtimāʿ basharī*); and the most elevated (*al-aʿlā*) is the *umma*, which is the end-point attainable by social association (*ijtimāʿ*). Are we permitted to claim that we have been an *umma* during the past stage of despotism (*istibdād*), which we have ended once and for all on this day? How so, when we have been prohibited from [proper] social association (*ijtimāʿ*) in every single one of its meanings, even in the family [...]. Today the end of this divisive despotism has come, and the delegates (*mabʿūthān*) elected by the Ottoman peoples (*shuʿūb*) have come together (*ijtimaʿa*), in order to act on their behalf concerning the establishment of their public interests (*maṣāliḥihā al-ʿāmma*), such as the legislation of laws (*qawānīn*) and the oversight of the ruling executives (*al-ḥukkām al-ʿāmilīn*). And by this association (*ijtimāʿ*) has been realized the formation (*takawwun*) of the umma."[355]

Particularly in such political usages of *umma*, the senses of 'society,' 'nation,' and 'the people' are often conflated, but what matters here is that this *umma* is not a divinely instituted community, but comes into existence through realization of the principle of social association and concurrence.

While Rida occasionally mentions the family not only as the smallest form of social association, but also as the smallest social unit of the overall umma – and thus as a certain mediator between individuals and society[356] – he more prominently conceives of the umma as a social body composed of individuals, thus sharing a common understanding of society in his time, which in Arabic was most explicitly conceptualized as *al-hayʾa al-ijtimāʿiyya*. In 1901, Rida pictures the Islamic umma as a "great body (*jism kabīr*), which has lost societal life (*al-ḥayāt al-ijtimāʿiyya*)."[357] Elsewhere, he attests that the roots of weakness and social illness (*al-marḍ al-ijtimāʿī*) had already become visible in the body of the Islamic community (*jism al-umma*) during Abbasid times.[358] For Rida, the reason God allegedly punishes a people as a whole for the wrongs of some individuals is precisely that "the umma in its mutual solidarity (*takāful*) is like the parts of one body (*ka-aʿḍāʾ al-jasad al-wāḥid*), so like the whole body suffers and is in pain when parts of it are afflicted, such is the case also with societies

355 Idem., "Iftitah Majlis," 860 f.
356 See, for example: Idem. 1905. "al-Hayat al-Zawjiyya." *al-Manar* 8/3: 92–100, here 94; idem., "ʿAqibat Harb," 342 (reprinted in idem., "al-Manar mundhu," 427); idem., "Munazara," *al-Manar* 30/8: 620.
357 Idem. 1900. "al-Haraka al-Islamiyya al-Hadira." *al-Manar* 3/10: 217–221, here 217.
358 Idem., "al-Khutba al-Raʾisiyya," 339.

(*umam*)."[359] In an article from 1905, which attends to "The Life and Death of Societies" ("Hayat al-Umam wa-Mawtuha") in greater detail, Rida elaborates on the relation of individuals to the whole social body. He begins this article with the following assertion:

"Bodies (*ajsām*) have a life and souls (*nufūs*) have a life differing from that of bodies, but the two of them are connected with each other. And individuals (*afrād*) have a life and societies (*umam*) have a life differing from that of individuals, but one of them depends on the other. [...] The life of society (*ḥayāt al-umma*) is an effect (*athar*) of the spirit (*rūh*) pervading its individuals (*afrādihā*), making them feel that the place (*makān*) of each one of them in the whole society (*majmūʿ al-umma*) is [like] the place of one of its limbs (*aʿḍāʾihi*) in its body (*jasadihi*), so that he for each of his deeds (*ʿamal*) takes into consideration his own benefit (*manfaʿat nafsihi*) and the benefit of society (*manfaʿat ummatihi*), just like the work of each part in the body (*ʿamal kull ʿuḍw fī al-badan*) is a means to preserve the life of the whole body."[360]

And in 1927, we read: "Since the whole society (*majmūʿ al-umma*) is tantamount to a spiritual body (*jism maʿnawī*) it inevitably occurs that the anomalous conditions of social illnesses (*ʿawāriḍ al-amrāḍ al-ijtimāʿiyya*) befall it, just like the anomalous conditions of physical illnesses (*ʿawāriḍ al-amrāḍ al-badaniyya*) befall the body of living creatures (*al-jism al-ḥayawāniyya*)."[361] It is based on this conception of society as a body that Rida repeatedly mentions the umma's need for doctors to cure its social diseases.

Since Rida's ideal society – the umma – is not solely the reified result of autonomous secular social association, but is also based on (a societal) religion and requires the continuous guidance of religious morals, it is in need of both social and spiritual doctors. In general, Rida distinguishes "two ways (*ṭarīqān*) for peoples (*umam*) to proceed in their social life (*ḥayātihā al-ijtimāʿiyya*), the way of religious guidance (*hidāya dīniyya*) combined with [theoretical] inspection (*naẓar*) and [empirical] experience (*tajriba*) and the way of inspection and experience without resorting to the guidance of religion. And history does not know of one people (*umma min al-umam*) that has advanced in social life with-

359 Idem., *Tafsir*, vol. 10: 120.

360 Idem. 1905. "Hayat al-Umam wa-Mawtuha." *al-Manar* 8/2: 67–71, here 67. Rida quotes this passage in his series "al-Muslimun wa-l-Qubt," which will be presented in the following subsection (idem. 1911. "al-Muslimun wa-l-Qubt (6)." *al-Manar* 14/4: 273–279, here 277).

361 Rashid Rida commenting upon Arslan, "al-Ziyy," 452, 452fn1. Rida here corrects and thus appropriates a sentence by Shakib Arslan, who had omitted a few words.

out religion."[362] In fact, as Rida maintains in 1906, "the life of a people (*umma*) that does not have societal doctors (*aṭbāʾ ijtimāʿiyīn*) and spiritual guides (*hudāt rūḥiyīn*) is below the life of cells in trees and [below] the life of herbs and shrubs in gardens."[363] This is because – in contrast to all other creatures, whose order (*niẓām*) comes about through the unconscious contributions of its individual parts to the whole – human beings require some individuals to take care of others and to facilitate personal and societal moral education (*al-tarbiya al-shakhṣiyya wa-l-ijtimāʿiyya*).[364] While Rida distinguishes between experts in religion and in society, we have seen that he integrates both fields in the Islamic religion and, relatedly, in the umma. Hence, experts on social association and societal doctors (sg. *ṭabīb ijtimāʿī*) must also be acquainted with the religious constituents and dispositions of the umma. Consequently, for Rida, only a societal doctor (*ṭabīb ijtimāʿī*) who is also knowledgeable about religion can cure the illnesses of society and reform society so that it becomes a true umma.[365]

In the above cases, Rida used *umma* to denote the whole social collectivity[366] made up of individuals who, based on common characteristics and shared interests, ought to cooperate in order to bring into existence – with the help of societal doctors and spiritual guides – the ideal society, the umma. Most of Rida's defining statements above stem from the first decade of *al-Manar*. This suggests that the usage of *umma* to express characteristics of society had been established by then – especially in view of the fact that in *al-Manar* the usage of *mujtamaʿ* and *al-hayʾa al-ijtimāʿiyya* to conceptualize society did not increase in later years. In tune with Rida's multiple senses of identity and his engagement on behalf of the independence and the proper functioning of different socio-political entities, this collectivity could comprise all Syrians, all Egyptians, all Ottomans, all Arabs, or all Muslims. For Rida, Islam was a constituent for all of these collectivities. While in his writings the *umma* as a stand-alone term predominantly refers to all Muslims, it is also remarkable that 'the Arab umma' occurs more

---

362 Rida, Rashid. 1903. "Masʾalat al-Nisaʾ." *al-Manar* 5/23: 881–889, here 881.

363 Idem. 1906. "Tatawwur al-Umam wa-Intiqaluha min Hal ila Hal." *al-Manar* 9/2: 120–130, here 121.

364 Ibid., 120.

365 For 'societal and spiritual doctors,' see, for example: idem., "al-ʿUlum wa-l-Funun," 806; idem., "al-Mutafarnijun," 344; idem. 1913. "Fatihat al-Sana al-Sabiʿa ʿAshara." *al-Manar* 17/1: 1–11. For *ʿulamāʾ al-ijtimāʿ* having to be familiar with religion, see above: 380.

366 Rida also uses *umma* to denote a particular sub-group representing – and in this sense being identical with – the overall social collectivity of the *umma*. In this regard, he repeatedly equates *umma* with the *ahl al-ḥall wa-l-ʿaqd* (see: Kerr, *Islamic*, 161, 163; see also: Rashid Rida commenting upon Abu al-Fadl, Muhammad. 1926. "al-Muʾtamar al-Islami al-ʿAmm li-l-Khilafa bi-Misr." *al-Manar* 27/6: 449–458, here 452fn1).

often in *al-Manar* than 'the Islamic umma,' and that 'the Egyptian umma' is clearly present even in the first volume of the journal.[367]

The following subsection, in contrast to the rather scattered instances collected here, presents Rida's work on *Muslims and Copts* in Egypt, in which *umma* denotes the idea of an overall Egyptian society.

4.2 The *Umma* as a National Society: *Al-Muslimun wa-l-Qubt*

Rida published his series of articles "Muslims and Copts and the Egyptian Conference" in 1911 as a book with the promising subtitle, "a collection of societal articles" (*majmūʿ maqālāt ijtimāʿiyya*).[368] The goal of the Egyptian Conference, which was held in Cairo in April 1911, was to assess the demands of a Coptic conference convened earlier that year in Asyut, and to discuss the social, religious, and political affairs of Egypt more generally. In this book, Rida clearly conceives of a national Egyptian society consisting of different religious communities. In line with our interest here, I will provide only a glimpse into how Rida conceives of the relation of the particular religious communities to Egyptian society as a whole,[369] and then shift the focus to his choice of words.

In later statements, Rida confirms a major assessment he made in *al-Muslimun wa-l-Qubt* – namely, that within Egyptian society, which remains religious overall, the Coptic community is superior in its societal integration. In the immediate aftermath of both conferences, Rida credits the Copts for their societal integration and deems it a positive effect of their conference to have awakened Muslims from their societal sleep (*nawmihim al-ijtimāʿī*).[370] The awakening of Muslims and their social reform remained a lifelong concern for Rida, of course. In 1928, he again deplores the lack of society among Muslims in Egypt: "the one force dominating all forces in this age is the force of the public opinion of society (*al-raʾy al-ʿāmm li-l-umma*); and the public opinion in Egypt continues to be religious (*mutadayyinan*), for Muslims just as for Copts and other Christians and Jews. Of all factions (*jamīʿa al-firaq*), the Christians are those clinging more strongly than the Muslims to their religious and social bond (*rābiṭatihim al-dīniyya wa-l-ijtimāʿiyya*), as we have explained previously in our article 'Muslims

367 See appendix, table 4d.

368 Rida, *al-Muslimun.*

369 For a contemporaneous Coptic view, see: Mikhail, Kyriakos. 1911. *Copts and Moslems under British control. A collection of facts and a résumé of authoritative opinions on the Coptic question.* London: Smith, Elder, and Co.

370 Rida, Rashid. 1911. "al-Akhbar wa-l-Araʾ." *al-Manar* 14/2: 155–160, here 159.

and Copts'."[371] It was thanks to their societal and religious integration, Rida suggests, that the Coptic community had acquired a disproportionately large share of economic resources and governmental positions[372] and had even come to form a communal society (*umma*) for themselves, independent of the body of Egyptian society as a whole (*jism al-umma al-miṣriyya*).[373]

However, Rida maintains, it cannot be possible that one religious faction – especially a minority – dominates the whole of society.[374] At the same time, he not only urges Muslims to strengthen their social integration as a community, but also foregrounds the Islamic character of Egyptian society as a whole. Rida rejects a socio-political role for Coptic Christianity but demands such a role for Islam, based on two arguments: empirically, because Muslims form the vast majority of the Egyptian population; and theoretically, because Islam as a social and a political bond (*jinsiyya ijtimāʿiyya wa-siyāsiyya*), in distinction to Islam as a religion (*dīn*), also comprises adherents of other religions living under its rule and treats them equally.[375] He stresses that Coptic citizens in general enjoy equal rights, as can be seen from the fact that Copts hold many senior government positions. However, Rida rejects – to pick one prominent topic of discussion – the Coptic demand to make Sunday a public holiday in addition to Friday. He argues that this demand not only has no basis in the Bible itself, but that it would also be impractical to have several weekly holidays. If there is only one weekly public holiday, it can only be Friday, since Islam is the religion of both the vast majority of the people and of the state. This is also why the Muslim Conference, according to Rida, was an *Egyptian* conference, concerned with the whole of society, not just with particular interests, as was the Coptic conference.[376]

---

371 Idem. 1928. "Aʿda' al-Islam al-Muharibun lahu fi hadha al-ʿAhd." *al-Manar* 29/2: 115–122, here 122.

372 Rida summarizes this assessment, which is elaborated at length in *al-Muslimun wa-l-Qubt* in: idem. 1931. "Munazara fi al-Jamiʿa al-Misriyya fi al-Madaniyyatayn al-Farʿuniyya wa-l-ʿArabiyya." *al-Manar* 31/6: 465–474, here 465.

373 Idem., *al-Muslimun*, 80.

374 Ibid., passim. The proceedings of the Egyptian Conference stress that the *umma* in its being a political order (*niẓām siyāsī*) must not be divided along religious lines; instead, its differences ought to express themselves in political parties (al-Lajna al-Tahdiriyya li-l-Mu'tamar al-Misri. 1911. "Taqrir al-Lajna al-Tahdiriyya li-l-Mu'tamar al-Misri al-Munʿaqad fi al-Qahira fi 29 Abril Sanna 1911." *al-Manar* 14/5: 353–372, here 354 f.)

375 Rida, *al-Muslimun*, 39 f.

376 For a more extensive summary of the contents of this book, with a different focus, see Ryad, *Islamic*, 106–116.

While Rida clearly operates with the ideas of (religious) community and (national) society in this work from 1911, the question remains as to which terms he uses to conceptualize these ideas. Recalling that previous research had suggested *al-hay'a al-ijtimāʿiyya* and *mujtamaʿ* as pertinent terms for 'society' during that period, it is remarkable that both of these terms are completely absent in this "collection of societal articles" (*maqālāt ijtimāʿiyya*) – which confirms the findings of chapters 7 and 8. This work also testifies to the rather broad semantic range of *umma* and also to alternative terms for conceptualizing society. In *Muslims and Copts*, Rida uses *umma* to refer to both a religious community and to the Egyptian nation and society overall. As a religious community, Rida uses *umma* synonymously with *milla*,[377] while his main alternative to *umma* in the sense of 'nation' is *qawm*. However, *umma* much more pertinently expresses the idea of a particular (national) society, since *qawm* is never once in the whole publication history of *al-Manar* attributed to conceptualize such a particular society (e.g., *al-qawm al-miṣrī*). The term *shaʿb* refers both to the collectivity of Muslims or Copts and to the Egyptian people. In many cases, *umma* could be translated as either 'the people,' 'the nation,' or 'society' – for example, when Rida summarizes the demand for a single weekly holiday for both the government (*al-ḥukūma*) and the *umma*.[378]

Unsurprisingly, I shall end this subsection by pointing out instances in which *umma* quite clearly refers to society as the overall social sphere and social order. Rida attributes the progress of Western peoples (*shuʿūb*) to the fact that elites care for the advancement of society (*tarqiyat al-umma*) by assisting it through organizations (*jamʿiyyāt*), companies (*sharikāt*), and the division of labor. On the basis of this division, Rida finds, all the relevant fields of society receive equal attention: when looking at the importance of religious education and services in Western society, one thinks that this is all that matters to them; the same goes for financial issues and the sciences.[379] The only way for "us" to progress, Rida maintains, is to assess the constituents of Egyptian society (*muqawwimāt ummatinā*) and its public interests (*maṣāliḥihā al-ʿāmma*) one by one.[380] He finds that Egyptian society does have welfare, educational, and religious societies (*jamʿiyyāt*), financial and agricultural corporations (*niqābāt*), trading and industrial companies (*sharikāt*), as well as provincial councils to make education universally accessible. Yet he sees their benefits as limited, especially since they are not connected with each other. Therefore, what is needed

377 See, for example, Rida, *al-Muslimun*, 11, 50.
378 Ibid., 61.
379 Ibid., 114 f.
380 Ibid., 115 f.

is a single connector ordering and overseeing society's public interests (*maṣālih al-umma al-ʿāmma*). The members of society must thus form a single body (*jism wāḥid*), with each one specializing in one task for the good of all the members. Rida expresses his hope that the Islamic Conference is that connector (*al-simṭ*), which is necessary for forming the social bond (*takwīn ʿaqdinā al-ijtimāʿī*), and that it will become the heart that gives life to all the members of society (*jamīʿ aʿḍāʾ al-umma*).[381]

The articles in *Muslims and Copts* demonstrate the double reference of *umma* to both a particular religious community and to society as a whole – two ideas that were not yet clearly terminologically distinguished. Relatedly, these articles illustrate that Rida infused his understanding of society as a whole with aspects that are now associated with 'community' and simultaneously imbued his understanding of community with aspects that are now associated with 'society.' Keeping this double reference of *umma* in mind, the final subsection points to the correspondence between *umma* and 'society' beyond *al-Manar*, taking its point of departure from contemporaneous Arabic translations of influential French socio-political writings.

4.3 *Umma* as 'Society' Beyond *al-Manar*

In the translation of Esquiros's *Émile* published in *al-Manar*, *société* in the sense of the overall social sphere is just as often rendered with *umma* as with *mujtamaʿ* – namely 15 times, and not least as the book's very last word.[382] In his translations of Demolins's *A quoi tient la supériorité des Anglo-Saxons* from 1899[383] and of Le Bon's *Psychologie des foules* from 1909,[384] Ahmad Fathi Zaghlul translates *société* mainly as *umma* and as *al-hay'a al-ijtimāʿiyya*, but also as *jamʿiyya* and *mujtamaʿ*. In a review of Demolins's work in *al-Manar*, *umma* is used for *société*,

381 Ibid., 116. On the conference having to fulfill this role, see also pages 125, 131.
382 Esquiros, *Émile*; idem., *al-Tarbiya*. The translator ʿAbd al-ʿAziz Muhammad once uses *mujtamaʿ* for a specific association, rendering *l'Académie des sciences* (Academy of Sciences) as *al-mujtamaʿ al-ʿilmī* (*akadīmiyā*) (Esquiros, *L'Émile*, 168; idem., "Amil," *al-Manar* 3/31: 778). While this again illustrates the different possible meanings of *mujtamaʿ*, Muhammad identified *mujtamaʿ* rather closely with the meaning of society as overall social sphere: he chose the Arabic term *mukhālaṭa* when the French *société* referred to the company of people one is with (idem., *L'Émile*, 159; idem., "Amil," *al-Manar* 3/30: 741 [page numbers in printed version are incorrect, page 741 actually is page 771]). In five cases ʿAbd al-ʿAziz Muhammad chose *qawm* to render *société*.
383 Demolins, *A quoi*; idem., *Sirr*.
384 Le Bon, *Psychologie*; idem., *Ruh*.

even where the full Arabic translation has *jamʿiyya*.[385] What is especially striking in the translations of Zaghlul is how flexibly he uses the term *umma* – not only for *nation* and *communauté*, but also for *population*, *race*, and *société*. The following paragraph discusses the extent to which these translations that render *société* as *umma* support the main argument of this study – that major authors in *al-Manar*, especially Rashid Rida, used *umma* to conceptualize society.

As a basic consideration, hardly any contemporaneous readers of the Arabic translation would have compared that translation with the French original, which is to say that the original *société* is not present to them when reading *umma*. In general, a translator may want to acquaint readers with new terms and concepts by providing the original terms or explaining the new meanings he seeks to convey with an established term. However, this has not been the case in the translations considered here. The fact that *umma* was used to render various terms that were differentiated in the French original may suggest that the Arabic language did not yet differentiate terminologically between concepts such as 'race' and 'society.' However, as Samah Selim has shown in her analysis of Zaghlul's translation of Le Bon's *Lois psychologiques de l'évolution des peuples*,[386] Zaghlul, whose "translation is remarkably faithful to the original,"[387] did occasionally use today's Arabic term for 'race' – *jins*. Selim argues that he preferred *umma* for *race* in order to bracket Le Bon's scientific-racial premises.[388] However, to add to Selim's perceptive analysis, I argue that Zaghlul also imbues *umma* with racial connotations by using the term in this new context. Similarly, the translation of *société* as *umma* not only blurs the first term's specificities in distinction from other terms rendered as *umma*, but also infuses *umma* with notions of *société*.

Translators of *umma* into English, in turn, limit themselves to 'nation,' 'community,' and 'people.' Indeed, so far I have come across only a single instance in which *umma* is, in passing, translated as 'society.'[389] However, a remark on the meanings of *umma* by Michael Gasper does play well into the argument of this study. Gasper, who suggests that *umma* should be translated as "Islamic moral

385 Al-Dimashqi, "al-Istiqlal."

386 Le Bon, *Lois*; idem., *Sirr*.

387 Selim, Samah. 2009. "Languages of Civilization: Nation, Translation and the Politics of Race in Colonial Egypt." *The Translator* 15/1 (Special Issue: Nation and Translation in the Middle East): 139–156, here 151.

388 Ibid., 152f.

389 Cornell, Vincent J. 2013. "Muḥammad ʿAbduh: A Sufi-Inspired Modernist?" In *Tradition and Modernity. Christian and Muslim Perspectives* ed. by David Marshall: 97–114. Washington, DC: Georgetown University Press, here 103.

community,"[390] has convincingly argued that Egyptians in the late nineteenth and early twentieth centuries infused the concept of *umma* with European notions of social and economic order. Hence, "the increasingly less precise ways in which Egyptians used the term *umma* at the time" were also the result of adhering to both an ideal of Islamic moral community and European notions of social order.[391] This perceptive remark can be qualified again, insofar as *umma* not only signified community imbued with societal aspects, but also society imbued with communal aspects.

Again, this is not to say that *umma* came to mean 'society.' Rather, in the Arabic saddle period, when no single term was yet established to conceptualize the modern idea of society, Islamic reformists rendered crucial aspects of the concept of 'society' with the classical Arabic-Islamic term *umma*.

390 Gasper, *The Power*, esp. 294.
391 Ibid., 119.

Chapter 11
Conclusion: Society, The Immanent Frame, and Modernity – Concepts, Spins, and Genealogies

1 Summary of This Study

Initially motivated by dissatisfaction with common depictions of Islam and modernity as separate entities, this study set out to discern 'society,' as the concept most constitutive of modernity, in the mouthpiece of Islamic reformism – the journal *al-Manar* (Cairo, 1898–1940). The introduction showed why I had to pre-configure the concept of 'society' based on European history and theory. Following the need for a heuristic Eurocentrism, chapter 2 sketched the evolution of the concept in European languages and worked out the normative core and central aspects of 'society.' As a bridge between the hegemonic understanding of modernity and that understanding presumably held by the Islamic reformists in *al-Manar*, chapter 3 introduced Charles Taylor's *A Secular Age*, which points to the most fundamental and thus most widely shared background understandings of modernity.

Following up on the assumptions about 'society' and modernity formulated in the first part, the second part substantiated the expectation that one could discern Arabic equivalents and alternatives to 'society' in the Islamic journal *al-Manar*. To this end, chapter 4 portrayed the socio-political and intellectual setting in which *al-Manar* was founded; chapter 5 introduced *al-Manar*, along with existing studies; and chapter 6 collected hints as to the evolution of terms conceptualizing society in the Arabic saddle period.

Based on the assumptions and expectations worked out in the first two parts, the third part presented the findings of this study in four chapters. Chapters 7 and 8 comprehensively analyzed the two supposedly most pertinent Arabic terms conceptualizing society in *al-Manar* – namely *al-hay'a al-ijtimāʿiyya* and *mujtamaʿ*. It transpired that both terms were established in the sense of 'society,' but that most authors who wrote regularly for *al-Manar* used them only reluctantly in this meaning and preferred *umma* instead. The following two chapters were then dedicated to the two regular contributors to *al-Manar* who most strikingly used or avoided *mujtamaʿ* in the modern meaning of 'society' – namely, the journal's editor, Rashid Rida, and his close collaborator, Rafiq al-ʿAzm. Chapter 9 showed that Rafiq al-ʿAzm indeed contributed a societal and secular perspective to the reformist discourse of *al-Manar*. Chapter 10 departed from the terms *ijtimāʿ* (human society, social association, etc.) and *ijtimāʿī* (social) to discern how Rida

https://doi.org/10.1515/9783110545845-012

addressed human beings' social association and whether he conceived of a distinct realm of 'the social' and of society. The findings of this last chapter consolidated the main argument of this study – namely, that Rida and other Islamic reformists used *umma* to conceptualize society, sharing central aspects of the concept of 'society.'

In the Arabic saddle period, then, the concept of 'society' was not yet crystallized in one basic term, but the idea of society was conceptualized with different terms, which competed over a shared semantic field. That Islamic reformists like Rashid Rida preferred *umma* over *al-hay'a al-ijtimāʿiyya* and *mujtamaʿ*, two terms with whose modern meaning they were quite familiar, was hardly an arbitrary choice. Rather, Rida preferred a term from the classical Islamic discursive tradition over terms popularized by Christian, somewhat secular authors. This is not to say that *umma* came to mean 'society,' but rather that the term, in one strand of its wide range of meanings, expressed central aspects of the idea of society, which may be conceptualized as 'society,' 'nation,' 'the people,' *société*, *Gesellschaft*, *Volk*, *al-hay'a al-ijtimāʿiyya*, *mujtamaʿ*, or *umma*. *Umma* conceptualized a particular answer to the modern problématique of socio-political order and thereby served as a *functional* equivalent to 'society,' but also shared in *substantial* aspects of 'society.'

The particularities might be summarized by alluding to rival concepts of 'society' also expressed by *umma* namely, 'the people,' 'nation,' and 'community.'[1] At its core, the Islamic concept of *umma* carried strong notions of a moral 'community' that intersected with aspects of 'society.' Since the society of the umma is genealogical and value-based, 'society' is closely linked to (an Islamic) 'nation,' a link also known in national-conservative European milieus (if we substitute 'Islamic' with 'Christian' or 'German,' for example). In a colonized context, moreover, the question of society was closely intertwined with the question of national independence, which further accounts for the overlap of 'society' and 'nation' in the concept of *umma*. That 'society' and 'the people' also overlapped in *umma* might be explained by the fact that the desire to create society in an authoritarian context also meant challenging authoritarian government in the name of 'the people.'

The substantial communalities with 'society' became most apparent when Rida posits *umma* as the object of sociological inquiry, to be constructed by individuals through their cooperation for mutual benefit, and as the reification of human beings' natural tendency toward social association – that is, of *ijtimāʿ*, which was already a basic term.

1 For the idealtypical distinction between these concepts, see above: chapter 2 section 2.

2 Modernity in Islamic Tradition: Spins on the Immanent Frame

Keeping the semantic range and normativity of *umma* in mind, Rashid Rida conceived of and constructed modernity in Islamic tradition in the following sense. Terminologically, Rida preferred this central term from the Islamic discursive tradition over against terms predominantly used by secular Christian thinkers to conceptualize the novel idea of society – namely *al-hay'a al-ijtimāʿiyya* and *mujtamaʿ*. Rida, more than Rafiq al-ʿAzm, took care not to legitimize a secular concept of 'society' as autonomous, but rather semantically confined it with the classical Arabic term *umma*. Ontologically, Rida denied that 'the social' (*al-ijtimāʿ*) alone could provide the ground beneath our feet, on which social and political order may be constructed. He insisted that the social had to be grounded in something beyond, namely God – even though he subsequently conceived of the social as largely autonomous. Epistemologically, Rida claimed that some knowledge and insights are only attainable through revelation; but he did not derive particular *premises* from religious sources. It was in Rida's *arguments* concerning socio-political order that religion really made a difference to secularist visions – above all, by allegedly providing moral guidance and an ethical dimension. The *umma* Rida envisioned was precisely that morally guided society which ought to be constructed via the social association of individuals who internalized Islamic teachings – teachings which, notably in their worldly dimension, also concerned non-Muslim members of society. This is modernity in Islamic tradition.

Once the religious, the social, and the political are conceptually distinguished, intellectuals can relate them to each other in different ways and continuously loosen or tighten the connection between them, also within an Islamic discourse. Rida widened the gap with secularist understandings by increasingly postulating the political as belonging to the alleged essence of the Islamic religion. However, he did not thereby essentially do away with the distinction between the religious and the political or the social. Rather, Rida gave way to a religio-political Islamism by locating the point of integration of the religious and the socio-political not in a distanced creator God, but in the worldly figure of the caliph. Such political Islamism is only possible based on the previous negation of a purely worldly political order (including a purely worldly Islam), the subsequent integration of a distinct political order into an alleged transcendent religious essence, and the resulting vision for transforming the immanent worldly order according to these transcendent principles.

Rafiq al-ʿAzm, in turn, clearly separated the religious from the political in his Islamic discourse – at least in the works from 1900 analyzed here, although he, too, seems to have tightened the relation between the two orders in other writings. Al-ʿAzm firmly departed from the premise of human beings' natural tendency toward social association and was almost exclusively interested in constructing the societal principles of Islam. In a secularist manner, he relegated Islamic belief to the conscience of individuals, delegated the reform of Islam as a religion to religious scholars, and himself elaborated Islam as a societal order. More than any other regular contributor to *al-Manar*, al-ʿAzm embraced the secularly connoted term *mujtamaʿ*. Moreover, he elaborated Islam as a societal order by engaging European socio-political trends. However, in this elaboration, he rarely referred to European sources; instead, from a modern secular and societal perspective, he appropriated classical Arabic-Islamic concepts. Al-ʿAzm thereby demonstrated that secular(ist) modernity can also be formulated from within Islamic tradition.

The fact that the Islamic discursive tradition and the very term *islām* were used to designate and elaborate both a religious and a socio-political order, whether separately or together, tends to blur the modern distinction between these realms. However, the flexibility of *islām* does not essentially undermine this distinction. Moreover, one should consider that the distinction of 'the religious' and 'the secular' in the first place was a distinction within Christianity. Under the hegemony of secularism, the two realms came to be more firmly separated, and 'Christianity' came to designate only the realm of the religious. Secularists demanded that *islām* should also be confined to the religious. Islamic reformists, in turn, were well aware of the Christian genealogy of 'the secular' and related colonialist claims to hegemony, and they preferred to express the distinction between the religious and the secular from within an Islamic discourse and hence used *islām* to designate both the religious and the secular. That said, even when analytically disentangling the double usage of *islām*, it seems true that Christian theologians and intellectuals have accepted and accommodated a secularist regime to a greater extent than Muslim thinkers.

Then again, we should keep in mind, firstly, that such (non-)accommodation is only of a temporary nature and, secondly, that a secularist regime is merely one of several modern secular options for the arrangement of the religious and the socio-political. While I do not want to dwell here on potential reasons why Christian thinkers have better accommodated the secularist regime, two related causes immediately come to mind – namely, the Christian genealogy of the secular and the secularist institutional makeover of predominantly Christian societies as an internal, rather than a colonially imposed, transformation. These two causes combined have made it easier for Christian thinkers, as compared to Islamic ones, to claim the secular – and even a secularist regime – as authentically their own. However, it took many Christian theologians, particularly Catholic ones, quite a while to accept the secularist arrangement, and, as shown in chapter 2 section 3, influential contemporary Christian theologians are once again negating the autonomy of the secular. Some even deny the existence of a secular realm as such and posit an overarching, godly reality that comprises the transcendent and the immanent. While proponents of a comprehensive integration – whether into a godly or a natural reality – may be the harbingers of a post-secular age, for now they, too, still operate with the basic modern categories of the religious and the socio-political, as fundamentally holds true for all modern interpretations of the world.

These modern interpretations – whether those of Rashid Rida or Rafiq al-ʿAzm, of Gustave Le Bon or Lord Cromer, of Niqula Haddad or Shibli Shumayyil – are all secular in that they share the understanding of an immanent frame and of human beings as rational individuals having to construct their society. Where they differ is, ontologically, in their reading of this immanent frame as either open or closed and – more concretely, and with relevance for socio-political order – in their envisioned points of connection between the immanent and the transcendent. The ontological dimension concerns the question of whether one believes in something beyond this immanent world or not. The answer to that question tends to remain relatively stable throughout one's life. This is not the case when it comes to the consequences drawn from one's basic reading of the immanent frame and its socio-political implications. It is not convincing to assess the modernity or secularity of a person according to their current view on the exact relation between the religious and the socio-political. Rafiq al-ʿAzm was not more modern and more secular in 1900, when he demanded the separation of the religious and the political, than in the 1920s, when he formulated his view of an Islamic government. Rida opposed a secularist stance, but he was not less modern or secular than Lord Cromer when he refuted Cromer's claim that Islam as a socio-political order was a failure, and instead validated such an order. If the characterization of particular persons or views as 'modern' or 'secular' ought to express a fundamental understanding of the world, we should stop equating modernity with particular modernist stances and secularity with secularist stances.

In this study, I have used Charles Taylor's open spin on the immanent frame as a bridge between my own closed reading, informed by secular theorization, and the Islamic reformists of *al-Manar*. As stated in the introduction, with my closed reading of the immanent frame, I am no exception among academics at European universities. Secular academic theories do make sense of a large portion of socio-political realities and views, because the secular university is located at the center of the hegemonic modern interpretation of the world. The authors in *al-Manar* advanced different, but equally modern, particular self-understandings. The idea of society, as most constitutive of the modern self-understanding, was not yet crystallized in a basic term, but it is nevertheless clearly discernible in our Islamic journal. The alternative vision of society and of modernity advanced by Rida informs us about the particularity of the hegemonic understanding. In this sense, modernity in Islamic tradition complements modernity in hegemonic Christian-secular tradition and enriches our understanding of modernity at large.

How should we, from within the modern self-understanding – whether in Islamic, Christian, secular, or other traditions – approach understandings that lie outside of or prior to the modern, wherever the latter's fringes are located exactly? The problem consists in its being tremendously difficult, if not utterly impossible, for us modern men and women to conceive of pre- or non-modern interpretations of the world without employing – if only in our minds – our particularly modern concepts. Thus, for example, if we say that "their" concept of 'religion' was fundamentally different from ours, we are already applying our present understanding of 'religion.' If we say that *umma* in the early nineteenth century did not connote society, but rather was a certain mixed form of 'society' and 'community,' we are projecting back onto the concept a later conceptual distinction. If we try to discern the political teachings of the prophet Muhammad, we assume that he had already conceived of the modern category of politics. Faced with this situation, we may either acknowledge our modern particularity and aspire to make sense of pre-modern phenomena and understandings only *for us*, or we may retrace the genealogy of our modern concepts in order to expand on and disorient their modern meanings.

Both strategies amount to subsuming other understandings under one's own. However, I can never fully place myself outside of the modern condition, any more than I can fully place myself outside of my own person. As a person, I can merely acknowledge the contingency and particularity of my own being and allow for, embrace, or try to project myself into alternative ways of being. As a scholar, to be reflectively modern means to acknowledge, to interrogate, and to disorient one's own modern(ist) particularity by uncovering alternative understandings.

Let me conclude, then, by sketching some concrete paths this study has pointed out for uncovering and making intelligible such alternative understandings.

3 Avenues for Future Research

Firstly, it would be worthwhile to discern in greater detail the conception of society put forward by Rashid Rida and Rafiq al-ʿAzm. We have seen that Rida thought of society as including all the members of a polity, and that he considered the modern division of labor as essential for the functioning of society. But how did Rida envision the interplay of the different members and tasks of society and their hierarchy? How exactly did he conceive of the social role of women and their political rights? Could we meaningfully identify further sub-fields of the social in his writings, such as the economic, the legal, the ethical, or the literary fields? And can we discern significant shifts in the presentation of these issues in Rida's writings over the course of 40 years?

Rafiq al-ʿAzm's œuvre as a whole, from which I presented two selected works in addition to several articles, merits additional research. This would allow us, for example, to test the hypothesis that al-ʿAzm's later works slightly reversed the secularist stance he formulated in 1900. Al-ʿAzm's earlier works would be of particular interest both for tracing the usage of *mujtamaʿ* and for discerning potential genealogies of his thought. It was striking that al-ʿAzm explicitly engaged European ideas but hardly referred to European sources in his writings. Discerning relevant sources from which al-ʿAzm appropriated secular(ist), anthropological, and sociological ideas would probably require attending to writings in Ottoman Turkish.

My analysis of *al-Manar* suggested some pertinent sources for the evolution of the modern meaning of *mujtamaʿ* as 'society' and the very idea of society beyond our Islamic journal. Niqula Haddad's pioneering book *ʿIlm al-Ijtimaʿ* (*Sociology*) would merit a closer analysis, both concerning the meanings of *mujtamaʿ* and *al-hayʾa al-ijtimāʿiyya* therein and concerning Haddad's conception of sociology and his exact sources in this regard. Expanding on this, it would be worthwhile to examine the reception of European sociology and the formulation of *ʿilm al-ijtimāʿ* by contemporaneous Arabic authors more broadly. Pertinent access points in this regard include the rival journals to *al-Manar* edited by Syrian Christians and known for their dissemination of European thought, above all *al-Muqtataf*, *al-Hilal*, and *al-Jamiʿa*, but also the mouthpiece of the Liberal Constitutionalist Party, *al-Siyasa*. In *al-Manar* it was reprints of articles from *al-Siyasa* that accounted for the most prominent usages of *mujtamaʿ* in original Arabic sources. Further research is also needed concerning the role of Arabic translations of French and English writings in the evolution of *mujtamaʿ* as 'society.' I have pointed out such influential translations as I came across them in *al-Manar*. A closer reading of these translations concerning their varying uses of *umma*, *mujtamaʿ*, *al-hayʾa al-ijtimāʿiyya*, etc. for rendering the original terms 'society' and *société* could further enlighten us as to the different meanings associated with these individual terms.

An obvious complement to synchronically expanding the basis of primary sources is to do so diachronically – that is, to trace the pertinent terms conceptualizing society and the social backward and forward in time. Concerning *ijtimāʿ*, it is of particular interest to discover when the term – which pre-modern philosophers had already used in the basic meaning of sociability and civil association – came to designate a societal sphere distinct from the political, and when thinkers started to derive normative claims from the alleged fact of human beings' natural tendency toward social association. The self-evident usage of *mujtamaʿ* in the sense of 'society' in the first volume of *al-Manar*, and even in articles from 1879 and 1884 quoted therein (see chapter 8 section 2), suggests that the term had already become available in this sense significantly earlier than is commonly assumed (see chapter 6 section 2). It would then be of interest to discern the scope of the social collectivity designated by *mujtamaʿ*, especially its first references to the whole social collectivity of a polity. When tracing the evolution of *mujtamaʿ* forward in time to discern the process of the crystallization of the idea of society in one basic concept, we should consider the continuing possibility – even after the firm establishment of *mujtamaʿ* – that the idea can also be conceptualized with other terms.

If it is worthwhile to consider *umma* as a major, enduring option in this regard,[2] it is still more relevant to trace the evolution of *umma* backward in time, so as to discern when this ubiquitous term in Arabic-Islamic discourse started to conceptualize aspects of the idea of society. In European languages, the concept of 'society' was coined and popularized by secular thinkers propagating the grounding of socio-political order in nature and the social (with the option of regrounding nature and the social in God). The theological roots of this secular vision notwithstanding, religious thinkers *re*acted to these secular coinages by gradually bringing forward their alternative conceptualizations of society (see chapter 2 section 3). The Islamic reformists of *al-Manar* also operated within a national setting (see chapter 4 section 1), catered to a modern society (see chap-

---

2 Thus, for example, Jamal al-Banna, the late brother of Hasan al-Banna, in a title from 2003, posited that Islam was religion (*dīn*) and society (*umma*), not world (*dunyā*) and state (*dawla*): al-Banna, Jamal. 2003. *al-Islam Din wa-Umma wa-laysa Dunyan wa-Dawla*. Cairo: Dar al-Fikr al-Islami. And Ridwan al-Sayyid, a prominent Lebanese theologian, intellectual, and journalist, terminologically updated a book title between 1984 and 2006; compare: al-Sayyid, Ridwan. 2006. *al-Jamaʿa wa-l-Mujtamaʿ wa-l-Dawla: Sultat al-Idiyulujiya fi al-Majal al-Siyasi al-ʿArabi al-Islami*. Beirut Dar al-Kitab al-ʿArabi; idem. 1984. *al-Umma wa-l-Jamaʿa wa-l-Sulta: Dirasa fi al-Fikr al-Siyasi al-ʿArabi al-Islami*. Beirut: Dar Iqra'.

ter 4 section 2), and were confronted with and engaged secularist visions of socio-political order (see chapter 4 section 3). It was in response to secularist stances that Rida formulated his understanding of the social having to be grounded in God and of society requiring religious foundations and guidance. However, while overt secular*ist* positions initially evolved in Europe and were also strongly discredited as such by Rida and other Islamic reformists, this does not exclude the possibility of a basic secular understanding having also evolved in the Islamic tradition. It is not only this study, but also other recent conceptual histories on Islamic contexts[3] that suggest a model of convergence of discursive traditions. Retracing the meanings of *umma*, along with *ijtimāʿ* or the conceptual pair *dīn* and *dunyā*, would be one means of discerning the evolution of the modern self-understanding within the Islamic discursive tradition.

Approaching Islamic conceptual and intellectual history via the concept of *umma* would mean, in a sense, following up on suggestions made by great scholars of Islamic studies some decades ago. In 1963, H.A.R. Gibb argued: "The key word for everything that has to do with Islamic culture is *Umma*, Community. It is in the historical development of this concept and its modalities that the true significance of Islamic history and culture must be sought."[4] Four years earlier, van Nieuwenhuijze had written: "The conclusion of this paper must be that the history of Islam can, in a way, be written as the history of the manner in which this primordially functional entity, the *umma*, has been realized under the prevailing conditions of the day, which have been its supposed co-ordinates. In the same manner, the position of Islam at a given moment can be studied in terms of the manner in which Muslims try to understand, and in understanding it, to realize, the *umma*."[5]

While Gibb and van Nieuwenhuijze rather straightforwardly and too exclusively identified *umma* with community, recent hints concerning the term's evolution in the centuries preceding the period of this study suggest it still more worthwhile to focus on the conceptual history and semantic range of *umma*. *Umma* did not simply acquire the modern meaning of 'the nation' – and possibly

3 See, for example, on analoguous developments of the concept of 'the state' and of the collective singular of 'history' in early modern French and Ottoman Turkish: Sigalas, Nikos. 2012. "Des histoires des sultans à l'histoire de l'État. Une enquête sur le temps du pouvoir ottoman (XVIe–XVIIIe siècles)." In *Les Ottomans et le temps* ed. by François Georgeon and Frédéric Hitzel: 99–128. Leiden/Boston: Brill.

4 Gibb, Hamilton A. R. 1963. "The Community in Islamic History." *Proceedings of the American Philosophical Society* 107/2: 173–176, here 173.

5 Van Nieuwenhuijze, C. A. O. 1959. "The Ummah: An Analytic Approach." *Studia Islamica* 10: 5–22, here 18; transliteration adjusted.

also 'society' – in reaction to the European idea of nation-states; comparing the concept of *umma* with that of *natio*, Ulrich Haarmann shows how the non-religious reference of *umma* to an ethnic group in the Middle Ages already conveyed an early sense of national conscience and national order.[6] This again suggests the convergence of discursive traditions in modernity, rather than the mere diffusion of European concepts.

For all the potential of conceptual history, one should finally also be aware of its limits – not least when it comes to understanding or even explaining socio-political developments. The lack of order of societies in Arab-Islamic countries today can hardly be explained by the insufficiency of local discursive traditions for conceptualizing such an order. After all, this study has shown that a conceptualization of society was clearly possible from within the Islamic discursive tradition. The vision of Islamic reformists might not have trickled down to the social imaginary of the whole populace, and it certainly did not lead to a factual reform of societal and political order. However, if the Islamic discursive tradition failed to order society in Arab countries, so also did liberal and socialist attempts. Thus, to understand or even explain the lack of order of societies in Arab countries, one has to complement intellectual and conceptual with other factors – not least demographic, educational, economic, political, and military ones.[7]

---

6 Haarmann, "Glaubensvolk," esp. 198; see also above: 183 f.

7 A recent multidisciplinary volume in that vein, which integrates multiple factors via the notion of citizenship, is: Meijer, Roel and Butenschøn, Nils (eds.). 2017. *The Crisis of Citizenship in the Arab World.* Leiden/Boston: Brill.

Bibliography

The bibliography consists of three parts:
a) Articles from *al-Manar*
b) Other Arabic Publications
c) Publications in Other Languages

a) Articles from *al-Manar*

> "The owners of newspapers and journals who aim at the progress of the nation (*tarqiyat al-umma*) in its societal life (*ḥayātihā al-ijtimāʿiyya*) are the persons most knowledgeable about the condition of society (*ḥāl al-umma*)."
> – Rashid Rida, 1902

ʿAbd al-Raziq, Mustafa. 1923. "Dhikra Rinan fi al-Jamiʿa al-Misriyya." *al-Manar* 24/5: 385–393.
ʿAbduh, Muhammad. 1906 [1882]. "al-Tamarrun wa-l-Iʿtiyad." *al-Manar* 9/8: 605–610.
—. 1899. "al-Quwa wa-l-Qanun." *al-Manar* 1/48: 917–923.
—. 1898. "Ma Akthar al-Qawl wa-Ma Aqall al-ʿAmal." *al-Manar* 1/9: 143–149.
—. 1898. "Muntadiyatuna al-ʿUmumiyya wa-Ahadithuha." *al-Manar* 1/20: 361–368.
—. 1898. "Wazifat al-Rusul (ʿAlayhim al-Salam) (Min Risalat al-Tawhid)." *al-Manar* 1/16: 286–294.
Abu al-ʿAyun. 1926. "Muharabat al-Bighaʾ." *al-Manar* 27/3: 233–235.
Abu al-Fadl, Muhammad. 1926. "al-Muʾtamar al-Islami al-ʿAmm li-l-Khilafa bi-Misr." *al-Manar* 27/6: 449–458.
Abu al-Kalam. 1923. "Wasf Thawrat al-Hind al-Siyasiyya al-Salbiyya wa-Intisaruha li-l-Khilafa wa-l-Dawla al-Turkiyya wa-l-Bilad al-ʿArabiyya (2)." *al-Manar* 24/2: 121–128.
Abu Rayya, Mahmud. 1934. "Kalima Khalisa li-Wijh Allah." *al-Manar* 34/3: 212–215.
Abu Shadi, Ahmad Zaki. 1917. "Taʾthir al-Sihafa fi Akhlaq al-Umma." *al-Manar* 19/8: 507–509.
Abu Zayd, Muhammad ʿAli. 1915. "al-Burhan ʿala Khuruj Tarik al-Salat wa-Maniʿ al-Zakat min al-Iman (3)." *al-Manar* 18/9: 662–672.
Adib Ghayr Maʿruf [an unknown writer]. 1939. "Tatawwur al-Islam." *al-Manar* 35/5: 49–60.
al-Afghani, Jamal al-Din. 1924. "al-Maqalat al-Jamaliyya (2): al-Sharq wa-l-Sharqiyun." *al-Manar* 25/8: 593–621.
—. 1922. "al-ʿIlla al-Haqiqiyya li-Saʿadat al-Insan." *al-Manar* 23/1: 37–45.
—. 1906. "Kitaban Siyasiyyan li-Hakim al-Islam al-Sayyid Jamal al-Din al-Afghani." *al-Manar* 10/11: 820–833.
—. 1900. "al-Hukuma al-Istibdadiyya [2]." *al-Manar* 3/26: 601–607.
Ahad Afadil al-Kuttab fi Dimashq al-Sham [a distinguished author from Damascus]. 1899. "al-Islah al-Islami." *al-Manar* 2/5: 65–72.
Ahad al-Kuttab min Suriya [an author from Syria] 1899. "Istinhad Himam (6)." *al-Manar* 2/13: 199–204.

https://doi.org/10.1515/9783110545845-013

—. 1899. "Istinhad Himam (13)." *al-Manar* 2/20: 312–316.
ʿAli, Amir. 1913. "al-Marʾa qabl al-Islam wa-baʿduhu." *al-Manar* 16/12: 933–941.
ʿAlim ʿAmil wa-Katib Fadil [an active scholar and a noble writer]. 1903. "Raʾy fi ʿIlm al-Kalam wa-Tariqa fi Ithbat al-Wahy." *al-Manar* 5/19: 726–759.
ʿAlim Azhari [a scholar from al-Azhar]. 1905. "Raʾy ʿAlim Azhari fi al-ʿUlamaʾ [2]." *al-Manar* 8/3: 110–114.
ʿAlim Kabir [a great scholar]. 1932. "Namudhaj min Kitab al-Injil wa-l-Salib." *al-Manar* 32/10: 745–752.
Amin, ʿAbdallah. 1935. "Naʿi Faqid al-Islam wa-l-Muslimin al-Sayyid al-Imam Muhammad Rashid Rida Munshiʾ al-Manar." *al-Manar* 35/2: 153–161.
Arafa, Muhammad. 1928. "al-Islah al-Haqiqi wa-l-Wajib li-l-Azhar." *al-Manar* 28/10: 758–765.
Arslan, Shakib. 1931. "Limadha Taʾakhkhara al-Muslimun, wa-Limadha Taqaddama Ghayruhum." *al-Manar* 31/5: 353–370, *al-Manar* 31/6: 449–464, *al-Manar* 31/7: 529–553.
—. 1929. "Madha Yuqal ʿan al-Islam fi Uruba (2)." *al-Manar* 30/1: 211–224.
—. 1928. "Azimat Kitab al-Salat fi Injlitira." *al-Manar* 29/3: 201–214.
—. 1927. "al-Ziyy al-Islami wa-l-Shaʿaʾir al-Islamiyya wa-l-Alqab al-ʿArabiyya ʿind Khawass Amrika." *al-Manar* 28/6: 450–454.
—. 1925. "al-Sufur wa-l-Hijab." *al-Manar* 26/4: 300–307.
al-Asram, Muhammad. 1907. "Uruba wa-l-Islam." *al-Manar* 10/10: 774–780.
Azad, Muhyi al-Din. 1922. "al-Khilafa al-Islamiyya; transl. ʿAbd al-Razzaq al-Mulih Abadi." *al-Manar* 23/1: 45–56, *al-Manar* 23/2: 102–106, *al-Manar* 23/3: 193–201, *al-Manar* 23/4: 282–289, *al-Manar* 23/5: 361–372, *al-Manar* 23/6: 466–471, *al-Manar* 23/7: 509–512, *al-Manar* 23/9: 691–702, *al-Manar* 23/10: 753–757.
al-ʿAzm, Rafiq. 1926. "al-Hukuma al-Islamiyya." *al-Manar* 26/7: 512–522.
—. 1910. "Asbab Suqut al-Dawla al-Ummawiyya." *al-Manar* 12/12: 933–947.
—. 1910. "Qadaʾ al-Fard wa-Qadaʾ al-Jamaʿa fi al-Islam." *al-Manar* 13/1: 33–49.
—. 1909. "al-Inqilab al-Maymun wa-Athr al-Sultan ʿAbd al-Hamid fi al-Dawla wa-Muqawimatuhu li-l-Dustur (Istidrak ʿala al-Manar)." *al-Manar* 12/5: 340–349.
—. 1907. "al-Jamiʿa al-Islamiyya." *al-Manar* 10/8: 589–594.
—. 1904. "Daʿf al-Muslimin bi-Mazj al-Siyasa bi-l-Din." *al-Manar* 7/17: 660–667.
—. 1904. "Hadha Awan al-ʿIbar." *al-Manar* 7/7: 269–271, *al-Manar* 7/8: 304–312.
—. 1904. "Kalima Thaniyya fi Ahl al-Dhimma." *al-Manar* 7/1: 11–17.
—. 1900. "Iqtirah ʿala al-Sadat al-ʿUlamaʾ fi Taqwim Iʿwijaj al-Wuʿʿaz wa-l-Khutabaʾ." *al-Manar* 2/44: 689–695.
—. 1899. "al-Islah al-Islami bi-ʿAdl al-Qawwam aw al-Takaful al-ʿAmm." *al-Manar* 2/6: 81–88.
—. 1899. "Kitab al-Durus al-Hikamiyya li-l-Nashiʾa al-Islamiyya." *al-Manar* 2/15: 225–227.
—. 1899. "Man al-Masʾul al-Hukuma am al-Shaʿb?." *al-Manar* 1/45: 866–872.
al-Baghdadi, ʿAbd al-Haqq. 1913. "al-ʿArab wa-l-ʿArabiyya: bi-Hima Salah al-Umma al-Islamiyya." *al-Manar* 16/10: 753–771.
Bahithat bi-l-Badiyya [pseudonym of Malak Hifni Nasif]. 1910. "al-Marʾa al-Misriyya wa-l-Marʾa al-Gharbiyya." *al-Manar* 13/4: 265–284.
al-Bakri, Muhammad Tawfiq. 1902. "al-Mustaqbal li-l-Islam." *al-Manar* 5/16: 601–634.
al-Banna, Hasan. 1940. "al-Marʾa al-Muslima (2)." *al-Manar* 35/10: 765–773.
—. 1940. "Mawqif al-ʿAlam al-Islami al-Siyasi al-Yawm," *al-Manar* 35/10: 747–750.

al-Battal, ʿAbd al-Samiʿ. 1936. "Faqid al-Islam al-Sayyid Muhammad Rashid Rida wa-Madrasat Dar al-Daʿwa wa-l-Irshad." *al-Manar* 35/3: 195–200.
Bin Fakhr al-Din, Ridaʾ al-Din. 1907. "Matalib Muslimi Rusya min Dawlatihim; transl. Musa ʿAbdallah al-Qazani." *al-Manar* 10/5: 367–377, *al-Manar* 10/6: 444–455.
al-Bitar, Muhammad Bahjat. 1926. "Kitab al-Mujaz fi al-Ijtimaʿ." *al-Manar* 27/4: 295–306, *al-Manar* 27/5: 354–362.
Chatelet, Monsieur. 1912. "al-Ghara ʿala al-ʿAlam al-Islami [translated from the French by al-Muʾayyad]." *al-Manar* 15/4: 259–269.
—. 1912. "al-Ghara ʿala al-ʿAlam al-Islami aw Fath al-ʿAlam al-Islami (10 [and 11])." *al-Manar* 15/10: 764–780.
Dabana, Niqula. 1899. "Asbab Inhitat al-Sharq (al-Hayʾa al-Ijtimaʿiyya al-Sharqiyya)." *al-Manar* 1/46: 886–889.
al-Dimashqi, Muhammad Efendi Kurd ʿAli. 1901. "al-Istiqlal wa-l-Ittikal." *al-Manar* 4/16: 601–615.
al-Dimashqi, Zaki Kiram. 1929. "Shuhadat ʿUlamaʾ al-Gharb al-Munsifin li-l-Islam wa-l-Nabi wa-l-Muslimin (1)." *al-Manar* 30/2: 140–144.
al-Dirdiri, Yahyi Ahmad. 1932. "Hadiyat al-Qurʾan." *al-Manar* 32/2: 102–109.
Esquiros, Alphonse. 1899–1906. "Amil al-Qarn al-Tasiʿ ʿAshar [; transl. ʿAbd al-ʿAziz Muhammad]." *al-Manar* 2/38: 598–603, *al-Manar* 2/42: 666–670, *al-Manar* 2/43: 679–682, *al-Manar* 3/11: 253–257, *al-Manar* 3/13: 294–301, *al-Manar* 3/11: 253–257, *al-Manar* 3/15: 345–351, *al-Manar* 3/18: 416–422, *al-Manar* 3/26: 607–610, *al-Manar* 3/30: 737–743, *al-Manar* 4/17: 659–668, *al-Manar* 4/23: 905–910, *al-Manar* 9/8: 626–628.
Fadil Hindi [a distinguished man from India]. 1899. "Mustaqbal al-Islam." *al-Manar* 1/41: 805–812.
Faruq, Sayf al-Rahman Rahmat Allah (Lord Headley). 1928. "Yaftarun ʿala Allah Kidhban." *al-Manar* 29/5: 344–351.
al-Fawiki, N. 1899. "al-Gharb al-Aqsa, Hal Yumkin Istirjaʿ Majd al-Sharq bi-Quwat al-Islam?." *al-Manar* 1/40: 794–801.
al-Ghamrawi, Muhammad Ahmad. 1926. "al-ʿIlm wa-l-Din (2)." *al-Manar* 27/7: 521–530.
Ghandi, Mahatma. 1926. "al-Sihha (4); transl. ʿAbd al-Razzaq." *al-Manar* 27/1: 48–54.
—. 1926. "al-Sihha (8); transl. ʿAbd al-Razzaq." *al-Manar* 27/8: 604–609.
Haʾ. ʿAyn. 1899. "Radd ʿala Bahith fi Kitab Sirr Taqaddum al-Inkliz al-Saksuniyin." *al-Manar* 2/30: 465–470.
al-Hadi, Shaykh bin Ahmad. 1905. "al-Manar al-Islami wa-l-Liwaʾ al-Watani." *al-Manar* 8/12: 478–479.
al-Hafiz, Ismaʿil Efendi. 1909. "Khutba li-ʿAyd al-Dustur." *al-Manar* 12/8: 547–551.
al-Harawi, Husayn. 1936. "al-Mustashriqun wa-l-Islam." *al-Manar* 35/4: 249–260, 267–279, 280–289.
Hifar, Muhammad Najib. 1911. "al-Ilhad fi al-Madaris al-ʿAlmaniyya." *al-Manar* 14/7: 544–545.
al-Hilal. 1914. "al-Sahyuniyya." *al-Manar* 17/5: 385–390.
Hurghrunj, Kristiyan Snuk. 1914. "al-Islam Yuqawim Nufudh al-Nasraniyya." *al-Manar* 17/3: 210–217.
Ibn Taymiyya, Taqi al-Din Ahmad. 1907. "Khilaf al-Umma fi-l-ʿIbadat wa-Madhhab Ahl al-Sunna wa-l-Jamaʿa." *al-Manar* 10/4: 265–279.

'Imran, Muhammad Basyuni. 1927. "Wujub al-Hajj." *al-Manar* 27/10: 778–781.

Jaridat al-Afkar al-'Arabiyya.1915. "al-Haqq wa-l-Quwa: Bahth Falsafi 'Anhuma bi-Munasibat al-Harb al-Hadira aw: Dars Daruri li-Nahnu al-Suriyin Khususan wa-l-Sharqiyin 'Umuman." *al-Manar* 18/2: 141–152.

Jaridat Umm al-Qura. 1929. "al-Mu'tamar al-Najdi al-Shuri al-'Amm." *al-Manar* 29/9: 696–711.

Katib min al-Bahrayn [an author from Bahrain]. 1910. "al-Bida' wa-l-Khurafat wa-l-Taqalid wa-l-'Adat 'ind al-Shi'a." *al-Manar* 13/4: 303–313.

al-Kawakibi, 'Abd al-Rahman. 1906. "Tijarat al-Raqiq wa-Ahkamuhu fi al-Islam." *al-Manar* 8/22: 854–861.

—. 1903. "Tatimmat al-Ijtima' al-Thani 'Ashar li-Jam'iyyat Umm al-Qura." *al-Manar* 5/22: 859–864.

—. 1902. "Baqiyyat al-Ijtima' al-Thalith li-Jam'iyyat Umm al-Qura." *al-Manar* 5/5: 183–190.

al-Khuli, Muhammad 'Abd al-'Aziz. 1926. "al-Irshad." *al-Manar* 27/4: 251–260.

—. 1921. "Tarikh Funun al-Hadith (5)." *al-Manar* 22/5: 353–369.

al-Lajna al-Tahdiriyya li-l-Mu'tamar al-Misri. 1911. "Taqrir al-Lajna al-Tahdiriyya li-l-Mu'tamar al-Misri al-Mun'aqad fi al-Qahira fi 29 Abril Sanna 1911." *al-Manar* 14/5: 353–372.

Lajnat Mashyakhat al-Azhar. 1920. "Taqrir Lajnat Mashyakhat al-Azhar al-Sharif al-Mu'allafa li-Fahs Mashru' Ta'mim al-Ta'lim al-Ula." *al-Manar* 21/7: 362–371.

—. 1920. "Taqrir Lajnat Mashyakhat al-Azhar al-Sharif al-Mu'allafa li-Fahs Mashru' Ta'mim al-Ta'lim al-Ula [2]." *al-Manar* 21/8: 423–427.

Le Bon, Gustave. 1920. "Namudhaj min Kitab al-Falsafa al-Siyasiyya; transl. 'Abd al-Basit Efendi Fath Allah al-Bayruni." *al-Manar* 21/7: 345–353.

al-Lihan, Mustafa Ahmad al-Rifa'i, 1935. "Zuhur al-Manar wa-Dalalatuhu." *al-Manar* 35/1: 77–79.

—. 1934. "Tafsir al-Manar li-'Alamat al-Dahr wa-Muslih al-'Asr." *al-Manar* 34/4: 284–289.

M. N. 1915. "Hal al-Muslimin al-Yawm wa-Jama'at al-Da'wa wa-l-Irshad." *al-Manar* 18/10: 793–799.

al-Maghribi, 'Abd al-Qadir. 1924. "Tazwij al-Muslim bi-Ghayr al-Muslima." *al-Manar* 25/2: 120–124.

al-Mahami, Hamuduh Efendi. 1898. "Taqwim al-Afkar." *al-Manar* 1/34: 661–665.

al-Mahami, Muhammad Fahmi Husayn. 1908. "al-'Amal." *al-Manar* 11/9: 673–680.

Majallat al-Fajr al-Tunisiyya. 1921. "al-Islam wa-Siyasat al-Hulafa'." *al-Manar* 22/9: 649–652.

al-Maqdisi, Muhammad Ruhi al-Khalidi. 1908. "al-Inqilab al-'Uthmani." *al-Manar* 11/9: 646–672.

—. 1908. "al-Inqilab al-'Uthmani wa-Turkiya al-Fata (3)." *al-Manar* 11/11: 842–859.

al-Maraghi, Muhammad Mustafa. 1936. "Khutbat al-Ustadh al-Akbar Shaykh al-Jami' al-Azhar." *al-Manar* 35/3: 186–188.

—. 1928. "Islah al-Azhar al-Sharif." *al-Manar* 29/5: 325–345.

al-Maraghi, Muhammad Mustafa et al. 1935. "Haflat al-Azhar bi-Shaykhihi al-Ustadh al-Akbar al-Shaykh Muhammad Mustafa al-Maraghi." *al-Manar* 35/2: 136–144.

al-Marghinani, Kamal al-Din. 1901. "al-Fiqh al-islami." *al-Manar* 4/4: 132–140.

al-Mawla, Muhammad Ahmad Jad. 1935. "Ma Ahwajuna fi hadha al-Zaman ila Hadayat al-Qur'an." *al-Manar* 35/5: 42–48.

al-Mughira, 'Abdallah. 1920. "Wasf Bilad al-'Arab al-Janubiyya allati Yusammuha al-Yunan al-'Arabiyya al-Sa'ida." *al-Manar* 21/8: 415–422.

Muhaysin, Hamid Mahmud. 1928. "al-'Uquba fi al-Islam laysat Taqriran li-Nazariyya al-Intiqam." *al-Manar* 29/4: 299–308.
Murasil al-Ahram fi Amrika. 1935. "Tafaqum Sharr al-Talaq fi Amrika." *al-Manar* 35/1: 78–79.
Muslim Ghayur [a zealous Muslim]. 1927. "al-Islah al-Islami fi al-Maghrib al-Aqsa (3)." *al-Manar* 28/3: 196–201.
—. 1927. "al-Islah al-Islami fi al-Maghrib al-Aqsa (4)." *al-Manar* 28/4: 285–288.
al-Nashashibi, Is'af. 1927. "al-'Arabiyya wa-Sha'iruha al-Akbar Ahmad Shuqi Bek." *al-Manar* 28/3: 213–224.
Nuwayhad, 'Ajaj. 1929. "Hal hadha al-Nahda Khadi'a li-Sultan al-'Ilm?." *al-Manar* 30/3: 193–211.
Qabani, 'Abd al-Qadir. 1909. "al-Duktur Shibli Efendi Shumayyil." *al-Manar* 12/8: 632–637.
al-Rafi'i, Mustafa Sadiq. 1928. "Khatar Hujum al-Kamaliyin 'ala al-Islam." *al-Manar* 29/6: 456–463.
Rida, Husayn Wasfi. 1910. "Taqriz al-Matbu'at al-Jadida." *al-Manar* 13/5: 374–383.
—. 1910. "al-Akhbar wa-l-Ara' (Dars 'ala Kitab al-Daris fi al-Madaris)." *al-Manar* 13/9: 697–709.
—. 1910. "Taqriz al-Matbu'at al-Jadida." *al-Manar* 13/2: 131–144.
—. 1908. "al-Suhuf fi al-Bilad al-'Uthmaniyya." *al-Manar* 11/8: 634–638.
Rida, Rashid. 1939. "al-Manar mundhu 'Ishrin Sanna." *al-Manar* 35/6: 450–462.
—. 1935. "Khitab al-Shaykh al-Akbar fi al-Jami' al-Azhar." *al-Manar* 35/1: 41–46.
—. 1935. "Kitab al-Wahy al-Muhammadi." *al-Manar* 35/1: 55–63.
—. 1935. "al-Mawlid al-Nabawi" *al-Manar* 34/7: 549–552.
—. 1935. "al-Tarbiya al-Islamiyya wa-l-Ta'lim al-Islami." *al-Manar* 34/7: 544–548.
—. 1934. "Dhikra al-Mawlid al-Nabawi." *al-Manar* 34/2: 129–139.
—. 1934. "Shahr Ramadan: Mawsim al-'Ibada al-Ruhiyya al-Badaniyya al-Ijtima'iyya." *al-Manar* 34/6: 473–474.
—. 1934. "Tafnid I'tirad Katib Juzwiti 'ala Kitab al-Wahy al-Muhammadi." *al-Manar* 34/2: 147–151.
—. 1934. "Taqariz Kitab al-Wahy al-Muhammadi." *al-Manar* 33/9: 697–710.
—. 1934. "Taqariz Kitab al-Wahy al-Muhammadi." *al-Manar* 33/10: 768–791.
—. 1933. "Da'irat al-Ma'arif al-Islamiyya." *al-Manar* 33/6: 474–478.
—. 1933. "al-Haja ila Hadhihi al-Tarjama." *al-Manar* 33/7: 536–542.
—. 1933. "al-'Ibra bi-Sirat al-Malik Faysal (3)." *al-Manar* 33/8: 631–634.
—. 1933. "'Ismat al-Anbiya'." *al-Manar* 33/8: 609–614.
—. 1933. "Majallat al-Manar Sanna 33." *al-Manar* 33/1: 78–79.
—. 1933. "al-Malik Faysal: al-'Ibra bi-Hayatihi wa-Wifatihi." *al-Manar* 33/6: 457–461.
—. 1933. "al-Malik Faysal al-Husayni al-Hashimi." *al-Manar* 33/5: 387–390.
—. 1933. "Mas'alat al-Tajnis al-Fransi." *al-Manar* 33/3: 224–230.
—. 1933. "al-Matbu'at al-Munkira fi al-Din." *al-Manar* 33/7: 513–535.
—. 1933. "Muqaddimat Kitab al-Wahy al-Muhammadi." *al-Manar* 33/4: 282–289.
—. 1933. "Muqaddimatuna li-Tasdir Kitab Naqd Mata'in fi al-Qur'an al-Karim." *al-Manar* 33/3: 193–210.
—. 1933. "Tahaddi al-'Alam bi-Ta'alim al-Wahy al-Muhammadi." *al-Manar* 33/2: 102–103.
—. 1933. "Taqriz al-Matbu'at al-Jadida." *al-Manar* 33/2: 141–150.
—. 1933. "Thawrat al-Mar'a al-Ibahiyya wa-Khataruha 'ala al-Usra fa-l-Umma." *al-Manar* 33/6: 462–472.

——. 1932. "Adhan Ibrahim al-Khalil bi-l-Hajj wa-Du'a'uhu li-Ahl al-Haram bi-l-Rizq." *al-Manar* 32/3: 217–221.
——. 1932. "Ahmad Shawqi Bek Amir al-Shu'ara'." *al-Manar* 32/9: 719–720.
——. 1932. "Fatawa al-Manar." *al-Manar* 32/4: 268–279.
——. 1932. "Muhammad Hafiz Bak Ibrahim Sha'ir Misr al-Ijtima'i." *al-Manar* 32/8: 625–630.
——. 1932. "al-Munazara bayna Ahl al-Sunna wa-l-Shi'a." *al-Manar* 32/2: 145–160.
——. 1932. "al-Mu'tamar al-Islami al-'Amm fi Bayt al-Muqaddas." *al-Manar* 32/2: 113–132.
——. 1932. "al-Mu'tamar al-Islami al-'Amm fi Bayt al-Muqaddas (2)." *al-Manar* 32/3: 193–208.
——. 1932. "al-Mu'tamar al-Islami al-'Amm fi Bayt al-Muqaddas (3)." *al-Manar* 32/4: 284–292.
——. 1932. "Nida' li-l-Jins al-Latif: Yawm al-Mawlid al-Nabawi al-Sharif." *al-Manar* 32/5: 352–400.
——. 1932. "Nida' li-l-Jins al-Latif [...]: al-Talaq." *al-Manar* 32/8: 607–624.
——. 1932. "al-Tajdid wa-l-Tajaddud wa-l-Mujaddidun (3)." *al-Manar* 32/3: 226–231.
——. 1931. "Fatawa al-Manar." *al-Manar* 31/10: 732–744.
——. 1931. "Ilhad fi al-Qur'an wa-Din Jadid bayna al-Batiniyya wa-l-Islam [4]: al-Sunan al-Kawniyya al-Ijtima'iyya wa-Nizam al-Kawn." *al-Manar* 32/1: 33–48.
——. 1931. "Munazara fi al-Jami'a al-Misriyya fi al-Madaniyyatayn al-Far'uniyya wa-l-'Arabiyya." *al-Manar* 31/6: 465–474.
——. 1931. "al-Tajdid wa-l-Tajaddud wa-l-Mujaddidun (2)." *al-Manar* 32/1: 49–60.
——. 1931. "al-Tajdid wa-l-Tajaddud wa-l-Mujaddidun." *al-Manar* 31/10: 770–777.
——. 1931. "Tasdir al-Tarikh." *al-Manar* 32/1: 2–14.
——. 1930. "Fatawa al-Manar." *al-Manar* 31/1: 46–58.
——. 1930. "al-Haqiqa wa-l-Tarikh." *al-Manar* 31/5: 371–389.
——. 1930. "Ilhad fi al-Qur'an wa-Din Jadid bayna al-Batiniyya wa-l-Islam [1]." *al-Manar* 31/9: 673–697.
——. 1930. "Israr Fransa 'ala Ikhraj al-Barbar min al-Islam." *al-Manar* 31/4: 309–317.
——. 1930. "Munazara fi Musawat al-Mar'a li-l-Rajul fi al-Huquq wa-l-Wajibat." *al-Manar* 30/7: 535–545.
——. 1930. "Munazara fi Musawat al-Mar'a li-l-Rajul fi al-Huquq wa-l-Wajibat (3) [and 4–6]." *al-Manar* 30/8: 610–624.
——. 1930. "Musawat al-Mar'a li-l-Rajul fi al-Huquq wa-l-Wajibat: al-Radd al-Tafsili fi Mawdu' al-Munazara (7)." *al-Manar* 30/9: 690–709.
——. 1929. "Fatihat al-Sanna al-Thalathin." *al-Manar* 30/1: 1–16.
——. 1929. "Hal al-Muslimin fi al-Sharq wa-l-Janub." *al-Manar* 29/10: 759–764.
——. 1929. "al-Ilhad wa-Du'atuhu fi Majallat al-Rabita al-Sharqiyya wa-l-Ustadh Ahmad Amin." *al-Manar* 29/9: 718–720.
——. 1929. "al-Istifta' fi Haqiqat al-Riba." *al-Manar* 30/4: 273–291.
——. 1929. "al-Jam' bayna Mas'alat al-Dhikran wa-l-Inath fi al-Madaris wa-Mas'alat al-Tajdid wa-l-Tajaddud." *al-Manar* 30/2: 115–127.
——. 1929. "Jami' Baris." *al-Manar* 29/10: 793–794.
——. 1929. "Muqaddimat Rasa'il al-Sunna wa-l-Shi'a." *al-Manar* 29/9: 671–686.
——. 1929. "Thawrat Filastin – Asbabuha wa-Nata'ijuha: Haqiqat fi Bayan Hal al-Yahud wa-l-Inkliz wa-l-'Arab wa-l-Ra'y fi Mustaqbal al-'Arab wa-l-Sharq." *al-Manar* 30/6: 450–468.

—. 1928. "A'da' al-Islam al-Muharibun lahu fi hadha al-'Ahd." *al-Manar* 29/2: 115–122.
—. 1928. "Fatihat al-Mujallad al-Tasi' al-'Ishrin min al-Manar." *al-Manar* 29/1: 1–8.
—. 1928. "Haqa'iq fi 'Adawat Malahidat al-Turk li-l-Islam." *al-Manar* 29/6: 464–474.
—. 1928. "al-Hukumat al-Ladiniyya li-l-Shu'ub al-Islamiyya al-A'jimiyya wa-'Awaqibuha fi al-Turk wa-l-Fars wa-l-Afghan." *al-Manar* 29/8: 635–636.
—. 1928. "al-Inqilab al-Madani al-Dini bi Bilad al-Afghan." *al-Manar* 29/7: 549–559.
—. 1928. "Iqtirah Ibtal al-Awqaf al-Ahliyya wa-Makan al-Din min al-Dawla al-Misriyya fi Qismayha al-Tashri'i wa-l-Tanfidhi." *al-Manar* 29/1: 75–78.
—. 1928. "al-Juz' al-Tasi' min Tafsir al-Qur'an al-Hakim." *al-Manar* 29/6: 450–455.
—. 1928. "al-Radd 'ala al-Za'im Muhammad 'Ali al-Hindi fi Mawdu' Malik al-Hijaz wa-Hukumatihi wa-Qawmihi wa-l-Khilafa (1)." *al-Manar* 29/3: 162–180.
—. 1928. "Rihlat Jalalat Malik al-Afghan (Aman Allah Khan)." *al-Manar* 28/10: 782–787.
—. 1928. "Taqriz al-Matbu'at al-Haditha." *al-Manar* 29/4: 317–320.
—. 1928. "Wifat Sayyid Amir 'Ali." *al-Manar* 29/5: 352–357.
—. 1927. "al-Matbu'at al-Haditha (Miftah al-Khataba wa-l-Wa'z)." *al-Manar* 28/5: 397–400.
—. 1927. "al-Murad bi-l-Ta'n fi al-Din – wa-Kawn Mukhalafat al-Qur'an Kufran." *al-Manar* 28/8: 578–583.
—. 1927. "Sa'd Zaghlul (1)." *al-Manar* 28/8: 584–592.
—. 1926. "Abna' al-'Alam al-Islami." *al-Manar* 27/6: 471–477.
—. 1926. "Ahwal al-'Alam al-Islami." *al-Manar* 27/1: 71–77.
—. 1926. "al-'Alam al-Islami." *al-Manar* 26/7: 540–547.
—. 1926. "al-Jama'a al-Islamiyya fi Berlin." *al-Manar* 27/4: 309–314.
—. 1926. "Jam'iyyat Tajdid al-Ilhad wa-l-Zandaqa wa-l-Ibahat al-Mutlaqa." *al-Manar* 27/5: 387–398.
—. 1926. "al-Ladiniyun fi Tunis wa-Misr wa-Kitab 'Ali 'Abd al-Raziq." *al-Manar* 26/7: 548–551.
—. 1926. "Tarbiyat Umara' al-'Arab qabl al-Islam wa-Kayfa Nastafid minha fi Hadhihi al-Ayam?." *al-Manar* 26/8: 600–612.
—. 1926. "al-Thawra al-Suriyya wa-l-Hukuma al-Fransiyya wa-l-Intiza' bayna al-Sharq wa-l-Gharb." *al-Manar* 26/8: 585–594.
—. 1925. "al-Din wa-l-Siyasa wa-Malahidat al-Mutafarnjin min al-'Arab wa-Ghayrihim." *al-Manar* 26/1: 47–59.
—. 1925. "Hukm Hay'a Kibar al-'Ulama' fi Kitab al-Islam wa-Usul al-Hukm." *al-Manar* 26/5: 363–382.
—. 1925. "al-Ighra' bayna al-Nasara wa-l-Muslimin." *al-Manar* 25/9: 709–713.
—. 1925. "al-Islam wa-Usul al-Hukm." *al-Manar* 26/3: 212–217, 230–232.
—. 1925. "Madi al-Azhar wa-Hadiruhu wa-Mustaqbaluhu (3)." *al-Manar* 26/1: 65–72.
—. 1925. "Madi al-Azhar wa-Hadiruhu wa-Mustaqbaluhu (4)." *al-Manar* 26/2: 123–131.
—. 1925. "al-Matbu'at al-Jadida." *al-Manar* 25/10: 797–799.
—. 1925. "Min 'Adhiri." *al-Manar* 26/4: 307–318.
—. 1925. "al-Muftirun fi Ramadan." *al-Manar* 25/10: 743–744.
—. 1925. "Rafiq al-'Azm: Wifatuhu wa-Tarjamatuhu." *al-Manar* 26/4: 288–300.
—. 1924. "Fatawa al-Manar: al-Tabshir wa-l-Mubashirun fi Nazar al-Muslimin." *al-Manar* 25/3: 188–194.
—. 1924. "Khitab 'Amm fima Yajib 'ala al-Muslimin li-Bayt Allah al-Haram." *al-Manar* 25/1: 33–63.

—. 1924. "Tajannus al-Muslim bi-Jinsiyya Tunafi al-Islam." *al-Manar* 25/1: 21–32.
—. 1923. "al-Ahkam al-Shar'iyya al-Muta'alliqa bi-l-Khilafa al-Islamiyya." *al-Manar* 24/1: 33–67.
—. 1923. "Ahwal al-'Alam al-Islami." *al-Manar* 24/10: 796–799.
—. 1923. "Fatihat al-Kitab al-Khilafa aw al-Imama al-'Uzma." *al-Manar* 24/6: 459–465.
—. 1923. "al-Istifta' fi Malik al-Hijaz." *al-Manar* 24/8: 593–618.
—. 1923. "al-Khilafa al-Islamiyya (3)." *al-Manar* 24/2: 98–120.
—. 1923. "al-Khilafa al-Islamiyya (5)." *al-Manar* 24/4: 257–272.
—. 1923. "al-Khilafa al-Islamiyya (6)." *al-Manar* 24/5: 345–365.
—. 1923. "Khitab Maftuh min Ruh al-Islam wa-l-Jami'a al-'Arabiyya ila al-Sha'b al-Inklizi wa-l-Hukuma al-Britaniyya." *al-Manar* 24/6: 441–448.
—. 1923. "Lughat al-Islam wa-l-Lugha al-Rasmiyya bayna al-Mamalik al-Islamiyya (1)." *al-Manar* 24/10: 753–765.
—. 1922. "al-Ihtifal bi-Dhikra al-Ustadh al-Imam (2)." *al-Manar* 23/8: 593–611.
—. 1922. "al-Islam wa-l-Nasraniyya." *al-Manar* 23/4: 267–272.
—. 1922. "al-Rihla al-Suriyya al-Thaniyya (10)." *al-Manar* 23/4: 313–317.
—. 1922. "al-Rihla al-Urubiyya (2)." *al-Manar* 23/4: 306–313.
—. 1922. "al-Rihla al-Urubiyya (4)." *al-Manar* 23/6: 441–459.
—. 1922. "al-Rihla al-Urubiyya [6]." *al-Manar* 23/8: 635–640.
—. 1922. "al-Rihla al-Urubiyya (7)." *al-Manar* 23/9: 696–702.
—. 1922. "Sa'id Halim Basha." *al-Manar* 23/2: 147–153.
—. 1922. "al-Watha'iq al-Rasmiyya li-l-Mas'ala al-'Arabiyya." *al-Manar* 23/8: 612–616.
—. 1921. "As'ila Maghribiyya min 'Asimat al-Bilad al-Isbaniyya." *al-Manar* 22/6: 429–442.
—. 1921. "al-Haqa'iq al-Jaliyya fi al-Mas'ala al-'Arabiyya." *al-Manar* 22/6: 442–479.
—. 1921. "al-Rihla al-Suriyya al-Thaniyya." *al-Manar* 22/5: 390–397.
—. 1921. "al-Rihla al-Suriyya al-Thaniyya (6)." *al-Manar* 22/8: 617–623.
—. 1921. "Watha'iq Tarikhiyya fi al-Mas'ala al-'Arabiyya." *al-Manar* 22/3: 232–240.
—. 1920. "'Aqibat Harb al-Madaniyya al-Urubiyya." *al-Manar* 21/7: 337–344.
—. 1920. "Istiqlal Suriya wa-l-'Iraq." *al-Manar* 21/8: 434–447.
—. 1920. "Tarjamat al-Tabib Muhammad Tawfiq Sidqi." *al-Manar* 21/9: 483–495.
—. 1919. "Bahithat al-Badiyya – Tatimmat Tarjamatiha." *al-Manar* 21/3: 163–168.
—. 1919. "al-Shaykh Muhammad Kamil al-Rafi'i (3)." *al-Manar* 21/6: 325–327.
—. 1919. "al-Tatawwur al-Siyasi wa-l-Dini wa-l-Ijtima'i bi-Misr." *al-Manar* 21/5: 274–277.
—. 1918. "al-Hala al-Siyasiyya fi al-Hijaz fi Awakhir Sanna 1334." *al-Manar* 20/6: 278–288.
—. 1918. "al-Mutafarnijun wa-l-Islah al-Islami (1)." *al-Manar* 20/8: 340–345.
—. 1918. "Radd al-Manar 'ala al-Naqid li-Dhikra al-Mawlid al-Nabawi." *al-Manar* 20/9: 395–403.
—. 1917. "Bida' al-Jum'a wa-l-Adhan wa-Khatm al-Salat wa-l-Janaza." *al-Manar* 19/9: 538–544.
—. 1917. "al-Duktur Shibli Shumayyil." *al-Manar* 19/10: 625–632.
—. 1917. "al-Jam'iyyat al-Ittihadiyya li-Takwin al-'Asabiyya al-Turkiyya." *al-Manar* 19/9: 555–562.
—. 1917. "Rihlat al-Hijaz (4)." *al-Manar* 20/2: 108–126.
—. 1917. "Taqriz al-Matbu'at al-Jadida." *al-Manar* 19/9: 574–576.
—. 1916. "Hal al-Muslimin al-Ijtima'iyya." *al-Manar* 19/2: 89–96, *al-Manar* 19/4: 244–256, *al-Manar* 19/5: 297–306.

—. 1916. "Hikam al-Siyam wa-Jinayat Tarikihi ʿala Anfusihim wa-ʿala al-Muslimin wa-l-Islam." *al-Manar* 19/2: 82–88.
—. 1916. "al-Intiqad ʿala al-Manar." *al-Manar* 19/4: 190–192.
—. 1916. "al-Sayyid ʿAbd al-Hamid al-Zahrawi." *al-Manar* 19/3: 169–182.
—. 1915. "Fasl fi Hikam Shahadat Ghayr al-Muslimin ʿala al-Muslimin." *al-Manar* 18/8: 575–583.
—. 1915. "Harb Umam al-Madaniyya La al-Milal al-Diniyya." *al-Manar* 18/10: 746–752.
—. 1915. "al-Islam fi Injiltirra." *al-Manar* 18/1: 73–79.
—. 1915. "Sufur al-Nisaʾ wa-Ikhtilatuhunna bi-l-Rijal wa-Fawda al-Adab bi-Misr." *al-Manar* 18/3: 227–233.
—. 1915. "Taqriz al-Matbuʿat al-Jadida." *al-Manar* 18/4: 315–320.
—. 1914. "Afdal al-Wasaʾil li-Inhad al-Saltana." *al-Manar* 17/4: 303–312.
—. 1914. "al-Akhbar wa-l-Araʾ." *al-Manar* 17/2: 153–160.
—. 1914. "Bab al-Murasala wa-l-Munazara." *al-Manar* 17/10: 793–800.
—. 1914. "Muhadarat al-Duktur Kristiyan Snuk Hurghrunj al-Hulandi fi al-Islam wa-Mustaqbal al-Muslimin." *al-Manar* 17/4: 268–272.
—. 1914. "Namudhaj min Inshaʾ Talabat Dar al-Daʿwa wa-l-Irshad." *al-Manar* 17/7: 545–555.
—. 1914. "al-Taʿrif bi-Kitab al-Iʿtisam." *al-Manar* 17/10: 745–749.
—. 1913. "Fatawa al-Manar." *al-Manar* 16/9: 675–688.
—. 1913. "Fatihat al-Sana al-Sabiʿa ʿAshara." *al-Manar* 17/1: 1–11.
—. 1913. "ʿIbar al-Harb al-Balqaniyya wa-Khatar al-Masʾala al-Sharqiyya." *al-Manar* 16/1: 54–63.
—. 1913. "al-Jihad aw al-Qital fi al-Islam." *al-Manar* 16/1: 25–28.
—. 1913. "Laʾihat al-Islah li-Wilayat al-Bayrut." *al-Manar* 16/4: 275–280.
—. 1913. "al-Majalla al-Misriyya al-Fransiyya wa-Raʾyuha fi al-Manar." *al-Manar* 16/8: 619.
—. 1913. "Namudhaj min Inshaʾ Talabat al-Sanna al-Tamhidiyya li-Madrasat Dar al-Daʿwa wa-l-Irshad." *al-Manar* 16/9: 709–715.
—. 1912. "Akhbar al-ʿAlam al-Islami." *al-Manar* 15/5: 386–391.
—. 1912. "Asʾila min al-Quqas." *al-Manar* 15/11: 826–832.
—. 1912. "Fatihat al-Mujallad al-Khamis ʿAshar." *al-Manar* 15/1: 1–8.
—. 1912. "Haflat al-Arbaʿin li-Taʾbin al-Marhum al-Sayyid Husayn Wasfi Rida." *al-Manar* 15/6: 466–480.
—. 1912. "Khatimat al-Maqalat: Shujun wa-Muhawarat (10)." *al-Manar* 15/1: 48–55.
—. 1912. "al-Khutba al-Raʾisiyya fi Nadwat al-ʿUlamaʾ bi-Lukunuhuʾ [Lucknow] al-Hind li-Sahib al-Manar (1)." *al-Manar* 15/5: 331–341.
—. 1912. "Taqriz al-Matbuʿat al-Jadida." *al-Manar* 15/12: 945–953.
—. 1912. "al-Tarbiya wa-Wajh al-Haja ilayha wa-Taqasimiha." *al-Manar* 15/5: 567–586.
—. 1911. "al-Akhbar wa-l-Araʾ." *al-Manar* 14/2: 155–160.
—. 1911. "ʿAridat al-Shukr min al-ʿUthmaniyin al-Mustakhdimin fi Afghanistan ila Amiriha." *al-Manar* 14/12: 943–944.
—. 1911. "Fatawa al-Manar." *al-Manar* 14/3: 178–190.
—. 1911. "Fatihat al-Mujallad al-Rabiʿ ʿAshar." *al-Manar* 14/1: 1–8.
—. 1911. "al-Ishtirakiyya wa-l-Din wa-l-Ilhad: Nasara al-Muqtataf al-Iman ʿala al-Taʿtil." *al-Manar* 13/12: 913–921.
—. 1911. "Munazarat ʿAlim Muslim li-Duʿat al-Brutistant fi Baghdad." *al-Manar* 14/12: 914–922.

—. 1911. "al-Muslimun wa-l-Qubt (1)." *al-Manar* 14/2: 108 – 114.
—. 1911. "al-Muslimun wa-l-Qubt (6)." *al-Manar* 14/4: 273 – 279.
—. 1911. "Nizam Madrasat Dar al-Da'wa wa-l-Irshad." *al-Manar* 14/10: 785 – 800.
—. 1911. "Radd al-Manar." *al-Manar* 14/10: 770 – 781.
—. 1911. "Ta'bin Riyad Basha." *al-Manar* 14/8: 633 – 635.
—. 1911. "Taqrir al-Lajna al-Tahdiriyya li-l-Mu'tamar al-Misri." *al-Manar* 14/6: 449 – 457.
—. 1911. "Taqriz al-Matbu'at al-Jadida." *al-Manar* 14/1: 71 – 74.
—. 1911. "al-'Ulum wa-l-Funun allati Tudarras fi Dar al-Da'wa wa-l-Irshad." *al-Manar* 14/11: 801 – 821.
—. 1910. "As'ila min Baris." *al-Manar* 13/10: 741 – 748.
—. 1910. "Fatihat al-Sanna al-Thalitha 'Ashar." *al-Manar* 13/1: 3 – 8.
—. 1910. "al-Ittihad al-Shamil wa-l-Ta'lim al-Shamil: Ayyahuma Yatawaqqif 'ala al-Akhar." *al-Manar* 13/4: 260 – 264.
—. 1910. "Quwat al-Ijtima' wa-l-Ta'awun." *al-Manar* 13/5: 345 – 348.
—. 1910. "al-Tarbiya al-Qawima wa-l-Siyasa al-Hikmiyya: al-Thiqqa wa-l-Zinna." *al-Manar* 13/8: 591 – 597.
—. 1909. "Din al-Mustaqbal wa-Hal Yakfur Man la-Hu Ra'y fihi." *al-Manar* 12/2: 93 – 95.
—. 1909. "Fatihat al-Sanna al-Thaniyya 'Ashara." *al-Manar* 12/1: 1 – 15.
—. 1909. "al-Hurriya wa-Istiqlal al-Fikr." *al-Manar* 12/2: 113 – 117.
—. 1909. "al-Ihtifal bi-'Id al-Dustur al-'Uthmani." *al-Manar* 12/6: 478 – 480.
—. 1909. "al-Jinsiyyat al-'Uthmaniyya wa-l-Lughatan al-'Arabiyya wa-l-Turkiyya." *al-Manar* 12/7: 501 – 512.
—. 1909. "Khitab Sahib al-Manar 'ala Tulab al-Kuliyya al-Amrikaniyya al-Muslimin fi Beirut." *al-Manar* 12/1: 16 – 18.
—. 1909. "al-Qada' wa-l-Qadr." *al-Manar* 12/3: 189 – 200.
—. 1908. "Athar 'Ilmiyya Adabiyya." *al-Manar* 11/7: 528 – 539.
—. 1908. "Athar 'Ilmiyya Adabiyya." *al-Manar* 11/8: 617 – 621.
—. 1908. "Fatihat al-Sanna al-Hadiyya 'Ashara." *al-Manar* 11/1: 1 – 6.
—. 1908. "Iftitah Majlis al-Mab'uthan." *al-Manar* 11/11: 860 – 872.
—. 1908. "al-Khutba al-Ula min Khutabina al-Islamiyya fi al-Diyar al-Suriyya." *al-Manar* 11/9: 641 – 646.
—. 1908. "Kitab Misr al-Haditha li-l-Lurd Krumir." *al-Manar* 11/2: 81 – 113.
—. 1908. "Kitaban Siyasiyyatan li-l-Ustadh al-Imam al-Shaykh Muhammad 'Abduh aw Matalib Misr min Inklitira." *al-Manar* 10/11: 834 – 848.
—. 1908. "Masab Misr bi-Qasim Bik Amin." *al-Manar* 11/3: 226 – 229.
—. 1908. "Muqaddimatuna li-Kitab al-Tarbiya al-Istiqlaliyya aw Amil al-Qarn al-Tasi' 'Ashar." al-*Manar* 11/6: 427 – 431.
—. 1908. "al-Mu'tamar al-Islami." *al-Manar* 11/3: 181 – 184.
—. 1908. "al-Qanun al-Asasi wa-l-Khatt al-Sultani bi-hi." *al-Manar* 11/6: 424 – 431.
—. 1908. "al-Qur'an wa-Najah Da'wat al-Nabi 'alayhi al-Salat wa-l-Salam wa-Ara' 'Ulama' Uruba fi Dhalik." *al-Manar* 11/1: 9 – 31.
—. 1908. "al-Radd 'ala Kitab al-Lurd Krumir." *al-Manar* 11/5: 354 – 360.
—. 1908. "al-Radd 'ala al-Lurd Krumir." *al-Manar* 11/3: 185 – 207.
—. 1908. "Ra'y Kibar Sasat al-Gharb fi al-Haraka al-Madaniyya al-Jadida fi al-Sharq." *al-Manar* 10/12: 916 – 919.

—. 1908. "Ra'y al-Shaykh Ahmad al-Manufi fi al-Islah wa-Rijalihi." *al-Manar* 10/12: 941–943.
—. 1908. "Taqriz al-Matbu'at al-Jadida." *al-Manar* 11/7: 528–539.
—. 1908. "Tarikh al-'Arab wa-l-Islam fi Silk al-Qisas wa-l-Riwayat." *al-Manar* 11/1: 64.
—. 1908. "Tatimmat al-Khutba al-Ula min Khutabina al-Islamiyya fi al-Diyar al-Suriyya (2)." *al-Manar* 11/10: 737–742.
—. 1907. "Athar 'Ilmiyya Adabiyya." *al-Manar* 10/5: 382–397.
—. 1907. "Bab al-Intiqad 'ala al-Manar." *al-Manar* 10/2: 160.
—. 1907. "Bahth fi al-Mu'tamar al-Islami li-Ta'aruf al-Muslimin wa-l-Bahth 'an Asbab Da'fihim wa-Tariq 'Alajihi wa-Tarikh al-Da'wa ilayhi." *al-Manar* 10/9: 673–682.
—. 1907–1928. "al-Da'wa ila Intiqad al-Manar." *al-Manar* 10/1: 9, *al-Manar* 11/1: 6–8, *al-Manar* 16/1: 9, *al-Manar* 17/1: 11, *al-Manar* 18/1: 31, *al-Manar* 19/1: 64, *al-Manar* 22/1: 74, *al-Manar* 24/1: 8, *al-Manar* 25/2: 160, *al-Manar* 29/1: 114.
—. 1907. "Fatihat al-Sanna al-'Ashira." *al-Manar* 10/1: 1–9.
—. 1907. "al-Haw wa-l-Huda aw al-Ladhdha wa-l-Manfa'a." *al-Manar* 10/2: 104–107.
—. 1907. "Hujjat al-Islam Abu Hamid al-Ghazali (3)." *al-Manar* 10/9: 694–705.
—. 1907. "al-Ihtifal bi-l-'Aqd al-Awwal min 'Umr al-Manar." *al-Manar* 10/9: 715–720.
—. 1907. "al-Jami'a al-Islamiyya." *al-Manar* 10/3: 200–234.
—. 1907. "Khutbat al-Duktur Diya' al-Din Ahmad." *al-Manar* 9/12: 933–939.
—. 1907. "Manafi' al-Urubiyin wa-Madarruhum fi al-Sharq." *al-Manar* 10/3: 192–199, *al-Manar* 10/4: 279–284, *al-Manar* 10/5: 340–344.
—. [1907]. "Muqaddimat al-Tab'a al-Thaniyya li-l-Mujallad al-Awwal min al-Manar." *al-Manar* 1/1–8.
—. 1907. "Sunan al-Ijtima' fi al-Hakimin wa-l-Mahkumin la-Hum wa-Jaza'uhum." *al-Manar* 10/2: 107–111.
—. 1907. "al-Ta'lim al-Dini." *al-Manar* 10/2: 123–128.
—. 1907. "Tamthil al-Qisas aw al-Tiyatru." *al-Manar* 10/1: 38–42.
—. 1907. "'Ulama' Tunis wa-Misr wa-Jami' al-Zaytuna wa-l-Azhar." *al-Manar* 10/1: 71–80.
—. 1906. "Abuna Adam wa-Madhhab Darwin." *al-Manar* 8/23: 920.
—. 1906. "al-Akhbar wa-l-Ara'." *al-Manar* 9/8: 636–640.
—. 1906. "al-'Aql wa-l-Qalb wa-l-Din." *al-Manar* 9/3: 186–195.
—. 1906. "Athar 'Ilmiyya Adabiyya." *al-Manar* 9/4: 309–316.
—. 1906. "[Athar 'Ilmiyya Adabiyya]." *al-Manar* 9/11: 872–879.
—. 1906. "al-Haqq, al-Batil wa-l-Quwa." *al-Manar* 9/1: 52–65.
—. 1906. "al-Iman Yazid wa-Yanqus." *al-Manar* 9/3: 196–204.
—. 1906. "al-Ma'arif fi Misr qabl al-Thawra al-'Urabiyya." *al-Manar* 9/7: 505–514.
—. 1906. "Maqalatan li-l-Ustadh al-Imam." *al-Manar* 9/4: 265–275.
—. 1906. "Muslimu al-Sin wa-l-Islam fi al-Yaban." *al-Manar* 8/22: 879–880.
—. 1906. "al-Shaykh Muhammad 'Abduh." *al-Manar* 9/7: 276–288.
—. 1906. "Tatimmat Sirat al-Ustadh al-Imam [2]." *al-Manar* 8/23: 891–901.
—. 1905. "al-Akhbar wa-l-Ara' (Mas'ala Makaduniyya)." *al-Manar* 8/19: 753–760.
—. 1905. "al-Akhbar wa-l-Ara'." *al-Manar* 7/21: 833–840.
—. 1905. "Athar 'Ilmiyya Adabiyya." *al-Manar* 8/7: 272–275.
—. 1905. "Athar 'Ilmiyya Adabiyya." *al-Manar* 8/11: 434–440.
—. 1905. "Athar 'Ilmiyya Adabiyya." *al-Manar* 8/13: 507–516.
—. 1905. "Bab al-Intiqad 'ala al-Manar." *al-Manar* 8/7: 279–280.

—. 1905. "Fatawa al-Manar." *al-Manar* 8/1: 18–24.
—. 1905. "Fatawa al-Manar." *al-Manar* 8/4: 150–155.
—. 1905. "al-Hayat al-Milliya bi-l-Tarbiya al-Ijtimaʿiyya." *al-Manar* 8/21: 811–819.
—. 1905. "Hayat al-Umam wa-Mawtuha." *al-Manar* 8/2: 67–71.
—. 1905. "al-Hayat al-Zawjiyya." *al-Manar* 8/3: 92–100.
—. 1905. "al-Hayat al-Zawjiyya (3)." *al-Manar* 8/5: 182–190.
—. 1905. "Khatimat al-Sanna al-Sabiʿa." *al-Manar* 7/24: 954–960.
—. 1905. "Mulakhkhas Sirat al-Ustadh al-Imam." *al-Manar* 8/10: 379–400.
—. 1905. "Rawabit al-Jinsiyya wa-l-Hayat al-Milliya wa-Falsafat al-Ijtimaʿ al-Bashari." *al-Manar* 8/20: 784–791.
—. 1905. "Taqrir Mashyakhat ʿUlamaʾ al-Iskandriyya: al-Ihsaʾ al-ʿAmm." *al-Manar* 8/21: 820–832.
—. 1905. "Tatimmat Mulakhkhas Sirat al-Ustadh al-Imam." *al-Manar* 8/11: 401–416.
—. 1905. "Tatimmat Sirat al-Ustadh al-Imam." *al-Manar* 8/13: 487–495.
—. 1904. "al-Asʾila wa-l-Ajwiba." *al-Manar* 6/23: 902–907.
—. 1904. "Athar ʿIlmiyya Adabiyya." *al-Manar* 7/13: 514–518.
—. 1904. "Bab al-Suʾal wa-l-Fatwa." *al-Manar* 7/12: 457–474.
—. 1904. "Bab al-Suʾal wa-l-Fatwa." *al-Manar* 6/22: 857–862.
—. 1904. "al-Ihtifal li-Tadhkar Taʾsis al-Dawla al-ʿAliyya." *al-Manar* 6/22: 875–880.
—. 1904. "Sabab Thanaʾ Riyad Basha ʿala al-Lurd Krumir." *al-Manar* 7/8: 317–320.
—. 1904. "Shubha ʿala al-Wahy." *al-Manar* 6/20: 788–792.
—. 1904. "al-Suʾal wa-l-Fatwa: Taʿaddud al-Zawjat." *al-Manar* 7/6: 231–240.
—. 1904. "al-Suʾal wa-l-Fatwa." *al-Manar* 7/10: 371–380.
—. 1904. "al-Taʿlim al-Islami fi Siraliyun." *al-Manar* 7/4: 153–159.
—. 1904. "al-Taqriz." *al-Manar* 7/4: 149–153.
—. 1904. "al-Taqriz." *al-Manar* 7/15: 596–600.
—. 1904. "al-Taqriz." *al-Manar* 6/21: 838–840.
—. 1904. "Taʾthir al-Jaraʾid wa-Haluha fi Misr." *al-Manar* 7/10: 399–400.
—. 1903. "Bayan al-Qurʾan wa-Balaghatuhu wa-ma Yawhim Ghayr Dhalik." *al-Manar* 6/12: 461–466.
—. 1903. "al-Ihtifal bi-Tadhkar ʿId al-Julus al-Sultani." *al-Manar* 6/12: 486–490.
—. 1903. "Masʾalat al-Nisaʾ." *al-Manar* 5/23: 881–889.
—. 1903. "Namudhaj min Dalaʾil al-Iʿjaz." *al-Manar* 6/11: 418–421.
—. 1903. "Raʾy fi Islah al-Muslimin aw Raʾyan." *al-Manar* 5/24: 921–930.
—. 1903. "al-Sultatan al-Diniyya wa-l-Madaniyya." *al-Manar* 5/22: 841–859.
—. 1902. "A-Yasumuna wa-la Yusilluna wa-hum Muʾminun?." *al-Manar* 5/17: 641–650.
—. 1902. "Bab al-ʿAqaʾid min al-Amali al-Diniyya." *al-Manar* 5/7: 245–252.
—. 1902. "Bab al-Asʾila wa-l-Ajwiba." *al-Manar* 5/18: 699–703.
—. 1902. "(al-Dars 36) Muhammad Rasul Allah wa-Khatim al-Nabiyin." *al-Manar* 5/9: 329–338.
—. 1902. "al-Hadaya wa-l-Taqariz." *al-Manar* 4/21: 836–840.
—. 1902. "al-Hadaya wa-l-Taqariz." *al-Manar* 5/14: 551–553.
—. 1902. "Masir al-Anam wa-Masir al-Islam." *al-Manar* 5/18: 681–693.
—. 1902. "Hurriyyat al-Jaraʾid wa-l-Shuʿur al-ʿAmm bi-l-Fadila fi Misr." *al-Manar* 5/1: 38–40.
—. 1902. "al-Idtihad fi al-Nasraniyya wa-l-Islam." *al-Manar* 5/11: 401–434.
—. 1902. "Khatimat al-Sanna al-Rabiʿa." *al-Manar* 4/24: 959–960.

—. 1902. "Masab ʿAzim bi-Wifat ʿAlim Hakim." *al-Manar* 5/6: 237–240.
—. 1902. "Mutill Qiraʾ al-Jaraʾid." *al-Manar* 4/23: 919–920.
—. 1902. "al-Umaraʾ wa-l-Hukkam Balaʾ al-Umma bihim." *al-Manar* 4/21: 809–813.
—. 1901. "al-Akhbar al-Tarikhiyya." *al-Manar* 4/13: 509–520.
—. 1901. "al-Akhbar al-Tarikhiyya." *al-Manar* 4/18: 714–720.
—. 1901. "Asʾila Diniyya wa-Ajwibatuha." *al-Manar* 4/6: 221–225.
—. 1901. "Bab al-Asʾila wa-l-Ajwiba al-Diniyya." *al-Manar* 4/13: 493–503.
—. 1901. "al-Dars 30: Wazaʾif al-Rusul ʿalayhim al-Salat wa-l-Salam." *al-Manar* 4/16: 615–619.
—. 1901. "al-Hadaya wa-l-Taqariz." *al-Manar* 4/16: 629–634.
—. 1901. "Ihtifal Madrasat al-Jamʿiyya al-Khayriyya al-Islamiyya bi-Misr." *al-Manar* 4/9: 347–350.
—. 1901. "al-Marʾa al-Jadida." *al-Manar* 3/32: 850–854.
—. 1901. "al-Marʾa al-Jadida: Tatimmat al-Taqariz." *al-Manar* 4/1: 26–34.
—. 1901. "al-Muhawarat bayna al-Muslih wa-l-Muqallid: al-Ijtihad wa-l-Wahda al-Islamiyya." *al-Manar* 4/6: 205–217.
—. 1901. "al-Muhawarat bayna al-Muslih wa-l-Muqallid (4)." *al-Manar* 3/32: 795–804.
—. 1901. "al-Rijal wa-l-Nisaʾ." *al-Manar* 4/13: 481–489.
—. 1901. "al-Shuʿur wa-l-Wijdan wa-Shaʿaʾir al-Umam wa-l-Adyan." *al-Manar* 4/17: 641–647.
—. 1901. "Tatimmat al-Dars 30 min Wazaʾif al-Rusul ʿalayhim al-Salam." *al-Manar* 4/18: 688–692.
—. 1900. "Athar ʿIlmiyya Adabiyya." *al-Manar* 3/3: 64–72.
—. 1900. "al-Dunya wa-l-Akhira (2)." *al-Manar* 3/7: 145–151.
—. 1900. "Fransa wa-l-Islam." *al-Manar* 3/7: 151–157.
—. 1900. "al-Haraka al-Islamiyya al-Hadira." *al-Manar* 3/10: 217–221.
—. 1900. "Hanutu wa-l-Islah al-Islami." *al-Manar* 3/15: 337–345.
—. 1900. "al-Hayra wa-l-Ghumma wa-Munashuʾhuma fi al-Umma." *al-Manar* 2/48: 753–758.
—. 1900. "Hikam al-Falasifa wa-Nawadiruhum." *al-Manar* 3/14: 326–327.
—. 1900. "al-ʿIlm wa-l-Jahl." *al-Manar* 3/24: 553–557.
—. 1900. "Istimaha wa-Tahniʾa." *al-Manar* 3/4: 96.
—. 1900. "Jamʿiyyat Shams al-Islam fi al-Qahira." *al-Manar* 2/48: 765–766.
—. 1900. "Kayfa Nantafiʿ bi-l-Mawalid wa-l-Mawasim." *al-Manar* 3/22: 525–527.
—. 1900. "Khatimat al-Sanna al-Thaniyya li-l-Manar." *al-Manar* 2/48: 767–768.
—. 1900. "Madaniyyat al-ʿArab." *al-Manar* 3/13: 289–294.
—. 1900. "Masʾalat Zayd wa-Zaynab: Idah wa-Khilasa." *al-Manar* 3/29: 714–720 [misprinted as 684–690].
—. 1900. "al-Mawalid wa-l-Muwasim." *al-Manar* 3/21: 501–502.
—. 1900. "al-Muhawarat bayna al-Muslih wa-l-Muqallid (al-Muhawara al-Ula)." *al-Manar* 3/28: 665–670 [misprinted as 635–640].
—. 1900. "al-Siyam wa-l-Tamaddun." *al-Manar* 2/43: 673–678.
—. 1900. "Ufkuha Ghariba." *al-Manar* 2/48.
—. 1900. "Tufuliyyat al-Umma wa-Ma fiha min al-Hayra wa-l-Ghumma." *al-Manar* 2/47: 737–740.
—. 1900. "al-Zakat wa-l-Tamaddun wa-l-Iman wa-l-Insaniyya." *al-Manar* 2/45: 705–713.
—. 1900. "al-Zakat wa-l-Tamaddun (2)." *al-Manar* 2/46: 722–725.
—. 1899. "al-Akhbar al-Tarikhiyya: al-Daʿwa ila al-Din." *al-Manar* 2/9: 140–144.

—. 1899. "Athar ʿIlmiyya Adabiyya." *al-Manar* 2/8: 123–125.
—. 1899. "Athar ʿIlmiyya Adabiyya." *al-Manar* 2/11: 173–174.
—. 1899. "Athar ʿIlmiyya Adabiyya: al-Kitaban al-Jalilan." *al-Manar* 2/18: 282–286.
—. 1899. "Ayyuha al-Fata." *al-Manar* 2/3: 43–46.
—. 1899. "Durus Jamʿiyyat Shams al-Islam (3)." *al-Manar* 2/30: 475–479.
—. 1899. "Falsafat al-Harb al-Hadira." *al-Manar* 2/32: 497–502.
—. 1899. "Hayat al-Islam fi Misr." *al-Manar* 2/9: 161–166.
—. 1899. "al-Hayat al-Milliya." *al-Manar* 2/20: 305–310.
—. 1899. "al-Islah al-Islami fi al-Jaraʾid." *al-Manar* 1/49: 949–956.
—. 1899. "al-Islam wa-l-Taraqqi." *al-Manar* 1/46: 885–886.
—. 1899. "al-Iʿtimad ʿala al-Nafs." *al-Manar* 2/9: 129–133.
—. 1899. "Izalat Shibha." *al-Manar* 2/16: 253–254.
—. 1899. "al-ʿIzz wa-l-Dhull." *al-Manar* 2/13: 193–199.
—. 1899. "al-Jamiʿa al-Islamiyya wa-Araʾ Kuttab al-Jaraʾid fiha." *al-Manar* 2/22: 337–345.
—. 1899. "al-Jinsiyya wa-l-Din al-Islami." *al-Manar* 2/21: 321–327.
—. 1899. "Kalima fi al-Hijab." *al-Manar* 2/24: 369–379.
—. 1899. "Khawariq al-ʿAdat wa-l-Khilaf fi al-Karamat." *al-Manar* 2/27: 417–422.
—. 1899. "Khitab al-Lurd Krumir fi al-Sudan." *al-Manar* 1/42: 827–828.
—. 1899. "Khitab Waʿzi li-l-Insan." *al-Manar* 2/1: 1–12.
—. 1899. "al-Kitaban al-Jalilan." *al-Manar* 2/18: 282–286.
—. 1899. "Muluk al-Muslimin wa-l-Tarikh." *al-Manar* 1/48: 929–930.
—. 1899. "al-Nahda al-Islamiyya fi Misr." *al-Manar* 2/16: 241–248.
—. 1899. "Ramadan al-Mubarak." *al-Manar* 1/43: 829–831.
—. 1899. "al-Sanaʾiʿ wa-l-Taʿlim wa-l-Tarbiya." *al-Manar* 1/47: 901–905.
—. 1899. "al-Shariʿa wa-l-Tabiʿa wa-l-Haqq wa-l-Batil." *al-Manar* 2/41: 641–648.
—. 1899. "Tahrif al-Kalam ʿan Mawadiʿihi: Radd ʿala Muslim Hurr al-Afkar." *al-Manar* 2/25: 385–391.
—. 1899. "Wamid Lamʿ fi Zalimat Bidaʿ." *al-Manar* 1/42: 828–829.
—. 1898. "al-Din wa-l-Madaniyya fi al-Sharq." *al-Manar* 1/14: 242–250.
—. 1898. "Istilahat Kuttab al-ʿAsr." *al-Manar* 1/1: 14–19.
—. 1898. "al-Ittihad." *al-Manar* 1/29: 547–551.
—. 1898. "al-Juyush al-Gharbiyya al-Maʿnawiyya." *al-Manar* 1/12: 299–308.
—. 1898. "Kayfa al-Sabil?!." *al-Manar* 1/7: 112–119.
—. 1898. "al-Khilafa wa-l-Khulafaʾ (1)." *al-Manar* 1/33: 628–633.
—. 1898. "Ma La Budda Minhu." *al-Manar* 1/30: 567–574.
—. 1898. "Mashruʿ Sikkat Hadid bayna Bur Saʿid wa-l-Basra." *al-Manar* 1/18: 318–331.
—. 1898. "Maʾthara Jalila." *al-Manar* 1/25: 481–482.
—. 1898. "al-Mawalid aw al-Maʿarid." *al-Manar* 1/5: 79–87.
—. 1898. "Munkarat al-Mawalid." *al-Manar* 1/6: 93–101.
—. 1898. "Nahdat Muslimi al-Hind." *al-Manar* 1/20: 369–371.
—. 1898. "al-Namima wa-l-Siʿaya." *al-Manar* 1/14: 236–242.
—. 1898. "al-Quwa fi al-Mal." *al-Manar* 1/13: 225–230.
—. 1898. "Raʾy fi Mawduʿ al-Manar [transl. from the Turkish]." *al-Manar* 1/24: 453–460.
—. 1898. "Risalat al-Tawhid." *al-Manar* 1/13: 231–233.
—. 1898. "Riwayat al-Yatim." *al-Manar* 1/7: 129–133.
—. 1898. "Sayhat Haqq." *al-Manar* 1/13: 217–225.

—. 1898. “al-Shiʿr wa-l-Shuʿaraʾ.” *al-Manar* 1/10: 170–177.
—. 1898. “Sultat Mashyakhat al-Tariq al-Ruhiyya.” *al-Manar* 1/22: 404–410.
—. 1898. “Tabsira wa-Dhikra li-Qawm Yuʿqilun: fi Bayan anna Saʿadat al-Umma fi al-Tahdhib.” *al-Manar* 1/4: 69–77.
Rida, Salih Mukhlis. 1920. “Taqriz al-Matbuʿat al-Jadida.” *al-Manar* 21/7: 389–391.
—. 1919. “Taqriz al-Matbuʿat al-Jadida.” *al-Manar* 21/6: 327–336.
—. 1913. “Taqriz al-Matbuʿat al-Jadida.” *al-Manar* 17/1: 63–67.
—. 1912. “al-Taqariz.” *al-Manar* 15/9: 703–716.
—. 1912. “al-Taqriz wa-l-Intiqad.” *al-Manar* 15/4: 305–312.
—. 1910. “al-Taqariz.” *al-Manar* 13/8: 634–635.
Saʿid, ʿAbd al-Hamid. 1930. “Nidaʾ ila Muluk al-Islam wa-Shuʿubihi Jamiʿan.” *al-Manar* 31/3: 205–218.
Saʿid, Muhammad. 1913. “al-Islam wa-Hurriyat al-ʿAqida wa-Kitab al-Daʿwa al-Islamiyya.” *al-Manar* 16/12: 929–932.
Saʾih Muhibb li-l-Manar. 1903. “Siraliyun.” *al-Manar* 6/19: 756–760.
al-Shatibi, Abu Ishaq. 1914. “Dukhul al-Ibtidaʿ fi al-ʿAdiyyat.” *al-Manar* 17/10: 753–772.
—. 1914 “Fasl.” *al-Manar* 17/6: 433–454, *al-Manar* 17/7: 513–534, *al-Manar* 17/8: 593–615.
—. 1913. “al-Bab al-Awwal min Kitab al-Iʿtisam.” *al-Manar* 17/1: 54–63.
Shaykh Mashayikh al-Turuq. 1905. “Islah al-Turuq al-Sufiyya.” *al-Manar* 8/9: 353–355.
Sidqi, Muhammad Tawfiq. 1915. “Madrasat Dar al-Daʿwa wa-l-Irshad, Durus Sunan al-Kaʾinat (7).” *al-Manar* 18/5: 353–371.
—. 1913. “Nazra fi Kutub al-ʿAhd al-Jadid wa-fi ʿAqaʾid al-Nasraniyya.” *al-Manar* 16/4: 281–299, *al-Manar* 16/5: 353–378, *al-Manar* 16/6: 433–449, *al-Manar* 16/7: 521–534, *al-Manar* 16/8: 588–600, *al-Manar* 16/9: 689–703, *al-Manar* 16/10: 777–789, *al-Manar* 16/11: 833–838.
—. 1912. “Bashaʾir ʿIsa wa-Muhammad fi al-ʿAhdayn al-ʿAtiq wa-l-Jadid (3).” *al-Manar* 15/7: 494–510.
—. 1910. “Hijab al-Marʾa fi al-Islam.” *al-Manar* 13/10: 771–778.
—. 1905. “al-Din fi Nazar al-ʿAql al-Sahih.” *al-Manar* 8/9: 330–335, *al-Manar* 8/11: 417–427, *al-Manar* 8/13: 495–500, *al-Manar* 8/18: 693–700, *al-Manar* 8/19: 721–744, *al-Manar* 8/20: 771–783.
Tahir, Muhammad. 1914. “Maqam ʿIsa (Yasuʿ) al-Masih ʿalayhi al-Salam fi al-Nasraniyya wa-l-Islam.” *al-Manar* 17/2: 142–147.
al-Taʿi, Abu Zabid. 1906. “Wasf al-Asad.” *al-Manar* 9/3: 214–218.
al-Tunisi, Muhammad al-Khidr. 1921. “al-Khayal fī l-Shiʿr al-ʿArabi (2).” *al-Manar* 22/3: 218–227.
al-ʿUrwa al-Wuthqa. 1906. “Madi al-Umma wa-Hadiruha wa-ʿAlaj ʿIlaliha.” *al-Manar* 9/9: 664–672.
—. 1901. “al-Fadaʾil wa-l-Radhaʾil [the title is Rida’s].” *al-Manar* 4/2: 41–50.
Wajdi, Muhammad Farid. 1902. “Kayfa Yakun al-Mustaqbal li-l-Muslimin.” *al-Manar* 5/17: 656–667.
al-Yafiʿi, Salih bin ʿAli. 1905. “Shakl Hukumat al-Islam wa-Daʿf al-Muslimin bi-Istibdad al-Hukkam.” *al-Manar* 7/23: 899–912.
—. 1904. “Asbab Daʿf al-Muslimin wa-ʿAlajuhu.” *al-Manar* 7/14: 540–550, *al-Manar* 7/15: 581–590.

Zaghlul, ʿUmar Khayri Efendi. 1899. "Kana Ya Ma Kana." *al-Manar* 2/23: 360 – 363.
al-Zahrawi, ʿAbd al-Hamid. 1908. "[Khadija Umm al-Muʾminin:] al-Fasl al-Awwal [wa-l-Thani wa-l-Thalith]." *al-Manar* 11/2: 145 – 160.
—. 1908. "[Khadija Umm al-Muʾminin:] al-Fasl al-Sabiʿ [wa-l-Thamin wa-l-Tasiʿ]." *al-Manar* 11/5: 383 – 451.
—. 1906. "Kayfa yakun al-Naqd? Kalam fi 'Kitab al-Taʿlim wa-l-Irshad' wa-Masaʾil Shatta." *al-Manar* 9/10: 788 – 795.
—. 1903 – 1904. "Nizam al-Hubb wa-l-Bughd." *al-Manar* 6/7: 270 – 274, *al-Manar* 6/8: 298 – 302, *al-Manar* 6/9: 335 – 341, *al-Manar* 6/13: 513 – 517, *al-Manar* 6/14: 552 – 558, *al-Manar* 6/16: 621 – 625, *al-Manar* 6/19: 745 – 752, *al-Manar* 6/20: 795 – 799, *al-Manar* 6/22: 863 – 869, *al-Manar* 6/23: 910 – 916, *al-Manar* 7/4: 147 – 149, *al-Manar* 7/5: 187 – 193, *al-Manar* 7/6: 229 – 233, *al-Manar* 7/7: 261 – 266, 271 – 275.
al-Zankluni, ʿAli Surur. 1931. "Naskh al-Shariʿa al-Muhammadiyya li-Ma Qabluha wa-Baʿthat Muhammad Khatim al-Nabiyin li-l-Nas Ajmaʿin." *al-Manar* 31/8: 608 – 618.

b) Other Arabic Publications

ليس العلم ما حفظ، العلم ما نفع

ʿAbd al-Raziq, ʿAli. 1925. *al-Islam wa-Usul al-Hukm: Bahth fi al-Khilafa wa-l-Hukuma fi al-Islam*. Cairo: Matbaʿat Misr.
ʿAbduh, Muhammad. 2006 [1881]. "al-Kutub al-ʿIlmiyya wa-Ghayruha." In Rashid Rida: *Tarikh al-Ustadh al-Imam al-Shaykh Muhammad ʿAbduh*, vol. 2: 153 – 157. Cairo: Dar al-Fadila.
—. 1993. *al-Aʿmal al-Kamila li-l-Imam al-Shaykh Muhammad ʿAbduh*; taḥqīq wa-taqdīm Muhammad ʿImara. 5 vols. Cairo: Dar al-Shuruq.
—. 1323 h [1905/1906]. *al-Islam wa-l-Nasraniyya maʿa al-ʿIlm wa-l-Madaniyya*. Cairo: Matbaʿat al-Manar.
Abu Hamdan, Samir. 1992. *al-Shaykh Rashid Rida wa-l-Khitab al-Islami al-Muʿtadil*. Beirut: al-Sharika al-ʿAlamiyya li-l-Kitab.
al-Afghani, Jamal al-Din. 2002. "al-Radd ʿala al-Dahriyin." In *Rasaʾil fi al-Falsafa wa-l-ʿIrfan* (= *al-Athar al-Kamila*, vol. 2): 127 – 198. Cairo: Maktabat al-Shuruq al-Duwaliyya.
al-Afghani, Jamal al-Din and ʿAbduh, Muhammad. 2002. *al-ʿUrwa al-Wuthqa*; ed. Sayyid Hadi Khusr Wishahi. Cairo: Maktabat al-Shuruq al-Duwaliyya.
al-ʿAjm, Rafiq (ed.). 2002. *Mawsuʿat Mustalahat al-Fikr al-ʿArabi wa-l-Islami al-Hadith wa-l-Muʿasir; al-Juzʾ al-Thani: 1890 – 1940*. Beirut: Maktabat Lubnan Nashirun.
Al Hamza, Khalid bin Fawzi bin ʿAbd al-Hamid. 1415 h. [1994/95]. *Muhammad Rashid Rida: Tawd wa-Islah, Daʿwa wa-Daʿiyya, 1282 – 1354 h.: Jihaduhu fi Khidmat al-ʿAqida wa-Athruhu fi al-Ittijahat al-Fikriyya al-Muʿasira*. Alexandria: Dar al-ʿUlamaʾ al-Salaf.
Amin, Qasim. 1901. *al-Marʾa al-Jadida*. Cairo: Matbaʿat al-Maʿarif.
—. 1899. *Tahrir al-Marʾa*. Cairo: Maktabat at-Taraqqi.
Amin, ʿUthman. 1944. *Muhammad ʿAbduh*. Cairo: Dar Ihyaʾ al-Kutub al-ʿArabiyya.
al-ʿAntabali, Ashraf ʿAyd. n.g. "Rafiq al-ʿAzm: Rajul al-Islah al-Siyasi wa-l-Fikri." In *Ikhwanwiki*. http://www.ikhwanwiki.com/index.php?title=رفيق_العظم.#.D8.A3.D9.88.D9.84.D8.A7_:_.D8.A7. D9.84.D9.85.D9.82.D8.AF.D9.85.D8.A9 (last accessed July 19, 2017).

Arslan, Shakib. 1937. *al-Sayyid Muhammad Rashid Rida aw Ikha' Arba'in Sanna*. Damascus: Matba'at Ibn Zaydun.

—. 1936. *Limadha Ta'akhkhara al-Muslimun wa-Limadha Taqaddama Ghayruhum*. Damascus: Matba'at Ibn Zaydun.

—. n.d. *Limadha Ta'akhkhara al-Muslimun wa-Limadha Taqaddama Ghayruhum*. Beirut: Dar Maktabat al-Hayat.

al-'Azm, Rafiq. 2012. *al-Bayyan fi al-Tamaddun wa-Asbab al-'Umran*; ed. 'Abd al-Rahman Hilali. Alexandria/Beirut/Cairo: Maktabat al-Iskandriyya/Dar al-Kitab al-Lubnani/Dar al-Kitab al-Misri.

—. 1988. *al-Durus al-Hikamiyya li-l-Nashi'a al-Islamiyya*; ed. Mahmud Radawi. al-Sa'udiyya: Jami'at al-Imam Muhammad Bin Sa'ud al-Islamiyya/Idarat al-Thaqafa wa-l-Nashr.

—. 1344 h. [1925]. *Majmu'at Athar Rafiq Bik al-'Azm; vol. 1: Kitab al-Sawanih al-Fikriyya fi al-Mabahith al-'Ilmiyya; Kitab Tarikh al-Siyasa al-Islamiyya; al-Jami'a al-'Uthmaniyya wa-l-'Asabiyya al-Turkiyya aw al-Ta'lif bayna al-Turk wa-l-'Arab; vol. 2: Khutab Rafiq Bik al-'Azm al-Tarikhiyya; Rasa'il Rafiq Bik al-'Azm; al-Jami'a al-Islamiyya wa-Uruba*; ed. by 'Uthman al-'Azm, with a biography by Rashid Rida. Cairo: Matba'at al-Manar.

—. 1912. *Risala fi Bayan Kayfiyyat Intishar al-Adyan*. Cairo: Matba'at al-Islam.

—. 1328 h. [1911/1912]. *al-Durus al-Hikamiyya li-l-Nashi'a al-Islamiyya*. Damascus: al-Matba'a al-Wataniyya.

—. 1910. *al-Khutab al-Ta'rikhiyya*. Cairo: Matba'at al-Manar.

—. 1327 h. [1909]. *Ashhar Mashahir al-Islam fi al-Harb wa-l-Siyasa*. Cairo: Matba'a Hindiyya.

—. 1907. *al-Jami'a al-Islamiyya wa-Uruba*. Cairo: Matba'a Hindiyya.

—. 1324 h. [1906]. *Qıwam-i Islam: Tanbih al-Afham ila Matalib al-Hayat al-Ijtima'iyya wa-l-Islam*; transl. Izmirli Hocazade Mehmed Ubeydallah. Cairo: n.g.

—. 1900. *Tanbih al-Afham ila Matalib al-Hayat al-Ijtima'iyya wa-l-Islam*. Cairo: Matba'at al-Mawsu'at.

—. 1317 h. [1899/1900]. *al-Durus al-Hikamiyya li-l-Nashi'a al-Islamiyya*. Cairo: Matba'at al-Mu'ayyad wa-l-Adab.

—. 1304 h. [1886/1887]. *Kitab al-Bayan fi al-Tamaddun wa-Asbab al-'Umran*. Cairo: al-Matba'a al-I'lamiyya.

al-Banna, Jamal. 2003. *al-Islam Din wa-Umma wa-laysa Dunyan wa-Dawla*. Cairo: Dar al-Fikr al-Islami.

al-Batush, Basam 'Abd al-Salam. 2007. *Rafiq al-'Azm: Mufakkiran wa-Muslihan; Dirasa fi Fikrihi wa-Dawrihi fi al-Haraka al-Islahiyya al-'Arabiyya*. 'Amman: Dar Kunuz al-Ma'rifa li-l-Nashr wa-l-Tawzi'.

—. 2004. *al-Fikr al-Ijtima'i fi Misr: Dirasa fi al-Khitab al-Ijtima'i al-Islami wa-l-Libarali wa-l-Yasari fi Misr Khilal Fitra ma bayna al-Harbayn al-'Alamiyyatayn*. al-Urdun: 'Alam al-Kutub al-Hadith.

Birbari, Nasim Efendi. 1897. "al-Susiyulujiyya ay 'Ilm al-Ijtima' al-Insani." *al-Muqtataf* 21/8: 574–579, 21/9: 674–679, 21/11: 825–830.

al-Bustani, Butrus. 2000 [1876]. *Da'irat al-Ma'arif: Encyclopedie Arabe*. Beirut: Dar al-Ma'rifa.

—. 1981 [1869]. "Khitab fi al-Hay'a al-Ijtima'iyya wa-l-Muqabala bayna al-'Awa'id al-'Arabiyya wa-l-Ifranjiyya." In *al-'Alim Butrus al-Bustani. Dirasa wa-Watha'iq* ed. by Jan Daya: 163–187. Beirut: Manshurat Majallat Fikr.

——. 1977 [1870]. *Muhit al-Muhit: Qamus Mutawwal li-l-Lugha al-ʿArabiyya*. Beirut: Maktabat Lubnan.

al-Bustani, Salim. n.d. *Iftitahat Majallat al-Jinan, vol. 2 (1872–1884)*, ed. Yusuf Qizman Khuri. Beirut: Dar al-Hamra.

Demolins, Edmond. 1899. *Sirr Taqaddum al-Injliz*; transl. Ahmad Fathi Zaghlul. Cairo: Matbaʿat al-Maʿarif.

al-Din, Hazim Zakariyya Muhyi. 2007. *Mafhum al-Sunan al-Ilahiyya fi al-Fikr al-Islami: al-Sayyid Muhammad Rashid Rida Namudhajan*. Damascus: Dar al-Nawadir li-l-Nashr wa-l-Tawziʿ.

Dughaym, Samih (ed.). 2000. *Mawsuʿat Mustalahat al-Fikr al-ʿArab wa-l-Islami al-Hadith wa-l-Muʿasir; al-Juzʾ al-Awwal: 1700–1890*. Beirut: Maktabat Lubnan Nashirun.

Esquiros, Alphonse. 1331 h. [1913]. al-Tarbiya al-Istiqlaliyya aw Amil al-Qarn al-Tasiʿa ʿAshar; transl. ʿAbd al-ʿAziz Muhammad. Cairo: Matbaʿat al-Manar.

al-Fahdawi, Khalid. 2007. *al-ʿAlama Muhammad Rashid Rida: ʿAsruhu, Tahdiyatuhu, Manhajuhu al-Islahi*. Damascus: Dar Safahat.

al-Fawal, Salah Mustafa. 2000. *al-Madkhal li-ʿIlm al-Ijtimaʿ al-Islami*. Cairo: Dar Gharuba li-l-Tibaʿa wa-l-Nashr wa-l-Tawziʿ.

Ghanim, Ibrahim al-Bayyumi and al-Jawhari, Salah al-Din (eds.). 2009. *al-Imam Muhammad ʿAbduh: Miʾat ʿAm ʿala Rahilihi, 1905–2005: Aʿmal wa-Munaqashat al-Nadwa al-Fikriyya allati Nazamatha Maktabat al-Iskandriyya 4–5.12.2005*. Cairo/Alexandria/Beirut: Dar al-Kitab al-Misri/Maktabat al-Iskandriyya/Dar al-Kitab al-Lubnani.

al-Haddad, Niqula. 2002 [1920]. *al-Ishtirakiyya*. n.g.: Dar al-Mada [?] li-l-Thaqafa wa-l-Nashr.

——. 1924–1925. *ʿIlm al-Ijtimaʿ: Hayat al-Hayʾa al-Ijtimaʿiyya wa-Tatawwuruha*. 2 vols. Cairo: al-Matbaʿa al-ʿAsriyya.

Hallaq, Muhammad Ratib. 1995. *ʿAbd al-Hamid al-Zahrawi: Dirasa fi Fikrihi*. Damascus: Ittihad al-Kuttab al-ʿArab.

Hava, J. G. 1915. *al-Faraʾid*. Beirut: Dar al-Mashriq.

Husayn, Taha. 1925. *Falsafat Ibn Khaldun al-Ijtimaʿiyya: Tahlil wa-Naqd*; transl. Muhammad ʿAbdallah ʿAnan. Cairo: Matbaʿat al-Iʿtimad.

Ibn Khaldun, ʿAbd al-Rahman. 2005. *al-Muqaddima*; ed. ʿAbd al-Salam al-Shaddadi. Casablanca: Bayt al-Funun wa-l-ʿUlum wa-l-Adab.

Ibn Taymiyya, Ahmad ibn ʿAbd al-Halim. 1349 h. [1930]. *Haqiqat Madhhab al-Ittihadiyin wa-Wahdat al-Wujud, wa-Bayan Butlanuhu bi-l-Barahin al-Naqliyya wa-l-ʿAqliyya*. Cairo: Matbaʿat al-Manar.

——. 1349 h. [1930]. *Kitab Madhhab al-Salaf al-Qawim fi Tahqiq Masʾalat Kalam Allah al-Karim: Majmuʿ Fatawa Ibn Taymiyya wa-Ma Haqqaqahu fi Mawadiʿ min Kutubihi wa-Muʾallafatihi*; ed. Rashid Rida. Cairo: Matbaʿat al-Manar.

ʿImara, Muhammad. 2011. *al-Shaykh Muhammad Rashid Rida wa-l-ʿAlmaniyya wa-l-Suhyuniyya wa-l-Taʾifiyya*. Cairo: Dar al-Salam li-l-Tibaʿa wa-l-Nashr wa-l-Tawziʿ wa-l-Tarjama.

Ismaʿil, Zaki Muhammad. 1981. *Nahwa ʿIlm al-Ijtimaʿ al-Islami*. Alexandria: Dar al-Matbuʿat al-Jadida.

Jawish, Fathulla. 1894. "al-Marʾa fi al-Hayʾa al-Ijtimaʿiyya." *Lisan al-Hal* 1601 (April 4): 4.

al-Kawtharani, Wajih. 1980. *Mukhtarat Siyasiyya min Majallat al-Manar*. Beirut: Dar al-Taliʿa.

Le Bon, Gustave. n.d. *al-Hadara al-Misriyya*; transl. Muhammad Sadiq Rustum. Cairo: al-Matbaʿa al-ʿAsriyya.

—. 2005 [1909]. *Ruh al-Ijtima'*; transl. Ahmad Fathi Zaghlul. Cairo: al-Majlis al-A'la li-l-Thaqafa.
—. 1913. *Sirr Tatawwur al-Umam*; transl. Ahmad Fathi Zaghlul. Cairo: Matba'at al-Ma'arif.
—. 1909. *Ruh al-Ijtima'*; transl. Ahmad Fathi Zaghlul. Cairo: Matba'at al-Sha'b.
Mahmud, Ra'd Muhammad. 2013. *al-Imam Muhammad Rashid Rida wa-Ikhtiyaratuhu al-Fiqhiyya min Khilal Tafsirihi al-Manar.* Baghdad: Diwan al-Waqf al-Sunni.
Maktabat al-Manar. 1914. *Fihris Maktabat al-Manar li-Ashabiha Rida wa-Khatib wa-Qatalan.* Cairo: Matba'at al-Manar.
Malla, Ahmad Salah. 2013. *Judhur al-Usuliyya al-Islamiyya fi Misr al-Mu'asira: Rashid Rida wa-Majallat al-Manar.* Cairo: Misr al-'Arabiyya li-l-Nashr wa-l-Tawzi'.
Musa, Salama. 1962 [1913]. *al-Ishtirakiyya.* Cairo: Salama Musa li-l-Nashr wa-l-Tawzi'.
Nassar, Nasif. 2009 [1975]. *Tariq al-Istiqlal al-Falsafi: Sabil al-Fikr al-'Arabi ila al-Hurriyya wa-l-Ibda'.* Beirut: Dar al-Tali'a.
—. 2003 [1978]. *Mafhum al-Umma bayna al-Din wa-l-Tarikh: Dirasa fi Madlul al-Umma fi al-Turath al-'Arabi al-Islami.* Beirut: Dar al-Tali'ya li-l-Tiba'a wa-l-Nashr.
—. 1995 [1970]. *Nahwa Mujtama' Jadid: Muqaddimat Asasiyya fi Naqd al-Mujtama' al-Ta'ifi.* Beirut: Dar al-Tali'a.
Qarni, 'Izzat. 2006. *Tarikh al-Fikr al-Siyasi wa-l-Ijtima'i fi Misr al-Haditha (1834–1914).* Cairo: al-Hay'a al-Misriyya al-'Amma li-l-Kitab.
al-Ra'i, al-Ab Basim. 2011. *al-Mujtama' wa-l-Dawla: Ashkaluhuma wa-Tahawwuluhuma fi al-Falsafa al-Siyasiyya al-Gharbiyya al-Mu'asira.* Beirut: Dar al-Farabi.
Rida, Rashid. 2008. *Muhawarat al-Muslih wa-l-Muqallid wa-l-Wahda al-Islamiyya.* Cairo/Minneapolis: Dar al-Nashr li-l-Jami'at/Dar Almanar.
—. 2007. *Nida' li-l-Jins al-Latif: fi Huquq al-Nisa' fi al-Islam wa-Hazzuhunna min al-Islah al-Muhammadi al-'Amm.* Cairo/Minneapolis: Dar al-Nashr li-l-Jami'at/Dar Almanar.
—. 1990. *Tafsir al-Qur'an al-Hakim (Tafsir al-Manar).* 12 vols. Cairo: al-Hay'a al-Misriyya al-'Amma li-l-Kitab.
—. 1406 h. [1985/86]. *al-Wahy al-Muhammadi: Thubut al-Nubuwa wa-l-Qur'an wa-Da'wat Shu'ub al-Madaniyya ila al-Islam Din al-Akhira li-l-Insaniyya wa-l-Salam.* Beirut: Mu'assasat 'Izz al-Din li-l-Tiba'a wa-l-Nashr.
—. 1983. *Muhammad Rashid Rida*; ikhtara al-nuṣūṣ wa-qaddamaha Adunis wa-Khalida Sa'id. Beirut: Dar al-'Ilm li-l-Milayin.
—. 1970–1971. *Fatawa al-Imam Muhammad Rashid Rida*; jama'aha wa-ḥaqqaqaha Salah al-Din al-Munajjid wa-Yusuf Q. Khuri. Beirut: Dar al-Kitab al-Jadid.
—. 1948–1961. *Tafsir al-Qur'an al-Hakim, al-Mushtahir bi-Tafsir al-Manar.* 12 vols. (various re-editions). Cairo: Maktabat al-Qahira.
—. 1933. *al-Wahy al-Muhammadi.* Cairo: Matba'at al-Manar.
—. 1926. *Tarikh al-Ustadh al-Shaykh Muhammad 'Abduh.* 3 vols. Cairo: Matba'at al-Manar.
—. 1922. *al-Khilafa aw al-Imama al-'Uzma: Mabahith shar'iyya siyasiyya ijtima'iyya islahiyya.* Cairo: Matba'at al-Manar.
—. 1329 h. [1911]. *al-Muslimun wa-l-Qubt wa-l-Mu'tamar al-Islami: Majmu' Maqalat Ijtima'iyya Nushirat fi al-Mu'ayyad wa l-Manar.* Cairo: Matba'at al-Manar.
—. 1322 h. [1904]. *Shubahat al-Nasara wa-Hujaj al-Islam: Maqalat fi al-Radd 'ala al-Nasara Tunshar fi Majallat 'al-Manar' al-Islami.* Cairo: Matba'at al-Manar.
Sa'b, Adib. 1995. *al-Din wa-l-Mujtama': Ru'ya Mustaqbaliyya.* Beirut: Dar al-Nahar.
al-Sa'id, Rif'at. 2003. *al-Zu'amat al-Siyasiyya al-Misriyya.* Cairo: Akhbar al-Yawm.

Salim, Salma Mirshaq. 2013. *Niqula al-Haddad: al-Adib al-'Alim*. Beirut: Dar al-Jadid.
al-Samahan, Faysal bin 'Abd al-'Aziz. 2011. *al-Imam al-Sayyid Muhammad Rashid Rida fi Mayadin al-Muwajaha*. Kuwayt: Maktabat Ahl al-Athr li-l-Nashr wa-l-Tawzi'.
al-Samaluti, Nabil. 2007. *Bina' al-Mujtama' al-Islami wa-Nuzumuhu*. Beirut: Dar wa-Maktabat al-Hilal.
—. 1970. *al-Manhaj al-Islami fi Dirasat al-Mujtama': Dirasat fi 'Ilm al-Ijtima' al-Islami*. Cairo: Dar al-Shuruq.
Sawa'i, Muhammad. 2013. *al-Hadatha wa-Mustalahat al-Nahda al-'Arabiyya fi al-Qarn al-Tasi'a 'Ashar: Dirasa fi Mufradat Ahmad Faris al-Shidyaq fi Jaridat "al-Jawa'ib"*. Beirut: al-Mu'assasa al-'Arabiyya li-l-Dirasat wa-l-Nashr.
—. 1999. *Azmat al-Mustalah al-'Arabi fi al-Qarn al-Tasi' 'Ashar: Muqaddima Tarikhiyya 'Amma*. Damascus/Beirut: al-Ma'had al-Fransi li-l-Dirasat al-'Arabiyya bi-Dimashq/Dar al-Gharb al-Islami.
al-Sayyid, Ridwan. 2006. *al-Jama'a wa-l-Mujtama' wa-l-Dawla: Sultat al-Idiyulujiya fi al-Majal al-Siyasi al-'Arabi al-Islami*. Beirut: Dar al-Kitab al-'Arabi.
—. 1984. *al-Umma wa-l-Jama'a wa-l-Sulta: Dirasa fi al-Fikr al-Siyasi al-'Arabi al-Islami*. Beirut: Dar Iqra'.
al-Sharabasi, Ahmad. 1977. *Rashid Rida: al-Sahafi, al-Mufassir, al-Sha'ir, al-Lughawi*. Cairo: al-Hay'a al-'Amma li Shu'un al-Matabi' al-Amiriyya.
—. 1976. *Rashid Rida: al-Adib al-Katib al-Islami*. Cairo: al-Hay'a al-'Amma li-Shu'un al-Matabi' al-Amiriyya.
—. 1970. *Rashid Rida, Sahib al-Manar: 'Asruhu wa-Hayatuhu wa-Masadir Thaqafatihi*. Cairo: Matabi' al-Ahram al-Tijariyya.
al-Shawabika, Ahmad. 1989. *Muhammad Rashid Rida wa-Dawruhu fi al-Hayat al-Fikriyya wa-l-Siyasiyya*. 'Amman: Dar 'Ammar.
Spencer, Herbert. 1308 h. [1890)]. *al-Tarbiya*; transl. Muhammad al-Siba'i. Cairo: al-Jarida.
al-Tuwayrani, Hasan Husni. 1891. *Maqala fi Ijmal al-Kalam 'ala Mas[']alat al-Khilafa bayna Ahl al-Islam*. Cairo: Matba'at al-Mahrusa.
—. 1888. *al-Nashr al-Zahri fi Rasa'il al-Nasr al-Dahri*. [Istanbul]: Mahmud Bey.
'Umar, Muhammad. 1320 h./1902. *Hadir al-Misriyin aw Sirr Ta'akhkhurihim*. Cairo: al-Muqtataf.
Wafi, 'Ali 'Abd al-Wahid. 1951. *al-Falsafa al-Ijtima'iyya li-Ibn Khaldun wa-Auguste Comte*. Cairo: Matba'at Lajnat al-Bayan al-'Arabi.
Wajdi, Muhammad Farid. 1971. *Da'irat Ma'arif al-Qarn al-'Ashrin*. Beirut: Dar al-Fikr.
Yasushi, Kusuji, Ibish, Yusuf Husayn and Khuri, Yusuf Quzma (eds.). 1998. *Fihris Majallat al-Manar, 1898–1935*. Beirut/Tokio: Turath/Mashru' Dirasat al-Hadara al-Islamiyya.
al-Zahrawi, 'Abd al-Hamid. 1995–1997. *al-A'mal al-Kamila*; i'dād wa-taḥqīq 'Abdallah Nubhan. 5 vols. Damascus: Wizarat al-Thaqafa.
—. 1328 h. [1910/11]. *Khadija Umm al-Mu'minin*. Cairo: Matba'at al-Manar.
Zajm, Zayn al-'Abidin Shams al-Din. 2007. *al-Dawla wa-l-Mujtama' fi Misr fi al-Qarn al-Tasi' 'Ashar*. Cairo: Dar al-Kutub.
Zaydan, Jurji. 1901–1906. *Tarikh al-Tamaddun al-Islami*. 5 vols. Cairo: Dar al-Hilal.

c) Publications in Other Languages

"I laughed and discovered something that has served me well since: the more we threaten thought and language with silence, or simply seek to demote them in our lives from the ludicrous pedestal on which our culture and background have placed them, then the more fertile, in their need to justify and assert themselves, they become. Reflection is never more exciting than when reflecting on the damage reflection does [...]."
– Tim Parks, *Teach Us to Sit Still*

Abaza, Mona. 1998. "Southeast Asia and the Middle East: Al-Manār and Islamic Modernity." In *From the Mediterranean to the Chinese Sea: Miscellaneous Notes* ed. by Claude Guillot, Denys Lombard and Roderich Ptak: 93–111. Wiesbaden: Harrasowitz.

Abbé Martinet, [Antoine]. 1850. *Religion in Society or The Solution of Great Problems: Placed within the Reach of Every Mind; translated from the French of the Abbé Martinet; with an introduction by John Hughes.* New York: D. & J. Sadler.

Abbey, Ruth. 2010. "*A Secular Age:* The Missing Question Mark." In *The Taylor Effect. Responding to a [sic] Secular Age* ed. by Ian Leask, Eoin Cassidy, Alan Kearns, Fainche Ryan and Mary Shanahan: 8–25. Newcastle upon Tyne: Cambridge Scholars Publishing.

ʿAbd al-Raziq, ʿAli. 1994 *L'Islam et les fondements du pouvoir*; transl. Abdou Filali-Ansary. Paris/Cairo: Éditions La Découverte/CEDEJ.

ʿAbd al-Raziq, ʿAli, Hans-Georg Ebert, Assem Hefny. 2010. *Der Islam und die Grundlagen der Herrschaft: Übersetzung und Kommentar des Werkes von Alî ʿAbd ar-Râziq.* Frankfurt a.M. et al.: Peter Lang.

ʿAbduh, Muhammad. 2002. "Laws Should Change in Accordance with the Conditions of Nations *and* The Theology of Unity." In *Modernist Islam, 1840–1940: A Sourcebook* ed. by Charles Kurzman: 50–60. Oxford/New York: Oxford University Press.

—. 1966. *The Theology of Unity*; transl. Ishaq Musaʾad and Kenneth Cragg. London: Allen & Uwin.

—. 1925. *Rissalat al Tawhid (Exposé de la religion musulmane).* Paris: Geuthner. trad. de l'arabe avec une introd. sur la vie et les idées du cheikh Mohammed Abdou par B. Michel et Moustapha Abdel Razik.

Abdul Rauf, Muhammad. 1967. "Some Notes on the Qur'anic use of the terms Islām and Imān." *The Muslim World* 57: 94–102.

Abdullahi, Ali Arazeem and Salawu, Bashir. 2012. "Ibn Khaldun: A Forgotten Sociologist?." *South African Review of Sociology* 43/3: 24–40.

Abou Sheishaa, Mohamed Ali Mohamed. 2001. "A Study of the Fatwa by Rashid Rida on the Translation of the Qurʾan." *Journal of the Society for Qurʾanic Studies* 1/1 https://www.academia.edu/6481246/A_STUDY_OF_THE_FATWA_BY_RASHID_RIDĀ_ON_THE_TRANSLATION_OF_THE_QURĀN (accessed Aug. 17, 2017).

Abu-Manneh, Butrus. 1980. "The Christians between Ottomanism and Syrian Nationalism: The Ideas of Butrus Al-Bustani." *International Journal of Middle East Studies* 11/3: 287–304.

Abushouk, Ahmed Ibrahim. 2007. "Al-Manār and the Ḥadhramī Elite in the Malay-Indonesian World: Challenge and Response." *Journal of the Royal Asiatic Society of Great Britain & Ireland* 17/3: 301–322.

Abu-ʿUksa, Wael. 2016. *Freedom in the Arab World: Concepts and Ideologies in Arabic Thought in the Nineteenth Century.* Cambridge: Cambridge University Press.

Abu-Zahra, Nadia. 2007. "Al-Manar (1898): A Journal Inspired by Afghani and ʿAbduh." *Maghreb Review* 32/2–3: 218–232.

Adal, Raja. 2008. "Constructing Transnational Islam. The East-West Network of Shakib Arslan." In *Intellectuals in the Modern Islamic World. Transmission, Transformation, Communication* ed. by Stéphane A. Dudoignon, Komatsu Hisao and Kosugi Yasushi: 176–210. London/New York: Routledge.

Adams, Charles. 1933. *Islam and Modernism in Egypt. A Study of the Reform Movement Inaugurated by Muḥammad ʿAbduh.* London: Oxford University Press.

al-Afghani, Sayyid Jamal al-Din. 2002. "Lecture on Teaching and Learning *and* Answer to Renan." In *Modernist Islam, 1840–1940: A Sourcebook* ed. by Charles Kurzman. 103–110. Oxford/New York: Oxford University Press.

Ahmad, Aziz. 1960. "Sayyid Aḥmad Khān, Jamāl al-dīn al-Afghānī and Muslim India." *Studia Islamica* 13: 55–78.

Ahmed, Jamal Mohammed. 1968. *The Intellectual Origins of Egyptian Nationalism.* London: Oxford University Press.

al-Ahsan, Abdullah. 1992. *Ummah or Nation? Identity Crisis in Contemporary Muslim Society.* Leicester: The Islamic Foundation.

Alatas, Syed Farid. 2006. "Ibn Khaldūn and Contemporary Sociology." *International Sociology* 21/6: 782–795.

—. 2014. *Applying Ibn Khaldūn: The Recovery of a Lost Tradition in Sociology.* London: Routledge.

Ali, Souad T. 2009. *A Religion, Not a State: Ali ʿAbd al-Raziq's Islamic Justification of Political Secularism.* Salt Lake City: The University of Utah Press.

Ameer, Ali. 1952 [1891]. *The Spirit of Islam: a History of the Evolution and Ideals of Islam; with a Life of the Prophet.* London: Christophers.

Amin, Qasim. 2000. *The Liberation of Women and The New Woman: Two Documents in the History of Egyptian Feminism*; transl. Samiha Sidhom Peterson. Cairo: American University in Cairo Press.

Amin, Osman. 1953. *Muhammad ʿAbduh*; transl. Charles Wendell. Washington, D.C.: American Council of Learned Societies.

al-Anani, Khalil. 2013. "The Power of the Jama'A [sic]: The Role of Hasan Al-Banna in Constructing the Muslim Brotherhood's Collective Identity." *Sociology of Islam* 1: 41–63.

Anderson, Benedict. 2006 [1982] *Imagined Communities. Reflections on the Origin and Spread of Nationalism.* London/New York: Verso.

Anjum, Ovamir. 2007. "Islam as a Discursive Tradition: Talal Asad and His Interlocutors." *Comparative Studies of South Asia, Africa and the Middle East* 27/3: 656–672.

Ansary, Tamim. 2009. *Destiny Disrupted. A History of the World Through Islamic Eyes.* New York: Public Affairs.

Appleby, Scott R. 2011. "Rethinking Fundamentalism in a Secular Age." In *Rethinking Secularism* ed. by Craig Calhoun, Mark Juergensmeyer and Jonathan VanAntwerpen: 225–247. Oxford: Oxford University Press.

Arjomand, Saïd Amir (ed.). 2014. *Social Theory and Regional Studies in the Global Age.* Albany: State University of New York Press.

—. 2014. "Introduction. The Challenge of Integrating Social Theory and Regional Studies." In *Social Theory and Regional Studies in the Global Age* ed. by Saïd Amir Arjomand: 1–20. Albany: State University of New York Press.

Arjomand, Saïd Amir and Schäfer, Wolfgang. 2014. "Foreword: Pangaea II: Global/Local Studies." In *Social Theory and Regional Studies in the Global Age* ed. by Saïd Amir Arjomand: xi–xii. Albany: State University of New York Press.

Arslan, Shakib. 1952. *Our Decline and Its Causes: A Diagnosis of the Symptoms of the Downfall of the Muslims*, transl. M. A. Shakoor. Lahore: Sh. Muhammad Ashraf.

Asad, Muhammad. 1980. *The Message of the Qur'ān*. Gibraltar: Dar al-Andalus.

Asad, Talal. 2009 [1986]. "The Idea of an Anthropology of Islam." *Qui Parle* 17/2: 1–30.

—. 2008 [2003]. *Formations of the Secular: Christianity, Islam, Modernity.* Stanford: Stanford University Press.

—. 1999. "Religion, Nation-State, Secularism." In *Nation and Religion: Perspectives on Europe and Asia* ed. by Peter van der Veer and Hartmut Lehmann: 178–196. Princeton, NJ: Princeton University Press.

—. 1997. "Europe against Islam: Islam in Europe." *The Muslim World* 87/2: 183–195.

—. 1993. *Genealogies of Religion: Discipline and Reasons of Power in Christianity and Islam.* Baltimore/London: The Johns Hopkins University Press.

—. 1986. *The Idea of an Anthropology of Islam.* Washington, D.C.: Centre for Contemporary Arab Studies, Georgetown University.

Avonius, Leena. 2014. "Building Nation and Society in the 1920s Dutch East Indies." In *A Global Conceptual History of Asia, 1860–1940* ed. by Hagen Schulz-Forberg: 129–148. London: Pickering & Chatto.

Ayalon, Ami. 2010. "The Press and Publishing." In *The New Cambridge History of Islam; vol. 6: Muslims and Modernity; Culture and Society since 1800* ed. by Robert W. Hefner: 572–596. Cambridge: Cambridge University Press.

—. 2008. "Private Publishing in the *Nahḍa*." *International Journal of Middle East Studies* 40: 561–577.

—. 1995. *The Press in the Arab Middle East: a History.* New York/Oxford: Oxford University Press.

—. 1987. *Language and Change in the Arab Middle East: The Evolution of Modern Political Discourse.* New York: Oxford University Press.

al-Azmeh, Aziz. 1996. *Islams and Modernities.* London/New York: Verso.

Azra, Azyumardi. 2008. "The Transmission of *al-Manār*'s Reformism to the Malay-Indonesian World: the Case of *al-Imām* and *al-Munīr*." In *Intellectuals in the Modern Islamic World. Transmission, Transformation, Communication* ed. by Stéphane A. Dudoignon, Komatsu Hisao and Kosugi Yasushi: 143–158. London/New York: Routledge.

Ba-Yunus, Ilyas and Ahmad, Farid. 1985. *Islamic Sociology: An Introduction.* London: Hodder & Stoughton.

Baali, Fuad. 1986. *Ilm al-Umran and Sociology: A Comparative Study.* Kuwait: Kulliyyat al-Adab, Jamiʿat al-Kuwayt.

Badawi, Muhammad Zaki. 1978. *The Reformers of Egypt.* London: The Muslim Institute.

Badran, Margot. 1995. *Feminists, Islam, and Nation: Gender and the Making of Modern Egypt.* Princeton: Princeton University Press.

Baer, Gabriel. 1969. *Studies in the Social History of Modern Egypt.* Chicago/London: The University of Chicago Press.

—. 1968. "Social Change in Egypt: 1800–1914." In *Political and Social Change in Modern Egypt. Historical Studies from the Ottoman Conquest to the United Arab Republic* ed. by P. M. Holt: 135–161. London: Oxford University Press.

Baker, Keith Michael. 2001. "Enlightenment and the Institution of Society: Notes for a Conceptual History." In *Civil Society: History and Possibilities* ed. by Sudipta Kaviraj and Sunil Khilnani: 84–104. Cambridge: Cambridge University Press.

—. 1995. "Aufklärung und die Erfindung der Gesellschaft." In *Nach der Aufklärung?* ed. by Wolfgang Klein and Waltraud Naumann-Beyer: 109–124. Berlin: Akademie Verlag.

—. 1992. "Enlightenment and the Institution of Society: Notes for a Conceptual History." In *Main Trends in Cultural History* ed. by W Tand W Velema: 95–120. Amsterdam/Atlanta: Rodopi.

Balagangadhara, S. N. 1994. *"The Heathen in his Blindness...:" Asia, the West, and the Dynamic of Religion.* Leiden: Brill.

Baneth, D. Z. 1971. "What did Muhammad Mean when he Called his Religion Islām? The Original Meaning of Aslama and its Derivatives." *Israel Oriental Studies* 1: 183–190.

al-Banna, Hasan and Wendell, Charles. 1978. *Five Tracts of Ḥasan Al-Bannāʾ (1906–1949): a Selection from the Majmūʿat Rasāʾil al-Imām al-Shahīd Ḥasan al-Bannāʾ.* Berkeley/LosAngeles: University of California Press.

al-Barghouti, Tamim. 2008. *The Umma and the Dawla: The Nation-State and the Arab Middle East.* London: Pluto Press.

Baring, Evelyn. 1908. *Modern Egypt.* 2 vols. London: Macmillan.

Baron, Beth. 2005. *Egypt as a Woman: Nationalism, Gender, and Politics.* Cairo: American University in Cairo Press.

—. 2005. "Women's Voluntary Social Welfare Organizations in Egypt." In *Gender, Religion and Change in the Middle East. Two Hundred Years of History* ed. by Inger Marie Okkenhaug and Ingvild Flaskerud: 85–102. Oxford/New York: Berg.

—. 1994. *The Women's Awakening in Egypt.* New Haven: Yale University Press.

Barre, Elizabeth A. 2012. "Muslim Imaginaries and Imaginary Muslims. Placing Islam in Conversation with *A Secular Age.*" *Journal of Religious Ethics* 40/1: 138–148.

Barthélemy, A. 1935. *Dictionnaire Arabe-Français: Dialectes de Syrie: Alep, Damas, Liban, Jérusalem.* Paris: Librairie Orientaliste Paul Geuthner.

Baudrillard, Jean. 1983. *In the Shadow of the Silent Majorities, or, The End of the Social and Other Essays.* New York: Semiotext(e).

Beckford, James A. 2012. "SSSR Presidential Address: Public Religions and the Postsecular: Critical Reflections." *Journal for the Scientific Study of Religion* 51/1: 1–19.

Behrent, Michael C. 2008. "The Mystical Body of Society: Religion and Association in Nineteenth-Century French Political Thought." *Journal of the History of Ideas* 69/2: 219–243.

Beinin, Joel. 1998. "Egypt, Society and Economy, 1923–1952." In *The Cambridge History of Egypt. Volume 2: Modern Egypt, from 1517 to the end of the twentieth century* ed. by M.W. Daly: 309–333. Cambridge: Cambridge University Press.

Beinin, Joel and Lockman, Zachary. 1998. *Workers on the Nile: Nationalism, Communism, Islam and the Egyptian Working Class, 1882–1954.* Cairo: The American University in Cairo Press.

Bell, David A. 2003. "Nation et Patrie, Société et Civilisation: Transformations du vocabulaire social français, 1700–1789." In *L'invention de la société: Nominalisme politique et*

science sociale au xviiie siècle ed. by Laurence Kaufmann and Jacques Guilhaumou: 99 – 120. Paris: École des Hautes Études en Sciences Sociales.
—. 2001. *The Cult of the Nation in France: Inventing Nationalism, 1680 – 1800.* Cambridge, Mass./London: Harvard University Press.
Belier, Wouter W. 1999. "The Sacred in the Social Sciences: On the Definition of Religion by the *Année sociologique* Group." In *The Pragmatics of Defining Religion: Contexts, Concepts and Contests* ed. by Jan G. Platvoet and Arie L. Molendijk: 173 – 206. Leiden/Boston/Köln: Brill.
Belot, P. J.-B. 1913. *Dictionnaire Français-Arabe; 4ième édition revue et corrigée; Seconde Partie.* Beyrouth: Imprimerie Catholique.
Benite, Zvi Ben-Dor. 2014. "Taking ʿAbduh to China: Chinese-Egyptian Intellectual Contact in the Early Twentieth Century." In *Global Muslims in the Age of Steam and Print* ed. by James L. Gelvin and Nile Green: 249 – 268. Berkeley/Los Angeles: University of California Press.
Bennett, Tony, Grossberg, Lawrence and Morris, Meaghan (eds.). 2005. *New Keywords. A Revised Vocabulary of Culture and Society.* Malden, Mass.: Blackwell.
Berger, Peter. 1999. "Introduction." In *The Desecularization of the World. Resurgent Religion and World Politics* ed. by Peter Berger: 1 – 18. Washington, D.C.: Ethics and Public Policy Center.
Berkes, Niyazi. 1936. "Sociology in Turkey." *American Journal of Sociology* 42/2: 238 – 246.
Berman, Nina. 2004. *Impossible Missions? German Economic, Military, and Humanitarian Efforts in Africa.* Lincoln: University of Nebraska Press.
von Bernhardi, Friedrich. 1912. *Vom heutigen Kriege*; vol. 1: *Grundlagen und Elemente des heutigen Krieges;* vol. 2: *Kampf und Kriegführung.* Berlin: E.S. Mittler & Sohn.
Beshara, Adel (ed.). 2011. *The Origins of Syrian Nationhood. Histories, Pioneers and Identity.* Oxon/New York: Routledge.
Biberstein Kazimirski, Albert de. [ca. 1900; original: Paris 1860]. *Qamus al-Lughatayn al-ʿArabiyya wa-l-Fransawiyya = Dictionnaire arabe-français : contenant toutes les racines de la langue arabe, leurs dérivés, tant dans l'idiome vulgaire que dans l'idiome littéral ainsi que les dialectes d'Alger et de Maroc; tome premier.* Beyrouth: Librairie du Liban.
Bielefeld, Ulrich. 2003. *Nation und Gesellschaft. Selbstthematisierungen in Frankreich und Deutschland.* Hamburg: Hamburger Edition.
Binder, Leonard. 1963. *Religion and Politics in Pakistan.* Berkeley/Los Angeles: University of California Press.
Blachère, Régis, Pellat, Charles, Chouémi, Moustafa and Denizeau, Claude. 1976. *Dictionnaire Arabe-Français-Anglais (Langue classique et moderne); tome troisième.* Paris: G.-P. Maisonneuve et Larose.
Black, Antony. 2011. *The History of Islamic Political Thought: from the Prophet to the Present.* Edinburgh: Edinburgh University Press.
—. 2001. "Concepts of Civil Society in Pre-Modern Europe." In *Civil Society: History and Possibilities* ed. by Sudipta Kaviraj and Sunil Khilnani: 33 – 38. Cambridge: Cambridge University Press.
Bluhm, Jutta E. 1997. "*al-Manār* and Aḥmad Soorkattie: Links in the Chain of Transmission of Muhammad ʿAbduh's Ideas to the Malay-Speaking World." In *Islam: Essays on Scripture, Thought and Society* ed. by Peter G. Riddell and Tony Street: 295 – 308. Leiden: Brill.

Bocthor, Ellious. 1828. *Dictionnaire français-arabe; revu et augmenté par A[rmand] Caussin de Perceva.* Paris: Didot.

Bond, Niall. 2009. "Gemeinschaft und Gesellschaft: The Reception of a Conceptual Dichotomy." *Contributions to the History of Concepts* 5/2: 162–186.

Booth, Marilyn. 2004. "[Review of:] Talal Asad, Formations of the Secular: Christianity, Islam, Modernity." *Bryn Mawr Review of Comparative Literature* 4/2, http://www.brynmawr.edu/bmrcl/Summer2004/Asad.html (accessed May 30, 2014).

Bormans, Maurice. 1975. "Le commentaire du Manar à propos du verset coranique sur l'amitié des Musulmans pour les Chrétiens (5, 82)." *IslamoChristiana* 1: 71–86.

Borutta, Manuel. 2010. "Genealogie der Säkularisierungstheorie: Zur Historisierung einer großen Erzählung der Moderne." *Geschichte und Gesellschaft* 36: 347–376.

Bossy, John. 1985. *Christianity in the West 1400–1700.* Oxford: Oxford University Press.

Botman, Selma. 1998. "The Liberal Age, 1923–1952." In *The Cambridge History of Egypt. Volume 2: Modern Egypt, from 1517 to the End of the Twentieth Century* ed. by M.W. Daly: 285–308. Cambridge: Cambridge University Press.

Bracke, Sarah and Fadil, Nadia. 2008. *Islam and Secular Modernity under Western Eyes: A Genealogy of a Constitutive Relationship.* San Domenico di Fiesole: European University Institute.

Branca-Rosoff, Sonia and Guilhaumou, Jacques. 1988. "De 'société' à 'socialisme' (Sieyès): l'invention néologique et son contexte discursif. Essai de colinguisme appliqué." *Langage et société* 83–84: 39–77.

Branford, Victor V. 1903. "On the Origin and Use of the Word 'Sociology,' and on the Relation of Sociological to Other Studies and to Practical Problems." *American Journal of Sociology* 9/2: 145–162.

Bremmer, Jan N. 2008. "Secularization. Notes Toward a Genealogy. In *Religion. Beyond a Concept* ed. by Hent de Vries: 432–437. New York: Fordham University Press.

Bruce, Steve. 2011. *Secularization: In Defence of an Unfashionable Theory.* Oxford: Oxford University Press.

Brunner, Rainer. 2016. "Lātinīya lā-dīnīya: Muḥammad Rašīd Riḍā über Arabisch und Türkisch im Zeitalter des Nationalismus." In *Osmanische Welten: Quellen und Fallstudien. Festschrift für Michael Ursinus*, ed. by Johannes Zimmermann, Christoph Herzog and Raoul Motika, 73–114. Bamberg: University of Bamberg Press.

—. 2001. "[Review of:] Yasushi, Kosugi; Ibis, Yusuf Husain; Huri, Yusuf Quzma (eds): *Fihris mağallat al-Manār, 1898–1935 – The Index of Al-Manar*. Beirut: Turāṯ/Tokio: Mašruʿ dirāsāt al-ḥaḍāra al-islāmīya/The Islamic Area Studies Project 1998." *Die Welt des Islams* 41/1: 132–133.

Brynjar, Lia. 2010 [1998]. *The Society of the Muslim Brothers in Egypt: the Rise of an Islamic Mass Movement, 1928–1942.* Reading: Ithaca Press.

Busool, Assad Nimer. 1976. "Shaykh Muḥammad Rashīd Riḍā's Relations with Jamāl al-Dīn al-Afghānī and Muḥammad ʿAbduh." *The Muslim World* 66/4: 272–286.

Buessow, Johann. 2015. "Re-imagining Islam in the Period of the First Modern Globalization: Muhammad ʿAbduh and his *Theology of Unity.*" In *A Global Middle East: Mobility, Materiality and Culture in the Modern Age, 1880–1940* ed. by Liat Kozma, Cyrus Schayegh and Avner Wishnitzer: 273–320. London: I.B. Tauris.

Burhanudin, Tajat. 2005. "Aspiring for Islamic Reform: Southeast Asian Requests for *Fatwās* in *al-Manār.*" *Islamic Law and Society* 12/1: 9–26.

Cabrera, Miguel A. 2005. “The Crisis of the Social and Post-social History.” *The European Legacy* 10/6: 611–620.

Casanova, José. 2012. “Religion, Secularization, and Sacralization.” In *Dynamics in the History of Religions between Asia and Europe. Encounters, Notions, and Comparative Perspectives* ed. by Volkhard Krech and Marion Steinicke: 453–460. Leiden/Boston: Brill.

—. 2011. “The Secular, Secularizations, Secularisms.” In *Rethinking Secularism* ed. by Craig Calhoun, Mark Juergensmeyer and Jonathan VanAntwerpen: 54–74. Oxford: Oxford University Press.

—. 2010. “A Secular Age. Dawn or Twilight?.” In *Varieties of Secularism in a Secular Age* ed. by Michael Warner, Jonathan VanAntwerpen and Craig Calhoun: 265–281. Cambridge, Mass.: Harvard University Press.

—. 2008. “Public Religions Revisited.” In *Religion. Beyond a Concept* ed. by Hent de Vries: 101–119. New York: Fordham University Press.

—. 2006. “Rethinking Secularization: A Global Comparative Perspective.” *The Hedgehog Review* 8/1–2: 7–22.

—. 2001. “Civil Society and Religion: Retrospective Reflections on Catholicism and Prospective Reflections on Islam.” *Social Research* 68/4: 1041–1080.

—. 1994. *Public Religions in the Modern World.* Chicago: The University of Chicago Press.

Castoriadis, Cornelius. 1987 [1975]. *The Imaginary Institution of Society*; transl. Kathleen Blamey. Cambridge, Mass.: MIT Press.

Chakrabarty, Dipesh. 2008. “In Defense of Provincializing Europe: A Response to Carola Dietze.” *History and Theory* 47/1: 85–96.

—. 2000. *Provincializing Europe: Postcolonial Thought and Historical Difference*; with a new preface by the author. Princeton, NJ: Princeton University Press.

Chalcraft, John. 2005. “Engaging the State: Peasants and Petitions in Egypt on the Eve of Colonial Rule.” *International Journal of Middle East Studies* 37/3: 303–325.

—. 2004. *The Striking Cabbies of Cairo and Other Stories: Crafts and Guilds in Egypt, 1863–1914.*

Chambers, Simone and Kymlicka, Will (eds.). 2002. *Alternative Conceptions of Civil Society.* Princeton: Princeton University Press.

—. 2002. “Introduction: Alternative Conceptions of Civil Society.” In *Alternative Conceptions of Civil Society* ed. by Simone Chambers and Will Kymlicka: 1–10. Princeton: Princeton University Press.

Chatterjee, Partha. 1990. “A Response to Taylor’s ‘Modes of Civil Society’.” *Public Culture* 3/1: 119–132.

Chidester, David. 1996. *Savage Systems: Colonialism and Comparative Religion in Southern Africa.* Charlottesivilee: University of Virginia Press.

Clark, J. C. D. 2012. “Secularization and Modernization: The Failure of a ‘Grand Narrative’.” *The Historical Journal* 55/1: 161–194.

Clark, Peter. 2000. *British Clubs and Societies.* Oxford: Clarendon.

Cleveland, William L. 1985. *Islam against the West: Shakib Arslan and the Campaign for Islamic Nationalism.* Austin: University of Texas Press.

Cole, Juan Ricardo. 2010. “Playing Muslim: Bonaparte’s Army of the Orient and Euro-Muslim Creolization.” In *The Age of Revolutions in Global Context, c. 1760–1840* ed. by David

Armitage and Sanjay Subrahmanyam: 125–143. Basingstoke/New York: Palgrave Macmillan.

—. 2008. *Napoleon's Egypt: Invading the Middle East.* New York: Palgrave Macmillan.

—. 1991. *Colonialism and Revolution in the Middle East: Social and Cultural Origins of Egypt's ʿUrabi Movement.* Princeton, N.J.: Princeton University Press.

—. 1983. "Rashid Rida on the Bahaʾi Faith: A Utilitarian Theory of the Spread of Religion." *Arab Studies Quarterly* 5: 276–291.

Commins, David. 2008. "Al-Manār and Popular Religion in Syria, 1898–1920." In *Intellectuals in the Islamic World: Transmission, transformation, and communication* ed. by Stéphane A. Dudoignon, Komatsu Hisao and Kosugi Yasushi: 40–54. London/New York: Routledge.

—. 1988. "Hasan al-Banna (1906–1949)." In *Pioneers of Islamic Revival* ed. by Ali Rahnema: 125–153. London/New Jersey: Zed Books.

Conermann, Stephan. 1996. *Muṣṭafā Maḥmūd (geb. 1921) und der modifizierte islamische Diskurs im modernen Ägypten.* Berlin: Klaus Schwarz.

Connolly, William E. 2010. "Belief, Spirituality, and Time." In *Varieties of Secularism in a Secular Age* ed. by Michael Warner, Jonathan VanAntwerpen and Craig Calhoun: 126–144. Cambridge, Mass.: Harvard University Press.

Conze, Werner. 1992 [1964]. "Nation und Gesellschaft. Zwei Grundbegriffe der revolutionären Epoche." In *Gesellschaft – Staat – Nation: Gesammelte Aufsätze* ed. by Ulrich Engelhardt, Reinhart Koselleck und Wolfgang Schieder: 341–354. Stuttgart: Ernst Klett.

—. 1992 [1958]. "Staat und Gesellschaft in der frührevolutionären Epoche Deutschlands." In *Gesellschaft – Staat – Nation: Gesammelte Aufsätze* ed. by *Ulrich Engelhardt, Reinhart Koselleck und Wolfgang Schieder:* 157–185. Stuttgart: Ernst Klett.

Cook, Michael. 2014. *Ancient Religions, Modern Politics. The Islamic Case in Comparative Perspective.* Princeton/Oxford: Princeton University Press.

Cooper, Clayton Sedgwick. 1914. *The Modernizing of the Orient.* New York: McBride, Nast & Company.

Cornell, Vincent J. 2013. "Muḥammad ʿAbduh: A Sufi-Inspired Modernist?" In *Tradition and Modernity. Christian and Muslim Perspectives* ed. by David Marshall: 97–114. Washington, DC: Georgetown University Press.

Corrado, Monica. 2011. *Mit Tradition in die Zukunft. Der taǧdīd-Diskurs in der Azhar und in ihrem Umfeld.* Würzburg: Ergon.

Crecelius, Daniel. 1998. "Egypt in the Eighteenth Century." In *The Cambridge History of Egypt. Volume 2: Modern Egypt, from 1517 to the End of the Twentieth Century* ed. by M.W. Daly: 59–86. Cambridge: Cambridge University Press.

Cuno, Kenneth M. 2010. "Egypt to c. 1919." In *The New Cambridge History of Islam. vol. 5: The Islamic World in the Age of Western Dominance* ed. by Francis Robinson: 79–106. New York: Cambridge University Press.

—. 2000. "Muhammad Ali and the Decline and Revival Thesis in Modern Egyptian History." In *Reform or Modernization? Egypt under Muhamed Ali. Symposium Organized by The Egyptian Society of Historical Studies, 9–11 March 1999* ed. by Raouf ʿAbbas: 93–119. Cairo: al-Majlis al-ʿAmm li-l-Thaqafa.

Dabla, Bashir Ahmad. 2007. "Muslim Political Thought in Colonial India: a Comparative Study of Sir Sayyid Ahmad Khan and Mawlana Abu al-Kalam Azad." In *Challenges to Religions*

and Islam: A Study of Muslim Movements, Personalities, Issues and Trends ed. by Hamid Naseem Rafiabadi, vol. 2: 788–815. New Delhi: Sarup & Sons.
Dallal, Ahmad S. 2010. "The Origins and Early Development of Islamic Reform." In *The New Cambridge History of Islam; vol. 6: Muslims and Modernity; Culture and Society since 1800* ed. by Robert W. Hefner: 107–147. Cambridge: Cambridge University Press.
—. 2000. "Appropriating the Past: Twentieth-Century Reconstruction of Pre-Modern Islamic Thought." *Islamic Law and Society* 7/3: 325–358.
Daly, M.W. 1998. "The British Occupation, 1882–1922." In *The Cambridge History of Egypt. Volume 2: Modern Egypt, from 1517 to the End of the Twentieth Century* ed. by M.W. Daly: 239–251. Cambridge: Cambridge University Press.
Davis, Charles. 1994. *Religion and the Making of Society: Essays in Social Theology.* Cambridge: Cambridge University Press.
el-Deeb, Mohamed Nagib. 2009. *Kulturgeschichte der Kaffeehäuser "makahi" in Kairo. Orte der sozialen und politischen Innovation im Ägypten des 19. und 20. Jahrhunderts.* Dissertation, Universität Freiburg.
Delanty, Gerard. 2006. "Modernity and the Escape from Eurocentrism." In *Handbook of Contemporary European Social Theory* ed. by Gerard Delanty: 266–278. London: Routledge.
Demolins, Edmond. [1923]. *Tafawwuq-i Angluksaksun marbut bi-čī'st?*; transl. ʿAli Dashti. Teheran: Husain KushanPur.
—. 1330 h. [1912]. *Anglosaksonların esbab-ı faikiyeti nedir?: Anglosaksonlar hakkında tedkikat-ı ictimaiye*; transl. A. Fuad. Dersaadet: Kitabhane-i Askeri/İbrahim Hilmi.
—. 1898. *Anglo-Saxon superiority: To what it is due*; transl. Louis Bertram Lavigne. London: Leadenhall.
—. 1897. *A quoi tient la supériorité des Anglo-Saxons.* Paris: Firmin-Didot.
Dietze, Carola. 2008. "Toward a History on Equal Terms: A Discussion of Provincializing Europe." *History and Theory* 47/1: 69–84.
Donzelot, Jacques. 1994 [1984]. *L'invention du social. Essai sur le déclin des passions politiques.* Paris: Éditions du Seuil.
—. 1988. "The Promotion of the Social." *Economy and Society* 17/3: 395–427.
Douglas, Ian Henderson. 1988. *Abul Kalam Azad: an Intellectual and Religious Biography*; ed. by Gail Minault and Christian W. Troll. Delhi: Oxford University Press.
Dozy, R. 1967 [1881]. *Supplément aux Dictionnaires Arabes; tome premier.* Leyde/Paris: Brill/G.-P. Maisonneuve et Larose.
Dressler, Markus. 2015. "Rereading Ziya Gökalp: Secularism and Reform of the Islamic State in the Late Young Turk Period." *International Journal of Middle East Studies* 47: 511–531.
Dubuisson, Daniel. 2003. *The Western Construction of Religion: Myths, Knowledge and Ideology*; transl. William Sayers. Baltimore: Johns Hopkins University Press.
Dudoignon, Stéphane A. 2008. "Echoes to al-Manār among the Muslims of the Russian Empire: a Prelimenary Research Note on Riza al-Din b. Fakhr al-Din and the Šūrā (1908–1918)." In *Intellectuals in the Modern Islamic World. Transmission, Transformation, Communication* ed. by Stéphane A. Dudoignon, Komatsu Hisao and Kosugi Yasushi: 85–116. London/New York: Routledge.
Dupont, Anne-Laure. 2008. "The Ottoman Revolution of 1908 as seen by al-Hilāl and al-Manār: The Triumph and Diversification of the Reformist Spirit." In *Liberal Thought in*

the Eastern Mediterraneaen: Late 19th Century until the 1960s ed. by Christoph Schumann: 123–146. Leiden: Brill.

—. 2006. *Ǧurǧī Zaydān (1861–1914): écrivain réformiste et témoin de la Renaissance arabe.* Damas: IFPO.

Dussel, Enrique. 1993. "Eurocentrism and Modernity." *Boundary* 2/3: 65–76.

Dykstra, Darrell. 1998. "The French Occupation of Egypt." In *The Cambridge History of Egypt. Volume 2: Modern Egypt, from 1517 to the End of the Twentieth Century* ed. by M. W. Daly: 113–138. Cambridge: Cambridge University Press.

Edipoğlu, Kerim. 2007. "Islamische Soziologie: Menschen- und Gesellschaftsbild." *Zeitschrift für Religionswissenschaft* 15/2: 131–153.

Egger, Vernon. 1986. *A Fabian in Egypt. Salamah Musa and the Rise of the Professional Classes in Egypt, 1909–1939.* Lanham: University Press of America.

Eisenstadt, Shmuel N. 2003. *Comparative Civilizations and Multiple Modernities.* 2 vols. Leiden: Brill.

—. 2000. "Multiple Modernities." *Daedalus* 129/1: 1–29.

—. (ed.). 1987. *Patterns of Modernity; vol. 1: The West; vol. 2: Beyond the West.* London: Frances Pinter.

El Shakry, Omnia. 2007. *The Great Social Laboratory: Subjects of Knowledge in Colonial and Postcolonial Egypt:* Stanford University Press.

Elias, Elias A. 1922. *Elias' Modern Dictionary Arabic-English.* Cairo: al-Matbaʿa al-ʿAsriyya bi-Misr.

Ellis, Marie-Therese Cecilia. 2007. *Empire or Umma. Writing Beyond the Nation in Moroccan Periodicals.* Dissertation, University of California, Berkeley.

ElShakry, Marwa. 2015. "Spencer's Arabic Readers." In *Global Spencerism: The Communication and Appropriation of a British Evolutionist* ed. by Bernard Lightman: 35–55. Leiden: Brill.

—. 2013. *Reading Darwin in Arabic, 1860–1950.* London: The University of Chicago Press.

Emon, Anver M. 2010. *Islamic Natural Law Theories.* New York: Oxford University Press.

Enayat, Hamid. 2005. *Modern Islamic Political Thought: the Response of the Shîʿî and the Sunnî Muslims to the Twentieth Century.* London: I.B. Tauris.

Ende, Werner. 1994. "Sollen Frauen schreiben lernen? Eine innerislamische Debatte und ihre Widerspiegelung in Al-Manār." In *Gedenkschrift Wolfgang Reuschel: Akten des III. Arabistischen Kolloquiums, Leipzig, 21.–22. November 1991* ed. by Dieter Bellmann: 49–57. Stuttgart: Steiner.

—. 1973. *Arabische Nation und islamische Geschichte: die Umayyaden im Urteil arabischer Au-toren des 20. Jahrhunderts.* Beirut/Wiesbaden: Orient-Institut der DMG/Franz Steiner.

—. 1969. "Waren Ǧamāladdīn al-Afġānī und Muḥammad ʿAbduh Agnostiker?." *ZDMG* Supplement 1/17: 650–659.

Endreß, Martin. 2011. "Postsäkulare Kultur'? Max Webers Soziologie und Habermas' Beitrag zur De-Säkularisierungsthese." In *Religionen verstehen. Zur Aktualität von Max Webers Religionssoziologie* ed. by Agathe Bienfait: 123–149. Wiesbaden: VS.

Ener, Mine. 2003. *Managing Egypt's Poor and the Politics of Benevolence, 1800–1952.* New Haven, CT: State University of New York Press.

Eppel, Michael. 2009. "Note About the Term Efendiyya in the History of the Middle East." *International Journal of Middle East Studies* 41: 535–539.

Esquiros, Alphonse. 1869. *L'Emile du dix-neuvième siècle.* Paris: Librairie Internationale.

Fabian, Johannes. 1983. *Time and the Other: How Anthropology Makes Its Object.* New York: Columbia University Press.

Fahmy, Khaled. 1998. "The Era of Muhammad ʿAli Pasha." In *The Cambridge History of Egypt. Volume 2: Modern Egypt, from 1517 to the End of the Twentieth Century* ed. by M.W. Daly: 139–179. Cambridge: Cambridge University Press.

—. 1997. *All the Pasha's Men. Mehmed Ali, His Army and the Making of Modern Egypt.* Cambridge: Cambridge University Press.

Fahmy, Ziad. 2011. *Ordinary Egyptians. Creating the Modern Nation through Popular Culture, 1870–1919.* Cairo: AUC Press.

Feil, Ernst. 1986–2007. *Religio* [different subtitles for the individual volumes]. 4 vols. Göttingen: Vandenhoeck & Ruprecht.

Fish, M. Steven. 2011. *Are Muslims Distinctive? A Look at the Evidence.* Oxford: Oxford University Press.

Fitzgerald, Timothy. 2007. "Introduction." In *Religion and the Secular. Historical and Colonial Formations* ed. by Timothy Fitzgerald: 1–24. London/Oakville: equinox.

—. 2000. *The Ideology of Religious Studies.* New York/Oxford: Oxford University Press.

Flores, Alexander. 1995. "Reform, Islam, Secularism : Farah Antûn and Muhammad Abduh." In *Entre reforme sociale et mouvement national : identité et modernisation en Egypte (1882–1962)* ed. by Alain Roussillon: 565–576. Cairo: CEDEJ.

Fulda, Daniel. 2016. "Sattelzeit. Karriere und Problematik eines kulturwissenschaftlichen Zentralbegriffs." In *Sattelzeit. Historiographiegeschichtliche Revisionen* ed. by Elisabeth Décultot and Daniel Fulda: 1–16. Berlin/Boston: De Gruyter.

Gaonkar, Dilip Parameshwar (ed.). 2001. *Alternative Modernities.* Durham, NC: Duke University Press.

Gasper, Michael Ezekiel. 2013. "Public Deliberations of the Self in *fin-de-siècle* Egypt." In *The Making of the Arab Intellectual (1880–1960): Empire, Public Sphere and the Colonial Coordinates of Selfhood* ed. by Dyala Hamzah: 40–62. London: Routledge.

—. 2009. *The Power of Representation. Publics, Peasants, and Islam in Egypt.* Stanford, CA: Stanford University Press.

Gautier, Claude. 1993. *L'invention de la société civile. Lectures anglo-écossaises: Mandeville, Smith, Ferguson.* Paris: Presses Universitaires de France.

Gen, Kasuya. 2008. "The Influence of al-Manār on Islamism in Turkey: the Case of Mehmed Âkif." In *Intellectuals in the Islamic World: Transmission, transformation, and communication* ed. by Stéphane A. Dudoignon, Komatsu Hisao and Kosugi Yasushi: 74–84. London/New York: Routledge.

Gershoni, Israel and Jankowski, James P. 1999. "Print Culture, Social Change, and the Process of Redefining Imagined Communities in Egypt. Response to the Review by Charles D. Smith of *Redefining the Egyptian Nation.*" *International Journal of Middle East Studies* 31/1: 81–94.

—. 1995. *Redefining the Egyptian Nation, 1930–1945.* Cambridge/New York: Cambridge University Press.

Gesink, Indira Falk. 2010. *Islamic Reform and Conservatism: Al-Azhar and the Evolution of Modern Sunni Islam.* London: I.B. Tauris.

Geulen, Christian. 2010. "Plädoyer für eine Geschichte der Grundbegriffe des 20. Jahrhunderts." *Zeithistorische Forschungen/Studies in Contemporary History* 1: 70–97.

Giannakis, Elias. 1983. "The Concept of Ummah." *Graeco-Arabica* 2: 100–111.

Gibb, Hamilton A. R. 1963. "The Community in Islamic History." *Proceedings of the American Philosophical Society* 107/2: 173–176.

Gilet, Julien. 2010. "al-Maktaba al-Shamela." In *Aldébaran, Collections numériques*, http://aldebaran.revues.orf/6597 (accessed Sep. 30, 2013).

Glaß, Dagmar. 2004. *Der Muqtaṭaf und seine Öffentlichkeit. Aufklärung, Räsonnement und Meinungsstreit in der frühen arabischen Zeitschriftenkommunikation. Erster Band: Analyse medialer und sozialer Strukturen. Zweiter Band: Streitgesprächsprotokolle.* Würzburg: Ergon.

—. 1994. "Popularizing Sciences through Arabic Journals in the Late 19th Century: How al-Muqtaṭaf Transformed Western Patterns." In *Changing Identities: The Transformation of Asian and African Societies under Colonialism* ed. by Joachim Heidrich: 323–364. Berlin: Das Arabische Buch.

Glei, Reinhold and Reichmuth, Stefan. 2012. "Religion between Last Judgement, Law and Faith: Koranic *dīn* and its Rendering in Latin Translations of the Koran." *Religion* 42/2: 247–271.

Godart, Gerard Clinton. 2008. "'Philosophy' or 'Religion'? The Confrontation with Foreign Categories in Late Nineteenth-Century Japan." *Journal of the History of Ideas* 69/1: 71–91.

Goldziher, Ignaz. 1920. *Die Richtungen der islamischen Koranauslegung.* Leiden: Brill.

Göle, Nilüfer. 2010. "The Civilizational, Spatial, and Sexual Powers of the Secular." In *Varieties of Secularism in a Secular Age* ed. by Michael Warner, Jonathan VanAntwerpen and Craig Calhoun: 243–264. Cambridge, Mass.: Harvard University Press.

Gosewinkel, Dieter. 2011. "Civil Society." In *European History Online (EGO), published by the Institute of European History (IEG), Mainz 2011-01-12*, http://www.ieg-ego.eu/gosewinkeld-2010-en (accessed March 20, 2015).

Gordon, Daniel. 1994. *Citizens without Sovereignty. Equality and Sociability in French Thought (1670–1789).* Princeton: Princeton University Press.

Gordon, Joel. 2010. "Egypt from c. 1919." In *The New Cambridge History of Islam. vol. 5: The Islamic World in the Age of Western Dominance* ed. by Francis Robinson: 372–401. New York: Cambridge University Press.

Gordon, Peter E. 2008. "The Place of the Sacred in the Absence of God: Charles Taylor's 'A Secular Age'." *Journal of the History of Ideas* 69/4: 647–673.

Gorski, Philip S. and Altınordu, Ateş. 2008. "After Secularization?." *Annual Review of Sociology* 34/1: 55–85.

Gramling, David. 2012. "'You Pray like we have Fun:' Toward a Phenomenology of Secular Islam." In *Migration and Religion: Christian Transatlantic Missions, Islamic Migration to Germany* ed. by Barbara Becker-Cantarino: 175–191. Amsterdam/New York: Rodopi.

Granfield, Patrick. 1982. "Aufkommen und Verschwinden des Begriffs 'societas perfecta'." *Concilium* 18: 460–464.

Greenfield, Liah. 1992. *Nationalism. Five Roads to Modernity.* Cambridge, Mass.: Harvard University Press.

Griffel, Frank. 2015. "What Do We Mean By 'Salafī'? Connecting Muḥammad ʿAbduh with Egypt's Nūr Party in Islam's Contemporary Intellectual History." *Die Welt des Islams* 55: 186–220.

Guilhaumou, Jacques. 2006. "Sieyès et le non-dit de la sociologie : du mot à la chose." *Revue d'Histoire des Sciences Humaines* 2/15: 117–134.

Haarmann, Ulrich. 1996. "Glaubensvolk und Nation im islamischen und lateinischen Mittelalter." In *Berichte und Abhandlungen* ed. by Berlin-Brandenburgische Akademie der Wissenschaften, vol. 2: 161–199. Berlin: Akademie-Verlag.

Habermas, Jürgen. 2008. "Ich bin alt, aber nicht fromm geworden [Gespräch mit Michael Funken]." In *Über Habermas. Gespräche mit Zeitgenossen* ed. by Michael Funken: 181–190. Darmstadt: WBG.

—. 2001. "Einleitung." In *Zwischen Naturalismus und Religion. Philosophische Aufsätze*: 7–14. Frankfurt a.M.: Suhrkamp.

—. 2001. *Glauben und Wissen. Friedenspreis des Deutschen Buchhandels 2001. Laudatio: Jan Philipp Reemtsma.* Frankfurt a.M.: Suhrkamp.

Haddad, Mahmoud. 2008. "The Manarists and Modernism. An Attempt to Fuse Society and Religion." In *Intellectuals in the Modern Islamic World. Transmission, Transformation, Communication* ed. by Stéphane A. Dudoignon, Komatsu Hisao and Kosugi Yasushi: 55–73. London/New York: Routledge.

—. 1997. "Arab Religious Nationalism in the Colonial Era: Rereading Rashīd Riḍā's Ideas on the Caliphate." *Journal of the American Oriental Society* 117/2: 253–277.

Haddad, Mohamed. 1997. "Les Œuvres de ʿAbduh: Histoire d'une manipulation." *Institut de Belles Lettres Arabes* 60/180: 197–222.

—. 1997. "ʿAbduh et ses lecteurs: Pour une histoire critique des 'lectures' de M. ʿAbduh." *Arabica* 45/1: 22–49.

Hallberg, Peter and Wittrock, Björn. 2006. "From *koinonìa politikè* to *societas civilis:* Birth, Disappearance and First Renaissance of the Concept." In *The Languages of Civil Society* ed. by Peter Wagner: 28–54. New York: Berghahn.

Hamzah, Dyala. 2013. "Introduction: the Making of the Arab Intellectual (1880–1960): Empire, Public Sphere and the Colonial Coordinates of Selfhood." In *The Making of the Arab Intellectual (1880–1960): Empire, Public Sphere and the Colonial Coordinates of Selfhood* ed. by Dyala Hamzah: 1–19. London: Routledge.

—. 2013. "From *ʿilm* to *Ṣiḥāfa* or the Politics of the Public Interest (*maṣlaḥa*): Muḥammad Rashīd Ridā and his Journal al-Manār." In *The Making of the Arab Intellectual (1880–1960): Empire, Public Sphere and the Colonial Coordinates of Selfhood* ed. by Dyala Hamzah: 90–127. London: Routledge.

—. 2008. "Muhammad Rashid Ridâ (1865–1935) or: The Importance of Being (a) Journalist." In *Religion and Its Other. Secular and Sacral Concepts and Practices in Interaction* ed. by Heike Bock, Jörg Feuchter and Michi Knecht: 40–63. Frankfurt/New York: Campus.

Hamzawy, Amr. 2004. "Exploring Theoretical and Programmatic Changes in Contemporary Islamist Discourse: The Journal *al-Manar al-Jadid.*" In *Transnational Political Islam. Religion, Ideology and Power* ed. by Azza Karam: 120–146. London/Sterling, Virginia: Pluto Press.

—. 2002. "Normative Dimensions of Contemporary Arab Debates on Civil Society. Between the Search for a New Formulation of Democracy and the Controversy over the Political Role of Religion." In *Civil Society in the Middle East* ed. by Amr Hamzawy: 10–46. Berlin: Schiler.

Hanafi, Hasan. 2002. "Alternative Conceptions of Civil Society: A Reflective Islamic Approach." In *Alternative Conceptions of Civil Society* ed. by Simone Chambers and Will Kymlicka: 171–189. Princeton: Princeton University Press.

Hanıoğlu, Şükrü. 2005. "Blueprints for a Future Society: Late Ottoman Materialists on Science, Religion, and Art." In *Late Ottoman Society: The Intellectual Legacy* ed. by Elisabeth Özdalga: 28–116. London/New York: RoutledgeCurzon.

Hanley, Will. 2013. "When did Egyptians stop being Ottomans? An Imperial Citizenship Case Study." In *Multilevel Citizenship* ed. by Willem Maas: 89–109. Philadelphia: Pennsylvania University Press.

Hanna, Nelly. 2003. *In Praise of Books. A Cultural History of Cairo's Middle Class, Sixteenth to Eighteenth Century.* Syracuse, NY: Syracuse University Press.

Hanna, Sami A. 1967. "al-Afghani: a Pioneer of Islamic Socialism." *The Muslim World* 57/1: 24–32.

Harrington, Austin. 2006. "Social Theory and Theology." In *Handbook of Contemporary European Social Theory* ed. by Gerard Delanty: 37–45. London: Routledge.

Hartmann, Martin. 1899. *The Arabic Press of Egypt.* London: Luzac & Co.

Hartung, Jan-Peter. 2013. "What Makes a "Muslim Intellectual"? On the Pros and Cons of a Category." *Middle East – Topics & Arguments* 1: 35–43.

Hasselblatt, Gunnar. 1968. *Herkunft und Auswirkungen der Apologetik Muhammed ʿAbduh's (1849–1905), untersucht an seiner Schrift: Islam und Christentum im Verhältnis zu Wissenschaft und Zivilisation.* Dissertation, Göttingen.

Hathaway, Jane. 2004. "Rewriting Eighteenth-Century Ottoman History." *Mediterranean Historical Review* 19/1: 29–53.

Hatina, Meir. 2010. *ʿUlamaʾ, Politics, and the Public Sphere: an Egyptian Perspective.* Salt Lake City: University of Utah Press.

—. 2007. "Religious Culture Contested: The Sufi Ritual of *dawsa* in Nineteenth-Century Cairo." *Die Welt des Islams* 47/1: 33–62.

Hauerwas, Stanley and Coles, Romand. 2010. "'Long Live the Weeds and the Wilderness Yet': *Reflections on A Secular Age.*" *Modern Theology* 26/3: 349–362.

Hoexter, Miriam, Eisenstadt, S. N. and Levtzion, Nehemia (eds.). 2002. *The Public Sphere in Muslim Societies.* Albany: State University of New York Press.

Horten, Max. 1915–1916. "Muhammad Abduh: Sein Leben und seine theologisch-philosophische Gedankenwelt." *Beiträge zur Kenntnis des Orients* 13: 83–114, *Beiträge zur Kenntnis des Orients* 14: 174–128.

Hourani, Albert. 1983 [1962]. *Arabic Thought in the Liberal Age, 1798–1939.* Cambridge/New York: Cambridge University Press.

—. 1981. "Sufism and Modern Islam: Rashid Rida." In *The Emergence of the Modern Middle East:* 90–102. Berkeley/Los Angeles: University of California Press.

—. 1977. "Rashid Rida and the Sufi orders: a footnote to Laoust." *Bulletin d'études orientales* 29: 231–241.

Howland, Douglas. 2001. *Translating the West: Language and Political Reason in Nineteenth-Century Japan.* Honolulu: University of Hawaii Press.

Humphreys, Stephen R. 2006. "The Historiography of the Middle East: Transforming a Field of Study." In *Middle East Historiographies. Narrating the Twentieth Century* ed. by Israel Gershoni, Amy Singer and Erdem Y. Hakan: 19–36. Seattle/London: University of Washington Press.

—. 1991. *Islamic History: A Framework for Inquiry.* Princeton, NJ: Princeton University Press.

Hunter, Robert F. 2000. "State-Society Relations in Nineteenth-Century Egypt: The Years of Transition, 1848–79." *Middle Eastern Studies* 36/3: 145–159.

Hurd, Elizabeth Shakman. 2010. "Appropriating Islam: The Islamic Other in the Consolidation of Western Modernity." *Critique: Critical Middle Eastern Studies* 12/1: 25–41.

—. 2008. *The Politics of Secularism in International Relations.* Princeton: Princeton University Press.

Hurgronje, Christiaan Snouck. 1957. *Selected Works of C. Snouck Hurgronje ed. in English and in French by G.-H- Bousquet and J. Schacht.* Leiden: Brill.

Husayn, Taha. 1917. *La philosophie sociale d'Ibn-Khaldoun.* Paris: A. Pedone.

Ibrahim, Bilal. 2013. *Freeing Philosophy from Metaphysics: Fakhr al-Dīn al-Rāzī's Philosophical Approach to the Study of Natural Phenomena.* PhD, McGill University, http://digitool.library.mcgill.ca/webclient/StreamGate?folder_id=0&dvs=1447165198658~26 (accessed Nov. 10, 2015).

Ibrahim, Yasir S. 2007. "Muḥammad ʿAbduh and Maqāṣid al-Sharīʿa." *The Maghreb Review* 32/1: 2–30.

—. 2006. "Rashīd Riḍā and Maqāṣid al-Sharīʿa." *Studia Islamica* 102–103: 157–198.

Izutsu, Toshihiko. 1966. *Ethico-Religious Concepts in the Qur'ān.* Montreal: McGill University Press.

—. 1965. *The Concept of Belief in Islamic Theology. A Semantic Analysis of îmān and islâm.* Toyko/Yokohama: The Keio Institute of Cultural and Linguistic Studies/Yurindo Publishing.

Işin, Ekrem. 2003. "Coffeehouses as Places of Conversation." In *The Illuminated Table, the Prosperous Hose. Food and Shelter in Ottoman Material Culture* ed. by Suraiya Faroqhi and Christoph K. Neumann: 199–208. Würzburg: Ergon.

Ivanyi, Katharina A. 2007. "Who's in Charge? The Tafsir al-Manar on Questions of Religious and Political Authority." *Maghreb Review* 32/2–3: 175–195.

ʿIzzat, ʿAbd al-ʿAziz. 1947. *Ibn-Khaldoun et sa science sociale.* Cairo: C. Tsoumas.

al-Jabarti, ʿAbdarrahman. 1994. *ʿAbd al-Raḥmān al-Jabarti's History of Egypt = ʿAjā'ib al-āthār fi'l-tarājim wa'l-akhbār*; ed. by Thomas Philipp and Moshe Perlmann. 3 vols. Stuttgart: Steiner.

—. 1975. *Al-Jabartī's chronicle of the first seven months of the French occupation of Egypt: Muḥarram-Rajab 1213, 15 June – December 1798 = Tārīkh muddat al-faransīs bi-miṣr*; edited and translated by S. Moreh. Leiden: Brill.

Jakobsen, Robert. 1959. "On Linguistic Aspects of Translation." In *On Translation* ed. by Reuben A. Brower: 232–239. Cambridge, Mass.: Harvard University Press.

Jeffery, Arthur. 1933. "Modernism in Islam. [Review of] *Islam and Modernism in Egypt. A Study of the Modern Reform Movement Inaugurated by Muhammad ʿAbduh* by Charles C. Adams." *The Journal of Religion* 13/4: 469–470.

Johnston, David. 2004. "A Turn in the Epistemology and Hermeneutics of Twentieth Century Uṣūl al-Fiqh." *Islamic Law and Society* 11/2: 233–282.

Jomier, Jacques. 1973. "Les raisons de l'adhésion du Sayyed Rashid Riḍā au nationalisme arabe." *Bulletin de l'Institut d'Égypte* 53: 53–61.

—. 1954. *Le Commentaire Coranique du Manār.* Paris: G.-P. Maisonneuve.

Joyce, Patrick. 2002. "Introduction." In *The Social in Question: New Bearings in History and the Social Sciences* ed. by Patrick Joyce: 1–18. London/New York: Routledge.

Juneja, Monica and Pernau, Margrit. 2009. "Lost In Translation? Transcending Boundaries in Comparative History." In *Comparative and Transnational History: Central European*

Approaches and New Perspectives ed. by Heinz-Gerhard Haupt and Jürgen Kocka: 105–132. New York/Oxford: Berghahn.

Jung, Dietrich. 2011. *Orientalists, Islamists and the Global Public Sphere: a Genealogy of the Modern Essentialist Image of Islam.* Sheffield/Oakville: Equinox.

Jung, Dietrich, and Kristine Sinclair. 2015. "Multiple Modernities, Modern Subjectivities and Social Order: Unity and difference in the rise of Islamic modernities." *Thesis Eleven* 130/1: 22–42.

Kamali, Masoud. 2001. "Civil Society and Islam: A Sociological Perspective." *European Journal of Sociology* 42/3: 457–482.

Karttunen, Klaus. 2014. "Sabhā-Samāj Society: Some Linguistic Considerations." In *A Global Conceptual History of Asia, 1860–1940* ed. by Hagen Schulz-Forberg: 75–90. London: Pickering & Chatto.

Krahl, Günther. 1964. *Deutsch-Arabisches Wörterbuch.* Leipzig: VEB.

Kaufmann, Laurence. 2003. "Le Dieu Social: Vers une socio-logie du nominalisme en Révolution." In *L'invention de la société: Nominalisme politique et science sociale au xviiie siècle* ed. by Laurence Kaufmann and Jacques Guilhaumou: 123–161. Paris: École des Hautes Études en Sciences Sociales.

[Kaufmann, Laurence and Guilhaumou, Jacques]. 2003. "Présentation." In *L'invention de la société: Nominalisme politique et science sociale au xviiie siècle* ed. by Laurence Kaufmann and Jacques Guilhaumou: 9–20. Paris: École des Hautes Études en Sciences Sociale.

Kaviraj, Sudipta. 2001. "In Search of Civil Society." In *Civil Society: History and Possibilities* ed. by Sudipta Kaviraj and Sunil Khilnani: 287–323. Cambridge: Cambridge University Press.

Kaviraj, Sudipta and Khilnani, Sunil. 2001. "Introduction: Ideas of Civil Society." In *Civil Society: History and Possibilities* ed. by Sudipta Kaviraj and Sunil Khilnani: 1–8. Cambridge: Cambridge University Press.

Kazi, Abdul Khaliq. 1966. "The Meaning of Īmān and Islām in the Qurʿān." *Islamic Studies* 5/3: 227–237.

Keddie, Nikki R. 1983. *An Islamic Response to Imperialism: Political and Religious Writings of Sayyid Jamāl ad-Dīn "al-Afghānī".* Berkeley: University of California Press.

Kedourie, Elie. 1966. *Afghani and Abduh. An Essay on Religious Unbelief and Political Activism in Islam.* London.

Kerr, Malcolm. 1968. "Notes on the Background of Arab Socialist Thought." *Journal of Contemporary History* 3/3: 145–159.

—. 1966. *Islamic Reform. The Political and Legal Theories of Muḥammad ʿAbduh and Rashīd Riḍā.* Berkeley, CA: University of California Press.

—. 1960. "Rashīd Riḍā and Islamic Legal Reform. An Ideological Analysis; Part I: Methodology; Part II: Application." *The Muslim World* 50: 99–108, 170–181.

Khoury, R. G. 1971. "Die Rolle der Übersetzungen in der modernen Renaissance des arabischen Schrifttums. Dargestellt am Beispiel Ägyptens." *Die Welt des Islams* 13/1: 1–10.

Khuri-Makdisi, Ilham. 2014. "The Conceptualization of the Social in Late Nineteenth- and Early Twentieth-Century Arabic Thought and Language." In *A Global Conceptual History of Asia, 1860–1940* ed. by Hagen Schulz-Forberg: 91–110. London: Pickering & Chatto.

—. 2014. “Fin-de-Siècle Egypt: A Nexus for Mediterranean and Global Radical Networks.” In *Global Muslims in the Age of Steam and Print* ed. by James L. Gelvin and Nile Green: 78–102. Berkeley/Los Angeles: University of California Press.

—. 2013. “Inscribing Socialism into the Nahḍa: al-Muqtaṭaf, al-Hilāl, and the Construction of a Leftist Reformist Worldview, 1880–1914.” In *The Making of the Arab Intellectual (1880–1960): Empire, Public Sphere and the Colonial Coordinates of Selfhood* ed. by Dyala Hamzah: 63–89. London: Routledge.

King, Richard. 1999. *Orientalism and Religion: Postcolonial Theory, India and the Mystic East.* London: Routledge.

Kinitz, Daniel. 2015. “Deviance as a Phenomenon of Secularity: Islam and Deviants in Twentieth-century Egypt – A Search for Sociological Explanations.” In *Multiple Secularities Beyond the West* ed. by Marian Burchardt, Monika Wohlrab-Sahr and Matthias Middell: 97–120. Boston/Berlin: DeGruyter.

Kırlı, Cengiz. 2004. “Coffehouses: Public Opinion in the Nineteenth-Centruy Ottoman Empire.” In *Public Islam and the Common Good* ed. by Armando Salvatore and Dale F. Eickelman: 75–98. Leiden/Boston: Brill.

Knöbl, Wolfgang. 2013. “Aufstieg und Fall der Modernisierungstheorie und des säkularen Bildes ‘moderner Gesellschaften’.” In *Moderne und Religion: Kontroversen um Modernität und Säkularisierung* ed. by Ulrich Willems, Detlef Pollack, Helene Basu, Thomas Gutmann and Ulrike Spohn: 75–116. Bielefeld: transcript.

Kocka, Jürgen. 2005. “Civil Society: Some remarks on the career of a concept.” In *Comparing Modernities. Pluralism versus Homogenity* ed. by Eliezer Ben-Rafael and Yitzhakq Sternberg: 141–149. Leiden/Boston: Brill.

Kocka, Jürgen and Haupt, Heinz-Gerhard. 2009. “Comparison and Beyond: Traditions, Scope, and Perspectives of Comparative History.” In *Comparative and Transnational History: Central European Approaches and New Perspectives* ed. by Heinz-Gerhard Haupt and Jürgen Kocka: 1–32. New York/Oxford: Berghahn.

Koenig, Matthias. 2016. “Beyond the Paradigm of Secularization?.” In *Working with A Secular Age. Interdisciplinary Perspectives on Charles Taylor’s Master Narrative* ed. by Florian Zemmin, Colin Jager and Guido Vanheeswijck: 23–48. Berlin/Boston: De Gruyter.

Koselleck, Reinhart. 2011. “Introduction (Einleitung) to the Geschichtliche Grundbegriffe.” *Contributions to the History of Concepts* 6/1: 6+ (accessed from Academic OneFile. Web. Jan 19, 2016).

—. 2006. “Sprachwandel und Ereignisgeschichte (erstmals erschienen 1989).” In *Begriffsgeschichten: Studien zur Semantik und Pragmatik der politischen und sozialen Sprache:* 32–55. Frankfurt a.M.: Suhrkamp.

—. 2004. *Futures Past. On the Semantics of Historical Time*; translated and with an introduction by Keith Tribe. New York: Columbia University Press.

—. 1998. “Social History and *Begriffsgeschichte.*” In *History of Concepts: Comparative Perspectives* ed. by Iain Hampsher-Monk, Karin Tilmans and Frank van Vree: 23–36. Amsterdam: Amsterdam University Press.

—. 1996. “A Response to Comments on the Geschichtliche Grundbegriffe.” In *The Meaning of Historical Terms and Concepts: New Studies on Begriffsgeschichte* ed. by Melvin Richter and Hartmut Lehmann: 59–70. Washington: German Historical Institute.

—. 1972. "Einleitung." In *Geschichtliche Grundbegriffe: Historisches Lexikon zur politisch-sozialen Sprache in Deutschland. Band 1: A-D* ed. by Otto Brunner, Werner Conze and Reinhart Koselleck: xiii–xvxii. Stuttgart: Ernst Klett.

Koselleck, Reinhart and Richter, Michaela. 2011. "Introduction and Prefaces to the 'Geschichtliche Grundbegriffe'." *Contributions to the History of Concepts* 6/1: 1–5, 7–25, 27–37.

Koselleck, Reinhart and Dipper, Christoph. 1998. "Begriffsgeschichte, Sozialgeschichte, begriffene Geschichte. Reinhart Koselleck im Gespräch mit Christoph Dipper." *Neue Politische Literatur* 51: 187–205.

Krämer, Gudrun. 2013. "Modern but not Secular: Religion, Identity and the *ordre public* in the Arab Middle East." *International Sociology* 28/6: 629–644.

—. 2010. *Hasan al-Banna.* Oxford: Oneworld.

Kudsi-Zadeh, A. Albert. 1972. "Afghānī and Freemasonry in Egypt." *Journal of the American Oriental Society* 92/1: 25–35.

Kuhlemann, Frank-Michael. 2002. *Bürgerlichkeit und Religion: Zur Sozial- und Mentalitätsgeschichte der evangelischen Pfarrer in Baden 1860–1914.* Göttingen: Vandenhoeck & Ruprecht.

Künstlinger, David. 1935. "'Islām', 'Muslim', 'aslama' im Kurān." *Rocznik Orientalistyczny* 11: 128–137.

Kurzman, Charles. 2002. *Modernist Islam, 1840–1940: A Sourcebook.* Oxford/New York: Oxford University Press.

Lane, Edward William. 1863–1893. *An Arabic-English Lexicon: Derived from the Best and most Copious Eastern Sources*; 8 vols., vols. 6–8 compiled by S. Lane-Poole. London: Williams & Norgate.

Langner, Joachim. 2015. "Religion in Motion and the Essence of Islam: Manifestations of the Global in Muhammad 'Abduh's Response to Farah Antūn." In *A Global Middle East: Mobility, Materiality and Culture in the Modern Age, 1880–1940* ed. by Liat Kozma, Cyrus Schayegh and Avner Wishnitzer: 356–364. London: I.B. Tauris.

Laoust, Henri. 1986 [1938]. *Le Califat dans la doctrine de Rašīd Riḍā. Traduction annotée d'al-Ḫilāfa au al-Imāma al-ʿuẓmà (Le Califat ou l'Imāma suprême).* Paris: Librairie d'Amérique et d'Orient.

—. 1932. "Le Réformisme orthodoxe des 'Salafiya' et les caractères généraux de son orientation actuelle." *Revue des Études Islamiques* 6: 175–224.

Latour, Bruno. 2002. "Gabriel Tarde and the End of the Social." In *The Social in Question: New Bearings in History and the Social Sciences* ed. by Patrick Joyce: 117–132. London/New York: Routledge.

Lauzière, Henry. 2016. *The Making of Salafism: Islamic Reform in the Twentieth Century.* New York: Columbia University Press.

—. 2016. "What We Mean Versus What They Meant by 'Salafi': A Reply to Frank Griffel." *Die Welt des Islams* 56: 89–96.

—. 2010. "The Construction of Salafiyya: Reconsidering Salafism from the Perspective of Conceptual History." *International Journal of Middle East Studies* 42: 369–389.

Le Bon, Gustave. 1912. *La Psychologie politique et la Défense sociale.* Paris: Ernest Flammarion.

—. 1900. *Psychologie des Foules.* Paris: Librairie Félix Alcan.

—. 1889. *Les premières civilisations.* Paris: Marpon et Flammarion.

—. 1884. *La civilisation des Arabes.* Paris: Firmin-Didot.
—. 1894. *Lois psychologiques de l'évolution des peuples.* Paris: Felix Alcan.
van Leeuwen, Richard. 2013. "Reformist Islam and Popular Beliefs: Rashīd Riḍā's Attack against the Cult of Shrines." In *Sources and Approaches Across Disciplines in Near Eastern Studies. Proceedings of the 24th Congress, Union Européenne des Arabisants et Islamistes, Leipzig 2008* ed. by Verena Klemm and Nuha al-Shaʿar: 141–154. Leuven/Paris/ Walpole, Mass.: Uitgeverij Peters/Departement Oosterse Studies.
—. 2012. "Mobility and Islamic Thought: The Syrian Journey of Rashīd Riḍā in 1908." In *Centre and Periphery within the Borders of Islam. Proceedings of the 23rd Congress of L'Union Européenne des Arabisants et Islamisants* ed. by Giuseppe Contu: 33–46. Leuven/Paris/Walpole, MA: Uitgeverij Peeters.
—. 2008. "Islamic Reformism and the Secular: Rashid Ridâ's Theory on Miracles." In *Religion and Its Other. Secular and Sacral Concepts and Practices in Interaction* ed. by Heike Bock, Jörg Feuchter and Michi Knecht: 64–78. Frankfurt/New York: Campus.
Leonhard, Jörn. 2004. "*Grundbegriffe* und *Sattelzeiten:* Languages and Discourses: Europäische und anglo-amerikanische Deutungen des Verhältnisses von Sprache und Geschichte." In *Interkultureller Transfer und nationaler Eigensinn. Europäische und anglo-amerikanische Perspektiven der Kulturwissenschaften* ed. by Rebekka Habermas and Rebekka von Mallinckrodt: 71–86. Göttingen: Wallstein.
—. 2001. *Liberalismus: Zur historischen Semantik eines europäischen Deutungsmusters.* München: Oldenbourg.
Lerner, David. 1958. *The Passing of Traditional Society. Modernizing the Middle East.* New York: The Free Press.
LeVine, Mark and Salvatore, Armando. 2009. "Religious Mobilization and the Public Sphere: Reflections on Alternative Genealogies." In *Publics, Politics and Participation. Locating the Public Sphere in the Middle East and North Africa* ed. by Seteney Shami: 65–90. New York: Social Science Research Council.
Lewis, Bernard. 2003. *What Went Wrong? Western Impact and Middle Eastern Response.* London: Phoenix.
—. 1988. *The Political Language of Islam.* Chicago, Ill. et al.: University of Chicago Press.
Lidzbarski, Mark. 1922. "Salām and Islām." *Zeitschrift für Semitistik und verwandte Gebiete* 1: 85–96.
Lightman, Bernard (ed.). 2015. *Global Spencerism: The Communication and Appropriation of a British Evolutionist.* Leiden: Brill.
Loeffler, Richard. 1988. *Islam in Practice: Religious Beliefs in a Persian Village.* New York: State University of New York Press.
Lomasky, Loren E. 2002. "Classical Liberalism and Civil Society." In *Alternative Conceptions of Civil Society* ed. by Simone Chambers and Will Kymlicka: 50–70. Princeton: Princeton University Press.
Lopez, Shaun T. 2005. "Madams, Murders, and the Media: Akhbar al-Hawadith and the Emergence of a Mass Culture in 1920s Egypt." In *Re-Envisioning Egypt 1919–1952* ed. by Arthur Goldschmidt, Amy J. Johnson and Barak A. Salmoni: 371–397. Cairo: The American University in Cairo Press.
Luizard, Pierre-Jean. 1995. "al-Azhar: Institution sunnite réformée." In *Entre reforme sociale et mouvement national: Identité et modernisation en Egypte (1882–1962)* ed. by Alain Roussillon: 519–547. Cairo: CEDEJ.

Madsen, Richard. 2011. "Secularism, Religious Change, and Social Conflict in Asia." In *Rethinking Secularism* ed. by Craig Calhoun, Mark Juergensmeyer and Jonathan VanAntwerpen: 248–269. Oxford: Oxford University Press.

Mahmood, Saba. 2010. "Can Secularism Be Other-wise?." In *Varieties of Secularism in a Secular Age* ed. by Michael Warner, Jonathan VanAntwerpen and Craig Calhoun: 282–299. Cambridge, Mass.: Harvard University Press.

Makdisi, Ussama. 2002. "After 1860: Debating Religion, Reform, and Nationalism in the Ottoman Empire." *International Journal of Middle East Studies* 34/4: 601–617.

March, Andrew F. 2011. "Law as a Vanishing Mediator in the Theological Ethics of Tariq Ramadan." *European Journal of Political Theory* 10/2: 177–201.

Martin, Xavier. 1989. "Révolution française et socialisation de l'individu." In *La Révolution française et les processus de socialisation de l'homme moderne* ed. by Claude Mazauric: 78–84. Paris: Messidor.

Massignon, Louis. 1946. "L'Umma et ses synonymes: notion de 'communauté sociale' en Islam." *Revue des Études Islamiques* 2: 151–157.

—. 1920. "La Presse Arabe." *Revue du Monde Musulman* 38: 210–216.

Masud, Muhammad Khalid. 2009. "Islamic Modernism." In *Islam and Modernity. Key Issues and Debates* ed. by Muhammad Khalid Masud, Armando Salvatore and Martin van Bruinessen: 237–260. Edinburgh: Edinburgh University Press.

Masud, Muhammad Khalid and Salvatore, Armando. 2009. "Western Scholars of Islam on the Issue of Modernity." In *Islam and Modernity. Key Issues and Debates* ed. by Muhammad Khalid Masud, Armando Salvatore and Martin van Bruinessen: 36–53. Edinburgh: Edinburgh University Press.

Masuzawa, Tomoko. 2011. "The University and the Advent of the Academic Secular: The State's Management of Public Instruction." In *After Secular Law* ed. by Winnifred Fallers Sullivan, Robert A. Yelle and Taussig-Rubbo. Mateo: 119–139. Stanford, CA: Stanford Law Books.

—. 2005. *The Invention of World Religions.* Chicago: Chicago University Press.

Maza, Sarah. 2003. *The Myth of the French Bourgeoisie: An Essay on the Social Imaginary, 1750–1850.* Cambridge, Mass.: Harvard University Press.

Meijer, Roel and Butenschøn, Nils (eds.). 2017. *The Crisis of Citizenship in the Arab World.* Leiden/Boston: Brill.

Mellor, Philip A. 2004. *Religion, Realism and Social Theory: Making Sense of Society.* London: Sage.

Meyer, Morakot Jewachinda. 2014. "Discordant Localizations of Modernity: Reflections on Concepts of the Economic and the Social in Siam during the Early Twentieth Century." In *A Global Conceptual History of Asia, 1860–1940* ed. by Hagen Schulz-Forberg: 149–168. London: Pickering & Chatto.

Mikhail, Kyriakos. 1911. *Copts and Moslems under British control. A collection of facts and a résumé of authoritative opinions on the Coptic question.* London: Smith, Elder, and Co.

Milbank, John. 1991. *Theology and Social Theory: Beyond Secular Reason.* Cambridge, Mass.: B. Blackwell.

Miller, James. 2008. "What Secular Age?." *International Journal of Politics, Culture, and Society* 21/1: 5–10.

Mitchell, Richard P. 1993 [1969]. *The Society of the Muslim Brothers.* New York: Oxford University Press.

Mitchell, Timothy. 2002. *Rule of Experts: Egypt, Techno-Politics, Modernity.* Berkeley/Los Angeles/London: University of California Press.

—. 1988. *Colonising Egypt.* Cambridge: Cambridge University Press.

Montgomery, Scott. 2000. *Science in Translation: Movements of Knowledge through Cultures and Time.* Chicago/London: The University of Chicago Press.

Moras, Joachim. 1930. *Ursprung und Entwicklung des Begriffs der Zivilisation in Frankreich (1756–1830).* Hamburg: Seminar für romanische Sprachen und Kultur.

Motzkin, Gabriel. 2005. "On the Notion of Historical (Dis)Continuity: Reinhart Koselleck's Construction of the Sattelzeit." *Contributions to the History of Concepts* 1/2: 145–158.

Moussalli, Ahmad S. 1995. "Modern Islamic Fundamentalist Discourses on Civil Society, Pluralism and Democracy." In *Civil Society in the Middle East* ed. by August Richard Norton: vol. 1: 79–119. Leiden/New York/Köln: Brill.

Musa, Salama. 1961. *The Education of Salama Musa*; translated by L. O. Schuman. Leiden: Brill.

Nassehi, Armin. 2001. "Moderne Gesellschaft." In *Klassische Gesellschaftsbegriffe der Soziologie* ed. by Georg Kneer, Armin Nassehi and Markus Schroer: 208–245. München: Wilhelm Fink.

Nietzsche, Friedrich. 1977. "Zur Genealogie der Moral." In *Sämtliche Werke. Kritische Studienausgabe*; ed. Giorgio Colli und Mazzino Montinari, vol. 5 München/Berlin: dtv/De Gruyter.

van Nispen Tot Sevenaer, Wouter. 2002. "Le commentaire coranique du Manâr. Un siècle plus tard." In *En hommage au père Jacques Jomier* ed. by Marie-Thérèse Urvoy: 247–257. Paris: Les Editions du Cerf.

—. 1996. *Activité humaine et agir de Dieu. Le concept de "Sunan de Dieu" dans le commentaire coranique du Manār.* Beirut: Dar al-Machreq.

Noorani, Yaseen. 2010. *Culture and Hegemony in the Colonial Middle East.* New York: Palgrave Macmillan.

Norton, August Richard (ed.). 1995. *Civil Society in the Middle East.* 2 vols. Leiden/New York/Köln: Brill.

Ophir, Adi. 2011. "Concept." *Political Concepts – A Critical Lexicon* 1, http://www.politicalconcepts.org/2011/concept (accessed March 20, 2015).

Outhwaite, William. 2006. *The Future of Society.* Oxford: Blackwell.

Özervarlı, M. S. 2010. "The Reconstruction of Islamic Social Thought in the Modern Period: Nursi's Approach to Religious Discourse in a Changing Society." *Asian Journal of Social Sciences* 38: 532–553.

—. 2007. "Transferring Traditional Islamic Disciplines into Modern Social Sciences in Late Ottoman Thought: The Attempts of Ziya Gokalp and Mehmed Serafeddin." *The Muslim World* 97: 317–330.

Pankoke, Eckart. 1977. "Fortschritt und Komplexität. Die Anfänge moderner Sozialwissenschaft in Deutschland." In *Studien zum Beginn der modernen Welt* ed. by Reinhart Koselleck: 352–376.

Pankhurst, Reza. 2014. *The Inevitable Caliphate? A History of the Struggle for Global Islamic Union, 1924 to Present.* New York: Oxford University Press.

Pannu, Paula. 2014. "From *Kerajaan* (Kingship) to *Masyarakat* (The People): Malay Articulations of Nationhood through Concepts of the 'Social' and the 'Economic',

1920–40." In *A Global Conceptual History of Asia, 1860–1940* ed. by Hagen Schulz-Forberg: 111–128. London: Pickering & Chatto.

Park, Myoung-Kyu. 2014. "How Concepts Met History in Korea's Complex Modernization: New Concepts of Economy and Society and their Impact." In *A Global Conceptual History of Asia, 1860–1940* ed. by Hagen Schulz-Forberg: 25–42. London: Pickering & Chatto.

Patel, Sujata. 2013. "Are the Theories of Multiple Modernities Eurocentric? The Problem of Colonialism and Its Knowledge(s)." In *Worlds of Difference* ed. by Saïd Amir Arjomand and Elisa Reis: 40–57. London et al.: Sage.

Patten, S. N. 1894. "The Organic Concept of Society." *Annals of the American Academy of Political and Social Science* 5: 88–93.

Pellitteri, Antonino. 1998. *Islam e riforma: l'ambito arabo-ottomano e l'opera di Rafīq bey al-ʿAẓm intellettuale damasceno riformatore (1865–1925)*. Palermo: n.g.

Pernau, Margrit. 2012. "Whither Conceptual History? From National to Entangled Histories." *Contributions to the History of Concepts*, 7/1: 1–11.

—. 2007. "Gab es eine indische Zivilgesellschaft im 19. Jahrhundert? Überlegungen zum Verhältnis von Globalgeschichte und historischer Semantik." *Traverse: Zeitschrift für Geschichte* 14/3: 51–65.

Pernau, Margrit and Sachsenmeier, Dominic (eds.). 2016. *Global Conceptual History: A Reader.* London et al.: Bloomsbury.

Pflitsch, Andreas. 2012. *Zweierlei Barbarei. Überlegungen zu Kultur, Moderne und Authentizität im Dreieck zwischen Europa, Russland und arabischem Nahen Osten.* Würzburg: Ergon.

Philipp, Thomas. 2014. *Jurji Zaydan and the Foundations of Arab Nationalism.* New York: Syracuse University Press.

—. 2010. "Progress and Liberal Thought in al-Hilāl, al-Manār, and al-Muqtaṭaf before World War I." In *Nationalism and Liberal Thought in the Arab East: Ideology and Practice* ed. by Christoph Schumann: 132–144. London: Routledge.

Philipp, Thomas [not identical with his just-listed namesake]. 2009. "Gesellschaft und Religion. Eine kritische Auseinandersetzung mit Habermas' Zeitdiagnose der postsäkularen Gesellschaft." *Berliner Journal für Soziologie* 19/1: 55–78.

Philippso[n], Ludwig. 1855. *The Development of the Religious Idea in Judaism, Christianity and Mahomedanism, considered in twelve lectures on the history and purport of Judaism, delivered in Magdeburg, 1847, by Dr. Ludwig Philippsohn*; translated from the German with notes by Anna Maria Goldsmid. London: Longman, Brown, Green and Longmans.

Pickstock, Catherine. 2002. "The Mediaeval Origins of Civil Society." In *The Social in Question: New Bearings in History and the Social Sciences* ed. by Patrick Joyce: 21–43. London/New York: Routledge.

Pieterse, Jan Nederveen. 2006. "Oriental Globalization." *Theory, Culture & Society* 23/2–3: 411–413.

Plessner, Helmuth. 1928. *Die Stufen des Organischen und der Mensch: Einleitung in die historische Anthropologie.* Berlin: De Gruyter.

Pollard, Lisa. 2014. "Egyptian by Association: Charitable States and Service Societies, circa 1850–1945." *International Journal of Middle East Studies* 46/2: 239–257.

—. 2005. *Nurturing the Nation: The Family Politics of Modernizing, Colonizing, and Liberating Egypt (1805–1923).* Berkeley: University of California Press.

Poovey, Mary. 2002. "The Liberal Civil Subject and the Social in Eighteenth-Century British Moral Philosophy." *Public Culture* 14/1: 125–145.

—. 2002. "The Liberal Civil Subject and the Social in Eighteenth-Century British Moral Philosophy." In *The Social in Question: New Bearings in History and the Social Sciences* ed. by Patrick Joyce: 44–61. London/New York: Routledge.

—. 1995. *Making a Social Body: British Cultural Formation.* Chicago: University of Chicago Press.

Quadri, Junaid. 2016. "Religion as Transcendence in Modern Islam: Tracking 'Religious Matters' into a Secular(izing) Age." In *Working with A Secular Age. Interdisciplinary Perspectives on Charles Taylor's Master Narrative; with an Afterword by Charles Taylor* ed. by Florian Zemmin, Colin Jager and Guido Vanheeswijck: 331–348. Berlin/Boston: De Gruyter.

Ramadan, Tariq. 2001. *Islam, the West and the Challenges of Modernity*; transl. Saïd Amghar. Leicester: The Islamic Foundation.

—. 1998. *Aux sources du renouveau musulman: d'al-Afghānī à Ḥassan al-Bannā. Un siècle de réformisme islamique.* Paris: Bayard Editions/Centurion.

—. 1998 [1994]. *Les musulmans dans la laïcité: responsabilités et droits des musulmans dans les sociétés occidentales.* Lyon: Tawhid.

Randeria, Shalini. 2009. "Entangled Histories of Uneven Modernities: Civil Society, Caste Councils, and Legal Pluralism in Postcolonial India." In *Comparative and Transnational History: Central European Approaches and New Perspectives* ed. by Heinz-Gerhard Haupt and Jürgen Kocka: 77–104. New York/Oxford: Berghahn.

Raouf, Abbas. 2005. "French Impact on the Egyptian Educational System under Muhammad Aly and Ismail." In *La France & l'Égypte à l'époque des vice-rois 1805–1882* ed. by Daniel Panzac and André Raymond: 91–99. Cairo: Institut français d'archéologie orientale.

Rebhan, Helga. 1986. *Geschichte und Funktion einiger politischer Termini im Arabischen des 19. Jahrhunderts (1798–1882).* Wiesbaden: Otto Harrassowitz.

Reid, Donald Malcolm. 1990. *Cairo University and the Making of Modern Egypt.* Cambridge: Cambridge University Press.

—. 1982. "*Arabic Thought in the Liberal Age* Twenty Years After." *International Journal of Middle East Studies* 14/4: 541–557.

—. 1975. *The Odyssey of Farah Antun: a Syrian Christian's Quest for Secularism.* Minneapolis [etc.]: Bibliotheca Islamica.

—. 1974. "The Syrian Christians and Early Socialism in the Arab World." *International Journal of Middle East Studies* 5/2: 177–193.

Richter, Melvin. 2005. "More Than a Two-Way Traffic: Analyzing, Translating, and Comparing Political Concepts from other Cultures." In *Redescriptions. Yearbook of Political Thought and Conceptual History* 9: 217–228.

—. 1995. *The History of Political and Social Concepts. A Critical Introduction.* New York/Oxford: Oxford University Press.

Rida, Rashid. 2008. *Christian Criticisms, Islamic Proofs. Rašīd Riḍā's Modernist Defence of Islam*; translation and analysis by Simon A. Wood. Oxford: Oneworld.

—. 1996. *The Muhammadan Revelation;* translated by Yusuf T. DeLorenzo. Alexandria: Al-Saadawi.

—. 1960. *The Revelation to Muhammad*; translated by Abdus-Samad Sharafuddin. Bhiwandi [India]: Ad-Darul-Qayyimah.

Riedel, Manfred. 1984. "'State' and 'Civil Society': Linguistic Context and Historical Origin." In: *Between Tradition and Revolution*. Cambridge: Cambridge University Press, 129–158.

—. 1975. "Gesellschaft, bürgerliche." In *Geschichtliche Grundbegriffe. Historisches Lexikon zur politisch-sozialen Sprache in Deutschland; Band 2 E-G* ed. by Otto Brunner, Werner Conze and Reinhart Koselleck: 719–800. Stuttgart: Klett.

—. 1975. "Gesellschaft, Gemeinschaft." In *Geschichtliche Grundbegriffe. Historisches Lexikon zur politisch-sozialen Sprache in Deutschland; Band 2 E-G* ed. by Otto Brunner, Werner Conze and Reinhart Koselleck: 801–862. Stuttgart: Klett.

Ringgren, Helmer. 1949. "Islam, ʾaslama and muslim." *Horae Soederblomianae* 2: 1–34.

Robson, James. 1954. "'Islām' as a Term." *The Muslim World* 44: 101–109.

Roussillon, Alain. 1996. "Sociologie et société en Egypte: le contournement des intellectuels par l'Etat." In *Les intellectuels et le pouvoir* ed. by T. Al-Bishri [et al.] ; réalisé en collaboration par le SEDEJ et le CEROAC et placé sous la direction de G. Dalanoue: 93–138. Cairo: CEDEJ.

—. 1995. "Introduction: La modernité disputée: Réforme sociale et politique en Egypte." In *Entre reforme sociale et mouvement national: Identité et modernisation en Egypte (1882–1962)* ed. by Alain Roussillon: 9–35. Cairo: CEDEJ.

—. 1995. "Réforme sociale et production des classes moyennes: Muhammad ʿUmar et 'l'arriération des Egyptiens'." In *Entre reforme sociale et mouvement national: Identité et modernisation en Egypte (1882–1962)* ed. by Alain Roussillon: 37–89. Cairo: CEDEJ.

—. 1992. "La représentation de l'identité par les discours fondateurs de la sociologie turque et égyptienne: Ziya Gökalp et ʿAli ʿAbd al-Wahid Wafi." In *Modernisation et mobilisation sociale II, Egypte-Turquie [Online]* ed. by CEDEJ. Cairo: CEDEJ – Égypte/Soudan. http://books.openedition.org/cedej/1047 (last accessed July 23, 2017).

—. 1991. "Projet colonial et traditions scientifiques : aux origines de la sociologie égyptienne." In *D'un Orient l'autre : les métamorphoses successives des perceptions et connaissances* ed. by CEDEJ: 347–388. Paris: Editions du CNRS et Idem.

Rueschemeyer, Dietrich and Skopcol, Theda (eds.). 1994. *States, Social Knowledge, and the Origins of Modern Social Policies*. Princeton, NJ: Princeton University Press.

Ryad, Umar. 2010. "Islamic Reformism and Great Britain: Rashīd Riḍā's Image As Reflected in the Journal Al-Manār in Cairo." *Islam and Christian Muslim Relations* 21/3: 263–285.

—. 2009. *Islamic Reformism and Christianity: A Critical Reading of the Works of Muhammad Rashīd Riḍā and His Associates (1898–1935)*. Leiden: Brill.

—. 2009. "A Printed Muslim Lighthouse in Cairo: *al-Manār*'s Early Years, Religious Aspiration and Reception (1898–1903)." *Arabica* 56/1: 27–60.

Ryzova, Lucie. 2014. *The Age of the Efendiyya: Passages to Modernity in National-Colonial Egypt*. Oxford: Oxford University Press.

—. 2005. "Egyptianizing Modernity through the 'New Effendiya': Social and Cultural Constructions of the Middle Class in Egypt under the Monarchy." In *Re-Envisioning Egypt 1919–1952* ed. by Arthur Goldschmidt, Amy J. Johnson and Barak A. Salmoni: 124–163. Cairo: The American University in Cairo Press.

Sachsenmeier, Dominic. 2014. "Notions of Society in Early Twentieth-Century China, 1900–25." In *A Global Conceptual History of Asia, 1860–1940* ed. by Hagen Schulz-Forberg: 61–74. London: Pickering & Chatto.

Sajid, Mehdi. 2013. “Rashīd Riḍā in Europe: A monomythic reading of his travel narrative.” In *Venturing beyond Borders: Reflections on Genre, Function and Boundaries in Middle Eastern Travel Writing* ed. by Bekim Agai, Olcay Akyıldız and Caspar Hillebrand: 179 – 202. Würzburg: Ergon.

Salama, Mohammad R. 2011. *Islam, Orientalism and Intellectual History: Modernity and the Politics of Exclusion since Ibn Khaldun.* London: I. B. Tauris.

Salvatore, Armando. 2013. “The Sociology of Islam: Precedents and Perspectives.” *Sociology of Islam* 1: 7 – 13.

—. 2007. *The Public Sphere: Liberal Modernity, Catholicism, Islam.* Basingstoke et al.: Palgrave Macmillan.

—. 2000. “The Islamic Reform Project in the Emerging Public Sphere: The (Meta-)Normative Redefinition of Shariʿa.” In *Between Europe and Islam: Shaping Modernity in a Transcultural Space* ed. by Armando Salvatore and Almut Höfert: 89 – 108. Brüssel/Berlin/Oxford: Presses Interuniversitaires Europeénnes.

Sawaie, Mohammed. 2000. “Rifaʿa Rafi al-Tahtawi and His Contribution to the Lexical Development of Modern Literary Arabic.” *International Journal of Middle East Studies* 32/3: 395 – 410.

Sayyid, Bobby S. 1997. *A Fundamental Fear: Eurocentrism and the Emergence of Islamism.* London/New York: Zed Books.

al-Sayyid, Mustapha K. 1995. “A Civil Society in Egypt?.” In *Civil Society in the Middle East* ed. by August Richard Norton: 269 – 293. Leiden/New York/Köln: Brill.

Schacht, Joseph. 1928. “Zur wahhābitischen Literatur.” *Zeitschrift für Semitistik und verwandte Gebiete* 6: 200 – 212.

Schaebler, Birgit. 2007. “Writing the Nation in the Arabic-Speaking World, Nationally and Transnationally.” In *Writing the Nation. A Global Perspective* ed. by Stefan Berger: 179 – 196. New York: Palgrave Macmillan.

Schalk, Peter (ed.). 2013. *Religion in Asien? Studien zur Anwendbarkeit des Religionsbegriffs.* Uppsala: Uppsala Universitet.

Scharbrodt, Oliver. 2007. “The Salafiyya and Sufism: Muhammad ʿAbduh and his Risalat al-Waridat (Treatise on Mystical Inspirations).” *Bulletin of the School of Oriental and African Studies* 70: 89 – 115.

Schielke, Samuli. 2012. “Being a Nonbeliever in a Time of Islamic Revival: Trajectories of Doubt and Certainty in Contemporary Egypt.” *International Journal of Middle East Studies* 44: 301 – 320.

—. 2007. “Hegemonic Encounters: Criticism of Saints-Day Festivals and the Formation of Mod ern Islam in Late 19th and Early 20th-Century Egypt.” *Die Welt des Islams* 47/3 – 4: 319 – 355.

Schulz-Forberg, Hagen. 2014. “Introduction: Global Conceptual History: Promises and Pitfalls of a New Research Agenda.” In *A Global Conceptual History of Asia, 1860 – 1940* ed. by Hagen Schulz-Forberg: 1 – 24. London: Pickering & Chatto.

—. (ed.). 2014. *A Global Conceptual History of Asia, 1860 – 1940.* London: Pickering & Chatto.

Schulze, Reinhard. 2016. “The Quest for the West in an Era of Globalization: Some Remarks on the Hidden Meaning of Charles Taylor’s Master Narrative.” In *Working with A Secular Age. Interdisciplinary Perspectives on Charles Taylor’s Master Narrative* ed. by Florian Zemmin, Colin Jager and Guido Vanheeswijck: 175 – 203. Berlin/Boston: De Gruyter.

—. 2015. *Der Koran und die Genealogie des Islam.* Basel: Schwabe Verlag.
—. 2013. "On Relating Religion to Society and Society to Religion." In *Debating Islam. Negotiating Religion, Europe, and the Self* ed. by Samuel M. Behloul, Susanne Leuenberger and Andreas Tunger-Zanetti: 333 – 356. Bielefeld: transcript.
—. 2010. "Die Dritte Unterscheidung: Islam, Religion und Säkularität." In *Religionen – Wahrheitsansprüche – Konflikte: Theologische Perspektiven* ed. by Walter Dietrich and Wolfgang Lienemann: 147 – 206. Zürich: TVZ.
—. 2000. "Is there an Islamic Modernity?." In *The Islamic World and the West: An Introduction to Political Cultures and International Relations* ed. by Kai Hafez: 21 – 32. Leiden: Brill.
—. 1997. "The Birth of Tradition and Modernity in 18th and 19th Century Islamic Culture: The Case of Printing." *Culture and History* 16: 29 – 72.
—. 1992. "Kolonisierung und Widerstand. Die ägyptischen Bauern-Revolten von 1919." In *Die ägyptische Gesellschaft im 20. Jahrhundert* ed. by Alexander Schölch and Helmut Mejcher: 11 – 41. Hamburg: Deutsches Orient-Institut.
Schweiker, William. 2009. "Our Religious Situation: Charles Taylor's *A Secular Age.*" *American Journal of Theology & Philosophy* 30/3: 323 – 329.
Schwinn, Thomas. 2009. "Multiple modernities: Konkurrierende Thesen und offene Fragen. Ein Literaturbericht in konstruktiver Absicht." *Zeitschrift für Soziologie* 38: 454 – 476.
Sedgwick, Mark J. 2010. *Muhammad Abduh.* Oxford: Oneworld.
Seferta, Yusuf H. R. 1985. "Rashid Rida's Quest for an Islamic Government." *Hamdard Islamicus* 8/35 – 50.
Seligman, Adam. 2002. "Civil Society as Idea and Ideal." In *Alternative Conceptions of Civil Society* ed. by Simone Chambers and Will Kymlicka: 13 – 33. Princeton: Princeton University Press.
Selim, Samah. 2009. "Languages of Civilization: Nation, Translation and the Politics of Race in Colonial Egypt." *The Translator* 15/1 (Special Issue: Nation and Translation in the Middle East): 139 – 156.
Senturk, Recep. 2007. "Intellectual Dependency: Late Ottoman Intellectuals between *fiqh* and Social Science." *Die Welt des Islams* 47/3 – 4: 283 – 318.
Shahin, Emad Eldin. 1993. *Through Muslim Eyes: M. Rashīd Riḍā and the West.* Herndon, Virginia: The International Institute of Islamic Thought.
—. 1989. "Muḥammad Rashīd Riḍā's Perspectives on the West as Reflected in *al-Manār.*" *The Muslim World* 79/2: 113 – 132.
Sharabi, Hisham. 1970. *Arab Intellectuals and the West: The Formative Years, 1875 – 1914.* Baltimore/London: The Johns Hopkins Press.
Shechter, Relli. 2006. *Smoking, Culture and Economy in the Middle East. The Egyptian Tobacco Market 1850 – 2000.* London/New York: I.B. Tauris.
Sheehi, Stephen. 2011. "Butrus al-Bustani. Syria's Ideologue of the Age." In *The Origins of Syrian Nationhood. Histories, Pioneers and Identity* ed. by Adel Beshara: 57 – 78. Oxon/New York: Routledge.
—. 2005. "Arabic Literary-Scientific Journals: Precedence for Globalization and the Creation of Modernity." *Comparative Studies of South Asia, Africa and the Middle East* 25/2: 438 – 448.

Sheehan, Jonathan. 2010. "When Was Disenchantment? History and the Secular Age." In *Varieties of Secularism in a Secular Age* ed. by Michael Warner, Jonathan VanAntwerpen and Craig Calhoun: 217–242. Cambridge, Mass.: Harvard University Press.

Sica, Alan. 2012. "A Selective History of Sociology." In *The Wiley-Blackwell Companion to Sociology* ed. by Georg Ritzer: 25–54. Chichester: Wiley-Blackwell.

Sigalas, Nikos. 2012. "Des histoires des sultans à l'histoire de l'État. Une enquête sur le temps du pouvoir ottoman (XVIe–XVIIIe siècles)." In *Les Ottomans et le temps* ed. by François Georgeon and Frédéric Hitzel: 99–128. Leiden/Boston: Brill.

Sirry, Mun'im. 2011. "Jamāl al-Dīn al-Qāsimī and the Salafi Approach to Sufism." *Die Welt des Islams* 51: 75–108.

Sirriyeh, Elizabeth. 2000. "Rashid Rida's Autobiography of the Syrian Years, 1865–1897." *Arabic and Middle Eastern Literatures* 3/2: 179–194.

Skovgaard-Petersen, Jakob. 2001. "Portrait of the Intellectual as a Young Man: Rašīd Riḍā's Muḥāwarāt al-muṣliḥ wa-al-muqallid (1906)." *Christian-Muslim Relations* 12/1: 93–104.

—. 1997. *Defining Islam for the Egyptian State: Muftis and Fatwas of the Dār al-Iftā.* Leiden/New York/Köln: Brill.

Small, A. W. 1895. "The Era of Sociology." *American Journal of Sociology* 1/1: 1–15.

Smith, Jane Idleman. 1975. *An Historical and Semantic Study of the Term 'islām' as seen in a Sequence of Qur'ān Commentaries.* Montana: Scholars Press of the University.

Smith, Wilfred Cantwell. 1981. "The Historical Development in Islām of the Concept of Islām as an Historical Development." In *On Understanding Islam. Selected Studies:* 41–77. The Hague et al.: Moutin Publishers.

Spencer, Herbert. 1861. *Education: Intellectual, Moral, And Physical.* New York: D. Appleton And Company.

Stephan, Johannes. 2016. "Reconsidering Transcendence/Immanence. Modernity's Modes of Narration in Nineteenth-Century Arabic Literary Tradition." In *Working with A Secular Age. Interdisciplinary Perspectives on Charles Taylor's Master Narrative* ed. by Florian Zemmin, Colin Jager and Guido Vanheeswijck: 349–367. Berlin/Boston: De Gruyter.

Stetkevych, Jaroslav. 1970. *The Modern Arabic Literary Language.* Chicago: Chicago University Press.

Stolz, Daniel A. 2012. "'By Virtue of your Knowledge': Scientific Materialism and the *fatwās* of Rashīd Riḍā." *Bulletin of the School of Oriental and African Studies* 75/2: 223–247.

Strauss, Claudia. 2006. "The Imaginary." *Anthropological Theory* 6/3: 322–344.

Suleiman, Yasir. 2003. *The Arabic Language and National Identity: A Study in Ideology.* Edinburgh: Edinburgh University Press.

Swan, George. 1911. "The Moslem Press in Egypt." *The Moslem World* 1: 147–154.

Tageldin, Shaden M. 2011. *Disarming Words. Empire and the Seductions of Translation in Egypt.* Berkeley, CA: University of California Press.

—. 2011. "Secularizing Islam: Carlyle, al-Sibāʿī, and the Translations of 'Religion' in British Egypt." *PMLA* 126/1: 123–139.

Tauber, Eliezer. 1998. "The Political Life of Rashīd Riḍā." *The Arabist: Budapest Studies in Arabic* 19–20: 261–272.

—. 1995. "Rashīd Riḍā and Fayṣal's Kingdom in Syria." *The Muslim World* 85: 235–245.

—. 1995. "Rashid Riḍā and Political Attitudes during World War I." *The Muslim World* 85/1–2: 107–121.

—. 1993. *The Emergence of the Arab Movements.* London: Frank Cass.

—. 1989. "Rashid Riḍā as Pan-Arabist before World War I." *The Muslim World* 79/2: 102–112.

Taylor, Charles. 2011. "Response." *The Australian Journal of Anthropology* 22: 125–133.

—. 2011. "Western Secularity." In *Rethinking Secularism* ed. by Craig Calhoun, Mark Juergensmeyer and Jonathan VanAntwerpen: 31–53. Oxford: Oxford University Press.

—. 2010. "Afterword: Apologia pro Libro suo." In *Varieties of Secularism in a Secular Age* ed. by Michael Warner, Jonathan VanAntwerpen and Craig Calhoun: 300–321. Cambridge, Mass.: Harvard University Press.

—. 2010. Challenging Issues about the Secular Age." *Modern Theology* 26/3: 404–416.

—. 2010. "Charles Taylor replies [to Tester, 'Multiculturalism']." *New Blackfriars* 91/1036: 677–679.

—. 2009. "The Polysemy of the Secular." *Social Research* 76/4: 1143–1166.

—. 2007. *A Secular Age*. Cambridge, Mass./London: The Belknap Press of Harvard University Press.

—. 2004. *Modern Social Imaginaries*. Durham/London: Duke University Press.

—. 2002. "Modern Social Imaginaries." *Public Culture* 14/1: 91–124.

—. 1999. *A Catholic Modernity? Charles Taylor's Marianist Award Lecture;* with responses by William M. Shea, Rosemary Luling Haughton, George Marsden, Jean Bethke Elshtain; edited and with an Introduction by James L. Heft, S. M. New York/Oxford: Oxford University Press.

—. 1998. "Modes of Secularism." In *Secularism and Its Critics* ed. by Rajeev Bhargava: 31–53. New Delhi: Oxford University Press.

—. 1995. "Two Theories of Modernity." *The Hastings Center Report* 24/2: 24–33.

—. 1993. *Modernity and the Rise of the Public Sphere*. Salt Lake City: University of Utah Press.

—. 1990. "Modes of Civil Society." *Public Culture* 3/1: 95–118.

Tayob, Abdulkader. 2009. *Religion in Modern Islamic Discourse*. London: Hurst.

Terrier, Jean and Wagner, Peter. 2006. "Civil Society and the Problématique of Political Modernity." In *The Languages of Civil Society* ed. by Peter Wagner: 9–27. New York: Berghahn.

Tester, Keith. 2010. "Multiculturalism, Catholicism and Us." *New Blackfriars* 91/1036: 665–676.

Thomas, Günter. 2016. "The Temptation of Religious Nostalgia. Protestant Readings of *A Secular Age*." In *Working with A Secular Age. Interdisciplinary Perspectives on Charles Taylor's Master Narrative* ed. by Florian Zemmin, Colin Jager and Guido Vanheeswijck: 49–70. Berlin/Boston: De Gruyter.

Thompson, Elizabeth F. 2015. "Rashid Rida and the 1920 Syrian-Arab Constitution: How the French Mandate Undermined Islamic Liberalism." In *The Routledge Handbook of the History of the Middle East Mandates* ed. by Cyrus Schayegh and Andrew Arsan: 244–257. London/New York: Routledge.

Thomson, William. 1937. "The Renascence of Islam." *The Harvard Theological Review* 30/2: 51–63.

Tian, Hailong. 2014. "Differing Translations, Contested Meanings: A Motor for the 1911 Revolution in China?." In *A Global Conceptual History of Asia, 1860–1940* ed. by Hagen Schulz-Forberg: 43–60. London: Pickering & Chatto.

Toledano, Ehud, R. 1998. "Social and Economic Reform in the Long Nineteenth Century." In *The Cambridge History of Egypt. Volume 2: Modern Egypt, from 1517 to the End of the Twentieth Century* ed. by M.W. Daly: 252–284. Cambridge: Cambridge University Press.

—. 1993. "Shemsigul: A Circassian Slave in Mid-Nineteenth-Century Cairo." In *Struggle and Survival in the Modern Middle East* ed. by Edmund Burke: 59–74. Berkeley, CA etc.: University of California Press.

Tomiche, Nada. 1968. "Notes sur la hiérarchie sociale en Égypte à l'époque de Muḥammad ʿAlī." In *Political and Social Change in Modern Egypt. Historical Studies from the Ottoman Conquest to the United Arab Republic* ed. by P. M. Holt: 249–263. London: Oxford University Press.

Tönnies, Ferdinand. 1887. *Gemeinschaft und Gesellschaft. Abhandlung des Communismus und des Socialismus als empirischer Culturformen.* Leipzig: Fues.

Tripp, Charles. 2006. *Islam and the Moral Economy. The Challenge of Capitalism.* Cambridge: Cambridge University Press.

Troll, Christian W. 1978. *Sayyid Ahmad Khan. A Reinterpretation of Muslim Theology.* New Delhi: Vikas Publishing House.

Troutt Powell, Eve M. 2006. "Will That Subaltern Ever Speak? Finding African Slaves in the Historiography of the Middle East." In *Middle East Historiographies. Narrating the Twentieth Century* ed. by Israel Gershoni, Amy Singer and Erdem Y. Hakan: 242–261. Seattle/London: University of Washington Press.

Touraine, Alain. 2005. "The End of the 'Social'." In *Comparing Modernities. Pluralism versus Homogenity* ed. by Eliezer Ben-Rafael and Yitzhak Sternberg: 229–244. Leiden/Boston: Brill.

—. 1980. "L'inutile idée de société." In *Philosopher:* les interrogations contemporarines ed. by R. Maggiori and C. Delacampagne: 237–245. Paris: Fayard.

—. 1965. *Sociologie de l'action.* Paris: Seuil.

Upson, Arthur T. 1915. "al-Manār as Open Court." *The Moslem World* 5: 291–295.

—. 1914. "A Glance at 'al-Manār'." *The Moslem World* 4: 392–395.

Vatikiotis, P. J. 1958. "Muhammad Abduh and the Quest for a Muslim Humanism." *Islamic Quarterly* 4/4: 145–161.

van der Veer, Peter. 2001. *Imperial Encounters: Religion and Modernity in India and Britain.* Princeton, N.J.: Princeton University Press.

van Nieuwenhuijze, C. A. O. 1959. "The Ummah: An Analytic Approach." *Studia Islamica* 10: 5–22.

Voll, John O. 1983. "Renewal and Reform in Islamic History: *Tajdid* and *Islah.*" In *Voices of Resurgent Islam* ed. by John L. Esposito: 32–47. New York/Oxford: Oxford University Press.

Wagner, Peter. 2014. "World-Sociology Beyond the Fragments. Oblivion and Advance in the Comparative Analysis of Modernities." In *Social Theory and Regional Studies in the Global Age* ed. by Saïd Amir Arjomand: 293–311. Albany: State University of New York Press.

—. 2008. *Modernity as Experience and Interpretation.* Cambridge: Polity.

—. 2006. "Social Theory and Political Philosophy." In *Handbook of Contemporary European Social Theory* ed. by Gerard Delanty: 25–36. London: Routledge.

—. 2001. *A History and Theory of the Social Sciences.* London: Sage.

—. 1990. *Sozialwissenschaften und Staat: Frankreich, Italien, Deutschland 1870–1980.* Frankfurt a.M.: Campus.

Wahba, Mourad Magdi. 1990. "The Meaning of Ishtirakiyah: Arab Perceptions of Socialism in the Nineteenth Century." *Alif: Journal of Comparative Poetics* 10: 42–55.

Walzer, Michael. 2002. "Equality and Civil Society." In *Alternative Conceptions of Civil Society* ed. by Simone Chambers and Will Kymlicka: 34–49. Princeton: Princeton University Press.

Watenpaugh, Keith David. 2006. *Being Modern in the Middle East. Revolution, Nationalism, Colo-nialism, and the Arab Middle Class.* Princeton, NJ: Princeton University Press.

Weismann, Itzchak. 2007. "The Sociology of 'Islamic Modernism': Muḥammad ʿAbduh, the National Public Sphere and the Colonial State." *The Maghreb Review* 32/1: 104–121.

Wendell, Charles. 1972. *The Evolution of the Egyptian National Image from its Origins to Ahmad Luṭfī al-Sayyid.* Berkeley: University of California Press.

Willis, John. 2010. "Debating the Caliphate: Islam and Nation in the Work of Rashid Rida and Abul Kalam Azad." *The International History Review* 32/4: 711–732.

Wilson, Samuel Graham. 1916. *Modern Movements among Moslems.* New York/Chicago: Fleming H. Revell.

Withington, Phil. 2010. *Society in Early Modern England. The Vernacular Origins of Some Powerful Ideas.* Cambridge/Malden, Mass.: Polity.

Wittrock, Björn, Wagner, Peter and Wollmann, Hellmut (eds.). 1990. *Social Sciences and Modern States.* Cambridge: Cambridge University Press.

Wood, Simon A. 2010. "Researching 'The Scripture of the Other': Niqula Ghabriyal's *Researches of the Mujtahids* and Rashid Rida's Rejoinder." *Comparative Islamic Studies* 6/1–2: 181–216.

Yared, Nazik Saba. 2002. *Secularism and the Arab World (1850–1939).* London: Saqi Books.

Yasushi, Kosugi. 2008. "Al-Manār Revisited. The 'lighthouse' of the Islamic revival." In *Intellectuals in the Modern Islamic World. Transmission, Transformation, Communication* ed. by Stéphane A. Dudoignon, Komatsu Hisao and Kosugi Yasushi: 3–39. London/New York: Routledge.

Younos, Farid. 2011. *Principles of Islamic Sociology.* Bloomington, IN: AuthorHouse.

Zachs, Fruma. 2014. "Growing Consciousness of the Child in Ottoman Syria in the 19th Century: Modes of Parenting and Education in the Middle Class." In *The Ottoman Middle East: Studies in Honor of Amnon Cohen* ed. by Eyal Ginio and Elie Podeh: 113–128. Leiden/Boston: Brill.

Zaman, Muhammad Qasim. 2004. "The ʿUlama of Contemporary Islam and their Conceptions of the Common Good." In *Public Islam and the Common Good* ed. by Armando Salvatore and Dale F. Eickelman: 129–156. Leiden/Boston: Brill.

Zaydan, Jurji. 1990. *The Autobiography of Jurji Zaidan: Including four Letters to his Son*; transl., ed. and introduced by Thomas Philipp. Washington: Three Continents Press.

Ze'evi, Dror. 2004. "Back to Napoleon? Thoughts on the Beginning of the Modern Era in the Middle East." *Mediterranean Historical Review* 19/1: 73–94.

Zemmin, Florian. 2018. "Wider die islamische Exzeptionalität: Zur (Inter-)Disziplinarität der Islamwissenschaft am Beispiel des Salafismus." In *Islam in der Moderne, Moderne im Islam. Eine Festschrift für Reinhard Schulze zum 65. Geburtstag* ed. by Florian Zemmin, Johannes Stephan and Monica Corrado: 159–186. Leiden/Boston: Brill.

—. 2016. “An Annotated Bibliography of Responses to *A Secular Age*.” In *Working with A Secular Age. Interdisciplinary Perspectives on Charles Taylor’s Master Narrative* ed. by Florian Zemmin, Colin Jager and Guido Vanheeswijck: 385–419. Berlin/Boston: De Gruyter.

—. 2016. “*A Secular Age* and Islamic Modernism.” In *Working with A Secular Age. Interdisciplinary Perspectives on Charles Taylor’s Master Narrative* ed. by Florian Zemmin, Colin Jager and Guido Vanheeswijck: 307–329. Berlin/Boston: De Gruyter.

—. 2016. “Modernity without Society? Observations on the term *mujtamaʿ* in the Islamic Journal *al-Manār* (Cairo, 1898–1940).” *Die Welt des Islams* 56/2: 223–247.

—. 2015. “Integrating Islamic Positions into European Public Discourse: The Paradigmatic Example of Tariq Ramadan.” *Journal of Religion in Europe* 8/1: 121–146.

—. 2011. *Islamische Verantwortungsethik im 17. Jahrhundert. Ein weberianisches Verständnis der Handlungsvorstellungen Kātib Čelebis (1609–1657).* Schenefeld: E. B. Braun.

Zemmin, Florian, Jager, Colin and Vanheeswijck, Guido (eds.). 2016. *Working with A Secular Age. Interdisciplinary Perspectives on Charles Taylor’s Master Narrative.* Berlin/Boston: De Gruyter.

Zisser, Eyal. 2011. “Rashid Rida: On the Way to Syrian Nationalism in the Shade of Islam and Arabism.” In *The Origins of Syrian Nationhood. Histories, Pioneers and Identity* ed. by Adel Beshara: 123–140. Oxon/New York: Routledge.

Zolondek, Leon. 1966. “Socio-Political Views of Salim al-Bustani (1848–1884).” *Middle Eastern Studies* 2/2: 144–156.

—. 1965. “Ash-Shaʿb in Arabic Political Literature of the 19th Century.” *Die Welt des Islams* 10/1–2: 1–16.

—. 1963. “The Language of the Muslim Reformers of the late Nineteenth Century.” *Islamic Culture* 37/3: 155–162.

Zubaida, Sami. 2005. “Islam and Secularization.” *Asian Journal of Social Sciences* 33/3: 438–448.

—. 2001. “Civil Society, Community, and Democracy in the Middle East.” In *Civil Society: History and Possibilities* ed. by Sudipta Kaviraj and Sunil Khilnani: 232–249. Cambridge: Cambridge University Press.

Appendix: Tables of Search Terms

As stated in the introduction, the search results produced by PowerGrep, while not in all cases fully accurate, are sufficient to give a broad overview of the distribution of terms in *al-Manar*. For the most pertinent terms for 'society' and the 'social' (*mujtamaʿ*, *al-hayʾa al-ijtimāʿiyya*, *ijtimāʿ*, *ijtimāʿī[ya]*), I have conducted an additional, more accurate search in Microsoft Word, and these results stem from that search. The quantitative findings recorded in the following tables show that remarkably few terms significantly increased or decreased in their usage over the lifespan of *al-Manar*. One should note that, except for the most frequent terms, a rise in usage in one volume is sometimes attributable to a single article. In other cases, the connection between a term's increased usage and certain events is rather obvious, as in the rise of *khilāfa* around the time of the controversial abolishment of the Ottoman caliphate in 1924. Some decreases in usage are due to certain volumes of *al-Manar* – particularly in the aftermath of the First World War – having been significantly thinner than usual.

To avoid over-interpreting decreasing usages in these volumes, the first table states the page numbers of the individual volumes. These page numbers are taken from the printed version and thus include the *Tafsir*. The following tables then group the most relevant terms thematically: table 2a has the most pertinent terms for 'society' and the 'social'; table 2b records the different meanings of *mujtamaʿ* and Rashid Rida's share of them; table 3 lists other terms addressing social collectivities; tables 4a–h record particular societies as conceptualized with these different terms. The following tables then record terms referring to different fields: the terms in table 5 refer to Islam, religion, and belief; those in table 6 to this world and the non-religious; those in table 7 to politics; those in table 8 to education and knowledge; those in table 9 to law or ethics; those in table 10 to civilization and progress; and those in table 11 to reform and its goals. Peculiarities of individual searches are noted beneath the individual tables.

https://doi.org/10.1515/9783110545845-014

Table 1: *Al-Manar:* Years of publication; number of issues; number of pages

Vol.	Month/Year Islamic calendar	Month/Year Gregorian calendar	Nr. of issues	Nr. of pages
1	10/1315–10/1316	02/1898–03/1899	49	956
2	10/1316–10/1317	03/1899–02/1900	48	768
3	11/1317–10/1318	03/1900–02/1901	33	864
4	11/1318–12/1319	02/1901–03/1902	24	960
5	01–12/1320	04/1902–03/1903	24	960
6	01–12/1321	03/1903–03/1904	24	960
7	01–12/1322	03/1904–02/1905	24	960
8	01–12/1323	03/1905–02/1906	24	960
9	01–12/1324	03/1906–02/1907	12	960
10	01–12/1325	03/1907–01/1908	12	960
11	01–12/1326	03/1908–01/1909	12	960
12	01–12/1327	02/1909–01/1910	12	960
13	01–12/1328	02/1910–01/1911	12	960
14	01–12/1329	01–12/1911	12	960
15	01–12/1330	01–12/1912	12	960
16	01–12/1331	01–11/1913	12	953
17	01–12/1332	12/1913–11/1914	12	971
18	03–12/1333	02–11/1915	10	800
19	08/1334–06/1335	06/1916–04/1917	10	640
20	10/1335–12/1336	07/1917–10/1918	10	448
21	03/1337–12/1338	12/1918–09/1920	10	560
22	03/1339–02/1340	12/1920–10/1921	10	800
23	05/1340–04/1341	01–12/1922	10	800
24	05/1341–03/1342	01–11/1923	10	800
25	06/1342–08/1343	01/1924–03/1925	10	800
26	09/1343–08/1344	04/1925–03/1926	10	800
27	09/1344–06/1345	04/1926–01/1927	10	800
28	08/1345–07/1346	03/1927–01/1928	10	800
29	09/1346–10/1347	03/1928–04/1929	10	800
30	01–11/1348	06/1929–05/1930	10	800
31	01/1349–02/1350	06/1930–07/1931	10	800
32	06/1350–09/1351	10/1931–12/1932	10	800
33	11/1351–12/1352	03/1933–04/1934	10	800
34	01/1353–01/1354	05/1934–05/1935	10	800
35	03/1354–08/1359	07/1935–09/1940*	10	779
Total incl. Tafsir				28880

*The first two issues of volume 35 appeared in 1935; issues 3 and 4 in 1936; issues 5 and 6 in 1939; and issues 7 to 10 in 1940.

Table 2a: The most pertinent terms for 'society' and the 'social'

Vol.	*hay'a ijtimā'iyya**	*mujtama'*	*mujtama' meaning 'society'*	*ijtimā'*	*ijtimā'ī (ya/yūn)*	*'ilm al-ijtimā'* **
1	13	23	9	88	37	5
2	5	21	15	92	47	13
3	3	17	16	78	35	7
4	2	17	14	58	69	4
5	3	8	3	117	63	5
6	1	5	2	65	17	0
7	2	3	1	69	41	1
8	3	13	4	61	51	7
9	8	13	5	72	56	0
10	7	17	15	106	86	3
11	16	20	17	83	74	3
12	2	6	5	89	57	3
13	6	10	6	62	67	5
14	2	1	0	81	84	3
15	6	6	3	67	87	3
16	4	13	11	46	54	1
17	3	4	1	71	54	0
18	2	9	9	17	33	1
19	2	0	0	26	67	0
20	1	1	1	21	20	0
21	3	7	6	29	51	1
22	0	7	4	49	69	0
23	12	2	0	82	104	2
24	1	2	1	45	71	0
25	2	3	0	39	43	1
26	4	9	7	38	37	2
27	3	9	7	66	40	13
28	1	6	6	32	39	2
29	1	31	28	62	51	4
30	0	5	1	32	51	0
31	1	6	4	35	25	1
32	1	8	6	72	60	3
33	0	4	4	45	52	5
34	0	2	1	42	33	0
35	6	28	25	30	71	0
Total	126	336	237	2067	1896	98
Tafsir	16	22	11	655	274	34
Total	142	358	248	2722	2170	132

*Including seven instances of *hay'at al-ijtimā'*; **including three instances of *al-'ilm al-ijtimā'ī*.

Table 2b: The different meanings of *mujtamaʿ* in *al-Manar* and Rashid Rida's share of them

Meaning of *mujtamaʿ*	**Total number of instances**	**Rida's share of them**
Assembly, collection, or convergence of something non-human	19	11 (57,8 %)
Place of assembly	12	5 (41.7 %)
Assembly, gathering, congregation, get-together	58	47 (81 %)
Unclear whether a place of assembly or the assembly itself is referred to	13	5 (38.4 %)
Club or association	8	4 (50 %)
Human society or society in general	138	38 (27.5 %)
Particular society or societies	110	11 (10 %)
Total	358	116 (32.4 %)

Table 3: Other terms addressing social collectivities

Vol.	*umma*	*milla*	*jam'iyya*	*jamā'a*	*sha'b*	*qawm*
1	498	219	86	79	97	291
2	462	211	199	34	78	221
3	267	154	184	39	51	178
4	299	125	108	118	40	220
5	397	219	261	79	47	288
6	242	155	59	114	72	280
7	387	150	84	82	44	180
8	322	179	58	60	54	188
9	361	217	84	174	41	205
10	400	194	86	114	51	219
11	376	118	170	54	60	281
12	460	167	246	92	56	172
13	266	126	147	128	50	182
14	346	169	243	180	100	241
15	275	167	265	96	88	209
16	335	145	242	148	92	191
17	209	176	105	173	93	198
18	109	101	26	93	38	137
19	229	100	115	54	39	110
20	84	38	27	80	46	90
21	223	123	127	73	119	112
22	333	130	44	126	117	156
23	423	122	169	256	128	119
24	359	138	71	213	185	152
25	272	159	61	141	100	126
26	201	156	112	141	73	181
27	188	94	94	151	63	164
28	168	110	111	195	112	152
29	211	129	99	135	141	149
30	212	128	91	85	90	124
31	249	94	93	137	67	126
32	187	138	145	98	67	138
33	194	126	57	111	82	121
34	149	85	33	72	43	114
35	155	84	30	112	43	133
Total	9848	4946	4132	4037	2667	6148
Tafsir	1738	306	90	598	282	3051
Total	11586	5252	4222	4635	2949	9199

Instances of *qawmī (ya)* are deduced from the results for *qawm*. Results for *qawm* in the journal, without counting the *Tafsir*, still include *yaqūm*, *muqawwima*. However, these instances are relatively few. In the *Tafsir*, they are not included, due to its being vocalized.

Tables 4a-h: References to particular societies by name:
4a: *al-hay'a al-ijtimāʿiyya*;
4b: *mujtamaʿ*;
4c: *ijtimāʿ*;
4d: *umma*;
4e: *shaʿb*;
4f: *jamʿiyya*;
4g–h: *milla*.

I have searched for *al-mujtamaʿ al-*, *al-umma al-*, *al-milla al-*, etc. This excludes instances such as *ummat al-miṣriyīn*. I list only those instances in which the attribute refers to a particular geographical, national, or religious entity, which excludes instances such as al-Jamʿiyya al-Khayriyya al-Islamiyya (The Islamic Benevolent Society). Also excluded are references to plural societies, for example, *al-mujtamaʿāt al-ʿarabiyya* (the Arab societies) or *al-umam al-islāmiyya* (the Islamic societies); this is both for technical reasons and because these references tend to be less normative and specific than references to one particular society or social order.

Table 4a: *Al-hayʾa al-ijtimāʿiyya* referring to particular societies

Vol.	*al-hayʾa al-ijtimāʿiyya*	*– al-sharqiyya* (Eastern –)	*– al-miṣriyya* (Egyptian –)	*– al-bashariyya* (human –)	*– al-islāmiyya* (Islamic –)	*– al-masīḥiyya* (Christian –)	*– al-yahūdiyya* (Jewish –)
1	13	2					
2	5						
3	3						
4	2						
5	3						
6	1						
7	2						
8	3						
9	8		1	2			
10	7	2	1			1	
11	16		1				
12	2						
13	6						
14	2						
15	6						
16	4						
17	3						1
18	2						
19	2						
20	1						
21	3						
22	0						
23	12				1		
24	1						
25	2						
26	4						
27	3						
28	1						
29	1						
30	0						
31	1						
32	1						
33	0						
34	0						
35	6	1					
Total	126	5	3	2	1	1	1
Tafsir	16	0	0	0	0	0	0
Total	142	5	3	2	1	1	1

Table 4b: *Mujtamaʿ* referring to particular societies

Vol.	*mujtamaʿ*	– *al-islāmī* (Islamic –)	– *al-ʿarabī* (Arab –)	– *al-turkī* (Turkish –)	– *al-sharqī* (Eastern –)	– *al-ūrūbī* (European –)
1	23				1	
2	21	4				
3	17					
4	17					
5	8					
6	5					
7	3					
8	13	1				
9	13					
10	17					
11	20					
12	6	1				
13	10					
14	1					
15	6					
16	13					
17	4					
18	9					1
19	0					
20	1					
21	7		1			
22	7	1				
23	2					
24	2					
25	3					
26	9	1				
27	9					
28	6					
29	31	4		2		
30	5					
31	6	2				
32	8		2			
33	4					
34	2					
35	28	4				
Total	336	18	3	2	1	1
Tafsir	22	0	0	0	0	0
Total	358	18	3	2	1	1

Table 4c: *Ijtimāʿ* referring to particular societies

Vol.	*ijtimāʿ*	*– al-islāmī* (Islamic –)	*– al-sharqī* (Eastern –)	*– al-amīrikī* (American –)	*– al-ʿarabī* (Arab –)
1	88				
2	92	1			
3	78				
4	58				
5	117				
6	65				
7	69				
8	61				
9	72				
10	106	1			
11	83				
12	89		1		
13	62				
14	81				
15	67				
16	46				
17	71				
18	17				
19	26				
20	21				
21	29				
22	49				
23	82				
24	45				
25	39				
26	38		1		1
27	66				
28	32			1	
29	62				
30	32				
31	35				
32	72				
33	45				
34	42				
35	30				
Total	2067	2	2	1	0
Tafsir	655	0	0	0	1
Total	2722	2	2	1	1

Table 4d: *Umma* referring to particular societies (continued on following page)

Vol.	*umma*	– *al-islāmiyya* (Islamic –)	– *al-ʿarabiyya* (Arab –)	– *al-miṣriyya* (Egyptian –)	– *al-ʿuthmāniyya* (Ottoman –)	– *al-turkiyya* (Turkish –)	– *al-inklīziyya* (English –)	Other*
1	498	4	1	9	4	1	1	15
2	462	17	2	2		2	1	4
3	267	25	9		3			2
4	299	10	1	2	1			5
5	397	12	3	12			3	15
6	242	4	3	5	1			6
7	387	17	5	5		1		6
8	322	7	2	4				4
9	361	11	4	2	1		1	4
10	400	17	6	5		1		5
11	376	3	3	3	22		1	4
12	460	11	4	1	20		5	4
13	266	8	6	5	1	1	2	
14	346	8	2	9	7		2	6
15	275	6	10		6		1	10
16	335	13	33		9	1		9
17	209	3	6	1	2			5
18	109	4			2			2
19	229	7	9	1	2	4	2	3
20	84	4	8	1				3
21	223		21	4	1			12
22	333	5	19	13		4		3
23	423	8	15	7	1	6		3
24	359	14	36	1		6		2
25	272	8	28	2		5	1	19
26	201	4	9			2		4
27	188	10	10	1	1			6
28	168	4	7	3				5
29	211	4	13	8			2	8
30	212	4	27	6			3	5
31	249	11	21	4		2	1	13
32	187	14	13	3				2
33	194	9	27	1				4
34	149	8	22	2			2	
35	155	6	10	2				3
Total	9848	300	395	124	84	36	28	201
Tafsir	1738	24	27	1	0	1	3	11

Table 4d: *Umma* referring to particular societies *(Continued)*

Vol.	***umma***	**– *al-islāmiyya* (Islamic –)**	**– *al-ʿarabiyya* (Arab –)**	**– *al-miṣriyya* (Egyptian –)**	**– *al-ʿuthmāniyya* (Ottoman –)**	**– *al-turkiyya* (Turkish –)**	**– *al-inklīziyya* (English –)**	**Other***
Total	11586	324	422	125	84	37	31	212

*Others are: *al-muḥammadiyya* (Muhammadan umma: 32, 9 of which in the *Tafsir*), *al-fransiyya* (French: 21), *al-britaniyya* (British: 19), *al-sūriyya* (Syrian: 16), *al-amīrīkiyya* (American: 14), *al-rūsiyya* (Russian: 13), *al-būlūniyya* (Polish: 10), *al-yabaniyya* (Japanese: 9), *al-yahūdiyya* (Jewish: 8), *al-afghāniyya* (Afghan: 8), *al-isrāʾīliyya* (Israeli: 7), *al-qubtiyya* (Coptic: 7), *al-almāniyya* (German: 7), *al-hindiyya* (Indian: 5), *al-fārisiyya* (Persian: 5), *al-sharqiyya* (Eastern: 5), *al-irāniyya* (Iranian: 4), *al-lubnāniyya* (Lebanese: 3), *al-masīḥiyya* (Christian: 2), *al-gharbiyya* (Western: 2), *al-maghribiyya* (Maghribi: 2), and, each with 1 occurence: *al-isbānyūliyya* (Spanish), *al-ṣīniyya* (Chinese), *al-ḥanafiyya* (Hanafitic), *al-naṣrāniyya* (Christian), *al-indūnīsiyya* (Indonesian), *al-habashiyya* (Ethiopian), *al-najdiyya* (Nejdi), *al-tūnisiyya* (Tunisian), *al-yūnāniyya* (Greek), *al-īṭāliyya* (Italian), *al-hūlāndiyya* (Dutch), and *al-bulghrāriyya* (Bulgarian).

Table 4e: *Sha'b* referring to particular societies (continued on following page)

Vol.	*sha'b*	– *al-islāmī* (Islamic –)	– *al-'arabī* (Arab –)	– *al-miṣriyya* (Egyptian –)	– *al-'uthmāniyya* (Ottoman –)	– *al-turkiyya* (Turkish –)	– *al-inklīziyya* (English –)	Other*
1	97			3				1
2	78		1				2	9
3	51					1		1
4	40		1			1		
5	47						1	3
6	72			1		1		
7	44	1					1	1
8	54			2			1	2
9	41							1
10	51							3
11	60		1	1				2
12	56		1			2	1	1
13	50			1				
14	100	1	1	1		2	1	1
15	88							2
16	92	1	9	1	1	2		4
17	93		2	1	1	1		9
18	38				1		1	4
19	39		2			5		2
20	46							6
21	119		4	4		2	1	7
22	117		2	6				3
23	128		1	6		14		18
24	185	3	4	2		15	7	8
25	100		4	2		11	1	5
26	73	1	2	2		6	1	6
27	63	2		2		2		
28	112			5		6	1	2
29	141	1		5		12	1	7
30	90	2		6		2	5	9
31	67	2	3	3		1		9
32	67			2		3	1	7
33	82		4	1		3		9
34	43		1			1		4
35	43	1		1			1	3
Total	2667	15	43	58	3	93	27	149
Tafsir	282	3	1	1	0	0	0	0

Table 4e: *Sha'b* referring to particular societies *(Continued)*

Vol.	*sha'b*	– *al-* *islāmī* (Islamic –)	– *al-* *'arabī* (Arab –)	– *al-* *miṣriyya* (Egyptian –)	– *al-* *'uthmāniyya* (Ottoman –)	– *al-* *turkiyya* (Turkish –)	– *al-* *inklīziyya* (English –)	Other*
Total	2949	18	44	59	3	93	27	149

*Others are: *al-sūrī* (Syrian: 17), *al-almānī* (German: 16), *al-afghānī* (Afghan: 10), *al-brīṭānī* (British: 9), *al-fransī* (French: 8), *al-hindī* (Indian: 8), *al-maghribī* (Maghribi: 7), *al-yahūdī* (Jewish: 7), *al-'irāqī* (Iraqi: 6), *al-farsī* (Persian: 5), *al-irānī* (Iranian: 5), *al-rūsī* (Russian: 5), *al-amīrikī* (American: 5), *al-isrā'īlī* (Israeli: 4), *al-fīlasṭīnī* (Palestinian: 3), *al-ḥijāzī* (Hejazi: 3), *al-armīnī* (Armenian: 3), *al-lubnānī* (Lebanese: 3), *al-jarmānī* (Germanic: 3), *al-sharqī* (the Eastern: 2), *al-yabānī* (Japanese: 2), *al-isbānyūlī* (Spanish: 2), *al-najdī* (Nejdi: 2), *al-tūnisī* (Tunisian: 2), and, each with 1 occurence: *al-yunānī* (Greek), *al-hūlāndī* (Dutch), *al-isbānī* (Spanish), *al-'irāqī* (Iraqi), *al-indūnīsī* (Indonesian), *al-barbarī* (Berber or barbarian), *al-ṣirbī* (Serbian), *al-saksūnī* (Saxon), *al-ūrūbī* (European), *al-urthūdūksī* (Orthodox), *al-kurdī* (Kurdish), and *al-farā'ūnī* (Pharaonic).

Table 4f: *Jam'iyya* referring to particular societies

Vol.	*jam'iyya*	*– al-basharīyya* (human –)	*– al-insāniyya* (human –)	*– al-islāmiyya* (Islamic –)	*– al-miṣriyya* (Egyptian –)	*– al-fransawiyya* (French –)
1	86	2			1	1
2	199					
3	184					
4	108			1		
5	261	1			1	
6	59					
7	84					
8	58	1		1		
9	84	1	1			
10	86					
11	170	1				
12	246	1				
13	147					
14	243					
15	265					
16	242			1		
17	105					
18	26					
19	115					
20	27					
21	127					
22	44					
23	169			3		
24	71			1		
25	61	2				
26	112					
27	94					
28	111					
29	99					
30	91					
31	93					
32	145					
33	57					
34	33					
35	30					
Total	4132	9	1	7	2	1
Tafsir	90	6	0	0	0	0
Total	4222	15	1	7	2	1

Table 4g: *Milla* referring to particular societies (continued on following page)

Vol.	*milla*	– *al-islāmiyya* (Islamic –)	– *al-miṣriyya* (Egyptian –)	– *al-ḥanafiyya* (Hanafitic –)	– *al-muḥammadiyya* (Muhammadan –)	– *al-masīḥiyya* (Christian –)	Other*
1	219			1			1
2	211	2		3		2	
3	154	1					
4	125	2		3			1
5	219	1					
6	155						
7	150	1		1			
8	179	2					
9	217	2					
10	194		1				
11	118						
12	167	2		1			1
13	126	1		1			
14	169	3					
15	167						
16	145	1					1
17	176						
18	101	1					
19	100						1
20	38						
21	123	1					
22	130			1			
23	122						
24	138	4			1		
25	159	2					
26	156	2			2		1
27	94	1			2		
28	110	1					1
29	129	1			1		
30	128	3		1		1	
31	94	3		1			
32	138	3					
33	126						
34	85	2					
35	84						
Total	4946	42	1	13	6	3	7
Tafsir	306	1	0	1	0	1	3

Table 4g: *Milla* referring to particular societies *(Continued)*

Vol.	*milla*	*– al-islāmiyya* (Islamic –)	*– al-miṣriyya* (Egyptian –)	*– al-ḥanafiyya* (Hanafitic –)	*– al-muḥammadiyya* (Muhammadan –)	*– al-masīḥiyya* (Christian –)	Other*
Total	5252	43	1	14	6	1	10

*Others are: *al-ʿuthmāniyya* (Ottoman: 2), *al-mūsawiyya* (Mosaic: 2), *al-turkiyya* (Turkish: 2), *al-ilāhiyya* (godly: 1), *al-naṣrāniyya* (Christian: 1), *al-qubṭiyya* (Coptic: 1), *al-fransawiyya* (French: 1).

Table 4h: *Milla* as the community or creed of a certain figure (continued on following page)

Vol.	*milla*	*millat Ibrahim*	*millat 'Abd al-Muttalib*	*millat al-Masih*	*millat Muhammad*	*millat al-islām*	Other*
1	219						
2	211						
3	154						
4	125						
5	219	2					
6	155	1					
7	150						
8	179						
9	217						
10	194						
11	118						
12	167	1					
13	126						
14	169						
15	167						
16	145						
17	176	1					
18	101	1					
19	100	3					
20	38						
21	123	1					
22	130						
23	122						
24	138						
25	159	1					
26	156						
27	94	1					
28	110	1					
29	129						

Table 4h: *Milla* as the community or creed of a certain figure *(Continued)*

Vol.	*milla*	*millat Ibrahim*	*millat 'Abd al-Muttalib*	*millat al-Masih*	*millat Muhammad*	*millat al-islām*	Other*
30	128	1					
31	94						
32	138	1					
33	126	2					
34	85	1					
35	84	6					
Total	4946	24	0	0	0	0	0
Tafsir	306	88	6	2	1	1	3
Total	5252	112	6	2	1	1	3

*Others are: *millat 'Īsā* (Jesus: 1), *millat Yahūd* (Jews: 1), *millat al-rusul* (prophets: 1).

Table 5: Terms referring to Islam, religion, and belief

Vol.	*islām*	*islāmī(ya)*	*dīnī(ya)*	*diyāna*	*adyān*	*īmān*
1	250	212	170	19	45	45
2	282	305	153	31	17	73
3	305	286	149	33	60	44
4	333	245	122	32	39	82
5	713	368	291	25	56	154
6	320	123	165	18	45	108
7	382	215	147	16	29	55
8	201	214	172	8	25	42
9	259	161	221	5	35	122
10	458	308	237	8	16	41
11	465	165	154	19	37	63
12	399	196	144	5	32	110
13	526	257	132	11	40	73
14	385	431	323	22	33	53
15	696	707	295	39	61	39
16	677	281	137	7	22	93
17	448	196	125	15	35	101
18	126	109	55	7	5	96
19	246	115	91	2	14	50
20	133	61	49	2	2	38
21	157	75	111	10	17	23
22	229	152	136	12	15	60
23	389	250	132	5	27	57
24	620	636	182	18	29	135
25	346	399	192	5	11	85
26	456	416	244	10	27	46
27	477	328	206	5	16	113
28	371	238	142	6	10	42
29	579	465	271	10	29	95
30	405	284	180	17	25	42
31	602	357	185	17	51	47
32	569	368	192	6	18	99
33	728	310	193	9	54	91
34	325	222	145	6	25	50
35	526	343	128	1	68	59
Total	14383	9798	5971	461	1070	2526
Tafsir	2649	291	500	49	158	2938
Total	17032	10089	6471	510	1228	5464

Dīn is not listed, because its search results are misleading insofar as they include too many irrelevant instances.

Table 6: Terms referring to this world and the non-religious

Vol.	*dunyā*	*dunyawī(ya)*	*dahrī*	*māddī*	*lādīnī(ya)*	*'almānī(ya)*
1	125	33	3	38	0	0
2	115	33	0	18	1	0
3	141	15	4	8	1	0
4	120	22	0	9	1	0
5	122	18	0	15	0	0
6	87	23	1	4	0	0
7	117	23	4	1	0	0
8	105	16	3	4	0	0
9	109	20	2	4	0	0
10	98	33	0	14	0	0
11	91	17	0	4	0	0
12	116	28	3	4	0	3
13	86	17	10	11	0	5
14	89	23	0	10	7	6
15	75	20	1	8	1	0
16	68	13	8	8	0	1
17	58	9	1	12	0	0
18	59	7	1	5	0	0
19	57	7	0	7	0	2
20	27	7	0	2	0	0
21	26	8	0	3	1	0
22	65	13	0	6	0	0
23	108	15	0	12	0	0
24	99	16	4	3	0	0
25	69	18	0	5	2	1
26	82	23	1	7	29	0
27	64	14	0	3	20	0
28	56	9	2	4	6	3
29	88	29	0	8	21	0
30	61	19	0	4	2	0
31	86	18	0	16	8	0
32	101	19	2	16	13	0
33	77	17	1	13	4	0
34	66	13	0	6	4	0
35	61	7	0	8	0	0
Total	2974	622	51	300	121	21
Tafsir	2000	219	1	218	2	0
Total	4974	841	52	518	123	21

Table 7: Terms referring to politics

Vol.	*siyāsa*	*dawla*	*ḥukūma**	*khilāfa*	*istiʿmār*	*shūrā*	*dīmuqrāṭiyya*
1	118	351	229	120	21	11	0
2	57	255	270	59	18	14	0
3	38	144	138	32	6	7	0
4	68	134	113	19	6	19	2
5	164	206	239	40	4	54	1
6	63	232	127	42	1	19	1
7	106	225	257	79	10	42	2
8	103	143	281	26	8	43	1
9	75	121	125	30	6	54	0
10	133	81	205	24	10	42	3
11	128	260	261	24	9	54	0
12	122	454	479	110	2	63	7
13	82	227	253	38	5	35	2
14	177	387	582	52	32	24	2
15	149	439	350	62	52	21	0
16	140	548	353	51	7	30	0
17	69	214	142	12	21	13	0
18	20	76	56	25	11	2	1
19	39	245	93	24	5	8	1
20	21	132	102	17	5	5	11
21	96	199	248	17	27	4	6
22	98	158	302	26	38	13	2
23	145	344	438	324	32	50	2
24	88	314	448	462	31	42	1
25	109	314	307	308	16	26	1
26	115	166	173	138	27	19	0
27	80	137	120	186	21	9	1
28	106	72	187	66	8	17	0
29	70	130	306	53	18	25	4
30	72	124	262	29	24	12	0
31	76	112	141	9	41	21	1
32	66	85	154	35	12	7	3
33	79	138	132	27	17	10	0
34	40	87	138	9	11	6	0
35	86	85	76	12	27	11	14
Total	3725	7339	8087	2587	589	832	69
Tafsir	186	255	155	94	32	123	3
Total	3911	7594	8242	2681	621	955	72

*Instances of *maḥkūma* are deducted from the search results for *ḥukūma*.

Table 8: Terms referring to education and knowledge

Volume	*ʿilmī*	*ʿaqlī*	*taʿlīm*	*tarbiya*	*falsafa*
1	68	34	245	228	15
2	65	56	304	251	10
3	80	30	211	162	18
4	80	25	224	167	27
5	105	80	371	187	124
6	59	25	196	106	12
7	63	42	160	91	24
8	52	39	247	131	29
9	53	48	253	97	26
10	181	47	242	132	75
11	56	27	209	150	28
12	41	24	175	89	14
13	70	58	158	87	38
14	104	16	298	120	18
15	75	41	217	180	34
16	39	39	136	61	18
17	37	28	95	36	17
18	47	21	25	21	20
19	57	21	26	31	19
20	20	6	20	15	2
21	44	13	117	18	15
22	43	26	112	69	16
23	47	24	55	35	16
24	37	14	42	33	24
25	33	17	59	13	5
26	74	23	69	68	19
27	101	56	41	23	15
28	81	15	69	36	6
29	81	32	126	29	34
30	62	33	99	41	12
31	52	34	64	21	10
32	87	46	105	83	15
33	82	51	104	42	38
34	58	24	36	47	5
35	90	31	59	31	34
Total	2324	1146	4969	2931	832
Tafsir	215	371	307	290	110
Total	2539	1517	5276	3221	942

ʿIlm and *ʿaql* are not included, as their search results contain too many other, less pertinent instances: the 36,058 hits for *ʿilm* include *ʿilmī(ya)*, *ʿulamāʾ*, *muʿallim*, *ʿalimtu*, *taʿallum*, among other terms; the 7,614 hits for *ʿaql* include *ʿaqlī(ya)*, *ʿuqalāʾ*, *ʿuqla*, among other terms.

Table 9: Terms referring to law or ethics

Vol.	*sharʿī*	*sharīʿa*	*qānūn*	*qānūnī*	*ʿibādāt*	*muʿāmalāt*
1	57	83	82	13	7	17
2	175	120	66	7	15	16
3	20	47	43	6	13	14
4	50	75	47	3	31	30
5	67	88	95	10	33	18
6	86	99	33	2	16	13
7	116	88	59	8	19	21
8	68	78	48	6	23	13
9	62	74	38	2	29	21
10	160	133	69	9	17	30
11	52	52	119	7	8	10
12	101	77	122	9	7	17
13	77	115	70	5	14	12
14	80	49	131	9	22	9
15	34	89	27	10	13	10
16	82	57	60	22	3	13
17	104	126	18	4	43	14
18	18	37	14	3	4	8
19	30	82	12	4	15	5
20	33	26	32	1	9	1
21	38	17	53	11	6	7
22	54	24	23	3	18	9
23	123	115	98	16	30	32
24	146	104	45	8	26	22
25	154	62	83	6	11	14
26	101	78	54	13	16	10
27	121	40	27	6	28	5
28	69	38	21	14	25	15
29	86	70	60	8	25	17
30	69	61	40	14	23	24
31	124	72	39	4	24	7
32	96	39	35	10	21	7
33	59	44	29	6	27	9
34	51	25	28	2	16	17
35	22	25	23	4	7	7
Total	2785	2409	1843	265	644	494
Tafsir	344	520	63	20	1473	132
Total	3129	2929	1906	285	2117	626

The search results for *fiqh* are not listed as they include other terms, esp. *fuqahāʾ*.

Table 10: Terms referring to civilization and progress (continued on following page)

Vol.	*ʿumrān*	*madanī(ya)**	*tamaddun* **	*ḥaḍāra*	*thaqāfa*	*taqad-dum* #	*tarqiya*	*taraqqin/al-taraqqī* ##
1	59	110	54	12	0	129	11	63
2	60	87	28	18	0	103	14	66
3	42	110	14	8	0	100	13	32
4	54	105	13	12	0	103	16	55
5	60	176	19	14	0	144	17	46
6	53	62	13	11	0	126	24	13
7	30	113	36	10	0	103	11	51
8	49	56	7	8	0	59	16	21
9	60	58	20	8	0	94	14	16
10	51	117	13	14	0	109	20	21
11	104	133	11	22	0	97	25	85
12	56	52	10	13	0	81	31	76
13	80	81	10	33	0	55	37	63
14	57	74	9	18	0	80	38	103
15	70	115	43	50	0	118	18	50
16	90	80	8	21	0	78	10	100
17	47	50	7	17	0	134	8	34
18	37	76	7	9	0	81	3	9
19	24	57	3	23	0	56	18	28
20	8	14	1	10	0	61	3	15
21	21	47	14	23	0	66	5	11
22	46	59	2	22	0	69	13	10
23	52	98	2	24	0	69	11	16
24	50	107	3	34	0	72	8	9
25	49	38	3	23	0	49	5	13
26	37	50	6	22	2	58	4	23
27	35	29	3	13	11	64	2	4
28	45	44	8	9	16	112	2	2
29	44	92	4	46	13	95	6	11
30	46	99	5	36	19	94	4	14
31	86	130	3	26	12	65	2	7
32	50	62	3	31	6	81	7	12
33	82	95	0	58	2	57	4	15
34	23	37	1	16	2	38	5	9
35	33	42	4	27	33	58	3	7
Total	1790	2755	387	741	116	2958	428	1047
Tafsir	137	241	1	97	4	36	24	65

Table 10: Terms referring to civilization and progress *(Continued)*

Vol.	*ʿumrān*	*madanī(ya)**	*tamaddun* **	*ḥaḍāra*	*thaqāfa*	*taqad-dum* #	*tarqiya*	*taraqqin/ al-taraqqī* ##
Total	1927	2996	388	838	120	2994	452	1112

*No precise statistics for the noun *madaniyya* can be given, as the feminine adjective is written identically; therefore, instances of the masculine adjective have also been included. **The numbers for *tamaddun* exclude instances where *tamaddun* is part of *mutamaddin* or *mutamaddan.* #The numbers for *taqaddum* exclude instances where *taqaddum* is part of *mutaqaddim* or *mutaqaddam.* ##The search results for *taraqqin* and *al-taraqqī* in the non-vocalized journal (without the *Tafsir*) also included instances of *tarqiya*; these have been deducted.

Table 11: Terms referring to reform and public interest as its goal

Vol.	*nahḍa*	*iṣlāḥ*	*tajdīd*	*maṣlaḥa*	*maṣāliḥ*	*ijtihād*
1	13	170	1	90	90	170
2	37	210	5	109	109	210
3	16	131	7	37	37	131
4	10	152	9	45	45	152
5	21	173	8	66	66	173
6	9	117	4	26	26	117
7	13	139	5	58	58	139
8	14	256	5	62	62	256
9	11	167	3	109	109	167
10	27	238	4	77	77	238
11	14	203	2	55	55	203
12	19	197	2	53	53	197
13	25	182	7	42	42	182
14	8	107	6	109	109	107
15	40	140	14	59	59	140
16	21	281	2	79	79	281
17	43	168	18	95	95	168
18	3	51	6	21	21	51
19	29	132	12	27	27	132
20	6	55	5	16	16	55
21	17	75	11	67	67	75
22	19	109	6	57	57	109
23	27	122	9	110	110	122
24	42	113	26	61	61	113
25	42	114	22	54	54	114
26	16	62	4	26	26	62
27	17	88	34	42	42	88
28	12	113	38	38	38	113
29	36	194	53	37	37	194
30	13	90	58	49	49	90
31	20	80	54	31	31	80
32	15	233	93	39	39	233
33	9	141	49	23	23	141
34	3	110	38	27	27	110
35	16	179	25	18	18	179
Total	683	5092	645	1849	1914	1848
Tafsir	6	477	33	408	477	490
Total	689	5569	678	2257	2391	2338

Index

Index of Persons and Journals

Included are individual historical actors, but not groups or organizations – for these, see the index of subjects. Authors of secondary sources are only included if these sources are crucial for an argument or are at least briefly evaluated. Authors of primary sources are listed more comprehensively. Journals and newspapers are italicized.

Abadi, ʿAbd al-Razzaq al-Mulih 239
ʿAbd al-Raziq, ʿAli 135 f., 172 f., 324 f.
ʿAbduh, Muhammad 14, 88, 96n16, 101 f., 115, 119, 125n166, 126n174, 129–133, 135, 138–140, 142 f., 145, 152–156, 158n117, 159, 165 f., 169, 173, 175n211, 180, 186, 194, 196, 213, 222, 226 f., 233 f., 246, 261 f., 265 f., 286, 293, 298, 308, 310, 321, 325, 331, 356, 362, 364 f., 369, 372, 377, 386 f., 390, 392, 400
Abu al-ʿUyun 289
Adams, Charles 143n38, 149, 152 f., 156, 157n112
al-Afghani, Jamal al-Din 34, 114, 132, 138, 155, 165 f., 222, 227, 228n130, 235, 261, 308, 310, 355n27, 362, 371, 390
al-Ahram 123, 125, 285, 308
ʿAli, Amir 214, 270, 292, 296
Amin, Qasim 134 f., 230, 370 f.
ʿAnan, Muhammad ʿAbdallah 259, 295 f.
Anderson, Benedict 46n38, 81, 96, 103n51
Antun, Farah 124, 132 f., 137, 273
ʿArafat, Muhammad 284
Arslan, Shakib 143–145, 271, 297 f., 376n171
Asad, Talal 6, 16n75, 183, 186 f., 232
Atatürk, Mustafa Kemal 296
Ayalon, Ami 178–183, 190
Azad, Muhyi al-Din 200, 239–244, 353 f.
al-ʿAzm, Haqqi 308
al-ʿAzm, Mahmud 307
al-ʿAzm, Rafiq 29–31, 134, 136, 143–145, 215–220, 259, 266, 270, 275, 280, 287 f., 293, 296 f., 302–349, 355, 371, 395, 410, 423, 425–427, 429
al-ʿAzm, ʿUthman 305 f.
al-Azmeh, Aziz 8, 89, 170 f.

Baker, Keith Michael 46, 57–64, 70, 389
al-Banna, Hasan 104, 140, 155, 267, 282, 298, 430n2
al-Banna, Jamal 430n2
al-Batush, Basam ʿAbd al-Salam 218, 220n91, 306 f., 309–311, 324n140, 325, 343
Behrent, Michael C. 62
Bell, David A. 44 f., 71
Belot, P. J.-B. 189, 360
Biberstein Kazimirski, Albert de 189
Bin Fakhr al-Din, Rida' al-Din 260, 293
Birbari, Nasim Efendi 123n155, 272n88
al-Bishri, ʿAbd al-ʿAziz 294
al-Bitar, Muhammad Bahjat 140, 289, 369, 383n216, 400n310
Black, Antony 11n50, 24n103
Bocthor, Ellious 189 f., 360
al-Bustani, Butrus 13, 192–195, 310
al-Bustani, Salim 194

Cabrera, Miguel A. 72
Casanova, José 5 f., 9, 55n85
Cole, Juan Ricardo 120 f., 166
Comte, Auguste 65–68

Dabana, Niqula 200, 237–239
Darwin, Charles 123
Davis, Charles 62 f., 70
Delanty, Gerard 24n99
Demolins, Edmond 128 f., 294 f., 339 f., 347, 360n64, 372n155, 420
Diderot and d'Alembert 58, 60

https://doi.org/10.1515/9783110545845-015

Dozy, R. 189 f., 350
Durkheim, Émile 65–70, 296, 311

Eisenstadt, Shmuel N. 2
Elias, Elias A. 190 f.
ElShakry, Marwa 123n154, 186n50, 350n1
Ende, Werner 306, 311
Esquiros, Alphonse 129, 231, 259 f., 271n81, 272n84, 278, 292 f., 360n64, 420

al-Fajr 297

Gasper, Michael Ezekiel 211n52, 421 f.
al-Ghazali 152, 166, 384
Gibb, Hamilton A. R. 431
Gökalp, Ziya 65, 131n207, 173n198
Goldziher, Ignaz 152

Haarmann, Ulrich 184n40, 432
Habermas, Jürgen 5 f., 121
Haddad, Mahmoud 142n27, 158n115, 175
Haddad, Mohamed 143n33, 154
Haddad, Niqula 124n162, 195, 237n186, 272–275, 294, 353n10, 369, 381, 427, 429
Hafiz, Isma'il Efendi 207–209
Hamzah, Dyala 149–151
Hanna, Nelly 109n81
Hanotaux, Gabriel 398, 400
al-Harawi, Husayn 270, 281 f., 295
Hatina, Meir 159n120
Hava, J. G. 190
al-Hilal 124, 126, 129, 133, 192, 245, 308, 353n10, 429
Hourani, Albert 153, 156–158
al-Huda 308
Hurgronje, Christiaan Snouck 184n40, 365n95, 391
Husayn, Taha 66, 214n72, 296, 311

Ibn Khaldun 66, 273, 288, 296n229, 356, 368 f., 375
Ibn Taymiyya 126 f., 152, 154, 199
al-Ittihad al-ʿUthmani 308

Jalal, ʿAtifa 230
al-Jamiʿa 124, 132, 137, 429
al-Jarida 102, 230
Jaridat al-Afkar 259n32, 260n33, 271n82, 277
Jaridat Misr 226
al-Jazaʾiri, Tahar 310
al-Jinan 192 f.
al-Jisr, Husayn 138 f.
Jung, Dietrich 4n13, 159 f., 169

Kamil, Mustafa 102
al-Kawakibi, ʿAbd al-Rahman 180, 252, 370
Kerr, Malcolm 161, 165 f., 416n366
Khuri-Makdisi, Ilham 13 f., 17 f., 20, 30, 170, 177, 187 f., 191, 195 f., 211, 350
Koselleck, Reinhart 39–44

Lane, Edward William 255 f., 355n23
Lauzière, Henry 15n72, 133n217, 159n119
Le Bon, Gustave 128, 130, 242, 259, 273, 295, 372, 420 f., 427
Lewis, Bernard 179 f., 312n67
Lisan al-Hal 231
al-Liwaʾ 102, 308
Lord Cromer 102, 156, 166n163, 200, 233–236, 247, 250, 362n77, 364, 371, 404, 427
Lord Headley 260n33, 297

al-Mahami, Muhammad 222 f., 229
Mahmood, Saba 83, 175
Majallat al-ʿIlm 213
Majallat al-Islam 125
Majallat al-ʿUlum al-Ijtimaʿiyya 369
al-Maraghi, Muhammad Mustafa 279 f., 285n164, 294n214
al-Mashriq 196
Massignon, Louis 152, 184n39
al-Mawsuʿat 336
Mitchell, Timothy 5, 130n203, 188
al-Mufid 128n182, 308
Muhammad, ʿAbd al-ʿAziz 129n194, 259, 420n382
Muhammad (Mehmet) ʿAli 94–100, 107–108, 111, 115, 119, 127, 181
Muhaysin, Hamid Mahmud 258, 290 f.
al-Muntaqid 136
al-Muqattam 123, 125, 221, 234, 237, 308

al-Muqtabas 308
al-Muqtataf 121, 123–126, 129 f., 134, 171n191, 192, 221, 273, 279, 308, 350, 429
Musa, Salama 13, 124n162

al-Nakdi, ʿArif 369
Napoleon Bonaparte 93–96
Nassar, Nasif 184, 247 f., 357n41
Nelson, Alfred 225 f.
Nimr, Faris 123 f., 134, 144, 221 f.

Ophir, Adi 19 f.

Pellitteri, Antonino 306, 336
Pernau, Margrit 12, 20 f., 23, 54
Philippson, Ludwig 409 f.
Plessner, Helmuth 227
Poovey, Mary 61, 212

Ramadan, Tariq 88n75, 104n60, 171n188, 357
Rebhan, Helga 179–183, 187 f., 190
Renan, Ernest 132, 165n155
Rida, Husayn Wasfi 134n220, 143, 230, 237n186, 278n118
Rida, Rashid 14, 16, 29–32, 66, 87, 89, 97, 102, 114, 117, 125, 126n174, 131–163, 166, 171–174, 199–215, 218–220, 222–231, 233–237, 239, 245–248, 250 f., 254–266, 270–273, 276–283, 285–287, 290–292, 294, 296–298, 300–303, 306–310, 314, 318, 320–322, 325, 337, 350–425, 427–429, 431
Rida, Salih Mukhlis 34n127, 143, 279, 308, 361n70, 371n147
Riedel, Manfred 47, 49 f., 52n68, 53n71, 61, 301n250

Saʿid, ʿAbd al-Hamid 289 f.
Saʿrruf, Yaqub 134
Sawaʿi, Muhammad (Sawaie, Mohammed) 99n31, 180–182
al-Sayyid, Ahmad Lutfi 102, 183n37
al-Sayyidat (wa-l-Banat/wa-l-Rijal) 273
Schulze, Reinhard 11n49, 24n100, 25n105, 186 f., 187n54
Schulz-Forberg, Hagen 12 f., 17–19, 22–25
al-Shatibi, Abu Ishaq 199, 224, 256
al-Shidyaq, Ahmad Faris 180–182
Shumayyil, Shibli 13, 124n162, 134, 144, 186n50, 195, 211, 273, 308, 371, 391, 427
Sidqi, Muhammad Tawfiq 143–145, 212 f., 257n17, 258n26, 260n33 f., 281
al-Siyasa 258 f., 290, 429
Smith, Jane Idleman 168 f.
Spencer, Herbert 123, 128–130, 207, 272n88, 372
Stetkevych, Jaroslav 186, 189

al-Tahtawi, Rifaʿa Rafʿa 180–182
Tauber, Eliezer 306–310
Taylor, Charles 25n108, 26 f., 64, 67, 72–89, 173, 379, 423, 427
Tayob, Abdulkader 165–167, 172 f.
Tharwat al-Funun 230
Tönnies, Ferdinand 53
Touraine, Alain 52, 70
al-Tuwayrani, Hasan Husni 187n54, 188n64

ʿUmar, Muhammad 129
Upson, Arthur 151 f.
al-ʿUrwa al-Wuthqa 138 f., 222, 261 f., 283, 362, 390

Van Leeuwen, Richard 174, 378n191
Van Nispen tot Sevenaer, Christiaan 160, 173 f., 377–380
Von Bernhardi, Friedrich 271n82, 277 f.

Wagner, Peter 3n8, 4n13, 24, 56, 64–69, 95n12, 381
Wajdi, Muhammad Farid 245n233, 266 f., 371
Weber, Max 65, 68 f.
Withington, Phil 45 f., 50, 58, 258

al-Yafiʿi, Salih bin ʿAli 311, 315–318, 320–322, 324, 347, 405
Yasushi, Kosogi (Kusuji) 32, 157
Yusuf, ʿAli 102, 125

Zaghlul, Ahmad Fathi 128 f., 242, 295, 420 f.

Zaghlul, Sa'd 102, 266n55
al-Zahrawi, 'Abd al-Hamid 143–145, 259, 294 f., 308, 371
Zaydan, Jurji 124, 132 f., 311
Ze'evi, Dror 95 f.
Zolondek, Leon 179 f., 182, 185, 249

Index of Non-English Terms

Only the most common modern English meaning in the context of *al-Manar* is stated in parentheses. Arabic adjectives are listed in their shorter male version only; this comprises the female version. English terms are included in the index of subjects.

'almānī (secular) 34, 88, 126, 502
'āmm (public) 256 f., 417
'aql (reason) 170, 224, 293, 314, 319, 321, 327, 331n170, 335, 344 f., 373, 392, 504

dahrī (temporal, secular) 165, 502
dawla (state) 216 f., 219, 267, 275 f., 278, 313, 319, 359, 395, 430n2, 503
dīmuqrāṭiyya (democracy) 315, 318, 503
dīn, pl. *adyān* (religion) 137, 147, 165n157, 167–170, 172 f., 202, 204, 208, 223, 225, 234 f., 263, 267, 279–281, 287, 298, 310, 313 f., 318 f., 323 f., 326, 331 f., 335, 344 f., 347, 358 f., 362, 365n94, 370, 373 f., 380, 386, 389–391, 393 f., 397–402, 405, 408, 418, 431, 501
dīnī (religious) 146 f., 168, 175, 262, 279, 284 f., 311, 320, 322, 362–365, 385, 387, 391, 393 f., 396–398, 400, 402–405, 415, 417, 501
diyāna (religion) 213, 501
dunyā (world) 209, 281, 287, 314, 319, 323 f., 390, 398 f., 401, 405, 431, 502
dunyawī (worldly) 214, 288, 314 f., 322, 330, 360, 391, 398 f., 403

effendiyya 109, 111–113, 115, 151

falsafa (philosophy) 137, 202 f., 362, 369, 371, 504

Gemeinschaft (community) 53, 247, 301n250
Gesellschaft (society) 47, 49, 53, 186n49, 247, 301n250, 381, 424

ḥaḍāra (culture) 205, 214, 246, 252, 284 f., 298, 393, 506 f.
al-hay'a al-ijtimā'iyya (social body, society) 14, 16 f., 29–31, 186n50, 187–189, 191–196, 199–203, 206–215, 219–241, 243–247, 250–253, 261–263, 268–272, 274 f., 285 f., 288, 291 f., 299 f., 338, 348, 350–352, 354 f., 380 f., 414, 420, 423–425, 429, 490
ḥukūma (government) 217, 220n91, 227, 238, 251 f., 276, 288, 313–315, 319, 322, 333, 398n305, 419, 503
ḥurriyya (freedom) 222, 327 f., 334 f., 340, 342

'ibādāt (religious matters) 172, 208, 224, 319, 392, 394–396, 399, 505
ijtihād (independent reasoning) 172, 225 f., 317–319, 337, 404, 508
ijtimā' (social association, society, gathering) 14, 29, 31, 34 f., 52, 128n184, 186n50, 187–191, 194, 203, 213, 215, 219, 240, 242 f., 244, 246, 248 f., 262–264, 268 f., 274, 276, 280, 287 f., 293, 302, 313, 327, 331 f., 334 f., 338, 340 f., 344, 348, 350–359, 362n75, 364, 365n94, 370 f., 376 f., 380, 381 f., 384, 386, 388–397, 399–402, 406–411, 413 f., 424 f., 430 f., 486
ijtimā'ī (social) 14, 31, 34, 116, 130, 136, 147 f., 174 f., 189, 191, 194, 204 f., 208, 212, 216, 234 f., 240, 242 f., 244, 262, 266–269, 280, 283, 285, 287, 290, 293, 303n1, 314–317, 319, 330, 336, 338, 341–344, 351, 353n10, 359–367, 369–

371, 376, 381, 384, 386 f., 388–396, 398–405, 407, 411–420, 486; see also: *al-hayʾa al-ijtimāʿiyya*, *al-masʾala al-ijtimāʿiyya*
ijtimāʿiyya (socialism) 52, 182 f., 353n10
ʿilm al-ijtimāʿ (sociology) 130, 191, 204, 224, 273, 367–369, 372–377, 380–384, 429, 486
īmān (belief) 34, 199, 202, 279, 309, 329, 341 f., 407 f., 501
intiẓām (order) 188, 213, 217, 219 f., 227, 261, 276
iqtiṣād (economy) 195, 366n100, 367, 370
ishtirākiyya (socialism) 51 f., 124, 183, 225n115, 238, 274, 279, 353n10
iṣlāḥ (reform) 14n71, 146 f., 175, 202 f., 224, 230 f., 234, 270 f., 279, 281 f., 287, 289, 321, 362, 365, 366n101, 388, 392 f., 395, 398n305, 399, 413, 508
istiʿmār (colonialism) 503

jamāʿa, pl. *jamāʿāt* (group of people, community) 53, 128n184, 188–190, 201, 221, 239 f., 242–244, 247 f., 265, 274, 281, 284, 288, 296, 301, 333, 353n10, 354, 360, 411, 488
al-jāmiʿa al-islāmiyya (Pan-Islamism) 233–235, 266
jamʿiyya, pl. *jamʿiyyāt* (society, association) 188–190, 194, 236, 242, 246–248, 258, 268, 331, 370, 414, 419–421, 488, 497
jinsiyya (nationalism) 156n109, 168, 225, 236, 309, 387 f., 403 f., 418
jumhūriyya (republic) 238, 295, 321, 331

koinonìa politkè (civil society) 49, 52

madanī (civil) 55, 146, 215, 262, 290, 292, 329, 340, 344, 356 f., 359n56, 360, 363, 365 f., 390 f., 395, 397, 398n305, 399–402, 407, 506 f.
madaniyya (civilization) 214, 221, 235, 237 f., 246, 252 f., 266, 283, 289, 296, 326, 331, 337 f., 343, 358, 364, 372, 392, 397, 399, 407 f., 506 f.
māddī (material) 203 f., 207, 209, 221, 289 f., 393, 399, 502
maqāṣid 171 f., 335, 343, 393, 396
al-masʾala al-ijtimāʿiyya (the social question) 306, 337 f., 407
maṣlaḥa, pl. *maṣāliḥ* (public interest) 150, 171 f., 194, 206, 208, 214 f., 217 f., 220, 265, 268, 278, 287 f., 314, 318 f., 330–332, 341 f., 375, 380, 391, 399, 405, 411, 413 f., 419 f., 508
mawlid, pl. *mawālid* (saint festival) 117, 257
milla (religious community) 247 f., 329, 341, 396, 403, 419, 488, 498–500
muʿāmalāt (social matters) 172, 287 f., 319, 336, 342, 380, 401, 505
mujtamaʿ (society, integrated collectivity) 14, 16 f., 19, 21, 29–31, 53, 55, 144, 175 f., 185–191, 194, 210, 216, 218 f., 227 f., 244, 247 f., 254–302, 324, 327, 330, 333 f., 341–344, 346–348, 351 f., 353n10, 354–356, 358 f., 376 f., 381, 384, 387, 409 f., 416, 419 f., 423–426, 429 f., 486 f., 491

nahḍa (Renaissance) 170, 192, 195, 508
niẓām (order) 99, 189, 191, 213, 215–217, 219 f., 223, 235, 241–243, 246, 262 f., 266, 271, 275, 279, 282, 285, 287, 290 f., 297, 313, 318, 333, 338, 348, 358 f., 364, 388 f., 392–395, 400–402, 411, 413, 416, 418n374

qānūn (law) 217, 221, 266, 288, 333 f., 342 f., 505
qawm (group of people) 194, 247, 259, 281, 294 f., 384, 388, 404, 411, 419 f., 488

salafiyya (Salafism) 15n72, 133, 158 f.
shaʿb (the people) 180, 182, 185, 200, 220, 238, 249, 252 f., 261–267, 269, 277, 301, 333, 358, 384, 412, 419, 488, 495 f.
sharʿ (revelation, religious law) 172 f., 216, 287 f., 292, 319, 321, 330, 333, 342 f.
sharīʿa/shariʿa (order, religious law) 171 f., 217, 241, 251, 288, 316–319, 322, 326 f., 333 f., 342 f., 345, 347, 385, 390, 393, 399 f., 403, 505
shūrā (consultation) 241, 317, 320 f., 323, 503

siyāsa (politics) 33 f., 204, 218, 263, 313–315, 317–319, 323, 358, 369 f., 392, 400, 413, 503
societas civilis (civil society) 49
société (society) 19, 44n23, 45, 49 f., 56–58, 60 f., 185, 189 f., 194 f., 257, 293n209, 294–296, 299, 301, 354, 360, 420 f., 424, 430
sociologie (sociology) 65
sunan allāh, sg. *sunnat allāh* (God's laws or ways) 173–175, 376–378, 382, 386, 389

al-takāful al-ʿāmm (mutual solidarity) 215 f., 218, 326, 334 f., 343, 348
taʿlīm (intellectual education) 33, 148, 150, 204, 224, 229, 231 f., 293, 504
tamaddun (civilization) 193, 217, 238, 246, 264, 285, 305, 358, 400, 506 f.
tanẓīm (ordering) 213, 216, 278, 289, 333
taqaddum (progress) 238, 340, 383, 506 f.
taqlīd (imitation) 156n109, 168, 172, 316, 337, 404
taraqqin/al-taraqqī (progress) 217, 228, 266, 280, 289, 293, 314, 318, 327, 361, 382–384, 506 f.
tarbiya (moral upbringing) 148, 204–208, 210, 219, 221, 224, 229, 231 f., 293, 344, 370, 380, 382 f., 416, 504
tarqiya (progress) 252, 361, 419, 506 f.
thaqāfa (culture) 34, 296, 298, 506 f.

ʿulamāʾ/ʿulamaʾ (scholars) 109–111, 149, 151, 207, 297, 310, 321, 337 f., 370, 382 f., 386, 413
umma/umma (nation, people, society, community) 1, 16 f., 30 f., 180, 182–185, 201–206, 209–212, 215–223, 232, 237, 240–244, 246 f., 249–253, 261–270, 272n88, 275, 277 f., 282, 284, 288, 295, 301 f., 314 f., 318–320, 326, 328, 330n164, 333, 341 f., 348, 350 f., 353–355, 358 f., 361, 366n101, 368, 370, 372 f., 376 f., 379–385, 387 f., 390, 392, 394, 396, 400, 403, 406 f., 409–425, 428–432, 488, 493 f.
ʿumrān (civilization) 137, 165n157, 276, 279 f., 288, 305, 326, 334, 338, 343, 350, 356, 359, 369, 374, 377, 380 f., 384, 392, 401, 407, 506 f.

waṭaniyya (patriotism) 238, 309, 387

Index of Subjects and English Terms

Abbasids 216
agriculture 100, 228 f., 276, 294
Alexandria 65n142, 94, 106, 115, 119, 121, 123 f., 139, 226, 273, 284, 290
Arab, Arabs 13, 54, 66, 97, 99, 112, 114, 121, 124n162, 127 f., 131 f., 134, 138, 151, 159, 179, 181, 183, 186, 192 f., 214, 220, 223, 230, 236, 248 f., 252, 255n7, 270, 273, 286, 295, 298, 306 f., 309, 312n68, 313–316, 343, 356, 360, 365n94, 370–372, 406, 416, 432, 491–496
Arabic 12, 16–19, 21 f., 27–30, 41, 51, 53–55, 88, 101, 111n91, 118 f., 121–130, 132, 136, 152, 160, 167, 175–192, 194 f., 209, 212, 230, 233, 239, 242, 253, 255, 258 f., 264, 273–275, 293, 295 f., 299–302, 306 f., 312, 324, 347 f., 350, 353n10, 358–360, 367, 369 f., 372–374, 376, 410, 414, 420–426, 429 f.
army 94, 98 f., 101, 144
associations 45 f., 105, 114–117, 189 f., 238, 242, 248, 296, 301 f., 355n27, 358, 361, 370
atheism 59, 85, 134
al-Azhar/Azhari 100, 110 f., 125, 230, 279 f., 284 f., 289 f., 294, 297, 324, 369

Beirut 13, 123, 136, 179, 192 f., 196, 223, 273, 369, 390n256
belief 5, 7, 34, 63, 74 f., 80, 84–86, 133 f., 151, 167, 169, 174, 184, 199, 202 f., 209, 263, 279, 282, 309, 314, 317, 328 f., 332, 341 f., 346 f., 383, 387, 389, 392, 399, 401, 404, 407 f., 426, 501

bureaucracy, bureaucratic, bureaucrats 3, 99 f., 105, 108, 112, 151

Cairo 13 f., 106, 108, 114, 119, 121, 123, 139, 179, 196, 225, 273, 288, 292, 294, 305, 308, 325, 336, 364, 417
Cairo University 65, 110, 370
caliphate 135, 160 f., 239, 241, 316, 324 f., 354
capitalism 3, 4n15, 54, 70, 81, 88, 103n51, 136n236, 274n102
Catholic, Catholicism 14n71, 27, 55n85, 62, 63n133, 73n7, 75, 89, 307
charity 115 f., 202
Christian, Christianity 7, 13, 24, 30, 34, 59 f., 63 f., 67, 73, 75, 83, 86–88, 119, 122–126, 130–134, 143 f., 149, 152, 161, 168 f., 171n191, 180, 182, 187, 190n73, 192, 194–196, 231 f., 234 f., 237, 245, 250, 275, 297 f., 308, 310 f., 313, 327, 339, 379, 391, 400, 403, 405, 417 f., 424–429, 490, 494, 498 f.
civilization 3, 13, 23 f., 29, 46, 60, 71, 74, 78 f., 83, 130, 133, 137, 139, 143, 146, 150, 157, 165, 168, 181, 193, 195 f., 205, 214, 217, 235, 237 f., 246, 252 f., 257, 266, 276, 279 f., 283, 285, 289, 296, 305, 312 f., 316, 326, 331, 335–338, 343–345, 350, 358, 364, 369, 372, 374, 377, 380 f., 384, 392 f., 397, 399–401, 406–408, 506
civil society 42, 46, 48–50, 52, 54–56, 60, 79, 117, 121n147, 221, 292
class 109, 112, 151, 246, 263
cohesion 81, 195, 228, 240, 242–244
colonialism 5, 9, 12, 23, 83, 87 f., 102, 105 f., 114, 127, 155, 159, 236, 242, 247, 286, 312n68, 345, 426
Communism 43, 104, 279, 353n10, 405
community 17, 52–54, 56, 96 f., 117, 151, 165, 183–185, 190, 201, 205, 209, 240, 242, 244, 247–249, 264, 280 f., 301, 315, 329, 332 f., 340 f., 348, 381, 387, 396, 400, 403, 414, 417–422, 424, 428, 431, 499 f.
conceptual history, research on concepts 1 f., 6 f., 9–14, 16–31, 39–49, 54, 81 f., 108 f., 121, 148, 159n119, 167, 172–175, 177–185, 421 f., 423 f., 428–432
constitution 43, 102–104, 184, 220n91, 221, 238, 241, 267, 289, 314, 318, 330, 333
convergence 1, 25, 167, 431 f.
cooperation 52, 194 f., 219, 222, 226–228, 278, 284, 321, 328 f., 340 f., 348, 353 f., 357, 387n235, 396, 406, 411 f., 424
Copts, Coptic 122, 417–420, 494, 499
corporation 45, 229, 370, 419
culture 34, 71, 78, 103, 128, 171, 192, 214, 246, 252, 284, 296, 298, 305, 326, 334, 343, 356, 431

Damascus 144, 225, 251, 270, 307, 325
Dar al-Daʿwa wa-l-Irshad (House of Proselytization and Guidance) 231, 239, 294, 375n167
decline paradigm 94–96, 127n177, 271, 280, 297, 315 f., 336, 344, 375, 377, 382–386
Deism 75, 79
democracy, democratic 42 f., 49, 54, 55n85, 79, 88 f., 104n60, 105, 135, 315, 318, 320, 324, 326
Dinshaway 102

economy 12 f., 67–69, 79, 87, 94 f., 100, 105–112, 120, 122, 136, 183, 195 f., 337 f., 365–367, 370, 395, 404 f., 422
education 33, 85, 101, 105, 107 f., 111–113, 121, 138, 147, 155, 156n109, 195 f., 204–208, 210 f., 219, 222, 224, 226, 229–232, 239, 271 f., 283, 293, 303n2, 305, 307, 316, 325, 328, 339 f., 344, 361, 367, 370, 372, 380, 382 f., 406, 416, 419, 504
effendiyya 109, 111–113, 115, 151
Egypt, Egyptian 5, 18, 28, 43, 86, 93–136, 138–140, 151, 178, 181, 221, 226, 230, 233–236, 246–249, 257–259, 273, 275, 279 f., 284, 286, 289, 298, 308, 317, 324, 336n200, 353, 371, 417–419, 422, 490, 493–499
England, English 2n5, 18, 23, 45, 101–103, 105, 208, 212, 235, 289, 296, 308, 312n68, 493–496

English language 16, 21f., 47n41, 53, 123, 126f., 181, 187, 189–192, 195, 209, 214, 252, 258, 263f., 277, 292, 301, 346, 429
Enlightenment 57–59, 68, 70
ethics, ethical 60f., 87, 152, 171, 221, 284, 339, 343f., 363, 368, 398, 406f., 425f., 505
Europe, European 1–14, 16, 18f., 22–28, 30f., 39, 41, 47f., 50, 53f., 63, 66f., 69, 85, 87f., 94–97, 99f., 105–108, 117–120, 122, 124, 126–132, 134, 138, 143, 151, 155f., 158–162, 168–170, 175, 177–179, 181f., 192–196, 204–208, 214, 221, 230, 234, 237, 242, 254, 257, 274, 280, 283, 286, 292f., 295–301, 309f., 312, 316f., 326f., 330, 335f., 338–340, 343–345, 347, 365n94, 367, 369, 372–376, 379f., 388, 390, 393, 395, 398–400, 405, 422–424, 426f., 429–432, 491, 496

the flock 219, 220n91, 252
France, French; see also: French language 2n5, 45, 50f., 62, 68, 71, 94–96, 98f., 101, 105, 129, 131, 145, 152, 181, 237, 266, 289, 307–309, 312n68, 389, 398, 402, 420f., 429, 494, 496f., 499
freedom 16, 58, 120, 157, 217, 319, 327, 334, 342, 352
Freemasonry 114f.
French language 16, 47n41, 56, 123, 126, 128, 136, 181, 189, 191f., 195, 242, 296, 307, 346f., 354, 360, 364
fullness 75
fundamentalism 82, 127, 158

Germany, German 2n5, 50, 65, 68, 277, 289, 381, 409, 494, 496
German language 39–42, 47n41, 53, 186n49
global(ization) 8f., 12, 50, 141f., 226
global (conceptual) history 3, 13, 17f., 23
global public sphere 4, 122
God 31, 50f., 56, 59, 61, 64, 80, 84, 86, 168f., 172–175, 183, 184n40, 196, 199, 202, 204, 207, 212, 215, 229, 240, 242, 244, 262, 281f., 287, 302, 313, 320, 328–335, 337, 342, 346, 351, 364, 367, 373, 376–384, 388f., 392f., 396, 398–402, 404–406, 408f., 414, 425, 427, 430f.
government, governmental 28, 52, 99–101, 103, 105, 107–110, 112f., 115f., 119f., 181, 195, 216–218, 220f., 227, 229, 238, 241, 249, 251f., 264, 266, 275n106, 276–278, 286–289, 293, 297, 307, 309, 313–315, 318–325, 327f., 332f., 335, 338, 345, 348, 366n101, 383n305, 398, 406, 413, 418f., 424, 427
guilds 108f., 116

hadith 138f., 147, 154, 229, 242, 282, 321f., 324, 329, 332
hegemony, hegemonic 1, 4, 6, 8, 16, 18f., 21, 24–26, 49, 52, 54, 64f., 70f., 75f., 83, 85, 87, 106, 118, 128, 131f., 136, 169, 178, 286, 301, 348, 359, 410, 423, 426–428
Hizb al-Lamarkaziya al-Idariya al-ʿUthmani (Ottoman Party for Administrative Decentralization) 134, 308
humanism, humanist 45, 75, 166

imagined community 96, 103n51, 183
immanence 76, 81, 279, 311, 322f., 326, 330, 345f., 376, 379, 398, 402, 405f., 425
immanent frame 72, 74f., 77, 79–82, 173, 209, 229, 346, 373, 379, 409, 427
independence 96, 102f., 107, 112, 159, 223, 226, 251, 266–269, 307, 309, 334f., 339f., 342, 383, 416, 424
India 23, 54, 140f., 165, 203, 213f., 228n131, 239, 259, 303n2, 311, 315, 353, 494, 496
individuals 27, 50f., 53f., 59, 62, 68, 80f., 85, 195, 201, 203f., 211, 213, 219, 222, 224, 227, 231, 240, 242f., 251, 263, 274, 281, 283, 287f., 290, 303n2, 328, 333, 339–343, 357, 359, 361, 379, 382, 384, 391f., 394f., 406–408, 410–416, 424–427
industry 106, 109, 229, 276, 294
infrastructure 99f., 108

intellectuals 5, 63, 87, 114, 120, 122, 128, 131, 134 f., 144, 147, 151, 221, 259, 271, 310 f., 322 f., 325 f., 337, 343, 347, 370, 374, 425 f.
Italian language 123, 181
Italy, Italian 68, 99, 181, 297, 405, 494

Jam'iyyat al-Shura al-'Uthmaniyya (Society of the Ottoman Council) 114, 144, 308
Japan 312n68, 313, 318, 321, 494, 496
Jesus 281, 399, 500
journalism, journalist 97, 111 f., 119–121, 125, 132–134, 138 f., 147–150, 192, 228, 361 f.

laws
– legal 49, 98n25, 161, 163, 171 f., 215–217, 235 f., 238 f., 251 f., 263, 266, 276 f., 285–293, 297, 300, 328, 333 f., 342–344, 399 f., 406 f., 413 f.
– natural 174, 186, 266, 331, 340, 377 f.
– social 4, 27, 31, 56, 64 f., 68 f., 123, 128, 173 f., 186n50, 204, 225, 241 f., 273 f., 279 f., 313, 330 f., 340, 351, 359, 373–381, 383 f., 386, 409
Lebanon, Lebanese 34, 119, 140, 192, 194 f., 210 f., 213, 223, 231, 247, 271, 277, 298, 309 f., 494, 496
liberal, liberalism 19n82, 48, 50, 55, 68–71, 104 f., 112, 120, 141n20, 169, 184, 258, 273, 290 f., 324, 339–341, 432
literacy 103, 114, 119–121

Mamluks 94, 98
masses 104, 207, 317, 322, 324, 409
material, materialism 43, 87, 93, 131, 133, 159, 162, 165 f., 203 f., 207, 209, 221, 289 f., 312, 358n51, 372, 393, 399
military 94, 98–101, 103, 105, 107, 118 f., 127, 225, 242, 305, 313, 365, 390, 393, 407
modernization 1–3, 93, 95, 99, 106, 127n177, 178, 286, 386
morals, morality 46, 61, 68, 81, 113, 135, 137, 146 f., 169, 174, 193, 203–210, 221–224, 227–232, 236, 246, 250, 264, 271, 279, 282–286, 288, 291, 328, 335–337, 339, 344, 358n51, 367, 371 f., 380, 382 f., 387 f., 391 f., 401, 403, 406–409, 415 f., 421 f., 424 f.
Muhammad (Prophet) 135, 147, 184n40, 204, 226, 235, 241, 281 f., 290, 294 f., 311, 314, 316 f., 319, 325, 331–334, 346, 378n191, 388, 390–393, 399, 404, 428
multiple modernities 2, 78, 83, 177
Muslim Brotherhood 104, 140, 155, 247, 306n19
mutual benefit 80 f., 117, 424

nation 13, 17, 28, 44–47, 49, 56, 67, 69, 93, 96 f., 100–103, 105, 113 f., 117, 122, 151, 158 f., 170 f., 183–185, 204–206, 215, 217, 232, 242, 246 f., 249, 251 f., 263–267, 277 f., 280, 284, 289, 297, 301, 306, 312 f., 315, 319 f., 326–330, 333 f., 342, 355, 361, 367, 375, 377–379, 381, 384, 388, 392, 394, 403, 411, 413 f., 417, 419, 421, 424, 431 f.
nationalism 43, 52, 54, 86, 96, 101–103, 109, 114, 116, 119, 128, 156n109, 183, 234, 236, 239, 270, 291, 308 f., 336n200, 387, 404 f., 411
nature 205, 271, 379, 408 f., 430
– human nature 50 f., 56, 74, 80, 195, 204, 215, 227 f., 262, 268, 274, 285, 302, 327, 332, 335, 340 f., 356 f., 364, 376, 379, 387, 409
normativity 10, 21 f., 27, 43, 46, 49, 57n95, 176, 266, 269, 351, 354, 359, 397, 425

order 4, 8, 10, 27 f., 30 f., 43, 45, 47, 50–52, 56, 59–64, 68 f., 71, 76, 79, 81 f., 86, 93, 100, 105, 110, 112, 118, 131 f., 135, 151, 164 f., 167, 169, 172, 174 f., 181, 185, 191 f., 194 f., 201, 208 f., 213–228, 231 f., 236–239, 241–246, 248 f., 251–254, 261–272, 275 f., 278–292, 295, 297–302, 312 f., 316 f., 320, 323 f., 327–333, 336–348, 351, 354 f., 358 f., 364, 371, 379, 385, 388 f., 391–395, 400–402, 404–406, 409, 411, 413, 416, 418n374, 419 f., 422, 424–427, 430–432

Ottoman Empire 95–99, 102, 105, 114, 141, 151, 221, 267, 307–309, 313, 413 f.

Paris 132, 138, 181, 222, 261
parliament(arian) 16, 103, 105, 120, 157, 182, 236, 242, 318, 413
peasants 102 f., 107 f., 110, 113, 116, 120 f.
the people 52, 56, 180, 185, 200, 207 f., 215, 217–221, 232, 238, 244, 249, 251 f., 262–269, 275n106, 277, 284, 287, 301, 314, 318, 320, 333–335, 348, 381, 410, 414, 419, 424
philosophy, philosophers, philosophical 29 f., 46, 59, 61, 66, 68, 130, 132, 160, 165n155, 199, 201–203, 206–208, 214, 227 f., 232, 250, 280, 283, 338, 350, 356, 359, 362 f., 368 f., 370–373, 408, 430
politics 29, 31, 33, 50, 101, 112, 120, 128, 132, 155, 163, 172 f., 175n211, 204, 212, 215–222, 228–230, 263, 271, 275–278, 291, 300, 308, 310 f., 313–315, 317–325, 346 f., 358, 369 f., 389, 392, 400, 402, 406, 413, 428, 503
the press 28, 103, 107, 111, 114, 117–122, 125, 130, 150, 220, 230 f., 239, 286, 305, 421
private 51, 115 f., 118 f., 126, 134, 169, 257, 314, 347
progress 13, 43, 46, 71, 87 f., 128 f., 132, 139, 150 f., 158, 162, 165, 175, 181, 209, 228, 230–232, 234 f., 238, 266, 277, 280, 288 f., 291–294, 305, 310, 312–316, 318, 326, 328, 330 f., 335, 338, 343 f., 355, 361, 364, 370, 377 f., 382–385, 388, 398, 400 f., 419, 506
Protestantism, Protestant 62, 74 f., 123 f., 160, 169, 192, 224, 273, 390n256
public interest 150, 154, 171 f., 205 f., 208, 215, 314, 318 f., 331, 341 f., 375, 414, 419 f., 508
public space 256 f.
public sphere 5, 53, 79, 84, 111, 114, 117 f., 121–123, 126, 134n221, 136, 138, 151, 171, 273, 275, 347, 410, 417

Qur'an, Qur'anic verses 87, 139, 142, 144, 147–149, 152, 154, 159 f., 167–170, 172, 179, 208, 226, 235, 237 f., 240, 264, 280 f., 288 f., 316 f., 320–324, 328–330, 334, 337, 346, 373–377, 379n195, 384, 388–393, 403, 407

reason 46, 68, 71, 87, 132, 170, 172, 174, 206–208, 314, 319, 321, 327, 330 f., 334 f., 337, 342, 344, 373, 375, 380, 406
Reformism, reformist 1, 14–16, 27–31, 86–89, 96, 113–116, 118, 130–136, 138, 143, 149–160, 164, 166 f., 169–175, 185, 195 f., 203, 209, 212, 214, 226, 228 f., 232–236, 239, 251, 262, 272, 277 f., 286, 292, 299, 302–304, 306 f., 310–312, 315 f., 322, 343, 345–347, 351, 364, 366 f., 371 f., 374–376, 379n195, 385, 387n235, 390, 406, 409, 422–424, 426 f., 430–432
revolution, revolutionary 42, 50 f., 68, 96, 102 f., 105, 115 f., 155, 180, 214, 308 f., 338
Russia 140 f., 293, 312n68, 494, 496

saddle period 27, 30, 39–43, 177 f., 410, 422–424
Salafism 15n72, 159
Saudi (Arabia) 154, 325, 326n150 f., 329n157, 330n164, 331n167, 397
secularism, secularist 1n1, 15, 27, 59, 86, 125 f., 132, 149, 158, 173, 206, 208, 229, 310 f., 324, 331, 347, 379, 385, 389, 425–427, 429, 431
secularity 1n1, 72–74, 76, 82–86, 88, 172, 427
Social Darwinism 170, 242, 271n82, 277, 377
social imaginary 72, 74, 77–82, 185, 432
Socialism, socialist 51 f., 86, 114, 124, 134, 182, 189, 195, 225, 238, 273 f., 279, 338–341, 353n10, 381, 395, 432
the social question 51, 68 f., 134, 306, 337 f., 347, 407
sociology, sociological, sociologist 4, 6, 8, 10, 27, 31, 52 f., 56, 64–70, 123n155, 127, 130, 131n207, 136 f., 166, 170, 174,

191, 224, 259, 273f., 294, 296, 303, 305, 324, 328, 330, 332, 348, 367–377, 379n198, 380–386, 424, 429
solidarity 54, 60, 117, 165, 215f., 218f., 225, 284, 326, 331f., 334f., 340–343, 345, 384, 388, 414
spiritual, spiritualism 74, 87, 159, 169, 201, 205, 209f., 262f., 284, 337, 339, 343–345, 358, 363, 366n102, 387, 390, 392–403, 405, 415f.
the state 27, 42, 45, 48–52, 54–56, 60n115, 62, 64, 79, 97, 100f., 105, 116f., 121f., 170f., 175, 183, 185, 216–220, 224, 275–278, 289, 300f., 318–320, 327f., 334, 347, 352, 359, 366, 401, 418, 431n3
subtraction story 64, 74, 87–89, 174
Sufi(s) 100, 116, 138, 147, 156, 161, 307
Syria, Syrian 97, 99, 111, 119, 122–126, 130f., 134, 138, 140f., 144, 151, 162, 182, 191f., 220, 259, 277, 307–309, 390n256, 391, 416, 429, 494, 496

tax 101, 107f., 120, 238
trade 100, 106–109, 228f., 251, 294
transcendence 61, 75f., 79, 81f., 84n56, 86, 167–169, 311, 322f., 346, 376, 379, 398, 402, 405f., 408f., 427
Tripolis 210f., 267
Turkey, Turkish 141, 214n72, 261, 295f., 309, 491, 493f., 495f., 499
Turkish language (incl. Ottoman Turkish) 96n15, 101, 119, 123, 131, 162, 178, 180f., 211, 219n90, 245n234, 307, 347, 390, 429, 431n3

ʿulamaʾ 107, 109–111, 149, 151, 297, 321, 337, 382f., 413
Umayyads 216, 306
unification, unity 31, 52, 69, 139, 165, 194, 210, 221f., 234f., 239, 242, 244, 249, 263, 265, 267, 281, 309, 317, 321, 324, 327–329, 334, 341f., 348, 352–354, 356, 357n39, 359, 362n75, 375, 378, 387–390, 396f., 406
ʿUrabi revolt 101, 119
USA, United States, North America 2n5, 84f., 230, 285, 312n68

Wahhabi movement 154
welfare 60, 115f., 248, 258, 267, 331, 419
the West, Western 1–3, 6, 8, 12, 15f., 18, 23f., 26f., 64, 69, 73f., 76, 78, 82–87, 95, 151, 155–161, 166, 168, 170, 180, 203, 206, 209, 217, 236, 238, 281, 285, 295f., 307n23, 310, 312, 316f., 320, 328, 335, 337, 345, 364, 391, 407, 409, 411, 419, 494
Westernization, Westernized 6n31, 16, 93, 151, 156–158, 160, 178, 203, 310, 364
women 68, 113, 115, 121, 134, 158, 162, 204f., 226, 230f., 238, 265, 271–273, 292, 298, 393, 429
workers 68, 107, 109, 112f., 121, 151, 205, 226, 228, 294, 338

www.ingramcontent.com/pod-product-compliance
Lightning Source LLC
Chambersburg PA
CBHW020602300426
44113CB00007B/481